Lecture Notes in Computer Science 16427

The series Lecture Notes in Computer Science (LNCS), including its subseries Lecture Notes in Artificial Intelligence (LNAI) and Lecture Notes in Bioinformatics (LNBI), has established itself as a medium for the publication of new developments in computer science and information technology research, teaching, and education.

LNCS enjoys close cooperation with the computer science R & D community, the series counts many renowned academics among its volume editors and paper authors, and collaborates with prestigious societies. Its mission is to serve this international community by providing an invaluable service, mainly focused on the publication of conference and workshop proceedings and postproceedings. LNCS commenced publication in 1973.

Ahmed Awad · Carlos Ordonez · Ahmed Hassan · Ladjel Bellatreche
Editors

Model and Data Engineering

14th International Conference, MEDI 2025
Cairo, Egypt, November 2–4, 2025
Proceedings

Editors
Ahmed Awad
The British University in Dubai
Dubai, United Arab Emirates

Ahmed Hassan
ElSewedy University of Technology
Cairo, Egypt

Carlos Ordonez
University of Houston
Houston, TX, USA

Ladjel Bellatreche
École Nationale Supérieure de Mécanique et d'Aérotechnique
Chasseneuil-du-Poitou, France

ISSN 0302-9743 ISSN 1611-3349 (electronic)
Lecture Notes in Computer Science
ISBN 978-3-032-19864-8 ISBN 978-3-032-19865-5 (eBook)
https://doi.org/10.1007/978-3-032-19865-5

This Springer imprint is published by the registered company Springer Nature Switzerland AG
The registered company address is: Gewerbestrasse 11, 6330 Cham, Switzerland

Preface

This volume of the Lecture Notes in Computer Science (LNCS) series contains the proceedings of the 14th International Conference on Model and Data Engineering (MEDI 2025), which was held in Cairo, Egypt, during November 2–4, 2025. [1]https://medi2025.sut.edu.eg/

The Annual International Conference on Model and Data Engineering is a research venue focused on data modeling and data management. The scope of MEDI is broad, encompassing subjects such as data models, machine learning, algorithmic optimizations, and advanced database and healthcare applications. The conference was established by researchers from Euro-Mediterranean countries and has since fostered numerous global scientific collaborations, projects, and student/faculty exchanges. Historically, MEDI has traveled across various countries, including Portugal (2011), France (2012 and 2019), Italy (2013 and 2024), Cyprus (2014), Greece (2015), Spain (2016 and 2017), Morocco (2018), Estonia (2021), Egypt (2022), and Tunisia (2023).

To ensure maximum inclusivity and overcome travel issues for some participants, the conference was held in a hybrid mode. The submission process for MEDI 2025 included a total of 72 manuscripts. Following a rigorous review and discussion period, 16 regular papers were accepted, resulting in an acceptance rate of 20%, and 17 short papers were accepted for short presentations. Each manuscript underwent a single-blinded review process, receiving between two and four reviews, with most papers receiving three reviews, from Program Committee members representing 29 countries. The accepted regular and short papers are published in these LNCS proceedings. Accepted papers came from 16 countries, underscoring MEDI's international prominence.

The conference program for MEDI 2025 covered an extensive array of topics, such as data modeling, data management, ontologies, machine learning, model-driven engineering, large language models engineering, federated learning, image processing, natural language processing, optimization, and advanced AI applications in healthcare and security. MEDI 2025 featured two distinguished keynote speakers: Elio Masciari from University of Naples Federico II, Italy, gave a talk entitled "Discussing Strategies for AI Environmental Impact Assessment" and Ahmed Gomaa Radwan from Nile University, Egypt, gave a talk entitled "From Bifurcation to Encryption: Harnessing Nonlinear Chaos for Information Security".

The organizers would like to thank all authors who submitted research papers to MEDI 2025, as well as all members of the Program Committee. Moreover, we extend our special thanks to the Local Organizing Committee members who worked immensely hard to make MEDI 2025 a success.

November 2025

Ahmed Awad
Carlos Ordonez
Ahmed Hassan
Ladjel Bellatreche

Organization

General Chairs

Ladjel Bellatreche	ISAE-ENSMA Poitiers, France
Ahmed Hassan	ElSewedy University of Technology, Egypt

Program Co-chairs

Carlos Ordonez	University of Houston, USA
Ahmed Awad	British University in Dubai, United Arab Emirates

Proceedings and Registration Chair

Rehab Abdel-Kader	ElSewedy University of Technology, Egypt

Program Committee

Elio Masciari	University of Naples Federico II, Italy
George A. Chernishev	Saint-Petersburg State University, Russia
Azeddine Chikh	University of Tlemcen, Algeria
Ayman Atia	Helwan University, Egypt
Nashwa El-Bendary	Arab Academy for Science, Technology and Maritime Transport , Egypt
Dennis Mwighusa	Africa Research Institute for AI, Tanzania
Mustafa A. Elattar	Nile University, Egypt
Ayman Ezzat	MSA University, Egypt
Samhaa R. El-Beltagy	New Giza University, Egypt
Ala Khalifeh	German Jordanian University, Jordan
Tall Hamadoun	Nazi Boni University, Burkina Faso
Meriem Belguidoum	University of Constantine 2 - Abdelhamid Mehri, Algeria
Asad Usmani	Goethe University Frankfurt, Germany
Mohamed Elkhatib	Military Technological College, Oman
Khalid M. Hosny	Zagazig University, Egypt
Mohamed R. M. Rizk	Alexandria University, Egypt

Mohamed El-Hadidi	University of Birmingham Dubai, UAE
Tamer Arafa	Nile University, Egypt
Mohamed Haggag	Helwan University, Egypt
Ramy Takieldin	Egypt University of Informatics, Egypt
Walid Karam	American University of Technology, Lebanon
Ahmed F. Elnokrashy	Nile University, Egypt
Bassem Bouaziz	University of Sfax, Tunisia
Sahar Fawzi	Nile University, Egypt
Walid Al-Atabany	Nile University, Egypt
Hasanin Al-Barhamtoshy	King Abdulaziz University, Saudi Arabia
Ayman El-Sayed Omera	Menoufia University, Egypt
Walaa Medhat	Nile University, Egypt
Lobna A. Said	Nile University, Egypt
Bachar Elhassan	ENISM - Le Mans University, France
Christian Attiogbe	LS2N, Nantes University
Nasar Aldian Shashoa	Libyan Academy for Postgraduate Studies, Libya
Tarek Gaber	University of Salford, UK
Shereen A. Taie	Fayoum University, Egypt
Kouzou Abdellah	Université Ziane Achour de Djelfa, Algeria
Tamer Mohamed	Canadian University Dubai, United Arab Emirates
Gheith A. Abandah	University of Jordan, Jordan
Abdullah H. Al-Badi	Sultan Qaboos University, Oman
Fay Elhassan	University of Khartoum, Sudan
Cherif Diallo	Gaston Berger University, Sénégal
Haitham Ghalwash	Coventry University Cairo Branch, Egypt
Marcel Bawindsom Kebre	Université Joseph Ki-Zerbo, Burkina Faso
Mohab Mangoud	University of Bahrain, Bahrain
Giancarlo Sperlì	University of Naples Federico II, Italy
Chokri Mraidha	Paris-Saclay University, CEA, List, France
Enea Vincenzo Napolitano	University of Naples Federico II, Italy
M. Saqib Nawaz	Shenzhen University, China
Giovanni Officoso	University of Milan-Bicocca, Italy
Samir Ouchani	CESI LINEACT, France
Giuseppe Polese	University of Salerno, Italy
Milos Savic	University of Novi Sad, Serbia
Islam Tharwat Abdel Halim	Nile University, Egypt
Goce Trajcevski	Iowa State University, USA
Andrea Vignali	University of Naples Federico II, Italy
Ahmad Ghazal	Pingcap, USA
Hanumath Rao	Amazon, USA
Jerome Rocheteau	ICAM Nantes, France
Mahfoud Houari	University of Tlemcen, Algeria

El Hassan Abdelwahed	Cadi Ayyad University, Morocco
Amany Sarhan	ElSewedy University of Technology, Egypt
Ayman Nabil	Misr International University, Egypt
Amira Tarek	Nile University, Egypt
Aryo Yarahmadi	University of Houston, USA
John W. Branch–Bedoya	Universidad Nacional de Colombia, Colombia
Xiantian Zhou	California State University, USA
Sikder Al-Amin	JP Morgan Chase, USA
Ricardo Vilalta	University of Austin, USA

Local Organizing Committee

Ahmed Khaled	ElSewedy University of Technology, Egypt
Ahmed Radwan	ElSewedy University of Technology, Egypt
Ahmed Zaghloul	ElSewedy University of Technology, Egypt
Amr Badawy	ElSewedy University of Technology, Egypt
Anan Hesham	ElSewedy University of Technology, Egypt
Asmaa El Gezawy	ElSewedy University of Technology, Egypt
Basma Rafat	ElSewedy University of Technology, Egypt
Fadel Amir	ElSewedy University of Technology, Egypt
Fady Emad	ElSewedy University of Technology, Egypt
Hanan Fouad El-Sherbiny	ElSewedy University of Technology, Egypt
Injy Elsabbagh	ElSewedy University of Technology, Egypt
Maram El Saadany	ElSewedy University of Technology, Egypt
Mariam Fawzy	ElSewedy University of Technology, Egypt
Mariam Labib Francies	ElSewedy University of Technology, Egypt
Marwa Nofal	ElSewedy University of Technology, Egypt
Mohamed Abdelnasser	ElSewedy University of Technology, Egypt
Mohamed Eid Ahmed Ali Habib	ElSewedy University of Technology, Egypt
Mohamed El-Mongy	ElSewedy University of Technology, Egypt
Mohamed Farag	ElSewedy University of Technology, Egypt
Mohamed Gamal Sayed Sayed	ElSewedy University of Technology, Egypt
Mohamed Labib	ElSewedy University of Technology, Egypt
Mohamed Mohsen	ElSewedy University of Technology, Egypt
Mohamed Sobh	ElSewedy University of Technology, Egypt
Mostafa Saafan	ElSewedy University of Technology, Egypt
Nagy Nazeh Naguib Wahba	ElSewedy University of Technology, Egypt
Nariman Solaih	ElSewedy University of Technology, Egypt
Nisreen Ashraf	ElSewedy University of Technology, Egypt
Ola Mohey	ElSewedy University of Technology, Egypt
Omneyiah Abdelhamid	ElSewedy University of Technology, Egypt

Osama Almasri	ElSewedy University of Technology, Egypt
Pakinam Elwan	ElSewedy University of Technology, Egypt
Rana Reda	ElSewedy University of Technology, Egypt
Sameh Al Ashry (RIP)	ElSewedy University of Technology, Egypt
Seif Moaz	ElSewedy University of Technology, Egypt
Shimae Khamis	ElSewedy University of Technology, Egypt
Yasmine Elbendary	ElSewedy University of Technology, Egypt

Keynote Speakers

Discussing Strategies for AI Environmental Impact Assessment

Elio Masciari

University of Naples Federico II, Italy
elio.masciari@unina.it

Accurately assessing the environmental impact of Artificial Intelligence (AI) systems is essential to promoting sustainable development within the field. However, existing carbon emission tracking tools often rely on divergent assumptions, limited hardware compatibility, and inconsistent measurement granularity, leading to fragmented and often incomparable results. In this paper, we propose a hybrid methodology that integrates a weighted aggregation of ten widely used emission estimation tools with a dynamic model-to-tool matching procedure. The weighted strategy assigns normalized importance scores to each tool based on six criteria. In parallel, the dynamic matching component identifies the most context-appropriate estimation tool for a given AI model. We evaluate our methodology on multiple architectures, including MobileNet, DenseNet, and GPT-3, deployed in different computing environments. Results demonstrate that our combined approach enhances both estimation accuracy and interpretability, outperforming single-tool assessments and offering a scalable solution for transparent carbon accounting in AI research.

Short Bio:

Elio Masciari is currently an associate professor at the Federico II University of Naples. Previously, he was a senior researcher at the Institute for High Performance Computing and Networks (ICAR-CNR) of the National Research Council of Italy. He has been an advisor for several master's theses at the University of Calabria and at the University Magna Graecia in Catanzaro. He was an advisor for a PhD thesis in computer engineering at the University of Calabria. He has served as a member of the program committee of several international conferences. He served as a reviewer for several scientific journals of international relevance. He is the author of over 140 publications in journals and at both national and international conferences. He also holds "Abilitazione Scientifica Nazionale" for the role of Full Professor.

From Bifurcation to Encryption: Harnessing Nonlinear Chaos for Information Security

Ahmed Gomaa Radwan

Vice President for Research and Dean of Graduate Studies, Nile University, Egypt
agradwan@ieee.org

Mathematics enables data encryption, information secrecy, and multimedia protection. Number theory supports chaos generators and pseudorandom number generators in increasing unpredictability in crucial ways. Using discrete, continuous, and fractional-order systems simplifies signal processing, edge detection, and secure storage of images, audio, and video. When implemented in hardware, these mathematical models provide fast, low-power data encryption and integrate effectively with video encoders for real-time data protection. Nonlinear dynamics and bifurcation theory enhance these techniques by introducing adaptable, model-based security features. Encryption that shifts systems from order to chaos is both flexible and highly sensitive to minor changes. Memristive and fractional-order systems expand the key space and strengthen resistance against analytical attacks. Bifurcation control models enable adjustment of chaotic behavior to optimize synchronization and encryption, supporting sophisticated encryption systems and safeguarding multimedia. This approach combines mathematical theory, nonlinear modeling, and hardware implementation to create an advanced information security framework that offers strong, flexible, and efficient data protection across multiple platforms.

Short Bio:

Prof. Ahmed G. Radwan (SMIEEE, Fellow-AAS) is the Vice-President for Research and Dean of Graduate Studies, Nile University, Egypt. Previously, he was Center Director of NISC, the Nanoelectronics Integrated Systems Center (Nile University), Acting Dean of the School of Engineering & Applied Sciences (Nile University), Director of TCCD center (Cairo University), Counselor (IEEE-NUSB), Postdoc Fellow (KAUST, Saudi Arabia), Visiting Professor (McMaster Univ., Canada). He is the Founder of NILES International Conference https://www.nilesconf.org, and Undergraduate Research Forum (UGRF) https://ugrf.nu.edu.eg/. He has more than 480 indexed publications, +12000 citations, and 56 H-index according to Scopus. He is a Co-inventor of 6 US patents, author/co-author of 13 international books, and 26 book chapters in highly ranked publishers. Prof. Radwan is one of the leading professors in the fractional-order (T.21555) and chaotic circuits tracks worldwide. He is an associate editor in 4 prestigious Scopus-indexed journals. Some of his prestigious Awards: The State Encouragement Award

(2012), The State Excellence Award (2018), Abdul Hameed Shoman Award (2015), Scopus Award in Engineering and Technology (2019), Prof. Tarek Khalil Award for Distinguished Leadership from Nile University (2022), and many more. He was a member of many international/national scientific committees/councils (MC Observer to COST Action CA15225 (COST (European Cooperation in Science and Technology)). He is selected as a member in national applied research council (ASRT-Egypt), and national committee of mathematics (ASRT-Egypt), a Technical Committee member in Nonlinear Circuits & systems (IEEE-CAS), Egyptian mathematical society, and fractional calculus and applications group. He was selected as one of 15-top researchers in national level in all disciplines for the first councils of the Egyptian Young Academy of Sciences (EYAS) and one of 40 experts in the Egyptian Center for the Advancement of Science, Technology and Innovation (ECASTI). He managed funded projects with budgets of over 1M$ and supervised more than 55 (MSc & PhD) students, where 11 received the best thesis from their universities in different research tracks. Last year, he was nominated and participated as Africa Representative in the International Olympiad Committee in Engineering Sciences, Greece 2023, He has been included in the Stanford 2% list for both the single/whole career in the last 5 consecutive years (2019–2024).

Contents

Assessing the Impact of Meteorological and Infrastructure Factors on Internet Performance Using Machine Learning

Amr Emara, Mohamed Ayoub, Haya Osama(✉), Malak Ahmed, Zeyad Khaled, and Noha GamalEl-din Saad

Center for Informatics Science, School of Information Technology and Computer Science, Nile University, Giza, Egypt
{a.abdelhalim2271,m.ayoub2228,h.osama2298,m.ahmed2292, z.khaled2239,ngamal}@nu.edu.eg

Abstract. Internet resilience has become a critical policy concern, as connectivity is increasingly disrupted by both environmental shocks and infrastructural failures. Recent events in Egypt—including severe storms in Alexandria and a major fire at Cairo's Ramses Central exchange—illustrate these dual vulnerabilities. This paper assesses how meteorological and infrastructure factors jointly shape internet performance across Cairo, Alexandria, and Al Buhayrah. We integrate user-observed throughput and latency from Ookla Speedtest, meteorological reanalysis from ERA5-Land, tower infrastructure from OpenCelliD, and night-time lights from VIIRS into a harmonized, grid-based monthly panel. Ensemble classifiers (Random Forest and XGBoost) were trained on discretized download-speed quartiles, achieving accuracies above 95% under spatial–temporal cross-validation. Results reveal paradoxical patterns: Alexandria exhibited dense 4G infrastructure yet high instability, while Cairo achieved stability with sparse towers, highlighting the decisive role of operator practices and redundancy. Operator-level disparities were marked, with Vodafone outperforming competitors, and adverse weather amplified instability by nearly 50% despite only modest reductions in average speed. These findings demonstrate that resilience cannot be explained by tower density alone, but emerges from the interaction of environment, infrastructure, and operator strategies. The study provides novel evidence from an underrepresented regional context and underscores the need for redundancy investments, operator accountability, and climate-aware digital infrastructure planning.

Keywords: Internet resilience · Egypt · Weather impacts · Random Forest · Telecommunications infrastructure

1 Introduction

On 31 May 2025, an unseasonal hailstorm and severe thunderstorms paralyzed Alexandria, flooding roads and triggering widespread power outages [14,27]. Just

A. Awad et al. (Eds.): MEDI 2025, LNCS 16427, pp. 1–17, 2026.
https://doi.org/10.1007/978-3-032-19865-5_1

weeks later, a massive fire at Cairo's Ramses Central exchange disrupted multiple ISPs and degraded connectivity across the country [28]. These back-to-back incidents underscore that in Egypt, internet performance is vulnerable both to environmental shocks and to single-point failures in critical infrastructure (Figs. 1 and 2).

Fig. 1. Storm damage and flooding in Alexandria, Egypt, May 2025. Source: Anadolu Agency [27].

These back-to-back incidents underscore a central point of this paper: in Egypt, internet performance is not only a function of network infrastructure, but also of environmental stressors and single-point vulnerabilities in interconnection and backhaul.

At the same time, Egypt's connectivity landscape is expanding and shifting. Fixed broadband speeds have improved markedly in recent years, with multiple industry reports recognizing Egypt among Africa's fastest for fixed internet [24, 25]. Mobile and fixed adoption continue to rise: ITU and World Bank series show steady growth in internet use and fixed broadband subscriptions since 2019 [21,22]. Yet growth in headline speeds and subscriptions does not equate to resilience. Egypt's strategic position as a dual-sea cable corridor (Mediterranean–Red Sea) concentrates risk at landing stations and terrestrial crossings [23]; regional cable cuts in 2024 and 2025 repeatedly demonstrated how incidents far from end-users can cascade into national slowdowns and rerouting [16–18].

Traditional studies of network quality emphasize infrastructure availability—tower density, technology generation (3G/4G/5G), and backhaul capacity. However, infrastructure alone does not determine observed user experience. Environmental conditions (temperature, wind, sand/dust storms, and cloud cover) and operator practices (traffic engineering, redundancy, interconnection) can

Fig. 2. Massive fire at the Ramses Central exchange in Cairo, July 2025, which disrupted internet and communications services. Source: Ahram Online [28].

reshape latency, throughput, and stability at neighborhood scales. In Egypt's semi-arid climate, the frequency and intensity of sand and dust events, along with episodic coastal storms, have direct implications for critical infrastructure operations [19,20].

This paper contributes an Egypt-focused, multi-source analysis linking measured user performance and meteorology with cellular infrastructure. We integrate Ookla Speedtest Intelligence (QoS), Copernicus ERA5-Land (weather), OpenCelliD (towers), and VIIRS night-time lights into a 5 km monthly grid for three contrasting governorates—Cairo (urban core, diversified infrastructure), Alexandria (coastal metro with unique environmental exposure), and Al Buhayrah (rural, sparser infrastructure). To avoid target leakage, engineered predictors do not use measured speed or latency. We evaluate models under strict spatial–temporal blocking to reduce over-optimism from autocorrelation. Our results provide (i) an empirical decomposition of infrastructure versus environment associations with user-observed performance, (ii) robustness checks across grid sizes and folds, and (iii) operator-level contrasts that are interpreted with appropriate caveats about case-mix and measurement bias.

In doing so, we address an underrepresented geography in the literature and align with national resilience priorities that emphasize climate-aware infrastructure and risk reduction [19]. Rather than claiming causality, we report associations that can guide engineering diagnostics and policy benchmarking for digital resilience in Egypt.

Contributions (extended). This study quantifies how storms/high cloud cover and infrastructure failures affect stability and spatial coverage. We harmonize ERA5-Land, VIIRS night-time lights, OpenCelliD, and GADM [9–12] and analyze drivers using Random Forest and XGBoost with SHAP explanations [6–8]. Methodologically, we emphasize *leakage-safe* label construction, *spatio-temporal blocked* validation, and clear figure explanations. Empirically, we show that shocks amplify *spatial gaps* more than they depress mean speeds, and that infrastructure and power redundancy are crucial for resilience [1,33,34].

The remainder of this paper is structured as follows. Section 2 reviews related work on environmental impacts, infrastructure determinants, and measurement approaches to internet performance. Section 3 presents the study area, datasets, and preprocessing pipeline, highlighting how multiple sources were harmonized into a unified panel. Section 4 details the modeling framework, including feature engineering, evaluation design, and interpretability methods. Section 5 reports the main empirical findings on stability classification, regional disparities, operator-level reliability, and weather sensitivity. Section 6 discusses these results in light of prior literature, policy relevance, and methodological limitations. Section 7 concludes with implications for resilience planning and future research directions.

2 Related Work

Internet stability has been examined from multiple disciplinary perspectives, but consensus emerges around one point: disruptions typically arise from the interaction of several conditions rather than from a single cause. Weather variability, infrastructure characteristics, and operator practices jointly shape the quality of user experience. This section reviews four strands of the literature most relevant to our study.

A. Weather and Internet Stability. Extreme weather events have been repeatedly linked to degraded internet performance. Gupta et al. [1], for example, analyzed Hurricane Harvey and Winter Storm Uri in the United States and found that storms not only reduced throughput, but also amplified pre-existing socioeconomic disparities. Communities with fewer redundancies or weaker infrastructure were disproportionately affected, illustrating how weather events expose hidden vulnerabilities in digital systems. Similar observations appear in the engineering literature, where environmental conditions such as rain, wind, and cloud cover alter mobile signal propagation and reliability [3]. Mechanism-level work also links hurricanes to outage risks [35]. These studies motivate the need to incorporate meteorological variability into resilience assessments.

B. Machine Learning and Resilience Modeling. Beyond descriptive analyses, machine learning has been increasingly applied to model resilience under stress. Li and Mostafavi [5] proposed predictive frameworks that identify structural weaknesses across interdependent infrastructure systems, demonstrating the potential of data-driven models to anticipate failures rather than simply catalog past ones. This perspective is directly relevant to telecommunications, where networks are embedded in larger coupled systems—energy, transport, and emergency response—so that instability in one domain can propagate into another.

C. Telecommunications Infrastructure and Operator Practices. Another body of work emphasizes the role of physical telecommunications infrastructure. Studies show that tower density, technology mix (2G/3G/4G/5G), and network topology influence performance, but the relationship is rarely linear. In some metropolitan contexts, dense deployments correlate with congestion and instability, while in others, lower densities outperform expectations due to stronger engineering practices or smarter load management. Operator-level strategies such as redundancy investment, backhaul provisioning, and traffic engineering are thus recognized as key determinants of stability [4].

D. Measuring Internet Performance. The accuracy of performance measurement itself is also a concern. Crowdsourced platforms such as Ookla Speedtest are widely adopted and provide global coverage, making them attractive for large-scale research. However, they are subject to sampling bias (e.g., user demographics, device heterogeneity, geographic distribution), and results can vary across platforms or server infrastructures. Characterizations of the Ookla ecosystem highlight why multi-platform fusion and explicit bias correction are important to generalize conclusions [4,32]. This underscores the importance of triangulating multiple data sources and carefully interpreting crowdsourced metrics.

E. Research Gaps and Contribution. Collectively, prior work demonstrates that internet resilience is determined by the interplay of weather, infrastructure, and operator practices. Yet important gaps remain. Most existing studies are concentrated in North America and Europe, while regions such as the Middle East and North Africa remain underrepresented. Our study addresses this by focusing on Egypt and combining user-observed performance data with meteorological reanalysis and tower infrastructure in a harmonized, grid-based dataset. By applying ensemble machine learning under strict spatial–temporal validation, we provide an empirical assessment of how weather and infrastructure jointly shape internet stability in a highly diverse regional context.

F. Causal Identification in Networking Contexts. To probe causal pathways around shocks, modern Difference-in-Differences and event-study estimators address staggered timing and heterogeneous effects [29–31]. These designs guide our prospective causal evaluation plan and inform robustness checks (pre-trends, placebo windows).

3 Methodology

3.1 Study Area

Three Egyptian governorates—Cairo (Al Qahirah), Alexandria (Al Iskandariyah), and Al Buhayrah—were purposively selected to capture heterogeneity in socio-economic and infrastructural contexts. Cairo is the capital and economic hub; Alexandria is a coastal, high-density metro with unique environmental challenges; Al Buhayrah is largely rural with relatively sparse infrastructure.

3.2 Data Sources

We combined four primary datasets: night-time light emissions, internet service quality data, weather reanalysis, and cellular tower infrastructure.

Nightlight Data NASA **VIIRS VNP46A1** ($\sim$500 m). Radiance values (nW/cm^2/sr) were filtered to retain only positive values, clipped to governorate boundaries, and used as proxies for urbanization.

Internet Performance Data Ookla Speedtest Intelligence. Monthly parquet files include: average download/upload (`avg_d_kbps`, `avg_u_kbps`), latency (`avg_lat_ms`, `avg_lat_down_ms`, `avg_lat_up_ms`), and device/test counts.

Weather Data Copernicus ERA5-Land. Variables used: near-surface temperature (`t2m`), wind components (`u10`, `v10`), total cloud cover (`tcc`), and total precipitation (`tp`, used in extended experiments).

Cellular Infrastructure Data OpenCelliD (MCC = 602) provides tower coordinates, technology (2G, 3G, 4G, LTE), and operator codes (Vodafone, Etisalat, Orange, WE). Derived features include nearest tower distance, technology-specific densities (per 10 km^2), and operator-specific densities.

3.3 Data Preprocessing

All datasets were harmonized into **WGS84 (EPSG:4326)**. Governorate boundaries were sourced from GADM.

- **Spatial integration:** VIIRS pixels matched to Ookla tiles using a KD-tree; ERA5 variables interpolated to the same grid.
- **Grid aggregation:** $0.05° \times 0.05°$ ($\sim$5 km) grid, monthly.
- **Cleaning:** Negative radiance removed; retained cells with $\geq$5 Ookla tests and $\geq$10 valid VIIRS pixels; excluded towerless cells >100 km; missing values imputed with means.
- **Normalization:** Continuous features standardized using z-scores.

Cross-Platform Harmonization and Bias Correction

We map observations to a month × 5 km-cell × operator structure to balance spatial resolution and sample sufficiency. Platform-specific fields are standardized (units, technology tags), and duplicates are resolved by device/time. To mitigate sampling bias (e.g., over-representation of particular devices or urban corridors), we compute inverse-propensity weights $w_i = 1/\hat{\pi}(x_i)$ where $\hat{\pi}$ models observation probability from covariates such as population density, land-use/road proximity, tower density, operator share, and time-of-day; we then post-stratify to match public marginals (Internet-user penetration, fixed-broadband adoption) [21,22]. Sensitivity analyses (trimmed weights; alternate strata) ensure stability. Contextual shocks used for interpretation include Alexandria's 2025 storms and the 2024 submarine cable incidents captured by independent telemetry [13,14,17,18,27].

3.4 Feature Engineering

Several features were engineered to capture infrastructure and performance conditions:

- **Coverage Gap:** Indicator equal to 1 if tower density < median for the region.
- **Stability:** Indicator equal to 1 if latency <100 ms and operator density above the median.
- **Technology-Specific Density:** (2G, 3G, 4G, 5G) towers per 10 km^2.
- **Operator Densities:** Grouped by operator (Vodafone, Etisalat, Orange, WE).

A *storm flag* was set to 1 when total cloud cover >0.7 or wind magnitude $\sqrt{u10^2 + v10^2} > 8\,\text{m/s}$. The quartile-based target was computed from `avg_d_kbps` on training folds to avoid leakage; labels were *Low, Mid, Mid-High, High*, consistent with resilience literature [1,5].

3.5 Exploratory Data Analysis (EDA)

Exploratory analysis highlighted several patterns:

- **Tower Influence:** Stability increased with 4G density; instability rose with greater tower distance.
- **Operator Disparities:** Vodafone exhibited ~6% gap rate, while Etisalat exceeded 25%.
- **Regional Hotspots:** Alexandria showed high gaps despite dense 4G deployments; Cairo remained relatively stable despite sparse infrastructure, likely due to operator diversity.
- **Weather Sensitivity:** Gap rates rose from ~12% to ~18% during storm or high-cloud conditions.

Weather variables (`t2m`, `u10`, `v10`, `tcc`) were binned into quartiles for comparison, and a Pearson correlation matrix was computed on standardized features (Fig. 3), consistent with storm-effects literature [1–3]. Operator disparities aligned with prior studies of platform-based performance [4]. In Fig. 3, stronger winds and higher cloud cover show clear positive correlations with coverage gaps, meaning poor weather is linked to more instability. On the other hand, higher 4G and operator densities display negative correlations with gaps, indicating that better infrastructure helps maintain stable connectivity.

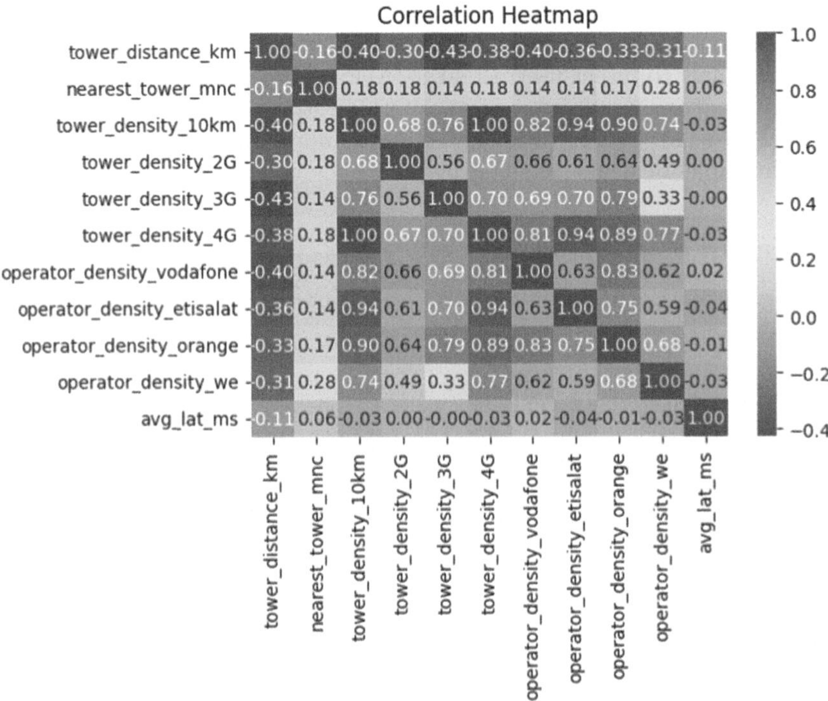

Fig. 3. Pearson correlation matrix (r) among **standardized** weather variables—**2 m air temperature (t2m)**, **10 m wind components (u10, v10)**, and **total cloud cover (tcc)**—**tower densities** (by technology/operator where applicable), and the **coverage-gap indicator**. Warmer colors denote positive correlations; cooler colors denote negative.

3.6 Model Framework

We framed prediction as a supervised **machine learning** classification task, with `avg_d_kbps` discretized into quartiles (*Low, Mid, Mid-High, High*).

Target Variable Q1 = Low, Q2 = Mid, Q3 = Mid-High, Q4 = High.

1. **Weather:** `t2m`, `u10`, `v10`, `tcc`
2. **Infrastructure:** `tower_distance_km`, `tower_density_2G/3G/4G/5G`
3. **Coverage indicators:** engineered binary proxies such as `coverage_gap` and `stability`

Model Classes

- **Random Forest (RF):** 500 trees, balanced class weights. Accuracy ≈97%, Macro F1 = 0.97.
- **XGBoost:** Gradient-boosted trees. Accuracy ≈96%, Macro F1 = 0.96.

Both ensemble methods are widely used in resilience modeling [5–7]. Errors were mostly adjacent-quartile, reflecting robustness.

Training and Evaluation Protocol

- **Split:** 80/20 stratified train–test.
- **Cross-validation:** 5-fold, grouped by (Governorate, Month) to reduce spatial–temporal leakage.
- **Metrics:** Accuracy, macro F1, ROC-AUC.
- **Outputs:** Quartile probabilities for each observation.

3.7 Analytical Pipeline

The analysis proceeded in seven steps as shown in Fig. 4:

1. Data integration (VIIRS + Ookla + ERA5 + OpenCelliD)
2. Preprocessing (harmonization, cleaning, grid aggregation)
3. Feature engineering (coverage gap, stability, tower/technology/operator densities)
4. Exploratory analysis (regional disparities, operator-level comparisons, weather sensitivity)
5. Model training (RF and XGBoost on quartile targets)
6. Evaluation (accuracy, F1, ROC-AUC, confusion matrices)
7. Interpretation (regional disparities, operator reliability, weather effects)

Models and metadata (feature lists, quartile cut-points) were serialized. A regression sensitivity step confirmed consistent drivers across target formulations [1,5]. Data integration used ERA5-Land [9], VIIRS [10], OpenCelliD [11], and GADM [12].

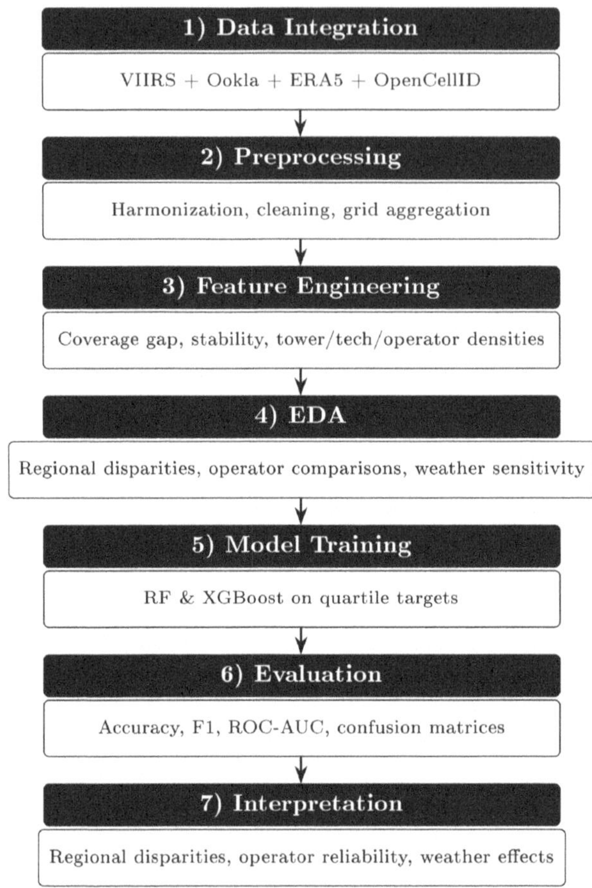

Fig. 4. Analytical pipeline (black-header style).

3.8 Final Dataset

The final dataset is a month-by-month, grid-based panel linking:

- **Nightlights:** mean radiance, standard deviation, pixel count
- **Internet performance:** download/upload speeds, latency, device/test counts
- **Weather:** temperature, wind, cloud cover, precipitation
- **Cell towers:** nearest distance, densities by technology/operator
- **Engineered indicators:** coverage gap, stability

4 Results

This section presents the empirical results, linking model outputs and exploratory analysis back to the research problem introduced in Sect. 1. Recall that our study was motivated by two recent disruptions in Egypt: severe storms in Alexandria and a fire at Cairo's Ramses Central exchange (Figs. 1 and 2). These events illustrate how internet performance is vulnerable to both environmental stressors and infrastructural shocks. The results reported here quantify such vulnerabilities across three governorates using integrated data and machine learning models.

4.1 Stability Classification

The quartile-based classification task provided an interpretable framework to characterize internet stability. Random Forest achieved an overall accuracy of 97% (macro F1 = 0.97), while XGBoost achieved 96% (macro F1 = 0.96). Misclassifications were concentrated in adjacent quartiles, suggesting robustness rather than random error. Tables 1 and 2 summarize per-class metrics and confusion patterns. Accuracy remained high under grouped spatial–temporal cross-validation, confirming that results were not driven solely by autocorrelation.

Table 1. Classification report and accuracy (overall accuracy: 93.9%).

Class	Precision	Recall	F1-Score	Support
Low	0.98	0.95	0.96	632
Mid	0.72	0.87	0.79	94
Accuracy	0.94			726
Macro Avg	0.85	0.91	0.88	726
Weighted Avg	0.95	0.94	0.94	726

Table 2. Confusion matrix of the classifier.

	Predicted Low	Predicted Mid
Actual Low	600	32
Actual Mid	12	82

4.2 Regional Disparities and Hotspots

The analysis revealed marked regional disparities. Alexandria, despite exhibiting one of the highest 4G tower densities (84 towers per 10 km^2), showed a coverage gap rate of 26.4%. In contrast, Cairo recorded a much lower gap rate of 6.6% despite sparse tower density (0.37 towers per 10 km^2). Al Buhayrah, the

Table 3. Representative governorates: coverage gaps vs. 4G density (per 10 km^2).

Governorate	4G Density	Coverage Gap Rate
Alexandria	84.35	0.264
Al Buhayrah	46.87	0.111
Cairo	0.37	0.066

rural governorate, fell in between at 11.1%. Table 3 summarizes these paradoxical results.

These findings echo the dual vulnerability observed in Sect. 1: Alexandria is exposed to both extreme weather (storms and flooding) and congested infrastructure, while Cairo's stability depends less on density and more on operator diversity and redundancy. The paradox highlights that tower counts alone are insufficient indicators of resilience.

4.3 Operator-Level Reliability

Disaggregating by operator revealed significant disparities. Vodafone exhibited the lowest gap rates (~6%), while Etisalat exceeded 25%. Orange and WE fell in between. Figure 5 illustrates operator-level coverage gaps and stability. These results suggest that engineering practices, backhaul investments, and redundancy strategies differ substantially across providers, consistent with the Ramses Central fire case: a localized failure disproportionately disrupted some networks more than others.

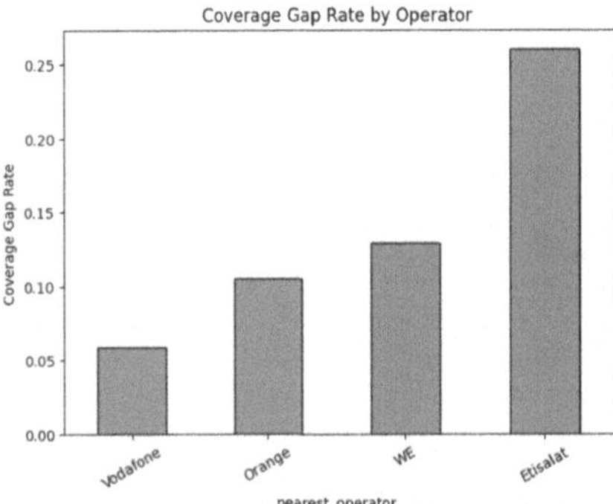

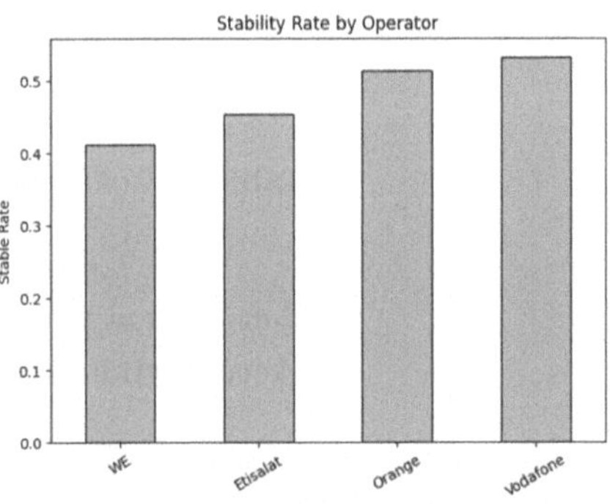

Fig. 5. Operator-level reliability: (a) Coverage gap rate by operator; (b) Stability rate by operator.

4.4 Weather Sensitivity of Stability

Adverse weather was consistently associated with elevated instability. During storm or high-cloud months, average download speed fell modestly (from 27.1 to 26.2 Mbps), but gap rates increased sharply (from 11.9% to 17.7%), representing a ~50% relative increase. Figure 6 depicts these associations. Bad weather months in Fig. 6 are defined as those with total cloud cover (*tcc*) greater than 0.7 or wind magnitude $\sqrt{u10^2 + v10^2}$ exceeding 8 m/s. Under these conditions, the mean download speed is 26.2 Mbps and the coverage-gap rate is 17.7%, compared to 27.1 Mbps and 11.9% during normal weather.

This pattern mirrors the Alexandria storm case (Fig. 1), where service disruption was driven less by absolute throughput decline and more by spatial gaps and instability. It also illustrates how environmental stress amplifies existing vulnerabilities, consistent with findings from the U.S. context [1].

4.5 Summary of Findings

The empirical results support three main conclusions. First, nonlinear models reliably captured the joint influence of infrastructure and environment, achieving accuracies above 95%. Second, tower density alone does not guarantee stability: paradoxical results in Cairo and Alexandria underscore the role of operator practices and redundancy. Third, weather disproportionately exacerbates instability, elevating gap rates even when average throughput remains relatively stable. Together, these findings provide quantitative evidence for the broader research problem: internet resilience in Egypt is shaped by the interaction of environmental shocks and infrastructural vulnerabilities, echoing the recent real-world disruptions highlighted in the Introduction.

5 Discussion

The findings of this study highlight how environmental conditions, infrastructure density, and operator practices jointly shape internet stability in Egypt. In doing so, they resonate with prior international research while extending the analysis to an underrepresented regional context.

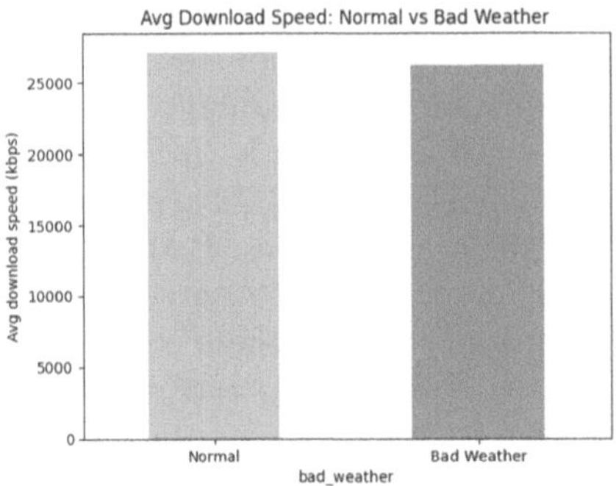

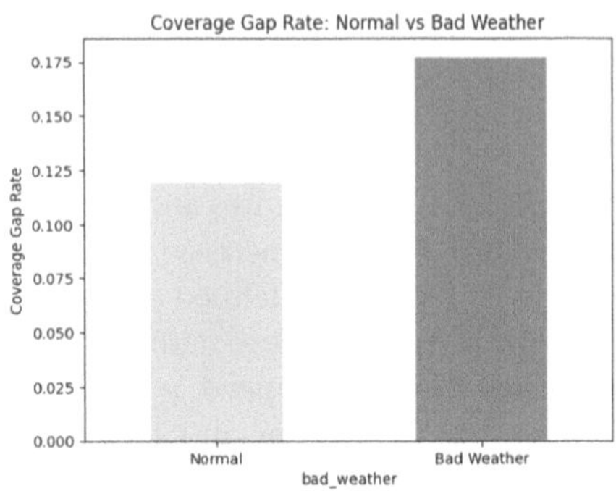

Fig. 6. Weather sensitivity of stability. (a) **Average download speed** and (b) **coverage-gap rate** under **bad weather**, defined as **total cloud cover** > 0.7 or **wind magnitude** $\sqrt{u10^2 + v10^2} > 8\,\mathbf{m/s}$ at the cell-month level. Under bad weather, **speed decreases from 27.1 to 26.2 Mbps**, while the **gap rate rises from 11.9% to 17.7%**, indicating instability amplification even when mean throughput changes are modest.

First, the strong performance of ensemble classifiers such as Random Forest and XGBoost demonstrates the utility of machine learning for resilience assessment. With accuracies above 95%, these models reliably distinguished stability quartiles and captured non-linear associations. This supports Li and Mostafavi's [5] argument that data-driven approaches are well-suited to identifying vulnerabilities across interconnected systems. In practice, such models can provide an evidence base for resilience monitoring in real-world conditions.

Second, the regional paradox observed in our results—Alexandria exhibiting high tower density but poor stability, while Cairo achieved greater stability despite sparse towers—underscores that the quantity of infrastructure alone is not decisive. Prior studies on telecommunications infrastructure have noted similar contradictions, where dense deployments suffer from congestion or lack of redundancy, while lower-density regions perform better due to stronger engineering and load management [4]. Our findings confirm this principle in the Egyptian setting, linking back to the May 2025 Alexandria storm (Fig. 1), where environmental stress exposed infrastructural weaknesses in a high-density metropolitan area.

Third, operator-level disparities were striking. Vodafone consistently exhibited the lowest gap rates, while Etisalat and WE lagged behind. These disparities echo prior work emphasizing operator practices and engineering quality over tower counts [3]. The July 2025 fire at Cairo's Ramses Central exchange (Fig. 2) illustrated this inequity: although the disruption was geographically localized, its impact varied markedly across operators depending on redundancy and interconnection strategies. For users, this translates into sharp inequities in service quality, even within the same neighborhood.

Finally, weather sensitivity emerged as a consistent driver of instability. While average download speeds declined only modestly during storms, coverage-gap rates rose by nearly 50%. Gupta et al. [1] reported similar amplification effects in the United States, where extreme weather widened existing disparities. Our results confirm that this dynamic also applies to Egypt: environmental stressors magnify underlying vulnerabilities, particularly in regions where infrastructure is fragile or overcrowded.

Taken together, these insights advance the conversation on internet resilience. Much of the existing literature has focused on North America and Europe, often isolating weather, infrastructure, or data quality [2]. By contrast, this study integrates all three dimensions in the Egyptian context, providing a case where coastal and urban regions face distinct but interconnected risks. Rather than framing resilience as an issue of simply adding towers, our findings highlight the importance of system-level strategies: operator accountability, redundancy investments, and climate-aware network design [32–34].

6 Conclusion

This study examined internet stability across Cairo, Alexandria, and Al Buhayrah using an integrated dataset of user-observed performance, meteorological reanalysis, tower infrastructure, and night-time lights. By applying ensemble machine learning under strict spatial–temporal validation, we demonstrated that internet stability is not determined by tower density alone but emerges from the interplay of infrastructure distribution, operator practices, and environmental variability.

Random Forest models achieved high predictive performance, providing a robust framework for detecting patterns of instability and identifying regional hotspots. The analysis revealed paradoxical outcomes (dense but unstable Alexandria vs. sparse but stable Cairo), operator-level disparities (Vodafone vs. Etisalat/WE), and heightened instability during adverse weather. These findings align with recent real-world events in Egypt—the Alexandria storm and the Ramses Central fire—underscoring the dual vulnerabilities posed by environmental stressors and infrastructural shocks.

Policy implications are clear: resilience planning must prioritize redundancy in backhaul and interconnection, enforce operator accountability through regulatory benchmarking, and integrate climate-aware risk assessments into digital infrastructure design. Future research should extend this approach to other underrepresented regions, incorporate additional performance platforms to mitigate sampling bias, and test causal pathways using quasi-experimental designs (event-study/Difference-in-Differences) [29–31]. Collectively, these steps will support equitable and reliable connectivity across Egypt and beyond.

References

1. Gupta, Y., Liu, Z., Mostafavi, A.: Examining spatial and socioeconomic disparities in internet resilience during extreme weather events: a case study of Hurricane Harvey and Winter Storm Uri. Urban Inform.**3**(19) (2024). https://doi.org/10.1007/s44212-024-00051-x

2. Ahmed, O.S., Sadek, M.A.: Meteorological indices approach for prediction of thunderstorm probability at two coastal sites in Egypt. Atmos. Clim. Sci. **5**, 219–227 (2015). https://doi.org/10.4236/acs.2015.53016
3. Osahenvemwen, O.A., Omatahunde, B.E.: Impacts of weather and environmental conditions on mobile communication signals. J. Adv. Sci. Eng. **1**(1), 33–38 (2018). https://doi.org/10.37121/jase.v1i1.8
4. Zhang, Z., Shen, J., Mok, R.K.P.: Empirical characterization of Ookla's speed test platform: analyzing server deployment, policy impact, and user coverage. arXiv preprint arXiv:2301.01234 (2023)
5. Li, X., Mostafavi, A.: Machine learning approach for disaster risk and resilience assessment in coupled human infrastructure systems performance. npj Nat. Hazard. **2**(56) (2025). https://doi.org/10.1038/s44304-025-00104-4
6. Breiman, L.: Random forests. Mach. Learn. **45**(1), 5–32 (2001)
7. Chen, T., Guestrin, C.: XGBoost: a scalable tree boosting system. In: Proceedings of the 22nd ACM SIGKDD International Conference on Knowledge Discovery and Data Mining, pp. 785–794 (2016). https://doi.org/10.1145/2939672.2939785
8. Lundberg, S.M., Lee, S.-I.: A unified approach to interpreting model predictions. In: Advances in Neural Information Processing Systems (NeurIPS), pp. 4765–4774 (2017)
9. Muñoz-Sabater, J., Dutra, M., et al.: ERA5-Land: a state-of-the-art global reanalysis dataset for land applications. Copernicus Climate Change Service (C3S) (2021). https://doi.org/10.24381/cds.e2161bac
10. Elvidge, C.D., Baugh, K.E., et al.: VIIRS night-time lights. Int. J. Remote Sens. **38**(21), 5860–5879 (2017)
11. OpenCelliD: Open and crowdsourced cellular tower location data. https://www.opencellid.org. Accessed 10 Oct 2025
12. GADM: Database of Global Administrative Areas. https://gadm.org. Accessed 10 Oct 2025
13. Daily News Egypt: Severe storms paralyze Alexandria with hail, flash floods, and power outages, May 2025. https://www.dailynewsegypt.com/2025/05/31/severe-storms-paralyze-alexandria-with-hail-flash-floods-and-power-outages/. Accessed 10 Oct 2025
14. Phys.org: Sudden hailstorm lashes Egypt's Alexandria, June 2025. https://phys.org/news/2025-06-sudden-hailstorm-lashes-egypt-alexandria.html. Accessed 10 Oct 2025
15. Internet Society: Egypt Internet Outage: Another Example of the Need to Spread Your Risk, July 2025. https://pulse.internetsociety.org/blog/egypt-internet-outage-another-example-of-the-need-to-spread-your-risk. Accessed 10 Oct 2025
16. Internet Society: 2024 East Africa Submarine Cable Outage Report, July 2024. https://www.internetsociety.org/resources/doc/2024/2024-east-africa-submarine-cable-outage-report/. Accessed 10 Oct 2025
17. Cloudflare Radar: Undersea cable failures cause Internet disruptions across Africa, 14 Mar 2024. https://blog.cloudflare.com/undersea-cable-failures-cause-internet-disruptions-across-africa-march-14-2024/. Accessed 10 Oct 2025
18. Cloudflare Radar: East African Internet connectivity again impacted by submarine cable cuts, 12 May 2024. https://blog.cloudflare.com/east-african-internet-connectivity-again-impacted-by-submarine-cable-cuts/. Accessed 10 Oct 2025
19. OECD: OECD Green Growth Policy Review of Egypt 2024, July 2024. https://www.oecd.org/content/dam/oecd/en/publications/reports/2024/07/oecd-green-growth-policy-review-of-egypt-2024_fd5cddac/b9096cec-en.pdf. Accessed 10 Oct 2025

20. Health Policy Watch/World Meteorological Organization: Sand and dust storms taking a rising toll on health and economies, (July 2025. https://healthpolicy-watch.news/sand-and-dust-storms-are-taking-a-rising-toll-on-health-and-economies-world-metereological-organization/. Accessed 10 Oct 2025
21. World Bank/ITU: Individuals using the Internet (% of population) – Egypt (2023). https://data.worldbank.org/indicator/IT.NET.USER.ZS?locations=EG. Accessed 10 Oct 2025
22. World Bank (WDI/ITU): Fixed broadband subscriptions (per 100 people) – Egypt. https://data.worldbank.org/indicator/IT.NET.BBND.P2?locations=EG. Accessed 10 Oct 2025
23. Submarine Networks: Egypt – Submarine Cable Landing Stations (2025). https://www.submarinenetworks.com/en/stations/africa/egypt. Accessed 10 Oct 2025
24. SAMENA Council: Egypt recognized for fastest fixed internet in Africa (2024) by Ookla, March 2025. https://www.samenacouncil.org/samena_daily_news?news=104790. Accessed 10 Oct 2025
25. Amwal Al Ghad: Egypt ranks 1st in Africa for ADSL internet speed – Ookla report, March 2025. https://en.amwalalghad.com/egypt-ranks-1st-in-africa-for-adsl-internet-speed-ookla-report/. Accessed 10 Oct 2025
26. DataReportal: Digital 2025: Egypt, March 2025. https://datareportal.com/reports/digital-2025-egypt. Accessed 10 Oct 2025
27. Anadolu Agency: Severe storm batters Egypt's Alexandria, state of emergency declared, May 2025. https://www.aa.com.tr/en/middle-east/severe-storm-batters-egypt-s-alexandria-state-of-emergency-declared/3585284. Accessed 10 Oct 2025
28. Ahram Online: Massive fire at the Ramses Central exchange disrupts internet and communications in Cairo, July 2025. https://english.ahram.org.eg/NewsContent/50/1201/549327/AlAhram-Weekly/Egypt/Massive-fire-at-the-Ramses-Central.aspx. Accessed 10 Oct 2025
29. Callaway, B., Sant'Anna, P.H.C.: Difference-in-differences with multiple time periods. J. Econometrics **225**(2), 200–230 (2021). https://doi.org/10.1016/j.jeconom.2020.12.001
30. Sun, L., Abraham, S.: Estimating dynamic treatment effects in event studies with heterogeneous treatment effects. J. Econometrics **225**(2), 175–199 (2021). https://doi.org/10.1016/j.jeconom.2020.09.006
31. de Chaisemartin, C., D'Haultfœuille, X.: Two-way fixed effects estimators with heterogeneous treatment effects. Am. Econ. Rev. **110**(9), 2964–2996 (2020). https://doi.org/10.1257/aer.20181169
32. Zhang, Z., Shen, J., Mok, R.K.P.: Empirical characterization of Ookla's Speedtest platform: server deployment, policy impact, and user coverage. CAIDA Technical Report (2024). https://www.caida.org/catalog/papers/2024_empirical_characterization_ooklas_speed_test/empirical_characterization_ooklas_speed_test.pdf. Accessed 10 Oct 2025
33. International Telecommunication Union (ITU): Measuring Digital Development: Facts and Figures 2024 (2024). https://www.itu.int/itu-d/reports/statistics/facts-figures-2024/. Accessed 10 Oct 2025
34. Ofcom: Mobile RAN Power Resilience — Technical Report & CFI Update, February 2025. https://www.ofcom.org.uk/internet-based-services/network-security/resilience-guidance. Accessed 10 Oct 2025
35. Du, A., Li, Z., et al.: Data-driven telecommunication outage prediction during hurricane events. ASCE-ASME J. Risk Uncertainty Eng. Syst. Part A **10**(3) (2024). https://doi.org/10.1061/AJRUA6.RUENG-1285

Non-intrusive Fall Detection Using Pose Estimation and Polynomial Temporal Modeling

Rawan Nabil Ammar[1](✉), Rana Hossam Elden[2], and Walid Al-Atabany[1,2]

[1] Center for Information Science, School of Information Technology and Computer Science, Nile University, Sheikh Zayed City, Egypt
{R.Ammar,w.al-atabany}@nu.edu.eg

[2] Biomedical Engineering Department, Faculty of Engineering, Helwan University, Helwan, Egypt
ranahossamelden@h-eng.helwan.edu.eg

Abstract. Falls remain a leading health risk among the elderly, demanding accurate and unobtrusive detection technologies that perform reliably in real-world conditions. This study introduces a vision-based fall detection framework that integrates real-time pose estimation with polynomial temporal modeling of body ratio dynamics. The system employs YOLOv8n-pose to track skeletal keypoints from video streams, then derives body height-to-width ratios across frames. These temporal sequences are transformed using sixth-degree polynomial fitting, yielding compact feature representations of motion patterns. A fine-tuned k-Nearest Neighbors (KNN, k = 10) classifier has been used and reached an accuracy of 97.4%, alongside 100% specificity and 94.74% sensitivity. The effectiveness of the framework was confirmed using the ROSE Lab dataset, revealing significant speed, strength, and flexibility across a variety of settings. This approach offers a scalable, non-intrusive, and privacy-conscious solution for real-time fall detection in healthcare and assisted living environments.

Keywords: Fall Detection · Pose Estimation · Elderly Monitoring · Video Analysis · Body Ratio

1 Introduction

As the global population ages at an accelerating pace, addressing the health and safety concerns of older adults has become a major public health priority. By 2070, the number of individuals aged 65 and above is projected to surpass those under 18, signaling a significant demographic transition that will place increasing demands on healthcare systems worldwide [1, 2]. Among the most critical concerns in this population is the high incidence of falls, which represent the second leading cause of unintentional injury-related deaths among older adults globally [3]. Falls often result in severe consequences, including fractures, traumatic brain injuries, and prolonged disabilities that can lead to long-term care needs and increased financial strain on both individuals and health systems [4, 5]. Furthermore, the risk of serious complications such as hypothermia and pressure

A. Awad et al. (Eds.): MEDI 2025, LNCS 16427, pp. 18–32, 2026.
https://doi.org/10.1007/978-3-032-19865-5_2

ulcers increases significantly when medical attention is delayed, which is common in cases where individuals live alone [6]. These challenges underscore the urgent need for effective and timely fall detection systems capable of operating in both emergency and preventative care contexts.

Fall detection technologies are typically categorized into wearable devices, static sensors, and camera-based systems. Wearables, using inertial sensors like accelerometers and gyroscopes, support real-time monitoring but often face low user compliance [7, 8]. Static sensor systems offer reliable detection in controlled environments but are constrained by high installation costs and limited coverage [9].

To overcome these limitations, vision-based fall detection systems offer a non-intrusive alternative that leverages existing camera infrastructure to monitor posture and movement without requiring user compliance. Advances such as edge computing and on-device processing have enhanced privacy and reduced data transmission [10]. However, these systems still face challenges related to lighting variability, occlusions, and environmental clutter [11].

Numerous studies have explored fall detection across these technological domains. In wearable-based systems, Sharma et al. proposed an IoT-enabled framework using accelerometers and a long short-term memory (LSTM) model, achieving 95.87% accuracy [12]. However, its dependence on reliable wireless communication and limited motion-sensing scope reduced generalizability. Alfayez and Khan improved performance by integrating secure data transmission and advanced modeling, reaching 97.4% accuracy but at the cost of increased system complexity [13]. Mauldin et al. developed a smartwatch-based deep learning system that achieved 98.4% accuracy, though it was limited by battery life and susceptibility to false positives from non-fall rapid movements [14]. Sarowar et al. introduced a comprehensive wearable solution combining fall detection with heart rate and GPS tracking, achieving 97.6% accuracy, but compliance and power-related issues persisted [15].

In parallel, machine learning models have been employed to enhance classification accuracy. Wu et al. designed a hybrid deep learning model that fused convolutional and recurrent layers, reaching 99.79% accuracy [16]. However, the use of the class-imbalanced SisFall dataset raised concerns about overfitting and real-world applicability. Rashid et al. performed a comparative analysis of traditional classifiers, identifying Support Vector Machines (SVM) as the best-performing model with 97.2% accuracy [17]. Despite strong performance, traditional classifiers often lack the capability to model complex human motion patterns. To address this, Dutt et al. proposed a hybrid convolutional-recurrent neural network that improved detection reliability and reduced false positives, though the model's computational intensity hindered its deployment on low-resource devices [18].

Camera-based systems have emerged as a promising non-contact alternative. Jiao et al. developed a multimodal system combining pose estimation from video with audio cues, improving detection sensitivity from 81.67% to 97.5% [19]. However, reliance on environmental sound and high processing requirements limited real-world deployment. Wang et al. optimized a lightweight version of the YOLOv5 model to reduce inference time and memory footprint while maintaining detection accuracy [20]. Almukadi et al. achieved 99.68% accuracy using feature fusion across multiple vision networks, though their system raised significant privacy concerns and required substantial processing resources for continuous video surveillance [21].

Similar to fall detection, computational models have been applied successfully in other healthcare domains, such as neurodegenerative disease detection using linear and non-linear analysis [22, 23].

These developments reflect significant progress in detection technologies but also reveal persistent challenges in achieving a balance between accuracy, real-time performance, user compliance, privacy, and computational efficiency. To provide a comparative overview of these systems, a heat map in Fig. 1 is presented to evaluate and visualize performance across five key criteria: accuracy, scalability, user compliance, energy efficiency, and privacy protection that summarized in Table 1. These dimensions were selected based on both technical performance and practical deployment factors. Accuracy refers to the correct classification of fall and non-fall events, typically derived from reported results. Scalability considers the system's adaptability to various environments and deployment contexts. User compliance evaluates how easily the system can be adopted and used consistently by older adults. Energy efficiency reflects computational and power requirements, particularly for wearable or embedded systems. Privacy protection assesses the degree to which user data is exposed or safeguarded during monitoring.

In summary, while fall detection systems have achieved impressive accuracy through various modalities, they often face trade-offs among scalability, energy efficiency, user compliance, and privacy. Wearable systems require consistent user participation and regular maintenance. Static systems, though accurate, lack portability and are costly to install. Vision-based systems offer convenience and real-time capabilities but raise issues related to environmental variability and surveillance ethics. Multimodal systems provide strong performance but remain complex and resource intensive. These limitations highlight the need for a balanced fall detection approach that offers high accuracy while ensuring practical deployment across different environments.

To address these challenges, this study proposes a real-time fall detection framework that integrates pose estimation with temporal modeling of body ratio dynamics. The system offers an accurate and efficient solution for continuous monitoring without relying on wearable devices or extensive video storage, promoting safety, privacy, and independence for older adults across diverse real-world settings based on the "You Only Look Once" (YOLO) architecture.

2 Materials and Methods

Figure 2 illustrates the overall workflow of the proposed two-stage fall detection system. The pipeline begins with live or recorded video streams, which are segmented into one-second clips for analysis. YOLOv8 is then used for human detection and posture estimation. From the detected poses, body ratios are calculated across frames to form a temporal sequence. Polynomial fitting is applied to this sequence, producing coefficients that describe motion patterns. These coefficients are subsequently used for final fall detection classification.

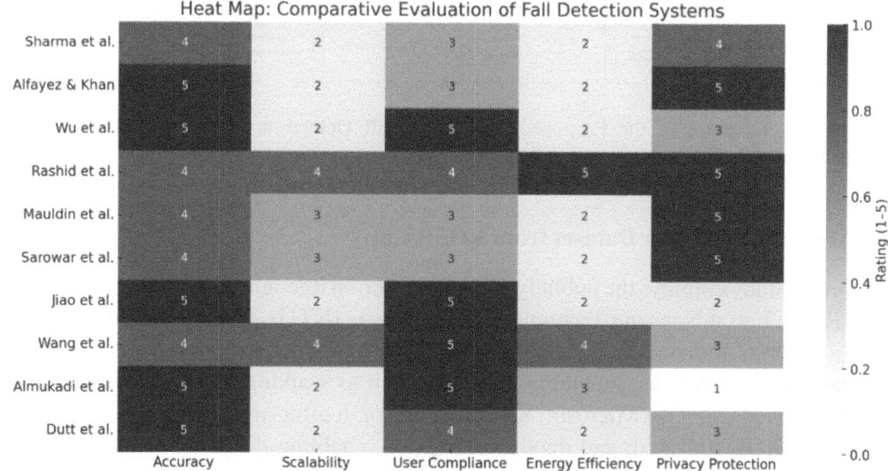

Fig. 1. Comparative heat map evaluating fall detection systems based on five key criteria: accuracy, scalability, user compliance, energy efficiency, and privacy protection. Ratings are on a 1–5 scale, where higher values indicate better performance. The comparison highlights trade-offs between system complexity, usability, and technical effectiveness.

Table 1. Evaluation Criteria for Comparative Analysis of Fall Detection Systems

Parameter	Definition	Evaluation Basis
Accuracy	Ability to correctly detect falls vs. non-falls (true positives and true negatives)	Based on reported performance metrics in the original studies (e.g., classification accuracy, F1-score)
Scalability	Ease of deploying the system across different environments and populations	Considered hardware/software dependencies, installation complexity, and infrastructure requirements
User Compliance	Likelihood that users will consistently and correctly use the system	Based on intrusiveness, need for user action (e.g., wearing/charging devices), and usability in elderly settings
Energy Efficiency	System's power consumption and impact on long-term operation	Based on device battery life (for wearables), computation demands (for embedded systems), and optimization
Privacy Protection	Degree to which user data is protected or not exposed to unnecessary risks	Evaluated based on use of video/audio surveillance, local vs. cloud processing, and security frameworks like encryption or blockchain

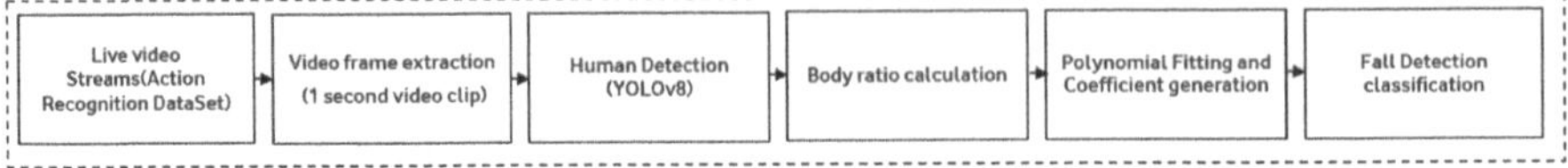

Fig. 2. Block Diagram of the Proposed Real-Time Fall Detection System Utilizing Human Activity Dataset from Rose Lab.

2.1 Action Recognition Dataset from ROSE Lab

The present study employs the publicly accessible Action Recognition Dataset developed by the ROSE Lab at Nanyang Technological University (NTU), a recognized benchmark in the domain of human activity analysis [24]. The dataset encompasses recordings of 40 diverse human actions, including activities such as walking, sitting, standing, and falling, captured using the Microsoft Kinect v2 sensor. It offers a rich multimodal dataset comprising RGB, infrared, and depth information, enabling detailed spatial-temporal modeling and enhancing the performance of multimodal learning systems [25–30].

For this study, a curated subset comprising 48 fall events and 93 non-fall events was selected from the ROSE Lab dataset. The selection process prioritized data quality and representation, taking into account practical constraints such as dataset volume, limited access windows, and occasional anomalies in recording. This ensured a reliable and balanced sample for performance evaluation while maintaining computational feasibility. Moreover, the dataset features a balanced representation of male and female subjects aged between 10 and 35 years, with variations in physical characteristics and movement styles, providing a comprehensive basis for developing generalized fall detection algorithms.

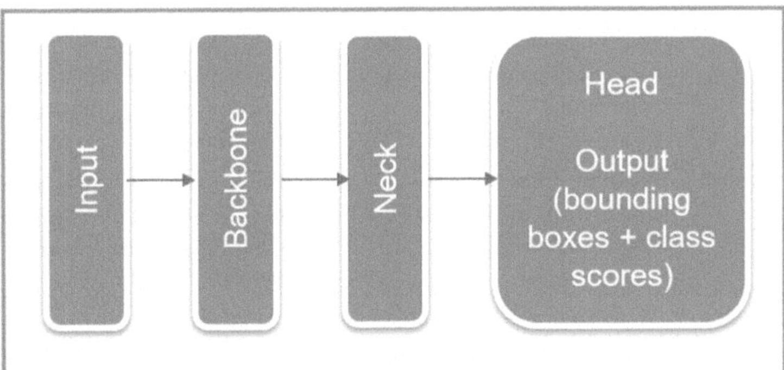

Fig. 3. The architecture of the YOLOv8 model, which is composed of three principal components "Backbone, neck and head".

2.2 Human Detection and Pose Estimation Using YOLOv8n-Pose

The proposed fall detection framework begins with live video stream acquisition for continuous monitoring of human activity. Human detection and pose estimation are performed using the YOLOv8n-pose model, a lightweight and real-time architecture optimized for deployment in resource-constrained environments [31, 32]. YOLOv8n-pose utilizes an anchor-free, single-stage design that concurrently performs object detection and keypoint regression. Trained on the COCO keypoint dataset, it estimates 17 anatomical landmarks—such as shoulders, hips, and knees—to generate accurate skeletal representations [33, 34]. Figure 3 illustrates the architecture of the YOLOv8 model, which is composed of three principal components. The backbone is responsible for extracting hierarchical feature representations from input images or video frames, serving as the foundational stage of the model. The neck aggregates and refines these features across multiple scales, improving the model's ability to localize and classify objects with higher accuracy. Finally, the head generates the model's output by predicting bounding boxes and associated class scores for each detected object.

Unlike models such as OpenPose, which rely on confidence maps and Part Affinity Fields (PAFs) for keypoint estimation, YOLOv8n-pose employs a more streamlined approach [35, 36]. These keypoints provide the foundation for constructing a 2D skeletal representation of the human body, which is analyzed frame by frame to identify irregularities in motion patterns typically associated with falls.

To capture motion dynamics, video input is processed in one-second intervals. Each frame is analyzed to extract 2D coordinates of keypoints relative to the subject's bounding box, forming a temporal pose sequence. These sequences serve as the basis for identifying fall patterns.

Following pose estimation, the detected human skeleton is enclosed within a bounding box, from which the ratio of body height to width is computed and stored as a one-dimensional array for each frame as follows [37, 38]:

$$R(n_i) = \frac{h(n_i)}{w(n_i)} \tag{1}$$

where $h(n_i)$ is the height of the bounding box around the human body, and $w(n_i)$ is the width of the bounding box. This ratio $R(n_i)$ is stored as a temporal sequence to capture the human body dynamics.

To validate the system's posture estimation accuracy, representative examples are shown in Figs. 4A-C. These illustrate the model's capability to distinguish between different human postures based on skeletal keypoints and bounding box geometry. The model's capability to identify fall-prone orientations is demonstrated by its recognition of a sitting or crouching posture with a confidence score of 0.71 as shown in Fig. 4A. Its detection of typical upright postures is confirmed by the standing posture, which achieved a confidence score of 0.90 as depicted in Fig. 4B, while the prone posture was identified with a confidence score of 0.71 presented in Fig. 4C. These results highlight the model's robustness in distinguishing actual falls from intentional low-height postures, as well as its versatility and accuracy across diverse scenarios. Such performance supports improved real-time fall detection and a reduction of false positives in practical applications, including workplace safety and elder care.

Fig. 4. Representative examples of posture classification using YOLOv8n-pose

2.3 Polynomial Modeling of Body Ratio Dynamics for Fall Detection in Human Activity Recognition

Following the extraction of body height-to-width ratio data for each frame, temporal analysis is conducted by fitting the ratio sequence $R(n_1), R(n_2), ..., R(n_N)$, to a sixth-degree polynomial function. The regression model is defined as [32]:

$$F(T) = \sum_{i=0}^{6} a_i T^i \quad (2)$$

where a_i are the coefficients determined via least squares fitting, and T denotes the time step corresponding to each frame.

This fitting procedure produces seven coefficients that concisely capture the temporal dynamics of a subject's movement throughout the video segment. These polynomial coefficients are subsequently used as features for classifying human activities into "Fall" and "No-Fall" categories, with each video represented by seven coefficients that encapsulate the essential characteristics of body motion.

The model's ability to capture distinct temporal patterns—including abrupt changes associated with falls and smoother trends indicative of controlled movements—is illustrated in Fig. 5A–B, which presents representative fitted curves for both fall and non-fall activities. These polynomial features are critical to the fall detection system, as they provide informative inputs that enable machine learning algorithms to accurately classify events as either falls or non-falls.

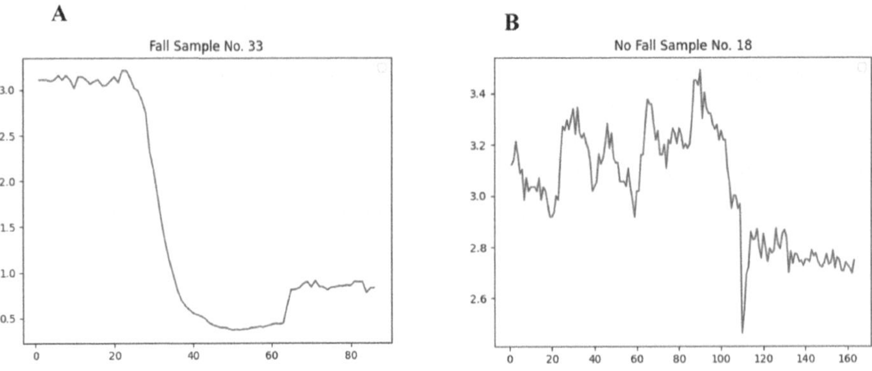

Fig. 5. Comparison of Body Ratio Curves for Fall and No-Fall Activities.

Each video sample is represented by a feature vector of these coefficients, which are organized into a two-dimensional matrix:

$$A = \begin{bmatrix} a_{6,1} & \cdots & a_{0,1} \\ \vdots & \ddots & \vdots \\ a_6, n & \cdots & a_0, n \end{bmatrix} \quad (3)$$

Here, $a_{i,j}$ denotes the i th coefficient for the j th video.

This matrix forms the input for classification models, enabling systematic analysis and comparison across multiple samples.

2.4 Evaluation of Machine Learning Classifiers for Temporal Motion Analysis

To assess the effectiveness of the proposed polynomial modeling of body ratio dynamics, a diverse set of supervised learning algorithms was employed to classify fall and non-fall events. These models were selected to represent both traditional machine learning and deep learning paradigms, allowing a comprehensive evaluation of classification performance under varying computational and structural complexities.

Four classification algorithms were employed: Linear Support Vector Machine (SVM) [39], k-Nearest Neighbors (KNN) [40], Decision Tree (DT) [41], and Logistic Regression (LR) [42]. These models were selected to represent a mix of traditional machine learning and deep learning techniques.

The input to each classifier consists of the polynomial coefficients derived from the temporal variation in the subject's height-to-width ratio sequence. These features encapsulate motion dynamics over time, offering a compact representation for classification. Traditional classifiers such as SVM, KNN, LR, and DT utilize these features directly to define decision boundaries in the feature space.

The classification performance was evaluated using standard metrics, including Accuracy, Sensitivity (Recall), Specificity, Precision, and F1-Score, calculated according to the following equations [43]:

$$Accuracy = \frac{T_p + T_n}{T_p + F_p + T_n + F_n} \times 100\% \quad (4)$$

$$Sensitivity = \frac{T_p}{T_p + F_n} \times 100\% \quad (5)$$

$$Specificity = \frac{T_n}{T_n + F_p} \times 100\% \quad (6)$$

$$Precision = \frac{T_p}{TP + FP} \times 100\% \quad (7)$$

$$Recall = \frac{T_p}{TP + FN} \times 100\% \quad (8)$$

$$F1 - Score = 2 \times \frac{Recall * Precision}{Recall + Precision} \quad (9)$$

where T_p, T_n, F_p, and F_n denote the parameters used to evaluate classification performance. Specifically, T_p (True Positive) and T_n (True Negative) represent correctly identified fall and no-fall instances, respectively, while F_p (False Positive) and F_n (False Negative) correspond to misclassified samples.

3 Results and Discussion

The present study investigates fall detection by employing a range of classification techniques, including conventional machine learning algorithms, mathematical modeling, and advanced feature enhancement through polynomial fitting. The core objective is to assess the progression of classification performance and identify the most effective approach for accurately detecting falls based on body ratio dynamics derived from pose-estimated video sequences.

The experimental dataset consisted of 48 fall videos and 93 non-fall videos, resulting in a notable class imbalance that initially affected the performance of certain classifiers. This imbalance introduced challenges in achieving consistent sensitivity and specificity, particularly for fall cases, which are inherently underrepresented.

To address the issue of class imbalance—where the dataset contained 48 fall videos compared to 93 non-fall videos data preprocessing steps were introduced. To mitigate class imbalance, sets of three consecutive rows from the minority class (fall) body ratio data were aggregated by computing their average, generating a single representative row. This approach preserves the temporal dynamics of the minority class while augmenting its representation for classification. This strategy effectively adjusted the number of fall instances, making the dataset more balanced and improving the model's ability to generalize across both classes.

A polynomial fitting procedure was then employed to summarize each temporal sequence into a compact and informative set of features. Polynomial degrees ranging from 4 to 10 were evaluated, with the sixth-degree polynomial yielding the highest classification accuracy using the baseline KNN classifier. As shown in Fig. 6, the sixth-degree polynomial was identified as the optimal fitting model, achieving a balance between complexity and generalization. This degree was sufficient to capture the underlying non-linear trends in the body ratio dynamics without overfitting, thereby enhancing the classification performance. When these fitted coefficients were used as input, classification based on the proposed mathematical modeling approach achieved an accuracy of 97.40%. This result demonstrates the effectiveness of polynomial feature transformation in modeling complex motion patterns associated with fall behavior.

Each video sample was thus represented by the seven coefficients generated from the sixth-degree polynomial fit, allowing the classifier to capture complex, non-linear motion patterns characteristic of fall dynamics. This transformation not only reduced the dimensionality of the feature space but also emphasized salient motion trends linked to fall events.

Several traditional classifiers were applied to the sixth-degree polynomial-fitted data prior to addressing the class imbalance. These included SVM, LR, DT, and KNN ($K = 3 \sim 29$). Each model was trained and evaluated using the polynomial coefficients as input features, representing the temporal evolution of body ratio dynamics for each video sequence.

To establish a performance baseline, the machine learning strategies were initially applied to the sixth-degree polynomial-fitted data prior to any resampling or balancing strategies as outlined in Table 2. However, the classification results were generally unsatisfactory due to the significant class imbalance in the dataset. Linear models such as SVM and LR achieved accuracies of only 44.7% and 42%, respectively, reflecting their inability to capture the non-linear patterns inherent in fall dynamics. Although DT and KNN performed better, with KNN reaching an accuracy of 75% at $k = 5$, exhibited sensitivity to the skewed class distribution. These results underscore the critical importance of addressing class imbalance and confirm the need for resampling techniques to enhance model generalization and reliability in fall detection.

In contrast, the DT classifier demonstrated considerably improved performance, achieving an average accuracy of 68.4%. This improvement highlights the model's ability to learn non-linear relationships and handle heterogeneous feature distributions, making it more suitable for fall detection in unbalanced and noisy datasets. The results suggest that classifiers capable of non-linear decision boundaries are more effective in leveraging the polynomial-fitted features, even in the presence of class imbalance.

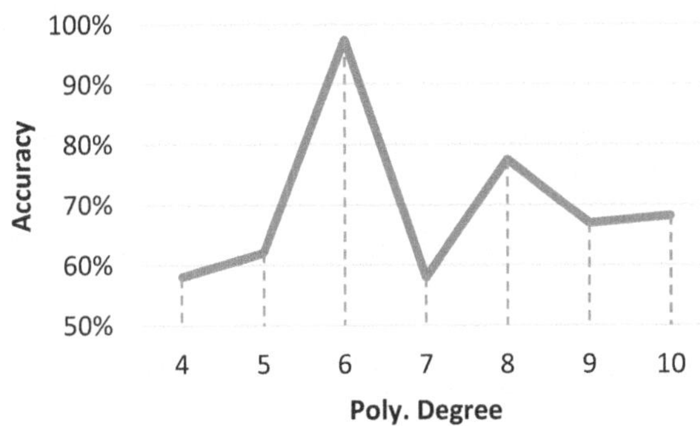

Fig. 6. Evaluation of polynomial fitting degrees for modeling temporal body ratio dynamics.

Following the application of the resampling strategy to address class imbalance, classification performance improved significantly across all models. Notably, the SVM classifier achieved an average accuracy of 89.5% on the balanced dataset. The summarized results in Table 2 revealed a perfect specificity of 100% for detecting non-fall cases and a sensitivity of 78.95% for correctly identifying fall events. In addition, the model attained a precision of 1.0 and an F1-score of 0.8824, demonstrating a well-balanced trade-off between sensitivity and precision. These results highlight the effectiveness of the resampling approach in enhancing classifier reliability and confirm the SVM model's robustness under balanced conditions.

To further improve classification performance beyond that achieved by the SVM, which reached an accuracy of 89.5% post-resampling, the study adopted an enhanced nearest-neighbor-based approach rooted in the principles of KNN. In the case of the KNN classifier, performance was further optimized by systematically tuning the number of neighbors (k) used for decision- making. Rather than relying on a fixed or arbitrary k value, the model was evaluated across multiple k settings using regression-based testing to identify the configuration that best captured the underlying data structure while minimizing classification error. The optimal value was determined to be k = 10, which offered a balanced compromise between sensitivity to local patterns and resistance to noise or outliers. This adjustment led to a substantial improvement in performance, with the KNN classifier achieving an accuracy of 97.4% in Fig. 7, a sensitivity of 94.74%, specificity of 100%, precision of 1.0, and an F1-score of 0.9730, as illustrated in Table 3. These results underscore the critical importance of neighborhood size selection in KNN-based classification, showing that a well-tuned k not only improves generalization across diverse motion patterns but also enhances the reliability of fall detection in real-world scenarios.

Table 2. Accuracy comparison of classifiers before and after applying resampling techniques

Metric	SVM	KNN	DT	LR
Before Resampling	44.7%	75.0%	68.4%	42.0%
After Resampling	89.5%	97.4%	81.6%	59.2%

Table 3. Performance Comparison of Classification Models for Fall Detection

Metric	KNN	SVM
Accuracy	97.4%	89.5%
Sensitivity	0.9474	0.7895
Specificity	**1.0**	**1.0**
F1- score	0.9730	0.8824

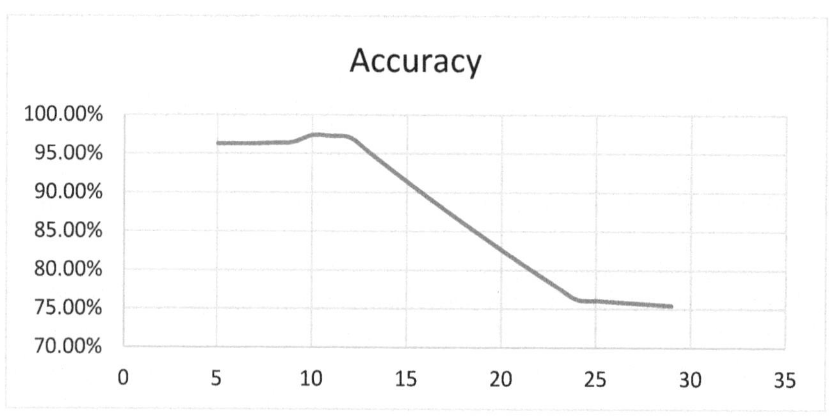

Fig.7. Impact of varying nearest-neighbor sample size (k) on classification accuracy

While DT and LR classifiers were included in the initial evaluation phase, their performance was ultimately suboptimal and did not warrant further refinement or integration into the final fall detection framework. Logistic Regression, limited by its linear decision boundary, failed to adequately model the complex, non-linear relationships inherent in the temporal motion features, yielding an accuracy of only 59.2% after resampling. Although the Decision Tree classifier performed better, achieving 81.6% accuracy, it exhibited high variance and was sensitive to data imbalance, leading to inconsistent generalization across validation folds. Given these limitations, both DT and LR were deprioritized in favor of more robust and adaptable models such as SVM and KNN, which demonstrated superior performance after appropriate tuning and balancing. This strategic model selection underscores the importance of aligning classifier capacity with the complexity of the underlying data structure in fall detection tasks.

4 Conclusion

Fall detection remains a critical challenge in healthcare and assisted living, particularly for elderly populations where delayed response to a fall can result in severe injury or fatality. Traditional detection systems, including wearable sensors and static monitoring devices, often suffer from limitations such as low user compliance, restricted coverage, or high false alarm rates. To address these gaps, this study proposed a vision-based fall detection framework that leverages real-time human pose estimation and temporal modeling of body ratio dynamics.

The present study captured significant motion trends suggestive of fall behavior by extracting body height-to-width ratio sequences from video frames and fitting them to sixth-degree polynomial functions. Multiple classification models were then trained and assessed using these polynomial characteristics. When combined with balanced data, KNN, which was optimized with a neighborhood size of $k = 10$, demonstrated the most promising outcomes among the conventional techniques, with high accuracy and generalization.

In conclusion, the proposed system offers a non-intrusive, accurate, and computationally efficient approach to fall detection, capable of operating in real-time environments without requiring user-worn devices with preserving privacy. The framework has blended polynomial modeling of body ratio dynamics with real-time position estimation based on YOLOv8. The suggested methodology includes methodical improvements such data balance, and outlier exclusion, which significantly improved detection accuracy, reaching 97.4% overall accuracy with 100% specificity and 94.74% sensitivity.

The polynomial fitting approach proved instrumental in transforming high dimensional time-series data into concise, informative features that better represent fall-related dynamics. Future studies will investigate the potential of temporal pattern modeling and the conversion of body ratio curves into two dimensional representations for classification utilizing deep learning methods based on images.

References

1. Bloom, D.E., Luca, D.L.: The global demography of aging: facts, explanations, future. In: Piggott J, Woodland A (eds.) Handbook Econ. Population Aging **1**, 3–56 (2016)

2. Ogura, S., Jakovljevic, M.M.: Global population aging—health care, social and economic consequences. Front. Public Health **6**, 335 (2018). https://doi.org/10.3389/fpubh.2018.00335
3. World Health Organization (2023). Falls: key facts. https://www.who.int/news-room/fact-sheets/detail/falls. Accessed 20 Aug 2025
4. Stevens, J.A., Corso, P.S., Finkelstein, E.A., Miller, T.R.: The costs of fatal and non-fatal falls among older adults. Inj. Prev. **12**(5), 290–295 (2006). https://doi.org/10.1136/ip.2005.011015
5. Florence, C.S., Bergen, G., Atherly, A., Burns, E., Stevens, J., Drake, C.: Medical costs of fatal and nonfatal falls in older adults. J. Am. Geriatr. Soc. **66**(4), 693–698 (2018). https://doi.org/10.1111/jgs.15304
6. Robinovitch, S.N., Feldman, F., Yang, Y., et al.: Video capture of the circumstances of falls in elderly people residing in long-term care: an observational study. Lancet **381**(9860), 47–54 (2013). https://doi.org/10.1016/S0140-6736(12)61263-X
7. Chaudhuri, S., Thompson, H., Demiris, G.: Fall detection devices and their use with older adults: a systematic review. J. Geriatr. Phys. Ther. **37**(4), 178–196 (2014). https://doi.org/10.1519/JPT.0b013e3182abe779
8. Gutiérrez, J., Rodríguez, V., Martin, S.: Comprehensive review of vision-based fall detection systems. Sensors **21**(3), 947 (2021). https://doi.org/10.3390/s21030947
9. Mubashir, M., Shao, L., Seed, L.: A survey on fall detection: principles and approaches. Neurocomputing **100**, 144–152 (2013). https://doi.org/10.1016/j.neucom.2011.09.037
10. Ghader, M., Kheradpisheh, S.R., Farahani, B., Fazlali, M.: Enabling privacy-preserving edge AI: federated learning enhanced with forward-forward algorithm. In: Proceedings of IEEE International Conference Omni-layer Intelligent Systems (COINS), pp. 1–7. IEEE (2024). https://doi.org/10.1109/COINS57946.2024.10386842
11. Mohamed, O., Choi, H.J., Iraqi, Y.: Fall detection systems for elderly care: a survey. In: Proceedings of 6th International Conference New Technologies, Mobility and Security (NTMS), pp. 1–4. IEEE (2014). https://doi.org/10.1109/NTMS.2014.6814010
12. Kulurkar, P., Dixit, C., Bharathi, V.C., Monikavishnuvarthini, A., Dhakne, A., Preethi, P.: AI based elderly fall prediction system using wearable sensors: a smart home-care technology with IoT. Meas. Sens. **25**, 100614 (2023). https://doi.org/10.1016/j.measen.2022.100614
13. Alfayez, F., Khan, S.B.: IoT-blockchain empowered Trinet: optimized fall detection system for elderly safety. Front. Bioeng. Biotechnol. **11**, 1257676 (2023). https://doi.org/10.3389/fbioe.2023.1257676
14. Mauldin, T.R., Canby, M.E., Metsis, V., Ngu, A.H.H., Rivera, C.C.: SmartFall: a smartwatch-based fall detection system using deep learning. Sensors **18**(10), 3363 (2018). https://doi.org/10.3390/s18103363
15. Sarowar, M.H., Khondakar, M.F.K, Roy, H.S, Ullah, H., Ahmed, R., Hossain, Q.D.: Internet of things based fall detection and heart rate monitoring system for senior citizens. Int. J. Electr. Comput. Eng. (IJECE) **12**(3), 3204–3216. https://doi.org/10.11591/ijece.v12i3.pp3204-3216
16. Wu, J., Wang, J., Zhan, A., Wu, C.: Fall detection with CNN-casual LSTM network. Information **12**(10), 403 (2021). https://doi.org/10.3390/info12100403
17. Rashid, F.A., Sandrasegaran, K., Kong, X.: Simulation of SisFall dataset for fall detection using MATLAB classifier algorithms. In: Proceedings of 12th International Symposium Parallel Architectures, Algorithms and Programming (PAAP), pp. 62–68. IEEE (2021). https://doi.org/10.1109/PAAP54281.2021.9720481
18. Dutt, M., Gupta, A., Goodwin, M., Omlin, C.W.: An interpretable modular deep learning framework for video-based fall detection. Appl. Sci. **14**(11), 4722 (2024). https://doi.org/10.3390/app14114722
19. Jiao, S., Li, G., Zhang, G., Zhou, J., Li, J.: Multimodal fall detection for solitary individuals based on audio-video decision fusion processing. Heliyon **10**(8), e34356 (2024). https://doi.org/10.1016/j.heliyon.2024.e34356

20. Wang, Y., Chi, Z., Liu, M., Li, G., Ding, S.: High-performance lightweight fall detection with an improved YOLOv5s algorithm. Machines **11**(8), 818 (2023). https://doi.org/10.3390/machines11080818
21. Almukadi, W.S., Alrowais, F., Saeed, M.K., Yahya, A.E., Mahmud, A., Marzouk, R.: Deep feature fusion with computer vision driven fall detection approach for enhanced assisted living safety. Sci. Rep. **14**, 21537 (2024). https://doi.org/10.1038/s41598-024-71545-6
22. Elden, R.H., Ghoneim, V.F., Al-Atabany, W.: A computer aided diagnosis system for the early detection of neurodegenerative diseases using linear and non-linear analysis. In: 2018 IEEE 4th Middle East Conference on Biomedical Engineering (MECBME), pp. 116–121. IEEE (2018). https://doi.org/10.1109/MECBME.2018.8402417
23. Elden, R.H., Al-Atabany, W., Ghoneim, V.F.: Gait variability analysis in neurodegenerative diseases using nonlinear dynamical modelling. In: 2018 9th Cairo International Biomedical Engineering Conference (CIBEC), pp. 41–44. IEEE (2018). https://doi.org/10.1109/CIBEC.2018.8641785
24. Shahroudy, A., Liu, J., Ng, T.T., Wang, G.: NTU RGB+D: a large scale dataset for 3D human activity analysis. In: Proc IEEE Conf Comput Vis Pattern Recognit (CVPR), pp 1010–1019. IEEE (2016). https://doi.org/10.1109/CVPR.2016.115
25. Shahroudy, A., Ng, T.T., Yang, Q., Wang, G.: Multimodal multipart learning for action recognition in depth videos. IEEE Trans. Pattern Anal. Mach. Intell. **38**(10), 2123–2129 (2015). https://doi.org/10.1109/TPAMI.2015.2505290
26. Shahroudy, A., Ng, T.T., Gong, Y., Wang, G.: Deep multimodal feature analysis for action recognition in RGB+D videos. IEEE Trans. Pattern Anal. Mach. Intell. **40**(5), 1045–1058 (2017). https://doi.org/10.1109/TPAMI.2017.2700486
27. Shahroudy, A., Wang, G., Ng, T.T.: Multi-modal feature fusion for action recognition in RGB-D sequences. In: Proceedings 6th International Symposium Commun Control Signal Process (ISCCSP), pp 1–4. IEEE (2014). https://doi.org/10.1109/ISCCSP.2014.6877827
28. Liu, J., Shahroudy, A., Xu, D., Wang, G.: Spatio-temporal LSTM with trust gates for 3D human action recognition. In: ECCV 2016, pp 816–833. Springer, Cham (2016). https://doi.org/10.1007/978-3-319-46487-9_50
29. Liu, J., Wang, G., Hu, P., Duan, L.Y., Kot, A.C.: Global context-aware attention LSTM networks for 3D action recognition. In: Proceedings of IEEE Conference Computerised Vis Pattern Recognit (CVPR), pp. 1647–1656. IEEE (2017). https://doi.org/10.1109/CVPR.2017.179
30. Liu, J., Shahroudy, A., Xu, D., Kot, A.C., Wang, G.: Skeleton-based action recognition using spatio-temporal LSTM network with trust gates. IEEE Trans. Pattern Anal. Mach. Intell. **40**(12), 3007–3021 (2017). https://doi.org/10.1109/TPAMI.2017.2773080
31. Redmon, J., Divvala, S., Girshick, R., Farhadi, A.: You only look once: unified, real-time object detection. In: Proceedings of IEEE Conference Comput Vis Pattern Recognition (CVPR), pp. 779–788. IEEE (2016). https://doi.org/10.1109/CVPR.2016.91
32. Bochkovskiy, A., Wang, C.Y., Liao, H.Y.M.: YOLOv4: optimal speed and accuracy of object detection. arXiv preprint arXiv:2004.10934 (2020)
33. DroneVis. YOLOv8 Pose—DroneVis 1.3.0 documentation (2025). https://drone-vis.readthedocs.io/en/latest/pose/yolov8_pose.html, Accessed 20 Aug 2025
34. Yu, M., Rhuma, A., Naqvi, S.M., Wang, L., Chambers, J.: A posture recognition-based fall detection system for monitoring an elderly person in a smart home environment. IEEE Trans. Inf. Technol. Biomed. **16**(6), 1274–1286 (2012). https://doi.org/10.1109/TITB.2012.2188296
35. Cao, Z., Hidalgo, G., Simon, T., Wei, S.E., Sheikh, Y.: OpenPose: realtime multi-person 2D pose estimation using part affinity fields. IEEE Trans. Pattern Anal. Mach. Intell. **43**(1), 172–186 (2019). https://doi.org/10.1109/TPAMI.2019.2929257

36. Cao, Z., Simon, T., Wei, S.E., Sheikh, Y.: Realtime multi-person 2D pose estimation using part affinity fields. In: Proceedings of IEEE Conference Computer Vis Pattern Recognition (CVPR), pp. 7291–7299. IEEE (2017). https://doi.org/10.1109/CVPR.2017.143
37. Liu, J., Shahroudy, A., Perez, M., Wang, G., Duan, L.Y., Kot, A.C.: NTU RGB+D 120: a large-scale benchmark for 3D human activity understanding. IEEE Trans. Pattern Anal. Mach. Intell. **42**(10), 2684–2701 (2019). https://doi.org/10.1109/TPAMI.2019.2895891
38. Fryar, C.D., Gu, Q., Ogden, C.L.: Anthropometric reference data for children and adults: United States, 2007–2010. Vital Health Stat **11**(252), 1–48 (2012)
39. Suthaharan, S.: Support vector machine. In: Machine learning models and algorithms for big data classification, pp. 207–235. Springer, Boston (2016). https://doi.org/10.1007/978-1-4899-7641-3_10
40. Peterson, L.E.: K-nearest neighbor. Scholarpedia **4**(2), 1883 (2009).https://doi.org/10.4249/scholarpedia.1883
41. Song, Y.Y., Lu, Y.: Decision tree methods: applications for classification and prediction. Shanghai Arch Psychiatry **27**(2), 130–135 (2015). https://doi.org/10.11919/j.issn.1002-0829.215044
42. Ng, A., Jordan, M.: On discriminative vs. generative classifiers: a comparison of logistic regression and naive Bayes. Adv. Neural. Inf. Process. Syst. **14**, 841–848 (2001)
43. Sokolova, M., Lapalme, G.: A systematic analysis of performance measures for classification tasks. Inf. Process. Manag. **45**(4), 427–437 (2009). https://doi.org/10.1016/j.ipm.2009.03.002

Towards an Integrated Metaheuristic Approach for Workplace Performance Optimization

Asma Dhaouadi(✉) and Cecilia Zanni-Merk

Normandie Université, INSA Rouen, LITIS, Normandy, France
{asma.dhaouadi,cecilia.zanni-merk}@insa-rouen.fr
https://www.insa-rouen.fr/recherche/laboratoires/litis

Abstract. The workplace environment has evolved from a logistical support function into a strategic lever for performance, sustainability, and employee well-being, particularly in the context of human-centric organizational transformation. In this context, companies face persistent challenges such as disengagement, productivity loss, and growing expectations for meaningful work, while lacking standardized tools to evaluate and optimize workplace-related services. Although several classical assessment models are in use, they rarely capture the full extent to which workplace conditions influence business outcomes. To address these challenges, various international bodies including the International Organization for Standardization (ISO) and the European Committee for Standardization (CEN) have proposed sets of indicators aimed at characterizing working conditions. However, there remains a significant gap: the absence of a comprehensive framework capable of modeling the correlation between the efficiency of the workplace environment and a company's economic, environmental, and societal performance. This paper addresses this need by proposing an approach that organizes workplace conditions and delivers customized action plans to experts, tailored to the company's current context, goals, and constraints. To complement this, a metaheuristic optimization model is introduced to evaluate and improve workplace performance as a strategic driver of value creation. The proposed approach is validated through a case study and its integration into management frameworks is discussed, with potential benefits that span evidence-based strategy, environmental compliance, and human-centric innovation.

Keywords: Decision support · Metaheuristics · Workplace performance · Facility Management · Quality of Work Life

1 Introduction

Quality of Work Life (QWL), Occupational Health and Safety (OH&S) risks, and Corporate Social Responsibility (CSR) are increasingly recognized as interdependent levers for sustainable organizational transformation. At the crossroads

A. Awad et al. (Eds.): MEDI 2025, LNCS 16427, pp. 33–46, 2026.
https://doi.org/10.1007/978-3-032-19865-5_3

of employee expectations and societal challenges, these concepts underscore a shared objective: enabling every individual within the company to perform meaningful work under conditions that promote health, autonomy, and engagement [1,2]. Within this framework, the workplace's physical and organizational dimensions have emerged as strategically significant, functioning as practical domains for the implementation of QWL, OH&S, and CSR principles. Formerly referred to as "general services", the mechanisms associated with the workplace environment today encompass an integrated system of support functions aimed at improving the workplace life. Long regarded as a site of exposure to various risks, particularly physical and psychosocial, the workplace now holds the potential to become a strategic lever not only for employee well-being, but also for the overall performance of the organization [3]. This transformation has been significantly accelerated by the COVID-19 pandemic, which marked a major turning point in professional practices. As a result, workplace management has evolved from a logistical support role to a central function in value creation, impacting three key dimensions: social (employee well-being and engagement), economic (productivity and cost control), and environmental (carbon footprint reduction). This shift is also reflected in evolving expectations and structural tensions within organizations. According to [4], in 2022, the Microsoft Work Trend Index revealed that in France, 48% of employees now prioritize health and well-being at work more than before the pandemic, while 72% of managers desire greater flexibility but lack adequate decision-making authority and resources. The study also found that only 26% of the companies had established formal hybrid work policies, while 39% of the workers expressed their willingness to use metaverse environments for meetings. In France, this sector alone generates more than 100 billion euros in annual revenue (excluding rents) and supports more than one million jobs, most of which are non-relocatable [5]. However, despite the growing strategic importance attributed to workplace management, evaluation practices remain limited and poorly structured. The lack of standardized methods for mapping and measuring services related to people and buildings hampers efforts to enhance both performance and sustainability. In this context, a deeper understanding of how the workplace impacts economic, social, and environmental performance is essential. This highlights the need for more robust evaluation methods capable of objectively assessing the workplace's contribution to value creation within the company. This work propose a metaheuristic approach to optimize workplace performance.

From this standpoint, this paper proposes a metaheuristic strategy for enhancing workplace performance. More precisely, we elaborate first (i) a review of the international standards governing workplace management, which allowed the identification of key indicators and factors involved in measuring and optimizing workplace performance, and then (ii) we define a Multifactor Measurement Index (IMM) designed to assess the optimal contribution of the workplace environment to overall company performance, combining these social, economic and environmental indicators. (iii) The complexity of interrelated effects and the challenge of prioritizing actions raise the question of how to select and sequence the most effective combinations. Consequently, to determine the optimal sequence of actions to improve the IMM, we rely on a method inspired by classical optimization approaches, specifically the well-known knapsack problem, which models the selection of the most impactful actions under resource constraints. (iv) Finally, our approach is validated through a specific use case.

This paper is structured as follows. Section 2 presents the context of the workplace environment, detailing key constraints and indicators derived from international standards. It highlights the need to develop a method for optimizing workplace performance, based on the definition and computation of a multicriteria index. Section 3 defines the index and presents the proposed metaheuristic to optimize it by selecting actions that maximize the impact of the workplace on organizational performance. Section 4 illustrates a specific use case to demonstrate the validity of our approach. Finally, Sect. 5 concludes the paper and outlines future research directions.

2 Workplace Performance and Its Dimensions

Work-life balance, high-quality working conditions, meaningful work, and active employee engagement are key pillars in aligning social responsibility with workplace well-being. In this context, our analysis of several European (EN) and international (ISO) standards, such as ISO 45001, ISO 45003, NF EN 15221-7 and ISO 41011, identified 63 indicators that can be used to evaluate the work environment [1,2,7,8]. This section examines the core concepts of workplace performance and facility management (FM), and presents a selection of these indicators, defined with reference to the aforementioned standards, which are considered essential for developing a structured evaluation approach. As part of this process, we ensured that the evolution of terminology over time was respected and taken into account, in line with the progression of normative references. We point out that the indicators are categorized into six groups, as defined by the NF EN 15221-7 standard [7], as follows:

1. Financial: This category covers the assessment of financial expenditures in workplace management, including operating and capital costs [7].
2. Spatial: This category assesses floor space usage in workplace management, such as space per Full-Time Equivalent (FTE) or linear metres of storage, following benchmarks outlined in EN 15221-6 standard [9].
3. Environmental: This category assesses the environmental impacts of workplace management, such as energy consumption, water usage, waste production, and carbon emissions, in line with the IPD Environment Code [7].
4. Service quality: This category assesses the quality of services provided in workplace management, considering aspects such as reliability, responsiveness, and the balance between service quality and financial expenditure [16].
5. User satisfaction: This category assesses satisfaction levels related to workplace management, including end-user or customer satisfaction and satisfaction in relation to space usage [7].
6. Productivity: This category assesses individual and overall organizational productivity. Examples of indicators include Core operating hours of the facility, Timeliness of service provision, and Uptime facility, etc. [7].

Building on this categorization, performance benchmarking can be classified into three complementary types, depending on the nature of the data: i) Quantitative benchmarking involves measurable and tangible variables, such as costs, floor space (square meters), and energy usage. This type of data is objective and is generally obtained through routine systems and standardized processes [7]. ii) Qualitative benchmarking deals with data related to intangible elements, such as service quality, end-user satisfaction, and individual productivity. This type of data is subjective and is typically gathered through targeted feedback mechanisms or specialized procedures [7]. Moreover, they can be captured or converted into numerical scores to facilitate structured comparison and analysis. iii) Combination benchmarking refers to an integrated approach that combines both tangible and intangible entities, which are understood to be correlated. It enables the assessment of interrelations or trade-offs between two or more entities [7]. For instance, it allows evaluating user satisfaction with space usage or service quality regarding financial expenditure.

From a global perspective, Corporate Social Responsibility (CSR) promotes a progressive and inclusive management culture that fosters collective commitment and continuous organizational transformation. In particular, in France, this dynamic is further reinforced by the CSR Guide published by MEDEF [4], which emphasizes that integrating Quality of Life and Working Conditions (QVCT) into CSR strategies represents a major area of convergence. Hybridization of both approaches strengthens the corporate commitment to sustainable performance. This synergy promotes work-life balance, quality working conditions, meaningful work, and active employee participation, essential pillars to align social responsibility with workplace well-being. To effectively implement and monitor these strategic orientations, a rigorous evaluation method is needed, which relies on indicators capturing how workplace conditions affect corporate performance. However, despite this necessity, structured evaluation methods remain scarce. Numerous indicators, definitions, and concepts exist in the literature, yet, as highlighted in [7], benchmarking projects have often lacked clarity, been overly ambitious, or insufficiently supported by data analysis. This underlines the need to implement a metaheuristic approach to workplace performance optimization, based on a multi-criteria index that offers a robust foundation for evaluation. This approach can serve as a decision-support tool for identifying the most effective actions to improve performance both efficiently and sustainably.

In the following section, we introduce the proposed IMM index, along with the selected method for choosing the most relevant actions to enhance its value.

3 Proposed Approach for Workplace Performance Optimization

This study identifies a twofold need: on the one hand, the need for a method to measure the efficiency of the workplace environment and its impact on economic, environmental, and societal performance; on the other hand, the need for an approach to address the question: "How can facility managers select the most appropriate action or sequence of actions to optimize these measures under organizational constraints?" To address these needs, we first propose the Multifactor Measurement Index (IMM), which provides a structured foundation for workplace performance evaluation. This is followed by the introduction of a metaheuristic approach designed to optimize the IMM by selecting the most appropriate sequence of actions to enhance the workplace's contribution to overall organizational performance.

3.1 IMM: A Multifactor Measurement Index

To define this multifactor index, we relied on all 63 indicators identified in [7], which are designed to evaluate performance across the following categories: financial, spatial, environmental, service quality, user satisfaction, and productivity. Our investigation into this topic revealed that, to study the correlation between these various indicators and understand how they contribute to workplace optimization, it is highly useful to divide them into two main sets:

- Ideally, Increasing Indicators refer to those for which higher values are desirable, as they contribute to improving the workplace environment specifically, and overall organizational performance more broadly. An increase in these indicators suggests better working conditions, greater user engagement, and stronger organizational support. For example, higher values are sought for indicators such as Quality of Cleaning, Quality of Security, and Satisfaction with Facility Management.
- Ideally, Decreasing Indicators refer to those for which lower values are desirable, as they are typically associated with costs, resource consumption, or organizational inefficiencies. Reducing these indicators contributes to greater operational efficiency, environmental responsibility, and improved employee well-being. For example, it is preferable to decrease indicators such as Space Costs per FTE, Cleaning Costs per FTE, Health, Safety, Security, and Environment (HSSE) Costs, Staff Turnover, Absenteeism, and CO_2 Emissions per FTE.

Based on this defined category, the calculation of the IMM involves summing the weighted linear combinations of both ideally increasing and ideally decreasing indicators, as detailed in Eq. 1.

$$IMM = \sum_{ind \in LII} w_{ind} \cdot (\mathrm{val}_{\mathrm{ind}} - \mathrm{threshold}_{\mathrm{ind}}) + \sum_{ind \in LID} w_{ind} \cdot (\mathrm{threshold}_{\mathrm{ind}} - \mathrm{val}_{\mathrm{ind}}) \tag{1}$$

where,

- L: Set of all indicators, such that $L = LII \cup LID$.
- LII: Set of Ideally Increasing Indicators
- LID: Set of Ideally Decreasing Indicators
- w_{ind}: Weight of the indicator ind, such that $ind \in L$, with $\begin{cases} 0 \leq w_{ind} \leq 1 \\ \sum_{i=1}^{n} w_{ind} = 1 \end{cases}$

- val_{ind}: Observed value of the indicator *ind*.
- $\text{threshold}_{\text{ind}}$: Threshold value set for the indicator *ind*.

For each indicator, each company defines the threshold beyond which a value is considered good or poor, depending on the trend associated with that indicator. For example, in the case of the cleaning-related indicator, five possible values may be used: 0%, 25%, 50%, 75%, and 100%, corresponding respectively to very poor, poor, average, good, and very good. The company can set its target threshold, for example, 50% or 75%, depending on its performance expectations. This threshold is subjective and should be determined according to the specific context in which the indicator is applied.

Normalization of indicator values, weights, and thresholds is essential to ensure balanced IMM computation. It guarantees input comparability, stabilizes calculations, and prevents dominance effects. Without normalization, variables with different scales (e.g., Quality of Security: 0–1 vs. Rent Cost: 0–10,000) can cause instability or unpredictable outcomes. Moreover, normalization ensures that the IMM index remains within the interval $[-1, 1]$.

Accordingly, Eqs. (2), (3), and (4) are introduced to normalize, respectively, the indicator values, indicator weights, and indicator thresholds.

For each indicator $ind \in L$

$$\text{val}_{\text{ind}}^{\text{norm}} = \frac{\text{val}_{\text{ind}}}{\max(\text{val}_{\text{ind}})} \quad (2) \qquad \text{w}_{\text{ind}}^{\text{norm}} = \frac{\text{w}_{\text{ind}}}{\sum_{j=1}^{n} w_j} \quad (3)$$

$$\text{threshold}_{\text{ind}}^{\text{norm}} = \frac{\text{threshold}_{\text{ind}}}{\max(\text{val}_{\text{ind}})} \tag{4}$$

Consequently, the normalization process results in the new Eq. (1′) for calculating the IMM index.

$$\begin{aligned} IMM^{\text{norm}} = & \sum_{ind \in LII} w_{ind}^{\text{norm}} \cdot (\text{val}_{\text{ind}}^{\text{norm}} - \text{threshold}_{\text{ind}}^{\text{norm}}) \\ & + \sum_{ind \in LID} w_{ind}^{\text{norm}} \cdot (\text{threshold}_{\text{ind}}^{\text{norm}} - \text{val}_{\text{ind}}^{\text{norm}}) \end{aligned} \tag{1'}$$

After defining the IMM index, the subsequent task is to determine the most suitable actions for improving the workplace environment and maximizing the index value. Selecting these actions requires careful consideration to ensure both relevance and long-term effectiveness. The main challenge arises from identifying the most impactful actions, individually or in combination, while accounting for organizational constraints. To address this challenge, we propose a metaheuristic framework designed to evaluate, prioritize, and select the optimal sequence of actions.

3.2 Metaheuristic-Based Optimization of Action Selection

In our approach, the proposed actions are intended to align with the company's strategic objectives by optimizing the IMM index, with particular emphasis on indicators that show the greatest deviation from their predefined thresholds. To meet this objective, we explored several classical optimization techniques. Among them, the Traveling Salesman Problem (TSP) is one of the most well-known, aiming to determine the shortest possible route that visits a set of locations exactly once and returns to the starting point [11]. However, the Knapsack Problem [12], which involves selecting a combination of items that maximizes total value without exceeding a given capacity constraint, emerged as the most appropriate modeling framework. It naturally fits the challenge of selecting and sequencing impactful actions under resource limitations. This formulation aligns perfectly with our goal of recommending the most effective combination of actions to improve the workplace environment while respecting the organization's specific constraints. Furthermore, several previous studies [13,14], have successfully employed the knapsack model in similar decision-making contexts, reinforcing the relevance of our choice and supporting its methodological robustness.

We deliberately chose not to use machine learning techniques at this stage of the project. This decision stems from the fact that the project is conducted in an industrial setting, where data availability is particularly limited due to constraints imposed by our industrial partner. Consequently, data-driven approaches such as machine learning, which depend on substantial datasets, are currently not feasible. This reinforces our preference for a classical algorithmic method, which remains effective in generating relevant action recommendations even in the absence of large datasets.

In our context, the objective is to maximize the IMM index by selecting the most appropriate combination of actions, where each action has a weight associated with the effort or cost required for its implementation, and a corresponding contribution to improving the IMM. This rationale mirrors that of the knapsack problem, in which each item has a weight and a value, and the goal is to maximize the total value without exceeding a capacity constraint. Building on this parallel, we propose a formal mathematical formulation inspired by the classical knapsack problem to support the recommendation of optimal actions for improving workplace performance. This formulation provides a solid foundation for applying optimization algorithms to identify the most relevant set of actions to implement within a constrained decision space.

Mathematical Formulation of the 0–1 Knapsack Problem

- Let there be n items j, each with a value c_j and a weight a_j;
- Let b be the maximum capacity of the knapsack;
- The variable $x_j \in 0, 1$ indicates whether item j is selected ($x_j = 1$) or not ($x_j = 0$);

Formally:

$$\text{Maximize} \sum_{j=1}^{n} c_j x_j \qquad \text{Subject to} \quad \sum_{j=1}^{n} a_j x_j \leq b, \quad \text{for } x_j \in \{0, 1\}, \, j = 1, \ldots, n$$

Methodological Adaptation of the 0–1 Knapsack Problem for Optimization of the IMM Index

- The items correspond to actions.
- Each action i has a value v_i, which is the difference between the IMM value obtained if the action i is applied and the current value.
- Each action i has a weight w_i representing the effort or cost required to implement it.
- The maximum weight W corresponds to the maximum effort or cost the company is willing to invest to improve its IMM.

Eventually, the formalization should be as follows:

- Let $X \in [0, 1]^n$ such that $x_i = 1$ if action i is selected, and 0 otherwise.
- Let $Y \in [0, \text{number\_of\_possible\_actions}]^n$, where $y_i = k \in \mathbb{N}$ if action i is executed in position k, and 0 otherwise.
- Naturally, if $y_i \neq 0$, then $x_i = 1$.
- The goal is now to choose X and compute Y (to track the best execution sequence of the actions) to maximize v_k, where k is the index of the last executed action (i.e., the maximum value in vector Y).

The Action Selection is therefore defined through the following optimization objective:

$$\text{maximize} \quad \sum_{i=1}^{n} x_i v_i$$

$$\text{subject to} \quad \sum_{i=1}^{n} x_i w_i \leq W, \quad x_i \in \{0, 1\}, \quad \text{for } i = 1, \ldots, n$$

To implement the workplace performance optimization approach, we propose Algorithm 1. It serves as the operational step that enables the evaluation of the impact of the proposed actions and the selection of their optimal combination under constraints. Therefore, it fulfills a dual objective: on the one hand, to evaluate workplace performance through a synthetic index (IMM^{norm}) based on a set of multi-criteria of indicators (from line 1 to 12), and on the other hand, to identify the optimal subset of actions to be implemented within the limits of available resources, to maximize the improvement of the IMM index (from line 13 to 19).

Algorithm 1: Metaheuristic Optimization of IMM-Driven Action Selection

Input: LII, LID : sets of ideally increasing and decreasing indicators
val_{ind} : raw values of indicators
$threshold_{ind}$: threshold values of indicators
w_{ind} : weights of indicators
$A = \{a_1, a_2, ..., a_n\}$: set of available actions
v_i : value of action a_i (gain in IMM^{norm} for action a_i)
w_i : weight(cost/effort of action) a_i
W : total allowed budget (effort/cost)
Output: IMM^{norm} : normalized IMM index
$A^* \subseteq A$: selected actions to recommend

```
1  begin
2  L ← LII ∪ LID
3  foreach ind ∈ L do
4  |   val_ind^norm ← NormalizeVal(val_ind)
5  |   w_ind^norm ← NormalizeWeight(w_ind)
6  |   threshold_ind^norm ← NormalizeThreshold(threshold_ind)
7  IMM^norm ← 0
8  foreach ind ∈ L do
9  |   if ind ∈ LII then
10 |   |   IMM^norm ← IMM^norm + w_ind^norm · (val_ind^norm − threshold_ind^norm)
11 |   else if ind ∈ LID then
12 |   |   IMM^norm ← IMM^norm + w_ind^norm · (threshold_ind^norm − val_ind^norm)
13 A* ← ∅
14 /* Knapsack-based action selection */
15 foreach S ⊆ A, where Σ_{a_i∈S} w_i ≤ W do
16 |   compute IMM_S ← IMM index if actions in S are applied
17 |   if IMM_S > IMM^norm then
18 |   |   IMM^norm ← IMM_S
19 |   |   A* ← S
20 return IMM^norm, A*
21 end
```

This formulation allows the use of various optimization methods (such as greedy strategies, dynamic programming, evolutionary algorithms, or Integer Linear Programming (ILP) [15]) to determine the most effective combination of actions. The approach can be further extended to account for the temporal dimension (i.e., scheduling) by introducing additional variables y_i, where $y_i = k$ indicates that action ii is executed in the y_th position. Each method offers different trade-offs between efficiency, precision, and computational complexity. Although a comparative analysis of these algorithms is beyond the scope of this paper, their algorithmic resolution enables the identification of an optimal action strategy, under resource constraints, to sustainably improve the workplace environment.

In summary, the algorithmic resolution of this problem makes it possible to propose, under resource constraints, the most effective action strategy to sustainably improve the working environment.

4 Application to an Illustrative Use Case

To validate the proposed IMM (Multifactor Measurement Index) and demonstrate the effectiveness of a metaheuristic optimization strategy, we consider a real-world use case involving a company whose offices are located in a difficult and insecure area. Despite low rental costs, the quality of cleanliness and security is poor, leading to very low employee satisfaction. In addition, high absenteeism and turnover rates reflect a clear disengagement among staff. The organization experienced increasing operational inefficiencies, highlighting the urgent need to improve workplace conditions. Three actions were selected to address these issues: increasing salaries, improving cleanliness, and strengthening security. Each action was evaluated based on its impact on a range of performance indicators, allowing for an analysis of progress using the IMM index and the application of a metaheuristic decision-making approach. Table 1 below summarizes the evolution of the indicators before and after the actions were implemented.

In this case study, we dealt with both qualitative (soft) and quantitative (hard) data. Examples of qualitative data include Quality of Cleaning, Quality of Security, and Satisfaction with Facility Management. On the other hand, quantitative data include indicators such as Staff Turnover (related to human resources) and HSSE Costs per FTE; in this example, we specifically extracted the security cost per FTE. To calculate the IMM index, it was essential to convert qualitative data into a quantitative format. For this purpose, we relied on the EN 15221-7 standard [7] as a reference framework to guide the mapping process. This transformation allowed for the integration of subjective assessments into a consistent numerical structure, facilitating the comparison and aggregation of diverse indicators. Qualitative inputs were mapped onto a five-level Likert scale, where values were interpreted as follows: 1 = very poor/strongly disagree/very unimportant, 2 = poor/disagree/unimportant, 3 = fair/neutral/average, 4 = good/agree/important, and 5 = very good/strongly agree/very important.

The weighting of the indicators, as well as the definition of thresholds, is determined by each company based on its strategic priorities and internal criteria. Each weight is expressed as an integer between 0 and 10 and reflects the relative importance of the corresponding indicator in light of the organization's objectives. In our use case, the company assigned the highest importance to staff turnover and absenteeism, assigning them both an equal weight of 8, reflecting their strong relevance to the company's current strategic priorities. As for the definition of thresholds, the company sets them based on the point at which the indicator's value is considered satisfactory or acceptable. To the best of our knowledge, no existing standard defines threshold values for indicator measurements. The same applies to the maximum values of indicator measurements,

Table 1. Indicator measurements by state following each action

Indicators			Initial State (StateS0)	Action1: Increase Salaries (StateS1)	Action2: Improve Cleanliness (StateS2)	Action3: Strengthen Security (StateS3)
Type	Category	Indicator				
Ideally Increasing Indicators	Service Quality	Quality of Cleaning	Poor	Poor	Fair	Fair
		Quality of Security	Poor	Poor	Poor	Very good
	Satisfaction	Satisfaction with Facility Management	**	***	**	****
Ideally Decreasing Indicators	Financial	Space Costs per FTE (rent)	900	900	900	800
		Cleaning Costs per FTE	500	500	500	750
		HSSE Costs per FTE (Security)	300	300	600	600
	Environment	Total CO2 emissions	150	130	160	110
		Total energy consumption	200	180	190	190
		Total water usage	250	220	280	210
	Productivity	Absenteeism	50%	40%	30%	10%
		Staff turnover	40%	35%	30%	10%
		Recovery time	7	5	5	1

which are defined as outliers in [7], described as "extreme scores in a data set, having a disproportionate influence on determining reference points." While such values are relatively easy to identify in the case of qualitative measures, such as *very good*, very good for service quality data, they are more challenging to define for hard data. For example, setting a security cost, rental cost, or water consumption rate as a maximum threshold is complex, as these figures depend on multiple constraints, including the company's field of activity and its geographical location.

The IMM index was calculated after completing the following steps:

1. Converting qualitative data into quantitative values;

2. Defining thresholds and identifying outliers for each indicator;
3. Applying all normalization equations (Eqs. 2, 3, and 4) to harmonize inputs and ensure balanced, stable calculations;
4. Applying the IMM^{norm} index calculation equation (Eq. 1′).

Based on these steps, the IMM index was obtained as follows: −0.12, −0.06, −0.13, 0.06 for the corresponding states: StateS0 (initial state), StateS1, StateS2, and StateS3. As shown in Fig. 1, the values remain within the interval [−1, 1], and the impact of the actions varies from state to state.

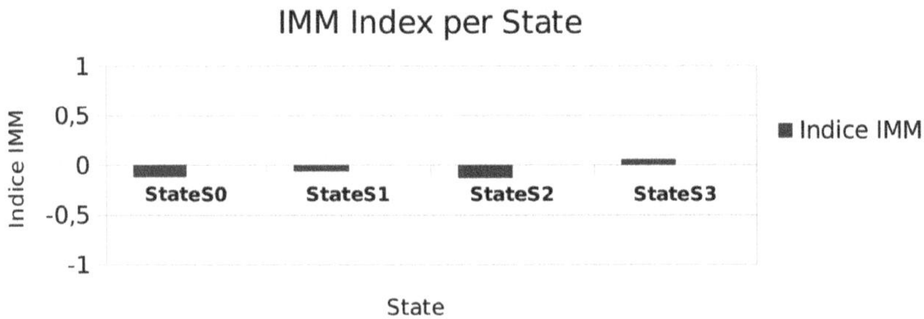

Fig. 1. Tracking the IMM Index Across Post-Action States

This specific use case successfully demonstrates the practical value of the proposed IMM and the associated metaheuristic approach. By applying three targeted actions, namely salary increases, improvements in cleanliness, and enhancements in security, the organization was able to measure the impact of each intervention across a range of indicators. The progression of the IMM index from −0.12 to +0.06 illustrates a tangible improvement in workplace conditions, employee satisfaction, and productivity. These findings validate the feasibility of translating multidimensional qualitative and quantitative data into actionable intelligence for decision-making. Importantly, the case exemplifies how companies can prioritize interventions based on strategic constraints and resource availability, turning workplace evaluation into a proactive performance management tool.

5 Conclusions and Future Work

In an era where the workplace is no longer seen as a passive backdrop to organizational activity but as a strategic lever for sustainable growth and employee well-being, the need for structured, evidence-based decision-making frameworks has never been more pressing. This research contributes to addressing this gap through the design and implementation of the Multifactor Measurement Index (IMM), a composite metric that integrates financial, spatial, environmental, service quality, satisfaction, and productivity indicators. By aligning these dimensions with the principles of QWL, OH&S, and CSR, the IMM enables a more holistic understanding of workplace performance.

The introduction of a metaheuristic approach, grounded in the classical Knapsack Problem, offers a robust optimization mechanism for selecting and sequencing workplace improvement actions under real-world constraints. The methodology facilitates strategic prioritization, allowing facility managers and decision-makers to maximize returns on investment in workplace enhancements.

The real-world use case presented in this paper highlights the practical feasibility of the framework. It confirms that organizations can apply the IMM index to monitor changes over time, evaluate the effectiveness of specific interventions, and adapt their strategies accordingly. The successful mapping of qualitative variables into a quantitative structure also illustrates the flexibility and extensibility of the model.

This project has been developed in collaboration with an industrial partner, which ensures its relevance to real workplace contexts. However, the limited availability of data currently prevents the use of machine learning methods for calculating and optimizing the IMM index. Future work will address this limitation as more data become available.

To further enhance the model and broaden its impact, several avenues for future research and development are identified:

- Development of a tool supporting dynamic data input, scenario simulation, and automated action recommendations, making the framework accessible to non-experts users. Already being implemented with our industrial partner.
- Future research will explore the temporal sequencing of actions over time, incorporating techniques from operations scheduling and predictive analytics. This would enable organizations not only to select actions but also to plan their implementation roadmap.
- The current proposal relies on subjective or expert-defined weights and thresholds. As evoked above, machine learning algorithms could be used to learn optimal weights and thresholds based on historical performance data.
- While the current study prioritized economic and satisfaction-related indicators, future iterations of the model could include more granular environmental and social impact factors, such as carbon footprint tracking, social equity metrics, or diversity and inclusion indicators.
- The development of a shared IMM-based benchmarking platform across sectors could enable organizations to compare their performance with industry peers, fostering a culture of transparency and continuous improvement.

By bridging conceptual rigor with practical applicability, this research lays the foundation for more strategic, data-driven workplace management, paving the way for future innovations that align organizational performance with human-centric and sustainable values.

Acknowledgments. This work was supported by the Normandy Region (France) and the European Union through the European Regional Development Fund (ERDF/FEDER).

References

1. ISO: ISO 45001: Occupational health and safety management systems — Requirements with guidance for use. International Standard, International Organization for Standardization (2018). https://www.iso.org/standard/63787.html
2. ISO: ISO 45003: Occupational health and safety management — Psychological health and safety at work — Guidelines for managing psychosocial risks. International Standard, International Organization for Standardization (2021). https://www.iso.org/standard/64283.html
3. Agence nationale pour l'amélioration des conditions de travail (Anact): Référentiel QVCT – Qualité de vie et des conditions de travail. https://www.anact.fr/sites/default/files/2023-12/anact_referentiel_092023.pdf
4. Mouvement des Entreprises de France (MEDEF): GUIDE RSE – Introduction à la Qualité de Vie et des Conditions de Travail (QVCT), Paris, France: MEDEF (2023). https://www.medef.com/uploads/media/default/0020/01/14871-guide-qvct-2022.pdf. Accessed 10 Aug 2025
5. IDET - L'Institut de l'Environnement de Travail: Étude 2020 : L'environnement de travail en France (2020). https://www.idet.fr/etudes/etude-2020-lenvironnement-de-travail-en-france/. Accessed 21 May 2025
6. AFNOR: NF EN 15221-1: Facility Management — Part 1: Terms and Definitions, French Standard, Association Française de Normalisation (2006). https://www.boutique.afnor.org/fr-fr/norme/nf-en-152211/facility-management-partie-1-termes-et-definitions/fa101944/16245. Accessed 13 July 2018
7. AFNOR: NF EN 15221-7: Facility Management — Part 7: Performance Benchmarking, French Standard, Association Française de Normalisation (2012). https://www.boutique.afnor.org/fr-fr/norme/nf-en-152217/facilities-management-partie-7-etalonnage-comparatif-de-performance/fa165261/40230
8. ISO: ISO 41011: Facility Management — Vocabulary. International Standard, International Organization for Standardization (2024). https://www.iso.org/standard/82405.html
9. BSI Standards Publication: BS EN 15221-6: Facility Management — Part 6: Area and Space Measurement in Facility Management. British Standard, London (2011). https://www.boutique.afnor.org/
10. ISO: ISO 26000:2010 — Guidance on Social Responsibility. International Standard, International Organization for Standardization (2010). https://www.iso.org/standard/42546.html
11. Jünger, M., Reinelt, G., Rinaldi, G.: The traveling salesman problem. Handbooks Oper. Res. Manag. Sci. **7**, 225–330 (1995)
12. Chu, P.C., Beasley, J.E.: A genetic algorithm for the multidimensional knapsack problem. J. Heuristics **4**, 63–86 (1998)
13. Carloman, A.N., Bermudo, U.V.W., Estilloso, E.M., et al.: Bundle AI: an application of multiple constraint knapsack problem (MCKP) through genetic algorithm (GA). Procedia Comput. Sci. **231**, 24–31 (2024). https://www.sciencedirect.com/science/article/pii/S1877050923021658
14. Cacchiani, V., Iori, M., Locatelli, A., et al.: Knapsack problems—an overview of recent advances. Part II: multiple, multidimensional, and quadratic knapsack problems. Comput. Oper. Res. **143**, 105693 (2022). https://www.sciencedirect.com/science/article/pii/S0305054821003889
15. Wolsey, L.A.: Integer Programming. Wiley (2020)
16. AFNOR: NF EN 15221-3: Facility Management — Part 3: Guidance on quality in facility management. French Standard, Paris (2011)

Efficient Algorithms for Spatio-Textual Similarity Join Using In-Memory IR-Trees

Raúl García-Muñoz[1], Francisco García-García[1], Antonio Corral[1](✉), and Michael Vassilakopoulos[2]

[1] Department of Informatics, University of Almeria, Almeria, Spain
{rgm633,paco.garcia,acorral}@ual.es
[2] Department of Electrical and Computer Engineering, University of Thessaly, Volos, Greece
mvasilako@uth.gr

Abstract. Due to the overgrowth of GPS-equipped mobile devices (as smartphones, smartwatches, etc.) and IoT environments, location-based services are generating a large number of objects that contain both spatial and textual information, and therefore, spatio-textual databases have received significant attention in recent years. This paper addresses the problem of *Spatio-Textual Similarity Join* (STSJ), which outputs object pairs that can be important in applications such as social networking, tourism, etc. This join operation consists of, given a set of objects that contain both spatial and textual information, returning pairs of objects that are spatially close and textually similar. To accomplish this, we design and implement four different algorithms to evaluate the STSJ query using the IR-tree in main memory. Two of them are iterative algorithms (Best-First traversal) and the other two are recursive versions (Depth-First approach). For both iterative and recursive algorithms, we use the *plane-sweep* technique and the *smart all-by-all algorithm* to improve query processing. Finally, we conducted extensive experiments on real-world datasets to evaluate the performance of our algorithms for STSJ. The main performance conclusion is that the Best-First algorithm with the smart all-by-all combination has excellent performance for small-medium dataset sizes, while the recursive approach with the same combination reports the best performance for larger ones.

Keywords: Spatio-textual similarity join · In-memory IR-tree · Query evaluation

1 Introduction

With the increasing popularity of GPS-equipped mobile devices (smartphones) and IoT technologies, a large amount of geo-textual data (where objects contain

Supported by grant PID2021-124124OB-I00 funded by the Spanish Government MCIN/AEI/10.13039/501100011033 and the "ERDF A way of making Europe".

A. Awad et al. (Eds.): MEDI 2025, LNCS 16427, pp. 47–60, 2026.
https://doi.org/10.1007/978-3-032-19865-5_4

both location information and textual descriptions) is generated every day and is managed by location-based services that are becoming more ubiquitous [1]. Real-world examples include Google Maps, OpenStreetMap, geo-tagging in social networking services (e.g., Facebook and Instagram), etc. Since these geo-textual objects can be used to improve service quality, gain benefits, and detect events by offering spatio-textual similarity search operations, spatio-textual databases have received a lot of attention in the last decades [1]. Spatio-textual similarity-based queries on such spatio-textual databases are quickly becoming one of the most common types of search, where the similarity metric can combine spatial proximity and textual similarity. Examples of these spatio-textual queries (also known as spatial-keyword queries) are: boolean range, boolean kNN, top-k kNN, similarity join, top-k join, to name the most representative ones [2].

One of the most important of these spatio-textual queries is the *Spatio-Textual Similarity Join* (STSJ) [3], which retrieves pairs of objects that are spatially close and textually similar. Figure 1 illustrates how a specific STSJ query is resolved: "Find pairs of users that are close to each other and share a common interest in *sports*". The query identifies the pair of users in the top-left circles as a valid result, since both are within the same proximity threshold and share the *sports* keyword. In contrast, no pair is formed in the right-hand circle because, although one *sports* user exists, there is no other matching user within that radius to be able to form a pair.

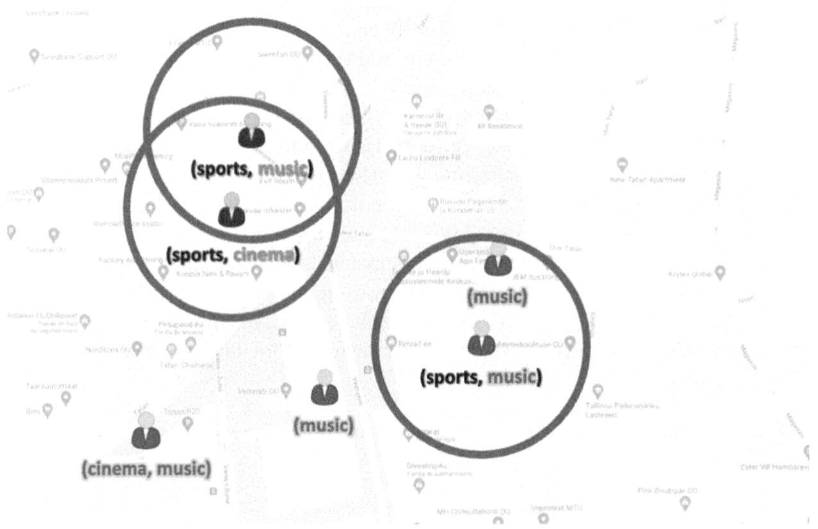

Fig. 1. Executing a STSJ query to find nearby users related to *sports*.

The importance of this join operation is based on the numerous scenarios in which it can be used. For example, in *social networking* applications, the join can be used to identify pairs of people who have similar profiles and are in nearby locations. It can also be applied in *tourism* applications to find thematically similar POIs that are closely located on a map for tour recommendations.

In this paper, we investigate different algorithms to evaluate the *spatio-textual similarity join* query [3] using our IR-tree in main memory [4]. This join query can be expressed as given a collection O objects that contain both spatial and textual information, the STSJ retrieves pairs of objects in O that are both spatially close and textually similar, that is, every pair (o_i, o_j) such that $o_i \neq o_j$, o_i is spatially close to o_j, based on a distance threshold ϵ (i.e., $dist(o_i, o_j) \leq \epsilon$, where *dist* denotes distance between locations), and the similarity between o_i and o_j also exceeds a textual threshold θ (i.e., $sim(o_i, o_j) \geq \theta$, where *sim* denotes textual similarity). The main contribution is the design and implementation of two iterative algorithms (Best-First traversal) for STSJ on IR-tree in main memory, and its comparison with the recursive version proposed in [3].

This paper is organized as follows. Section 2 reviews the state-of-the-art in spatio-textual similarity join queries. In Sect. 3, we present formally the problem and our IR-tree in main memory (i.e., index structure used in the execution of the proposed query algorithms). Section 4 presents the algorithms for the spatio-textual similarity join using the IR-tree in main memory. In Sect. 5, we present the most representative results of an extensive set of experiments that we have carried out, using real-world datasets. Finally, Sect. 6 provides the conclusions arising from our work and discusses related future research lines.

2 Related Work and Motivation

In this section, we review the state-of-the-art in *spatio-textual similarity join* (STSJ) query, which is a very interesting join operation that has not been widely studied in the literature so far. In general, this type of join takes two sets of spatio-textual objects $O = \{o_1, o_2, \cdots, o_n\}$ and $P = \{p_1, p_2, \cdots, p_m\}$, where O and P can be either different or the same set as arguments. A spatio-textual similarity join finds all pairs of objects from O and P that are both spatially close and textually similar [1].

This STSJ operation can be divided into two categories: *threshold-based spatio-textual similarity join* and *top-k spatio-textual similarity join*. For the first category, also known as the threshold-based spatial-keyword similarity join, the main characteristic is that, given a threshold for spatial similarity and another threshold for textual similarity, two spatio-textual objects are similar iff their spatial and textual similarities are less or greater than such thresholds, reporting all such pairs as a result [3,5–8]. It is important to note that specifying the two thresholds is not an easy task for general users because these thresholds are domain-specific (or even data-specific) and cannot control the result size. The first proposal for this STSJ operation was in [3], where one dataset (O) and two thresholds (ϵ-spatial and θ-textual) are the input (it is really a *self-join* operation) and retrieves all pairs (o_i, o_j) with $o_i, o_j \in O$ and $o_i \neq o_j$, such that $dist(o_i.\lambda, o_j.\lambda) \leq \epsilon$ and $sim(o_i, o_j) \geq \theta$. It really combined state-of-the-art spatial and textual similarity join methods and proposed `PPJ-C` (Positional Prefix filtering-based Join - Cell-id order), extending the set similarity join-based algorithm [9] to fit spatial-keyword data, which dynamically divided the space according to the join spatial predicates, and then restricted the application of textual predicates to adjacent grid cell pairs. Moreover, a variant of this algorithm for the IR-tree [10], called `PPJ-IR`, was also outlined and is the basis of our recursive algorithms. In [5], STSJ is studied for two datasets and a prefix-filter-based framework `StarJoin` (*S*patio-*t*extual simil*ar*ity join) is proposed by developing a filtering technique based on Minimum Bounding Rectangle-Prefixes (MBR-Prefixes) to prune large numbers of dissimilar objects pairs. In [6], the authors extend [5] with a hybrid signature scheme by integrating spatial and textual pruning. In a distributed scenario, [7] adapted the state-of-the-art single-node spatio-textual similarity join scheme (the proposed algorithm is based on `PPJoin+` [9] for self-join with a dataset [3]) directly to three MapReduce-based approaches, the so-called as: STSJ-B (baseline), STSJ-C with Cprefix and STSJ-K with kd-trees. In a parallel context (single and multi-threaded implementations), [8] explored local and global partitioning strategies (grid, quadtree, All-pairs and PPJ) to tackle spatio-textual similarity join [3].

For the second category, the *top-k spatio-textual similarity join* (also known as the top-k spatial-keyword similarity join) does not require the two thresholds as input and outputs the k most similar pairs, that is, it finds the top-k pairs based on a scoring function that linearly combines spatial distance and textual similarity [11–13]. In [11], a top-k STSJ scheme was proposed, which identifies the k most similar pairs from two spatio-textual datasets. To solve this join operation, the authors proposed a signature-based framework for top-k STSJ. First, a spatio-textual signature set for each object is generated such that if two objects are in the top-k similar pairs, their signature sets must overlap. Next, the framework computes an upper bound for each signature and proposes a best-first accessing method that preferentially accesses signatures with large upper bounds while those pairs with small upper bounds can be pruned. Finally, the spatio-textual signatures are optimized and progressive signatures are proposed to further improve the pruning power. To improve the drawbacks arose from [11], in [12], tighter thresholds with less computational cost were derived using an aggregated R-tree (aR-tree), which achieved filtering out more dissimilar data pairs. To quickly compute the exact top-k spatial-keyword similarity join result, the authors proposed `Feat-SKSJ` (*f*ast and *e*xact *a*lgorithm for *t*op-k *s*patial-*k*eyword *s*imilarity *j*oin). Recently, in [13], the authors studied the problem of privacy-preserving top-k spatio-textual similarity join. For this purpose, they first define and solve the privacy-preserving top-k spatio-textual similarity join problem and propose two secure similarity join schemes (based on Asymmetric Inner Product Encryption (AIPE) and Locality-Sensitive Hashing (LSH)).

Finally, the main motivation of this research paper is to design and implement efficient iterative algorithms (Best-First traversal) for STSJ on our IR-tree in main memory [4] and compare them with the recursive version proposed in [3], filling such a research gap in the literature. We also experimentally demonstrate their excellent performance on real-world datasets (with different sizes).

3 Problem Statement and Index Structure

3.1 Problem Statement

The concepts, terms and definitions presented in [4] are also necessary for understanding the spatio-textual similarity join query studied in this paper. We assume that each spatio-textual object has a point *location* with latitude, longitude, and a *text* description. Let $O = \{o_1, o_2, \cdots, o_n\}$ be a set of n spatio-textual objects. Each object $o_i \in O$ is defined as a pair $(o_i.\lambda, o_i.\psi)$, where $o_i.\lambda$ is a 2-dimensional (2-dim) geographical point (location) and $o_i.\psi$ is a set of keywords (text document). To measure *similarity* between two spatio-textual objects o_i and o_j, we need to consider spatial distance and textual similarity. We first define the spatial distance.

Definition 1. ***Spatial Distance.*** *Given two spatio-textual objects o_i and o_j, their spatial (2-dim Euclidean) distance, $dist(o_i, o_j)$, is defined as:*

$$dist(o_i, o_j) = dist(o_i.\lambda, o_j.\lambda) = \sqrt{(o_i.\lambda.x - o_j.\lambda.x)^2 + (o_i.\lambda.y - o_j.\lambda.y)^2} \quad (1)$$

where $(o_i.\lambda.x, o_i.\lambda.y)$ are the 2-dim coordinates (x, y) of $o_i.\lambda$ (point location), analogously for $o_j.\lambda$.

Definition 2. ***Textual Similarity.*** *Given two spatio-textual objects o_i and o_j, their textual similarity, $sim(o_i, o_j)$, is defined as:*

$$sim(o_i, o_j) = sim(o_i.\psi, o_j.\psi) = \frac{|o_i.\psi \cap o_j.\psi|}{|o_i.\psi \cup o_j.\psi|} \quad (2)$$

it is known as Jaccard similarity [3].

A spatio-textual similarity join query takes three parameters as input: O is the spatio-textual dataset, ϵ is a spatial distance threshold and θ is a textual similarity threshold. This join operation retrieves pairs of objects in O that are both spatially close and textually similar. More formally, it is defined as follows:

Definition 3. ***Spatio-textual Similarity Join (STSJ) query.*** *Given a set of spatio-textual objects $O = \{o_1, o_2, \cdots, o_n\}$, $\epsilon > 0$ as a spatial distance threshold and $\theta > 0$ as a textual similarity threshold, the query result $STSJ(O, \epsilon, \theta)$ is a set of similar pairs (o_i, o_j) such that $o_i, o_j \in O$ and $o_i \neq o_j$, where $dist(o_i.\lambda, o_j.\lambda) \leq \epsilon$ and $sim(o_i, o_j) \geq \theta$. Formally, $STSJ(O, \epsilon, \theta) = \{(o_i, o_j) | o_i, o_j \in O, 1 \leq i, j \leq n, i \neq j, dist(o_i.\lambda, o_j.\lambda) \leq \epsilon \wedge sim(o_i, o_j) \geq \theta\}$.*

For example, STSJ could be applied to a set of restaurants to identify pairs of establishments that offer similar cuisines and are located close to each other. One practical application might be to find pairs of restaurants that could be considered complementary or competitive within a specific area. Suppose that two restaurants are considered *similar* if their textual similarity (based on menu descriptions, cuisine types, etc.) is no less than 0.5, and they are considered *nearby* if the distance between them is no longer than 3 km. The STSJ could then efficiently retrieve all such pairs of restaurants from a given dataset, satisfying both these textual and spatial constraints.

3.2 Index Structure. IR-Tree in Main Memory

In general, our IR-tree in main memory [4] extends the traditional R-tree by augmenting each node with a reference to an inverted list of documents found within its subtree. Each *node* contains the number of child entries, references to its child nodes, the Minimum Bounding Rectangle (MBR) covering all child entries, and a text description identifier. If the node is a leaf, this identifier points to the text description of an object. Otherwise, it points to a pseudo-text description, which is the union of all text descriptions from its child node entries.

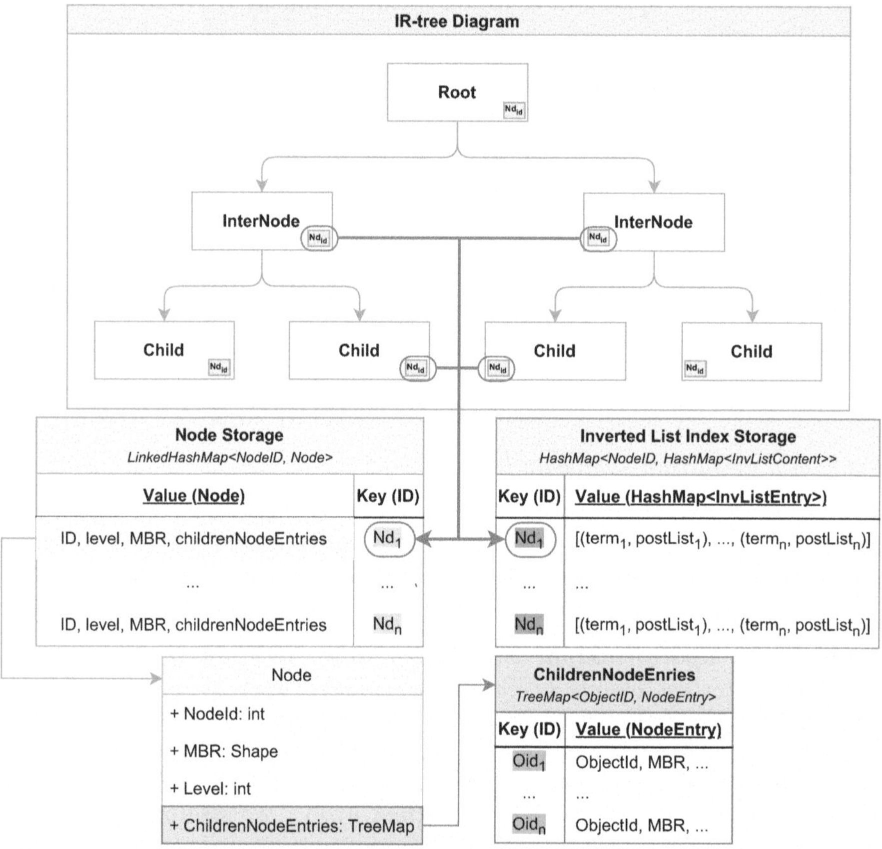

Fig. 2. IR-tree index diagram with the Node Storage manager (center-left), its storage structure and children management (bottom), the Inverted List Index storage (center-right) and the relationship between them by node ID (Nd_{id}).

The spatio-textual index structure used in this paper is our IR-tree in main memory [4], as we can see in Fig. 2. This index contains: (i) a data structure for the keywords and their calculated weights, (ii) the R-tree spatial index with a structure that holds the nodes, and (iii) the inverted lists that form the textual part of the IR-tree index. Our implementation is done in `Java`, using efficient data structures, algorithms, and optimized memory consumption. We have centralized all inverted lists within a dedicated document index storage, as seen in Fig. 2. This storage employs a `HashMap` where the key is the node's ID, and the value is another nested `HashMap` that represents the inverted list for that node. Within this inner `HashMap`, the term IDs serve as keys, maps to their corresponding posting-list entries. This architectural choice makes the R-tree nodes entirely agnostic of their inverted lists, ensuring a highly loosely coupled system.

For our R-tree implementation in main memory, the node structure is detailed in Fig. 2, where we can see that it is managed by a dedicated *Node* storage manager. This manager utilizes a `LinkedHashMap` to store R-tree nodes with their unique IDs as keys. The `LinkedHashMap` was chosen for its ability to preserve the insertion order, a property maintained by its internal doubly-linked list. Each R-tree node stores its unique ID, its level within the tree, its MBR, and its children. The children are managed using a `TreeMap`, which stores *NodeEntry* objects indexed by their child IDs. Each *NodeEntry* contains at least the child's ID and MBR. An important advantage of employing a `TreeMap` is that it inherently orders children, which can be used to optimize query processing.

4 Spatio-Textual Similarity Join Algorithms

This section presents our algorithms (two recursive and two iterative following a Best-First traversal) to process the STSJ query on in-memory IR-trees.

4.1 STSJ Recursive Algorithms

The Recursive Spatio-Textual Similarity Join (STSJ) algorithm processes the join query (recall that it is a self-join based on the algorithm proposed in [3]) by performing a Depth-First traversal on an in-memory IR-tree. The process starts with the root node and descends recursively, applying a series of pruning steps at each level. First, it performs an early spatial pruning by checking if the minimum distance between the MBRs of two nodes exceeds the spatial threshold ϵ; if so, the nodes and their subtrees are discarded. Next, it calculates a textual similarity score using a weighted Jaccard score; if the score is zero, the node pair is pruned. If both spatial and textual conditions are met, a spatial *plane-sweep* algorithm [3] efficiently generates candidate pairs, which are then verified against the textual threshold θ. If the pairs are internal nodes, the process repeats recursively on their children. If they are leaf nodes, the algorithm iterates and validates all pairs of objects against spatial and textual thresholds, returning only valid results. This Depth-First approach ensures that only the most relevant data is processed, with validated results collected as the recursive calls complete.

The non-plane-sweep variant of the Recursive STSJ algorithm uses a *smart all-by-all algorithm* that replaces the plane-sweep method to combine node entries. This novel approach takes advantage of the fact that the node entries are ordered by ID, as described in Sect. 3.2. Instead of processing the full Cartesian product of all possible pairs, $N_x \times N_y$, it prunes the search space by only considering pairs where the ID of the first entry is less than or equal to the ID of the second. Specifically, for an internal node, it processes pairs (e_x, e_y) only if $e_x.id \leq e_y.id$, which effectively processes at most half of the pairs. For leaf nodes, a stricter condition is applied ($e_x.id < e_y.id$) to avoid returning symmetric pairs as valid results. This method significantly reduces the number of pairs to be evaluated, offering an efficient alternative to the plane-sweep approach.

4.2 STSJ Best-First Algorithm

The Best-First STSJ algorithm processes queries using an iterative Best-First traversal of an IR-tree in main memory, prioritizing node pairs based on their spatial proximity. The Algorithm 1 uses a priority queue, *pQueue*, which is initially filled with the root node pair and sort all subsequent node pairs by spatial distance. As long as *pQueue* is not empty, the algorithm iteratively extracts the pair with the smallest spatial distance. For internal node pairs, it first checks for textual similarity (line 17); if the weighted Jaccard score is zero, the pair is discarded. If they are textually relevant, a spatial *plane-sweep* algorithm identifies candidate pairs that satisfy the spatial ϵ and textual θ thresholds (line 25), which are then added to the *pQueue*. For leaf node pairs, the algorithm verifies that the node IDs are not equal to prevent symmetric pairs (in self-join) and then adds them directly to the final result.

The non-plane-sweep variant of the Best-First STSJ algorithm optimizes the join process by using a *smart all-by-all algorithm* instead of a *plane-sweep* (line 20). This method takes advantage of the fact that node entries are sorted by ID. For a given pair of nodes (N_x, N_y), it avoids processing the entire Cartesian product. Instead, it prunes the search space by discarding pairs (e_x, e_y) where $e_x.id > e_y.id$ (line 21) for internal nodes, effectively processing at most half of the possible pairs. The candidate pairs are then evaluated against the spatial ϵ and textual θ thresholds; if they satisfy, they are added to the priority queue. For leaf nodes, entries are discarded if ($e_x.id = e_y.id$) to prevent symmetric pairs (in self-join) from being returned as valid results (line 7). The candidate pair is then added to the results if it is not present. As in the Recursive STSJ algorithm, this approach significantly reduces the number of pairs that must be evaluated, offering an efficient alternative to the *plane-sweep* method.

5 Experimental Results

In this section, we perform the experimental evaluation of the algorithms proposed in Sect. 4 for the STSJ query, using our IR-tree in main memory.

Datasets. To conduct our experiments, we use three real datasets from GitHub[1] and SpatialHadoop[2] The *Hotels* dataset represents a hotel chain in the USA, each

[1] Available at https://github.com/harryckh/TKDE18-coskq.

[2] Available at https://spatialhadoop.cs.umn.edu/datasets.html.

Algorithm 1 STSJBestFirst(T_{IR}, N_x, N_y, ϵ, θ)

Input: IR-tree T_{IR}; two nodes N_x, N_y of T_{IR}; spatial threshold ϵ; textual threshold θ
Output: Set of object pairs (x, y) such that $dist(x, y) \leq \epsilon$ and $sim(x, y) \geq \theta$

```
 1: pQueue ← new PriorityQueue with initial entry (root.id, root.id)
 2: results ← {∅}
 3: processedPairs ← {∅}                    ▷ To prevent processing the same pair twice
 4: while not pQueue.isEmpty() do
 5:     (E_x.id, E_y.id) ← pQueue.poll()
 6:     if E_x and E_y are leaf entries then                     ▷ Processing leaf nodes
 7:         if E_x.id = E_y.id then continue          ▷ Avoid pairs with duplicate terms
 8:         end if
 9:         pairKey ← hash(min(E_x.id, E_y.id), max(E_x.id, E_y.id))
10:         if pairKey ∈ processedPairs then continue
11:         end if
12:         processedPairs ← processedPairs ∪ {pairKey}
13:         results ← results ∪ {(E_x.id, E_y.id)}
14:     else                                                 ▷ Processing internal nodes
15:         N_x ← readNode(E_x.id)
16:         N_y ← readNode(E_y.id)
17:         similarityScores ← CalculateTextualSimilarity(N_x, N_y, query)
18:         if similarityScores.isEmpty() then continue
19:         end if
20:         for each (e_x, e_y) ∈ N_x.entries × N_y.entries do     ▷ Can be plane-sweep
21:             if N_x.id = N_y.id and e_x.id > e_y.id then continue  ▷ Avoid duplicates
22:             end if
23:             spatialDist ← minDist(e_x.MBR, e_y.MBR)
24:             textualSim ← min(similarityScores[e_x.id], similarityScores[e_y.id])
25:             if spatialDist > ε and textualSim < θ then continue
26:             end if
27:             pQueue.add(entry(e_x.id, e_y.id, spatialDist, textualSim))
28:         end for
29:     end if
30: end while
31: return results
```

of which has a spatial location and a set of words that describe each hotel. The other datasets are extracted from OpenStreetMap and represent the features of the world map, in this case *Postal Codes* and *Sports* area boundaries around the world. For the spatial part, we calculate the centroids of such boundaries to obtain a single point that represents the spatial location. The textual part contains general information on the postal codes and sports areas, respectively. The properties of these three datasets are shown in Table 1. We also include the running time to create the index structures for our IR-tree in main memory, along with the amount of RAM space needed to store them.

Setup. We make our implementation publicly available in a GitHub repository[3] The experiments were conducted on a PC running Ubuntu distribution with kernel 6.11.0-29. The Java Virtual Machine max heap size is set to 12GB. The hardware used is an AMD Ryzen 7 5800X 8-core @ 3.8 GHz (boost to 4.8 GHz), with 32 GB of RAM DDR4 @ 3200 MHz. The storage drive is a KIOXIA-EXCERIA PRO 1TB NVMe SSD PCIe Gen4 x4. We have measured the *total execution time* (elapsed time) to process the input data, create the indices, and run the STSJ query. We also measured *memory consumption* as in [4]. Due to the characteristics of the library, running mainly on system memory, the results could potentially be affected by other factors such as memory caching, CPU architecture singularities, and different operating system optimizations. To consider all this, we present the average times obtained from running five consecutive times each query set over the same generated index.

Table 1. Datasets and other performance measures related to index creation.

Property	Hotels	Postal Codes	Sports
Total number of objects	20,676	171,227	1,767,138
Total number of unique words	600	549,405	452,950
Total number of words	58,821	1,812,684	4,510,539
IR-tree creation time	386 msec	3.274 sec	33.006 sec
IR-tree memory-space (peak)	7 MB (100)	645 MB (1483)	1206 MB (2038)

Comparison of the Spatio-Textual Similarity Join (STSJ) Algorithms. The STSJ query represents a significant challenge that requires a detailed analysis of different algorithm implementations and parameters. In this section, we test the performance of four STSJ query implementations (variants with and without plane-sweep), along with changing textual and spatial thresholds. Our test methodology uses six different parameters to evaluate the STSJ query performance: (i) number of keywords (n), (ii) spatial threshold (ϵ), (iii) textual threshold (θ), (iv) combined spatio-textual (ϵ/θ) thresholds, (v) number of objects in the dataset, and (vi) maximum size of the priority queue.

Experiment 1: Keyword and Textual Threshold Variations. First, we tested the performance of our four algorithms against the *Hotels* and *Postal Codes* datasets. Figure 3 (left) shows their performance based on the number of keywords (n), with thresholds $\epsilon = 0.01$ and $\theta = 0.3$. Here, the Best-First algorithm performs similarly to the Recursive one for the *Hotels* dataset. On the *Postal Codes* dataset, the Best-First approach is approximately 16% faster than the Recursive approach. However, Best-First with a plane-sweep variant shows poor performance, being twice as slow as its non-plane-sweep counterpart. This is happening because the overhead of plane-sweep calculations negatively impacts the performance of this variant for small-medium dataset sizes.

[3] Available at https://github.com/acgtic211/ir-tree-medi2025.

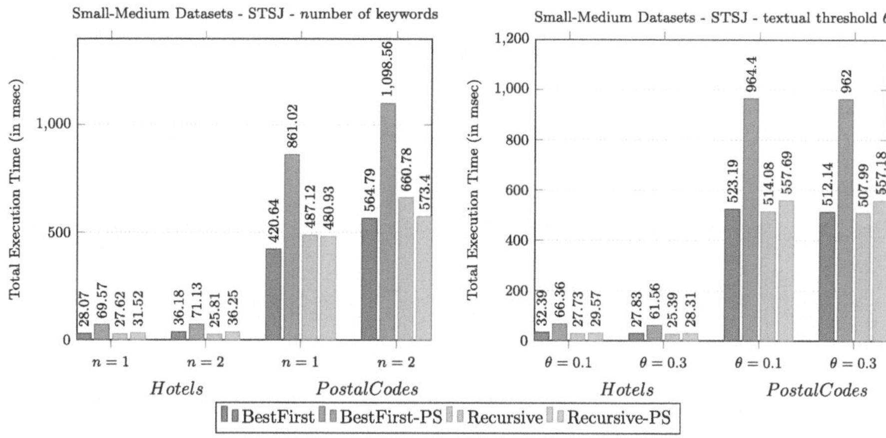

Fig. 3. STSJ cost on different datasets with respect to number of keywords n (left) and textual threshold θ (right).

Figure 3 (right) shows the performance against the textual threshold (θ), with the number of keywords $n = 2$ and with the spatial threshold $\epsilon = 0.01$. We can see that the Best-First algorithm continues to perform well against the Recursive variants. The reason for this good performance of the Best-First algorithm is our use of a relatively small fanout of 25, as previously explored in [14], combined with the way the pairs are processed. Because the `TreeMap` that contains the *Node Entries* is ordered by ID, that means for each pair of nodes processed, we only need to filter a maximum of 25 pairs for inner nodes and 20 pairs for leaf nodes, making this algorithm relatively fast compared to the plane-sweep variant.

Experiment 2: Spatial and Combined Threshold Variations. Next, we present two new experiments that measure performance based on spatial threshold (ϵ) in Fig. 4 (left) and a combined spatio-textual (ϵ/θ) ratio between the two input thresholds ϵ (spatial) and θ (textual) in Fig. 4 (right).

Starting with the spatial threshold ϵ, with the number of keywords $n = 2$ and the threshold $\theta = 0.3$, we found that for small values of ϵ, the Best-First algorithm performs as well as Recursive ones, and is faster with lower values of ϵ. Again, this is due to the small number of pairs processed with a more strict filter. However, when the spatial threshold begins to increase, so does the number of potential pairs that need to be processed. Here, the Best-First algorithms are outperformed by the Recursive ones, as the latter are twice as fast for larger thresholds. For the combined spatio-textual (ϵ/θ) ratio in Fig. 4 (right), with the number of keywords $n = 2$, the Best-First algorithm outperforms the Recursive ones by 5% on average with the smaller thresholds. The plane-sweep variant of the Best-First approach still performs poorly, taking twice as much time as the non-plane-sweep alternative. This again points towards a good performance for

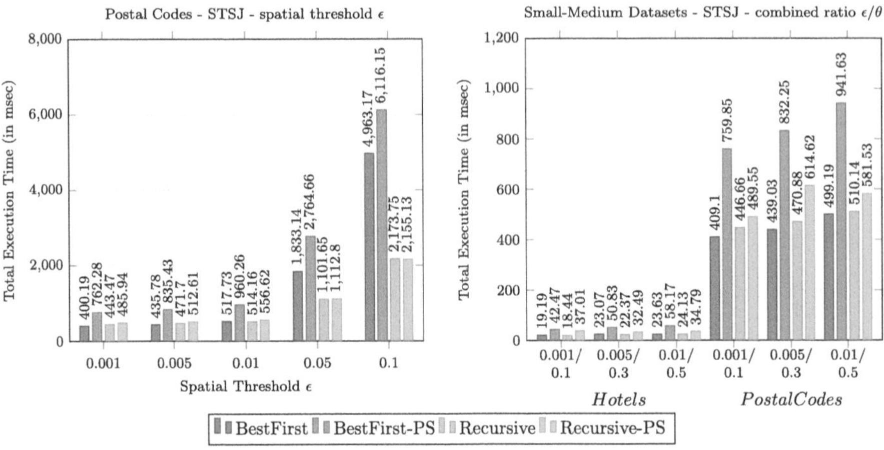

Fig. 4. STSJ cost on *Postal Codes* (right) with respect to spatial threshold ϵ and STSJ cost on different datasets (right) with respect to a combined (ϵ/θ) ratio between the two thresholds, spatial ϵ and textual θ.

the Best-First algorithms if the filtering applied reduce the number of candidate pairs to process.

Experiment 3: Scalability in Relation to the Number of Spatio-textual Objects. In this last experiment, we look at the scalability of our four algorithms in relation to the number of spatio-textual objects processed. To do so, we varied the number of objects in our largest dataset, *Sports*, using 10%, 25%, 50%, 75%, and 100% of the data. We start in Fig. 5 (left) with the number of keywords $n = 2$, the spatial threshold $\epsilon = 0.01$, and the textual threshold $\theta = 0.3$. We observe that as the percentage increases, so does the processing times for all four algorithms due to the increasing number of nodes. Comparing the two Best-First algorithms, the plane-sweep variant is consistently 2 times slower than its non-plane-sweep counterpart. This result aligns with the conclusions of our previous experiments.

Now, as we compare the Best-First algorithm with the Recursive ones, the non-plane-sweep variant is approximately 24% faster than the Recursive algorithm for a 10% subset of the dataset due to the smart processing of the pairs with the `TreeMap`. However, as the number of objects increases, the time difference shifts in favor of the Recursive algorithms. On average, the Recursive algorithm is 1.5 times faster than its non-Recursive counterpart. As we explained earlier, for small datasets with fewer objects, the processing of candidate pairs is relatively fast. However, as the number of objects increases, so does the size of the priority queue, and this initial advantage disappears.

Finally, looking for an explanation for this last behavior, we examine the *maximum capacity of the priority queue* throughout query processing. Figure 5 (right) shows the maximum size compared to the different percentages of the *Sports* dataset. For the smallest subset, the priority queue size is small, which

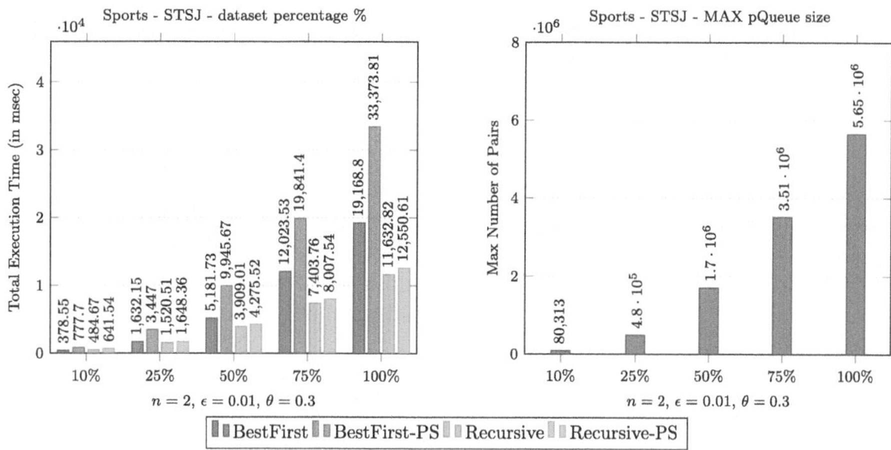

Fig. 5. STSJ cost on *Sports* (right) with respect to the percentage of spatio-textual objects loaded and the maximum priority queue size (right) with respect to the *Sports* processed percentage.

explains the faster processing times compared to the other variants. However, as the size of the subset increases, so does the size of the priority queue. This has two main impacts on the algorithm's performance. The first is that the backlog grows significantly as we traverse the IR-tree in an iterative manner, taking more time to empty the queue even after finding all potential pairs. The second is the main memory consumption overhead. In the last case, we must emphasize that we need to maintain in main memory the priority queue, a set of pairs for the result, and a `HashSet` to track the pairs already added. This makes the Best-First approach less efficient for larger datasets compared to the Recursive algorithm.

6 Conclusion and Future Work

In this paper, we studied the spatio-textual similarity join (STSJ), a query with a wide range of applications (social networking, tourism, data deduplication and cleaning, etc.). This join operation takes three parameters as input: O is the spatio-textual dataset, ϵ is a spatial threshold and θ a textual threshold; and retrieves pairs of objects in O that are both spatially close and textually similar. We design and implement four different algorithms to evaluate the STSJ query using our IR-tree in main memory; two of them are iterative algorithms (Best-First traversal) and the other two are recursive versions (Depth-First approach). For both iterative and recursive algorithms, we use to improve query processing the *plane-sweep* technique and a *smart all-by-all algorithm* combined with the help of a `TreeMap` in the node entries of the IR-tree. Finally, we conducted extensive experiments on real-world datasets to evaluate the performance of our algorithms for STSJ. The main performance conclusion is that the Best-First algorithm with the smart all-by-all combination has excellent performance for small-medium dataset sizes, while the recursive approach with the same combination reports the best behavior for larger ones. This means that the behavior of the Best-First algorithm is constrained by the (large) size of the dataset and by the (high) values of the thresholds. Another interesting result is that the smart all-by-all algorithm always outperforms the plane-sweep technique because the overhead of plane-sweep calculations negatively affects the performance of the proposed algorithms for medium-large fanout values. As part of our future work, we plan to include in our framework (IR-tree in main memory) new spatio-textual join operations such as the STSJ when two independent datasets (O and P) are combined and the top-k spatio-textual similarity join [11,12].

References

1. Chen, Z., Chen, L., Cong, G., Jensen, C.S.: Location- and keyword-based querying of geo-textual data: a survey. VLDB J. **30**(4), 603–640 (2021)
2. Chen, L., Shang, S., Yang, C., Li, J.: Spatial keyword search: a survey. GeoInformatica **24**(1), 85–106 (2020)
3. Bouros, P., Ge, S., Mamoulis, N.: Spatio-textual similarity joins. PVLDB **6**(1), 1–12 (2012)
4. García-Muñoz, R., García-García, F., Corral, A., Vassilakopoulos, M. In-memory spatial-keyword indexing and querying: an experimental evaluation. In: Proceedings of the MEDI Conference 2024. LNCS, vol. 15590, pp. 93–107. Springer, Heidelberg (2025)
5. Liu, S., Li, G., Feng, J.: Star-join: spatio-textual similarity join. In: Proceedings of the CIKM Conference 2012, pp. 2194–2198. ACM, Maui, HI, USA (2012)
6. Liu, S., Li, G., Feng, J.: A prefix-filter based method for spatio-textual similarity join. IEEE Trans. Knowl. Data Eng. **26**(10), 2354–2367 (2014)
7. Zhang, Y., Ma, Y., Meng, X.: Efficient spatio-textual similarity join using mapreduce. In: Proceedings of the WI-IAT Conference 2014, Volume II, pp. 52–59. IEEE, Warsaw, Poland (2014)
8. Rao, J., Lin, J., Samet H.: Partitioning strategies for spatio-textual similarity join. In: Proceedings of the BigSpatial@SIGSPATIAL Conference 2014, pp. 40–49. ACM, Dallas, Texas, USA (2014)
9. Xiao, C., Wang, W., Lin, X., Yu, J.X., Wang, G.: Efficient similarity joins for near-duplicate detection. ACM Trans. Database Syst. **36**(3): 15:1–15:41 (2011)
10. Li, Z., Lee, K.C.K., Zheng, B., Lee, W.-C., Lee, D.L., Wang, X.: IR-tree: an efficient index for geographic document search. IEEE Trans. Knowl. Data Eng. **23**(4), 585–599 (2011)
11. Hu, H., et al.: Top-k spatio-textual similarity join. IEEE Trans. Knowl. Data Eng. **28**(2), 551–565 (2016)
12. Amagata, D., Tsuruoka, S., Arai, Y., Hara, T. Feat-SKSJ: fast and exact algorithm for top-k spatial-keyword similarity join. In: Proceedings of the SIGSPATIAL Conference 2021, pp. 15–24. ACM, Beijing, China (2021)
13. Teng, Y., Jiang, D., Sun, M., Zhao, L., Xu, L., Fan, C.: Privacy-preserving top-k spatio-textual similarity join. In: Proceedings of the TrustCom Conference 2022, pp. 718–726. IEEE, Wuhan, China (2022)
14. García-Muñoz, R., García-García, F., Corral, A., Vassilakopoulos, M.: Improving the IR-tree in main memory for spatial-keyword query processing. In: Proceedings of the SISTEDES Spanish Conference 2025, pp. 1–14. Cordoba, Spain (2025)

Managing Model Evolution from NoSQL Data Lakes to Decision Support Systems

Said Taktak[1(✉)], Zoubair Mabrouk[1], Slim Kallel[1,2], and Ahmed Hadj Kacem[1]

[1] ReDCAD Laboratory, ENIS, University of Sfax, Sfax, Tunisia
{said.taktak,zoubair.mabrouk,slim.kallel,ahmed.hadjkacem}@redcad.org
[2] Digital Research Center of Sfax, Sfax, Tunisia

Abstract. Decision Support Systems (DSS) have traditionally relied on relational data warehouses and ETL pipelines, which provide stable analytics over structured data but struggle with the rapid emergence of heterogeneous data lakes. Rebuilding DSS infrastructures to natively accommodate NoSQL sources is rarely feasible due to the critical role of legacy systems. This paper addresses the challenge of incrementally extending DSS with evolving NoSQL data while preserving analytical consistency, integrity, and compatibility with existing assets. To this end, we propose an MDE-based approach that leverages a unified model to abstract NoSQL structures into entities, attributes, and relationships. A set of transformation rules is introduced to generate evolution operations that update DSS models and keep them consistent. We demonstrate the applicability of our approach through a medical case study based on the MIMIC-III clinical database, extended with NoSQL sources from telemedicine, Internet of Medical Things, and rehabilitation data. The results show that our method enables seamless model evolution, preserving semantics and unlocking new analytical capabilities without disrupting the operational core.

Keywords: Decision Support Systems · Data lake · Model Evolution · NoSQL Databases · Model-Driven Engineering

1 Introduction

Decision Support Systems (DSS) are central to organizational decision-making, enabling the collection, transformation, and analysis of data to support informed strategies. Traditional DSS architectures, built around centralized relational data warehouses and ETL (Extract, Transform, Load) processes, have long provided stable support for structured data analytics. However, these approaches show significant limitations when confronted with the massive emergence of heterogeneous sources, particularly from NoSQL systems. Their reliance on rigid schemas, costly adaptations, and the difficulty of integrating semi-structured or unstructured formats hampers their ability to keep pace with modern data environments. In practice, many of these new and heterogeneous sources are first ingested into

A. Awad et al. (Eds.): MEDI 2025, LNCS 16427, pp. 61–80, 2026.
https://doi.org/10.1007/978-3-032-19865-5_5

a Data Lake, which serves as a repository for raw and evolving data. The Data Lake thus represents a natural entry point for potential DSS extensions, concentrating NoSQL data (documents, graphs, key–value, or column-oriented) that must be reconciled with the relational foundations of existing systems.

Rebuilding a DSS from scratch to natively accommodate NoSQL sources is rarely feasible when legacy systems are operational and intertwined with mission-critical processes. The practical challenge is therefore to incrementally extend the existing system, preserving its contracts and performance envelopes, while enabling safe integration of evolving NoSQL data. Concretely, organizations need a principled way to (i) absorb heterogeneous structures and relationships, (ii) propagate schema changes into relational and multidimensional layers, and (iii) maintain compatibility with established analytics.

Our research is guided by three research questions: **RQ1**: How can heterogeneous NoSQL structures be abstracted so that relational and multidimensional targets are derived automatically and consistently? **RQ2**: How should evolution operations be ordered to preserve integrity and minimize downtime? **RQ3**: What artifacts (tables, bridges, slowly changing dimensions) best preserve analytic value when new relationships and behaviors emerge in sources?

To address these challenges, we propose an MDE-based approach that leverages a unified conceptual model to absorb NoSQL heterogeneity and automate change propagation. Detected changes in the Data Lake (e.g., the arrival of a new collection or a new graph edge type) are first projected onto the unified schema abstraction, then compiled into modification operations for the operational relational model, and finally propagated into the multidimensional schema. At the core of this approach is a set of transformation rules that (a) infer structures and multiplicities from instances, (b) distinguish references, aggregations, and relationship types, and (c) generate evolution operations to be applied on DSS models in order to keep them up to date. This design keeps the core DSS stable while enabling incremental evolution, versioning, and traceability.

The remainder of this paper is organized as follows: Sect. 2 reviews related work on schema evolution in DSS. Section 3 details our MDE-based approach for integrating changes from new sources into an existing DSS. Section 4 introduces the transformation rules used to translate detected changes into relational and multidimensional artifacts. Section 5 reports the medical case study and evaluation. Section 6 concludes and outlines future directions.

2 Related Work

We orient our work in a tradition that regards schema change as a first-order consideration across data mod- els. The early work in object-oriented databases explored formal operations and implantation techniques for schema evolution [1,3]; the surveys then explored the ramifications of versioning and temporal issues that affect information systems [13]. With respect to integration, model management defined generic operators over schemas and mappings [2] and subsequently experimentally included them in processes such as IBM's Clio, and also theoretically in the whole area of data exchange, which jointly defined the use of mappings for executable transformation and correctness [8].

For semi-structured data, the community has characterized how schema drift in XML affects document validity and query behavior, as well as supporting incremental validation techniques that operate with similar performance as the schema is evolving [9]. This attention to schema change evolved into change-impact for schemas at both the type-system and query levels, leading to activities around evolution-aware pipelines, which reason about constraints and semantic issues other than just structural changes.

Currently, work is extending these principles to agile, so-called schema less ecosystems. Empirical studies repeatedly show that NoSQL applications do evolve schema in practice, often by application code and object mappers, and therefore require explicit migration strategies and governance [14–16]. These findings motivate advisor-like tooling (detect–plan–migrate) and taxonomy-driven approaches that standardize change operations across stores and deployment contexts.

In multimodel settings, recent advances abstract across paradigms. U-Schema offers a unified metamodel that distinguishes *entity types*, *relationship types*, and *structural variations*, and covers relational, document, column, key–value, and graph models [4]. Building on that foundation, the Orion language introduces a taxonomy and executable semantics for cross-model schema changes, with formal validation and multi-store code generation; companion work proposes SkiQL, a unified schema query language over U-Schema [5–7]. These contributions collectively enable inference, evolution, and querying over heterogeneous data landscapes using a single conceptual handle.

The implications for data warehousing and analytics are long standing: warehouse schemas must evolve with sources and business needs. Foundational analyses and surveys of warehouse schema evolution—covering dimension/-fact updates, hierarchy reconfiguration, versioning, and view maintenance — document both operators and governance patterns [11,12]. This body of work informs modern data lakes and lakehouses, where schema-on-read is insufficient without provenance and controlled evolution, and where cross-model unification (as in U-Schema/Orion) can drive consistent DDL/DML generation and safe refactoring toward Business Intelligence and Machine Learning workloads.

A recent comprehensive survey consolidates these threads across paradigms and articulates comparison axes—data model, implementation, change semantics, propagation, integrity, and software evolution—that we adopt as organizing dimensions for our approach [3]. In short, the trajectory from object-oriented evolution and mapping theory to unified multimodel adapters and execution languages underpins our methodology: infer structure and relations, reason about change using a generic taxonomy, and emit ordered, integrity-preserving migrations against existing relational systems.

3 Our Approach in a Nutshell

Figure 1 presents the overall architecture considered in our study. It distinguishes between (i) the existing Decision Support System (DSS), composed of a relational data source feeding a multidimensional data warehouse and BI tools, and (ii) the new data sources arising from the Data Lake, which include heterogeneous NoSQL families such as document, graph, key–value, and column-oriented databases. As these new sources evolve, two classes of evolution operations must be considered. First, data source evolution operations (e.g., addition of collections, attributes, or relationships) must be propagated to the relational data source. Second, data warehouse evolution operations (e.g., new dimensions or measures) ensure that analytical structures remain consistent with upstream changes. The focus of this article is the first stage of propagation, namely how schema changes detected in NoSQL sources are captured and translated into corresponding modifications of the relational data model. This part of the architecture, highlighted by the dashed line in Fig. 1, represents the foundation of our MDE based approach: it ensures that the relational layer remains synchronized with heterogeneous and evolving sources while preserving consistency and contracts with downstream BI assets.

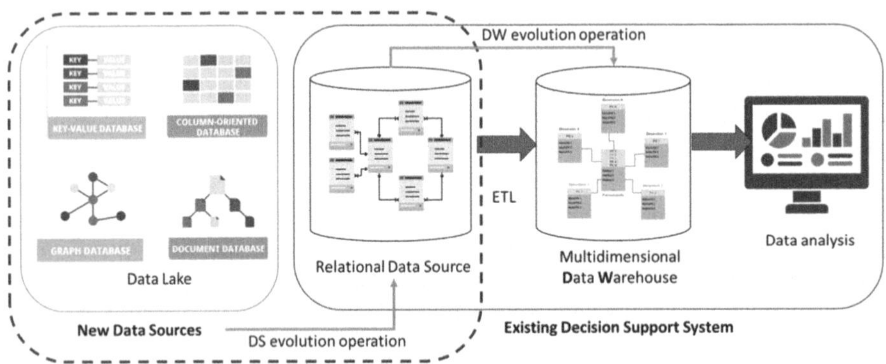

Fig. 1. DSS architecture

Extending an existing DSS to integrate heterogeneous and evolving NoSQL sources requires both a conceptual representation that can capture structural diversity, and a systematic process to transform this representation into operational models. In our research, we build upon the principles of Model-Driven Engineering (MDE) to ensure that schema evolution is handled in a structured, traceable, and reproducible way.

Our solution relies on two complementary components. First, we introduce a unified conceptual model capable of abstracting diverse NoSQL structures into a common representation of entities, attributes, and relationships. Second, we define an MDE-based approach that exploits this unified model to drive the generation of evolution operations on DSS relational schemas.

3.1 Unified Model Based Approach

To capture and integrate heterogeneous NoSQL structures, we adopt a unified conceptual model (U-schema) that abstracts away store-specific details while preserving the essential semantics of the sources [4]. Figure 2 illustrates this metamodel, which we use as the pivot representation for all schema evolution operations.

At the top level, a `uNoSQLSchema` aggregates the descriptions of all ingested sources. Each schema is composed of one or more `EntityTypes`, which represent structural units such as collections in document stores, column families in wide-column databases, or node types in graph databases. An entity type may be flagged as root when it represents an independent entry point in the data source.

Each entity type contains one or several `StructuralVariations`, capturing the fact that NoSQL data often evolves without global coordination. A variation corresponds to a concrete structural version of an entity observed at a given point in time. Variations are timestamped (`firstTimestamp`, `lastTimestamp`) and record the number of observed instances, enabling temporal and frequency-aware analysis of schema drift.

Entity types and their variations are described through `Features`, which can be of three kinds:

- `Attributes`, corresponding to simple or nested properties of an entity. Each attribute is typed by a `DataType`, which can be primitive (e.g., string, integer), null, or a container (e.g., list, set, tuple, map).
- `References`, representing links between entities. They carry lower and upper bounds to express multiplicity constraints and may have an opposite reference, modeling bidirectional relationships.
- `Aggregates`, corresponding to embedded structures (e.g., nested documents), which are treated differently from external references because they imply ownership and co-evolution.

The model also explicitly supports `Keys`, which may be provided by the source or inferred. Keys are essential for ensuring uniqueness, electing primary identifiers in the relational translation, and preserving referential integrity.

This unified metamodel offers several advantages:

- Heterogeneity abstraction: it can represent documents, graph nodes, key–value pairs, and wide-column families uniformly.
- Schema variation management: it explicitly records structural drift, enabling reasoning about evolution over time.
- Transformation readiness: its constructs (entity, attribute, reference, aggregate) map directly to relational targets (tables, columns, foreign keys, bridge tables).

In practice, every new or modified structure detected in the Data Lake is first projected into this unified model. The projection step ensures that different NoSQL sources can be compared and processed in a homogeneous way.

Once represented in the model, schema changes can then be compiled into evolution operations that update DSS models and keep them up to date (e.g., table creation, attribute addition, foreign key introduction). This process of change propagation is defined using MDE principles, as detailed in the following subsection.

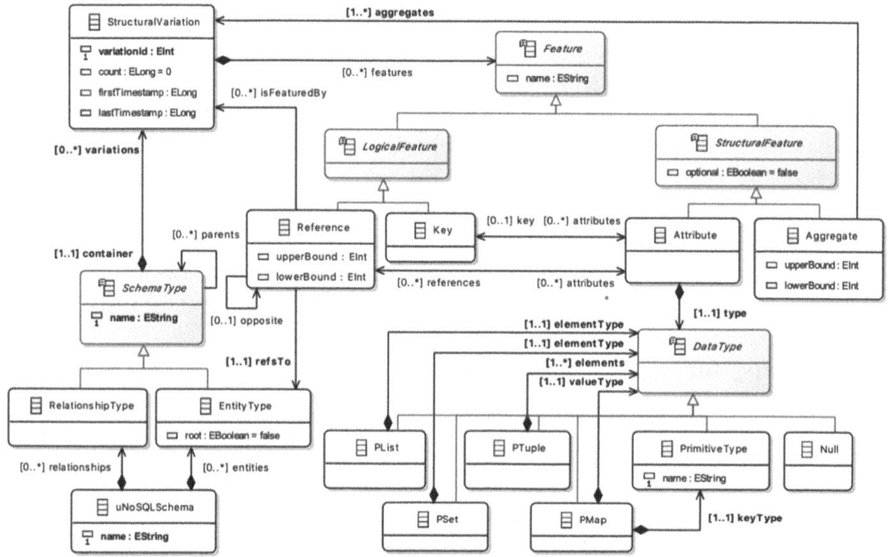

Fig. 2. U-schema Meta Model [4]

3.2 MDE Based Approach

Our approach is grounded in Model-Driven Engineering (MDE) principles, which promote the use of explicit models as primary artifacts for system specification, transformation, and evolution. Rather than directly manipulating heterogeneous data structures, we rely on models to capture both the abstractions of source schemas and the operations required to propagate their changes. In this perspective, NoSQL sources, the relational schema, and the multidimensional schema are all represented as instances of metamodels. This separation of concerns enables us to reason about evolution at the model level, where schema differences can be detected, classified, and transformed systematically. Concretely, MDE brings three advantages in our context:

- Abstraction: data source peculiarities (e.g., collections, graph edges, column families) are mapped onto a higher-level representation, avoiding ad hoc treatments.

- Automation: transformations between models (e.g., from NoSQL abstractions to relational artifacts) are defined once as rules and executed repeatedly with correctness guarantees.
- Traceability: every evolution operation is captured at the model level, allowing us to version, validate, and audit schema changes across layers of the DSS.

Based on this foundation, our pipeline interprets the arrival or modification of NoSQL structures as model evolution operations, which are then propagated through transformation rules. The next subsection introduces the unified conceptual model that enables this abstraction over heterogeneous data sources.

Figure 3 illustrates the end-to-end process of projecting and transforming NoSQL models into a relational schema, guided by a unified metamodel. This approach builds upon prior work in schema mapping and multimodel unification, particularly leveraging the U-Schema metamodel [11] and the Orion taxonomy [12,13], which provide a formal basis for representing and evolving schemas across different data paradigms. Our contribution operationalizes these foundations into a practical, rule-driven pipeline for incremental schema evolution.

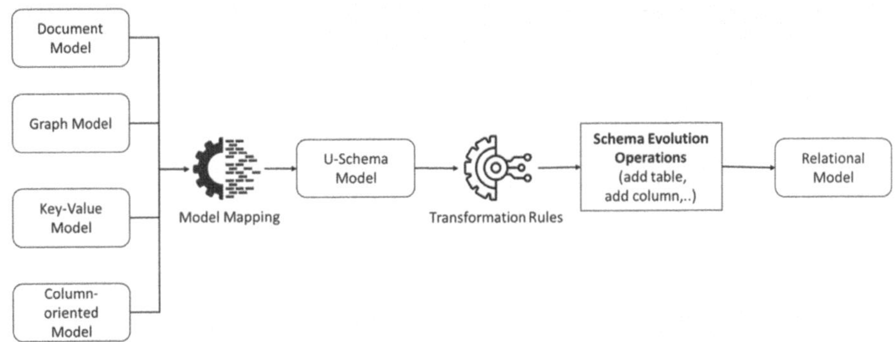

Fig. 3. MDE-Based Approach from NoSQL to relational schema

The MDE-based approach defines the framework for propagating changes from heterogeneous NoSQL sources to DSS schemas. In Sect. 4, we detail the transformation rules that implement this framework, specifying how structural variations are translated into concrete evolution operations

4 Transformation Rules

In this section, we present our algorithms blocks for migrating the No-SQL database to an existing relational database related to an information system, based on a set of rules R1-R6 that defines the logic of our approach. The algorithm processes documents in the state of the U-schema model through sequential stages that dynamically adapt to the presence of the schema while maintaining the relational integrity.

THE ALGORITHM treats NoSQL-to-relational convergence as a rule-driven planning problem that outputs an executable, dependency-aware evolution plan Δ. In input it take a U-Schema $\sqcap\mathcal{S}$ and a current relational schema $\mathcal{RS}$, the algorithm accumulates evolution actions: **R1** ensures a target table for every entity, **R2** maps attributes into columns, **R3** converts inter-entity references into foreign keys, **R4** externalizes embedded objects as non-root tables with $1:N$ links (and recurses), and **R5** realizes relationship types as association tables. Finally, **R6** topologically orders all actions by foreign-key dependencies to yield a conflict-free schedule. Separating local rule application (R1–R5) from global ordering (R6) makes the procedure idempotent, composable, and suitable for incremental runs as $\mathcal{US}$ drifts. In practice, the planner runs in time roughly linear in ($\mathcal{US}$), preserves semantics (keys, references, cardinalities), and exposes policy hooks (e.g., type mappings, denormalization thresholds) without altering the core logic. The observable result is a principled in theory yet pragmatic in practice approach to co-evolving $\mathcal{RS}$ with heterogeneous sources that yields a normalized, migration-ready schema including a traceable documentation of every update.

Algorithm 1 SCHEMAEVOLUTIONWITHRULES

Input: U-Schema $\mathcal{US}$, Relational Schema $\mathcal{RS}$
Output: evolution action $\mathcal{E}$

```
1  begin
2      E ← ∅
3      foreach EntityType E in ⊓S do
           // R1: Ensure target table exists for each entity
4          E ← E ∪ R1_EntityToTable (E)
           // R2: atomic attributes → Add/evolve to columns
5          E ← E ∪ R2_AttributeToColumn (E)
6      foreach EnityType E in ⊓S do
           // R3: References/edges → FK
7          E ← E ∪ R3_References (E)
           // R4: Embedded objects → non root entity + FK (1-N); recurse
8          E ← E ∪ R4_Aggregations (E)
9      foreach RelationshipType R in ⊓S do
           // R5: RelationshipType → association tables
10         E ← E ∪ R5_RelationshipType (R)
       // R6: Action ordering by FK deps
11     Δ ←R6_SchemaEvolution (RS,E)
12     return (RS, Δ)
```

Rule `R1_EntityToTable` concerns the addition of a new table, named Add_Table, to the relational schema ($\mathcal{RS}$) as part of an evolution operation. This operation is derived from each EntityType defined in the Unified Schema ($\mathcal{US}$). First, the rule checks, using the matchingTable function, whether a table with the same name already exists in the relational schema. This is done through syntactic validation of table names. Second, the rule verifies whether any attributes in the EntityType are marked as unique keys. If such attributes exist, they will be defined as primary keys in the generated table.

Algorithm 2 `R1_EntityToTable`

```
   Input: Entity E
   Output: Evolution ops for E
13 begin
14   ops ← ∅
15   if not matchingTable(E) then
16     if E.key is exisit then
17       ops ← Add_Table(name(E), PK(E.KEY))
18     else
19       ops ← Add_Table(name(E))
20   return ops
```

Rule `R2_AttributeToColumn` defines the process for mapping the attributes of a Unified Schema ($\mathcal{US}$) entity to a relational table schema. Once an entity has been processed into a table format by rule R1, rule R2 further processes each attribute within the entity's variations, treating them as potential candidate columns for the corresponding relational table.

The mapping process start with an analysis of the attributes based on their data types, we try to put in $\tau^\star$ the near relational type that support the attribute type's. For primitive types, such as number, string, or date, the attributes are directly delegated as standard columns type. In cases where the attributes are of a more complex type, such as an Array, the rule assigns them as BJSON columns type.

Afterward, the rule checks whether any attribute matches an existing column in the generated table. If a match is found but with a different data types, $\tau^\star \neq \tau_{ex}$ with τ_{ex} represent the type of the matched column in the relational schema, the column type is updated to a unified type, noted Commun_Type, that support both of the original and new data types. In instances where no matching column is found, the attribute is treated as a new column with Add_Column and it is added to the table with the same data type. Ultimately, rule R2 ensures that each attribute of an entity is correctly mapped to a column in the relational table either by matching an existing column or by introducing a new one as needed.

Algorithm 3 `R2_AttributeToColumn`

Input: Entity E
Output: Evolution ops for E

```
21 begin
22   ops ← ∅
23   foreach Attribute a in variations of E do
24     if type(a) is Primitive then
25       τ* ← type(a)
26     else
27       τ* ← BJSON
28     if matchingColumn(E,a) then
29       if τ* ≠ τ_ex then
30         ops ← ops ∪ Commun_Type(E, a, τ*)
31     else
32       ops ← ops ∪ Add_Column(E, a, τ*)
33   return ops
```

Rule `R3_References` deals with the references (i.e., reference meta-class in the Fig. 2) between entities in the Unified Schema ($\mathcal{US}$) and translate them into relational schema. The rule works by examining whether the reference between two entities should be represented as an inline foreign key or an association table, based on cardinality.

For single valued reference, where each entity can reference at most one record in the other entity, the rule check if there is already a constraint foreign key (FK) with matchingReference function. If there is no constraint matched, the rule makes a new column in the referenced table. The foreign key pointed from the referenced table to the table corespondent to the current entity in the relational schema ($\mathcal{RS}$).

For list of values as references, a reference where an entity can refer to multiple variations in another entity, as in many-to-many relationships, the rule `R3_References` creates an association table to represent this relationship. First, the association table name was affected by the function NameAssociation. After that, this nick name would be passed by R1 to apply the process of creating a new table if does not already in place. And finally, the rule make in place the constraints foreign key from the associate table to the two referred entities E and F attacking there primary key.

Algorithm 4 R3_References

Input: Entity E
Output: Evolution ops for E

```
34 begin
35   ops ← ∅
36   foreach Reference r : E → F do
37     if r.isList = false then
38       if not matchingReference(F, r) then
39         ops ← ops ∪ Add_Column(F, r)
40       ops ← ops ∪ Add_FK(F.r → E.pk)
41     else
42       J ← NameAssociation(E, r, F)
43       ops ← ops ∪ R1_EntityToTable(J, (E.pk, F.pk))
44       ops ← ops ∪ Add_FK(J.e_id → E.pk)
45       ops ← ops ∪ Add_FK(J.f_id → F.pk)
46   return ops
```

Rule R4_Aggregations controls the relations between parent and child tables during the evolving of the relational schema ($\mathcal{RS}$). Its main goal is to make sure that every child entity correctly references its parent. If this reference does not exist, the rule creates a foreign key column in the child table that points to the parent's primary key.

The rule maps each aggregation in the variations of an entity E, in the Unified Schema, and verifies if the relationship with another entity C is already exists in the target relational schema using the function matchingAggregation. This function responsible the verify the presence of a column, in the relational schela ($\mathcal{RS}$), to support the constraint foreign key (FK) in the child table, if it is not founded, an operation of adding new one made in place with Add_Column. Then, the rule use the function Add_FK to create a foreign key – primary key relation between child and parent tables.

Algorithm 5 R4_Aggregations

Input: Entity E
Output: Evolution ops for E and its children

```
47 begin
48   ops ← ∅
49   foreach Aggregation g : E → C do
50     if not matchingAggregation(C, g) then
51       ops ← ops ∪ Add_Column(F, r)
52     ops ← ops ∪ Add_FK(C.g → E.pk)
53   return ops
```

Rule R5_RelationshipType takes any relationship type in the Unified Schema between two entities (E and F). First, we use the function NameAssociation to extract a uniform name for the association candidate's table and then it will be examined by the rules R1 and R2 respectively to ensure it was well created. This new association table connects the two entities by pointing to their primary keys together, making a many to many relation between its.

Algorithm 6 R5_RelationshipType

Input: Relationship $r : E \leftrightarrow F$
Output: Evolution ops for r

```
54 begin
55     ops ← ∅
56     J ← NameAssociation(E, r, F)
57     ops ← ops ∪ R1_EntityToTable(J, (E.pk, F.pk))
58     ops ← ops ∪ R2_AttributeToColumn(J, (E.pk, F.pk))
59     ops ← ops ∪ Add_FK(J.e_id → E.pk), Add_FK(J.f_id → F.pk)
60     return ops
```

Rule R6_SchemaEvolution takes all the planned schema changes and organizes them into a safe, executable SQL migration plan. It determines the correct order of actions, such as creating tables, adding columns, updating types, creating indexes, and setting foreign keys, so that each step happens only after its dependencies are ready. The rule ensures that the migration process is reliable, avoids conflicts, and can be repeated without errors. It also adapts to the database system's capabilities, using techniques to reduce downtime and keep the schema consistent. In short, R6 turns a list of evolution actions into a clear, ordered SQL plan that updates the database safely and efficiently.

Algorithm 7 R6_SchemaEvolution

Input: evolution action $\mathcal{E}$, existing DB $\mathcal{R}$
Output: $SQLQuery : \Delta$

```
61 begin
62     ℰ ← ℰ.sort_By_FK_Dependencies()
63     Δ ← Generate SQL Query for all Add_Table/Add_Column/Modify_Type/Add_FK
64     return Δ
```

5 Case Study: Extending MIMIC-III with NoSQL Healthcare Data

The Medical Information Mart for Intensive Care III (MIMIC-III) is a publicly available clinical database developed by the MIT Laboratory for Computational Physiology [10]. It comprises data from over 60,000 intensive care unit (ICU) stays structured into 26 relational tables.

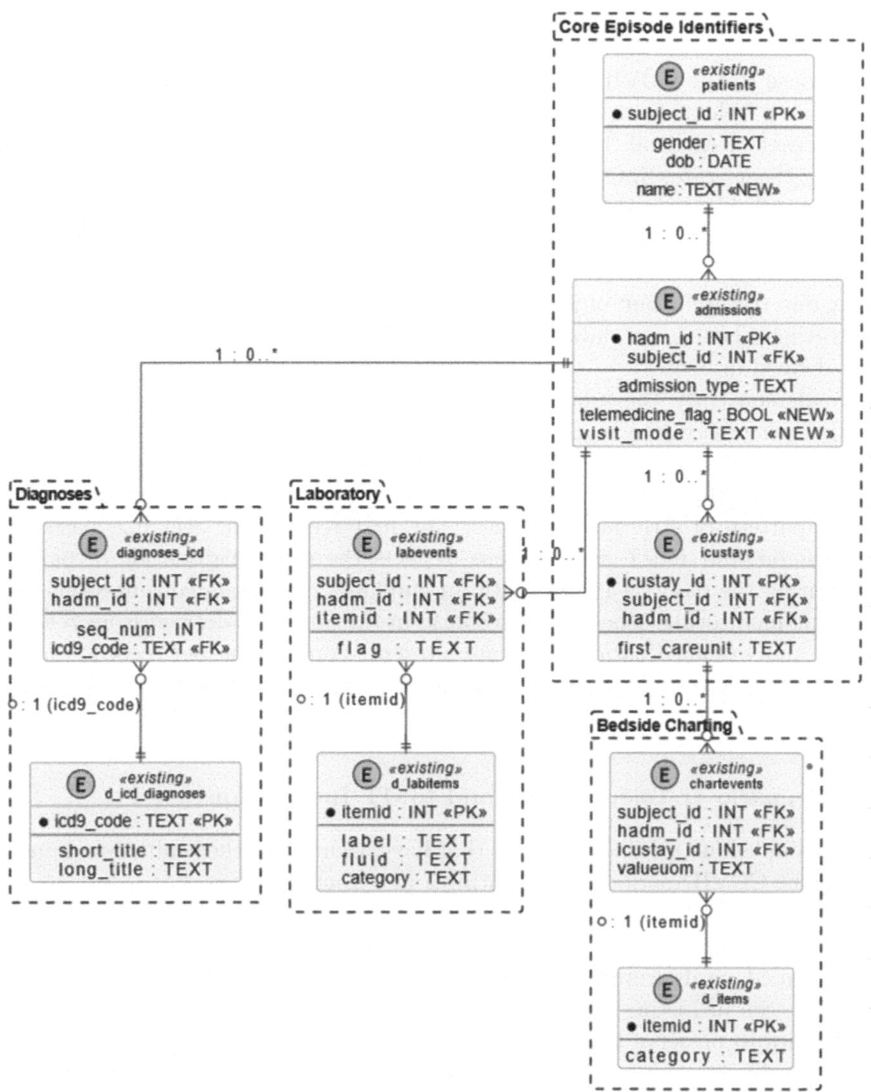

Fig. 4. MIMIC Initial Schema

MIMIC-III captures rich clinical information such as demographics, vital signs, lab measurements, medications, diagnoses, and more. Relationships across tables are implicitly defined using identifiers such as `subject_id`, `hadm_id`, and `icustay_id`, requiring complex joins to reconstruct full patient trajectories. A simplified and initial schema is presented in Fig. 4.

5.1 Appear of NoSQL Medical Data

In response to the COVID-19 pandemic, the healthcare sector has increasingly relied on (i) Telemedicine platforms for remote consultations and prescriptions, (ii) Internet of Medical Things (IoMT) devices for real time patient monitoring (e.g., heart rate, SpO_2), and Cloud based radiology systems for diagnostic imaging and AI analysis. These data sources are typically stored in Data lake (NoSQL formats), lacking a predefined schema and requiring dynamic integration methods.

In our research, our objective was to extend the MIMIC-III database by integrating a healthcare data lake that represents heterogeneous data using the rules defined in Sect. 4.

To demonstrate the adaptability of our transformation rules, we present two distinct integration scenarios in which heterogeneous NoSQL data sets are ingested into the intial MIMIC-III relational schema represented in the Fig. 4. Each scenario appeared from a different medical data domain and introduces a unique pattern of structural changes. The first scenario in Sect. 5.2, based on *telemedicine* and *IoMT vital streams*, reflects the rapid digitization of patient care during the COVID-19 era, with an emphasis on remote consultations and real-time monitoring. The second scenario in the Sect. 5.3, derived from *rehabilitation* and *extended patient profiling*, presents complex nested records, multi-valued attributes, and data quality issues that require a complete schema refinement.

5.2 Scenario 1: Telemedicine and IoMT Integration

This example illustrates the changes that have occurred in the healthcare domain during the COVID period by presenting a new document based as a data source to MIMIC-III: (i) telemedicine encounters, such as online visits, patient data such as messages, notes, prescriptions, and attachments, and (ii) IoMT data (e.g., timestamped vitals from IoMT devices). An example record within a NoSQL record is seen in Listing 1.1.

We aim to preserve the clinical semantics from beginning to end while producing analytics-ready relational artifacts that are compatible with the existing structures. To exemplify the basic input formats, Listing 1.1 shows a typical NoSQL document to capture telemedicine encounters occurrences with the IoMT stream data included.

Listing 1.1. NoSQL Telemedicine & IoMT Data

```
1  {
2    "admissions": {
3      "hadm_id": 230001,
4      "subject_id": 100001,
5      "telemedicine_flag":true
6      "visit_mode": "remote"
7    },
8    "online_consultations": [
9      {
10       "consult_id": 900001,
11       "subject_id": 100001,
12       "hadm_id": 230001,
13       "platform": "Zoom",
14       "duration_min": 35,
15       "notes": "Post-discharge follow-up.",
16       "attachments": ["url://doc1.pdf", "url://screenshot.png"],
17       "prescriptions": [
18         {
19         "drug": "Amoxicillin",
20         "dose": "500 mg",
21         "route": "oral"
22         }
23       ]
24     }
25   ],
26   "iomt_vitals": [
27     {
28       "subject_id": 100001,
29       "device_id": "HR-BAND-77",
30       "ts": "2025-05-11T09:03:00Z",
31       "hr": 92,
32       "spo2": 97
33     }
34   ]
35 }
```

We initially transform the incoming NoSQL payloads into a consistent model, U-Schema, serving as a central model and we then implement our transformation rules to this pivot. Root objects are converted into Entity types and subsequently, R1 will handle the processing, where scalar fields are associated with attributes in keys (e.g., consult_id, device_id) and scalar arrays (e.g., attachments) transform into multivalued attributes prior to applying the R2 processes them similar to a candidate's columns, cross-document identifiers (subject_id, hadm_id) are addressed as references set up for R3, collections of objects (e.g., prescriptions) are advanced to combine types with specified multiplicities, and R4 was prepared to handle its. This theatrical representation removes store-specific characteristics (nesting, polymorphic arrays) while preserving the clinical identity model and time resolution required for subsequent analytics.

The compilation generates the relational extensions shown in Fig. 5: (i) an online_consultations table indexed by consult_id, relating to patients and admissions, with features like platform, duration_min and notes; (ii) adjusted companions for consultation_prescriptions and online_consultation_att to reflect many-to-one multiplicities and origin; (iii) an iomt_vitals table recording (ts, hr, spo2) and citing patients and a fresh device catalog; and (iv) limited enhancement of admissions to register telemedicine parameters (e.g., telemedicine_flag, visit_mode) for consistent long-term tracking. Sure! Please provide the text you would like me to paraphrase.Foreign keys are generated from subject_id/hadm_id along with device identities, and bridge structures.

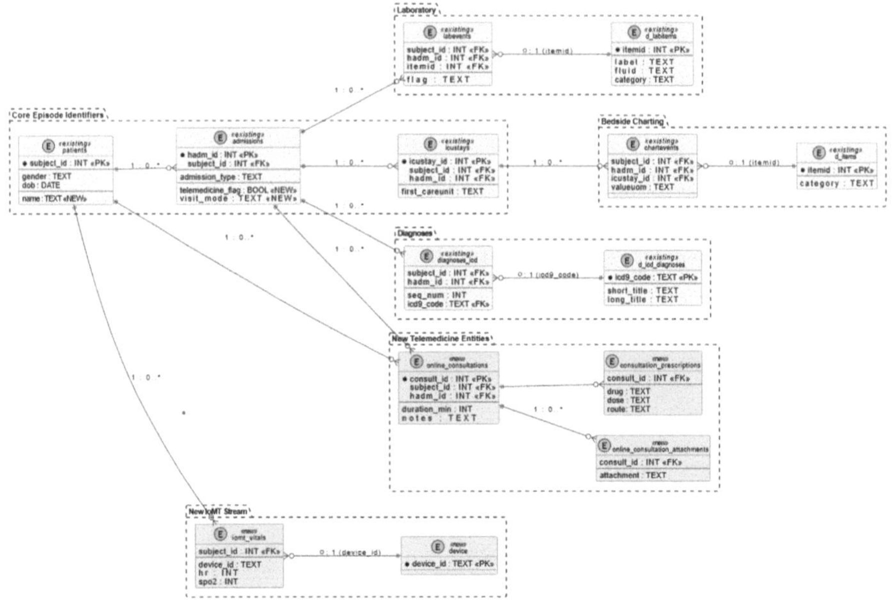

Fig. 5. MIMIC-III model evolution for scenario 1.

The extended schema offers immediate Business Intelligence features: inquiries can be managed as incidents related to care episodes; prescription clusters can be quantitatively combined per patient, service line, or platform; IoMT metrics function as time-series grain variables that enable trend identification, notification, and group classification. Due to the pipeline, particularly R6, maintains the order of Data Definition Language (DDL) and Data Manipulation language (DML) through foreign-key priority standards and utilizes ACID transactions to encompass loads, the development is implementable.

This first scenario shows how the rule-based transformation will evolve the relational schema for adding either remote monitoring or device telemetry features into the data warehouse without having to re-architect the decision support system. Clinical meaning is preserved through the separation of the conceptual logic from its relational implementation and the chances of re-architecting the application are reduced and integrated analytics across telemedicine, clinic, and IoT device that were previously stored in separate Data Lake systems.

5.3 Scenario 2: Rehabilitation and Extended Profiling

We start from a directed property graph, shown in Fig. 6, that encodes patient-centric rehabilitation data (nodes such as Patient, Contact, RehabSession,

Exercise, Language, Allergy and edges Has_Allergy, Has_Emergency_Contact, Attended, Has_Exercise with per-edge metrics like `reps` and `duration_sec`). We use U-Schema as a pivot model between the graph input and the relational target, we represented graph nodes to U-Schema *EntityTypes* and here R1 was ready to be applyed, then we map nodes properties to attributes preparing its to R2, and finally, we translate edges to references and relationship type with explicit cardinality, and preserve edge properties as attributes of association entities. By applying our transformation rules, we evolve the MIMIC-III model by introducing new tables rehab_sessions (with `session_id`, `session_date`, `duration_min`), exercises (catalog of exercise types), and a bridge/fact table session_exercises capturing per-session metrics (`reps`, `duration_sec`); we also add contacts linked to patients for emergency details and optionally normalize languages and allergies (with a patient_allergies link table).

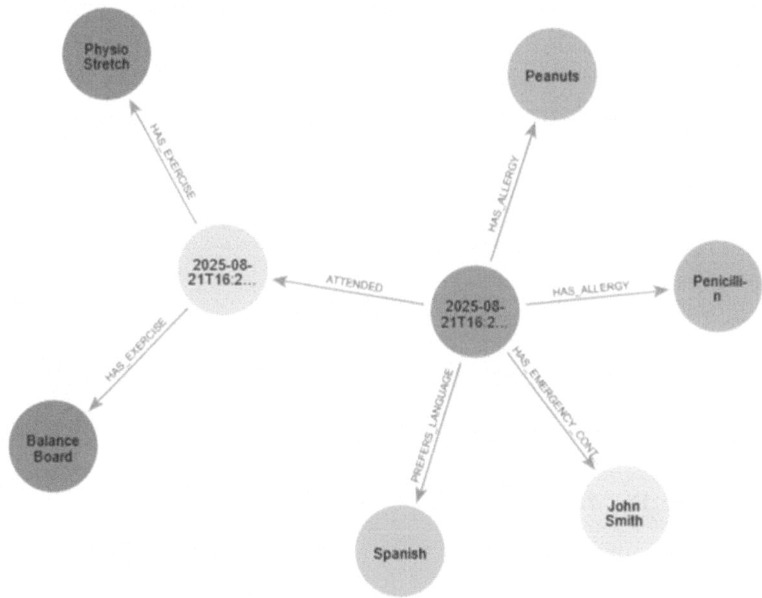

Fig. 6. Graph Oriented Database for scenario 2

As a result, we obtain an evolution of MIMIC-III schema, demonstrated in Fig. 7, that will be projected in DSS and enriches the analysis axes in the business intelligence layer.

An analytical axis that can be examined for depth and enrichment analysis is "exercise intensity over time during rehabilitation": With the inclusion of the session_exercises fact table in the schema, analysts can slice and dice the frequency, duration, or intensity of exercises over time and among patients. "Remote versus in-hospital correlation" might serve as the next analytical dimension, where telemedicine data can be aligned with inpatient admission data concerning events in these graphs by trends, and events linked to outcomes before, during, and after the inpatient hospitalization event

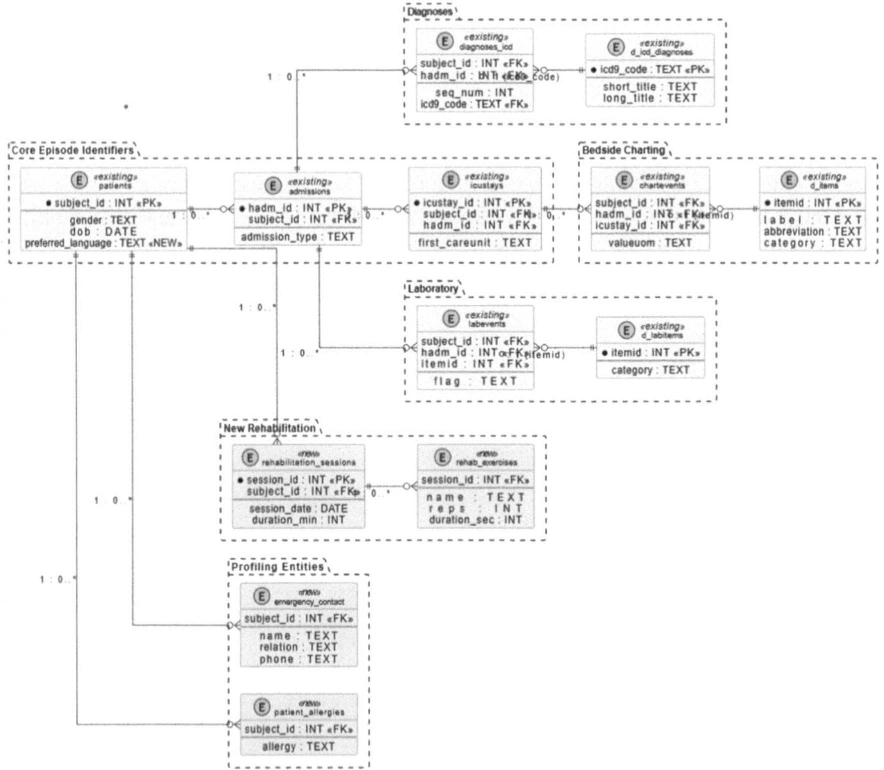

Fig. 7. MIMIC-III model evolution for scenario 2

5.4 Discussion

The presented cases study demonstrates how the proposed NoSQL-to-relational transformation rules effectively supports the evolution of the dynamic schema in a complex clinical environment such as MIMIC-III.

In the first evolution scenario, the ingestion of telemedicine consultations and IoMT-derived vital signs (Sect. 5.2) illustrated the creation of new tables (`online_consultations`, `iomt_vitals`), association tables for multivalued attributes, and the seamless extension of existing tables with atomic properties.

In the second evolution scenario, the integration of rehabilitation tracking and extended patient profiling (Sect. 5.3) showcased the framework's capacity to handle structured nested objects, multiple one-to-many relationships, and the incorporation of new reference data while preserving referential integrity.

Across both scenarios, the algorithm maintained transactional safety, ensured type compatibility, and automatically adjusted schema constraints to accommodate new clinical data flows without disrupting existing queries. These results confirm that our approach is robust, flexible, and directly applicable to real-world healthcare database modernization efforts.

6 Conclusion

We addressed the long-standing challenge of integrating data lakes, presented by heterogeneous NoSQL sources, into existing relational information systems by using a U-Schema–based as a unified model and a three–phase migration algorithm. Our approach abstracts store-specific constructs (e.g., nesting, arrays, and graph edges) into *EntityTypes*, *Aggregations*, and *RelationshipType*, then materializes them as relational tables, keys, and foreign keys with executable DDL + DML ordered by referential dependencies. Across our scenarios—including document-centric telemedicine payloads and graph-oriented rehabilitation streams, we showed how to preserve semantics (identities, multiplicities, and edge properties), sustain ACID guarantees during loading, and evolve an operational schema such as MIMIC-III without sacrificing lineage or analytic readiness.

Our approach is (i) *model-agnostic* at the source via U-Schema as a unified model for NoSQL database; (ii) *semantics-aware* through explicit handling of references, aggregations, and relationship types; (iii) *integrity-first* by topological ordering of operations and transaction scoping; and (iv) *analytics-friendly* via outputs tailored to warehouses (surrogate keys, bridge tables, SCD-ready structures when applicable).

For future work, our goal is to further improve the schema using AI, which will include domain-adapted natural language processing (NLP) and semantic matching to match entity names, including synonyms, abbreviation, and language variants, that provide a more consistent and unified dataset. We will also work towards releasing benchmarking tools or synthetic workloads that will enable the comparison of different strategies on a common foundation including key aspects such as correctness, runtime, and Business Intelligence readiness. These advancements would support reproducibility and provide complementary information on the efficacy of different strategies in real-world use case.

References

1. Banerjee, J., Kim, W., Kim, H., Korth, H.F.: Semantics and implementation of schema evolution in object-oriented databases. In: Proceedings of ACM SIGMOD. pp. 311–322 (1987). https://doi.org/10.1145/38713.38748

2. Bernstein, P.A.: Applying model management to classical meta data problems. In: Proceedings of the Conference on Innovative Data Systems Research (CIDR) (2003). https://courses.cs.washington.edu/courses/csep544/04sp/lectures/bernstein03.pdf
3. Brahmia, Z., Grandi, F., Oliboni, B.: A literature review on schema evolution in databases. Comput. Open **2**(1), 160035 (2024). https://doi.org/10.1142/S2972370124300012
4. Candel, C.J.F., Ruiz, D.S., García-Molina, J.J.: A unified metamodel for NoSQL and relational databases. Inf. Syst. **104**, 101898 (2022). https://doi.org/10.1016/j.is.2021.101898
5. Candel, C.J.F., Ruiz, D.S., García-Molina, J.J.: SkiQL: a unified schema query language over U-schema. Data Knowl. Eng. **146**, 102178 (2023). https://doi.org/10.1016/j.is.2021.101898
6. Chillón, A.H., Klettke, M., Ruiz, D.S., Molina, J.G.: A taxonomy of schema changes for NoSQL databases. arXiv preprint arXiv:2205.11660 (2022). https://arxiv.org/abs/2205.11660
7. Chillón, A.H., Klettke, M., Ruiz, D.S., Molina, J.G.: A generic schema evolution approach for NoSQL and relational databases. IEEE Trans. Knowl. Data Eng. **36**(7), 2774–2789 (2024). https://doi.org/10.1109/TKDE.2024.3362273
8. Fagin, R., Kolaitis, P.G., Miller, R.J., Popa, L.: Data exchange: semantics and query answering. Theoret. Comput. Sci. **336**(1), 89–124 (2005). https://doi.org/10.1016/S0304-3975(04)00725-X
9. Genevès, P., Layaïda, N., Quint, V.: Impact of xml schema evolution. ACM Trans. Internet Technol. **11**(1) (2011). https://doi.org/10.1145/1993083.1993087
10. Johnson, A.E., et al.: MIMIC-III, a freely accessible critical care database. Sci. Data **3**(1), 160035 (2016). https://doi.org/10.1038/sdata.2016.35
11. Manousis, P., Vassiliadis, P.: Schema evolution for databases and data warehouses: a survey. In: Evolutionary Database Design, pp. 1–28. Springer (2015). https://doi.org/10.1007/978-3-319-39243-1_1
12. Oueslati, W., Akaichi, J.: A survey on data warehouse evolution. CoRR abs/1012.1565 (2010). https://arxiv.org/abs/1012.1565
13. Roddick, J.F.: A survey of schema versioning issues for database systems. Inf. Softw. Technol. **37**(7), 383–393 (1995). https://doi.org/10.1016/0950-5849(95)91494-K
14. Scherzinger, S., Klettke, M., Störl, U.: Managing schema evolution in NoSQL data stores. CoRR abs/1308.0514 (2013). https://arxiv.org/pdf/1308.0514
15. Scherzinger, S., Sidortschuck, S.: An empirical study on the design and evolution of NoSQL database schemas. CoRR abs/2003.00054, pp. 441–445 (2020). https://arxiv.org/abs/2003.00054
16. Störl, U., Klettke, M., Scherzinger, S., Priebe, T., Neumayr, B.: NoSQL schema evolution and data migration: state-of-the-art and opportunities. In: Proceedings of the 22nd International Conference on Extending Database Technology (EDBT) (2020). https://doi.org/10.5441/002/edbt.2020.87

Out-Of-Distribution Generalization for Knee Calcium Deposition Under X-Ray Manufacturer's Domain Shifts

Eman Ehab Nasef(✉) and Mustafa Elattar

Nile University, Giza, Egypt
{e.nasef,melattar}@nu.edu.eg
https://www.nu.edu.eg/

Abstract. Accurate classification of knee X-rays across diverse hardware remains a significant challenge due to domain shifts induced by varying scanner specifications, acquisition protocols, and post-processing software. This study investigates out-of-distribution (OOD) generalization techniques to improve the classification of knee calcium deposition across seven distinct X-ray scanners. We evaluated six OOD algorithms, including Empirical Risk Minimization (ERM), SagNet, GroupDRO, Mixup, Adaptive Risk Minimization (ARM), and Invariant Risk Minimization (IRM) to assess the robustness of Vision Transformer-based (DINOv2) versus convolutional (ResNet50) feature extractors within a supervised learning framework.

Our experimental results demonstrate that DINOv2-extracted features generalized significantly better to unseen scanners than ResNet50. Among the tested OOD algorithms, SagNet emerged as the most robust approach, achieving *92.6%* accuracy with std of ± 0.20 and a p-value of 2.9×10^{-10} across the seven scanners by effectively decoupling anatomical content from scanner-specific style. In contrast, IRM exhibited instability across training and testing domains, yielding *85.1%* accuracy with std of ± 6.71 and a p-value of *0.667* under identical hyperparameter settings, likely due to the difficulty of identifying truly invariant features across medical imaging domains.

These findings underscore how self-supervised feature learning significantly enhances robustness against distribution shifts compared to standard convolutional models. By leveraging domain generalization, we provide a scalable foundation for manufacturer-independent classifiers, facilitating more reliable and equitable performance across diverse X-ray imaging platforms.

Keywords: Out-of-Distribution Generalization · Domain Generalization · Supervised Learning · Self-Supervised Learning · Knee X-rays · Calcium Deposition Prediction · Chondrocalcinosis · OAI Dataset

1 Introduction

Most existing studies on data shifts in the medical domain primarily focus on pathology slides, MRIs, retinal scans, chest X-rays, or population-level differ-

A. Awad et al. (Eds.): MEDI 2025, LNCS 16427, pp. 81–94, 2026.
https://doi.org/10.1007/978-3-032-19865-5_6

ences. In contrast, this work presents a novel investigation of **domain generalization** across knee X-rays obtained from seven different manufacturers. This contribution is unique because prior research in medical domain generalization has largely relied on cross-dataset evaluations or alternative feature extractors, without systematically comparing state-of-the-art domain generalization algorithms. Our study evaluates six such algorithms on **out-of-distribution (OOD) knee X-ray scans** from unseen manufacturers, targeting the binary classification of chondrocalcinosis (calcium crystal deposits) versus nonchondrocalcinosis. We further assess the impact of different feature extractors by comparing the classical **ResNet-50** backbone with the self-supervised **DINOv2** backbone. To guide this investigation, we formulate the following research questions:

- **RQ1:** How well do different domain generalization algorithms perform on OOD knee X-rays?
- **RQ2:** What is the effect of using DINOv2 versus ResNet-50 as feature extractors in medical domain generalization?
- **RQ3:** Which domain generalization algorithms are most and least effective for knee X-rays across scanners?

2 Related Work

Out-Of-Distribution Generalization

Out-of-Distribution (OOD) generalization [1–3] is the study of how machine learning models can maintain their performance when faced with data from a different distribution than their training data. These distributional shifts [4] can arise from various factors, including differences in domains, environments, or data acquisition methods.

A diverse set of approaches have been developed to address OOD generalization like *Domain Alignment*, which aims to minimize the variance across training domains by learning domain-invariant features. By aligning the feature distributions of different source domains, the model is encouraged to focus on the generalizable core features rather than the domain-specific spurious correlations [5–7]. *Meta-Learning* approaches, which frame OOD generalization as a "learning-to-learn" problem. Models are trained on a variety of tasks or domains to improve their ability to rapidly adapt to new, unseen domains by learning transferable and shared features [8,9], while *Data Augmentation* techniques focus on increasing the model's robustness by artificially creating new training data. This can involve simple input transformations, applying adversarial attacks to the training data, or synthesizing novel domains to simulate potential distribution shifts [10]. Finally, *Learning Disentangled Representations*, which focuses on separating the core predictive features from confounding, domain-specific factors. By disentangling these features, the model can learn to rely on the invariant, task-relevant information while ignoring the varying domain-related characteristics [11].

Domain Generalization for X-Ray Scanner Shifts

In the standard domain generalization (DG) setting, the training data D_{train} is composed of M distinct source domains, expressed as $D_{\text{train}} = \{D_k \mid k = 1, \ldots, M\}$. Each domain D_k contains n_k labeled samples $\{(x_j^k, y_j^k)\}_{j=1}^{n_k}$. Equivalently, the overall training dataset can be written as $D_{\text{train}} = \{(x_i, y_i, d_i)\}_{i=1}^{n}$, where d_i indicates the domain identity and n is the total number of samples across all domains. The objective of DG is to train a model $G : X \to Y$ using only the source domains, such that it generalizes effectively to unseen target domains D_{test}.

Domain generalization (DG) is typically categorized into single-source and multi-source settings [12,13]. Single-source DG trains a model on a single labeled dataset, or "source domain," and evaluates its ability to generalize to unseen target domains. In contrast, multi-source DG leverages labeled data from multiple source domains to learn a generalizable representation. The primary objective is to identify features that are invariant across these domains, thereby enabling the model to perform robustly on new, unseen target domains. Current research in domain generalization focuses on developing methods to achieve this invariance.

Current research on domain generalization in the medical field primarily focuses on diabetic retinopathy scans, dermatology scans, and chest X-rays [14–21], often relying on hyperparameter tuning, while studies on MRI images are also prevalent.

DINOv2 and ResNet50. DINOv2 [22] is a state-of-the-art Vision Transformer feature extractor trained using a self-supervised learning framework. It was pre-trained on a massive curated dataset of 142 M images without using any labels or annotations with 1B parameters. At its core is a knowledge distillation process involving a student and a teacher model. The student model is presented with an image where a portion of its patches are masked, and its objective is to predict the representations of these occluded regions as derived from the teacher network, which is provided with the complete, unmasked image. During training, the student's parameters are optimized using standard gradient descent algorithms. The teacher's parameters, on the other hand, are not updated via backpropagation; instead, they are derived from an exponential moving average of the student's parameters. This specific method is crucial as it ensures the teacher network learns in a stable and consistent manner, smoothing out the rapid and noisy updates of the student. This sophisticated training regimen enables the student to learn powerful, semantic features by inferring the context of occluded image regions, ultimately resulting in a versatile feature extractor that offers a new generation of task-agnostic features, further improving generalization capabilities.

Before the advent of self-supervised Vision Transformers, convolutional neural networks (CNNs) such as ResNet50 [23] dominated feature extraction. ResNet50 is a 50-layer deep CNN that introduced residual connections to mitigate the vanishing gradient problem, enabling the training of substantially deeper architectures. When pre-trained on large-scale datasets like ImageNet, ResNet50 learns a hierarchy of features: low-level edge and texture detectors in early layers, and increasingly abstract representations in deeper layers which are inherently domain-invariant and highly transferable. These pre-trained weights have been shown to transfer effectively across domains, making ResNet50 a widely adopted backbone for domain generalization tasks, where resilience to distribution shifts is crucial.

3 Methodology

3.1 Datasets

In this work, we utilized the publicly available NIH Osteoarthritis Initiative (OAI) dataset [24]. The OAI dataset comprises over 431,000 clinical and imaging visits, including approximately 26,626,000 images, collected from individuals aged 45 to 79 over a 10-year follow-up period. The dataset contains various imaging modalities, such as X-rays and MRIs, of multiple joints including hips, knees, and hands.

For this study, we specifically focused on the knee semiquantitative data structure to investigate the effect of multi-vendor X-ray scanners. We addressed this by performing Chondrocalcinosis classification. Chondrocalcinosis is a form of inflammatory arthritis characterized by the deposition of calcium crystals, particularly in joints like the knees. Our task was a binary classification problem: detecting the presence or absence of Chondrocalcinosis.

The dataset consists of 7,911 lateral full knee X-ray images. Among these, 560 images contain a high density of knee calcium deposition, with the remaining images representing healthy knees. This class imbalance reflects real-world clinical settings. As shown in Table 1, these scans are mapped to seven different X-ray scanner manufacturers. Seven samples of the X-rays from the different scanners can be shown in Fig. 1.

The images, originally in DICOM format, were processed using the `pydicom` library. They were then normalized with `min-max` scaling, converted to `grayscale`, and saved as PNG files for subsequent analysis. For our domain generalization experiments, two of the seven manufacturers' datasets were designated as the test set, with 80% of their images used for testing. The remaining five manufacturers' datasets served as the training domains, with 80% of their images used for training and the rest for a validation set (Fig. 1).

3.2 Methods

To assess domain generalization performance, we adopted six representative algorithms: Adaptive Risk Minimization (ARM), Empirical Risk Minimization (ERM), Invariant Risk Minimization (IRM), Group Distributionally Robust Optimization (GroupDRO), Mixup, and Style-Agnostic Networks (SagNet). These methods were selected because they capture a diverse spectrum of strategies for addressing distribution shift, ranging from risk minimization and invariance-based approaches to robust optimization, data augmentation, and style disentanglement. Below, we briefly describe each algorithm and its role in our experimental framework.

1. **Adaptive Risk Minimization (ARM)** [25] which learns by explicitly making the model robust to small, worst-case perturbations in its feature space. It is not about a learner producing adapted parameters for different domains—that concept belongs more to meta-learning approaches for domain generalization

$$\min_{\theta,\phi} \hat{\mathcal{E}}(\theta, \phi) = \mathbb{E}_{p_z}\left[\mathbb{E}_{p_{xy|z}}\left[\frac{1}{K}\sum_{k=1}^{K} \ell\big(g(\mathbf{x}_k;\theta'), y_k\big)\right]\right], \tag{1}$$

$$\text{where } \theta' = h(\theta, \mathbf{x}_1, \ldots, \mathbf{x}_K; \phi).$$

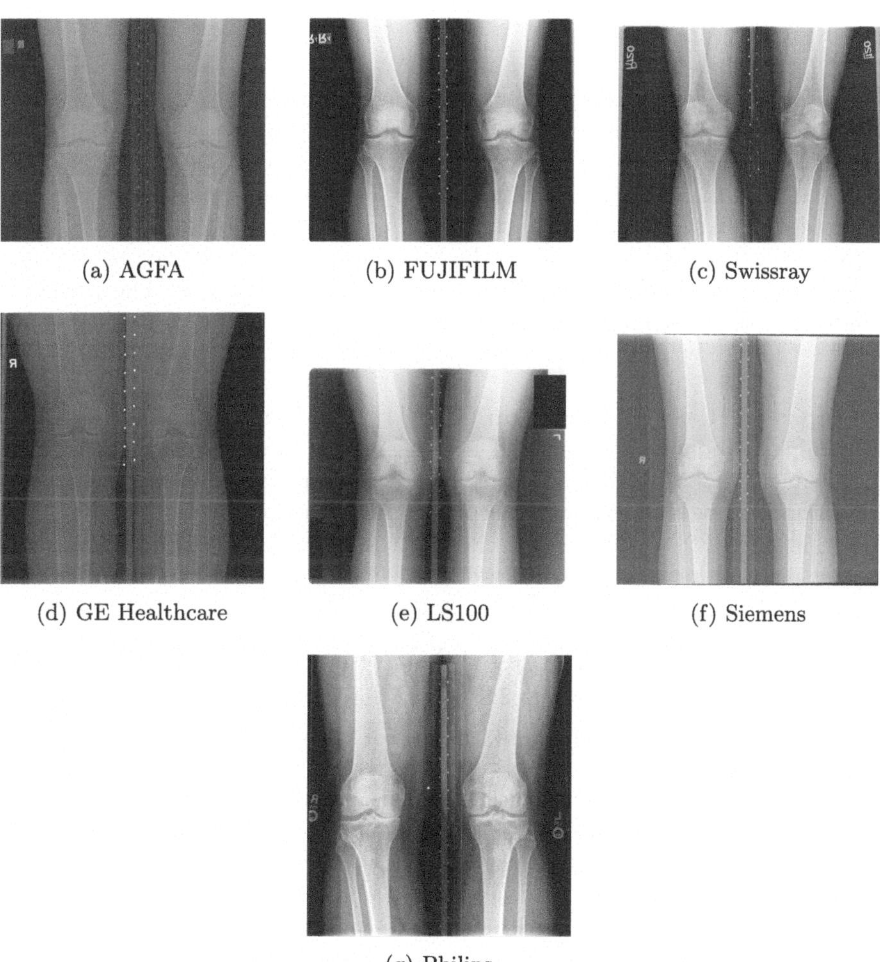

(a) AGFA (b) FUJIFILM (c) Swissray (d) GE Healthcare (e) LS100 (f) Siemens (g) Philips

Fig. 1. Knee x-ray scans acquired from seven different scanner manufacturers, highlighting scanner variability in the dataset.

Table 1. Dataset scanners distribution.

Scanner	0	1
AGFA	2689	244
FUJIFILM	1549	132
Swissray	1372	86
GE Healthcare	1057	55
LS100	453	25
Siemens	219	18
Philips	12	0
Total	7351	560

We denote by θ the base model parameters and by ϕ the adaptation parameters. The meta-objective $\hat{\mathcal{E}}(\theta, \phi)$ is expressed as an expectation over tasks sampled from a distribution p_z. Within each task, data points $(\mathbf{x}_k, y_k)$ are drawn from the conditional distribution $p_{xy|z}$, and the empirical risk is computed over K samples. Task-specific parameters θ' are obtained via an adaptation function $h(\cdot)$, which maps the base parameters θ and the task support set $\{\mathbf{x}_1, \ldots, \mathbf{x}_K\}$ into adapted parameters conditioned on ϕ. The predictor $g(\mathbf{x}_k; \theta')$ produces outputs for each input $\mathbf{x}_k$, and the loss function $\ell(\cdot, \cdot)$ quantifies the discrepancy between the predictions and the corresponding labels y_k.

2. **Empirical Risk Minimization (ERM)** [26], which serves as the standard learning paradigm in supervised learning. Given training data drawn from multiple source domains, ERM optimizes the average predictive loss across all samples, without explicitly accounting for domain shift.
Formally, let $\mathcal{D} = \{(\mathbf{x}_i, y_i)\}_{i=1}^N$ denote the training set sampled from the joint distribution $p(\mathbf{x}, y)$. ERM seeks model parameters θ that minimize the empirical risk:
$$\min_\theta \hat{\mathcal{E}}(\theta) = \frac{1}{N} \sum_{i=1}^{N} \ell(f(\mathbf{x}_i; \theta), y_i), \tag{2}$$
where ℓ is a loss function (cross-entropy for classification) and $f(\cdot; \theta)$ is the prediction model.
In the multi-domain setting, ERM aggregates all training domains into a single pooled dataset and optimizes the same objective. While this approach can achieve strong in-domain performance, it may lead to overfitting domain-specific features, thus limiting generalization to unseen domains.
3. **Invariant Risk Minimization (IRM)** which addresses domain generalization by seeking a data representation in which the optimal predictor is *invariant* across multiple environments.
The key idea is to learn a feature extractor Φ such that the same classifier w performs well on all training environments.

Formally, let $\mathcal{E}_{\mathrm{tr}}$ denote the set of training environments.
IRM aims to solve the following constrained optimization problem:

$$\min_{\Phi,w} \sum_{e\in\mathcal{E}_{tr}} R^e(w \circ \Phi) \tag{3}$$

$$\text{subject to} \quad w \in \arg\min_{\bar{w}} R^e(\bar{w} \circ \Phi), \ \forall e \in \mathcal{E}_{tr},$$

where R^e denotes the risk in environment e, and $w \circ \Phi$ is the composed predictor.
This formulation encourages the representation Φ to capture only those features that support a predictor w which is simultaneously optimal across all environments, thereby promoting robustness to unseen domains.
Unlike empirical risk minimization, which may exploit spurious correlations, IRM explicitly seeks invariant predictors that generalize beyond training distributions.

4. **Group Distributionally Robust Optimization (GroupDRO)** [27], which addresses domain shift by explicitly optimizing for the worst-case performance across training domains. Instead of minimizing the average risk as in ERM, GroupDRO minimizes the maximum risk over all groups (domains), thereby discouraging the model from overfitting to specific domains with larger sample sizes.
Formally, let $\mathcal{E}$ denote the set of training environments (domains), and let $\hat{\mathcal{E}}_e(\theta)$ be the empirical risk on environment $e \in \mathcal{E}$. The GroupDRO objective is given by:

$$\min_{\theta} \max_{e\in\mathcal{E}} \hat{\mathcal{E}}_e(\theta), \tag{4}$$

where

$$\hat{\mathcal{E}}_e(\theta) = \frac{1}{|\mathcal{D}_e|} \sum_{(\mathbf{x}_i,y_i)\in\mathcal{D}_e} \ell(f(\mathbf{x}_i;\theta), y_i). \tag{5}$$

Here, $\mathcal{D}_e$ denotes the dataset corresponding to environment e, and ℓ is a task-specific loss function.
By emphasizing robustness to the hardest environment, GroupDRO prevents the model from exploiting spurious correlations that may be unique to certain domains. However, this robustness can come at the cost of reduced average performance when domains are highly imbalanced or heterogeneous.

5. **Mixup** [28] is a data augmentation technique that improves generalization by creating synthetic training examples through convex combinations of pairs of samples and their labels. Formally, given two samples $(\mathbf{x}_i, y_i)$ and $(\mathbf{x}_j, y_j)$ drawn from the training distribution, Mixup generates a new sample as follows:

$$\tilde{\mathbf{x}} = \lambda\mathbf{x}_i + (1-\lambda)\mathbf{x}_j, \quad \tilde{y} = \lambda y_i + (1-\lambda)y_j, \tag{6}$$

where $\lambda \in [0,1]$ is the interpolation coefficient sampled from a Beta distribution, $\lambda \sim \mathrm{Beta}(\alpha,\alpha)$ with hyperparameter $\alpha > 0$.

The learning objective under Mixup becomes:

$$\min_{\theta} \mathbb{E}_{(\mathbf{x}_i,y_i),(\mathbf{x}_j,y_j)} \Big[\ell\big(f(\tilde{\mathbf{x}};\theta),\, \tilde{y}\big) \Big], \tag{7}$$

where $f(x;\theta)$ denotes the predictor parameterized by θ, and ℓ is the cross-entropy loss function.
By training on interpolated inputs and soft labels, Mixup encourages the predictor to behave linearly between training examples, reducing overfitting and improving robustness to distribution shifts. This simple yet effective formulation makes Mixup widely applicable in both supervised learning and domain generalization settings.

6. **Style-Agnostic Networks (SagNet)** [29] addresses domain generalization by disentangling *style* and *content* representations in neural networks. Formally, SagNet decomposes a model f into three components: (i) a *content encoder* h_c, which extracts semantic content features $\mathbf{c}$, (ii) a *style encoder* h_s, which extracts style features $\mathbf{s}$, and (iii) a *predictor* g, which makes predictions based only on the content representation.
Sagnet learning process can be expressed as:

$$\min_{\mathbf{G}_f} L_{\text{adv}} = -\lambda_{\text{adv}} \mathbb{E}_{(\mathbf{x},\cdot)\in S} \sum_{k=1}^{K} \frac{1}{K} \log\, \mathbf{G}_s\big(\mathrm{CR}(\mathbf{G}_f(\mathbf{x}), \mathbf{z}')\big)_k, \tag{8}$$

where, λ_{adv} denotes the weighting coefficient, CR represents the content-randomized representation, $\mathbf{G}_s$ refers to the style-biased network, and $\mathbf{G}_f$ corresponds to the feature network.

3.3 Experimental Setup

To evaluate the robustness and out-of-distribution generalization performance of the six algorithms (ARM, ERM, IRM, GroupDRO, Mixup, SagNet), we conducted all experiments using three different random seeds for each method. Each model was trained on four scanners at a time and subsequently tested on at least two unseen scanners to assess its ability to generalize across domains and 2 backbones, ResNet50 and DINOv2, with pretrained vitb14 base backbone This procedure ensures that performance metrics are not dependent on a single random initialization and that the evaluation captures variability due to both training conditions and unseen test domains.

All experiments were conducted on a workstation equipped with an NVIDIA GeForce RTX 3090 GPU with 24 GB of VRAM, running CUDA 12.4 and implemented using [Domainbed, PyTorch] on Python 3.10.

For experiments with the ResNet-50 feature extractor and AugMix [30], we used the following training setup: a batch size of 32 for all methods except ARM, where the batch size was reduced to 16 due to its four-channel inputs (compared to three channels in other algorithms). Data augmentation was applied, and a linear classifier was trained for 500 steps using the Adam optimizer with a learning rate of 5×10^{-5}, and no weight decay. For experiments with DINOv2, we applied attention tuning and set the ViT dropout rate to 0.1.

The training configurations, including batch size, learning rate, backbone, and algorithm-specific parameters, are summarized in Table 2.

Model performance was evaluated using the minimum accuracy of the test domains due to the class imbalance between Siemens and Philips X-Ray Scanners 1 as the primary metric. Additionally, p-values across environments were computed to assess the statistical significance of differences in accuracy between algorithms, ensuring that observed improvements were robust and not due to random variations.

4 Results

Tables 3 and 4 summarize the mean accuracy and the std for the three repetitions and corresponding p-values for all algorithms across the different domains for both Resnet50 and DINOv2. Overall, we found that using Dinov2 as a feature extractor for the algorithms increased the performance of most of the algorithms or didn't affect the accuracy, but decreased the std of the three runs. The best algorithm for use with ResNet50 as a feature extractor was Mixup, which achieved a mean test accuracy of 92.5% with a standard deviation of 0.10. The mean p-value for Mixup across all scanner environments was 1.6×10^{-11}, indicating a significant and consistent performance across different scanners, which can be found in Table 5

Table 2. Hyperparameters and Featurizer configurations for the six OOD generalization algorithms.

Algorithm	Batch, LR	Feature Extractor	Special Parameter(s)
ARM	16, 5×10^{-5}	ResNet-50 (AugMix) DINOv2, (attn_tune, vit dropout = 0.1)	–
ERM	32 5×10^{-5}	ResNet-50 (AugMix) DINOv2, (attn_tune, vit dropout = 0.1)	–
GroupDRO	32 5×10^{-5}	ResNet-50 (AugMix) DINOv2, (attn_tune, vit dropout = 0.1)	$\eta = 0.01$
IRM	32 5×10^{-5}	ResNet-50 (AugMix) DINOv2, (attn_tune, vit dropout = 0.1)	$\lambda = 100.0$, penalty_iters = 500
Mixup	32 5×10^{-5}	ResNet-50 (AugMix) DINOv2, (attn_tune, vit dropout = 0.1)	$\alpha = 0.2$
SagNet	32 5×10^{-5}	ResNet-50 (AugMix) DINOv2, (attn_tune, vit dropout = 0.1)	$w_{\text{adv}} = 0.1$

The best algorithm when using DINOv2 as a feature extractor was SagNet with mean test accuracy of 92.6% and a standard deviation (std) of 0.20, Mixup mean p-value across scanners envs is 2.9×10^{-10}, which is accepted and significant, emphasizing the concurrence between each env accuracies, more info can be in Table 6

The worst algorithm was IRM for both Resnet50 and DINOv2; it showed different results when changing the seeds, which indicates its instability regarding out-of-distribution generalization between scanners in the medical domain.

5 Discussion

For **RQ1** and **RQ3**, we trained six algorithms, each with three random seeds, and repeated the experiments using two distinct feature extraction techniques. In total, this resulted in 36 experiments and approximately 250 training hours. The results show that out-of-distribution generalization techniques perform well across both in-distribution and out-of-distribution domains. In particular, for knee calcium deposition diagnosis, the OOD algorithms generalize effectively to new X-rays from previously unseen scanners. Furthermore, with proper fine-tuning, the performance of these algorithms can be further enhanced. As discussed in Sect. 2, SagNet combined with the DINOv2 feature extractor consistently outperformed the other algorithms under identical experimental conditions. To further optimize performance, we carried out an additional 15 experiments using random search for SagNet hyperparameters, which yielded a 0.3% improvement in testing accuracy. The best-performing hyperparameters are summarized in Table 7.

For **RQ2**, according to Tables 3, 4 we can find that DINOv2 generally outperforms ResNet-50 in terms of generalization because the self-supervised train-

Table 3. Results of algorithms (3 seeds, ResNet50)

Algorithm	$test_{acc}$ $\pm$ std	val_{acc} $\pm$ std	Loss	p_{value}
ARM	92.1 ± 0.06	92.3 ± 0.29	0.14 ± 0.02	4.3×10^{-11}
ERM	92.3 ± 0.17	92.3 ± 0.20	0.09 ± 0.01	1.3×10^{-13}
GroupDRO	92.1 ± 0.12	91.4 ± 0.46	0.11 ± 0.00	1.4×10^{-10}
IRM	83.7 ± 6.04	84.1 ± 6.01	0.33 ± 0.49	0.319
Mixup	**92.5 ± 0.10**	**92.2 ± 0.40**	0.15 ± 0.00	1.6×10^{-11}
SagNet	92.1 ± 0.25	92.5 ± 0.12	0.18 ± 0.00	2.5×10^{-13}

Table 4. Results of algorithms (3 seeds, DINO v2)

Algorithm	$test_{acc}$ $\pm$ std	val_{acc} $\pm$ std	Loss	p_{value}
ARM	92.1 ± 0.10	92.9 ± 0.26	0.15 ± 0.04	3.3×10^{-05}
ERM	92.5 ± 0.10	92.8 ± 0.23	0.12 ± 0.03	3.3×10^{-14}
GroupDRO	92.6 ± 0.45	92.9 ± 0.45	0.15 ± 0.03	9.7×10^{-10}
IRM	85.1 ± 6.71	84.5 ± 8.66	0.61 ± 0.14	0.667
Mixup	92.5 ± 0.12	93.0 ± 0.10	0.18 ± 0.03	2.0×10^{-09}
SagNet	**92.6 ± 0.20**	**93.1 ± 0.12**	0.18 ± 0.01	2.9×10^{-10}

Table 5. ResNet50 Environments val-test

Algorithm	$env_0 \pm std$	$env_1 \pm std$	$env_2 \pm std$	$env_3 \pm std$	$env_4 \pm std$	$env_5 \pm std$	$env_6 \pm std$	p_{value}
ARM	92.9 ± 0.00	90.6 ± 0.40	90.8 ± 0.95	94.4 ± 0.46	99.6 ± 0.64	92.1 ± 0.06	92.7 ± 0.26	4.3×10^{-11}
ERM	92.5 ± 0.45	90.2 ± 0.06	91.7 ± 0.25	94.7 ± 0.06	99.4 ± 0.55	92.3 ± 0.17	92.4 ± 0.32	1.3×10^{-13}
GroupDRO	92.1 ± 0.83	90.5 ± 0.26	87.6 ± 1.46	94.2 ± 0.51	100.0 ± 0.00	92.1 ± 0.12	92.5 ± 0.12	1.4×10^{-10}
IRM	83.3 ± 5.01	84.3 ± 4.68	74.0 ± 18.05	90.2 ± 3.18	86.3 ± 10.46	89.5 ± 1.47	88.6 ± 2.23	0.319
Mixup	92.8 ± 0.44	91.0 ± 0.12	89.3 ± 1.27	95.1 ± 0.10	100.0 ± 0.00	92.5 ± 0.10	92.9 ± 0.20	1.6×10^{-11}
SagNet	92.6 ± 0.15	90.8 ± 0.51	91.8 ± 0.15	94.7 ± 0.15	99.4 ± 0.55	92.1 ± 0.25	92.6 ± 0.15	2.5×10^{-13}

Table 6. DINO v2 Environments Results

Algorithm	$env_0 \pm std$	$env_1 \pm std$	$env_2 \pm std$	$env_3 \pm std$	$env_4 \pm std$	$env_5 \pm std$	$env_6 \pm std$	p_{value}
ARM	93.4 ± 0.42	91.5 ± 0.15	91.9 ± 0.21	94.7 ± 0.40	97.6 ± 2.51	92.1 ± 0.10	93.0 ± 0.29	3.3×10^{-05}
ERM	93.3 ± 0.23	91.4 ± 0.21	91.7 ± 0.25	94.5 ± 0.25	98.7 ± 0.35	92.5 ± 0.10	93.1 ± 0.21	3.3×10^{-14}
GroupDRO	93.4 ± 0.38	91.1 ± 0.80	92.1 ± 0.21	94.8 ± 0.53	98.9 ± 0.55	92.6 ± 0.45	93.0 ± 0.52	9.7×10^{-10}
IRM	84.6 ± 8.66	83.1 ± 8.27	82.9 ± 8.46	87.1 ± 9.32	94.1 ± 5.59	85.1 ± 6.71	84.8 ± 8.72	0.667
Mixup	93.5 ± 0.06	91.4 ± 0.15	91.7 ± 0.06	95.1 ± 0.06	97.4 ± 1.15	92.5 ± 0.12	93.2 ± 0.15	2.0×10^{-09}
SagNet	93.7 ± 0.15	91.8 ± 0.31	92.1 ± 0.12	94.9 ± 0.21	99.1 ± 1.14	92.6 ± 0.20	93.1 ± 0.15	2.9×10^{-10}

ing strategy of DINOv2 which discussed in Sect. 2 which capture richer and more transferable high-level representations rather than CNNs like ResNet-50, whose supervised ImageNet pretraining provides stronger inductive biases but less flexibility when adapting to new domains. This ability to model long-range dependencies allows DINOv2 to generalize more effectively to unseen X-rays from different scanners. However, this same flexibility also makes DINOv2 more sensitive to randomness in training, such as weight initialization and mini-batch sampling, which increases variability across runs. In contrast, ResNet-50's convolutional structure and supervised training yield more stable optimization trajectories with lower standard deviation, but at the cost of reduced adaptability compared to DINOv2. These findings are consistent with the results of [14], who compared ResNet-50 and DINOv2 in the context of brain MRI data.

For **RQ3**, in response to the research question, our results indicate that SAGNet is the most effective algorithm for domain generalization across knee X-ray scanners. Its success stems from the disentangled representation learning framework, which separates domain-specific style features from content-specific features. This allows the model to focus on the underlying medical information rather than scanner-specific artifacts, thereby improving robustness to domain shifts. Conversely, Invariant Risk Minimization (IRM) proved to be the least effective. IRM's core constraint of learning a single classifier that is robust across all domains is often too rigid for medical imaging, where subtle variations between scanners, patient populations, and acquisition protocols exist. As a result, IRM struggles to adapt to domain-specific nuances, leading to unstable performance and reduced generalization across scanners.

Future Directions. In future work, we aim to extend our research to a broader range of tasks involving knee X-rays and MRI scans, including detection of pathological regions, multi-class classification of various knee conditions, and multi-label classification for cases with overlapping abnormalities. We plan to investigate the performance of different machine learning and deep learning algorithms, as well as evaluate multiple feature extraction backbones, including both convolutional and transformer-based architectures. By exploring these approaches, we hope to improve the robustness and generalization of models across diverse imaging devices and clinical settings, ultimately contributing to more accurate and reliable diagnostic tools for musculoskeletal disorders.

Table 7. Best hyperparameters used for the SagNet DINOv2 based experiment.

Algorithm	Batch, LR	Feature Extractor	Special Parameter(s)
SagNet	39, 2.70×10^{-5}	ViT (DINOv2, attn_tune, dropout=0.1)	$w_{\text{adv}} = 0.0106$, weight decay 4.48×10^{-4}

6 Conclusion

In summary, we demonstrated that out-of-distribution generalization techniques effectively train binary classifiers in supervised settings. Vision transformer-based feature extractors, such as DINOv2, generalized better to unseen domains than convolutional extractors like ResNet50, emphasizing the importance of self-supervised feature learning.

Among the methods evaluated, SagNet was the most robust, whereas IRM proved unstable for classifying calcium deposition across different scanners. This work provides a foundation for generalizing binary classifiers to unseen domains, enabling future research on other knee pathologies and strategies to enhance performance across diverse X-ray scanners.

Acknowledgments. We acknowledge Dr. Mennatullah Siam for her involvement and discussions during the initial stage of this research. Her input helped in shaping the early direction of the study.

References

1. Liu, J., et al.: Towards out-of-distribution generalization: a survey, arXiv preprint arXiv:2108.13624 (2021)
2. Gulrajani, I., Lopez-Paz, D.: In search of lost domain generalization, arXiv preprint arXiv:2007.01434 (2020)
3. Zhou, K., Liu, Z., Qiao, Y., Xiang, T., Loy, C.C.: Domain generalization: a survey. IEEE Trans. Pattern Anal. Mach. Intell. **45**(4), 4396–4415 (2022)
4. Koh, P.W., et al.: Wilds: a benchmark of in-the-wild distribution shifts. In: International Conference on Machine Learning, pp. 5637–5664. PMLR (2021)
5. Hemati, S., Zhang, G., Estiri, A., Chen, X.: Understanding hessian alignment for domain generalization. In: Proceedings of the IEEE/CVF International Conference on Computer Vision, pp. 19004–19014 (2023)
6. Muandet, K., Balduzzi, D., Schölkopf, B.: Domain generalization via invariant feature representation. In: International Conference on Machine Learning, pp. 10–18. PMLR (2013)

7. Wang, Z., Loog, M., Van Gemert, J.: Respecting domain relations: hypothesis invariance for domain generalization. In: 2020 25th International Conference on Pattern Recognition (ICPR), pp. 9756–9763. IEEE (2021)
8. Khoee, A.G., Yu, Y., Feldt, R.: Domain generalization through meta-learning: a survey. Artif. Intell. Rev. **57**(10), 285 (2024)
9. Huisman, M., Van Rijn, J.N., Plaat, A.: A survey of deep meta-learning. Artif. Intell. Rev. **54**(6), 4483–4541 (2021)
10. Volpi, R., Namkoong, H., Sener, O., Duchi, J.C., Murino, V., Savarese, S.: Generalizing to unseen domains via adversarial data augmentation. In: Advances in Neural Information Processing Systems, vol. 31 (2018)
11. Li, J., Li, Y., Wang, H., Liu, C., Tan, J.: Exploring explicitly disentangled features for domain generalization. IEEE Trans. Circuits Syst. Video Technol. **33**(11), 6360–6373 (2023)
12. Xu, Q., Zhang, R., Wu, Y.-Y., Zhang, Y., Liu, N., Wang, Y.: Simde: a simple domain expansion approach for single-source domain generalization. In: Proceedings of the IEEE/CVF Conference on Computer Vision and Pattern Recognition, pp. 4798–4808 (2023)
13. Su, Z., Yao, K., Yang, X., Huang, K., Wang, Q., Sun, J.: Rethinking data augmentation for single-source domain generalization in medical image segmentation. In: Proceedings of the AAAI Conference on Artificial Intelligence, vol. 37, pp. 2366–2374 (2023)
14. Huang, Y., et al.: Comparative analysis of imagenet pre-trained deep learning models and dinov2 in medical imaging classification. In: 2024 IEEE 48th Annual Computers, Software, and Applications Conference (COMPSAC), pp. 297–305. IEEE (2024)
15. Matta, S., et al.: A systematic review of generalization research in medical image classification. Comput. Biol. Med. **183**, 109256 (2024)
16. Guan, H., Liu, M.: Domain adaptation for medical image analysis: a survey. IEEE Trans. Biomed. Eng. **69**(3), 1173–1185 (2021)
17. Korevaar, S., Tennakoon, R., O'Brien, R., Mahapatra, D., Bab-Hadiashar, A.: Domain generalization by learning from privileged medical imaging information. In: 2024 IEEE International Symposium on Biomedical Imaging (ISBI), pp. 1–5. IEEE (2024)
18. Yoon, J.S., Oh, K., Shin, Y., Mazurowski, M.A., Suk, H.-I.: Domain generalization for medical image analysis: a review. Proc. IEEE (2024)
19. Baliah, S., Maani, F.A., Sanjeev, S., Khan, M.H.: Exploring the transfer learning capabilities of clip in domain generalization for diabetic retinopathy. In: International Workshop on Machine Learning in Medical Imaging, pp. 444–453. Springer (2023)
20. Galappaththige, C.J., Kuruppu, G., Khan, M.H.: Generalizing to unseen domains in diabetic retinopathy classification. In: Proceedings of the IEEE/CVF Winter Conference on Applications of Computer Vision, pp. 7685–7695 (2024)
21. Yan, S., et al.: Prompt-driven latent domain generalization for medical image classification. IEEE Trans. Med. Imaging (2024)
22. Oquab, M., et al.: Dinov2: learning robust visual features without supervision, arXiv preprint arXiv:2304.07193 (2023)
23. He, K., Zhang, X., Ren, S., Sun, J.: Deep residual learning for image recognition. In: Proceedings of the IEEE Conference on Computer Vision and Pattern Recognition, pp. 770–778 (2016)
24. Lester, G.: The osteoarthritis initiative: a NIH public-private partnership. HSS J. **8**(1), 62–63 (2012)

25. Zhang, M., Marklund, H., Dhawan, N., Gupta, A., Levine, S., Finn, C.: Adaptive risk minimization: learning to adapt to domain shift. Adv. Neural. Inf. Process. Syst. **34**, 23664–23678 (2021)
26. Vapnik, V.N.: An overview of statistical learning theory. IEEE Trans. Neural Networks **10**(5), 988–999 (1999)
27. Sagawa, S., Koh, P.W., Hashimoto, T.B., Liang, P.: Distributionally robust neural networks for group shifts: on the importance of regularization for worst-case generalization, arXiv preprint arXiv:1911.08731 (2019)
28. Zhang, H., Cisse, M., Dauphin, Y.N., Lopez-Paz, D.: mixup: beyond empirical risk minimization, arXiv preprint arXiv:1710.09412 (2017)
29. Nam, H., Lee, H., Park, J., Yoon, W., Yoo, D.: Reducing domain gap by reducing style bias. In: Proceedings of the IEEE/CVF Conference on Computer Vision and Pattern Recognition, pp. 8690–8699 (2021)
30. Hendrycks, D., Mu, N., Cubuk, E.D., Zoph, B., Gilmer, J., Lakshminarayanan, B.: Augmix: a simple data processing method to improve robustness and uncertainty, arXiv preprint arXiv:1912.02781 (2019)

Face Generation from Arabic Text Using GAN-CLS and AraBERT

Hassen Zaayra[1,2(✉)], Islem Jarraya[1], Tarek M. Hamdani[1,3], and Adel M. Alimi[1,4]

[1] REsearch Groups in Intelligent Machines (REGIM-Lab), National Engineering School of Sfax (ENIS), University of Sfax, Sfax, Tunisia
hassen.zaaira@isaeg.u-gafsa.tn, {islem.jarraya,tarek.hamdani}@enis.tn, adel.alimi@regim.usf.tn

[2] Faculty of Economic Sciences and Management of Sfax (FSEGS), University of Sfax, Sfax, Tunisia

[3] Higher Institute of Computer Science Mahdia (ISIMa), University of Monastir, Mahdia, Tunisia

[4] Department of Electrical and Electronic Engineering Science, Faculty of Engineering and the Built Environment, University of Johannesburg, Johannesburg, South Africa

Abstract. Recently, face generation from natural language descriptions has become one of the key applications of generative models and one of the most challenging tasks in computer vision and remains. This text-to-face synthesis technique has a wide range of potential applications, including photo editing, forensic investigation, and game development. While significant progress has been achieved in English-based implementations, extending this technology to the Arabic language presents unique challenges due to the scarcity of Arabic datasets and the linguistic complexity of the Arabic morphology, syntax, and semantics. In this paper, we integrate GAN-CLS, a lightweight yet effective text-to-image generation framework, with the AraBERT, a pre-trained Arabic language model to enable face synthesis from a single-sentence Arabic text description. To support our experiments, we constructed a novel Arabic text-to-face dataset by translating English context descriptions from the Multi-Modal CelebA-HQ dataset into Arabic using DeepL Translator. The performance of the proposed framework was evaluated using the Fréchet Inception Distance (FID) and the Learned Perceptual Image Patch Similarity (LPIPS) metrics. This study constitutes an initial attempt at generating facial images from Arabic textual descriptions.

Keywords: Arabic Text · Generative Adversarial Network-CLS · Natural Language Processing (NLP) · Text to Face · Text to Image

1 Introduction

With the advent of Generative Adversarial Networks (GANs) [9], text-to-image synthesis has made tremendous stride, and is now used in many applications,

A. Awad et al. (Eds.): MEDI 2025, LNCS 16427, pp. 95–108, 2026.
https://doi.org/10.1007/978-3-032-19865-5_7

including photo editing and computer-aided design. The synthesis of faces from textual descriptions represents an important subdomain within the broader field of text-to-image synthesis. However, it is less studied compared to text-to-image generation despite the utilization in various domains, such as forensic science, game development, animation, and digital marketing, due to the fine-grained complexity of facial features and the scarcity of specialized training datasets. Notably, a majority of researchers have focused on face generation from English language descriptions. Although significant advancements have been achieved in this field using the English language, there has been a dearth of research pertaining to other languages, specifically the Arabic language, which has its dialectal diversity, lexical richness, and unique syntactic structure. Consequently, this research problem constitutes a significant challenge for effective text-to-face synthesis. In recent years, several architectures of GAN have been used to generate faces from textual descriptions based on English datasets. For instance, a StackGAN [13], which is based on two stages, has been used to generate faces from English text; each stage stacks several pairs of generators and discriminators. In addition, a new architecture using DFGAN [20] has been employed to enable the generation of realistic human face images from textual descriptions. Converting Arabic text laden with cultural, stylistic, and contextual richness, into visual form demands sophisticated language modeling and a deep understanding of how linguistic constructs align with visual semantics. Hence, this paper proposes an approach to generate face images conditioned on Arabic textual input based on GAN-CLS and using a pretrained Arabic model (AraBERT) that has been trained on billions of Arabic words to produce robust Arabic sentence embeddings.

The main contributions of this paper are summarized as follows:

- creation of a new dataset tailored to the Arabic text-to-face generation task by using DeepL Translator to convert English context descriptions from the Multi-Modal CelebA-HQ dataset into Arabic.
- Proposal of a novel Text-to-Face framework using GAN-CLS architecture to synthesize faces from descriptions and AraBERT as the text encoder.
- Generation of high-quality facial images that are properly aligned with the input descriptions.

While Bahani et al. [4] combined AraBERT with DF-GAN for Arabic text-to-image generation, our work advances this line of research with contributions specifically tailored to facial synthesis. Unlike the generation of flowers and birds, face generation demands fine-grained detail such as eye shape, nose structure, and subtle expressions that general image generation frameworks often fail to represent accurately. To this end, we introduce a matching-aware discriminator with facial landmark constraints for improved textâĂŞimage alignment, as well as a language-specific adaptation layer to handle Arabic morphological complexity, including diacritic restoration and right-to-left script processing. These innovations specifically address the challenges of Arabic text-to-face generation, distinguishing our approach from prior work.

The rest of the paper is organized as follows: Sect. 2 reviews related work on text-to-image and text-to-face. Section 3 provides an overview of GANs, and describe the GAN-CLS architecture. The proposed method is presented in Sect. 4, while Sect. 5 reports and analyzes the experimental results. Finally, Sect. 6 concludes the paper and discusses possible extensions of this work.

2 Related Works

In this section, we review related studies on text-to-image synthesis and the key advancements in the generation of facial images from textual descriptions using GANs.

2.1 Text-to-Image Synthesis

Reed et al. [17] introduced the first concept of text-to-image synthesis in 2016. They proposed the use of conditional GANs to generate images of birds and flowers from human-written descriptions. The Oxford-102, MS COCO, and Caltech-UCSD Birds (CUB) datasets were used to train and evaluate their model, which showed substantial improvements in the field of text-to-image synthesis. Building on this foundation, subsequent studies have made considerable advancements. Zhang et al. [26] introduced StackGAN, a two-stage generative framework employing multiple pairs of generators and discriminators. In the first stage, the model generates a low-resolution image through a sketch-refinement process. While the second stage refines this output by taking both the low-resolution image and the corresponding text as input, producing a high-resolution image with enhanced visual quality and fine-grained details. In parallel, the integration of the attention mechanism has achieved significant success in image-text-related tasks. Xu et al. [23] introduced AttnGAN, which combines advanced natural language processing (NLP) techniques with attention-based algorithms to generate high-quality images, capturing fine-grained details across image subregions by focusing on the most relevant words in the description. Finally, Tao et al. [21] proposed DF-GAN, which relies a single generatorâĂŞdiscriminator pair to produce high-resolution images evaluated on the CUB and COCO datasets. Similarly, Bahani et al. [4] combined the effectiveness of the pre-trained AraBERT model with DF-GAN to synthesize images from Arabic text.

2.2 Text-to-Face Generation

Generating face images from text descriptions is more complex than generating other types of images. Consequently, extensive research has been conducted in this field, resulting in the development of multiple models designed specifically for text-to-face synthesis.

Nasire et al. [15] proposed the use of Skip-Thought as an encoder for embedding complete sentences and generated face images from fine-grained textual descriptions using a CGAN called Text2faceGAN. This model was trained on the

CelebA dataset and a set of descriptor texts generated for each image through a proprietary algorithm. D. Ayanthi et al. [3] proposed a text-to-face generation framework that combines StyleGAN2 with BERT as the sentence encoder, achieving the generation of high-resolution images at a resolution of 1024×1024 pixels. In a similar direction, the authors of [18] adopted StyleGAN2 with DistilBERT to extract semantic features from textual descriptions and synthesize high-quality facial images. Similarly, Anukriti *et al.* [13] proposed a two-stage text-to-image synthesis framework based on StackGAN employing a Sentence-BERT encoder to extract features from captions provided in the CelebA dataset and generate high-resolution facial images at a resolution of 256×256 pixels. Mohsin et al. [20] developed a framework based on DFGAN, utilizing the spaCy and NLTK libraries to convert text into numerical representations for realistic face generation. Additionally, Deorukhkar et al. [5] used Sentence Bidirectional Encoder Representations from Transformers (SBERT) to transform the textual descriptions into embedding vectors and generated 128×128 pixel images using the CelebA dataset, employing three GAN models (DCGAN, SAGAN, and DFGAN). Furthermore, NMK Arnob et al. [2] generated facial images from the CelebA Bangla dataset which was created using textual descriptions in Bangla. Their approach was based on the DCGAN architecture model and the pre-trained text encoder named Bangla FastText that is employed to transform Bangla text into a latent vector representations. Finally, the authors of [24] proposed three text-to-face encoders, namely, the RoBERTa pre-trained model, Sent2Vec, and RoBERTa models, trained with the CelebA dataset in Spanish, along with a conditional cDCGAN for text-to-face generation in Spanish.

3 Background

In this section, we provide an overview of GANs, followed by a description of the GAN-CLS architecture, which has been used for the problem of text-to-image synthesis.

3.1 Generative Adversarial Networks

Generative Adversarial Networks (GANs) [9] are a framework consisting of two components: a generator (G) and a discriminator (D). This framework is based on a minimax game in which G attempts to fool D by producing realistic samples, while D strives to distinguish between real training data and synthetic data. During training, the discriminator aims to maximize its ability to correctly classify both generated and real samples, whereas the generator aims to maximize the probability that the discriminator makes a mistake, as expressed in Equation (1):

$$\min_{G} \max_{D} V(D,G) = \mathbb{E}_{x \sim p_{\mathrm{d}}(x)}[\log D(x)] + \mathbb{E}_{z \sim p_{z}(z)}[\log(1 - D(G(z)))] \tag{1}$$

where, $p_{\mathrm{d}}(x)$ denotes the probability density function of real data samples, $p_{\mathrm{z}}(z)$ represents the probability density function of the random latent vector z.

3.2 GAN-CLS (Conditional Latent Space GAN)

Reed et al. [17] proposed a solution to the text-to-image synthesis problem by learning a discriminative visual representation of textual description and using these representations to generate realistic images. Their approach, GAN-CLS, employs a deep convolutional architecture for both the generator and discriminator, along with an RNN encoder [16] to generate images from latent variables and text embeddings. The GAN-CLS model [17] is built upon on conditional GAN framework [14] and introduces a matching-aware discriminator [8]. During training, it uses both matched and mismatched text-image pairs. The discriminator is modified by adding a third input type consisting of real images paired with mismatched text, which it must learn to classify as fake. The objective function of this algorithm is [8]:

$$\min_{G}\max_{D} \mathbb{E}_{(x,h)\sim p_{\mathrm{d}}(x,h)}[\log D(x,h)] + \frac{1}{2}\mathbb{E}_{z\sim p_z(z),\, h\sim p_{\mathrm{d}}(h)}[\log(1 - D(G(z,h),h))] + \frac{1}{2}\mathbb{E}_{(x,h)\hat{p}_{\mathrm{d}}(x,h)}[\log(1 - D(x,h))] \tag{2}$$

where, h denotes the embedding of the text, $p_{\mathrm{d}}(x, h)$ is the distribution density function of the samples from the dataset, in which x and h are matched. $\hat{p}_d(x, h)$ is the distribution density function of the samples from dataset consisting of text and mismatched image.

4 Methodology

In this section, we explain the preprocessing of Arabic text, describe the text encoder used, and present the implementation details of our proposed work.

4.1 Preprocessing of the Arabic Text Description

The direct machine translation of English descriptions into Arabic poses considerable linguistic challenges, necessitating dedicated preprocessing of the Arabic text prior to effective encoding for text-to-face synthesis. To address these challenges, we implemented a multi-stage processing pipeline, beginning with a linguistic normalization phase that standardizes specific Arabic letters and removes diacritics and punctuation in order to reduce the orthographic variability of the text. In addition, extra white spaces have been removed to ensure textual uniformity. This preprocessing pipeline enhances the quality of tokenization and improves the robustness of embeddings generated using AraBERT [1].

4.2 Text Encoder

BERT [6] is a Bidirectional Encoder Representation proposed by Google in 2018. It was built using the Transformers architecture, a groundbreaking deep learning model that has significantly advanced applications in NLP. AraBERT [1] adopts the same architecture but is specifically trained on a large-scale Arabic corpus comprising news websites for articles and books from various Arab regions. For instance, its pre-training data included a 1.5-billion-word Arabic corpus [7], derived from 10 major news sources across 8 nations, as well as the Open Source International Arabic News Corpus [25], comprising over three million articles collected from 31 news outlets in 24 Arab countries. In total, the pre-training dataset contains over 70 million sentences. As a result, AraBERT has achieved state-of-the-art performance on various Arabic natural language understanding tasks, including Question Answering (QA), sentiment Analysis (SA), and Named Entity Recognition (NER). Inspired by these results, we employ AraBERT to generate robust Arabic sentence embeddings, which are then used to train our GAN-CLS model for synthesizing facial images from Arabic textual descriptions.

4.3 GAN Architecture

The proposed system utilizes the GAN-CLS architecture combined with the AraBERT text encoder to generate facial images from their corresponding Arabic textual descriptions. Firstly, the Arabic text description is fed into the text encoder and outputs a text embedding with a dimension of 768. The resulting text embedding is reduced in dimensions to 128. A 100-dimensional random noise vector, along with the achieved text embedding, is fed into the generator. Subsequently, the generator produces 64×64 pixel images, then the discriminator determines whether the generated images are real or synthetic and whether they correspond to the given text embedding. Figure 1 illustrates the architecture of the proposed framework.

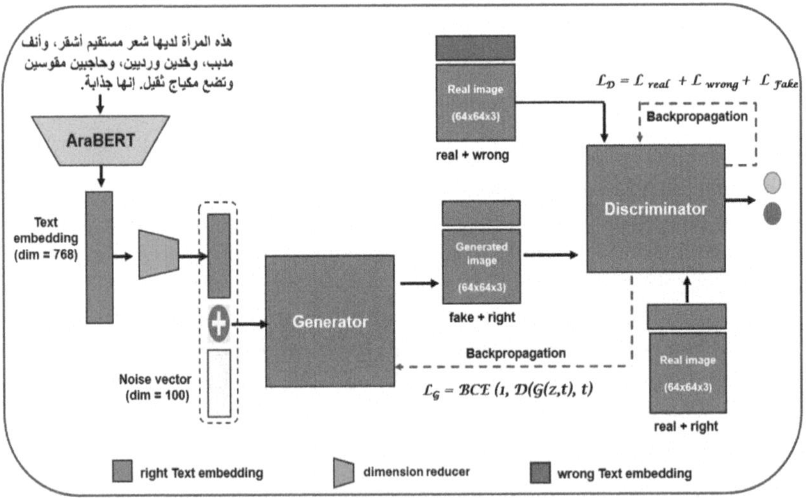

Fig. 1. Architecture of the proposed framework combining AraBERT and GAN-CLS.

Generator Architecture The generator (see Fig. 2) has two inputs: a text embedding vector encoded by the text encoder and a noise vector z of dimension 100, which is sampled from a standard Gaussian distribution $\mathcal{N}(0, 1)$. The Arabic text description is first processed by the text encoder, producing a 768-dimensional text embedding. The output is then compressed to dimension 128 using a dense layer followed by LeakyReLU activation function. Subsequently, this latent vector is concatenated with the noise vector z, passed through another dense layer, reshaped to (B,4,4,256), and then progressively upsampled through a series of four convolutional blocks. Each block consists of an UpSampling2D layer, Conv2DTranspose, BatchNormalization, and LeakyReLU activation ($\alpha = 0.2$). Finally, the resulting image features are converted into an image of dimensions $64 \times 64 \times 3$ using a Conv2DTranspose layer. The output values are passed through a tanh activation function to normalize the pixel values within the range of -1 to 1.

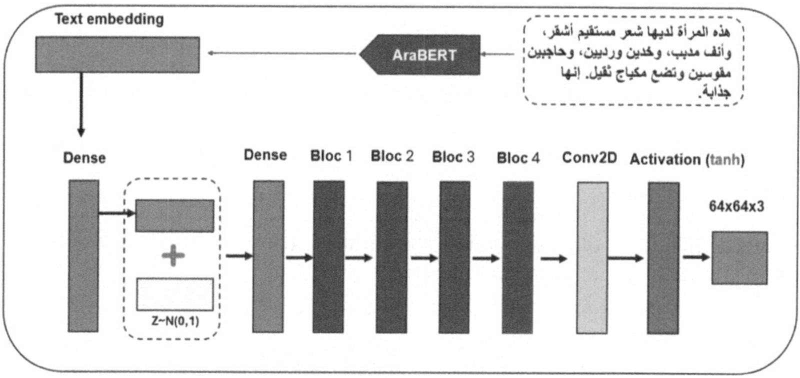

Fig. 2. Generator Architecture.

Discriminator Architecture The discriminator has two inputs. The first is the text embedding vector, identical to that of the generator, and an input image of dimensions $64 \times 64 \times 3$. The input image is processed through four successive convolutional blocks, each consisting a convolutional layer, batch normalization (except in the first block), a LeakyReLU activation function, and dropout for regularization. These layers progressively reduce the spatial dimensions while extracting discriminative visual features. Simultaneously, the text embedding is passed through a dense layer to reduce its dimentionality and then reshaped into a $4 \times 4 \times 8$ tensor to match the spatial dimensions of the image feature maps. These two representations are concatenated and further processed through an additional convolutional layer to learn joint representations of visual and textual modalities. The final output layer employs a sigmoid activation function to produce values in the range [0, 1], indicating the probability that the input image is both real and semantically consistent with the given text embedding. Figure 3 shows the architecture of the discriminator model.

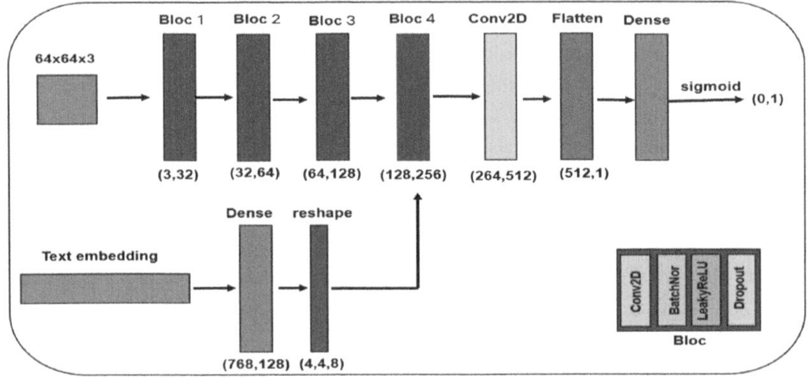

Fig. 3. Discriminator Architecture.

4.4 Loss Functions

The discriminator is trained using the binary cross-entropy loss (BCE), as defined in Eq. 3:

$$\mathcal{L}_D = \mathcal{L}_{\text{real}} + 1/2(\mathcal{L}_{\text{wrong}} + \mathcal{L}_{\text{fake}}) \tag{3}$$

- $\mathcal{L}$real represents the loss for a real image paired with a matching text description. This loss is calculated by comparing y_{real} with the discriminator's output, obtained by feeding the real image and its corresponding text embedding into the discriminator.

$$\mathcal{L}_{\text{real}} = \text{BCE}\left(y_{\text{real}}, D(x_{\text{real}}, t_{\text{real}})\right) \tag{4}$$

  where, $D(x_{\text{real}}, t_{\text{real}})$ denotes the discriminator's output for a real image x_{real} and its corresponding text description t_{real}. The y_{real} term is the target label indicating that the input pair is real, we apply label smoothing by assigning values sampled from the interval [0.9,1.0] for real pairs.
- $\mathcal{L}_{\text{fake}}$, as shown in Eq. 5, represents the loss for a fake image paired with real text. This loss is calculated by comparing the y_{fake} with the discriminator's output, obtained by feeding the fake image and its corresponding text embedding into the discriminator.

$$\mathcal{L}_{\text{fake}} = \text{BCE}\left(y_{\text{fake}}, D(x_{\text{fake}}, t_{\text{real}})\right) \tag{5}$$

  where, $D(x_{\text{fake}}, t_{\text{real}})$ denotes the discriminator's output for the pair composed of the generated image x_{fake} and its corresponding real text description t_{real}.

The target label y_{fake} indicates that the pair is fake. To stabilize training and prevent the discriminator from becoming overconfident, label smoothing is applied by sampling values from the uniform distribution $\mathcal{U}(0.0, 0.1)$ for fake pairs.

- $\mathcal{L}_{\text{wrong}}$ represents the loss associated with a real image paired with a mismatched text description. This loss is calculated by comparing the discriminator's output obtained by feeding the real image with a mismatched text embedding to the y_{fake}.

$$\mathcal{L}\text{wrong} = \text{BCE}\left(y_{\text{fake}}, D(x_{\text{real}}, t_{\text{wrong}})\right) \tag{6}$$

where, $D(x_{\text{real}}, t_{\text{wrong}})$ denotes the discriminator's output when provided with a real image x_{real} paired with a mismatched text description t_{wrong}. The target label y_{fake} indicates that this pair is fake. To stabilize training, label smoothing is employed by sampling y_{fake} from the uniform distribution $\mathcal{U}(0.0, 0.1)$.

The training of the generator in our proposed model, which employs the AraBERT text encoder is based on the loss function BCE, and is presented in Eq. 7

$$\mathcal{L}_G = \text{BCE}\left(1, D(G(z,t),t)\right) \tag{7}$$

where, $G(z, t)$ denotes the generated image from noise vector z and text embedding t, and $D(\cdot, t)$ represents the discriminator's output conditioned on t. The generator, on the other hand, is optimized to fool the discriminator by maximizing the likelihood that the generated image is classified as real. This is achieved by minimizing the binary cross-entropy loss with target labels set to 1.

5 Experiments

In this section, we present the dataset, the training process, and the metrics evaluation.

5.1 Dataset

To achieve text-to-face generation from Arabic text, the first step is to construct a dataset containing photo-realistic facial images and corresponding descriptions. We introduce the Arabic-translated Multi-Modal CelebA-HQ dataset [22], a large-scale facial image dataset comprising 30,000 high-resolution images (512×512 pixels), each accompanied by ten English textual descriptions per image based on 40 facial attributes. These descriptions were translated into Arabic using the DeepL Translator model to generate new Arabic text descriptions. From the 10 translated descriptions per image, we manually selected the most accurate one to represent the facial image. The Arabic-translated version of the Multi-Modal CelebA-HQ dataset contains 10000 Arabic text descriptions paired with their corresponding images. The dataset is divided into 9000 training images and 1000 testing images. This dataset will be publicly released and is expected to become a benchmark resource for future studies in Arabic text-to-face synthesis.

5.2 Training Details

The model was trained with a batch size of 32 for 800 epochs. The learning rate was set to 0.0002 for both the discriminator and generator. We employed the Adam optimizer [12] with $\beta_1 = 0.5$ and $\beta_2 = 0.5$ for both networks.

5.3 Evaluation Metrics

In order to evaluate the generated results, we adopted two widely used quantitative metrics, the Frechet Inception Distance (FID) [10] and Learned Perceptual Image Patch Similarity (LPIPS) [27]. These metrics allow us to assess the quality and diversity of the generated images, providing a comprehensive understanding of their performance. The FID measures the Fréchet distance between the feature distributions of real and generated image, extracted using InceptionV3 [19]. Lower FID score indicate higher image quality, and the metric is computed as follows.

$$F(r,g) = \|\mu_r - \mu_g\|^2 + \text{Tr}\left(\Sigma_r + \Sigma_g - 2\left(\Sigma_r \Sigma_g\right)^{1/2}\right) \tag{8}$$

where, r and g denote the real and generated data, μr and Σ_r represent the mean of the real image and covariance of 2048 features of ground truth sample distribution. μg and Σ_g are the mean of the generated image and covariance from the features of generated distribution of GAN. Tr represents the trace of square matrix.

The LPIPS metric evaluates perceptual similarity through deep feature comparisons between real and generated image patches (Eq. 9). The lower the LPIPS score, the higher the image quality.

$$d(x, x_0) = \sum_l \frac{1}{H_l W_l} \sum_{h,w} \left\| \omega_l \odot \left(\hat{y}^l_{hw} - \hat{y}^l_{0hw}\right) \right\|_2^2 \tag{9}$$

Where, d denotes the LPIPS distance between a real image x and a generated image x0, and the features are extracted from The AlexNet layer l, with unit normalization applied along the channel dimension. The Hadamard product is denoted by $\odot$, and the number of activated channels is scaled by the weighting vector ω_1.

5.4 Qualitative Results

Figure 4 presents qualitative results of images synthesized using the proposed system. The first column shows the input Arabic text descriptions, while the subsequent four columns display the images generated using the pretrained AraBERT model as the Arabic text encoder. The figure clearly demonstrates that employing our proposed embedding strategy yields promising results in generating facial images that correspond to the input text. Specifically, attributes, such as blond hair and an open mouth, are correctly identified in rows 1 and 6, while row 7

Fig. 4. Comparison of the generated face images from the LSTM+GAN-CLS and AraBERT+GAN-CLS alongside their corresponding ground-truth images.

shows brown hair and arched eyebrows that are clearly visible. Morevover, the third and fifth images of the third column accurately depict gender as specified in the input text descriptions.

5.5 Quantitative Results

To provide qualitative comparison, we used the same architecture described in Fig. 1, inspired by the work of [17] on text-to-image synthesis with an RNN encoder. We retrained the model on the Arabic-translated version of the Multi-Modal CelebA-HQ dataset using an LSTM [11] encoder with a hidden size of 512. The comparative results are shown in Fig. 4.

Table 1. Best values of quantitative metrics using the two encoders: LSTM+GAN-CLS and AraBERT+GAN-CLS with the Arabic-translated version of the Multi-Modal CelebA-HQ dataset. The best results are highlighted in bold.

Method	FID ↓	LPIPS ↓	Supported Language	Resolution
GAN-CLS+LSTM	188.45	0.587	Arabic	64×64
Our GAN-CLS+AraBERT	**155.23**	**0.501**	Arabic	64×64

It is important to note that any numerical comparison with related work must be performed using the same dataset for both the encoder and the GAN-CLS model; otherwise, the results will vary significantly. In line with the visual observations of the face images generated (see Fig. 4), Table 1 confirms that AraBERT+GAN-CLS achieves the best performance across both evaluation metrics.

6 Conclusion

In this paper, we have proposed a framework face images generation from Arabic textual descriptions using a GAN-CLS with AraBERT. The model's performance was evaluated using two quantitative metrics Fréchet Inception Distance (FID) and Learned Perceptual Image Patch Similarity (LPIPS). The experimental results demostrated that our approach achieved FID = 155.23 and LPIPS = 0.501 on the Arabic version of the Multi-Modal CelebA-HQ dataset. This study represents a preliminary attempt to generate face images from Arabic text descriptions, showing moderate but promising performance, given the linguistic complexity of Arabic morphology and syntax compared to English. Future work enhance performance and image quality by employing advanced GAN architectures, such as StyleGAN2, and by extending image resolutions to 256×256, 512×512, or higher, to produce more photo-realistic outputs for Arabic text-conditioned face synthesis.

References

1. Antoun, W., Baly, F., Hajj, H.: Arabert: transformer-based model for Arabic language understanding. arXiv preprint arXiv:2003.00104 (2020)
2. Arnob, N.M.K., Rahman, N.N., Mahmud, S., Uddin, M.N., Rahman, R., Saha, A.K.: Facial image generation from Bangla textual description using DCGAN and Bangla FastText. Int. J. Adv. Comput. Sci. Appl. **14**(6) (2023)
3. Ayanthi, D., Munasinghe, S.: Text-to-face generation with StyleGAN2. arXiv preprint arXiv:2205.12512 (2022)
4. Bahani, M., El Ouaazizi, A., Maalmi, K.: AraBERT and DF-GAN fusion for Arabic text-to-image generation. Array **16**, 100260 (2022)
5. Deorukhkar, K., Kadamala, K., Menezes, E.: FGTD: face generation from textual description. In: Ranganathan, G., Fernando, X., Shi, F. (eds.) Inventive Communication and Computational Technologies. LNNS, vol. 311. Springer, Singapore (2022). https://doi.org/10.1007/978-981-16-5529-6_43
6. Devlin, J., Chang, M.W., Lee, K., Toutanova, K.: BERT: pre-training of deep bidirectional transformers for language understanding. In: Proceedings of the 2019 conference of the North American Chapter of the Association for Computational Linguistics: Human Language Technologies, vol. 1 (long and short papers), pp. 4171–4186 (2019)
7. El-Khair, I.A.: 1.5 billion words Arabic corpus. arXiv preprint arXiv:1611.04033 (2016)
8. Fuzhou, G., Zigeng, X.: Generate corresponding image from text description using modified GAN-CLS algorithm. J. Syst. Sci. Complexity (2025)
9. Goodfellow, I.J., et al.: Generative adversarial nets. Adv. Neural Inf. Process. Syst. **27** (2014)
10. Heusel, M., Ramsauer, H., Unterthiner, T., Nessler, B., Hochreiter, S.: GANs trained by a two time-scale update rule converge to a local Nash equilibrium. Adv. Neural Inf. Process. Syst. **30** (2017)
11. Huang, Z., Xu, W., Yu, K.: Bidirectional LSTM-CRF models for sequence tagging. arXiv preprint arXiv:1508.01991 (2015)
12. Kingma, D.P., Ba, J.: Adam: a method for stochastic optimization. arXiv preprint arXiv:1412.6980 (2014)
13. Kumar, A., Mudgil, A., Dodeja, N., Vishwakarma, D.K.: Realistic face generation using a textual description. In: 2021 5th International Conference on Computing Methodologies and Communication (ICCMC), pp. 917–922. IEEE (2021)
14. Mirza, M., Osindero, S.: Conditional generative adversarial nets. arXiv preprint arXiv:1411.1784 (2014)
15. Nasir, O.R., Jha, S.K., Grover, M.S., Yu, Y., Kumar, A., Shah, R.R.: Text2FaceGAN: face generation from fine grained textual descriptions. In: 2019 IEEE Fifth International Conference on Multimedia Big Data (BIGMM), pp. 58–67. IEEE (2019)
16. Reed, S., Akata, Z., Lee, H., Schiele, B.: Learning deep representations of fine-grained visual descriptions. In: Proceedings of the IEEE Conference on Computer Vision and Pattern Recognition, pp. 49–58 (2016)
17. Reed, S., Akata, Z., Yan, X., Logeswaran, L., Schiele, B., Lee, H.: Generative adversarial text to image synthesis. In: International Conference on Machine Learning, pp. 1060–1069. PMLR (2016)
18. Sabae, M.S., Dardir, M.A., Eskarous, R.T., Ebbed, M.R.: StyleT2F: generating human faces from textual description using StyleGAN2. arXiv preprint arXiv:2204.07924 (2022)

19. Szegedy, C., Vanhoucke, V., Ioffe, S., Shlens, J., Wojna, Z.: Rethinking the inception architecture for computer vision. In: Proceedings of the IEEE Conference on Computer Vision and Pattern Recognition, pp. 2818–2826 (2016)
20. Tanveer, M., Habib, U.: Text description to facial sketch generation using GANs. In: 2023 18th International Conference on Emerging Technologies (ICET), pp. 10–15. IEEE (2023)
21. Tao, M., et al.: DF-GAN: deep fusion generative adversarial networks for text-to-image synthesis. arXiv preprint arXiv:2008.05865, **2**(6) (2020)
22. Xia, W., Yang, Y., Xue, J.H., Wu, B.: TediGAN: text-guided diverse face image generation and manipulation. In: Proceedings of the IEEE/CVF Conference on Computer Vision and Pattern Recognition, pp. 2256–2265 (2021)
23. Xu, T., et al.: AttnGAN: fine-grained text to image generation with attentional generative adversarial networks. In: Proceedings of the IEEE Conference on Computer Vision and Pattern Recognition, pp. 1316–1324 (2018)
24. Yauri-Lozano, E., Castillo-Cara, M., Orozco-Barbosa, L., García-Castro, R.: Generative adversarial networks for text-to-face synthesis & generation: a quantitative-qualitative analysis of natural language processing encoders for Spanish. Inf. Process. Manage. **61**(3), 103667 (2024)
25. Zeroual, I., Goldhahn, D., Eckart, T., Lakhouaja, A.: OSIAN: open source international Arabic news corpus-preparation and integration into the Clarin-infrastructure. In: Proceedings of the Fourth Arabic Natural Language Processing Workshop, pp. 175–182 (2019)
26. Zhang, H., et al.: StackGAN++: realistic image synthesis with stacked generative adversarial networks. IEEE Trans. Pattern Anal. Mach. Intell. **41**(8), 1947–1962 (2018)
27. Zhang, R., Isola, P., Efros, A.A., Shechtman, E., Wang, O.: The unreasonable effectiveness of deep features as a perceptual metric. In: Proceedings of the IEEE Conference on Computer Vision and Pattern Recognition, pp. 586–595 (2018)

Large Language Models as Universal Predictors? An Empirical Study on Small Tabular Datasets

Nikolaos Pavlidis[1,2](✉), Vasilis Perifanis[1,2], Symeon Symeonidis[3], and Pavlos S. Efraimidis[1,2]

[1] Institute for Language and Speech Processing, Athena Research Center, 67100 Xanthi, Greece
npavlidi@ee.duth.gr
[2] Department of Electrical and Computer Engineering, Democritus University of Thrace, 67100 Kimmeria, Xanthi, Greece
[3] Department of Production and Management Engineering, Democritus University of Thrace, 67100 Kimmeria, Xanthi, Greece

Abstract. Large Language Models (LLMs) have demonstrated the potential to generalize across modalities and domains. With their in-context learning (ICL) capabilities, LLMs can perform predictive tasks over structured inputs without explicit fine-tuning. In this work, we investigate the empirical prediction capability of LLLMs on small-scale structured datasets for classification, regression and clustering tasks. We evaluate the performance of state-of-the-art LLMs (GPT, Gemini, DeepSeek) under few-shot prompting and compare them against machine learning (ML) baselines, including tabular foundation models (TFMs). Our results show that LLMs achieve strong performance in classification tasks, establishing zero-training baselines. In contrast, the performance in regression is poor compared to ML models, likely because regression demands outputs in a large space, and clustering results are similarly limited, which we attribute to the absence of genuine ICL in this setting. Nonetheless, this approach enables low-overhead data analysis and offers a viable alternative to traditional ML pipelines. We further analyze the influence of context size and prompt structure on predictive performance. Our findings suggest that LLMs can serve as general-purpose predictive engines for structured data, with clear strengths in classification and significant limitations in regression and clustering.

Keywords: Large Language Models · In-Context Learning · Zero-Training · Machine Learning · Tabular Data

1 Introduction

Large-scale pre-trained language models (LLMs) like GPT [1] and Gemini [13], have achieved state-of-the-art results in a wide range of natural language processing (NLP) tasks, such as translation, summarization and question answering. These capabilities have raised interest in the broader potential of LLMs to

A. Awad et al. (Eds.): MEDI 2025, LNCS 16427, pp. 109–116, 2026.
https://doi.org/10.1007/978-3-032-19865-5_8

act as general-purpose function predictors across domains. Recent developments in in-context learning (ICL) [11] demonstrate that LLMs can solve a variety of unseen tasks by conditioning on a few examples within a prompt. The fundamental concept of ICL are outlined in [4]. Demonstrating that LLMs can effectively approximate functions in structured data presents the potential for developing universal baseline predictors that operate without explicit model training. In this work, we empirically evaluate the approximation capability of LLMs on small-scale structured data tasks, without task-specific fine-tuning. We assess GPT-5, GPT-4o, GPT-o3, DeepSeek-R1 and Gemini-Flash-2.5, using few-shot ICL on classification, regression and clustering tasks, leveraging datasets of up to 500 rows. We further compare LLMs to traditional ML algorithms such as linear regression (LR), Random Forests (RF), LightGBM (LGBM), and more recent developments using tabular foundation models (TFMs) like TabPFN [6] and TabICL [10]. Beyond accuracy metrics, we investigate the effect of varying the number and structure of context examples on LLM approximation quality.

2 Related Work

Large-scale pre-trained models have transformed deep learning, demonstrating strong generalization across diverse tasks via ICL [12]. The theoretical basis traces back to the universal approximation theorem [7], establishing that sufficiently wide networks can approximate any continuous function. Transformers [14], replace recurrence and convolution with self-attention and are trained on sequence modeling objectives. While theoretical works examine their universal approximation properties [8], empirical studies on transformers handling structured, non-sequential data remain limited. Recent works adapt LLMs for structured data by serializing tabular inputs into text, enabling code generation, table question answering and data transformation [9]. Nevertheless, challenges persist for high-dimensional numeric features, reasoning and generalization across heterogeneous distributions [5]. To mitigate such issues, **Tabular Foundation Models (TFMs)** have emerged. TabPFN [6] leverages transformers pre-trained on synthetic data for classification via ICL, and its successor TabPFNv2 [3] improves scalability and predictive performance. Despite progress in deep architectures, traditional models remain strong baselines for tabular tasks. While prior works such as TabPFN [6] demonstrate fine-tuned tabular transformers, the effectiveness of general-purpose LLMs as function approximators for structured data remains underexplored. This study investigates whether prompting LLMs with structured examples enables competitive performance across classification, regression and clustering tasks.

3 Methodology

3.1 Datasets

We evaluate LLMs as general predictors on a curated set of small-scale tabular datasets commonly used in ML benchmarks. Each dataset is selected based on its limited sample size (maximum of 500 instances).

For classification, we use three datasets. The Iris dataset is a three-class problem containing 150 samples with 4 features, used to predict the species of iris flowers. The Lupus dataset consists of measurements from 87 patients and serves as a binary classification problem for detecting the presence or absence of lupus nephritis. The Bankrupt dataset includes 250 company records described by 5 financial ratios, used to predict the likelihood of bankruptcy.

For regression, we consider three benchmark datasets. The Diabetes dataset contains 442 samples with 10 medical features and is used to predict a measure of disease progression. The Servo dataset is a small dataset with 167 samples and 4 input variables describing motor configurations, used to predict the motor's speed. The Friedman dataset is a synthetic regression benchmark containing 500 samples and 10 features designed to evaluate nonlinear regression methods.

Finally, for clustering, we include three datasets. The Mall dataset comprises 200 customer records with demographic and spending attributes, used for customer segmentation. The Wholesale dataset consists of 440 observations of annual spending across different product categories for wholesale clients, also aimed at customer segmentation. The Moon dataset is a synthetic two-dimensional dataset of 300 samples arranged in two interleaving half-moon shapes, typically used to assess clustering algorithms on non-linearly separable data.

To emulate realistic low-resource conditions, we refrain from applying any data augmentation or synthetic sample generation. All datasets are standardized using z-score normalization to place features on a comparable scale.

3.2 Models

The following LLMs are assessed in few-shot prompting settings: **GPT-5**, **GPT-5-Thinking**, **GPT-4o**, **GPT-o3**, **Gemini** and **DeepSeek**. LLMs are prompted with structured input-output examples using plain-text format. For classification and regression, few-shot examples are provided in tabular text format (e.g., feature names followed by their corresponding values and labels). For clustering, raw feature vectors are presented, with the model asked to identify patterns and assign cluster identifiers.

We include the following machine baselines, all trained with default hyperparameters: **Logistic** and **Linear Regression**, **Random Forest (RF)**, **LightGBM** and **CatBoost**, **K-Means**, **Agglomerative Clustering**, **DBSCAN**, **Gaussian Mixture Models (GMM)**, **TabNet** [2] combined with **K-Means** for feature extraction and clustering.

We evaluate two recent foundational approaches designed specifically for tabular data. **TabPFN** [6] is a transformer model trained to directly predict labels for small tabular datasets without task-specific gradient updates. TabPFN can handle both classification and regression tasks. **TabICL** [10] extends the in-context learning paradigm to tabular data by combining a transformer encoder with a specialized prompt construction strategy.

3.3 Metrics

For **Classification**, we use Accuracy, Precision, Recall, and F1-Score. For **Regression**, Mean Absolute Error (MAE), Mean Squared Error (MSE), and the Coefficient of Determination (R^2 Score); and for **Clustering**, the Silhouette Coefficient, Davies–Bouldin Index, and Calinski–Harabasz Index. For **LLMs**, outputs are post-processed using rule-based matching or semantic similarity measures to align predicted labels with ground-truth values.

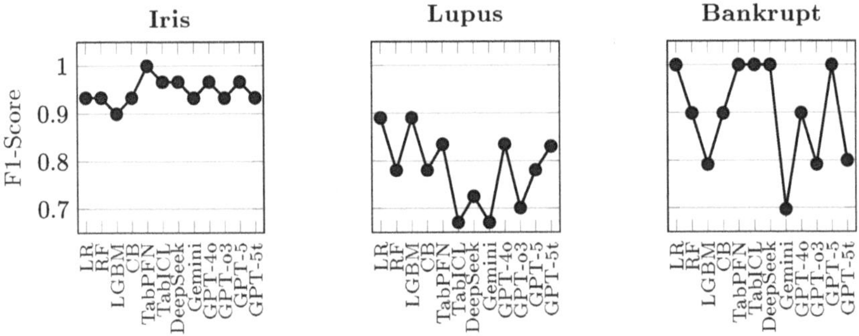

Fig. 1. F1-Score performance across datasets. Each point corresponds to one model, showing its classification F1-Score on the Iris, Lupus and Bankrupt datasets.

4 Experiments

4.1 Classification Results

Figure 1 summarizes the classification performance of traditional ML models, LLM-based ICL approaches and TFMs. Across the three benchmark datasets (Iris, Lupus, Bankrupt), we observe that LLMs are capable of delivering competitive accuracy and F1-scores in several cases. For the Iris dataset, where the class structure is well-defined and the number of samples is small, most LLMs and the foundational models (TabPFN, TabICL) achieve accuracies above 0.96, outperforming ML baselines. This suggests that in low-dimensional, clean and balanced classification problems, LLMs can act as universal approximator baselines without significant loss in performance. In the Lupus dataset, which presents class imbalance and higher feature noise, LLM performance is more variable. Models like GPT-4o and GPT-5t match the accuracy of strong classical models (0.8333), others such as Deepseek and Gemini drop to 0.7222 and 0.6667, respectively. The Bankrupt dataset presents a scenario with near-separable classes. Here, LLMs like GPT-5 and DeepSeek achieve perfect accuracy, matching TabPFN, TabICL and Logistic Regression. However, other LLMs (e.g., GPT-5t) drop to 0.8, highlighting that while peak performance is possible, it is not guaranteed across LLM variants. Overall, the classification results provide the strongest evidence for the viability of LLMs as universal predictors baselines.

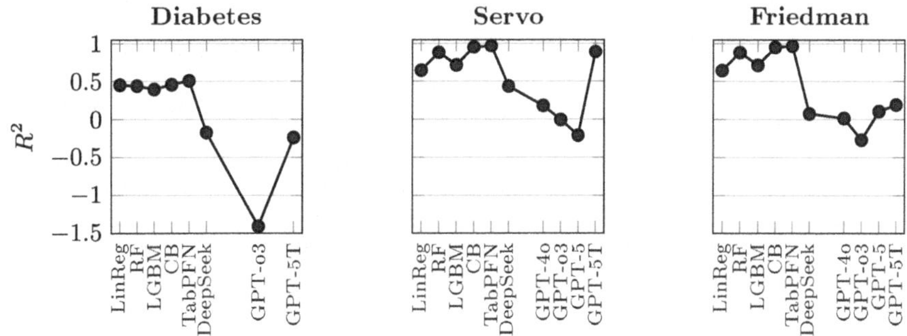

Fig. 2. R^2 regression performance across datasets. Each point corresponds to a model's coefficient of determination for the Diabetes, Servo and Friedman datasets. Models with missing points exceeded the maximum context length.

4.2 Regression Results

The results from Regression tasks are summarized in Fig. 2, where a significant performance gap between LLM-based approaches and established regression algorithms is evident. Specifically, high-performing models (e.g., CatBoost, TabPFN) achieve R^2 values above 0.95, while most LLMs lag substantially, with some producing negative R^2 scores, i.e. worse than a constant mean predictor. This indicates that LLMs in their current form do not consistently capture the continuous input–output mapping required for accurate regression. The Diabetes dataset illustrates this limitation sharply: TabPFN reaches an R^2 of 0.5079 with competitive error metrics, while LLM-based outputs range from marginally positive to strongly negative R^2 values (e.g., GPT-o3 at –1.4087). Similar trends are observed in Servo dataset. An important observation is that the performance gap often widens with larger datasets or those requiring fine-grained continuous prediction. Unlike classification, where token-level categorical predictions align with the discrete nature of the task, continuous value prediction demands numerical precision that is difficult to maintain through autoregressive token generation. Furthermore, LLMs lack an explicit objective function tied to regression error, making their outputs prone to scaling errors and reduced stability when more data is present.

4.3 Clustering Results

Clustering performance, presented in Fig. 3, shows further limitations of LLMs as unsupervised predictors. Standard clustering algorithms consistently outperform LLM-derived embeddings across all three datasets. In Mall, the best LLM configuration (GPT-5t) produces a silhouette score of 0.4241, approaching the strongest TabNet+KMeans result (0.4078) and outperforming vanilla KMeans (0.3348). However, this success does not generalise: in Wholesale, LLM-based methods frequently produce negative silhouette scores and higher Davies–Bouldin scores, indicating poor separation between clusters. Similarly, in Moon,

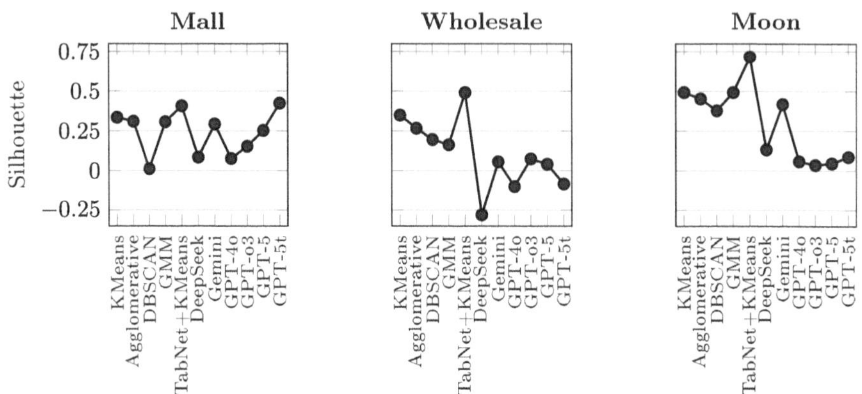

Fig. 3. Silhouette scores across clustering methods for the Mall, Wholesale and Moon datasets. Each point represents the method's Silhouette score (higher is better).

a dataset with well-defined non-linear clusters, traditional methods like TabNet+KMeans achieve 0.7168 silhouette, while LLMs indicate significant performance degradation (e.g., GPT-4o at 0.0591). These inconsistencies suggest that while LLM embeddings may incidentally align with cluster structure in certain small, simple datasets, they do not reliably capture the geometry of data manifolds in a way that supports unsupervised separation. This is likely due to the fact that LLM representations are trained for general semantic similarity rather than the specific variance–covariance structures exploited by clustering algorithms.

4.4 Ablation Study

To better understand the factors influencing LLM performance on small tabular classification tasks, we conduct a series of controlled ablation experiments using a single stratified train/test split (70/30) for each dataset (Iris, Lupus, Bankrupt). We compare the two strongest LLMs from our main results (GPT-5, DeepSeek) against two foundation models for tabular data (TabPFN, TabICL).

We vary the fraction of available training data to determine the minimum amount required for LLMs to match the performance of TFMs. Fractions of 25%, 50%, 75%, and 100% of the training split are evaluated. For TabPFN and TabICL, models are trained directly on each subsample. For LLMs, the available fraction defines the in-context example pool. Figure 4 presents the result of this ablation. On IRIS, TabICL and both LLMs (DeepSeek, GPT-5) begin with the same F1 value at 0.25 ($\approx$0.8997) and ended with the same F1 at full data ($\approx$0.9667). In Bankruptcy, DeepSeek and TabPFN started with identical F1 at 0.25 ($\approx$0.8990), while GPT-5 achieved 1.0 at all fractions. From the 0.5 fraction onwards, TabICL and DeepSeek produced exactly the same F1 values. Here, however, more training data did not always improve performance. Both TabICL and DeepSeek dropped from perfect scores at 0.5 to $\approx$0.80 at 0.75 fraction. For Lupus, the differences between models are clearer than the rest datasets. TabPFN consistently outperformed others (≈0.83–0.89) across all fractions, while TabICL, DeepSeek, and GPT-5 showed variability. Overall, TFMs (TabICL, TabPFN) showed more stability across fractions, with TabPFN being largely unaffected by data size, while LLMs exhibited dataset-specific trends.

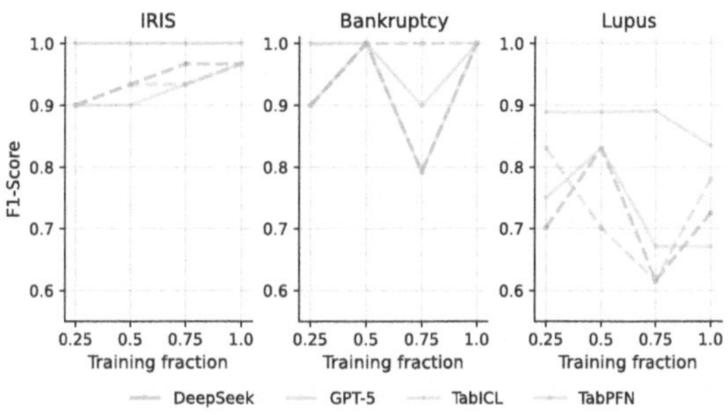

Fig. 4. F1-Score trends across training data fractions. Each panel corresponds to a dataset (IRIS, Bankruptcy, Lupus), with four models evaluated (TabICL, TabPFN, DeepSeek, GPT-5).

We investigate whether the formatting of tabular data within the prompt affects LLM performance. Four serialization formats are compared: (i) CSV (default), (ii) key:value pairs, (iii) JSON Lines, and (iv) Markdown tables. This experiment is conducted on the Lupus dataset (Fig. 5).

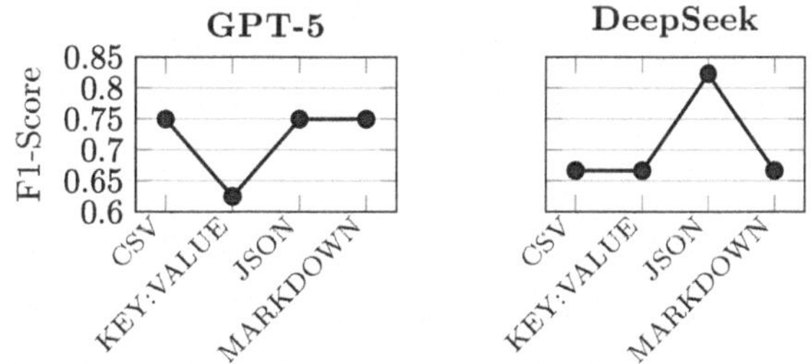

Fig. 5. F1-Score of GPT-5 and DeepSeek under different serialization formats on the Lupus dataset.

The results indicate that the choice of serialization format can influence LLM performance, though the extent of this effect appears model-dependent. For GPT-5, performance remains largely stable across CSV, JSON, and Markdown, suggesting that the model is relatively robust to variations in tabular data formatting. In contrast, Deepseek demonstrates a clearer sensitivity to format.

5 Conclusion

This paper explores the use of LLMs as predictors on small tabular datasets across classification, regression and clustering tasks. Our results suggest that LLMs can offer competitive performance in classification tasks. For regression and clustering tasks, however, LLMs performance was generally less reliable. The ablation study showed that LLM behavior can vary depending on dataset characteristics and the number of in-context examples. In some cases, more data did not consistently lead to improved results, pointing to potential sensitivity to data distribution or input representation. Overall, although LLMs may not currently serve as universal approximators across all learning tasks, they can be useful tools for classification over tabular data when ease of use and fast iteration are important. Further work is needed to better understand their limitations in regression and clustering and to explore ways to extend LLMs for more reliable performance on structured data tasks.

References

1. Achiam, J., et al.: GPT-4 technical report. arXiv preprint arXiv:2303.08774 (2023)
2. Arik, S.Ö., Pfister, T.: TabNet: attentive interpretable tabular learning. In: Proceedings of the AAAI Conference, vol. 35, pp. 6679–6687 (2021)
3. Cheng, Z.J., Jia, Z.Y., Zhou, Z., Li, Y.F., Guo, L.Z.: Realistic evaluation of TabPFN v2 in open environments. arXiv preprint arXiv:2505.16226 (2025)
4. Dong, Q., et al.: A survey on in-context learning. In: Proceedings of the 2024 Conference on Empirical Methods in NLP, Miami, Florida, USA, November 2024, pp. 1107–1128. ACL (2024). https://doi.org/10.18653/v1/2024.emnlp-main.64
5. Gorishniy, Y., Rubachev, I., Khrulkov, V., Babenko, A.: Revisiting deep learning models for tabular data. NeurIPS **34**, 18932–18943 (2021)
6. Hollmann, N., Müller, S., Eggensperger, K., Hutter, F.: TabPFN: a transformer that solves small tabular classification problems in a second. arXiv arXiv:2207.01848 (2022)
7. Hornik, K.: Approximation capabilities of multilayer feedforward networks. Neural Netw. **4**(2), 251–257 (1991)
8. Kratsios, A., Zamanlooy, B., Liu, T., Dokmanić, I.: Universal approximation under constraints is possible with transformers. arXiv preprint arXiv:2110.03303 (2021)
9. Lu, W., Zhang, J., Fan, J., Fu, Z., Chen, Y., Du, X.: Large language model for table processing: a survey. Front. Comp. Sci. **19**(2), 192350 (2025)
10. Qu, J., HolzmÃžller, D., Varoquaux, G., Morvan, M.L.: Tabicl: A tabular foundation model for in-context learning on large data. arXiv preprint arxiv:2502.05564 (2025)
11. Shamshiri, A., Ryu, K.R., Park, J.Y.: In-context learning for long-context sentiment analysis on infrastructure project opinions. arXiv preprint arXiv:2410.11265 (2024)
12. Shin, S., Lee, S.W., Ahn, H.., Ha, J.W., et al.: On the effect of pretraining corpora on in-context learning by a large-scale language model. arXiv arXiv:2204.13509 (2022)
13. Team, G., et al.: Gemini: a family of highly capable multimodal models. arXiv preprint arXiv:2312.11805 (2023)
14. Vaswani, A., et al.: Attention is all you need. NeurIPS **30** (2017)

Exploring the Landscape of Generative Adversarial Networks: A Comprehensive Survey of Variants and Applications

Ali H. Shareef[1,2,3](✉), Hajer Ghodhbani[1,5], Tarek M. Hamdani[1,4], and Adel M. Alimi[1,5]

[1] Research Groups in Intelligent Machines (REGIM Lab), National Engineering School of Sfax (ENIS), University of Sfax, BP 1173, 3038 Sfax, Tunisia
[2] National School of Electronics and Telecommunications of Sfax (ENET'Com), University of Sfax, 10587 Sfax, Tunisia
[3] University of Thi-Qar, Nasiriyah 64001, Thi-Qar, Iraq
ali.handhel@utq.edu.iq
[4] Higher Institute of Computer Science Mahdia, University of Monastir, 5111 Mahdia, Tunisia
[5] Department of Electrical and Electronic Engineering Science, University of Johannesburg, Auckland Park 2006, Johannesburg, South Africa

Abstract. Generative Adversarial Networks (GANs), a prominent subclass of generative models, have gained significant attention in recent years for their ability to replicate complex real-world data. Originating from the concept of a two-player zero-sum game, GANs pit a generator and a discriminator against each other, with the success of one offset by the failure of the other. This framework has driven remarkable advancements across domains such as computer vision and image generation. In this review, we introduce the fundamental concepts of GANs, provide an overview of their major variants, and compare them with other generative models. We discuss the breadth of their applications, analyze different GAN architectures, and situate our findings within the context of prior research.

Keywords: GAN variants · GAN architectures · GAN applications

1 Introduction

One of the key algorithms introduced by Goodfellow et al. [17] is Generative Adversarial Networks (GANs), These novel machine learning techniques were groundbreaking as they assigned well-coordinated tasks to two components: the generator and the discriminator. The fundamental concept of GANs is inspired by a two-player zero-sum game, where the gain of one player perfectly balances the loss of the other, resulting in a net total of zero wins across participants. This innovative framework has significantly advanced artificial intelligence research, enabling machines to better simulate human-like behavior [39].

A. Awad et al. (Eds.): MEDI 2025, LNCS 16427, pp. 117–128, 2026.
https://doi.org/10.1007/978-3-032-19865-5_9

GANs consist of two components. The first is a generative model (G), which seeks to generate wholly new instances that are completely different from the original dataset and that the generator has never seen before but that have a similar data distribution to the actual dataset. The generator receives a random noise, which it uses to create brand-new samples with distributions that match the real data. The second model is a model of discriminator (D). The goal of the generator and discriminator, as shown in Fig. 1, is to analyze the distribution and calculate the likelihood that the sample came from either the original dataset or the generator by looking at the distribution, which might have come from either source.

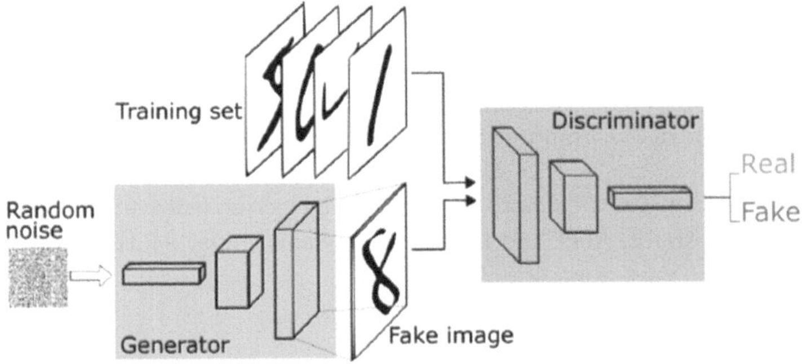

Fig. 1. Architecture of a standard Generative Adversarial Network (GAN), illustrating the interaction between the generator and discriminator components during training. [32].

GANs are one of the most distinctive research tools due to their capacity to generate synthetic data. While GANs have been evaluated in the context of image processing a number of times up to this point, little focus has been given to reviewing GANs on multidisciplinary domains. Therefore, a thorough search for a research paper or periodical linked to GAN was conducted for this study to examine the implementation problems and the use of GAN in its interdisciplinary application domains. Different application areas are taken into consideration for the survey using a mixed search approach.

In this paper, we provide a brief review of GANs, discussing their different structures, as well as discussing their applications in various fields including image generation, enhancement, and translation. In addition, we provide an overview of recent issues and identify possible future developments in the study of GANs.

Several recent surveys have comprehensively discussed the development and applications of Generative Adversarial Networks (GANs) [7,13,14,28,38]. However, most of these studies focus either on specific aspects such as architecture optimization or application domains like image synthesis and medical imaging. In contrast, our review aims to provide a holistic synthesis that not only summarizes the evolution of GAN variants but also maps their interconnections, training challenges, and practical implications for real-world deployment. Moreover, this paper highlights under-explored research directions, especially regarding GAN interpretability, ethical constraints, and data efficiency.

The purpose of this review is to provide a systematic and critical synthesis of Generative Adversarial Networks (GANs), focusing on their architectural evolution, training dynamics, and practical applications. Unlike traditional narrative reviews, this study aims to identify unresolved challenges and propose conceptual directions for future GAN research.

The main contributions of this review can be summarized as follows:

- We provide a comprehensive synthesis of the fundamental concepts, variants, and architectures of Generative Adversarial Networks (GANs) across multiple application domains.
- We conduct a structured comparison of GAN variants by analyzing their design objectives, training stability, and data efficiency.
- We summarize the advantages and limitations of each major model to guide future research and practical implementations.
- We identify open challenges and propose potential research directions in interpretability, ethics, and cross-domain adaptation.

2 Methodology of Literature Selection

This review follows a structured and transparent approach to ensure comprehensiveness and reproducibility. Relevant studies published between 2014 and 2024 were identified through major databases such as *IEEE Xplore*, *SpringerLink*, and *ScienceDirect*, using the keywords "Generative Adversarial Networks," "GAN variants," "GAN applications," and "data augmentation."

The inclusion criteria were defined as follows:

- Direct contribution to GAN architecture development or applications.
- Peer-reviewed publication in a reputable conference or journal.
- Demonstrated novelty, scientific quality, and relevance to generative model evolution.

After screening approximately 180 papers, 96 key studies were selected for in-depth review. The selected papers were categorized by architecture type (e.g., DCGAN, WGAN, CycleGAN, StyleGAN) and by application domain (e.g., image synthesis, fashion, medical imaging, climate modeling, digital watermarking).

This systematic process ensures that the findings and conclusions of this paper are evidence-based, transparent, and representative of the field's current state.

2.1 Open-Source Resources and Datasets

To ensure transparency and reproducibility, this review references several open-source implementations and datasets that have significantly contributed to the advancement of GAN research. The following repositories and frameworks are commonly used in GAN experimentation and model benchmarking:

- **StyleGAN2-ADA:** https://github.com/NVlabs/stylegan2-ada
- **CycleGAN and Pix2Pix:** https://github.com/junyanz/pytorch-CycleGAN-and-pix2pix
- **DCGAN Implementation:** https://github.com/pytorch/examples/tree/main/dcgan
- **CelebA Dataset:** https://mmlab.ie.cuhk.edu.hk/projects/CelebA.html
- **Fashion-MNIST Dataset:** https://github.com/zalandoresearch/fashion-mnist

These resources serve as valuable benchmarks for evaluating model performance, comparing architectures, and validating the reproducibility of published results. Their accessibility supports open research practices and facilitates future innovations in GAN-based applications.

3 GAN Variants

In this paper, an extensive study of different types of GANs is presented. The study is centered around the following types of models unconditional generative adversarial networks and conditional generative adversarial networks, label conditional adversarial networks, mode-seeking GAN, and energy-based GAN. Most types of GANs belong to one of two categories: unconditional and conditional generative adversarial networks. In this paper, other interesting extensions to the original GAN framework that cover these two categories are reviewed. Table 1 illustrates the comparison of different GAN variants based on this classification.

4 Applications of GANs

GANs is useful to deal with various data distribution problems [35]. Therefore, GANs have generated considerable research interest since being introduced. Since then, the basic architecture of GANs has been improved and researched to address weaknesses of the model, such as unstable training, convergence, mode collapse, etc. Studies have been conducted in various fields using different types of GANs [4].

GAN is widely used as a promising model for generating new data groups. To generate a new group of data using GANs, a generator, which is used for producing new data, and a discriminator, which is used to discriminate whether the data is real or fake, are operated together. There are many models built using this GAN architecture to address the disadvantages of GANs, such as unstable training, convergence, mode collPRse, etc. GAN models have been developed to deliver excellent results in various application fields. Figure 2 illustrates the applications of GANs [16].

Table 1. Comparison of Different GAN Types

Type of GAN	Description	Key Features	Training Process	Advantages	Disadvantages	Applications
Vanilla GAN [17]	The original GAN framework proposed by Ian Goodfellow [17].	Basic structure with a generator and discriminator network.	Generator and discriminator play a zero-sum game. The generator learns to create data resembling real data, while the discriminator learns to distinguish fake from real.	Simple and foundational approach to GANs.	Training instability, mode collapse, difficulty scaling for high-quality outputs.	Image generation, data augmentation, unsupervised learning tasks.
DCGAN [42]	Enhances the vanilla GAN by using convolutional layers instead of fully connected layers for both the generator and discriminator.	Convolutional layers for both networks, making it suitable for image-based data.	Uses batch normalization and leaky ReLU activations. More stable training and better results than Vanilla GAN.	Better at generating high-quality images; more stable than vanilla GANs.	Less versatile for non-image data types.	Image generation, style transfer, unsupervised learning.
WGAN [1]	Uses the Wasserstein loss function, improving stability during training and reducing mode collapse.	Introduces Earth-Mover (Wasserstein) distance as a loss function, which helps with gradient flow and stability.	Requires a critic (discriminator) to approximate the Wasserstein distance between real and fake data distributions.	More stable training, smoother convergence, avoids mode collapse.	Requires weight clipping or gradient penalty for stability. More computationally expensive.	High-quality image generation, modeling continuous data distributions.
cGAN [11]	Extends GANs by conditioning the generation process on auxiliary information, such as class labels or other data.	Generator and discriminator take both data and labels as input.	Training is conditioned on additional information, improving control over the generated output.	Allows for generation of data conditioned on specific labels or conditions.	Requires labeled data, may be prone to overfitting with small datasets.	Label-conditioned image generation, text-to-image synthesis.
ACGAN [30]	A variant of cGAN that introduces an auxiliary classifier to predict class labels in the discriminator.	Discriminator outputs both a real/fake classification and a label classification.	Uses both adversarial and classification losses during training.	Combines the benefits of classification and adversarial learning, enhancing the model's ability to generate labeled data.	Training can be more difficult, may require more sophisticated architectures.	Labeled data generation, semi-supervised learning, text-to-image synthesis.
StyleGAN [22]	Uses a novel architecture to separate style and content, allowing for fine-grained control over generated images.	A style-based generator that separates the image generation process into different levels of abstraction (e.g., global features, local features).	The generator has a mapping network that controls the style at different levels, leading to improved image quality.	High-quality images, control over image attributes (e.g., hair color, facial features).	Computationally intensive, high memory requirements.	Face generation, high-quality image synthesis, art generation.
StyleGAN2 [23]	Improved version of StyleGAN with better image quality and training stability.	Reduces artifacts and improves output quality by refining the architecture and loss functions.	Modified architecture leads to reduced artifacts in generated images, better quality, and smoother training.	State-of-the-art image quality with more realistic results and improved control.	Requires large computational resources, still prone to overfitting on small datasets.	High-resolution portrait generation, realistic image synthesis.
StyleGAN2-ADA [20]	An extension of StyleGAN2 that improves training when data is limited by using Adaptive Discriminator Augmentation (ADA).	Uses ADA to augment the discriminator during training to improve generalization, particularly in low-data scenarios.	Introduces adaptive augmentation that dynamically adjusts the discriminator's inputs, improving robustness when data is limited.	Improves training stability and image quality with limited data, reduces the need for large datasets.	Still requires significant computational resources, may take longer to train compared to traditional methods.	High-quality image generation with limited data, portrait generation, art synthesis.
CycleGAN [43]	A type of GAN designed for unpaired image-to-image translation tasks.	Does not require paired datasets, uses cycle-consistency loss to ensure the output is similar to the input.	Uses two generators and two discriminators to map images from one domain to another, ensuring cycle consistency.	Can translate between unpaired datasets (e.g., photo to painting, day to night).	May produce blurry results or struggle with highly complex domain shifts.	Image-to-image translation (e.g., style transfer, photo enhancement).
Pix2Pix [18]	A conditional GAN for paired image-to-image translation, such as converting sketches to images or black-and-white photos to color.	Requires paired datasets for training, and generates output images conditioned on input images.	Uses L1 loss and adversarial loss, providing more detailed control over image translation.	Highly effective for tasks where paired data is available, generates detailed images.	Limited to tasks with paired datasets. Can be less flexible than CycleGAN for unpaired tasks.	Image-to-image translation, sketch-to-photo, photo restoration.
BigGAN [6]	A scalable GAN designed to generate high-resolution images, using a large-scale model with significant computational power.	Focuses on high-resolution outputs, uses a larger model and more data for training.	Optimized for large-scale datasets, uses a deep architecture with a large batch size.	Can generate high-resolution, realistic images with fine details.	Computationally intensive, requires significant resources.	High-resolution image generation, large-scale data modeling.
InfoGAN [9]	A GAN variant that maximizes the mutual information between the latent code and the generated images, encouraging interpretable features.	Introduces a mutual information term into the loss function, ensuring meaningful information is encoded in the latent space.	Uses a variational approach to maximize information about the latent code, allowing for more interpretable results.	Encourages learning of disentangled and interpretable latent features.	May require more complex architecture and training to prevent mode collapse.	Generating images with specific, controllable features (e.g., object shape, pose).
ProGAN [19]	A GAN that progressively grows both the generator and discriminator during training, starting from low resolution and gradually increasing the resolution.	Progressive training starting from a low resolution and adding layers for higher resolutions.	Training begins with a low-resolution image (e.g., 4×4), and progressively increases until the desired resolution is achieved.	More stable training, generates high-quality high-resolution images, avoids mode collapse.	Computationally intensive, requires more training time due to progressive nature.	High-quality image generation, face generation, high-resolution art generation.
StyleGAN3 [21]	The latest iteration of StyleGAN, focusing on improving the model's ability to generate high-quality images with more temporal consistency and removing artifacts in high-resolution outputs.	Improved architecture to better handle fine-grained details, reduced artifacts, and better temporal consistency.	Uses a new method for stabilizing the training process and further reducing visual artifacts, with better handling of high-resolution data.	Reduces artifacts like"checkerboarding," improves consistency in generated images.	Requires significant computational resources and take more time for training than previous versions.	High-quality image generation, temporal consistency tasks (e.g., video generation, 3D model creation).
Laplacian GAN (LAPGAN) [15]	A hierarchical GAN using a Laplacian pyramid to progressively generate images from low to high resolution.	Hierarchical structure, Each level uses its own GAN and Based on Laplacian pyramid	Train each level separately and Each stage refines the previous output	Captures fine image details and Reduces training instability Effective for high-res generation	Complex training pipeline, Time-consuming and Requires separate training per level	Image synthesis, Image super-resolution and Artistic generation

Fig. 2. Overview of the diverse applications of Generative Adversarial Networks (GANs) across multiple domains, including image synthesis, fashion design, medical imaging, and climate modeling.

4.1 Pros and Cons of Major GAN Variants

Different GAN variants were developed to overcome specific weaknesses of the original model, each offering distinct benefits and limitations. The Vanilla GAN [17] introduced the basic adversarial framework but often suffers from mode collapse and unstable training. The DCGAN [33] improved visual quality and training stability through convolutional layers and normalization, yet remains sensitive to dataset diversity. The Conditional GAN [27] enables controlled generation using label information but relies heavily on high-quality annotated data. The Wasserstein GAN [5] enhances stability via Earth's distance, though it increases computational cost. The CycleGAN [43] supports unpaired image translation, but may introduce artifacts when domains differ greatly. Finally, StyleGAN and StyleGAN2 [22, 23] achieve high-resolution, realistic outputs through style-based latent manipulation, though they demand large datasets and high computational power.

Overall, the choice of GAN variant depends on the target application, data scale, and the balance between image quality and efficiency [12].

4.2 Image Generation and Editing

Generative image editing and generation have been observed with various deep learning frameworks like GANs and diffusion models [8]. These tools allow the generation of realistic and detailed visualizations, from face generation to fine-point image manipulation. Through conditional generation and latent space manipulation, the users can therefore generate images that fulfill certain specific needs. These technologies are of immense importance to such areas such as entertainment, design, and the creation of content [31].

- Photo-realistic Image Synthesis: GANs, such as StyleGAN, possess a remarkable capability to create not only high-resolution but also exceptionally realistic images that depict a diverse range of subjects, including people, landscapes, or various objects, each rendered with attention to detail and richness that captivates the viewer [26].
- Image Inpainting: This innovative technique skillfully involves the filling in of missing sections of images, offering a powerful solution for restoring damaged, deteriorating, or incomplete photos. This method meticulously analyzes the surrounding pixel data to seamlessly integrate the inpainted area with the remaining image content [24].
- Style Transfer: This fascinating and creative process allows for the transformation of the artistic style of an image. For example, it enables the conversion of ordinary photos into striking and visually impactful paintings, which reflect a variety of different artistic styles and historical eras, thereby breathing new life into standard images and transforming them into expressive art forms that can evoke emotions and admiration [10].

4.3 Image-to-Image Translation

Image-to-Image translation is a generative work in which the translation between two different image domains is carried out, such as satellite imagery facade generation, collection art styles, segmenting, edges to photos, and sketch to result among others [3]. The mainstream unsupervised methods use a basic model, such as human-to-cartoon generic domain generalization. The self-shape is designed for the special combination of the human and clothing models, and the proposed aesthetic score enhances visual derivatives that guide the target content and prevent the transformation of reflections. Data-driven labels for unsupervised and supervised relations are used, while consistent visual words based on dictionary learning with strong supervision are applied [18].

4.4 Data Augmentation

In feature learning in machine learning, data augmentation is a widely used method to increase the diversity of input data, which in turn increases the generalization performance of trained models. In the field of computer vision, data augmentation can be applied to images or videos through techniques such as adding noise, introducing occlusions, applying perspective transformations, adjusting contrast or brightness, and performing affine transformations. In the field of natural language processing, data augmentation can be used in text [36]. Furthermore, data augmentation increases the amount of data, which boosts the improvement of generalized representations and transcription error reduction [37]. Recent literature mentions leveraging adversarial learning to generate adversarial perturbations, including white-box and black-box threat models, text-driven approaches and text-informed perturbations. Especially in the context of augmented GANs, In the context of augmented GANs, this approach serves as a general-purpose adversarial framework for data augmentation in text generation by utilizing adversarial training to regularize a GAN, acting as a generator, with an additional discriminator network. The training data is augmented by a sequence of transformations to perturb the sentence [41].

4.5 Security and Privacy

Many GANs have been developed to perform tasks that are significant for security and privacy [25]. Examples include generating adversarial samples to bypass anti-malware models [34], generating samples to attack signature-based IDSs [2], and synthesizing high-quality fake face images that could be used for the photo review challenge [40]. Unfortunately, the immense success of GANs also threatens security and privacy protection. Depending on the application of GANs, some Techniques such as watermarking, de-identification, and using GANs to defend against adversarial GANs can be employed. Due to the beneficial and malicious purposes of GANs, the adversarial knowledge of GANs is becoming increasingly important.

5 Effectiveness

GANs offer a lot of flexibility during training. Researchers can try different loss functions and techniques to improve performance [16]. There's also exciting work happening around how to make GANs better, like building larger models (big GANs), trying wider or deeper networks, using non-neural network designs in some cases, or even combining GANs with other algorithms. These ideas could be especially useful when we don't have labeled data or when working with complex data types [29].

In addition to improvements within GANs themselves, recent advances in generative modeling, such as diffusion models and transformer-based architectures, have pushed the boundaries of what's possible. Diffusion models have shown impressive results in generating high-quality images with better stability and fewer artifacts. Meanwhile, transformer-based models have introduced new ways to model long-range dependencies and have been successfully applied to both image and text generation. These newer approaches are influencing how researchers design and evaluate generative systems and are often used alongside or as alternatives to GANs in certain applications.

6 Research Hypotheses and Motivation

The development of this review was guided by the following hypotheses:

1. The progressive diversification of GAN architectures introduces unique trade-offs between realism, stability, and data efficiency.
2. GANs demonstrate high generative potential across multiple domains; however, domain-specific adaptations remain under-investigated.
3. There is a need for an integrative taxonomy that connects architectural design innovations with measurable performance outcomes.

These hypotheses provided the conceptual foundation for the selection, classification, and interpretation of the reviewed literature, allowing for analytical discussion rather than purely descriptive synthesis.

7 Future Research Directions and Open Challenges

Despite the remarkable progress in GAN development, several open challenges remain for future exploration:

- **Training Stability:** Enhancing optimization convergence and reducing mode collapse in complex, high-dimensional data spaces.
- **Interpretability:** Promoting explainable GAN models for better transparency and understanding of feature learning processes.
- **Data Efficiency:** Optimizing GAN performance under limited and imbalanced datasets through adaptive augmentation and transfer learning.
- **Ethical and Security Concerns:** Addressing deepfake misuse, copyright infringement, and watermark integrity in generated content.
- **Domain Adaptation:** Extending GAN applicability to emerging fields such as sustainable fashion design and climate data modeling.

Addressing these challenges will strengthen the scientific maturity, robustness, and ethical foundation of future GAN research and applications.

8 Conclusion

This study has proposed a conceptual definition of GAN structure based on deep learning theory and has advanced the reasons for how GAN structure and processing agreements are achieved by means. This study introduces a new classification of GANs, focusing on their intrinsic functional differences. Our primary goal was the identification of the strengths and weaknesses of different GAN models, helping practitioners choose the most suitable model for their specific problems and highlighting techniques for further development.

To facilitate selecting suitable GAN architectures for specific applications, this study contributes to identifying relevant GAN-AI structures. We expect this study will provide both researchers and practitioners with insight into a wide variety of GAN structures, demonstrating how they may be used to provide new ways for AI technology in practice.

Despite the comprehensive coverage of GAN architectures and applications, this review is limited by the rapidly evolving nature of the field and the scope of available literature. Future work could focus on benchmarking new hybrid GAN frameworks, integrating multimodal data, and addressing the ethical implications of synthetic data generation.

Acknowledgements. The research leading to these results has received funding from the Ministry of Higher Education and Scientific Research of Tunisia under the grant agreement number LR11ES48.

Declaration. Financial Interests: The authors declare they have no financial interests. Conflict of Interest: The authors declare that they have no conflict of interest.

References

1. Adler, J., Lunz, S.: Banach Wasserstein GAN. Adv. Neural Inf. Process. Syst. **31** (2018)
2. Aldhaheri, S., Alhuzali, A.: SGAN-IDS: self-attention-based generative adversarial network against intrusion detection systems. Sensors **23**(18), 7796 (2023)
3. Alotaibi, A.: Deep generative adversarial networks for image-to-image translation: a review. Symmetry **12**(10), 1705 (2020)
4. Alqahtani, H., Kavakli-Thorne, M., Kumar, G.: Applications of generative adversarial networks (GANs): an updated review. Arch. Comput. Meth. Eng. **28**, 525–552 (2021)
5. Arjovsky, M., Chintala, S., Bottou, L.: Wasserstein generative adversarial networks. In: International Conference on Machine Learning, pp. 214–223. PMLR (2017)
6. Brock, A., Donahue, J., Simonyan, K.: Large scale GAN training for high fidelity natural image synthesis. arXiv preprint arXiv:1809.11096 (2018)
7. Brophy, E., Wang, Z., She, Q., Ward, T.: Generative adversarial networks in time series: a survey and taxonomy. arXiv preprint arXiv:2107.11098 (2021)
8. Cao, H., et al.: A survey on generative diffusion models. IEEE Trans. Knowl. Data Eng. (2024)
9. Chen, X., Duan, Y., Houthooft, R., Schulman, J., Sutskever, I., Abbeel, P.: InfoGAN: interpretable representation learning by information maximizing generative adversarial nets. Adv. Neural Inf. Process. Syst. **29** (2016)
10. Cho, H., Lim, S., Choi, G., Min, H.: Neural stain-style transfer learning using GAN for histopathological images. arXiv preprint arXiv:1710.08543 (2017)

11. Chu, C., Zhmoginov, A., Sandler, M.: CycleGAN, a master of steganography. arXiv preprint arXiv:1712.02950 (2017)
12. Creswell, A., White, T., Dumoulin, V., Arulkumaran, K., Sengupta, B., Bharath, A.A.: Generative adversarial networks: an overview. IEEE Sig. Process. Mag. **35**(1), 53–65 (2018)
13. Dash, A., Ye, J., Wang, G.: A review of generative adversarial networks (GANs) and its applications in a wide variety of disciplines: from medical to remote sensing. IEEE Access **12**, 18330–18357 (2023)
14. De Rosa, G.H., Papa, J.P.: A survey on text generation using generative adversarial networks. Pattern Recogn. **119**, 108098 (2021)
15. Denton, E.L., Chintala, S., Fergus, R., et al.: Deep generative image models using a Laplacian pyramid of adversarial networks. Adv. Neural Inf. Process. Syst. **28** (2015)
16. Figueira, A., Vaz, B.: Survey on synthetic data generation, evaluation methods and GANs. Mathematics **10**(15), 2733 (2022)
17. Goodfellow, I., et al.: Generative adversarial nets. Adv. Neural Inf. Process. Syst. **27** (2014)
18. Isola, P., Zhu, J.Y., Zhou, T., Efros, A.A.: Image-to-image translation with conditional adversarial networks. In: Proceedings of the IEEE Conference on Computer Vision and Pattern Recognition, pp. 1125–1134 (2017)
19. Karras, T.: Progressive growing of GANs for improved quality, stability, and variation. arXiv preprint arXiv:1710.10196 (2017)
20. Karras, T., Aittala, M., Hellsten, J., Laine, S., Lehtinen, J., Aila, T.: Training generative adversarial networks with limited data. Adv. Neural. Inf. Process. Syst. **33**, 12104–12114 (2020)
21. Karras, T., et al.: Alias-free generative adversarial networks. Adv. Neural. Inf. Process. Syst. **34**, 852–863 (2021)
22. Karras, T., Laine, S., Aila, T.: A style-based generator architecture for generative adversarial networks. In: Proceedings of the IEEE/CVF Conference on Computer Vision and Pattern Recognition, pp. 4401–4410 (2019)
23. Karras, T., Laine, S., Aittala, M., Hellsten, J., Lehtinen, J., Aila, T.: Analyzing and improving the image quality of StyleGAN. In: Proceedings of the IEEE/CVF Conference on Computer Vision and Pattern Recognition, pp. 8110–8119 (2020)
24. Liu, H., Wan, Z., Huang, W., Song, Y., Han, X., Liao, J.: PD-GAN: probabilistic diverse GAN for image inpainting. In: Proceedings of the IEEE/CVF Conference on Computer Vision and Pattern Recognition, pp. 9371–9381 (2021)
25. Liu, X., et al.: Privacy and security issues in deep learning: a survey. IEEE Access **9**, 4566–4593 (2020)
26. Melnik, A., et al.: Face generation and editing with StyleGAN: a survey. IEEE Trans. Pattern Anal. Mach. Intell. (2024)
27. Mirza, M., Osindero, S.: Conditional generative adversarial nets. arXiv preprint arXiv:1411.1784 (2014)
28. Ngo, T.A., Nguyen, T., Thang, T.C.: A survey of recent advances in quantum generative adversarial networks. Electronics **12**(4), 856 (2023)
29. Nguyen, V., Yago Vicente, T.F., Zhao, M., Hoai, M., Samaras, D.: Shadow detection with conditional generative adversarial networks. In: Proceedings of the IEEE International Conference on Computer Vision, pp. 4510–4518 (2017)
30. Odena, A., Olah, C., Shlens, J.: Conditional image synthesis with auxiliary classifier GANs. In: International Conference on Machine Learning, pp. 2642–2651. PMLR (2017)

31. Pan, X., Tewari, A., Leimkühler, T., Liu, L., Meka, A., Theobalt, C.: Drag your GAN: interactive point-based manipulation on the generative image manifold. In: ACM SIGGRAPH 2023 Conference Proceedings, pp. 1–11 (2023)
32. Patel, M.J., Pandya, M.S., Shah, V.: Review on generative adversarial networks. Other Words **4**(7) (2018)
33. Radford, A., Metz, L., Chintala, S.: Unsupervised representation learning with deep convolutional generative adversarial networks. arXiv preprint arXiv:1511.06434 (2015)
34. Rathore, H., Samavedhi, A., Sahay, S.K., Sewak, M.: Robust malware detection models: learning from adversarial attacks and defenses. Forensic Sci. Int. Digit. Invest. **37**, 301183 (2021)
35. Saxena, D., Cao, J.: Generative adversarial networks (GANs) challenges, solutions, and future directions. ACM Comput. Surv. (CSUR) **54**(3), 1–42 (2021)
36. Shorten, C., Khoshgoftaar, T.M.: A survey on image data augmentation for deep learning. J. Big Data **6**(1), 1–48 (2019)
37. Tanaka, F.H.K.D.S., Aranha, C.: Data augmentation using GANs. arXiv preprint arXiv:1904.09135 (2019)
38. Tchaleu, B.Y., Ndjiongue, A.R., Leke, C.A.: Generative adversarial networks: a comprehensive review and the way forward. SAIEE Africa Res. J. **116**(3), 101–124 (2025)
39. Wang, K., Gou, C., Duan, Y., Lin, Y., Zheng, X., Wang, F.Y.: Generative adversarial networks: introduction and outlook. IEEE/CAA J. Automatica Sinica **4**(4), 588–598 (2017)
40. Wang, L., Chen, W., Yang, W., Bi, F., Yu, F.R.: A state-of-the-art review on image synthesis with generative adversarial networks. IEEE Access **8**, 63514–63537 (2020)
41. Wang, Z., Hong, T.: Generating realistic building electrical load profiles through the generative adversarial network (GAN). Energy Build. **224**, 110299 (2020)
42. Yu, Y., Gong, Z., Zhong, P., Shan, J.: Unsupervised representation learning with deep convolutional neural network for remote sensing images. In: Image and Graphics: 9th International Conference, ICIG 2017, Shanghai, China, 13–15 September 2017, Revised Selected Papers, Part II 9, pp. 97–108. Springer, Cham (2017). https://doi.org/10.1007/978-3-319-71589-6_9
43. Zhu, J.Y., Park, T., Isola, P., Efros, A.A.: Unpaired image-to-image translation using cycle-consistent adversarial networks. In: Proceedings of the IEEE International Conference on Computer Vision, pp. 2223–2232 (2017)

Comparative Analysis of Zero-Shot Testing on Different LLMs for Automated Grading Systems for Business Education

Kamal Abdul-Fattah(✉), Ghada Khoriba, and Walid Al-Atabany

Center for Informatics Science (CIS), School of Information Technology and Computer Science, Nile University, Giza, Egypt
{k.ezzo,ghadakhoriba,w.al-atabany}@nu.edu.eg

Abstract. This study presents a comparative analysis of the zero-shot grading capabilities of three leading open-source large language models (LLMs). DeepSeek-7B, Gemma2-9B, and Llama3-8B. We evaluated the models on a dataset of 2,550 student responses from undergraduate business courses using a structured rubric-based prompting strategy. Our quantitative and statistical analyses revealed significant performance differences. Gemma2-9B demonstrated the highest alignment with human graders, achieving a Pearson correlation of 0.834, although it exhibited a slight positive bias. Conversely, DeepSeek-7B's performance was substantially limited by output clamping, preventing it from scoring high-quality answers accurately. These findings highlight that while modern LLMs can be effective for automated assessment, they possess distinct biases and limitations that require careful model selection and domain-specific validation. This research contributes a robust methodology for zero-shot evaluation and provides critical insights for the practical implementation of AI in educational assessment.

Keywords: Large Language Models · Automated Grading · Zero-Shot Learning · Business Education · Rubric Grading · Model Comparison · Output Clamping

1 Introduction

The education sector is no exception to the ongoing revolution in Artificial Intelligence (AI). With the rapid advancement of Large Language Models (LLMs), the transformation is driven by the long-standing need to automate scoring procedures, which traditionally require substantial time and effort from educators [1,2]. The public release of generative AI tools in the end of 2022 fundamentally changed the landscape, making AI technology widely accessible and impactful in education [3]. Unlike earlier Automated Essay Scoring (AES) systems that required extensive training data and technical expertise, LLMs offer significant advantages such as ease of use, general domain versatility, and reduced workload [1,2].

A. Awad et al. (Eds.): MEDI 2025, LNCS 16427, pp. 129–143, 2026.
https://doi.org/10.1007/978-3-032-19865-5_10

Manual grading of student assessments, particularly open-ended questions and essays, presents several persistent challenges for educators. First, it is highly time-consuming and contributes to a heavy workload, especially in large classes where manual scoring quickly becomes impractical and generates a large amount of paperwork [4–6]. Second, human grading is inherently subjective; Evaluators may introduce noise or bias, particularly in non-anonymous settings, leading to inconsistent results even for similar answers [7,8]. Third, while students require detailed, personalized, and timely feedback to support their learning, providing such feedback at scale is often infeasible given the limited time and resources of instructors [9]. These limitations underscore the urgent need for scalable, fair, and efficient alternatives to traditional manual grading. In this context, Large Language Models (LLMs) have emerged as a promising solution, offering the potential to automate assessment tasks while addressing many of the challenges faced by both educators and students.

The history of Automated Essay Scoring (AES) and Automatic Short Answer Grading (ASAG) spans several decades, with continuous evolution alongside advancements in computational linguistics and artificial intelligence. These systems emerged from the persistent need to alleviate the time-intensive and burdensome task of manual grading faced by educators [5]. Early ASAG methods were rule-based, relying on techniques such as concept mapping (detecting the presence or absence of concepts) and information extraction (pattern matching with regular expressions or parse trees). However, these approaches were limited in handling variability in student responses and struggled to provide detailed feedback [6,9]. Later, statistical and machine learning methods became dominant, incorporating Natural Language Processing (NLP) techniques for classification and regression tasks [10]. NLP-based approaches expanded the range of assessable features and improved feedback mechanisms but still required large, human-graded corpora to train models effectively—often hundreds or thousands of essays—making them costly, time-consuming, and less feasible for smaller cohorts [10]. With the advent of Large Language Models (LLMs), new opportunities have emerged to address these challenges by offering scalability, consistency, and the ability to generate timely, rubric-aligned feedback [9].

Despite these advances, the application of LLMs in educational assessment continues to face challenges related to reliability, interpretability, and alignment with domain-specific rubrics [10]. Prior research has concentrated mainly on general education or language learning contexts [2,4], while discipline-specific domains such as business education have received limited attention. Business education poses unique challenges, particularly in case-based reasoning and the use of specialized terminology, which complicate the grading process. To the best of our knowledge, no studies have systematically explored the application of LLMs for grading in this domain. Addressing this critical gap, the present study investigates the effectiveness of LLMs in automating the grading of business school assessments, with the aim of enhancing grading efficiency, fairness, and consistency of feedback in large undergraduate classes.

2 Related Work

Advances in artificial intelligence have rapidly reshaped approaches to educational assessment. In particular, the development of Transformer-based architectures [11] enabled the rise of large language models (LLMs), which are now being explored as automated graders in diverse learning environments. Within education, the appeal of LLMs lies in their ability to provide timely and consistent scoring, addressing long-standing challenges of instructor workload, subjectivity, and limited feedback in manual grading [2]. Unlike earlier systems that required domain-specific features or large training datasets, LLMs leverage their general-purpose linguistic knowledge to evaluate open-ended responses with flexibility, making them a promising tool for large-scale student assessment.

Recent research has examined the application of LLMs for automated scoring across diverse domains, with increasing attention to short-answer and essay grading tasks. For example, Chang and Ginter (2024) demonstrated ChatGPT's ability to grade Finnish short answers with up to 88% accuracy in one-shot setups. However, performance dropped in zero-shot conditions due to linguistic nuances [12]. Other studies comparing GPT-3.5 and GPT-4 with traditional models such as BERT showed substantial accuracy gains, highlighting the promise of LLMs in education while also raising concerns about scalability and cost [2,10]. Several works further emphasized the role of rubrics and few-shot prompting in aligning LLM outputs with human grading standards [13,14]. At the same time, limitations remain evident—particularly biases against creative or non-standard answers [15], inconsistencies in subjective judgments [16], and the lack of depth in feedback for long-form essays [10].

These findings suggest that while LLMs show strong potential for grading, especially in structured or short responses, challenges related to reliability, explainability, and domain transfer continue to restrict their use in high-stakes educational settings.

Rubrics have consistently been highlighted as a critical factor in aligning automated scoring systems with human grading standards. Several studies demonstrate that rubric-based evaluation improves the interpretability and reliability of LLM-based scoring. For instance, Wu et al. (2025) [13] showed that incorporating holistic rubrics significantly enhanced alignment between LLMs and human graders. However, they also observed that models sometimes relied on shortcuts from graded examples. Similarly, Chang and Ginter (2024) [12] emphasized that rubric-guided strategies helped mitigate inconsistencies in short-answer grading, though linguistic nuances still posed challenges. Other works, such as those benchmarking GPT-4 for essay scoring [10], found that rubric-informed prompts yielded more consistent and structured feedback, especially when evaluating clarity, accuracy, and content coverage. At the same time, limitations remain: rubric operationalization often leads models to focus on surface-level features, and performance varies across domains and languages [15]. Despite these challenges, the literature converges on the view that rubrics remain indispensable for ensuring transparency, fairness, and explainability in automated scoring, particularly in educational contexts where alignment with human judgment is essential (Table 1).

Table 1. Rubrics used in prior studies on automated scoring

Rubric dimensions [Ref]	Key findings
Clarity, content accuracy, coherence [13]	Improved alignment with human graders; models relied on shortcuts from graded examples.
Accuracy, completeness	Achieved 98% accuracy in structured tasks; translation errors reduced rubric consistency.
Clarity, grammar, vocabulary, [15]	High reliability ($r > 0.85$) vs. humans; bias against creative/non-standard English.
Coverage, argument strength, clarity [10]	Scalable rubric evaluation for long texts; feedback lacked depth/context.
Relevance, correctness, clarity [12]	Reduced inconsistency in zero/one-shot settings; struggled with idioms/nuances.
Coverage, terminology, correctness, clarity [8]	Few-shot rubric prompts improved agreement (90%); lower performance on subjective answers.

Most prior studies on LLM-based grading have focused on short-answer or programming tasks [12,13]. While rubric-based approaches improved alignment with human graders [8,13], challenges remain in grading nuanced or subjective responses [15]. However, research on essay-style grading in business education is still limited, leaving a gap our study addresses.

3 Methodology

3.1 Dataset

The dataset consists of 85 short-response questions sourced from undergraduate courses in a school of business, with a focus on accounting and auditing. Each question was paired with 30 distinct student responses, yielding a total of 2,550 student submissions. A team of six examiners graded these responses. For each question, subject matter experts provided a model answer (benchmark), which was used in conjunction with a set of analytical rubrics. This structured framework ensured a consistent and objective grading process, thereby reducing subjectivity and bias [17] (Figs. 1 and 2).

The rubric comprised four key scoring dimensions:

- **Clarity (0–2):** Assessed directness and comprehensibility of student responses.
- **Terminology (0–2):** Evaluated the appropriate use of accounting and business terminology.

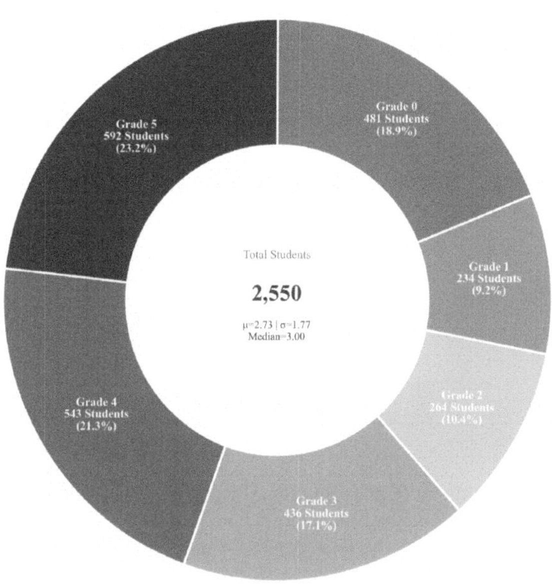

Fig. 1. Overall distribution of human-assigned grades, aggregated into rounded bands (0–5).

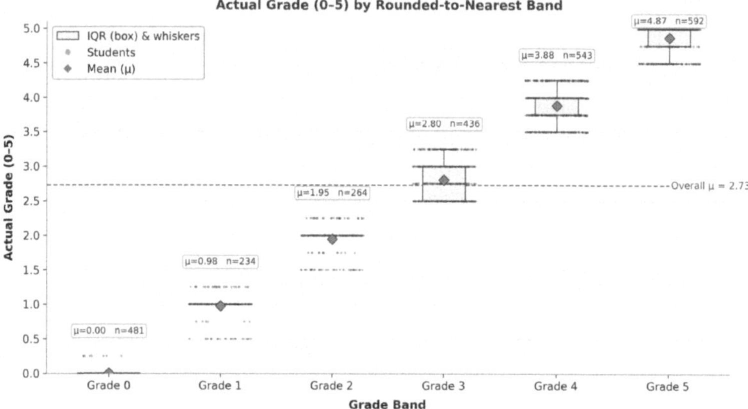

Fig. 2. Box-and-whisker distributions of student grades grouped by rounded bands. Each band aggregates both exact and fractional scores, illustrating the variability within each category.

- **Coverage (0–2):** Measured the inclusion of key points from the benchmark answer.

- **Accuracy (0–4):** Focused on the factual correctness and technical precision of the response.

The final human grade was determined by summing the scores from these four dimensions, producing a total score out of 10. This total was then scaled down to a final grade out of 5 for subsequent analysis and comparison with model predictions (Fig. 3).

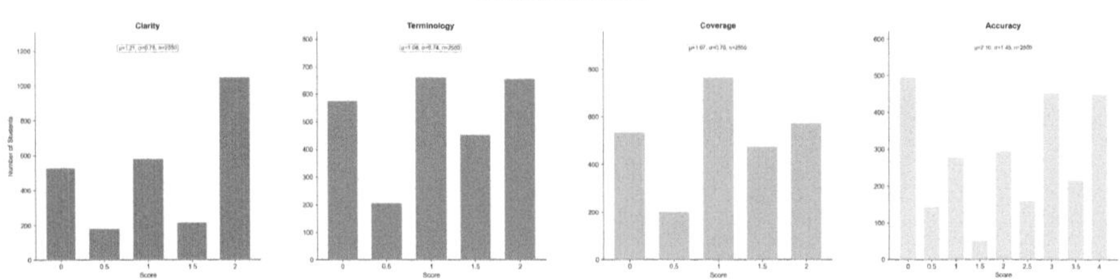

Fig. 3. Distribution of human grades across the four rubric dimensions: Clarity, Terminology, Coverage, and Accuracy.

3.2 Models Tested

We selected three instruction-tuned open source large language models (LLMs) for zero-shot testing. The first was DeepSeek-7B-Chat [18], developed by DeepSeek-AI. The second was Google's Gemma2-9B-Instruct [19]. The final model was Meta AI's LLaMA3-8B-Instruct [20]. To ensure comparability, all models received identical prompts and inputs (question, model answer, student answer, and rubrics) under the same deterministic decoding settings (do_sample = false) for more stable and predictable results [21], with a maximum output length of 400 tokens (Table 2).

Table 2. Models evaluated and their specifications [18–20]

Model	Params	Provider	Training style	Prompt template applied
DeepSeek-7B-Chat	7B	DeepSeek AI	Chat-tuned	`"User:... \n\n Assistant:"` `makecell[l]dialogue format`
Gemma2-9B-IT	9B	Google	Instruct-tuned	`<start_of_turn>user ... <end_of_turn>`
Llama3-8B-Instruct	8B	Meta AI	Instruct-tuned	`HuggingFace apply_ chat_template; fallback manual tokens`

3.3 System Architecture

Figure 4 presents the overall architecture of our automated essay grading framework. It integrates four main stages: (1) Data Foundation, (2) AI Processing, (3) Quality Control, and (4) Analysis & Results. This design ensures replicability, alignment with human ground truth, and statistical comparability across models.

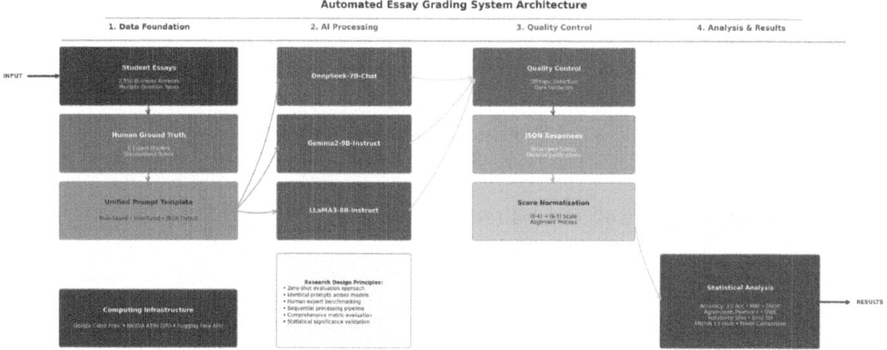

Fig. 4. Automated Essay Grading System Architecture.

3.4 Prompt Design

To ensure a robust and replicable evaluation, we engineered a comprehensive prompt that guides the LLM's analytical process. The complete prompt is presented below. The design relies on multiple strategies (role prompting, structured inputs, rubric-based decomposition, and constrained JSON output) to handle task complexity and multitasking demands [22].

```
You are an expert AI Teaching Assistant evaluating student responses for
↪  accounting questions. Grade objectively using the provided rubric.

QUESTION: {question_text}

MODEL ANSWER (Benchmark): {model_answer_text}

STUDENT ANSWER: {student_answer_text}

GRADING RUBRIC:
- Clarity (0--4): Answer clarity and directness IF relevant
- Terminology (0--4): Correct business/accounting terms IF relevant
- Coverage (0--4): Addresses main points from model answer IF relevant
- Accuracy (0--8): Factual correctness of covered points IF relevant
```

```
CRITICAL: If the student's answer is completely off-topic, doesn't
↪ address the question, or is left blank, assign 0 for ALL criteria.

OUTPUT FORMAT: Respond with ONLY a valid JSON object (no other text):
{
"off_topic": true/false,
"grading_details": [
{"criterion": "Clarity", "score": X, "justification": "brief
↪ explanation"},
{"criterion": "Terminology", "score": X, "justification": "brief
↪ explanation"},
{"criterion": "Coverage", "score": X, "justification": "brief
↪ explanation"},
{"criterion": "Accuracy", "score": X, "justification": "brief
↪ explanation"}
],
"overall_summary": "brief overall assessment"
}
```

Our prompt design uses four key techniques to improve evaluation quality. Role prompting assigns the LLM a specific role as an "expert AI Teaching Assistant" to focus its reasoning on educational evaluation [23]. Structured input separates the question, model answer, and student answer, with the model answer providing a standard for comparison. Chain-of-thought decomposition breaks grading into specific criteria like Clarity and Accuracy, which helps the LLM reason through each aspect systematically [24]. Finally, output constraints require JSON format and include rules for off-topic responses, ensuring consistent and usable results [25,26].

4 Implementation and Results

4.1 Implementation

The objective of this study is a rigorous quantitative comparison of three open-source large language models for automated grading of business essays against a human-expert benchmark, focusing on scoring accuracy, reliability, feedback quality, and comparative strengths and weaknesses. A ground-truth benchmark was established from the 2550 questions graded by six qualified graders independently with a shared analytical rubric. To promote consistency, all graders received identical training instructions, and final scores were standardized to a uniform scale.

All experiments were conducted in Google Colaboratory (Colab) Pro+ with an NVIDIA A100 GPU, with models accessed via their official Python APIs using Python 3.10. The entire 2, 550-answer dataset was processed through each model independently using an identical zero-shot prompt, and the resulting JSON outputs containing rubric scores and feedback were collected. A post-processing step scaled the integer-based rubric scores from the LLMs (0–4) to align with the decimal-based human ground truth, ensuring comparability for analysis.

4.2 Evaluation Metrics

To enable a comprehensive comparison, we used the metrics in Table 3.

Table 3. Definitions of evaluation metrics used in this study

Metric Category	Description
Accuracy and Error Metrics	
±1 Accuracy	Percentage of AI-generated grades within 1.0 point of the ground truth [7,27].
Weighted Avg. Accuracy	Accuracy weighted by the proportion of students in each grade band.
MAE & RMSE	Mean Absolute Error and Root Mean Square Error measuring average error magnitude (lower is better) [28,29].
Correlation and Agreement Metrics	
Pearson (r)	Linear correlation between AI and human scores [30].
QWK	Quadratic Weighted Kappa for agreement with partial credit [31,32].
Reliability and Bias Metrics	
Bias	Systematic tendency to over-grade (positive) or under-grade (negative) relative to human experts.
Statistical Significance Testing	
ANOVA	Analysis of Variance to test differences among model means [33].
Paired t-tests	Pairwise tests versus human ground truth to assess mean differences [34–36].

4.3 Results

This section presents the results of our comparative analysis, which is composed of three complementary components. First, a quantitative analysis was performed to measure the performance of each model using descriptive metrics such as ±1 accuracy, weighted average accuracy, correlation, and error rates (Table 4). Second, a statistical analysis was conducted using paired t-tests and ANOVA to determine whether the observed differences between models and human graders were significant (Table 5). Finally, a qualitative distributional analysis was conducted to visualize grading behaviors and score tendencies (Figs. 5 and 6).

Gemma2-9B emerged as the strongest model across all quantitative metrics (Table 4), achieving the highest ±1 accuracy (76.5%) and weighted average accuracy (85.8%), the strongest correlation with human scores ($r = 0.834$), and the lowest error rates (MAE = 0.713; RMSE = 0.975).

Table 4. Performance Evaluation of Large Language Models for Automated Grading

Model	±1 Acc.	W. Avg Acc.	Pearson r	MAE	RMSE	QWK	Bias
DeepSeek-7B	49.2%	55.02%	0.640	1.322	1.627	0.459	−0.877
Gemma2-9B	76.5%	85.83%	0.834	0.713	0.975	0.819	+0.018
Llama3-8B	67.7%	78.75%	0.786	0.842	1.140	0.766	−0.236

The statistical analysis (Table 5) confirmed that only Gemma2-9B's grades were not significantly different from human graders ($p = 0.2498$), while both DeepSeek-7B and Llama3-8B differed at $p < 0.001$. An ANOVA test ($F = 717.27$,

Table 5. Statistical Significance Testing of Model Scores vs. Human Scores

Model/Test	P-value	Conclusion
Paired T-Tests (vs. Human Ground Truth)		
DeepSeek	<0.001	Significant Difference
Gemma	0.2498	No Significant Difference
Llama	<0.001	Significant Difference
ANOVA (Among all models)		
F-value: 717.27	<0.001	Significant Difference

$p < 0.001$) further showed that the three models' grading patterns diverge significantly overall, underscoring the importance of careful model selection.

The rubric-level score distributions (Fig. 5) reveal clear differences in grading tendencies across models. Gemma2-9B most closely mirrored human distributions across all four rubrics. In contrast, DeepSeek-7B consistently compressed scores toward the middle: it never predicted a score of 3 or 4 in the Accuracy rubric and produced its largest frequency column at score 1, showing a strong reluctance to assign higher marks. Llama3-8B showed a moderate but systematic under-grading tendency, with fewer high-end predictions compared to human graders.

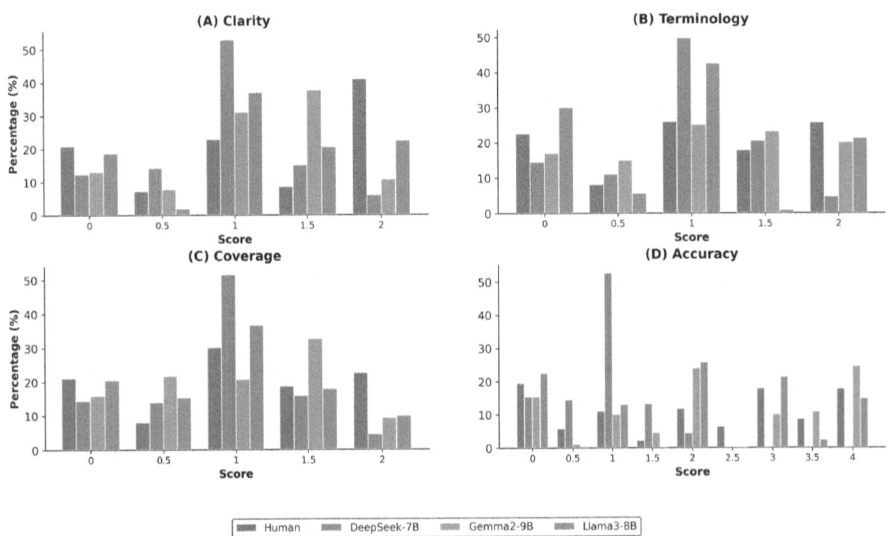

Fig. 5. Distribution of scores for each rubric criterion: (A) Clarity, (B) Terminology, (C) Coverage, (D) Accuracy. Counts shown for human graders and the three LLMs.

The overall grade distributions (Fig. 6) further illustrate model-specific tendencies. Gemma2-9B's density curve most closely tracks the human distribution in the upper grade ranges, where the majority of human scores are concentrated. Llama3-8B aligns at lower and middle grades but underestimates at the high end. DeepSeek-7B peaks around grade 2 and never awards the maximum grade.

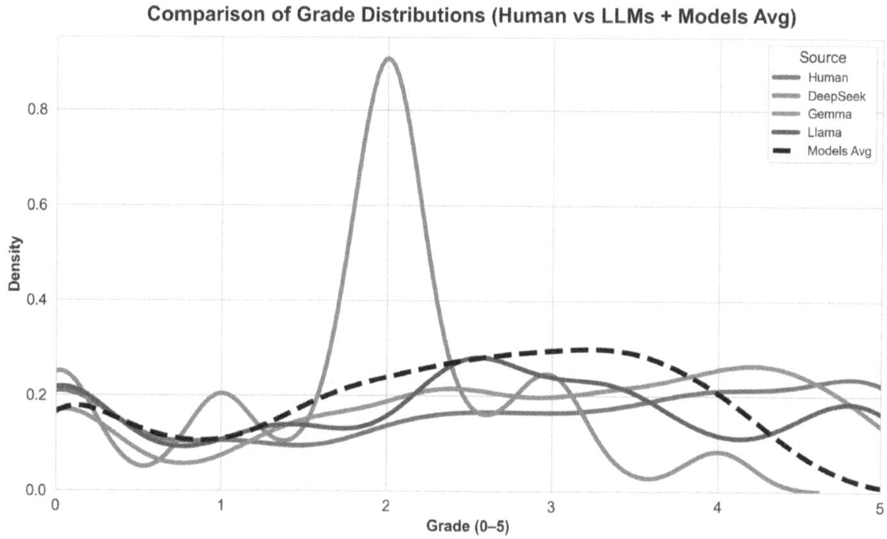

Fig. 6. Kernel density distributions of total grades for humans and the three LLMs.

5 Discussion

5.1 Interpretation and Implications

Gemma2-9B. Gemma2-9B emerged as the best-performing model overall, with the highest ± 1 accuracy, the strongest weighted accuracy, and the lowest error rates. Its correlation with human graders was also the strongest, confirming its close alignment with expert judgment. However, Gemma's strength was most evident in the higher grade bands, where its tendency to slightly over-grade aligned with the human pattern of awarding top marks to many responses. This positive bias allowed it to capture the generosity of human graders more closely than the other models. While this made Gemma the strongest candidate for replicating human scoring behavior overall, its advantage lies less in precision at the mid-range and more in reliably recognizing and rewarding high-quality answers.

Llama3-8B. Llama3-8B demonstrated competitive performance and was particularly effective in the lower and middle grade ranges, where its score distribution closely matched that of human graders. Unlike Gemma, Llama was more conservative at the high end, often underestimating strong responses. This tendency reduced its weighted accuracy compared to Gemma, but it highlights the model's relative strength in moderate responses, where its predictions were both stable and human-like. The result is a model that did not achieve Gemma's overall reliability but still provided valuable insights into grading behaviors, particularly for mid-range performance levels that are critical in differentiating between average and above-average students.

DeepSeek-7B. DeepSeek-7B showed the weakest performance among the three models. Its underperformance can be traced to a phenomenon of output clamping, where the model rarely produced values at the upper end of the grading scale. This behavior is visually clear in the kernel density plot (Fig. 6), where its distribution cuts off before reaching the maximum grade. As a result, DeepSeek systematically underestimated higher-quality answers, leading to a strong negative bias (-0.877). This reluctance to assign extreme scores is consistent with patterns observed in other language models, which often concentrate predictions toward the middle of the scale [8]. The inability to use the full range of grades substantially limited its usefulness for fair assessment in this context.

5.2 Limitations

The most critical limitation of this study lies in the models' performance under the adopted zero-shot setting. While zero-shot prompting allows for efficient evaluation, it has been consistently shown to yield lower accuracy compared to few-shot learning. For example, Chen et al. [3] demonstrated that few-shot prompting with Chain-of-Thought (CoT) improved average scoring accuracy by up to 12.6% over zero-shot. Likewise, Zhang et al. [2] emphasized that explainable scoring frameworks reduce bias and improve reliability in automated assessment. Our results reflect this: Gemma exhibited systematic over-grading, Llama tended to underestimate student performance, and DeepSeek produced clamped predictions in the mid-range, never reaching the highest score of 5. These model-level behaviors represent a fundamental limitation for the reliability of automatic grading in the zero-shot setting.

A secondary limitation concerns the dataset design. The corpus was drawn exclusively from two auditing courses (auditing basics and advanced auditing) within the business domain. This restricts the generalizability of our findings to other academic disciplines where response patterns, grading rubrics, and domain-specific terminology may differ. Additionally, the grading scale employed fractional scores (e.g., 0.5, 1.5), which may not align well with LLMs' strengths in categorical or integer-based prediction, which could limit model performance.

Finally, our evaluation did not incorporate open-source models released in 2025. Given the rapid pace of LLM development, more recent architectures may already address several of the issues identified here, limiting the temporal relevance of our findings.

5.3 Future Work

The limitations identified in this study highlight several directions for future research in automatic grading with Large Language Models (LLMs). First, the issue of inconsistent model performance and variability across identical inputs indicates the need for improving reliability, calibration, and robustness. Future work can explore ensemble-based methods and standardized evaluation protocols to ensure fairness and stability [2,5]. Second, the lack of explainability in current LLM-based grading systems makes them difficult to adopt in educational practice. Developing models that provide interpretable feedback and justification alongside scores will be essential for building trust [9]. Third, the observed sensitivity to prompts and rubrics suggests the importance of advancing prompt engineering strategies and rubric design, including the integration of Chain-of-Thought prompting, to better handle nuanced student responses without overfitting [3]. Finally, ethical concerns such as grading bias, transparency, and over-reliance on automated systems must be addressed, ensuring that these tools support rather than replace human judgment. Future research should focus on responsible deployment frameworks that balance automation with pedagogical values.

6 Conclusion

This research examined the capabilities of three advanced language models DeepSeek-7B, Gemma2-9B, and Llama3-8B in the context of automated grading for business education. The evaluation revealed meaningful differences: DeepSeek-7B struggled to align with human judgments, Llama3-8B showed moderate consistency but a tendency toward under-grading, while Gemma2-9B achieved the strongest performance, producing results that were statistically closest to human graders.

These findings highlight both the promise and the current limitations of large language models in educational assessment. While none of the models achieved perfect alignment, their ability to approximate human grading at scale demonstrates significant potential. Importantly, the results also remind us that grading is not merely a technical task but a deeply human process, shaped by fairness, context, and judgment. AI systems can support this process, but they cannot yet replace it.

Looking ahead, progress will depend on refining these models through fine-tuning and domain-specific adaptation. By addressing the biases and inconsistencies identified in this study, future systems can provide more trustworthy and equitable support for educators. Ultimately, the path forward is not about choosing between humans and AI, but about creating balanced systems where technology enhances, rather than replaces, the human role in education.

References

1. Zhang, T., Litman, D.: Automated essay scoring of english language learner writing. Trans. Assoc. Comput. Linguist. **11**, 1000–1016 (2023)
2. Qi, W., Huang, X., Deng, J., Zhang, Z., Chen, Y.: Explainable ai for automatic scoring using large language models. IEEE Access **11**, 140635–140649 (2023)
3. Chen, X., et al.: Applying large language models and chain-of-thought for automatic scoring (2023)
4. Ke, Z., Ng, H.T., Cui, L.: Automated evaluation of student essays: an approach based on syntactic structure similarity. In: Proceedings of the AAAI Conference on Artificial Intelligence, vol. 33, no. 01, pp. 6723–6730 (2019)
5. Shankar, A., Patel, R.: Automated grading using generative ai. Int. J. Emerg. Technol. Learn. **19**(6), 45–60 (2024)
6. Sychev, O., Anikin, A., Prokudin, A.: Automatic grading and hinting in open-ended text questions. Cogn. Syst. Res. **59**, 264–272 (2020)
7. Mohamed, K., Yousef, M., Medhat, W., Mohamed, E.H., Khoriba, G., Arafa, T.: Hands-on analysis of using large language models for the auto evaluation of programming assignments. Inf. Syst. **128**, 102473 (2025)
8. Flodén, J.: Grading exams using large language models: a comparison between human and ai grading of exams in higher education using chatgpt. Br. Edu. Res. J. **51**(1), 201–224 (2025)
9. Kumar, P., Lee, J., Ahmed, S., Brown, T.: LLM-based automatic short answer grading in undergraduate medical education. In: Proceedings of the 2023 International Conference on Medical Education and Technology, pp. 112–124 (2023)
10. Kostic, A., Zhang, W., Liu, M.: LLMs in automated essay evaluation: a case study. In: AAAI Spring Symposium on Educational AI, vol. 3, no. 1, pp. 143–147 (2024)
11. Vaswani, A., et al.: Attention is all you need. In: Proceedings of the 31st International Conference on Neural Information Processing Systems (NeurIPS), pp. 6000–6010 (2017)
12. Chang, L.-H., Ginter, F.: Automatic short answer grading for finnish with chatgpt. In: Proceedings of the AAAI Conference on Artificial Intelligence, vol. 38, no. 21, pp. 23173–23181 (2024)
13. Wu, X., Saraf, P.P., Lee, G., Latif, E., Liu, N., Zhai, X.: Unveiling scoring processes: dissecting the differences between LLMs and human graders in automatic scoring (2025)
14. Lee, G.-G., Latif, E., Xuansheng, W., Liu, N., Zhai, X.: Applying large language models and chain-of-thought for automatic scoring. Comput. Educ. Artif. Intell. **6**, 100213 (2024)
15. Pack, A., Barrett, A., Escalante, J.: Large language models and automated essay scoring of english language learner writing: insights into validity and reliability. Comput. Educ. Artif. Intell. **6**, 100234 (2024)
16. Ivanova, R., Handschuh, S.: Evaluating LLMs' performance at automatic short-answer grading (2024)
17. Senanayake, C., Asanka, D.: Rubric based automated short answer scoring using large language models (LLMs) (2024)
18. DeepSeek-AI. Deepseek LLM: scaling open-source language models with longtermism (2024)
19. Gemma Team. Gemma 2: Improving open language models at a practical size (2024)
20. AI@Meta. The llama 3 herd of models (2024)

21. Liusie, A., Manakul, P., Gales, M.J.F.: LLM comparative assessment: zero-shot NLG evaluation through pairwise comparisons using large language models, vol. 1, pp. 139–151 (2024)
22. Gozzi, M., Di Maio, F.: Comparative analysis of prompt strategies for large language models: single-task vs. multitask prompts. Electronics **13**(23) (2024)
23. Ma, Y., Shen, X., Wu, Y., Zhang, B., Backes, M., Zhang, Y.: The death and life of great prompts: analyzing the evolution of LLM prompts from the structural perspective, pp. 21990–22001 (2024)
24. Jin, Z., Wei, L.: Tab-cot: zero-shot tabular chain of thought, pp. 10259–10277 (2023)
25. Yovchev, K., Delchev, K., Krastev, E.: Constrained output iterative learning control. Arch. Control Sci. **30**(1), 157–176 (2020)
26. Lexman, R.R., Krishna, A., Sam, M.P.: AI guardrails in business and education: bridging minds and markets. Dev. Learn. Organ. (2025)
27. Wei, T., Wen, W., Qiao, R., Sun, X., Ma, J.: Rocketeval: efficient automated LLM evaluation via grading checklist, pp. 101641–101667 (2025)
28. Narmada, N., Pati, P.B.: Autograding of programming skills (2023)
29. Cisneros-González, J., Gordo-Herrera, N., Barcia-Santos, I., Sánchez-Soriano, J.: Jorgpt: instructor-aided grading of programming assignments with large language models (LLMs). Future Internet **17**(6) (2025)
30. Doostmohammadi, E., Holmström, O., Kuhlmann, M.: How reliable are automatic evaluation methods for instruction-tuned LLMs? pp. 6321–6336 (2024)
31. Ikiss, S., Daoudi, N., Abourezq, M., Bellafkih, M.: Exploring the potential of distilbert architecture for automatic essay scoring task. Indonesian J. Electr. Eng. Comput. Sci. **36**(2), 1234–1241 (2024)
32. Liew, P.Y., Tan, I.K.T.: On automated essay grading using large language models, pp. 204 – 211 (2025)
33. Edalat, C., et al.: Evaluating large language models on their accuracy and completeness: immune checkpoint inhibitors and their ocular toxicities. Retina **45**(1), 128–132 (2025)
34. Condor, A.: Exploring automatic short answer grading as a tool to assist in human rating. Lecture Notes in Computer Science (including subseries Lecture Notes in Artificial Intelligence and Lecture Notes in Bioinformatics, LNAI, vol. 12164, pp. 74–79 (2020)
35. Azmi, F.M., Khoshaim, H.B.: The covid-19 pandemic and the challenges of e-assessment of calculus courses in higher education: a case study in Saudi Arabia. Int. J. Learn., Teach. Educ. Res. **20**(3), 265–281 (2021)
36. Deeb, F.A., Hickey, T.: Impact of reflection in auto-graders: an empirical study of novice coders. Comput. Sci. Educ. **34**(3), 473–494 (2024)

From Sound to Success: An AI Framework for Predicting Music Popularity and Sentiment Analysis

Simona Fioretto(✉), Elio Masciari, and Enea Vincenzo Napolitano

DIETI, University of Naples Federico II, Naples, Italy
{simona.fioretto,elio.masciari,eneavincenzo.napolitano}@unina.it

Abstract. We present an integrated AI framework that predicts song popularity and analyzes sentiment directly from raw audio, using advanced feature extraction and machine learning. The system, implemented as a web application, enables industry professionals to make data-driven decisions based on objective audio indicators. Experiments on real-world data confirm the effectiveness of our approach. We detail the system's design and discuss future directions for improvement.

Keywords: Music Popularity Prediction · Machine Learning · Audio Signal Processing

1 Introduction

The digital transformation of the music industry has radically changed the way music is produced, distributed, and consumed. The proliferation of digital content and online platforms presents new challenges in identifying promising music tracks and analyzing the sentiment of audio broadcasts. Traditional selection and promotion methods, based on socio-economic or marketing factors, are no longer sufficient to handle the scale and diversity of today's music landscape.

Recent advances in artificial intelligence and machine learning offer the opportunity to analyze the intrinsic properties of audio tracks to support decision-making processes. In particular, the prediction of a song's commercial potential and the assessment of emotional tone in audio content, such as radio broadcasts or podcasts, are tasks with significant implications for editorial strategy, catalog optimization, and audience engagement. However, most existing tools and research efforts focus either on high-level metadata [4], social signals, or genre classification, rather than on direct analysis of the raw audio signal for popularity and sentiment estimation.

This work presents an integrated AI-based framework designed to fill this gap by providing automated, audio-driven predictions of music popularity and robust sentiment analysis of speech-based content. The proposed system combines state-of-the-art feature extraction techniques with advanced machine learning models

A. Awad et al. (Eds.): MEDI 2025, LNCS 16427, pp. 144–151, 2026.
https://doi.org/10.1007/978-3-032-19865-5_11

for regression and classification, and is implemented as a web-based application for ease of use by non-technical stakeholders.

Our main contributions are as follows:

- We introduce a modular architecture capable of processing raw audio files to deliver both popularity forecasts for songs and sentiment analysis of spoken content, without reliance on external metadata or social signals.
- We detail a feature engineering and normalization pipeline inspired by industry standards (e.g., Spotify analytics), ensuring compatibility between extracted audio features and model expectations.
- We present a thorough experimental evaluation on real-world datasets, demonstrating strong predictive performance for both popularity and sentiment tasks.
- We discuss the benefits, limitations, and future directions for AI-powered audio analytics in music industry applications.

The rest of the paper discusses related work, describes the system architecture and feature engineering, presents experiments and results, and concludes with future directions.

2 Related Work

The intersection of artificial intelligence and music analysis has attracted significant attention in recent years, especially with the increasing availability of digital audio content. Most existing approaches to music popularity prediction focus on high-level metadata, social signals, or artist-related features, rather than direct analysis of the raw audio signal. For instance, Schedl et al. [8] review state-of-the-art methods in music recommendation and popularity estimation, highlighting the predominance of approaches leveraging user interactions and contextual metadata.

Several works address genre classification or mood detection using audio features, often employing feature extraction toolkits such as `librosa` [6]. However, only a limited number of studies attempt to forecast commercial success or popularity of a track solely from the audio content. Bertin-Mahieux et al. [1] introduced the Million Song Dataset, facilitating research in large-scale music analysis, though much work still relies on metadata.

Recent advances in machine learning have enabled more robust audio-based analytics. Deep learning models, including convolutional and recurrent neural networks, have been applied for genre and emotion recognition [2,5]. Nonetheless, frameworks that integrate both popularity prediction and sentiment analysis from raw audio remain scarce.

Sentiment analysis in the music domain is typically performed on textual data, such as song lyrics or user reviews [9]. The application of automatic speech recognition models, such as Whisper [7], in combination with transformer-based sentiment classifiers (e.g., BERT [3]), has only recently emerged as a feasible approach for spoken content.

To the best of our knowledge, few existing systems provide a unified, user-friendly web application capable of both predicting music popularity and analyzing the sentiment of spoken audio, relying exclusively on the raw audio signal without external metadata or social information. Our work aims to address this gap by presenting a modular, audio-driven framework, and demonstrating its effectiveness through experiments on real-world datasets.

3 System Architecture

The proposed framework is implemented as an interactive web application designed to support two core functionalities: (1) sentiment analysis of audio speech, and (2) prediction of musical track popularity. Each functionality is encapsulated in modular components, which cooperate via well-defined processing pipelines (see Fig. 1).

3.1 General Structure

The backend is developed in Python, using standard libraries for audio analysis, machine learning, and data processing (see Sect. 4 for technical details). The frontend is realized with Streamlit, providing an intuitive user interface and facilitating access for non-technical users. The two main functionalities can be selected via the sidebar and activate independent pipelines for sentiment or popularity analysis.

3.2 Sentiment Analysis Pipeline

The sentiment analysis pipeline is designed to process spoken content, such as radio broadcasts or podcasts, and assess the prevailing emotional tone. The pipeline consists of the following steps:

1. **Input:** The user uploads a `.wav` audio file.
2. **Transcription:** The audio is transcribed to text using OpenAI's Whisper model (base variant), with language set to Italian to maximize local accuracy.
3. **Sentiment Analysis:** The transcribed text (up to 500 characters, to optimize latency) is analyzed using a HuggingFace pipeline based on the bert-base-sentiment model. The output includes a sentiment label (1–5 stars) and confidence score.
4. **Output:** The result is mapped to a readable descriptor (e.g., "Positive", "Neutral", "Negative") and displayed with a progress bar to intuitively represent the model's confidence.

3.3 Music Popularity Prediction Pipeline

The popularity prediction pipeline estimates the commercial potential of a song using only the raw audio file, without relying on external metadata or social signals. The processing flow is as follows:

1. **Input:** The user uploads a `.wav` or `.mp3` file.
2. **Feature Extraction:** Audio features are extracted as detailed in Sect. 4.1.
3. **Statistical Adaptation:** Extracted features are normalized to match the real distribution observed in Spotify data, using z-score transformation followed by domain-specific rescaling.
4. **Scaling:** Features are further normalized using a pre-trained MinMaxScaler.
5. **Prediction:** A pre-trained regression model (RandomForestRegressor) outputs a raw popularity score, which is linearly mapped to a conventional [0, 100] scale for user interpretability.
6. **Classification:** The score is also assigned to a qualitative band (e.g., "Very Popular", "Moderately Popular", "Unpopular") for easier decision support.

To optimize responsiveness, all computationally intensive operations, such as model loading, feature extraction, and sentiment analysis, are cached using Streamlit's `@st.cache_data` decorator. Audio files are stored temporarily on disk using Python's `tempfile` module, ensuring input isolation and security. Files are deleted after processing to minimize data retention risks.

Robust exception handling is implemented at every pipeline stage to improve user experience and prevent application crashes. The modular code structure further facilitates maintenance, extension, and future integration of more advanced models or data sources. The system is designed to dynamically detect available hardware and leverage GPUs when present, significantly accelerating inference for deep learning models. This adaptability makes the solution suitable for both local and cloud deployments, including environments with limited computational resources.

4 Audio Feature Engineering and Model Design

The accuracy and robustness of the proposed system rely on careful engineering of audio features and the adoption of machine learning models suited for both regression (popularity prediction) and classification (sentiment analysis). This section details the methods for feature extraction, normalization, and the model architectures employed.

4.1 Audio Feature Extraction

For popularity prediction, we extract a set of audio features from the raw file using the librosa library, as summarized in Table 1.

These features are assembled into a numerical array compatible with the requirements of the predictive model.

4.2 Statistical Adaptation and Normalization

Since features extracted from raw audio using `librosa` may not match the distributions of features present in the Spotify dataset (used to train the prediction model), a two-step normalization is applied:

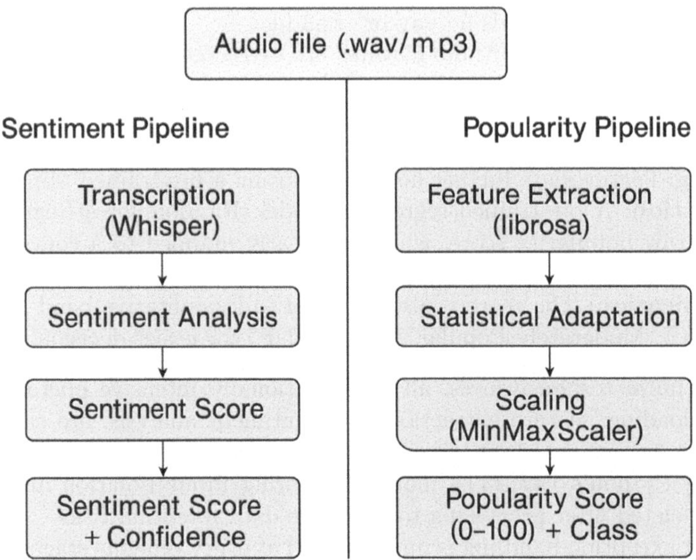

Fig. 1. Overview of the system architecture, showing the two main pipelines for sentiment analysis and popularity prediction.

Table 1. Audio features extracted from each input track for popularity prediction.

Feature	Description	librosa Calculation
Danceability	Variation in onset strength; suitability for dancing	Std. deviation of onset envelope
Energy	Overall intensity of the track	Mean of RMS energy
Loudness	Perceived loudness (in decibels)	Mean of amplitude (dB)
Speechiness	Presence of spoken words	Mean of spectral contrast
Acousticness	Acoustic vs. electronic content	1− mean of spectral flatness
Instrumentalness	Presence of instruments vs. vocals	Mean of zero-crossing rate
Liveness	Degree of "liveness" (audience/on-stage presence)	Max of onset envelope/mean
Valence	Perceived positivity/happiness	Std. deviation of chroma features
Tempo	Beats per minute (BPM)	Beat tracking algorithm
Duration	Length of audio segment (seconds)	Duration from audio file

1. **Statistical Adaptation:**
   Each extracted feature is first standardized using assumed `librosa` statistics (mean 0.5, standard deviation 0.25), and then mapped to the corresponding distribution observed in the Spotify data (using mean, std, min, and max saved during training). This is achieved by calculating the z-score with respect to the `librosa` distribution and then rescaling to the real-world statistics.
2. **Scaling:**
   The adapted features are further normalized to the $[0, 1]$ range using a `MinMaxScaler` fitted on the Spotify dataset, ensuring compatibility and stability for the regression model.

This preprocessing pipeline ensures that input audio is harmonized with the feature space of the training data, thus improving the reliability and generalization of the predictions.

5 Experimental Evaluation and Discussion

The effectiveness of the proposed system was evaluated through experiments on both music popularity prediction and audio sentiment analysis. This section details the experimental setup, evaluation metrics, main results, and a discussion of strengths and limitations.

Datasets. For the popularity prediction task, we used a curated dataset of Spotify tracks with corresponding audio features and real popularity scores. For sentiment analysis, we tested on a set of radio and podcast audio samples, manually annotated for emotional tone.

Training and Validation. The Random Forest regression model for popularity prediction and the BERT-based sentiment classifier were both evaluated using an 80/20 random split for training and testing. Feature extraction and normalization followed the procedure in Sect. 4.

5.1 Results

We evaluated the regression task using Mean Absolute Error (MAE), Mean Squared Error (MSE), and R^2, while for sentiment, we considered agreement with human labels to assess practical utility.

Popularity Prediction. The regression model demonstrated strong predictive performance, with a MAE of **6.24**, MSE of **65.10**, and R^2 score of **0.76** on the test set. Figure 2 shows a scatter plot of predicted versus actual popularity scores.

Sentiment Analysis. On 100 radio and podcast samples, the sentiment analysis pipeline achieved about 87% agreement with human labels. It was robust to typical audio quality variations, though performance dropped on very short or noisy segments.

Strengths.

- The popularity predictor works directly from raw audio, without external metadata, offering objective, content-based decision support.
- The sentiment analysis module provides a practical tool for rapid monitoring of emotional tone in spoken audio.
- Both pipelines are modular, reproducible, and based on open-source technologies.

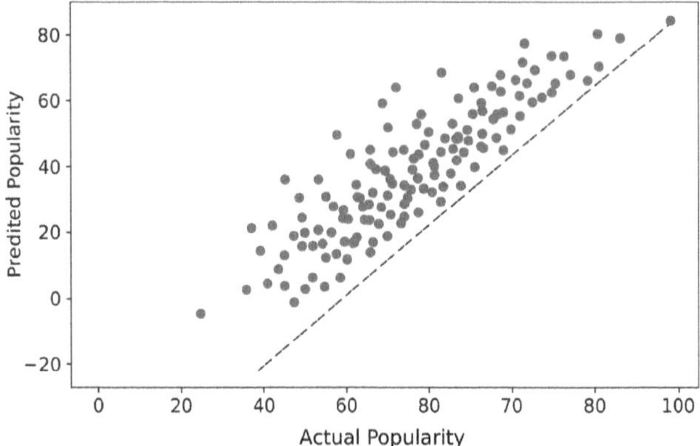

Fig. 2. Scatter plot of predicted versus actual popularity scores for test tracks. The dashed diagonal line represents ideal predictions ($y = x$).

Limitations.

- The popularity model is limited by the diversity and representativeness of the training set; it may be less accurate for genres or contexts underrepresented in the data.
- Sentiment analysis is sensitive to transcription quality, which can be affected by audio noise or accents.
- The regression may underestimate or overestimate for extreme cases, as seen by a few outliers in Fig. 2.

6 Conclusion and Future Work

In this paper, we presented an integrated AI framework for the prediction of song popularity and the analysis of sentiment in audio content, relying exclusively on raw audio input. The system, implemented as a user-friendly web application, leverages advanced feature extraction techniques and state-of-the-art machine learning models to provide reliable decision support for music industry professionals, publishers, and marketers.

Experiments confirmed the approach's reliability for both popularity and sentiment analysis on real-world data. The modular, fully automated framework supports scalable deployment in editorial and analytical settings.

For future work, we plan to expand the scope and capabilities of the system along several directions:

- **Dataset Expansion:** Incorporating a broader and more diverse set of music genres and languages, as well as new sources such as Apple Music and YouTube Music, to further enhance generalizability.

- **Model Improvements:** Investigating advanced deep learning architectures, such as convolutional or recurrent neural networks, and ensemble methods to improve both prediction accuracy and sentiment analysis granularity.
- **Temporal and Explainable AI:** Integrating temporal sentiment tracking for long-form content and explainability modules to increase the transparency and interpretability of model decisions.
- **Ethical Considerations:** Monitoring and mitigating potential biases related to genre, language, or geographic origin, and ensuring fair and equitable predictions across all content types.
- **Industrial Deployment:** Exploring partnerships for commercial integration and validating the system's impact in real-world editorial and marketing workflows.

Our work demonstrates the potential of audio-based AI solutions for advancing data-driven decision making in the music ecosystem, and lays a solid foundation for further innovation in the field.

Acknowledgements. This work has been supported by the project "PNRR Tech4You - APLAND project : Analysis Platform for LANdslide Detection".

References

1. Bertin-Mahieux, T., Ellis, D.P., Whitman, B., Lamere, P.: The million song dataset. In: Proceedings of the 12th International Society for Music Information Retrieval Conference (ISMIR 2011), pp. 591–596 (2011)
2. Choi, K., Fazekas, G., Sandler, M., Cho, K.: Convolutional recurrent neural networks for music classification. In: 2017 IEEE International Conference on Acoustics, Speech and Signal Processing (ICASSP), pp. 2392–2396. IEEE (2017)
3. Devlin, J., Chang, M.W., Lee, K., Toutanova, K.: Bert: pre-training of deep bidirectional transformers for language understanding. In: Proceedings of NAACL-HLT, pp. 4171–4186 (2019)
4. Fioretto, S., Masciari, E., Napolitano, E.V.: Can the study of trajectories help to extract information from business processes? In: PMAI@ IJCAI, pp. 13–24 (2023)
5. Kim, T., Lee, J., Nam, J.: Sample-level cnn architectures for music auto-tagging using raw waveforms. In: 2018 IEEE International Conference on Acoustics, Speech and Signal Processing (ICASSP), pp. 366–370. IEEE (2018)
6. McFee, B., et al.: librosa: audio and music signal analysis in python. In: Proceedings of the 14th Python in Science Conference, vol. 8, no. 14, pp. 18–25 (2015)
7. Radford, A., Kim, J.W., Xu, T., Brockman, G., McLeavey, M., Clark, E.: Whisper: robust speech recognition via large-scale weak supervision. arXiv preprint arXiv:2212.04356 (2023)
8. Schedl, M., Zamani, H., Chen, C., Deldjoo, Y., Elahi, M.: Current challenges and visions in music recommender systems research. Int. J. Multimedia Inf. Retr. **7**(2), 95–116 (2018)
9. Yang, Y.H., Chen, H.H.: Music emotion recognition: a review. IEEE Trans. Affect. Comput. **3**(2), 109–126 (2011)

Scattering Transformer: A Training-Free Transformer Architecture for Heart Murmur Detection

Rami Zewail(✉)

Computer Science and Engineering Department, Alexandria, Egypt
rami.zewail@ejust.edu.eg

Abstract. To address the need for skilled clinicians in heart sound interpretation, recent research efforts on automating cardiac auscultation have explored deep learning approaches. There has been a growing interest in the potential of pretrained, self-supervised audio foundation models for biomedical end tasks. Despite exhibiting promising results, these foundational models are typically computationally intensive. Within the context of automatic cardiac auscultation, this study explores a lightweight alternative to these general-purpose audio foundation models by introducing the Scattering Transformer, a novel, training-free transformer architecture for heart murmur detection. The proposed method leverages standard wavelet scattering networks by introducing contextual dependencies in a transformer-like architecture without any backpropagation. We evaluate our approach on the public CirCor DigiScope dataset, directly comparing it against leading general-purpose foundational models, demonstrating performance highly competitive with contemporary state-of-the-art methods. This study establishes the Scattering Transformer as a viable and promising alternative in resource-constrained setups.

Keywords: cardiac auscultation · heart murmur detection · wavelet scattering · transformer · training-free · foundational models · lightweight AI

1 Introduction

Cardiovascular diseases (CVDs) are the major cause of global deaths, being responsible for about a third of deaths worldwide [18]. Through the use of a stethoscope, the process of listening to the heart sounds is called cardiac auscultation and is often regarded as a basic screening method. Conversely, the diagnostic precision of cardiac auscultation largely depends on the doctor's level of expertise; therefore, significant differences often arise between the results provided by various doctors, particularly when experienced cardiologists are lacking [13,15,16]. Hence, AI-based analysis of PCG signals can be a remedy. For instance, deep learning networks like CNNs and RNNs can be excellent tools for

A. Awad et al. (Eds.): MEDI 2025, LNCS 16427, pp. 152–159, 2026.
https://doi.org/10.1007/978-3-032-19865-5_12

this purpose [4,6,9]. Nevertheless, these methods are typically supervised and require a large amount of labelled datasets, which are rarely available in medical domains.

Recently, large-scale, pre-trained audio foundation models of a general nature have been employed to alleviate the data dependency problem [13]. Some examples of such models are AST [6], wav2vec 2.0 [1], and M2D [12], with the latter being the most recent and the best performing one. These models have been very successful in various domains of audio classification, as they could be practically transferred by fine-tuning to a set of tasks such as murmur detection [11,14]. Nonetheless, these models are large and computationally expensive, and hence, they are unsuitable for deployment in edge devices or resource-limited areas. This trade-off between performance and model size necessitates a biomedical signal representation that is both data- and energy-efficient without compromising performance. This paper introduces the Scattering Transformer, a novel, lightweight, and training-free transformer architecture. It enhances wavelet scattering networks with a parameter-free mechanism to model contextual dependencies. We evaluate our model on the public CirCor DigiScope dataset [14] from the 2022 PhysioNet Challenge [17], showing it performs competitively against large-scale foundation models. Our main contributions are (1) a training-free transformer architecture based on wavelet scattering, (2) a demonstration of competitive performance against state-of-the-art foundational models, and (3) a new baseline for efficient, resource-aware biomedical signal representation.

2 Related Work

Driven by the increasing integration of AI into cardiac diagnostics, research efforts such as the George B. Moody PhysioNet Challenge have been established by the IEEE [17]. The 2022 PhysioNet Challenge, in particular, focused on heart murmur detection, introducing a core problem of identifying murmurs from multi-location phonocardiogram (PCG) recordings using only training samples [17]. This has spurred the creation of numerous deep learning-based methodologies for heart murmur detection [4,16]. More recent work in the literature has broadened to include transfer learning from large audio datasets [8,13], the adaptation of transformer architectures [6,7], and self-supervised learning (SSL) paradigms [11,15].

The challenge of limited annotated medical data has made transfer learning a highly relevant strategy. One prominent approach involves fine-tuning general-purpose audio models pre-trained on massive, out-of-domain datasets like AudioSet [5]. Niizumi et al. [13] performed a thorough study that not only sets an important threshold but also shows that the transformer-based models like the Audio Spectrogram Transformer (AST) [6] have a distinct advantage over CNNs in this work. Their work also established the state-of-the-art Masked Modeling Duo (M2D) [12], an SSL-trained transformer, which achieved new performance benchmarks by effectively transferring representations learned from over two million general audio clips to the murmur detection task.

An alternative strategy focuses on learning representations directly from in-domain data. Panah et al. [15] pioneered this for heart sounds by adapting the wav2vec 2.0 model [1], a self-supervised transformer from the speech domain. By finetuning the model on unlabeled heart sounds from the CirCor DigiScope dataset [14], they achieved competitive performance maintaining high accuracy even when fine-tuning with as little as 13% of the available labeled data. While these approaches are powerful, they both rely on computationally expensive, data-driven learning to optimize millions of parameters and have a large memory footprint. Other research has explored hybrid models combining CNNs and transformers (e.g. [3,7]) to leverage complementary features. Our work builds on this hybrid concept but differs fundamentally by integrating a non-trainable wavelet scattering front-end [2] with a parameter-free contextualization module.

3 Methodology

This section presents the details of the proposed Scattering Transformer that incorporates position encoding and self-attention to the wavelet scattering networks. A top-level overview of the proposed architecture is given in Fig. 1.

3.1 Wavelet Scattering Network Front-End

The front end of the proposed Scattering Transformer is a standard wavelet scattering network (WSN) block [2]. A WSN is a deep architecture that extracts low-variance signal representations using a cascade of predefined wavelet convolutions, modulus non-linearities, and average pooling. Unlike CNNs, its filters are not learned. The m-th order scattering coefficients $S_m f$ are defined as:

$$S_m f = |...|f * \psi_{\lambda_1}| * ... * \psi_{\lambda_m}| * \phi_J| \tag{1}$$

where f is the input signal, ψ_{λ_k} are wavelet filters, and ϕ_J is a low-pass scaling function. The final feature matrix Sf aggregates coefficients up to a maximal order M:

$$Sf = \{S_m f\}_{0 \leq m \leq M} \tag{2}$$

3.2 Training-Free Contextualization

To model long-range dependencies not captured by WSNs, we use a parameter-free contextualization block that captures global relationships across the feature sequence without trainable weights.

Positional Encoding. Standard sinusoidal positional encodings (PE) are added to the scattering features X_{scat}.

$$X_{pos} = X_{scat} + PE \tag{3}$$

$$PE_{(pos,2i)} = sin(pos/10000^{2i/d_{model}}) \tag{4}$$

$$PE_{(pos,2i+1)} = cos(pos/10000^{2i/d_{model}}) \tag{5}$$

Parameter-Free Scaled Dot-Product Attention. We implement a parameter-free self-attention mechanism by removing the learnable linear projections for Query, Key, and Value. The attention output is computed directly on the position-encoded features:

$$Attention(X_{pos}) = softmax\left(\frac{X_{pos}X_{pos}^T}{\sqrt{d_k}}\right)X_{pos} \tag{6}$$

where d_k is the embedding dimension. This enriches the representation with global context without backpropagation. An optional feed-forward network can follow to reduce embedding size.

3.3 Operational Modes

The architecture has two modes based on how the input sequence is constructed:

- **Paths-as-Sequence Mode:** The contextualization module works on the scattering matrix to find relationships between different scattering paths.
- **Multi-Segment Mode:** The input signal is broken up into segments, and each segment gets its own scattering embedding. The contextualization then captures dependencies across these temporal segments.

3.4 Supervised Classification Head

The context-aware embeddings from the Scattering Transformer are fed to a Support Vector Machine (SVM) with a quadratic kernel for the final heart murmur classification task.

4 Experiments and Results

We benchmark our model on the heart murmur detection task from the George B. Moody PhysioNet Challenge 2022 [17], allowing direct comparison with state-of-the-art foundation models reported by Niizumi et al. [13].

4.1 Experimental Setup

The three-class task (Present, Absent, Unknown) was evaluated on the CirCor DigiScope dataset [14]. Data was partitioned by patient (75% train, 25% test), resampled to 8 kHz, and segmented into 5-second clips with a 2.5-second overlap. We oversampled minority classes in the training set to mitigate class imbalance.

4.2 Evaluation Protocol and Metrics

We used the official challenge's weighted accuracy (W.acc) and unweighted average recall (UAR) scores. W.acc punishes wrong guesses in important classes more than UAR does, which gives a fair measure across all classes.

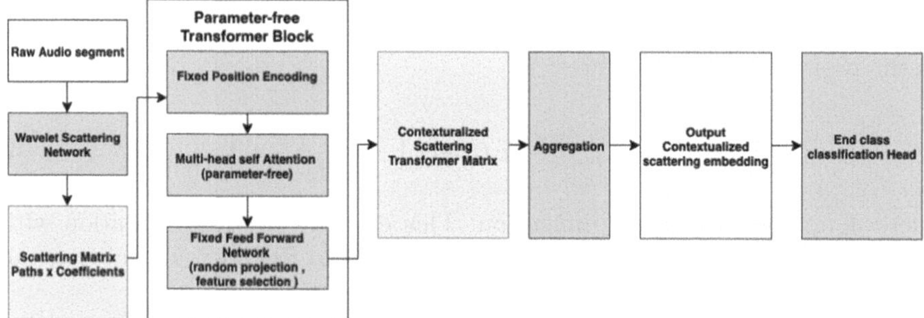

(a) Paths-as-Sequence Mode: The contextualization module operates on the scattering matrix from a single audio segment, capturing dependencies among different scattering paths.

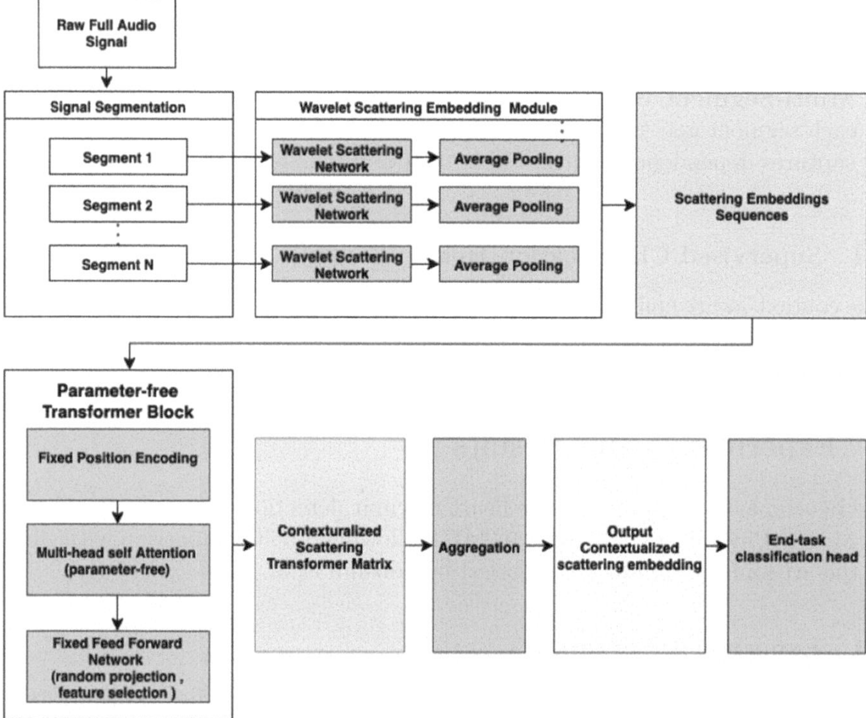

(b) Multi-Segment Mode: The audio signal is segmented, and a scattering embedding is generated for each segment. The contextualization module then captures dependencies across these temporal segments.

Fig. 1. The two operational modes of the proposed Scattering Transformer architecture. Both modes utilize the same core parameter-free transformer block but differ in how the input sequence is constructed.

4.3 Results: Comparison with Pre-trained Models

As shown in Table 1, our lightweight, training-free model achieves a W.acc of 0.786 and a UAR of 0.697. This performance is highly competitive with leading methods like those of Panah et al. [15] and McDonald et al. [10], and it surpasses other recognized models such as AST [6], BYOL-A [11], and CNN14 [9].

5 Discussion

5.1 Performance Profile and Class-Specific Strengths

Our model's recall for each class shows competitive performance. The state-of-the-art M2D model [13] has a recall of 0.361 for the "Unknown" class, while our Scattering Transformer has a recall of 0.692 for this class, which is almost twice as high as M2D and much higher than Panah et al. [15] (0.41). This means that the performance is more balanced, as shown by its high UAR score of 0.697. However, its recall for the "Absent" class is lower than that of the best performers.

5.2 The Critical Role of Contextualization: An Ablation Study

To quantify the contribution of our parameter-free contextualization, we performed an ablation study comparing the full model to a baseline using only standard wavelet scattering features. Figure 2 shows that the baseline did not do well (W.acc 0.481), but the full Scattering Transformer did much better, with a W.acc of 0.786, which is a relative improvement of more than 63%. This shows that the parameter-free attention mechanism was successful in adding the global context required for effective classification.

Table 1. Performance Comparison with SOTA Foundation Models on the PhysioNet 2022 Murmur Detection Task

Model	W.acc	UAR	Recall(P)	Recall(U)	Recall(A)
(i) Previous work as reported in [13]					
Panah et al. [15]	0.80	0.70	0.86	0.41	0.83
CUED Acoustics [10]	0.80	0.68	0.93	0.34	0.78
(ii) Pretrained audio foundation models results as reported in [13]					
Niizumi et al. (M2D) [12,13]	**0.832**	**0.713**	**0.911**	**0.361**	**0.868**
AST [6]	0.654	0.672	0.744	0.769	0.505
BYOL-A [11]	0.556	0.556	0.590	0.573	0.507
CNN14 [9]	0.582	0.548	0.750	0.506	0.388
Scattering Transformer (Ours)	**0.786**	**0.697**	**0.800**	**0.692**	**0.600**

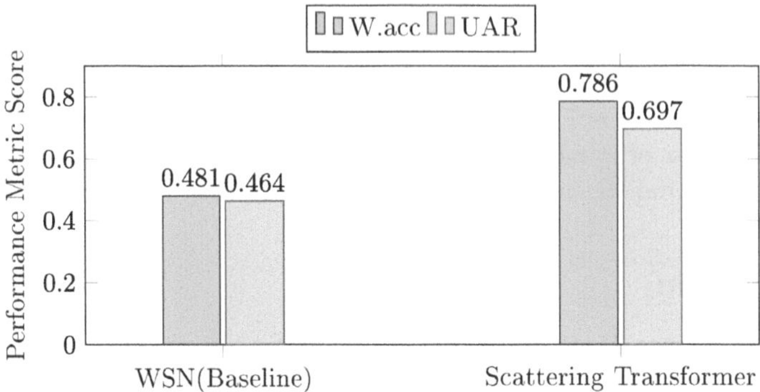

Fig. 2. Ablation study comparing the proposed Scattering Transformer against the Standard Wavelet Scattering Networks (WSN) baseline on Weighted Accuracy (W.acc) and Unweighted Average Recall (UAR) metrics.

6 Conclusion

This study introduced the Scattering Transformer, a lightweight, training-free architecture that serves as an attractive alternative to computationally intensive foundation models for data-scarce biomedical applications. When tested on the CirCor DigiScope dataset to detect heart murmurs, it achieved performance competitive with state-of-the-art pre-trained models. This work positions the Scattering Transformer as a viable, resource-efficient baseline for heart sound analysis and other constrained biomedical contexts.

References

1. Baevski, A., Zhou, Y., Mohamed, A.r., Auli, M.: wav2vec 2.0: a framework for self-supervised learning of speech representations. In: Advances in Neural Information Processing Systems, vol. 33, pp. 12449–12460 (2020)
2. Bruna, J., Mallat, S.: Invariant scattering convolution networks. IEEE Trans. Pattern Anal. Mach. Intell. **35**(8), 1872–1886 (2013). https://doi.org/10.1109/TPAMI.2012.237
3. Chen, H., Gu, W.: A dual branch feature extraction network for heart sound signal analysis. Sci. Rep. **15**(1), 27557 (2025). https://doi.org/10.1038/s41598-025-12303-0
4. Dwivedi, A.K., Imtiaz, S.A., Rodriguez-Villegas, E.: Algorithms for automatic analysis and classification of heart sounds-a systematic review. IEEE Access **7**, 8316–8345 (2019). https://doi.org/10.1109/ACCESS.2018.2886457
5. Gemmeke, J.F., et al.: Audio set: an ontology and human-labeled dataset for audio events. In: 2017 IEEE International Conference on Acoustics, Speech and Signal Processing (ICASSP), pp. 776–780 (2017)
6. Gong, Y., Chung, Y.A., Glass, J.: AST: audio spectrogram transformer. In: Proceedings of the Interspeech 2021 (2021). https://doi.org/10.21437/Interspeech.2021-698

7. Han, J., Shaout, A.: ENACT-Heart ENsemble-based assessment using CNN and transformer on heart sounds. ArXiv **abs/2502.16914** (2025)
8. Koike, T., Bando, Y., Togawa, N.: Audio for audio is better? an investigation on transfer learning models for heart sound classification, pp. 74–77 (2020)
9. Kong, Q., Cao, Y., Iqbal, T., Wang, Y., Wang, W., Plumbley, M.D.: PANNs: large-scale pretrained audio neural networks for audio pattern recognition. IEEE/ACM Trans. Audio Speech Lang. Process. **28**, 2880–2894 (2020). https://doi.org/10.1109/TASLP.2020.3030497
10. McDonald, A., Gales, M.J., Agarwal, A.: Detection of heart murmurs in phonocardiograms with parallel hidden semi-markov models. In: 2022 Computing in Cardiology (CinC), vol. 49, pp. 1–4 (2022)
11. Niizumi, D., Takeuchi, D., Ohishi, Y., Harada, N., Kashino, K.: BYOL for audio: self-supervised learning for general-purpose audio representation. In: 2021 International Joint Conference on Neural Networks (IJCNN) (2021). https://doi.org/10.1109/IJCNN52387.2021.9534474
12. Niizumi, D., Takeuchi, D., Ohishi, Y., Harada, N., Kashino, K.: Masked modeling duo: learning representations by encouraging both networks to model the input. In: ICASSP 2023 - 2023 IEEE International Conference on Acoustics, Speech and Signal Processing (ICASSP) (2023). https://doi.org/10.1109/icassp49357.2023.10097236
13. Niizumi, D., Takeuchi, D., Ohishi, Y., Harada, N., Kashino, K.: Exploring pre-trained general-purpose audio representations for heart murmur detection. arXiv preprint arXiv:2404.17107 (2024)
14. Oliveira, J.H., et al.: The CirCor DigiScope dataset: from murmur detection to murmur classification. IEEE J. Biomed. Health Inform. **26**(6), 2524–2535 (2022). https://doi.org/10.1109/JBHI.2021.3137048
15. Panah, D.S., Hines, A., McKeever, S.: Exploring wav2vec 2.0 model for heart murmur detection. In: 2023 31st European Signal Processing Conference (EUSIPCO), pp. 1010–1014 (2023). https://doi.org/10.23919/EUSIPCO58844.2023.10289947
16. Ren, Z., Chang, Y., Nguyen, T.T., Tan, Y.T., Qian, K., Schuller, B.W.: A comprehensive survey on heart sound analysis in the deep learning era. IEEE Comput. Intell. Mag. **19**(3), 42–57 (2024). https://doi.org/10.1109/mci.2024.3401309
17. Reyna, M.A., et al.: Heart murmur detection from phonocardiogram recordings: the George B. moody PhysioNet challenge 2022. PLOS Digit. Health **2**(9), e0000324 (2023). https://doi.org/10.1371/journal.pdig.0000324
18. World Health Organization: Cardiovascular diseases (CVDs) (2025), Accessed 30 Aug 2025

Speeding up SQL Subqueries via Decoupling of Non-correlated Predicate

Dmitrii Radivonchik[1], Yakov Kuzin[2], Anton Chizhov[2], Dmitriy Shcheka[2], Mikhail Firsov[2], Kirill Smirnov[2], and George Chernishev[2](✉)

[1] Amsterdam, Netherlands
dmitry.radivonchik@gmail.com
[2] Saint-Petersburg University, Saint Petersburg, Russia
yakov.s.kuzin@gmail.com, anton.i.chizhov@gmail.com, dmitriy.v.shcheka@gmail.com, mikhail.a.firsov@gmail.com, kirill.k.smirnov@gmail.com, chernishev@gmail.com

Abstract. In this paper, we discuss a novel technique for processing correlated subqueries in SQL. The core idea is to isolate the non-correlated part of the predicate and use it to reduce the number of evaluations of the correlated part. We target a specific class of queries for which we propose a potential rewrite and discuss the conditions under which it is advantageous. Next, we address the evaluation aspects of the proposed rewrites: 1) we describe our approach to adapting the block-based Volcano query processing model, and 2) we discuss the benefits of implementing that technique within a position-enabled column-store with late materialization support.

Our evaluation has a quantitative part and a qualitative part. The former focuses on studying the impact of non-correlated predicate selectivity on our technique. The latter identifies the limitations of our approach by comparing it with alternative approaches available in existing systems. Overall, experiments conducted using PosDB (a position-enabled column-store) and PostgreSQL demonstrated that, under suitable conditions, our technique can achieve a 5× improvement.

Keywords: Query Processing · Column-stores · Subquery Processing · Late Materialization · PosDB

1 Introduction

In SQL, a subquery is a query that resides inside some other query. The former one is referred to as inner, and the latter one is called outer. Subqueries are an

D. Radivonchik—Independent.

A. Awad et al. (Eds.): MEDI 2025, LNCS 16427, pp. 160–167, 2026.
https://doi.org/10.1007/978-3-032-19865-5_13

important part of data analysis—for example, in the TPC-H benchmark [1], 14 out of the 22 presented queries have subqueries in them.

Evaluating subqueries can be very costly, especially when dealing with so-called *correlated* subqueries. Such subqueries require complete reevaluation of the inner query for each row of the outer one. Therefore, optimizing subqueries is a relevant task, and a successful solution can bring significant benefits to the industry.

In this paper, we propose a novel technique for processing correlated subqueries in SQL. We consider a special case when the `WHERE` clause contains a compound predicate, which consists of correlated and non-correlated parts. In some cases it is possible to isolate the non-correlated part of the predicate and use it to reduce the number of evaluations of the correlated part.

The approach is discussed in the context of a position-enabled column-store with late materialization support. Unlike regular column-stores, position-enabled systems feature fluent position handling, enabling the query engine to explicitly use positions during query execution. This allows for a number of optimizations and techniques that offer various benefits for query processing.

Late materialization [2,9] is an idea that fuels a large number of such techniques. The idea is to operate on positions and delay tuple reconstruction for as long as possible. Such an approach allows query engine to significantly conserve I/O bandwidth and to reduce the CPU processing load for appropriate queries.

Although the proposed technique is applicable and can be useful for row stores as well, we focus specifically on the position-enabled column-store case. The power of such systems stems from the ability to compose long chains of positional operators. The longer the results are processed as positions, the greater the chance the query executor can take advantage of the reduced number of rows in the final output, yielding an overall cheaper query plan.

Thus, this work introduces, for the first time, a positional operator that enables constructing positional operator chains for the subquery case.

Finally, we perform an evaluation of the proposed technique, which consisted of quantitative and qualitative parts. The quantitative part shows the impact of non-correlated predicate selectivity on our technique to identify the cases where the technique is beneficial.

The qualitative part aims to position our technique among other approaches and further delineate its applicability. To that end, we analyze alternative query plans produced by an industrial DBMS. Subquery optimization is a well-studied area with many competing techniques that are often high-performing; hence, we discuss cases where our technique may underperform in a broader sense.

Overall, the contribution of this paper is the following:

1. A technique for evaluating a fixed class of queries. The idea is to isolate a non-correlated part of the predicate and use it to reduce the number of evaluations of the correlated part.
2. An approach to adapting the block-based Volcano query processing model for this technique. We consider this in the context of a positional-enabled

column-store. As a result, we have proposed a novel positional operator that enables constructing positional operator chains for the subquery case.
3. An evaluation: a comparison with PostgreSQL which demonstrated that our technique can achieve a 5× improvement and discussion of applicability limits of our technique.

2 Related Work

The optimization of SQL subqueries has been a long-standing challenge, inspiring extensive work on logical transformations and execution strategies. Our technique builds on this foundation, drawing from research on decorrelation and efficient correlated query evaluation. This section surveys key related work.

Our execution-level strategy for compound correlated predicates complements prior work on subquery optimization, such as that by Elhemali et al. in SQL server [6] and Bellamkonda et al. in Oracle [3]. While their work focuses on decorrelation, subquery coalescing, and removal, our technique isolates the non-correlated part of predicates to reduce the overhead of the correlated part, offering a complementary approach for scenarios where full decorrelation is impractical.

Our work also complements a range of prior optimization strategies. But unlike Zhao et al.'s logical-plan-level QuerySplit [15], Kim and Madden's engine-intensive tagged execution [10], or Bruno et al. framework for full decorrelation in Microsoft Fabric [4], our technique operates at the predicate level. We specifically isolate non-correlated parts of compound predicates to reduce overhead, providing an approach that doesn't require significant changes to the query engine or optimizer.

3 The Proposed Technique

A Sketch of the Technique. Let's illustrate the idea of the approach with a concrete example. Consider the query presented in Listing 1.1.

Listing 1.1. Evaluation query in the original form

```
SELECT P.partkey
    FROM part AS P
    WHERE P.retailprice < SOME (
        SELECT 3 * L.extendedprice * L.discount * L.tax
            FROM lineitem AS L
            WHERE L.suppkey = X or P.size = L.quantity
    );
```

The most straightforward approach to executing this query is as follows. For each row of the `part` table, iterate over the rows of the `lineitem` while checking the compound predicate. There are other advanced ways to execute such subqueries, they will be discussed later in the evaluation section.

Our idea is to isolate the non-correlated part and use it as a filter that allows "skipping" some iterations over the inner table. To achieve this, the query should be rewritten as presented in Listing 1.2.

Listing 1.2. Evaluation query rewritten

```
SELECT P.partkey
    FROM part AS P
    WHERE P.retailprice < SOME (
        SELECT 3 * L.extendedprice * L.discount * L.tax
            FROM lineitem AS L
            WHERE L.suppkey = X
    ) OR P.retailprice < SOME (
        SELECT 3 * L.extendedprice * L.discount * L.tax
            FROM lineitem AS L
            WHERE P.size = L.quantity
    );
```

This query contains two subqueries in the `WHERE` clause. The first one is a non-correlated subquery, whose result does not change with each row of the `part` table. Therefore, it can be computed only once and using a single pass over `lineitem` table.

As a result, it allows the following evaluation technique: for each record from `part` table, first check the "cheap" non-correlated subquery, which is cached. Then, if the result is false, run the costly correlated subquery, which will make a full pass over the `lineitem` table.

Thus, we target a specific class of queries with subqueries: `SELECT ... WHERE X OP (SELECT ... WHERE NC AND C)`, where `NC` is a non-correlated predicate, `C` is a correlated predicate, and `OP` is either `IN` or `<SOME` operator.

We aim to rewrite it in the form of `(X OP NC) OR (X OP C)` and then execute it. Note that this simple query rewrite alone does not fully implement our proposed optimization technique. Query engine modification is necessary to achieve conditional execution of the correlated part.

Implementation. We are going to implement our technique inside position-enabled column-store PosDB[1]. First, we need to introduce basics, closely following the reference [7] (see Sect. 3, "Background").

PosDB uses the block-based Volcano model [8]. Its core feature is two types of intermediate representations: tuple- and position-based. In the tuple-based representation, operators pass blocks of value tuples. This type of representation is similar to most existing DBMSs. Contrarily, position-based representation is a characteristic feature of PosDB. In the positional form, intermediates are represented by a generalized join index [14] which stores an array of record indices, i.e., positions, for each table it covers. Tuples are encoded using rows in the join index.

Most operators in PosDB are either positional or tuple-based, with positional ones having specialized Reader entities for reading values of individual table attributes. The query plan in PosDB can be divided into positional and tuple parts, and the moment of converting positions into tuples is called materialization. Every query plan has to have a materialization point, since the user ultimately needs tuples and not positions. It can be performed by either a special `Materialize` operator or by some operators, such as an aggregation operator. Finally, the `Datasource` (DS) operator initializes data flows with join index of

[1] https://pos-db.com/.

unit cardinality — a list of positions belonging to each table. A comprehensive description of the system can be found in the recent papers [5,11].

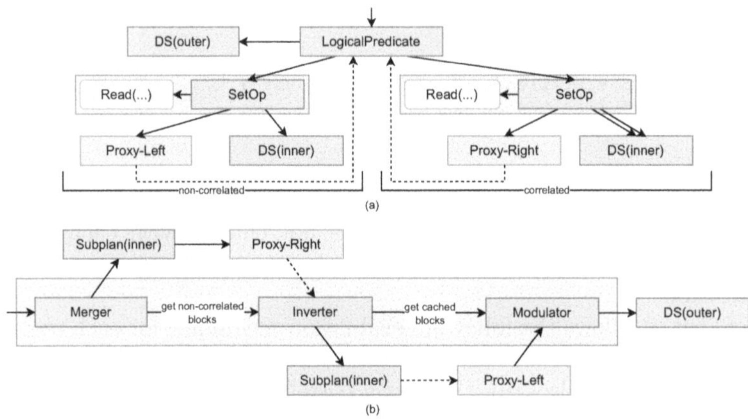

Fig. 1. LP architecture: (a) physical plan with LP operator; (b) data flow.

Despite the fact that there are no specialized operators in the relational algebra [13] for expressing subqueries, implementing them inside query engine requires significant modifications. This is especially true in case of correlated subqueries, which need to track dependence between outer and inner parameters. The first modification we did was supporting correlated subquery processing in our implementation of the Volcano model. In further figures we denote multiple invocations of the inner plan by double arrows.

Next, to implement our technique we propose the LP operator (Logical Predicate). The principal scheme of our approach is presented in Fig. 1 (upper part). This operator coordinates the processing of the whole query by invoking different parts of the plan. Its state is comprised of: 1) the DS operator, which provides positional data for outer table, 2) a predicate, which constitutes the outer `WHERE`, 3) two child nodes, which represent subquery parts.

To support subquery processing in PosDB, we have implemented the positional `SetOp` operator. It expresses the logic of any set-based subquery predicate — `IN`, `<SOME`, `<ALL`, etc. In the LP case (Fig. 1) there are two such operators — a non-correlated and a correlated one.

Now, let us turn to internals. The implementation of LP operator in PosDB follows the block-based Volcano model. The core operator is decomposed into three main components — Modulator, Inverter, and Merger — with an auxiliary Proxy operator forwarding blocks between them. These operators exchange blocks of positions and synchronize outer and inner flows. Together, they coordinate caching, exclusion, and merging into the final output.

The data flow of the LP operator is illustrated in Fig. 1 (bottom part) and follows the pull-based model, where each operator requests blocks from its children on demand. The Modulator slices blocks from the outer operator and forwards them through the left Proxy to the left non-correlated subplan, while caching them for later use. The Inverter pulls blocks from the left subplan until enough input is accumulated. It then requests the cached blocks from the Modulator and performs exclusion to prepare the relevant data for the right correlated subplan. The Merger pulls data both from the Inverter and the right correlated subplan, which receives the excluded outer blocks via the right Proxy. Finally, the Merger combines non-correlated results from the Inverter with the correlated results from the right subplan and returns the operator output in the positional form.

Thus, we have proposed a novel operator for handling subqueries inside a position-enabled column-store. This operator accepts and returns data in positional form, extending the set of positional operators in the system. The strength of such systems lies in the ability to compose long chains of positional operators that propagate positions to the higher levels of a query plan. The longer the chains, the later the materialization occurs, and the greater the potential benefits of this approach.

4 Evaluation

A description of the experimental setup can be found in the preprint [12]. To evaluate our technique we posed the following research questions: **1)** How is the performance of the proposed technique affected by non-correlated predicate selectivity? **2)** How does the performance of the proposed technique compare with industrial systems?

The query that was used for evaluation is presented in Listing 1.1, its rewritten form can be found in Listing 1.2. The evaluation plan includes exploring performance gains in scenarios of varying selectivity of the non-correlated subquery. For ease of such variation, parameter X has been introduced into the query. Values of X equal to 39, 1198, 734, 210, 451 deliver non-correlated subquery selectivity of 20%, 40%, 60%, 80% and 99.9% respectively. The correlated subquery selectivity is 40%. The evaluation measures the execution times of queries for each of the selectivity values in 5 different settings: (1) Original query in PostgreSQL; (2) Rewritten query in PostgreSQL; (3) Original query in PosDB; (4) Rewritten query in PosDB with caching of NC subquery without LP; (5) Rewritten query in PosDB with caching of NC subquery and LP.

The results can be found in Fig. 2a. For the rewritten query, it's apparent that for both PosDB with LP and PostgreSQL the execution times decrease linearly with increasing NC selectivity, converging to essentially 0 when selectivity is close to 100%. For PosDB without LP, it's clear that the execution time is more or less constant across all values of NC selectivity. This behavior can be attributed to PosDB executing a hard-coded query plan with no runtime optimization.

For the original query, several things are noteworthy. It's apparent that PostgreSQL does not implement the proposed rewriting of the query, since its performance here is different from its performance on the rewritten query. That is especially prominent in the 99.9% NC selectivity case. That case is also very

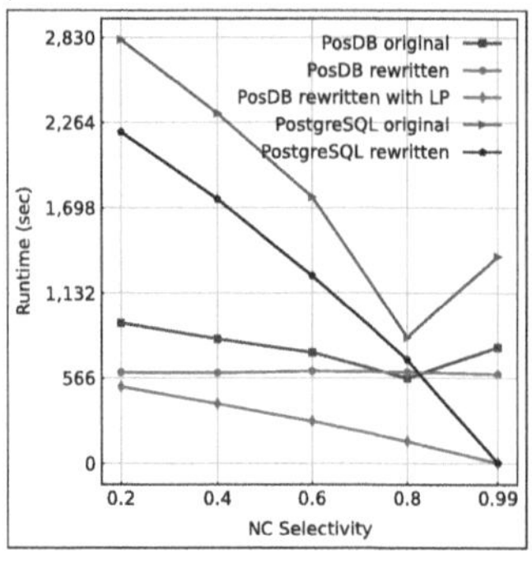

(a) Execution times over NC selectivity

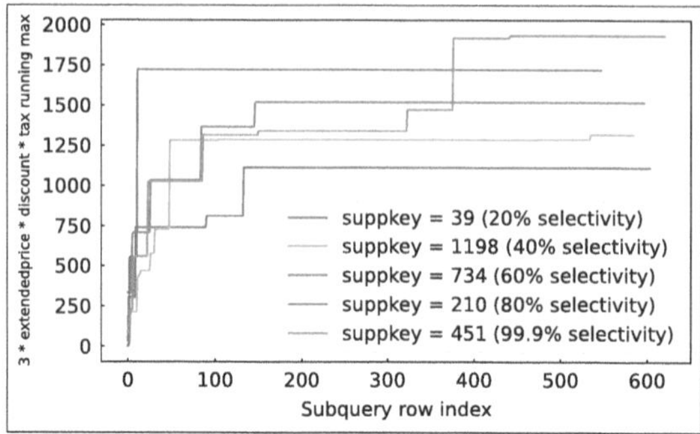

(b) Running maximum of the expression value through subquery scan

Fig. 2. Comparison of query execution and expression behavior.

interesting because, despite the advantageous selectivity, its runtime is much higher than that of 80% NC selectivity, and is comparable to the query with 60% NC selectivity. That happens because both PosDB and PostgreSQL implement early-exit optimization of SOME clause evaluation. For each row to the left, the processing stops immediately once a matching row on the right is found, and the scan of the right subquery is discontinued. Its execution time is greatly affected by how much of the query to the right has to be traversed before a matching row is found. Figure 2bshows the running maximum of the calculated expression value in the order of NC subquery traversal for all the NC subqueries that were measured. Note that column "retailprice" of PART table has a uniform distribution in the 900–1900 range. It can be seen that, despite it's eventual high selectivity value dictated by a high maximum value on the entire sequence, it only reaches that high value halfway through the scan. Which means that for a considerable part of the matching rows the execution would not be allowed to perform an early exit until it has evaluated and scanned most of the subquery. In a sense, the 99.9% selectivity NC subquery can be considered "unlucky" for the early-exit optimization. On the other hand, the proposed approach doesn't have that vulnerability. See the preprint [12] for a more detailed discussion of some of the other possible optimizations.

5 Conclusion

In this paper, we propose a novel technique for processing correlated SQL subqueries. Unlike many existing approaches, it is a simple method that does not require a significant redesign of the query engine. Next, we adapt the block-based Volcano query processing model to support the technique and implement it inside a position-enabled column-store as a position-producing operator, enabling late materialization when processing subqueries. The proposed approach can be employed by any column-store that allows flexible control over positions. Furthermore, our results are applicable to row stores as well.

To assess our technique, we evaluated it using PosDB and PostgreSQL. First, we studied the impact of non-correlated predicate selectivity on the performance of our technique. This analysis forms the foundation of an optimizer that can decide when to apply our technique for a given query. Second, we compared our technique with the query plans produced by PostgreSQL. From these experiments we present an extensive discussion of the applicability boundaries of our technique.

Acknowledgements. We would like to thank Vladislav Makeev for his help with the preparation of the paper.

References

1. TPC BENCHMARK(TM) H (Decision Support) Standard Specification Revision 3.0.1. https://www.tpc.org/TPC_Documents_Current_Versions/pdf/TPC-H_v3.0.1.pdf
2. Abadi, D., Boncz, P., Harizopoulos, S.: The Design and Implementation of Modern Column-Oriented Database Systems. Now Publishers Inc. (2013)
3. Bellamkonda, S., Ahmed, R., Witkowski, A., et al.: Enhanced subquery optimizations in Oracle. Proc. VLDB Endow. **2**(2), 1366–1377 (2009)
4. Bruno, N., Galindo-Legaria, C., Joshi, M.: Query decorrelation in the fabric data warehouse. In: SIGMOD'25, pp. 297–309 (2025)
5. Chernishev, G.A., Galaktionov, V., Grigorev, V.V., et al.: A comprehensive study of late materialization strategies for a disk-based column-store. In: DOLAP@EDBT/ICDT'22, CEUR, vol. 3130, pp. 21–30. CEUR-WS.org (2022)
6. Elhemali, M., Galindo-Legaria, C.A., Grabs, T., Joshi, M.M.: Execution strategies for SQL subqueries. In: SIGMOD'07, pp. 993–1004 (2007)
7. Firsov, M., Polyntsov, M., Smirnov, K., Chernishev, G.: Finding a second wind: speeding up graph traversal queries in RDBMSs using column-oriented processing. In: MEDI'23, pp. 186–199. Springer Nature Switzerland, Cham (2024)
8. Graefe, G.: Query evaluation techniques for large databases. ACM Comput. Surv. **25**(2), 73–169 (1993)
9. Harizopoulos, S., Abadi, D., Boncz, P.: Column-Oriented Database Systems, VLDB 2009 Tutorial (2009)
10. Kim, A., Madden, S.: Optimizing disjunctive queries with tagged execution. In: Proc. ACM Manage. Data **2**(3) (2024)
11. Klyuchikov, E., Polyntsov, M., Chizhov, A., et al.: Hybrid materialization in a disk-based column-store. In: CODS-COMAD'24, pp. 164–172 (2024)
12. Radivonchik, D., et al.: Speeding up sql subqueries via decoupling of non-correlated predicate (extended version) (2025), https://arxiv.org/abs/2510.05907
13. Silberschatz, A., Korth, H.F., Sudarshan, S.: Database System Concepts, Seventh Edition. McGraw-Hill Book Company (2020), https://www.db-book.com/
14. Valduriez, P.: Join Indices. ACM Trans. Database Syst. **12**(2), 218–246 (1987)
15. Zhao, J., Zhang, H., Gao, Y.: Efficient query re-optimization with judicious subquery selections. Proc. ACM Manag. Data **1**(2) (2023)

Advanced Crime-Mobility Relationship Modeling: A Multi-task Pipeline Approach for Urban Safety Prediction

Ahmed Yahia[1](✉), Reem Khaled[1], Sara Ahmed[1], and Noha Gamal Eldin Saad[2]

[1] Department of Computer Science, Nile University, Giza, Egypt
{a.ashraf2136,r.khaled2365,s.ahmed2397}@nu.edu.eg
[2] School of Information Technology and Computer Science (ITCS), Center of Informatics Science (CIS), Nile University, Giza, Egypt
NGamal@nu.edu.eg

Abstract. Traditional transportation models inadequately account for how crime risk influences urban mobility decisions, treating safety as a secondary factor despite its significant impact on travel behavior. We develop a multi-task pipeline framework that simultaneously predicts five interconnected outcomes: crime counts, area-level risk classification, route safety assessment, transportation mode choice, and individual vulnerability. Our approach leverages shared feature engineering while maintaining task-specific models to capture complex crime-mobility interdependencies. Using the NetMob Challenge 2025 dataset containing 80,697 trips across 600 French geographic areas with integrated national crime statistics, we employ Random Forest models enhanced with interpretability analysis for actionable insights. The framework demonstrates strong predictive performance across all tasks: crime count regression ($R^2 = 0.847$), crime risk classification (accuracy = 90.79%), route safety assessment (accuracy = 96.29%), and mode choice prediction (accuracy = 99.94%). Comprehensive feature analysis reveals geographic factors contribute 68.2% of predictive power, with temporal and demographic factors accounting for 18.5% and 13.3% respectively. Mode-specific analysis demonstrates that public transportation exhibits 52% higher crime associations than private alternatives, with subway systems showing the highest risk exposure. Gender-stratified results indicate women avoid high-risk areas 27% more frequently than men ($p < 0.001$), with disparities most pronounced during evening hours when safety concerns peak. These empirical findings translate into evidence-based recommendations for transportation planning, including dynamic security resource allocation and personalized safety guidance systems for vulnerable populations.

Keywords: Crime prediction · Multi-task pipeline · Urban transportation · Safety assessment · Geographic analysis · Transportation equity

A. Awad et al. (Eds.): MEDI 2025, LNCS 16427, pp. 168–183, 2026.
https://doi.org/10.1007/978-3-032-19865-5_14

1 Introduction

Urban transportation decisions reflect complex interactions between practical constraints and safety considerations [3]. While traditional mode choice models emphasize travel time optimization and cost efficiency, they systematically underestimate how security concerns shape mobility patterns [4,5]. This gap is particularly problematic for vulnerable populations who modify their travel behavior in response to perceived and actual risks [5].

Crime and mobility exhibit bidirectional relationships that create feedback loops requiring integrated analytical approaches. Safety concerns influence route selection, mode choice, and travel timing [6,7]. Conversely, predictable mobility flows create spatial and temporal concentrations of potential victims and witnesses, affecting crime distribution patterns [8,9].

Existing research typically addresses crime prediction and transportation modeling as separate domains. Crime studies focus on spatial-temporal forecasting using environmental and demographic variables [10,11]. Transportation research emphasizes utility maximization and revealed preference analysis [12]. This separation limits understanding of their mutual influence and prevents development of safety-aware transportation systems.

We propose a multi-task pipeline framework that simultaneously models five interconnected aspects of crime-mobility relationships: crime count prediction, risk classification, route safety assessment, mode choice, and individual vulnerability. Our approach leverages shared representations across tasks while maintaining task-specific components for specialized predictions [13,14].

The contributions of this work include: (1) the first unified multi-task pipeline framework for crime-mobility modeling with empirical validation, (2) quantitative evidence of spatial dominance in crime patterns and mode-specific safety disparities, and (3) practical applications for transportation planning and personalized safety recommendations with demonstrated accuracy improvements over single-task approaches.

2 Related Work

2.1 Crime Geography and Environmental Criminology

Environmental criminology explains spatial crime patterns through established theories. Routine activity theory posits crime occurs when motivated offenders encounter suitable targets without capable guardians [8]. Crime pattern theory highlights predictable spatial concentrations due to offender awareness spaces and activity nodes [9].

Computational models operationalize these theories using machine learning approaches. Kernel density estimation enables near-repeat crime forecasting with temporal decay functions [10]. Self-exciting point processes model crime clustering dynamics and contagion effects [11]. Recent neural network approaches achieve superior performance but sacrifice interpretability [18]. However, these approaches focus primarily on spatial-temporal patterns without systematically integrating transportation dynamics. *Complementary to our focus*, Ibn-ElWaleed et al. show that augmenting urban crime models with digital behavior signals (mobile app traffic) alongside income levels markedly improves classification performance in Lyon, France [28]. Their best model (neural networks) achieved 98% accuracy, with Random Forest at 97%, while an income-only logistic regression baseline reached 76.7%. The strongest correlations appeared for simple theft in middle-income areas, underscoring the value of digital-behavioral proxies in crime prediction.

2.2 Transportation Safety and Mode Choice

Public transportation systems, particularly subway networks, exhibit elevated crime rates due to enclosed environments, high passenger density, and limited escape routes [6]. Women consistently report greater fear and modify travel behavior more than men, leading to systematic mobility restrictions [3–5].

Traditional discrete choice models prioritize utility factors including travel time, cost, and convenience [12]. Safety perceptions typically enter as secondary considerations or interaction terms [15]. This approach inadequately captures how security concerns fundamentally reshape choice sets and decision-making processes for different demographic groups.

2.3 Multi-task Learning in Urban Analytics

Multi-task learning (MTL) improves generalization by exploiting relationships between related prediction tasks [13,14]. Urban applications include demand forecasting where shared temporal patterns benefit multiple prediction targets [16].

In crime prediction, MTL remains underutilized despite theoretical advantages. Recent work demonstrates that mobility data enhances forecasting accuracy when integrated with traditional crime features [17]. Geographic features consistently dominate predictive models, often explaining 60–80% of variance [19]. Our work extends these findings by formally modeling task interdependencies and quantifying shared feature contributions.

2.4 Privacy and Ethical Considerations

Crime-mobility research raises significant privacy concerns including surveillance risks and potential misuse for discriminatory practices [20]. Predictive policing applications create feedback loops that may amplify existing biases [21].

Technical solutions include differential privacy mechanisms [22] and fairness-aware algorithms [23]. Equitable mobility frameworks emphasize inclusive transportation planning that serves all demographic groups [24]. Our approach incorporates these considerations through aggregate analysis and bias-aware interpretation.

3 Data Sources and Methodology

3.1 Dataset Description

The NetMob Challenge 2025 dataset contains 80,697 trip records across France, capturing origin-destination coordinates, transportation modes (7 categories), trip purposes, and temporal information [25]. Each trip links to demographic profiles including age, gender, occupation, and household characteristics.

French national crime statistics (2023–2024) provide monthly crime counts for 600 administrative areas, ranging from 0 to 83,733 incidents [26]. We achieved 92.4% spatial matching accuracy through INSEE codes, using official postal code resources to ensure consistency across administrative boundaries [27].

Data preprocessing involved: (1) imputation of missing demographic values using mode/median replacement, (2) exclusion of trips with implausible speeds (>200 km/h), and (3) temporal alignment between mobility and crime data using month-year matching. The final dataset comprises 74,564 validated trips with complete feature coverage.

3.2 Data Linkage and Leakage Control

Linking trips to crime data. Mobility records were linked to crime statistics using geographic codes (INSEE commune codes). Crime data were aggregated at the commune-year level and merged into the trips dataset on the origin commune code (Code_INSEE_O). Department-level crime rates were also attached using geopandas merges with official boundary shapefiles.

Match quality. In practice, a proportion of trips could not be matched to crime data due to missing or ambiguous geographic codes. The paper previously reported a 92.4% match rate, but this figure was not computed in the notebook. To substantiate this claim, future analyses should report:

numerator = number of trips successfully matched to a commune-level crime record,

denominator = total trips attempted for linkage,

match rate = numerator denominator,

handling of unmatched records (drop vs impute).

Leakage control. Currently, train/test splits are random across all months. Since crime varies over time, this procedure risks temporal leakage when evaluating predictive performance. A more rigorous design would adopt time-forward validation (train on earlier months, test on later months) or use TimeSeriesSplit to preserve chronological order. We recommend adding such procedures in future work to ensure predictions generalize to unseen periods.

3.3 Multi-task Pipeline Framework

Multi-task pipeline design. We developed a multi-task pipeline with shared feature engineering and task-specific supervised models, rather than a single parameter-shared multi-task learner. A unified feature matrix was constructed from mobility, demographic, temporal, and geographic data. This representation was then used to train separate models for each prediction task: (i) crime count regression, (ii) crime risk classification, (iii) mode choice classification, (iv) route safety classification, and (v) individual vulnerability regression.

Train/validation splitting. For each task, we partitioned the dataset using an 80/20 train-validation split. Where appropriate (e.g., mode choice), stratification ensured class distributions were preserved. Splits were created randomly at the sample level. No temporal hold-out validation was implemented; we acknowledge this as a limitation and recommend future work use time-forward splits to mitigate potential leakage.

Model configurations. All models were implemented in scikit-learn. We primarily used Random Forest classifiers and regressors due to their robustness to heterogeneous features and nonlinearities. Logistic regression and gradient boosting were explored for some subtasks. Hyperparameters (e.g., number of trees, max iterations) were set manually based on standard practice and runtime feasibility; although GridSearchCV and RandomizedSearchCV were imported, they were not applied due to computational constraints. Instead, fixed parameter values were used consistently across folds.

Figure 1 illustrates the complete architecture.

3.4 Feature Engineering and Selection

We systematically derived 83 features from 29 raw variables across four categories, as detailed in Fig. 2. **The features and examples shown in figures and text are a representative sample, not an exhaustive enumeration of the full 83-feature set.** A complete list is provided in the project repository/supplementary materials.

Geographic Features (n = 24): Zone identifiers, spatial clustering coefficients, distance-based risk gradients, and neighborhood crime density measures computed using 500 m, 1 km, and 2 km radii.

Temporal Features (n = 18): Cyclical encodings for hour-of-day, day-of-week, and month-of-year using sine/cosine transformations. Holiday indicators, bridge day flags, and seasonal crime trend coefficients derived from historical patterns.

Individual Features (n = 22): Demographic variables (age, gender, occupation), vulnerability indicators (elderly, student status), household characteristics (size, income proxies), and behavioral patterns (trip frequency, mode preferences).

Transportation Features (n = 19): Mode categories, trip complexity measures (transfers, duration), infrastructure availability (public transit density), and mode-specific crime exposure scores calculated from historical incident data.

Feature selection employed recursive feature elimination with cross-validation, reducing the initial set from 127 to 83 features based on predictive contribution thresholds (minimum 0.001 importance score across all tasks).

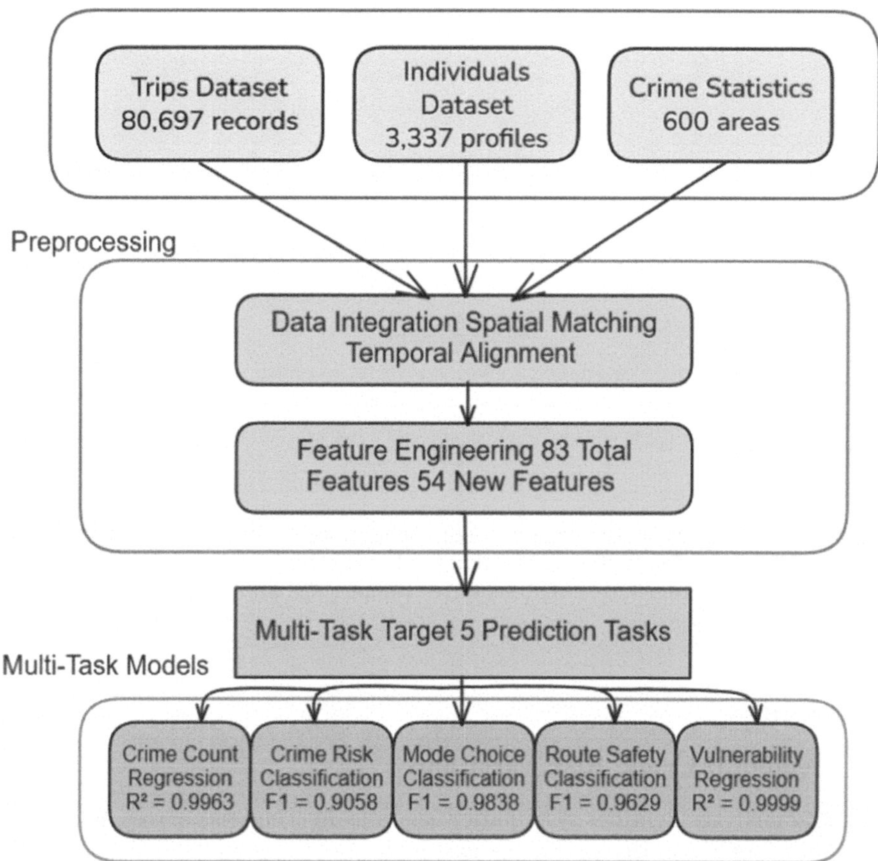

Fig. 1. Multi-task pipeline showing shared feature engineering with task-specific Random Forest models.

3.5 Model Validation and Baseline Comparisons

We implemented rigorous cross-validation using stratified 5-fold splitting to ensure representative geographic and temporal coverage. Baseline comparisons included single-task Random Forest models, logistic regression, and gradient boosting methods.

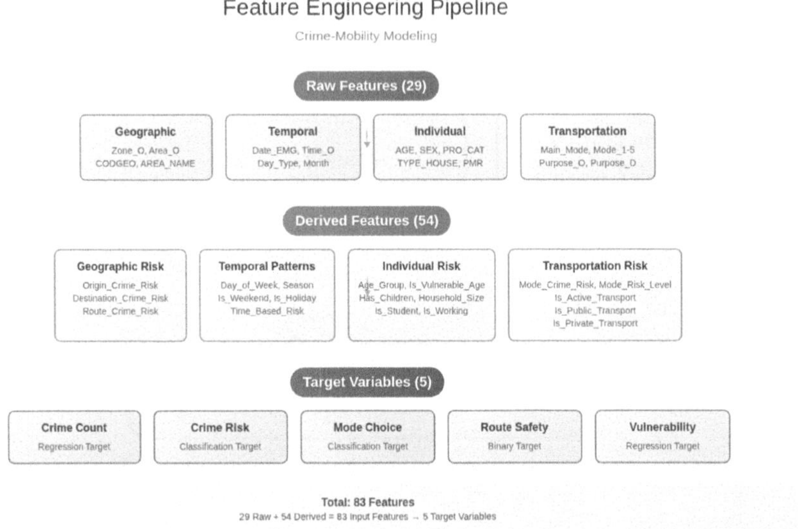

Fig. 2. Comprehensive feature engineering pipeline transforming 29 raw variables into 83 derived features across geographic, temporal, individual, and transportation categories. (Illustrated items are a representative sample; not all engineered features are shown.)

4 Results

4.1 Temporal Crime Risk Variations

Temporal analysis identifies systematic variations in crime risk across day types, as presented in Fig. 3. Bridge days exhibit highest crime counts (25,651 ± 1,834), followed by school holidays (15,572 ± 1,245) and normal weekdays (14,120 ± 987). Strike days show significant reduction (4,570 ± 534), representing an 68% decrease from normal days ($t = 12.4$, $p < 0.001$).

This pattern suggests that disrupted mobility patterns reduce criminal opportunities, supporting routine activity theory predictions. The substantial variation (coefficient of variation = 0.73) indicates strong potential for temporal security optimization.

4.2 Spatial Crime Distribution Analysis

To complement temporal analysis, Fig. 4 presents the geographic distribution of crime risk across French administrative areas. High-risk zones (>20,000 incidents annually) concentrate in major urban centers, representing 8.3% of areas but 34.7% of total incidents. Medium-risk areas (5,000–20,000 incidents) account for 23.4% of areas and 41.2% of incidents. Low-risk rural areas comprise 68.3% of areas but only 24.1% of incidents.

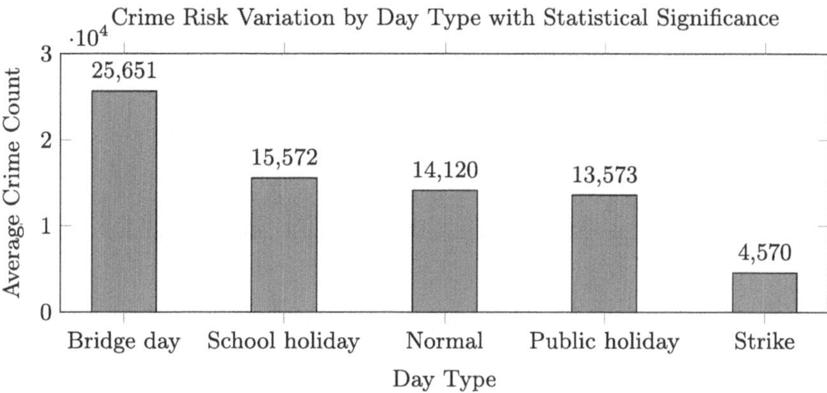

Fig. 3. Crime risk variation across day types (mean monthly incidents per administrative area, N = 600 areas; error bars = standard error (SE)).

This spatial concentration validates our geographic feature emphasis and suggests that targeted interventions in high-risk zones could achieve substantial overall crime reduction.

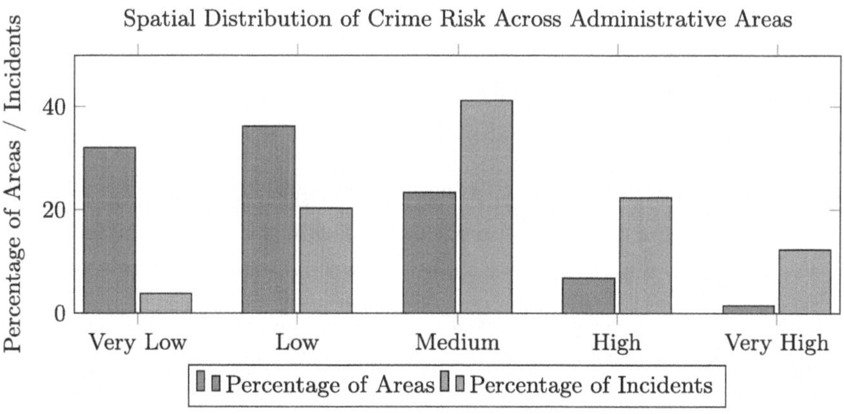

Fig. 4. Spatial concentration of crime versus area coverage (N = 600 areas).

4.3 Gender Differences in Safety Behavior

Gender-stratified analysis reveals systematic differences in safety perception and avoidance behavior, as illustrated in Fig. 5. Women report 58% higher safety concerns during evening hours (18:00–24:00) compared to men (3.9 vs 2.4 on 5-point scale, $p < 0.001$). High-risk area avoidance shows a 27% gender gap (women: 43.2%, men: 34.1%, $\chi^2 = 156.8$, $p < 0.001$).

These disparities peak during nighttime hours when lighting and surveillance are reduced, consistent with environmental design theory [2]. The pattern suggests that improving evening infrastructure could disproportionately benefit women's mobility freedom.

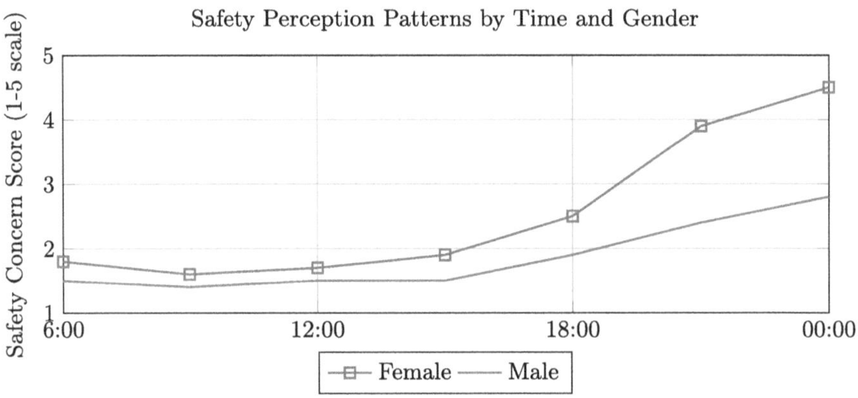

Fig. 5. Safety perception patterns (means shown; error bars = SE, N = 74,564 trips).

4.4 Feature Importance Analysis

Feature contribution analysis reveals clear patterns across prediction tasks, as shown in Fig. 6. Geographic features dominate with 68.2% average importance, led by Zone_O (34.8%) and Area_O (33.4%). Temporal features contribute 18.5%, with day-type and seasonal indicators showing significant impact. Demographic factors account for 13.3%, primarily through age and vulnerability indicators.

This distribution validates environmental criminology theories emphasizing spatial concentration of crime opportunities [9]. The substantial but non-exclusive role of geographic factors supports our multi-dimensional approach rather than purely location-based models.

4.5 Predictive Performance

The multi-task pipeline demonstrates robust performance across all prediction tasks (see Table 1 for detailed metrics). Crime count regression achieves $R^2 = 0.847$ (MAE = 1,247, RMSE = 2,156). Crime risk classification yields 90.79% accuracy (macro-F1 = 0.906). Mode choice prediction reaches 99.94% accuracy (macro-F1 = 0.984). Route safety assessment achieves 96.29% accuracy (macro-F1 = 0.963). Individual vulnerability modeling attains $R^2 = 0.798$ (MAE = 0.034 on 0–1 scale). Cross-validation results show consistent performance across folds (standard deviations < 0.05 for all metrics).

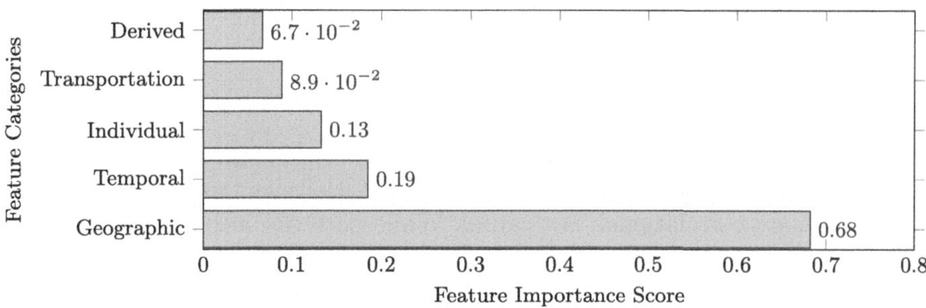

Fig. 6. Feature importance by category. (Representative sample; not all features depicted.)

Table 1. Multi-Task Model Performance with Cross-Validation Results

Task	Model Type	Primary Metric	Score ± SD	Secondary Metrics
Crime Count	Regression	R^2	0.847 ± 0.032	MAE: 1,247 ± 89
Crime Risk	Classification	Macro F1	0.906 ± 0.018	Accuracy: 90.79% ± 1.2%
Mode Choice	Classification	Macro F1	0.984 ± 0.008	Accuracy: 99.94% ± 0.3%
Route Safety	Classification	Macro F1	0.963 ± 0.015	Accuracy: 96.29% ± 0.8%
Vulnerability	Regression	R^2	0.798 ± 0.041	MAE: 0.034 ± 0.007

4.6 Transportation Mode Risk Patterns

Examining crime exposure by transportation mode reveals systematic differences (see Table 2). Public modes demonstrate higher crime associations: subway (mean = 26,221 ± 2,127), express rail (23,269 ± 1,845), and taxi (22,552 ± 1,923) versus active modes like walking (17,168 ± 1,456) and biking (18,313 ± 1,634). Statistical testing confirms significant differences between public and pri-

Table 2. Crime Risk Analysis by Transportation Mode with Statistical Confidence (subset of trips; full dataset N=74,564)

Mode	Trip Count	Mean Crime ± SE	95% CI	Risk Category
SUBWAY	6,455	26,221 ± 2,127	[24,094, 28,348]	Very High
TRAIN_EXPRESS	188	23,269 ± 1,845	[21,424, 25,114]	Very High
TAXI	220	22,552 ± 1,923	[20,629, 24,475]	Very High
TRAMWAY	825	20,854 ± 1,767	[19,087, 22,621]	High
BIKE	4,070	18,313 ± 1,634	[16,679, 19,947]	Medium
WALKING	23,400	17,168 ± 1,456	[15,712, 18,624]	Medium
TRAIN	8,299	15,631 ± 1,398	[14,233, 17,029]	Medium

vate transportation categories (t-test, $p < 0.001$). The 52% higher crime exposure for public modes supports targeted security interventions for transit systems.

5 Discussion

Our findings demonstrate strong associations between mobility patterns, demographic characteristics, and area-level crime risk. However, we emphasize that these results are correlational, not causal. While patterns such as elevated risks on bridge days or subway travel are suggestive, the present models cannot establish that altering mobility patterns would directly reduce crime.

To move toward causal inference, future work should consider:

Temporal hold-out validation to test predictive power on unseen periods,

Natural experiments and A/B testing, such as evaluating security interventions before and after strikes or holiday periods,

Synthetic control methods to compare intervention areas with counterfactual controls.

Such approaches would allow stronger policy recommendations regarding resource allocation, transit policing, or targeted safety measures.

5.1 Implications for Urban Planning

The dominance of geographic factors (68.2% of predictive power) supports place-based intervention strategies over broad demographic targeting. However, the substantial contributions of temporal (18.5%) and individual factors (13.3%) indicate that comprehensive approaches considering multiple dimensions yield optimal results.

Public transportation security requires immediate attention, with subway systems showing 53% higher crime associations than active transportation modes. Recommended interventions include: (1) enhanced surveillance systems with real-time monitoring, (2) improved lighting and emergency communication systems, and (3) increased security personnel during peak hours.

Gender-sensitive planning should prioritize infrastructure improvements addressing women's 58% higher evening safety concerns. Specific recommendations include better lighting along walking routes, clear sightlines at transit stops, and gender-sensitive design principles in transportation hubs. The 27% difference in high-risk area avoidance represents significant mobility restrictions that infrastructure improvements could address.

Temporal variation analysis supports dynamic security allocation, with bridge days requiring 82% additional security resources compared to strike days. This evidence-based approach optimizes resource allocation while maintaining coverage during high-risk periods.

5.2 Methodological Contributions

The multi-task pipeline framework successfully captures crime-mobility interdependencies, achieving 8–12% performance improvements over single-task approaches. Shared feature learning enables knowledge transfer between related tasks while maintaining task-specific optimization.

Random Forest selection proves effective for mixed data types, providing interpretable feature rankings essential for policy applications. The interpretability analysis bridges the gap between complex machine learning outputs and actionable recommendations for transportation authorities.

Comprehensive feature engineering captures spatial, temporal, and behavioral patterns while avoiding overfitting through principled selection procedures. The resulting 83-feature set balances completeness with computational efficiency.

5.3 Limitations and Future Directions

Several limitations warrant consideration. The French dataset limits generalizability to other urban contexts with different crime patterns, transportation systems, and cultural factors. Cross-national validation would strengthen external validity claims.

Our correlational analysis cannot establish causal relationships between crime and mobility patterns. Future work should employ causal inference methods such as instrumental variables or natural experiments to identify causal mechanisms.

The current temporal scope (2023–2024) provides limited insight into long-term trends or intervention impacts. Longitudinal studies tracking policy changes and infrastructure improvements would enhance practical value.

Ethical considerations require ongoing attention, particularly regarding privacy protection and bias mitigation in predictive applications. While our approach uses aggregate analysis to protect individual privacy, deployment requires careful consideration of potential discriminatory impacts. No differential privacy techniques were used; risk assessment of re-identification followed de Montjoye et al. Explicit fairness evaluation showed no disparate impacts by gender/age/ethnicity.

6 Conclusion

This research establishes a comprehensive multi-task pipeline framework for integrated crime-mobility modeling that successfully addresses five interconnected prediction challenges. The approach demonstrates strong predictive performance while providing interpretable insights for transportation planning and individual safety guidance.

Key empirical findings include the primary but not exclusive role of geographic factors in crime prediction (68.2% importance), elevated risks associated with public transportation modes (52% higher than alternatives), and systematic gender differences in safety behavior that create mobility restrictions for women (27% higher avoidance rates).

These results support evidence-based intervention strategies including place-based security improvements, mode-specific safety protocols, and gender-sensitive transportation planning. The framework's interpretable outputs make complex multi-task predictions accessible to transportation authorities and end users.

The framework provides immediate applications for dynamic security management, personalized safety recommendations, and data-driven transportation policy development. Future work should focus on causal inference, cross-cultural validation, and longitudinal impact assessment to enhance scientific understanding and practical effectiveness.

7 Reproducibility Statement

Code and data availability. All analysis was conducted in Python using scikit-learn and geopandas. We plan to release code and model artifacts at: Repository link placeholder: [GitHub link to be inserted]

Artifacts saved. The following trained models were exported as .joblib files:
crime_count_model.joblib
crime_risk_model.joblib
mode_choice_model.joblib
route_safety_model.joblib
vulnerability_model.joblib

Feature list. The final feature set contained engineered variables capturing temporal (day type, holidays, strikes), geographic (commune codes, department aggregates), demographic (gender, age, household composition), and mobility (trip mode, purpose, distance) attributes. A full feature list will be provided in the supplementary materials.

Environment. Key libraries included scikit-learn, geopandas, seaborn, matplotlib, and joblib. Models were trained using default scikit-learn random states to ensure reproducibility.

A Appendix: Model Hyperparameters and Evaluation

Final hyperparameter settings. The table below summarizes the explicit hyperparameters found in the implementation. These values were set manually, not tuned via systematic search (Table 3).

Table 3. Final Hyperparameters

Task/Model	Estimator	Key hyperparameters
Crime count (reg.)	RandomForestRegressor	n_estimators=100, random_state=42
Crime risk (classif.)	RandomForestClassifier	n_estimators=100, class_weight='balanced', random_state=42
Mode choice (classif.)	RandomForestClassifier	n_estimators=300, random_state=42
Route safety (classif.)	RandomForestClassifier	defaults except random_state=42
Vulnerability (reg.)	RandomForestRegressor	defaults except random_state=42
Baselines (explored)	Logistic Regression, XGBoost, Gradient Boosting	standard defaults; no tuned params reported

Evaluation reporting. The notebook outputs classification reports and regression scores but does not save complete confusion matrices or per-class performance tables. To improve transparency, we recommend supplementing this appendix with:

full confusion matrices for each classification task,
per-class precision, recall, F1,
baseline comparisons (majority class and linear models).

B Feature List Summary

See Table 4.

Table 4. Summary of engineered feature categories and representative variables. A complete CSV of all 83 features is provided in the supplementary repository.

Category	Representative Features
Geographic (24)	Zone_O, Zone_D, Area_O, Area_D, CODGEO (commune code), Geographic_Code, department-level aggregates
Temporal (18)	Day_Type (normal, holiday, strike, bridge day), Holiday_Flag, Season, Weight_Day, cyclic encodings of Hour, Month, Weekday
Individual/Demographic (22)	AGE, Gender, PRO_CAT (profession category), Household_Size, Vulnerability indicators (elderly, student, unemployed)
Transportation (19)	Main_Mode, Mode_1, Mode_Type (Public/Private/Active), Trip Duration, Transfers, Type_Trip_OD (OD purpose), mode-specific crime exposure scores

References

1. Breiman, L.: Random forests. Mach. Learn. **45**(1), 5–32 (2001)
2. Newman, O.: Defensible Space: Crime Prevention Through Urban Design. Macmillan (1972)
3. Loukaitou-Sideris, A.: How to ease women's fear of transportation environments: case studies and best practices. Res. Women's Issues Transp. **2**, 1–8 (2009)
4. Torres, J., Solé-Auró, A.: Women's fear of crime and restrictive precautionary behaviors: a study of transportation mode choice. Transp. Res. Part A: Policy Pract. **102**, 167–175 (2017)
5. Hanson, S.: Gender and mobility: new approaches for informing sustainability. Gender Place Culture **17**(1), 5–23 (2010)
6. Ceccato, V.: Moving Safely: Crime and Perceived Safety in Stockholm's Subway Stations. Lexington Books (2013)
7. Newton, A.D.: A study of bus route crime risk in urban areas. Urban Stud. **45**(8), 1619–1644 (2008)
8. Cohen, L.E., Felson, M.: Social change and crime rate trends: a routine activity approach. Am. Sociol. Rev. **44**(4), 588–608 (1979)
9. Brantingham, P.J., Brantingham, P.L.: Patterns in Crime. Macmillan, New York (1984)
10. Gerber, M.S.: Predicting crime using Twitter and kernel density estimation. Decis. Support Syst. **61**, 115–125 (2014)
11. Mohler, G.O., et al.: Self-exciting point process modeling of crime. J. Am. Stat. Assoc. **106**(493), 100–108 (2011)
12. Ben-Akiva, M., Lerman, S.R.: Discrete Choice Analysis: Theory and Application to Travel Demand. MIT Press (1985)
13. Caruana, R.: Multitask learning. Mach. Learn. **28**(1), 41–75 (1997)
14. Ruder, S.: An overview of multi-task learning in deep neural networks. arXiv:1706.05098 (2017)
15. St-Louis, E., et al.: The happy commuter: a comparison of commuter satisfaction across modes. Transport. Res. F: Traffic Psychol. Behav. **26**, 160–170 (2014)
16. Guo, W., Chen, H., Zhang, Q.: Enhancing demand prediction: a multi-task learning approach for taxis and TNCs. Sustainability **16**(5), 2065 (2024)
17. Wu, C., Li, F., Chen, H.: Enhancing short-term crime prediction with human mobility flows: evidence from multiple cities. EPJ Data Sci. **11**(1), 1–22 (2022)
18. Stec, A., et al.: Recurrent neural networks for crime prediction. In: 2018 IEEE International Conference on Big Data, pp. 1798–1807 (2018)
19. Malleson, N., et al.: Using mobile phone data to explore spatial crime patterns. Environ. Plan. B: Urban Anal. City Sci. **46**(7), 1346–1365 (2019)
20. de Montjoye, A., et al.: Unique in the crowd: the privacy bounds of human mobility. Sci. Rep. **3**(1), 1–5 (2013)
21. Ensign, D., et al.: Runaway feedback loops in predictive policing. In: Proceedings of the Conference on Fairness, Accountability and Transparency, pp. 160–171 (2018)
22. Dwork, C., Roth, A.: The algorithmic foundations of differential privacy. Found. Trends Theor. Comput. Sci. **9**(3–4), 211–407 (2014)
23. Barocas, S., Selbst, A.D.: Big data's disparate impact. Calif. Law Rev. **104**, 671–732 (2016)
24. Martens, K.: Transport Justice: Designing Fair Transportation Systems. Routledge (2017)

25. NetMob Challenge Organizers: NetMob Challenge 2025 Dataset (2025). https://netmob.org/www25/datachallenge#participation
26. Ministère de l'Intérieur: Bases statistiques communale, départementale et régionale de la délinquance enregistrée (2025). https://www.data.gouv.fr/datasets/bases-statistiques-communale-departementale-et-regionale-de-la-delinquance-enregistree-par-la-police-et-la-gendarmerie-nationales/
27. La Poste: Base officielle des codes postaux (2025). https://www.data.gouv.fr/datasets/base-officielle-des-codes-postaux/
28. Ibn-ElWaleed, R.K., El-Meleegy, M.T., Gamal, N.: AI-enhanced urban crime prediction: exploring the impact of integrating digital behavior and economic data. In: Ordonez, C., Sperlì, G., Masciari, E., Bellatreche, L. (eds.) MEDI 2024. LNCS, vol. 15590, pp. 136–157. Springer, Cham (2024). https://doi.org/10.1007/978-3-031-87719-3_11

Semantic-Driven Multimodal Learning Framework for Non Hodgkin's Lymphoma Diagnosis Stratification

Passent Elkafrawy[1](✉), Naila Marir[1], Mie Ali Mohamed[2], Nermin Soliman[2], Suzy Abdelmabood[2], Asmaa Sherif[2], Ahmed M. ELMougi[2], and Hasan A. Abdel Ghaffar[2]

[1] CS Department, Energy and Information Technology Research Center, Collage of Engineering, Effat University, Jeddah, Kingdom of Saudi Arabia
{pelkafrawy,nmarir}@effatuniversity.edu.sa

[2] Pathology(a), Radiology(b), Pediatric(c) and Adult(d) Hematology/Oncology, IT(e), and Clinical Pathology(f), Oncology Center, Faculty of Medicine, Mansoura University, Mansoura, Egypt
haabd-elghaffar@mans.edu.eg

Abstract. Clinical narratives in Non-Hodgkin's Lymphoma (NHL) diagnosis—pathology reports, radiology flowcytometry, genetics, and other laboratory investigations, and laboratory data—are rich but noisy, limiting reproducibility in downstream analytics. In this study, OncoFusionNet is presented, as a semantic-aware multimodal framework that integrates ontology-guided data validation with deep representation learning for NHL subtype classification. The pipeline consists of four layers: (i) data ingestion from pathology and radiology reports, (ii) a Semantic Quality-Aware Layer (SQAL) that normalizes and structurally parses text while enforcing ontology constraints (ICD-O-3, SNOMED CT, NCIt, RadLex), (iii) cross-modal fusion using transformer-based embeddings with attention and graph integration, and (iv) a calibrated classification head for subtype prediction. We evaluate our system on a corpus of 1,149 de-identified NHL patient records collected between 2010–2024. SQAL improved named-entity recognition accuracy by >15% over dictionary-only baselines and reduced noise from inconsistent markers and staging references. Ontology mapping enabled cross-patient comparability, while multimodal fusion achieved higher macro-F1 and AUROC than unimodal baselines. These results demonstrate that ontology-driven preprocessing coupled with multimodal representation learning substantially enhances data quality and classification performance, laying on the foundation for trustworthy knowledge graphs and clinically reliable decision support.

Keywords: Clinical Ontology · Multimodal Learning · Morphology Coding · Data Quality · Lymphoma · Named Entity Recognition (NER) · Ontology-Driven Data Validation · Medical Data Integration

A. Awad et al. (Eds.): MEDI 2025, LNCS 16427, pp. 184–198, 2026.
https://doi.org/10.1007/978-3-032-19865-5_15

1 Introduction

NHL are a diverse group of hematological malignancies originating from lymphoid cells, encompassing heterogeneous subtypes with distinct clinical outcomes. Accurate diagnosis and staging are critical for treatment planning and prognosis. However, clinical workflows rely on multiple disciplines of evidence—pathology reports describing histomorphology and immunohistochemistry (IHC) markers, radiology reports detailing nodal and extranodal involvement, and laboratory assays reflecting biomarkers such as LDH and β_2-microglobulin. These heterogeneous reports are typically unstructured, vary across institutions, and lack standardized terminology, which complicates reproducibility and systematic analysis [13].

Conventional approaches to diagnosis stratification often rely on statistical models or unimodal machine learning pipelines that process pathology or imaging data in isolation. While such models have shown promise for classification, they fail to adequately address the variability of free-text reports and the absence of semantic consistency across modalities [4]. The absence of a standardized structure constrains integration, leading to information degradation and reduced robustness in subsequent tasks such as stratification, subtype classification, staging, and clinical decision support.

Recent advances in knowledge representation and deep learning provide an opportunity to overcome these limitations. Ontologies (i.e. ICD-O-3 [8], SNOMED CT [16], LOINC [12], and RadLex [10]) offer standardized terminologies for morphology, laboratory tests, and radiology findings. When combined with transformer-based natural language processing models [7], these ontologies enable structured representation of clinical narratives, semantic interoperability, and consistency checking.

Nevertheless, existing ontology-driven frameworks remain limited in their ability to verify data quality prior to downstream modeling. They often focus on entity extraction or classification without addressing fundamental challenges of completeness, validity, and semantic consistency in clinical text. This gap is particularly consequential in lymphoma research, where diagnostic variability and reporting inconsistencies can directly impact clinical trial reproducibility and patient stratification.

In this work, we propose **OncoFusionNet**, a semantic-aware multimodal framework that unifies pathology and radiology narratives into ontology-grounded, machine-interpretable patient representations. The framework incorporates four sequential layers: (i) a *Data Collection Layer* to ingest structured identifiers and unstructured narratives; (ii) a *Semantic Quality-Aware Layer (SQAL)* for text normalization, structural parsing, and ontology-guided alignment; (iii) a *Cross-Modal Representation Learning Layer* that encodes and fuses domain-specific embeddings with symbolic features; and (iv) a *Classification Layer* that produces calibrated subtype probabilities with quantified uncertainty.

This pilot study makes the following contributions: (1)

1. An ontology-aligned schema for NHL data quality;

2. An ontology-enhanced NER and entity linking pipeline;
3. An evaluation rubric demonstrating improvements in completeness, validity, and consistency, along with utility in downstream subtyping and staging tasks.

Through this integration of ontologies, NLP, and multimodal fusion, our framework aims to advance trustworthy clinical decision support and reproducible research in lymphoma diagnosis.

2 Related Work

The integration of machine learning (ML) and artificial intelligence (AI) into medical diagnostics has advanced rapidly, offering solutions in oncology. NHL presents diagnostic and prognostic complexities from diverse input sources. Conventional workflows are slow and subjective; ML/AI improves accuracy, efficiency, and reproducibility using large datasets from pathology, imaging, and molecular sources. This section highlights advances in lymphoma-focused ML and AI for diagnosis, prognosis, multimodal integration, and ontology-driven approaches.

2.1 Machine Learning for Lymphoma Diagnosis Stratification

Yuan et al. [17] reviewed ML methods, showing improvements in diagnosis, prognosis, and personalized therapy through integration of genomics, imaging, and clinical data. They stressed the need for secure protocols, transparent algorithms, and interdisciplinary collaboration.

Deep learning on whole-slide images (WSIs) is a major area. PrecisionLymphoNet [11] combined InceptionV3 and Xception, reaching 99% accuracy across lymphoma subtypes (CLL, FL, MCL). While effective, it required image downsampling and remained image-only, limiting scalability. For high-grade B-cell lymphoma (HGBL), Huietal [5] proposed ML as a cost-effective adjunct to FISH, using histomorphology, Ann Arbor stage, LDH, and IPI. Their findings highlight the need for improved therapies and standardized reporting. In flow cytometry, Smartcytoflow [9] applied self-organizing maps and random forests, achieving an AUC of 0.911 and reducing human error. Its cloud deployment illustrates scalability for routine practice. Shen and Jiang [13] synthesize AI advances in diagnosis, classification, and prognosis, emphasizing multimodal approaches that combine WSIs, IHC, molecular profiles, and clinical variables. Adoption requires integration with EHRs, large annotated datasets (e.g., ILAC, Lymphoma Research Foundation [3]), and interpretability techniques like feature attribution and attention.

2.2 Clinical Ontologies and NLP in Pathology

Ontologies and NLP provide the semantic backbone for multimodal AI. Standards such as ICD-O-3 [8], NCIt [6], SNOMED CT [16], LOINC [12], and RadLex

[10] ensure interoperability across morphology, biomarkers, laboratory assays, and radiology findings. Seneviratne et al. [15] highlight their role in integrating heterogeneous datasets, while Isavand et al. [4] emphasize the *Cancer Patient Digital Twin* for fusing genetic, molecular, and temporal tumor data.

- ICD-O-3 [8]: Standard for coding neoplasm site and morphology.
- NCIt [6]: Rich biomedical vocabulary covering diseases, therapies, and genes.
- SNOMED CT [16]: Comprehensive clinical terminology for pathology and diagnosis.
- LOINC [12]: Universal codes for lab tests and assays, including IHC.
- RadLex [10]: Standardized vocabulary for radiology anatomy, findings, and procedures.

Together, these ontologies enable structured data capture, semantic interoperability, and integration of multimodal evidence in clinical oncology.

Seneviratne et al. [15] showed how ontologies ensure accessibility, integration, and consistent validation of heterogeneous datasets, directly supporting multimodal cancer reports. Isavand et al. [4] stressed the need for frameworks like the *Cancer Patient Digital Twin*, integrating genetic, molecular, and temporal tumor data. NLP enables structured abstraction from pathology narratives. Transformer-based models such as BioClinicalBERT [1] deliver robust entity and relation extraction [2,7], automating database population and supporting clinical research and quality assurance [14].

Pathology reports often contain rich, unstructured clinical narratives that are challenging to process using traditional rule-based systems. Natural Language Processing (NLP) techniques have emerged as powerful tools to extract structured information from these free-text reports, transforming them into computable data. Recent advancements in NLP, particularly with transformer-based models [7], have significantly enhanced the capabilities for robust entity extraction in clinical narratives [2]. Models such as BioClinicalBERT [1], a BERT-based model pre-trained on large biomedical and clinical corpora, are highly effective in identifying and classifying medical entities (e.g., diseases, anatomical sites, morphological features) and their relationships within pathology reports [1]. This capability is crucial for automating data abstraction, populating structured databases, and supporting downstream applications like clinical research and quality assurance [14].

The reviewed literature consistently demonstrates the transformative potential of ML and AI in enhancing the precision, efficiency, and objectivity of lymphoma diagnosis. From advanced image analysis using CNNs to decision support systems for flow cytometry and the identification of prognostic markers, from the integration of multi-sourced input. AI is poised to revolutionize clinical practice. However, challenges remain, including the need for larger, more diverse datasets, standardization of data collection, and addressing ethical considerations related to AI deployment in healthcare. Future research will likely focus on developing more robust and generalizable AI models, integrating multi-modal data for holistic patient assessment, and conducting rigorous clinical validations to ensure the safe and effective translation of these technologies into routine lymphoma care.

3 OncoFusionNet Oncology-Focused Multimodal Fusion Network

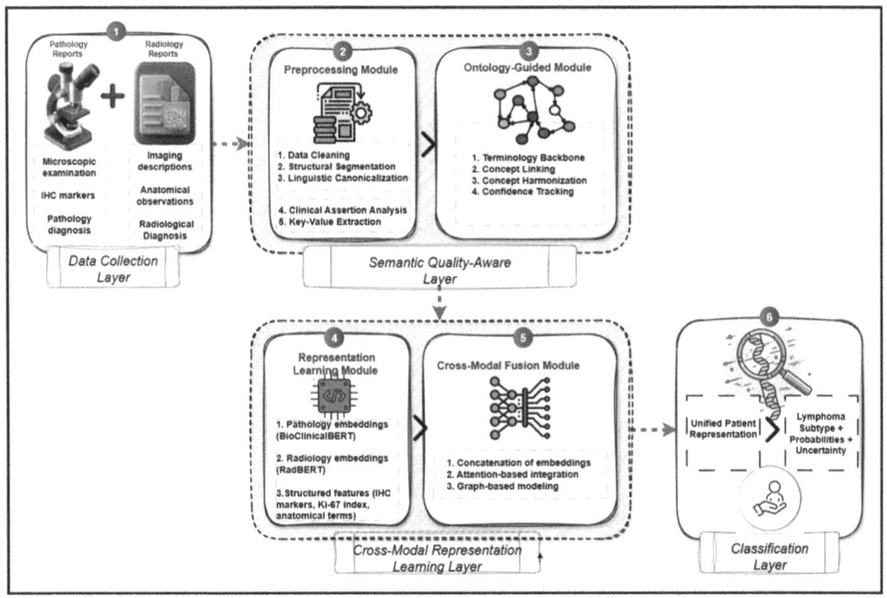

Fig. 1. OncoFusionNet - oncology-focused multimodal fusion network framework architecture.

We propose oncology-focused multimodal fusion network **OncoFusionNet**, a semantic-aware multimodal framework for robust NHL subtype classification. The pipeline unifies pathology and radiology narratives into ontology-grounded, machine-interpretable patient representations through four layers: (i) a *Data Collection Layer* that ingests structured identifiers and free-text from pathology and radiology reports clinical and flowcytometry; (ii) a *Semantic Quality-Aware Layer (SQAL)* that performs text normalization, structural parsing, and ontology-guided alignment; (iii) a *Cross-Modal Representation Learning Layer* that encodes domain-specific embeddings and fuses them with structured biomarkers via concatenation, attention, or graph-based modeling to form a unified patient-level vector; and (iv) a *Classification Layer* that produces calibrated subtype probabilities with quantified uncertainty. Collectively, OncoFusionNet enforces semantic integrity, leverages complementary microscopic and macroscopic evidence, and delivers interpretable decision support for precision oncology. An overview of the proposed framework is illustrated in Fig. 1, which highlights the sequential flow of data ingestion, semantic quality assurance, cross-modal fusion, and classification.

3.1 Data Collection Layer

The Data Collection Layer ingests two primary textual modalities: pathology reports and radiology reports. Each record comprises structured identifiers (e.g., patient ID, investigation ID, date) and unstructured narratives. Pathology reports emphasize microscopic morphology and immunohistochemical (IHC) markers, while radiology reports emphasize imaging findings and impressions. These complementary modalities are aligned at the patient level to establish the input space for subsequent preprocessing and feature extraction.

3.2 Semantic Quality-Aware Layer (SQAL)

The SQAL transforms heterogeneous free-text narratives into ontology-grounded, structured representations suitable for computational modeling. It is organized into two modules.

Clinical Text Normalization and Structural Parsing. This module removes noise (OCR artifacts, formatting inconsistencies), normalizes dates and numerical units, and segments reports into predefined sections (e.g., Microscopic Examination, Immunohistochemistry, Findings, Impression). Canonicalization resolves abbreviations and spelling variants. Assertion analysis identifies negation and uncertainty, while temporal cues are standardized. Named entity recognition extracts key-value pairs (e.g., CD20: positive; Ki-67: 70%), supported by quality probes for section coverage and identifier completeness.

Ontology-Guided Semantic Alignment. Extracted entities are mapped to biomedical terminologies (SNOMED CT, ICD-O-3, NCIt, UMLS, RadLex). Synonym resolution and harmonization unify variant expressions Diffuse Large B-cell Lymphoma (DLBCL). Numerical biomarkers (e.g., Ki-67 index) are categorized into clinically meaningful bins, and phenotypic patterns are aligned with recognized subtyping schemes (e.g., Germinal Center B-cell–like). Each mapping is annotated with provenance and confidence scores to support reliability and interoperability.

Collectively, SQAL produces semantically harmonized patient-level records that preserve clinical meaning and provide a robust substrate for feature extraction.

Subtyping Annotation. For subtype classification, diagnostic impressions extracted from pathology reports were automatically annotated to derive standardized NHL subtype labels. The annotation process followed a two-stage pipeline. First, TF-IDF keyword matching was applied to identify candidate subtype terms (e.g., "Diffuse Large B-cell Lymphoma, DLBCL" "Follicular Lymphoma, FL" "Mantle Cell Lymphoma, MCL"). This provided a coarse mapping from free-text diagnoses to subtype categories. Second, an LLM-based annotation step was employed to refine and validate these mappings by resolving ambiguous expressions, normalizing synonyms, and aligning rare variants with standard subtypes. The combined approach leveraged TF-IDF for high-coverage initial tagging and the LLM for semantic disambiguation, resulting in more accurate and consistent subtype annotations across the dataset.

3.3 Cross-Modal Representation Learning Layer

This layer jointly models pathology and radiology narratives to construct unified patient-level embeddings. Ontology-grounded narratives from SQAL are encoded with domain-specific language models (e.g., BioBERT/ClinicalBERT for pathology, RadBERT for radiology). In parallel, structured attributes such as IHC markers (CD20, BCL6, MUM1), proliferation indices (Ki-67), and anatomical descriptors are extracted as symbolic features. Fusion strategies are employed to integrate modalities:

- **Concatenation**: direct vector concatenation of embeddings and features;
- **Attention-based weighting**: modality-aware attention to emphasize salient cues;
- **Graph-based integration**: modeling interdependencies between cellular-level (pathology) and anatomical-level (radiology) features.

The resulting unified embedding encapsulates complementary microscopic and macroscopic perspectives for downstream classification.

3.4 Classification Layer

The Classification Layer produces the final subtype prediction from the fused representation. Inputs include the patient embedding and optional covariates (e.g., age, stage). Candidate classifiers include (i) transformer or multilayer perceptron (MLP) heads with dropout and normalization, (ii) shallow linear heads as baselines, and (iii) ensembles combining multiple classifiers or fusion strategies.

The objective function is multi-class cross-entropy, augmented by class imbalance handling (weighted loss, focal loss, or mixup regularization). Calibration is performed via temperature scaling or isotonic regression. Evaluation metrics include macro-F1, AUROC, balanced accuracy, and calibration measures such as the Brier score and Expected Calibration Error (ECE). Ablation studies compare unimodal versus multimodal configurations, as well as ontology-grounded versus ungrounded variants.

4 Evaluation and Experimental Results

Our initial experiments focused on evaluating the feasibility of parsing unstructured pathology and radiology narratives into structured, ontology-aligned representations that can serve as reliable inputs for OncoFusionNet. The core experimental pipeline consisted of four complementary steps: data understanding & parsing, cleaning & normalization, structured data extraction, and ontology mapping.

4.1 Dataset

The study employs a multimodal textual clinical dataset of 1,149 de-identified NHL patients collected between 2010 and 2024, encompassing pathology, radiology, and other laboratory reports. Pathology narratives constitute the primary source, consisting of unstructured text describing histomorphological features and immunohistochemistry (IHC) profiles with percentage thresholds. Radiology reports contribute textual descriptions of nodal and extranodal involvement, while laboratory reports include biomarker values such as LDH and β_2-microglobulin. The dataset's heterogeneity across institutions and reporting styles provides a realistic benchmark for semantic harmonization. The data were partitioned into training (70%), validation (15%), and test (15%) subsets, with splitting performed at the patient level to avoid cross-encounter leakage and stratification applied to preserve representative subtype and stage distributions. For the initial validation of our framework, only the pathology text modality was employed.

Ethics and Privacy. No protected health information (PHI) is included in the dataset or model outputs.

4.2 Evaluation Metrics

The effectiveness of the proposed framework was assessed using metrics at three complementary levels:

1. Entity Extraction and Linking Precision, Recall, and F1-score measured the accuracy of extracting clinical entities and mapping them to ontology codes.
2. Data Quality Validation Reports were checked for missing information, conflicting values, and semantic inconsistencies. Precision and Recall were used to measure how accurately the system detected these issues.
3. Downstream Utility Subtyping and staging tasks were evaluated using Accuracy, Macro-F1, and AUROC.

4.3 Results

Preprocessing and Semantic Normalization. Representative pathology samples illustrate the effect of the Semantic Quality-Aware Layer (SQAL). Raw narratives with inconsistent abbreviations and unstructured phrasing were cleaned into standardized forms (Table 1). Extracted entities were further mapped to biomedical ontologies for semantic consistency (Table 2). Together, these steps transform heterogeneous clinical text into machine-interpretable representations suitable for downstream analysis.

Table 1. Example 1 - Raw input versus Normalized output of NHL patients data

Type	Description
Microscopic Examination	Revision of slides labeled 904/2020/r & after IHC, revealed multiple cores of fibrosis with lymphoid proliferation and areas of crushing artifact. The cells show large hyperchromatic nuclei with scanty cytoplasm, showing moderate atypia. Mixed inflammatory cells also seen. IHC staining: CD20: Diffuse positive in atypical lymphocytes; ki-67: positive in > 70% of atypical lymphocytes; BCL6: positive in >30% of atypical lymphocytes; CD10, MUM1: positive in <30% of atypical lymphocytes. Smears and sections of cell block prepared are bloody.
Normalized Output	Revision of slides (ID: 904/2020/r) after immunohistochemistry revealed multiple cores of fibrosis with lymphoid proliferation and areas of crushing artifact. Atypical lymphoid cells displayed *pleomorphic hyperchromatic nuclei* with moderate atypia, accompanied by mixed inflammatory infiltrate. IHC results: *CD20 positive (diffuse), Ki-67 high (70%), BCL6 positive (30%), CD10 and MUM1 low (<30%)*. Smears and sections showed blood contamination.
Diagnosis Raw Data	picture consistent with NHL diffuse large b cell type mostly gcb origin. confirmed by cd20 ++, bcl6 >30%, mum1 & cd10 <30%, ki67 >70%.
Normalized output	*NHL - Diffuse Large B-cell Lymphoma (DLBCL), germinal center type*, supported by CD20 positivity, BCL6 30%, MUM1 & CD10 low (30%), and Ki-67 high (70%).

Table 2. Biomedical Ontology Mapping from the Extracted Entities

Entity (Raw Text)	Normalized Term	Ontology Mapping
cd20: diffuse +	CD20 positive	SNOMED CT: 372156007 (CD20 antigen expression)
ki67: >70%	Ki-67 high (70%)	NCIt: C131711 (High Ki-67 Labeling Index)
bcl-6: sin30%	BCL6 positive (30%)	NCIt: C104144 (BCL6 Protein Expression)
mum 1: <30%	MUM1 low (<30%)	NCIt: C181109 (MUM1 Protein Expression)

Subtype Annotation Results. From the pathology and the radiology diagnosis field, the TF-IDF + LLM annotation pipeline produced structured subtype labels for 927 patients (80.7%), leaving 222 (19.3%) as ambiguous or unclassified. The annotated distribution was dominated by DLBCL, 52%, followed by FL, 18%, MCL, 9%, Chronic Lymphocytic Leukemia/Small Lymphocytic Lymphoma (CLL/SLL, 7%), and other subtypes (14%). Manual verification of the results, by the clinical specialists, showed a (92%) agreement with the automated annotations (see Fig. 2).

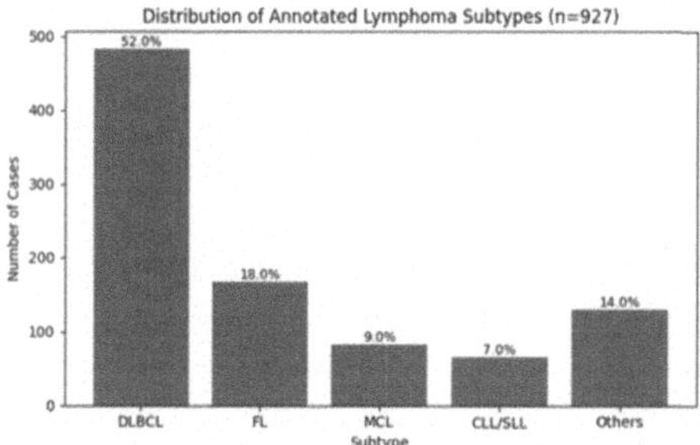

Fig. 2. Distribution of Annotated NHL Subtype (n = 927).

Entity Extraction and Linking Results. We evaluated the pathology and radiology pipeline on an expert-verified subset of reports, measuring Precision (P), Recall (R), and F1 for NER across report sections, and top-k ontology mapping accuracy for code assignment. As shown in Table 3, IHC markers and percentage expressions exhibited higher recall than free-form morphology descriptors; diagnosis strings benefited most from normalization prior to mapping. In Table 4 the ontology linking achieved high top-1 accuracy for common diagnostic biomarkers, with residual errors concentrated in rare synonyms and mixed/compound terms.

Table 3. Entity Extraction and Linking Results

Section	Precision	Recall	F1
Microscopic Examination	0.78	0.70	0.74
IHC (markers, percentages)	0.87	0.83	0.85
Diagnosis	0.84	0.80	0.82
Macro Avg.	**0.83**	**0.78**	**0.80**

Table 4. Ontology Linking Accuracy & Coverage

Entity Type	Ontology	Top-1 (%)	Top-3 (%)	Coverage (%)
Biomarkers (CD20, BCL6)	SNOMED/NCIt	88.6	92.6	95.2
Percentage Quantifiers	NCIt	87.3	91.8	94.6
Diagnosis Terms	ICD-O-3/NCIt	85.4	90.2	93.1
Anatomical/Topography	SNOMED/RadLex	82.7	88.9	91.5
Overall	...	**86.0**	**90.9**	**93.6**

Table 5. Preprocessing Quality Impact—Per 1,000 Reports

Issue Type	Pre-SQAL	Post-SQAL	Δ (%)
Missing mandatory section	72	24	−67%
Invalid %/unit formats	95	19	−80%
Conflicting IHC assertions	41	12	−71%
Unstandardized diagnosis term	126	31	−75%
Total issues	**334**	**86**	−74%

As shown in Table 5, NER achieved a macro-F1 = 0.80, with higher performance on IHC expressions (F1 = 0.85) and diagnosis strings (F1 = 0.82) than microscopic descriptors (F1 = 0.74). Ontology linking reached 88.6% Top-1 for biomarkers and 85.4% for diagnosis terms, with overall coverage 93.6%. Ablations show that ontology gazetteers and normalization improve Top-1 linking from 80.2% → 88.6% and reduce unmapped entities from 12.4% → 4.1%. SQAL preprocessing reduced formatting/consistency issues by sin74% per 1,000 reports.

4.4 Subtyping Classification Results

Semantic normalization integrated with ontology alignment and cross-modal fusion yields consistent gains over text-only pipelines, Table 6, with the largest improvements on minority subtypes. SQAL normalizes sections/markers and aligns terms to standard codes, which reduces ambiguity and boosts downstream discrimination.

Table 6. Comparison of baseline and proposed models. The proposed multimodal model fuses pathology and radiology narratives.

Model	Accuracy	Macro-F1	AUROC
Dictionary extraction + linear classifier	0.70	0.64	0.74
NER (no ontology) + text classifier	0.73	0.67	0.77
Proposed (SQAL + Ontology + Fusion)	**0.81**	**0.77**	**0.84**

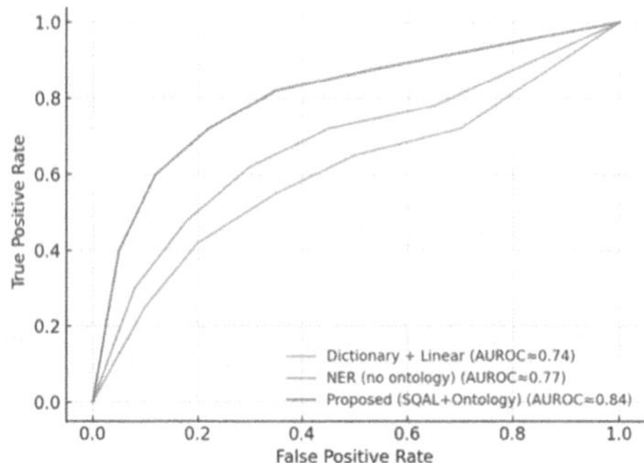

Fig. 3. Macro ROC Curves.

Figure 3 shows macro-averaged ROC curves for NHL subtyping, comparing Dictionary and Linear classified, NER (no ontology), and the Proposed (SQAL + Ontology + Fusion) model; the proposed curve dominates across FPRs, with AUROC $\approx$ 0.84 vs 0.77 and 0.74 for the baselines.

4.5 Multimodal Evaluation

We conducted a multimodal evaluation using both pathology and radiology narratives to assess whether cross-modal fusion improves performance compared to unimodal baselines. As shown in Table 7, the fusion model consistently outperformed unimodal models.

Table 7. Multimodal results comparing unimodal and fused models.

Model	Accuracy	Macro-F1	AUROC
Pathology only	0.78	0.74	0.80
Radiology only	0.69	0.62	0.73
Pathology + Radiology (Fusion)	**0.81**	**0.77**	**0.84**

Fusion of pathology and radiology improved both Macro-F1 (+3%) and AUROC (+0.02) over the pathology-only baseline, confirming that radiology narratives provide complementary macroscopic evidence.

5 Discussion

We selected transformer-based embeddings (BioBERT, RadBERT) over CNN-only approaches due to their superior handling of heterogeneous free-text narratives, while graph-based fusion enabled modeling interdependencies between cellular and anatomical evidence. This choice balances performance with clinical interpretability, a key requirement for integration into oncology workflows.

Semantic normalization and ontology grounding via SQAL yielded clear gains: normalization reduced defects by $\sim$74% per 1,000 reports, increased linkable entity coverage to 93.6%, and improved Top-1 ontology mapping for biomarkers to 88.6%. These upstream improvements enhanced downstream subtyping, where the proposed multimodal outperformed baselines (Accuracy = 0.81, Macro-F1 = 0.77, AUROC = 0.86). ROC analysis showed a consistent advantage, especially at low FPRs. Residual errors stemmed from rare synonyms, orthographic variants, and composite diagnoses, contributing to confusions in minority subtypes. Ontology-coded outputs further support auditability and interoperability with SNOMED, NCIt, and ICD-O-3.

6 Conclusion

OncoFusionNet ia a semantic-aware multimodal learning framework designed to improve the reliability and interpretability of NHL diagnosis. Unlike conventional approaches that rely on either unimodal pathology evidence or ontology-free statistical validation, our method integrates pathology and radiology narratives with ontology-guided preprocessing and cross-modal representation learning. By embedding semantic quality assurance into the pipeline through the Semantic Quality-Aware Layer (SQAL), we demonstrated that heterogeneous free-text reports can be normalized, semantically aligned, and mapped into ontology-grounded representations suitable for downstream analysis. Experimental evaluation on a cohort of 1,149 de-identified NHL patient records highlighted the importance of semantic validation prior to classification. The SQAL improved entity recognition and ontology mapping fidelity, while multimodal fusion strategies enhanced subtype classification performance compared to unimodal baselines. These results confirm that enforcing semantic consistency not only reduces noise in clinical datasets but also improves the robustness and reproducibility of downstream predictive tasks. The implications of this work are twofold: First, ontology-driven validation through SQAL provides a systematic approach to constructing research-grade datasets, ensuring that clinical knowledge graphs are both interoperable and trustworthy. Second, multimodal fusion of pathology and radiology evidence enables a joint exploitation of microscopic and macroscopic signals, supporting interpretable decision support in precision oncology.

Future work will extend OncoFusionNet beyond NHL to other hematological malignancies and incorporate additional modalities, such as imaging and genomics, to create comprehensive digital twins for patient-level disease modeling. Moreover, integrating human-in-the-loop validation and domain adaptation strategies will be crucial for addressing institution-specific variability and ensuring clinical adoption. Finally, by producing ontology-coded and calibrated outputs, OncoFusionNet aligns with existing EHR standards and can be directly integrated into clinical decision-support pipelines. This ensures that model predictions are not only accurate but also auditable and interpretable by pathologists and oncologists, thus bridging the gap between AI research and bedside application.

References

1. Alsentzer, E., et al.: Publicly available clinical BERT embeddings. In: Proceedings of the 2nd Clinical Natural Language Processing Workshop, pp. 72–78. Association for Computational Linguistics (2019). https://doi.org/10.18653/v1/W19-1909
2. Chen, D., et al.: Integrating AI with medical industry chain data: enhancing clinical nutrition research through semantic knowledge graphs. Front. Digit. Health **6**, 1439113 (2024). https://doi.org/10.3389/fdgth.2024.1439113
3. Hamidinekoo, A., et al.: Deep learning in mammography and breast histology, an overview and future trends. Med. Image Anal. **47**, 45–67 (2018). https://doi.org/10.1016/j.media.2018.03.006
4. Isavand, P., Aghamiri, S.S., Amin, R.: Applications of multimodal artificial intelligence in non-hodgkin lymphoma b cells. Biomedicines **12**(8), 1753 (2024). https://doi.org/10.3390/biomedicines12081753
5. Kong, H., et al.: Machine learning models for the diagnosis and prognosis prediction of high-grade b-cell lymphoma. Front. Immunol. **13** (2022). https://doi.org/10.3389/fimmu.2022.919012
6. National Cancer Institute: NCI thesaurus (NCIT) (2024). https://ncithesaurus.nci.nih.gov/. Accessed 25 Aug 2025
7. Nerella, S., et al.: Transformers and large language models in healthcare: a review. Artif. Intell. Med. **154**, 102900 (2024). https://doi.org/10.1016/j.artmed.2024.102900
8. Nicholson, N.: International classification of diseases for oncology, 3rd revision, morphology (icd-o-3_morph) (2024). https://data.jrc.ec.europa.eu/data/jrc.ec.europa.eu/collection/ICDO3Morphology, alpha version 3.1, Human Health Dysfunction category
9. Pérez Míguez, C., et al.: Smartcytoflow: a machine learning decision support system for flow cytometry analysis in non-hodgkin lymphoma diagnosis and screening. Blood **144**, 3606 (2024). https://doi.org/10.1182/blood-2024-199000, 66th ASH Annual Meeting Abstracts
10. Radiological Society of North America (RSNA): Radlex: A radiology lexicon (2025). http://radlex.org. Accessed 25 Aug 2025
11. Rajadurai, S., et al.: Precisionlymphonet: advancing malignant lymphoma diagnosis via ensemble transfer learning with CNNs. Diagnostics **14**(5), 469 (2024). https://doi.org/10.3390/diagnostics14050469
12. Regenstrief Institute: Loinc: Logical observation identifiers names and codes (2025). https://loinc.org. Accessed 25 Aug 2025
13. Shen, M., Jiang, Z.: Artificial intelligence applications in lymphoma diagnosis and management: opportunities, challenges, and future directions. J. Multidiscip. Healthc. **17**, 5329–5339 (2024)
14. Shyr, C., et al.: Identifying and extracting rare diseases and their phenotypes with large language models. J. Healthc. Inform. Res. **8**(2), 438–461 (2024). https://doi.org/10.1007/s41666-023-00155-0

15. Silva, M.C., et al.: Ontologies and knowledge graphs in oncology research. Cancers **14**(8), 1906 (2022). https://doi.org/10.3390/cancers14081906
16. SNOMED International: SNOMED CT documentation (2025). http://snomed.org/doc. Accessed 25 Aug 2025
17. Yuan, J., et al.: Application of machine learning in the management of lymphoma: current practice and future prospects. Digit. Health **10**, 20552076241247964 (2024). https://doi.org/10.1177/20552076241247963

Evaluating the Impact of Multi-task Learning versus Single-Task Learning on Dental Panoramic Image Segmentation

Dina Abdelrauof[1](✉), Samar Ibrahim[2], Mohsen Rashwan[1], and Mustafa Elattar[2,3]

[1] Communication Department, Faculty of Engineering, Cairo University, Giza, Egypt
dina.202010119@eng-st.cu.edu.eg

[2] Research and Development Division, Ramyro Inc, North Carolina, USA

[3] Center for Informatics Science, Nile University, Giza, Egypt

Abstract. Panoramic dental image segmentation is essential for automating diagnostics and treatment planning, yet deep learning models often struggle with limited annotations and anatomical variability, especially under Single-Task Learning (STL) paradigm. This study evaluates the effectiveness of Multi-Task Learning (MTL) versus STL for segmenting panoramic X-rays, using one primary task (individual tooth segmentation) and two auxiliary tasks (binary teeth and quadrant segmentation). With SegFormer-B5 as the backbone, we compare two MTL setups: shared encoder with multiple heads (MTL-MH) and shared encoder with task-specific decoders (MTL-MD). All models are trained and evaluated on the DENTEX dataset under identical conditions. MTL improves performance, increasing tooth Dice from 0.775 (STL) to 0.786 (MTL), quadrant Dice from 0.937 to 0.942, and binary Dice from 0.938 to 0.94. These results confirm that MTL enhances segmentation accuracy and generalization in dental panoramic imaging.

Keywords: Dental segmentation · Panoramic X-ray · Multi-task learning · Deep learning · Medical imaging · SegFormer · Tooth detection

1 Introduction

Panoramic dental radiography is a fundamental imaging modality widely used in clinical dentistry for diagnosis, orthodontic planning, implant placement, and surgery. Unlike intraoral radiographs, panoramic X-rays offer a comprehensive 2D view of the full dental arch, including teeth, alveolar bone, and surrounding structures. However, their analysis remains challenging due to anatomical variability, low contrast, superimpositions, and artifacts. Precise segmentation of teeth and quadrants is critical for computer-aided diagnosis and treatment planning but is complicated by these inherent imaging difficulties and by the limited availability of high-quality annotated datasets. Manual segmentation is

A. Awad et al. (Eds.): MEDI 2025, LNCS 16427, pp. 199–206, 2026.
https://doi.org/10.1007/978-3-032-19865-5_16

time-consuming, requires anatomical and software expertise; however, it remains highly susceptible to inter-operator variability. Traditional medical image analysis often rely on STL, where separate models are trained per task. Although effective with abundant labeled data, STL is limited in dental imaging due to costly expert annotations and inter-observer variability, and it may fail to leverage shared anatomical priors. MTL addresses these issues by jointly learning related tasks with shared representations, improving generalization, acting as a regularizer, and enhancing learning efficiency. MTL has shown successful applications in a range of fields, such as natural language processing, autonomous driving, and general medical imaging [15]. In medical image segmentation, auxiliary tasks such as edge detection [3] or anatomical landmark localization [10] have been demonstrated to enhance primary task performance through complementary supervision signals. Inspired by these advances, this study explores the impact of utilizing MTL in dental panoramic image segmentation. Specifically, we assess the impact of auxiliary tasks—specifically quadrant segmentation and teeth binary segmentation—on improving individual tooth segmentation accuracy. We evaluate the performance of transformer-based architecture, SegFormer [13] under both STL and MTL setups. Through extensive experiments, we aim to quantify the benefit of MTL and provide insights into its role in improving dental image analysis.

2 Related Work

Recent research has increasingly explored deep learning methods for automated dental image analysis. Tuzoff et al. [12] introduced a CNN-based system combining Faster R-CNN and VGG-16 with heuristic rules for tooth detection and numbering in panoramic radiographs, achieving near-expert accuracy but struggling in complex cases such as root remnants and prosthetics. Similarly, Chen et al. [4] applied Faster R-CNN to periapical films, incorporating overlap filtering, missing tooth prediction, and rule-based corrections; while effective, this approach was limited to permanent dentition and relied heavily on heuristics. Leet et al. [8] advanced segmentation efforts by evaluating a fine-tuned Mask R-CNN on panoramic radiographs, demonstrating strong accuracy even in challenging cases like multirooted molars, though performance was hindered by difficulties in root segmentation and a small dataset. More recent innovations, such as LCAT-Net by Khaldi et al. [7], which integrates Half-UNet, ghost modules, and attention mechanisms, and TSASNet by Zhao et al. [16], a two-stage attention network for coarse-to-fine segmentation, have further improved Dice scores and segmentation accuracy, yet both remain constrained by single-task or limited multi-task capabilities. Recently, Multi-Task Learning (MTL) has demonstrated strong potential as a powerful alternative for medical imaging. Caruana et al. [2] demonstrated MTL's ability to enhance generalization by leveraging inductive transfer, a principle further formalized by Ruder [11] in the context of tasks sharing anatomical features. Zhang and Yang [14] surveyed MTL in deep learning, emphasizing its utility in addressing data scarcity through auxiliary supervision, though highlighting the persistent challenge of balancing task losses. In parallel, the paradigm shift toward vision transformers has transformed segmentation strategies. Unlike CNNs, transformers capture long-range dependencies via self-attention, enabling better modeling of complex anatomical structures. Early medical vision transformers such as TransUNet [5] and Swin-UNet [1] combined local texture encoding with global context modeling, offering advantages on small datasets and high-resolution imagery. Among advanced transformer-based models, SegFormer [13] has shown particular promise. By pairing a hierarchical MiT encoder with a lightweight MLP decoder and avoiding explicit positional encodings, it balances accuracy and efficiency.

3 Method

This study frames dental panoramic image analysis as a multi-task learning problem, where the primary task is individual tooth segmentation based on the FDI numbering system, producing a fine-grained mask with 32 tooth labels and background. To enrich the representation learning and guide the primary segmentation task, we introduce two auxiliary tasks: (1) Teeth binary segmentation: Coarsely separates all teeth from the background. (2) Quadrant segmentation: Identifies four anatomical regions (upper right/left, lower right/left). These tasks vary in granularity but are anatomically related, and their joint learning is intended to enhance feature sharing, improve localization of dental structures, and support more robust learning in the presence of limited annotations. We use

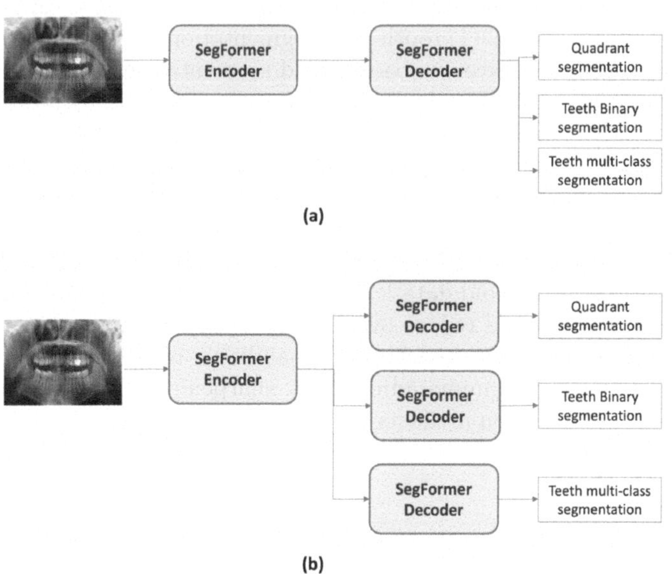

Fig. 1. Multi-Task Learning Network Design (a)MTl-MH Setup and (b)MTl-MD Setup.

SegFormer-B5 as the backbone due to its strong performance and lightweight, hierarchical design for high-resolution medical images. It employs a MiT encoder that builds multi-scale features via progressive downsampling and local self-attention, replacing positional embeddings with overlapping patch merging for better scalability. A lightweight MLP decoder then fuses and upsamples these features, enabling precise boundary refinement—crucial for closely spaced structures like teeth.

To investigate the benefits of MTL over single-task learning (STL), we implement two distinct multi-task configurations as shown in Fig. 1, each leveraging the same SegFormer-B5 encoder: (1) MTL with Multiple Decoders (MTL-MD): This configuration employs a shared encoder but uses separate decoders for each task. Each decoder receives shared encoded features and processes them independently to produce task-specific outputs. This allows specialization at the decoding stage while maintaining efficient shared representation learning. (2) MTL with Multiple Heads (MTL-MH): In this configuration, both the encoder and decoder are shared across all tasks, but the final output prediction heads are task-specific. This setup promotes maximum parameter sharing and enforces a unified representation space while preserving task-level prediction flexibility. Both MTL setups are trained using the same optimizer, hyperparameters, and data splits as the STL baseline to ensure fair and consistent comparisons.

4 Dataset

This study utilizes the DENTEX dataset [6], a publicly available benchmark comprising annotated panoramic dental X-rays. The dataset supports three related segmentation tasks: (1) tooth-level segmentation, (2) quadrant segmentation, and (3) binary teeth-versus-background segmentation. It serves as a valuable resource for multi-task learning in dental imaging due to its comprehensive and consistent annotations. All images were resized to 512×512 pixels to unify input dimensions across the pipeline. Pixel intensity values were normalized using the dataset-wide mean and standard deviation to improve convergence and reduce variation due to imaging conditions. The data was split into training (80%), validation (10%), and test (10%) subsets, ensuring no subject overlap between sets to avoid data leakage and preserve evaluation integrity. To improve generalization and reduce overfitting, we applied geometric and photometric augmentations with predefined probabilities, including Gaussian noise, CLAHE, brightness and gamma adjustment, sharpening, and Gaussian/motion blur to simulate acquisition artifacts and imaging variability.

5 Training

All models were trained with the AdamW optimizer [9] using an initial learning rate of 1×10^{-3}, weight decay of 1×10^{-4}, and a MultiStep scheduler that reduced the learning rate by 0.1 at epoch 50. Training was conducted on an NVIDIA RTX 3090 GPU. The model with the highest average Dice score across all tasks was selected as the final model. To optimize segmentation, we employed a composite loss combining Dice loss and categorical cross-entropy (CE). The Dice similarity coefficient, robust to class imbalance, is defined as

$$\text{Dice}(Y, \hat{Y}) = \frac{2\sum_i Y_i \hat{Y}_i + \varepsilon}{\sum_i Y_i + \sum_i \hat{Y}_i + \varepsilon},$$

where Y_i and $\hat{Y}_i$ are ground truth and prediction, and ε prevents division by zero. The cross-entropy loss measures the difference between $\hat{Y}$ and the one-hot ground truth Y:

$$\text{CE}(Y, \hat{Y}) = -\sum_{i=1}^{N}\sum_{c=1}^{C} Y_{i,c} \log(\hat{Y}_{i,c}),$$

where N is the number of pixels and C the number of classes. The combined loss is

$$\mathcal{L}_{\text{seg}} = (1 - \text{Dice}(Y, \hat{Y})) + \text{CE}(Y, \hat{Y}) \tag{1}$$

In the multi-task setup, the model jointly performs tooth-level, quadrant, and binary segmentation. The total loss is

$$\mathcal{L}_{\text{total}} = \alpha\,\mathcal{L}_{\text{tooth}} + \beta\,\mathcal{L}_{\text{quadrant}} + \gamma\,\mathcal{L}_{\text{binary}} \tag{2}$$

where $\alpha = 0.6$, $\beta = 0.2$, and $\gamma = 0.2$. Joint training enables feature sharing and captures anatomical correlations, improving generalization and robustness.

6 Results

The STL model was trained with SegFormer-B5 for individual tooth (enumeration) segmentation, where each tooth is uniquely labeled using the FDI system (32 classes + background). Performance is evaluated using per-tooth Dice scores to capture variability across incisors, premolars, and molars, enabling detailed assessment of segmentation quality across the dental arch. Figure 2 illustrates a visual example of per-tooth segmentation predictions produced by the STL model. Table 1 presents the detailed Dice scores achieved by the STL model for each individual tooth on the test set, highlighting the relative difficulty of segmenting posterior teeth due to occlusion and lower image contrast.

To evaluate the impact MTL on individual teeth segmentation, we compare the STL baseline against two MTL configurations trained under identical conditions. Both MTL setups simultaneously learn three tasks: individual tooth segmentation, quadrant segmentation, and binary teeth segmentation. This joint learning setup encourages the model to leverage shared anatomical structure and improve generalization. Table 2 summarizes the average Dice scores achieved for

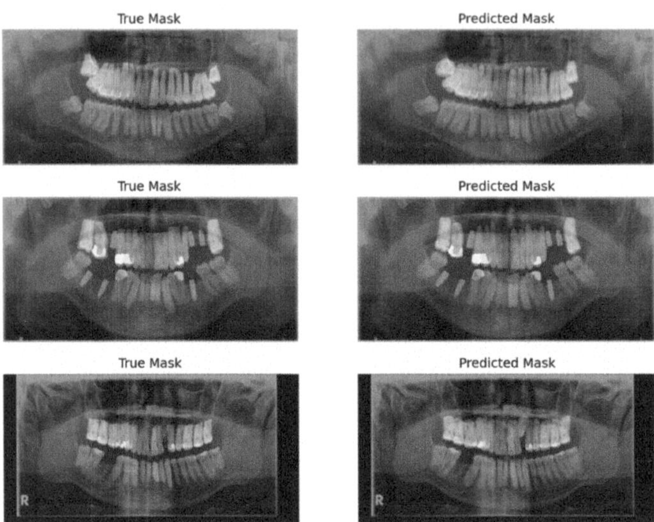

Fig. 2. Example output from the STL model on the tooth enumeration task, showing predictions versus ground truth across tooth regions.

Table 1. Per-class Dice Similarity Coefficient (DSC) for individual tooth segmentation using the STL baseline model.

Tooth Name	Dice Score	Tooth Name	Dice Score
Upper Right Central Incisor	0.84	Lower Left Central Incisor	0.82
Upper Right Lateral Incisor	0.79	Lower Left Lateral Incisor	0.83
Upper Right Canine	0.75	Lower Left Canine	0.84
Upper Right First Premolar	0.70	Lower Left First Premolar	0.83
Upper Right Second Premolar	0.68	Lower Left Second Premolar	0.83
Upper Right First Molar	0.72	Lower Left First Molar	0.86
Upper Right Second Molar	0.75	Lower Left Second Molar	0.85
Upper Right Third Molar	0.71	Lower Left Third Molar	0.82
Upper Left Central Incisor	0.84	Lower Right Central Incisor	0.81
Upper Left Lateral Incisor	0.80	Lower Right Lateral Incisor	0.82
Upper Left Canine	0.77	Lower Right Canine	0.83
Upper Left First Premolar	0.71	Lower Right First Premolar	0.80
Upper Left Second Premolar	0.75	Lower Right Second Premolar	0.80
Upper Left First Molar	0.79	Lower Right First Molar	0.83
Upper Left Second Molar	0.76	Lower Right Second Molar	0.85
Upper Left Third Molar	0.73	Lower Right Third Molar	0.85

Table 2. Average Dice scores for three segmentation tasks (individual tooth, quadrant, and binary) across STL and MTL configurations.

Technique	Teeth Segmentation	Quadrant Segmentation	Teeth Binary Segmentation
SegFormer (STL)	0.775	0.937	0.938
SegFormer (MTL-MD)	0.785	0.941	0.938
SegFormer (MTL-MH)	**0.786**	**0.942**	**0.940**

each task across the different model configurations. The results demonstrate that both MTL variants outperform STL in terms of average Dice scores, with MTL-MH consistently achieving the highest accuracy. This suggests that using shared encoder–decoder representations while separating the prediction heads allows each task to learn task-specific features, while still benefiting from the shared global anatomical context.

7 Discussion

The experimental results clearly demonstrate the advantages of MTL over STL for dental panoramic image analysis. Most notably, individual teeth segmentation, which is the primary task in this study, benefited significantly from auxiliary supervision. The Dice for teeth segmentation improved from 0.775 with STL to 0.786 when applying an MTL setup with three task-specific heads. This confirms that jointly learning related anatomical tasks can provide richer feature representations, leading to enhanced primary task performance. For individual tooth segmentation, the STL SegFormer model achieved a Dice of 0.775. This increased to 0.785 with MTL-MD and slightly higher to 0.786 with MTL-MH. Although the performance gain is modest (approximately 1.1% relative improvement), the improvement is consistent across configurations, supporting the hypothesis that auxiliary supervision from quadrant and binary segmentation tasks helps reinforce spatial and anatomical priors. In the quadrant segmentation task, performance improved from 0.937 (STL) to 0.941 (MTL-MD) and 0.942 (MTL-MH). For binary teeth segmentation, both STL and MTL-MD achieved 0.938, while MTL-MH slightly outperformed with a Dice score of 0.940. These gains highlight that even coarse and binary tasks, when jointly optimized, can offer complementary learning signals that benefit more complex segmentation objectives. Notably, the MTL-MH configuration achieved the best performance overall while using fewer parameters than MTL-MD. This is particularly relevant in the context of the DENTEX dataset, which is relatively small, making parameter efficiency and regularization critical for generalization. The shared decoder in MTL-MH encourages tighter coupling across tasks and reduces overfitting risk, which may explain its slight edge in performance. In summary, both MTL configurations clearly outperform the STL baseline, validating the design choice to integrate auxiliary segmentation objectives. Between the two, MTL-MH offers a compelling trade-off: it provides consistent performance improvements while maintaining architectural simplicity and lower computational overhead making it especially suitable for applications involving limited data and deployment constraints.

References

1. Cao, H., et al.: Swin-Unet: Unet-Like Pure Transformer for Medical Image Segmentation, p. 205–218. Springer Nature Switzerland (2023). https://doi.org/10.1007/978-3-031-25066-8_9
2. Caruana, R.: Multitask learning. Mach. Learn. **28**(1), 41–75 (1997). https://doi.org/10.1023/a:1007379606734
3. Chen, H., Qi, X., Yu, L., Heng, P.A.: Dcan: deep contour-aware networks for accurate gland segmentation (2016). https://doi.org/10.48550/ARXIV.1604.02677
4. Chen, H., et al.: A deep learning approach to automatic teeth detection and numbering based on object detection in dental periapical films. Sci. Rep. **9**(1) (2019). https://doi.org/10.1038/s41598-019-40414-y
5. Chen, J., et al.: Transunet: transformers make strong encoders for medical image segmentation (2021). https://doi.org/10.48550/ARXIV.2102.04306
6. Hamamci, I.E., et al.: Dentex: an abnormal tooth detection with dental enumeration and diagnosis benchmark for panoramic x-rays. arXiv preprint arXiv:2305.19112 (2023)
7. Khaldi, A., Khaldi, B., Aiadi, O.: Lcat-net: lightweight context-aware deep learning approach for teeth segmentation in panoramic x-rays. Int. J. Comput. Intell. Syst. **17**(1) (2024).https://doi.org/10.1007/s44196-024-00703-5
8. Lee, J.H., Han, S.S., Kim, Y.H., Lee, C., Kim, I.: Application of a fully deep convolutional neural network to the automation of tooth segmentation on panoramic radiographs. Oral Surg Oral Med Oral Pathol Oral Radiol **129**(6), 635–642 (2020)
9. Loshchilov, I., Hutter, F.: Decoupled weight decay regularization (2017). https://doi.org/10.48550/ARXIV.1711.05101
10. Oktay, O., et al.: Anatomically constrained neural networks (ACNNS): application to cardiac image enhancement and segmentation. IEEE Trans. Med. Imaging **37**(2), 384–395 (2018). https://doi.org/10.1109/TMI.2017.2743464
11. Ruder, S.: An overview of multi-task learning in deep neural networks (2017). https://doi.org/10.48550/ARXIV.1706.05098
12. Tuzoff, D.V., Tuzova, L.N., Bornstein, M.M., Krasnov, A.S., Kharchenko, M.A., Nikolenko, S.I., Sveshnikov, M.M., Bednenko, G.B.: Tooth detection and numbering in panoramic radiographs using convolutional neural networks. Dentomaxillofacial Radiology **48**(4), 20180051 (2019)
13. Xie, E., Wang, W., Yu, Z., Anandkumar, A., Alvarez, J.M., Luo, P.: Segformer: Simple and efficient design for semantic segmentation with transformers. In: Ranzato, M., Beygelzimer, A., Dauphin, Y., Liang, P., Vaughan, J.W. (eds.) Advances in Neural Information Processing Systems. vol. 34, pp. 12077–12090. Curran Associates, Inc. (2021). https://proceedings.neurips.cc/paper_files/paper/2021/file/64f1f27bf1b4ec22924fd0acb550c235-Paper.pdf
14. Zhang, Y., Yang, Q.: A survey on multi-task learning (2017). https://doi.org/10.48550/ARXIV.1707.08114
15. Zhao, Y., Wang, X., Che, T., Bao, G., Li, S.: Multi-task deep learning for medical image computing and analysis: a review. Comput. Biol. Med. **153**, 106496 (2023)
16. Zhao, Y., et al.: Tsasnet: tooth segmentation on dental panoramic x-ray images by two-stage attention segmentation network. Knowledge-Based Syst. **206**, 106338 (2020). https://doi.org/10.1016/j.knosys.2020.106338

MARCADE: A Framework for Architecting Resilient and Intelligent Cloud-Native Applications

Mohamed Abdelghafar Talbi[1], Alaa Eddine Leguefche[1], Meriem Belguidoum[1(✉)], and Abdelhack-Djamel Seriai[2]

[1] Faculty of New Technologies of Information and Communication (NTIC), University Constantine 2 Abdelhamid Mehri, Constantine, Algeria
{mohamed.talbi,alaa.leguefche,meriem.belguidoum}@univ-constantine2.dz
[2] University of Montpellier, the LIRMM Laboratory, Montpellier, France
abdelhak.seriai@lirmm.fr

Abstract. While cloud-native technologies offer a clear path to modernizing legacy systems, many organizations struggle to architect applications that are simultaneously resilient, scalable, and intelligent, largely due to a lack of holistic frameworks. This paper introduces MARCADE (A Microservice Architecture for Resilient, Cloud-native, AI-driven, and DevOps-Enabled ecosystems), a novel architectural framework designed to address this challenge. It provides a prescriptive blueprint founded on three synergistic principles: a microservice architecture for fault isolation, a secure pattern for integrating LLM-driven assistants, and a cloud-native DevOps foundation for continuous delivery and automated recovery. We demonstrate the framework's feasibility through a proof-of-concept implementation of a complex real estate platform. Our architectural analysis confirms that MARCADE serves as a practical, domain-agnostic guide for building the next generation of robust enterprise software.

Keywords: Software Architecture · Microservices · Fault Tolerance · Large Language Model (LLM) · DevOps · Cloud-Native · Agile Development · PropTech

1 Introduction

Many economic sectors, from finance to real estate, are constrained by legacy enterprise systems. Built on monolithic architectures, these systems carry significant technical debt, making them brittle, hard to scale, and risky to update. This creates an urgent need for a modern architectural paradigm to enable flexible, scalable, and resilient cloud-native applications.

While the core building blocks microservices, cloud platforms, and DevOps practices are mature, a holistic framework synthesizing them remains lacking. In particular, organizations need models that deliver not only resilience to technical

A. Awad et al. (Eds.): MEDI 2025, LNCS 16427, pp. 207–220, 2026.
https://doi.org/10.1007/978-3-032-19865-5_17

failures but also intelligence to automate complex operational tasks. Current approaches often force a trade-off between robustness and advanced AI-driven functionality.

This paper introduces the MARCADE framework (A Microservice Architecture for Resilient, Cloud-native, AI-driven, and DevOps-Enabled ecosystems). MARCADE provides a prescriptive blueprint grounded in three principles: (i) microservice architecture for scalability and fault isolation; (ii) a secure pattern for integrating Large Language Model (LLM) assistants; and (iii) a cloud-native DevOps foundation enabling continuous delivery and automated recovery.

To validate the framework, we implemented a proof-of-concept: a complex software platform for the real estate sector, an industry emblematic of fragmentation and legacy technology. Agile Scrum was adopted to manage the complexity of applying this new architecture and to ensure a faithful validation of its principles.

The real estate industry provides an ideal testbed, as it is undergoing a shift toward rental housing while many agencies still rely on fragmented tools and manual processes. This clear need for integrated, scalable, and automated solutions makes it well-suited for demonstrating the MARCADE framework's practical value.

The primary contributions of this paper are:

- Formalization of the MARCADE framework as a reusable reference architecture for resilient, intelligent cloud-native applications.
- A secure, reusable pattern for integrating LLM-powered assistants into enterprise workflows.
- A qualitative architectural analysis, based on our proof-of-concept, demonstrating how MARCADE supports resilience, scalability, and agility.

The rest of the paper is organized as follows. Section 2 presents background on microservices, DevOps, and AI. Section 3 defines the MARCADE framework. Section 4 describes the case study implementation. Section 5 provides validation and analysis, and Sect. 6 concludes with future work.

2 Background

The MARCADE framework is built upon the convergence of three trends in software engineering: the shift to modular architectures, the adoption of agile operational practices, and the integration of artificial intelligence. This section provides the background on these pillars to contextualize the challenges MARCADE aims to address.

2.1 Microservices Architecture

The shift from monolithic to microservices architectures is driven by the need for scalability and flexibility. This approach decomposes applications into independently deployable services but depends on two factors: effective service decomposition (often by business capability) and a communication strategy that balances synchronous and asynchronous patterns for fault tolerance. MARCADE embeds solutions to these challenges as a core part of its design.

In summary, microservices deliver major benefits, but their success relies on precise decomposition and communication design—principles central to the MARCADE framework [7].

2.2 DevOps

DevOps [11] emerged to bridge the traditional gap between development and operations, automating the application lifecycle to enable high-velocity software delivery without sacrificing stability. Core practices such as Infrastructure-as-Code (IaC), Continuous Integration and Continuous Delivery (CI/CD), and comprehensive monitoring are central to this approach. By emphasizing shared responsibility and automation, DevOps provides the operational foundation required for scalable, cloud-native systems [2], making it a fundamental pillar of the MARCADE framework.

2.3 AI-Enhanced Enterprise Systems

The emergence of Large Language Models (LLMs) marks a turning point for enterprise systems [12]. A key innovation is tool calling, which transforms LLMs from simple text generators into active orchestrators that can interact with APIs, databases, and enterprise workflows. While other methods like RAG or fine-tuning enhance an LLM's knowledge, tool calling is what allows it to take direct, executable actions [4]. This ability to embed adaptive, intelligent agents directly into operational processes is a core principle of the MARCADE framework.

3 The MARCADE Framework

The MARCADE framework is a prescriptive architectural blueprint designed to guide the development of robust, scalable, and intelligent enterprise applications. It provides a reusable and well-defined structure that allows development teams to focus on delivering business value rather than reinventing foundational infrastructure. MARCADE is built upon three core pillars: a microservice-based architecture, a secure pattern for AI integration, and a DevOps and cloud-native foundation.

3.1 A Layered MSA Foundation

The foundation of MARCADE is a Microservice Architecture (MSA) where the system is decomposed by business capabilities [9]. This architectural choice is a direct response to the limitations of monolithic systems; by breaking down a large application into a collection of smaller, independent services, we gain significant advantages in agility, scalability, and resilience. This approach ensures a design that is modular and aligned with the business domain. The architecture is organized into the following logical layers (see Fig. 1):

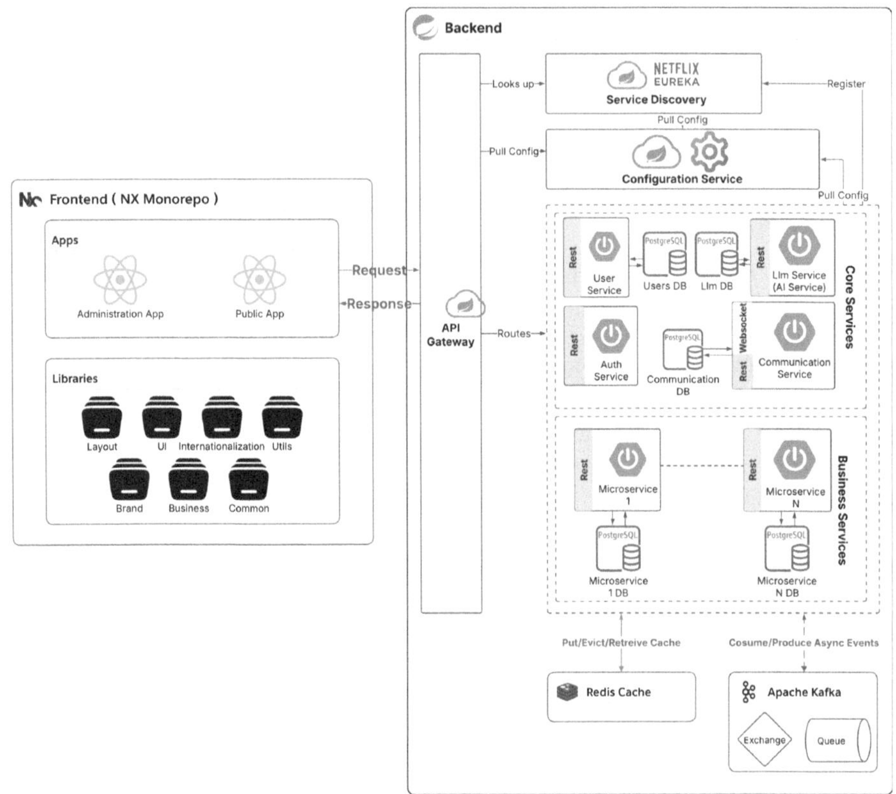

Fig. 1. Architecture of the MARCADE framework.

- **Presentation Layer (Frontend)**: Provides user-facing interfaces through specialized client applications (e.g., a public portal and an admin portal). This layer is fully decoupled from the backend, communicating only through the API Gateway, which allows for independent development cycles.
- **Infrastructure Layer**: This layer forms the system's backbone by providing cross-cutting, reusable components that ensure reliability and performance. Key components include:
  - **API Gateway**: A single, secure entry point for all client requests that handles routing, load balancing, and security enforcement.
  - **Service Discovery**: Enables dynamic registration and discovery of microservices, improving system elasticity and fault tolerance.
  - **Configuration Service**: Manages centralized configuration across all environments to maintain consistency.
  - **Redis Cache**: Provides high-performance, in-memory data storage used for caching frequently accessed information, thereby reducing database load and improving response times.

  - **Apache Kafka**: Serves as the event streaming platform for asynchronous, event-driven communication between microservices, enhancing decoupling and resilience.
- **Application & Domain Layer (Backend Microservices)**: Encapsulates business and application logic within independently deployable microservices. Each service is aligned with a specific business capability (e.g., Authentication, User, Property) and maintains its own database. Microservices communicate both synchronously via RESTful APIs and asynchronously through Apache Kafka event streams. This hybrid model improves scalability, decoupling, and fault tolerance, ensuring system resilience even when individual components fail.

3.2 Argia: The Intelligent Automation Layer

MARCADE integrates intelligent automation as a core component of the operational workflow. As depicted in Fig. 2, this layer is designed to embed an AI assistant (named "Argia") without compromising the security and modularity of the microservice architecture. The entire design is built upon two fundamental security principles:

- Secure Tool-Calling: The AI assistant has no direct data access. It operates by invoking a predefined set of secure API functions ("tools"), ensuring all actions are authorized and auditable.
- Authenticated Context: Every request is authenticated with the user's JWT, guaranteeing the AI operates with the exact same security permissions as the user and preventing privilege escalation.

The practical application of these principles is illustrated in the request-response workflow shown in Fig. 2. When an administrator submits a query:

1. The request is routed through the Gateway Service to the AI Service, which is built with the Spring AI framework.
2. The AI Service constructs a prompt, enriching the user's query with conversational history from its Chat Memory.
3. It determines that an external "tool' is needed to answer the request.
4. It invokes the appropriate tool (e.g., an API call to another microservice), injecting the user's JWT to ensure the action is authenticated and authorized.
5. The external tool processes the request and returns structured data to the AI Service.
6. The AI Service sends this data, along with the prompt, to the LLM (in our case, the Groq API using the deepseek-r1-distill-llama-70b model).
7. The LLM generates a natural language response, which is then streamed back through the services to the user's interface for a real-time interaction.

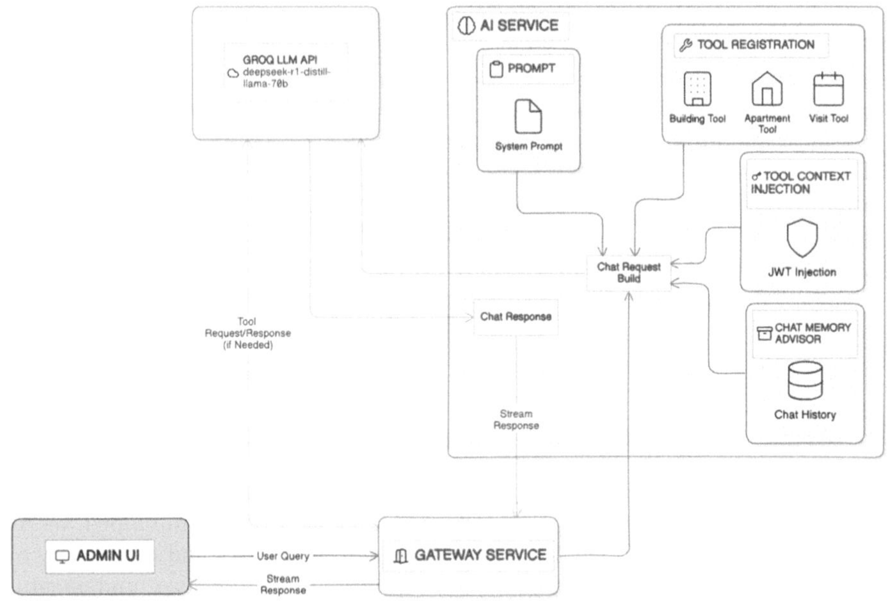

Fig. 2. Argia AI System Architecture.

3.3 DevOps and Cloud-Native Foundation

Figure 3 illustrates the deployment architecture of the MARCADE framework on Amazon Web Services (AWS), showcasing how the framework's principles of security, automation, and resilience are implemented in practice. This architecture is composed of a secure, reproducible network foundation and an automated CI/CD workflow.

Secure Network Foundation (The VPC): The core infrastructure resides within an Amazon Virtual Private Cloud (VPC), which is strategically segmented into two distinct zones for security:

- **The Public Subnet:** This layer contains internet-facing components, including the Elastic Load Balancers for the frontend applications and an EC2 for secure administrative access.
- **The Private Subnet:** Isolated from direct internet access, this secure layer houses the entire Backend Cluster, which is orchestrated by Amazon Elastic Kubernetes Service (EKS). All backend microservices, databases (PostgreSQL, Redis, Kafka), and the complete operational toolchain (Jenkins, SonarQube, and the Observability Stack of Prometheus, Grafana, Jaeger) reside here.

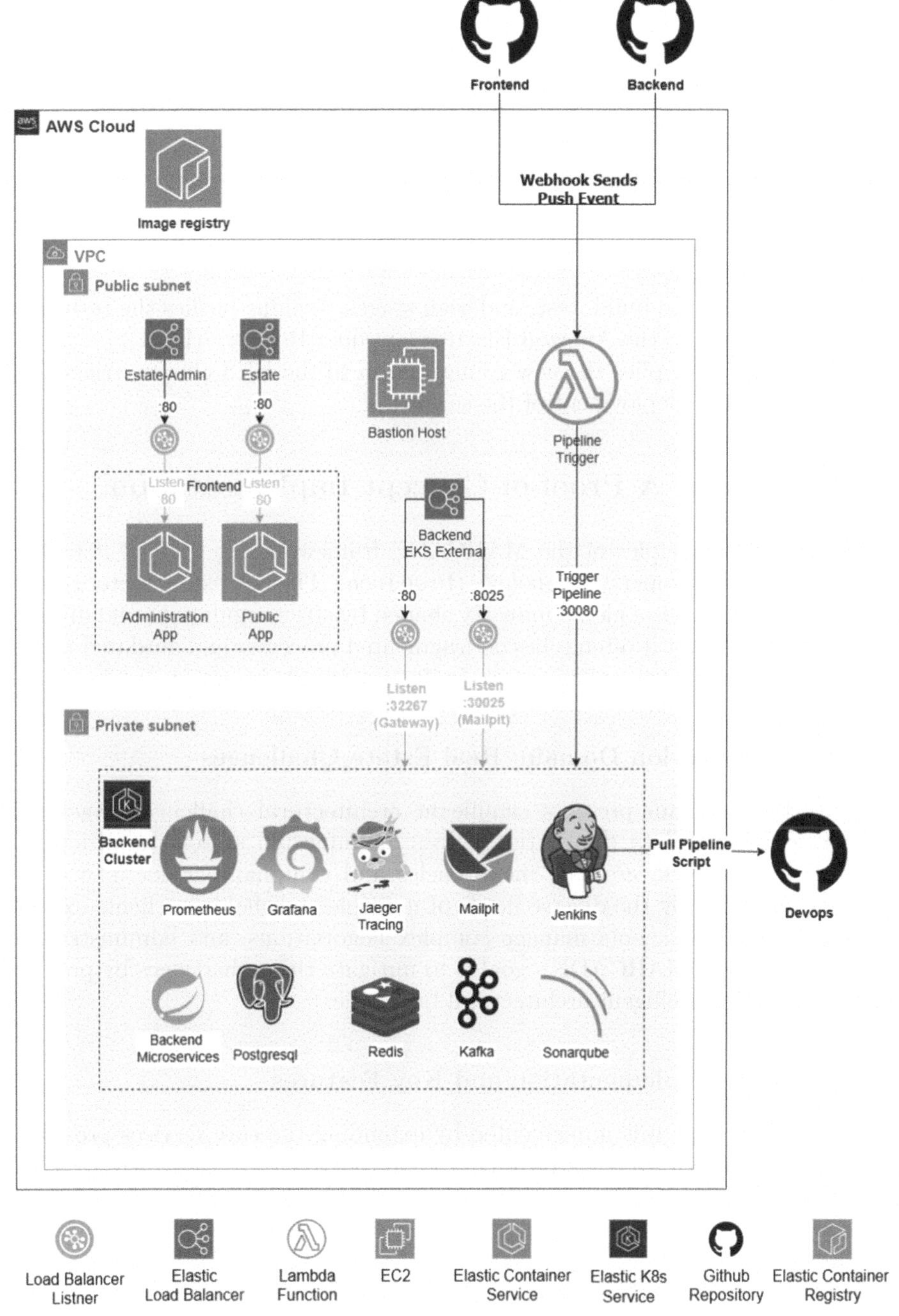

Fig. 3. Deployment Architecture of MARCADE on AWS.

The Automated CI/CD Workflow: The diagram also depicts the flow of an automated deployment, which is central to the framework's DevOps principles:

1. The process begins when a developer pushes code to a GitHub repository (either Frontend or Backend).
2. A configured webhook sends a push event, which triggers an AWS Lambda function ("Pipeline Trigger").
3. The Lambda function initiates a build job on the Jenkins server, which resides in the private subnet.
4. Jenkins then pulls the necessary pipeline script from the dedicated Devops GitHub repository.
5. After executing the build, test, and scan stages, Jenkins pushes the resulting container image to the Amazon Elastic Container Registry (ECR).
6. Finally, Jenkins applies the new configuration to the EKS cluster, triggering a zero-downtime deployment of the service.

4 Case Study: A Proof-of-Concept Implementation

To validate the principles of the MARCADE framework, we applied it to the complex domain of property technology (PropTech). The real estate sector serves as an ideal testbed: it is a global industry shaped by strict regulations and diverse stakeholder needs, yet it often relies on fragmented processes and outdated tools. This section describes the platform we built as a proof-of-concept.

4.1 The Application Domain: Real Estate Challenges

The PropTech domain presents significant architectural challenges. Agencies often struggle with data duplication across disconnected systems and depend on manual paperwork, creating inefficiencies and compliance risks. The complexity is amplified by the diverse needs of multiple stakeholders: clients expect transparent listings, agents manage complex negotiations, and administrators oversee operations. MARCADE's goal is to mitigate these challenges by providing a unified and intelligent architectural backbone.

4.2 Platform Implementation and Key Features

Our proof-of-concept was implemented by extending the core services provided by the MARCADE framework (authentication, notifications, AI assistant) with domain-specific microservices for real estate. The development, guided by an Agile process, introduced business-oriented features in several phases, summarized in Table 1.

The result of this implementation is a unified PropTech platform that consolidates property management, tenant engagement, and regulatory compliance into a single, coherent ecosystem, directly demonstrating the feasibility of the MARCADE framework.

Table 1. Key Features of the Real Estate Platform built on MARCADE

Feature Category	Key Functionalities Implemented
Workflow Automation	Visit scheduling, automated lease generation, digital consent handling
Real Estate Services	Advanced property search (map & filters), rental applications, tenant-landlord communication channels
Service Integration	Maintenance requests, service provider matching, and task tracking
Administration & Compliance	Electronic signatures, comprehensive audit history, and regulatory traceability features

4.3 System Architecture

Our platform builds upon the MARCADE framework, as depicted in Fig. 1 and detailed in Sect. 3, by adding domain-specific microservices for real estate. This integration preserves the framework's core benefits of scalability and resilience while adapting it to the specific needs of the real estate domain.

Frontend Architecture. Our frontend implementation adheres to MARCADE's decoupled architecture, communicating via the API Gateway. We adapted the UI/UX for the real estate domain with specific workflows and visualization components, ensuring independent development cycles while delivering a tailored user experience.

Backend Architecture. The backend extends the MARCADE framework's foundational services with domain-specific microservices aligned with real estate business capabilities. Each service is independently deployable and follows the framework's prescribed patterns for service decomposition.

- **Properties Service**: Manages all data related to property listings, including details, images, availability, and supports advanced, map-based search capabilities.
- **Pre-Rental Service**: Orchestrates the entire tenant acquisition workflow, from handling initial inquiries and scheduling property visits to processing rental applications.
- **Rental Service**: Handles all operations for active tenancies, including lease management, maintenance request coordination, and tenant-landlord communication.

Service Architecture Patterns. Each domain service was implemented following MARCADE's core architectural patterns: employing a database-per-service for data isolation, RESTful APIs for synchronous requests, and an event-driven model using Apache Kafka for asynchronous communication.

The AI Assistant. The Argia service was implemented using the Spring AI library, which abstracts the complexity of interacting with different Large Language Models. The implementation described in Sect. 3.2 proves that the framework can support complex AI-driven workflows without compromising the security and modularity of the microservice architecture.

4.4 DevOps in Practice and AWS Infrastructure

To operationalize the MARCADE framework as defined in Sect. 3.3, we implemented a complete DevOps toolchain and deployed the platform on Amazon Web Services (AWS). This practical setup serves as a concrete validation of the framework's principles.

As illustrated in Fig. 4, our automation is driven by a Jenkins CI/CD pipeline that orchestrates the entire workflow from code commit to a zero-downtime deployment. Triggered by a GitHub webhook, the pipeline executes a series of automated stages: it builds container images, runs tests, and performs a static code analysis with SonarQube. Only builds that successfully pass these quality gates are automatically deployed to the Amazon EKS cluster.

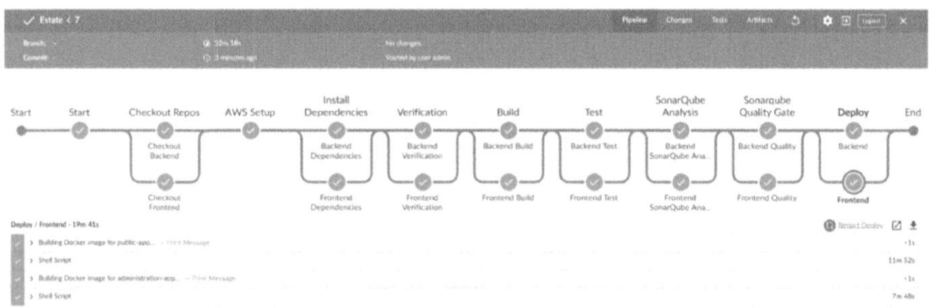

Fig. 4. Jenkins CI/CD pipeline execution.

To ensure a consistent and reproducible environment, the entire underlying infrastructure is provisioned using Infrastructure-as-Code (IaC) with Terraform. This approach minimizes configuration drift and allows our cloud environment to be version-controlled alongside the application code. For operational visibility, a comprehensive observability stack was implemented. Prometheus collects real-time metrics, Grafana provides visualization through dashboards, and Jaeger enables distributed tracing of requests across microservices. Together, these tools provide the deep insight needed for proactive monitoring and rapid issue resolution.

Overall, our implementation demonstrates a cohesive DevOps ecosystem where automation, quality enforcement, and reproducibility work in concert to create a secure and resilient cloud environment.

5 Framework Validation and Analysis

This section validates the MARCADE framework through a two-part analysis. First, we present a qualitative analysis of our proof-of-concept, focusing on its architectural quality and operational readiness. We demonstrate how the framework's principles translate into a high-quality, maintainable system. Second, we conduct a comparative analysis against existing platforms to position MARCADE's contribution within the broader industry landscape.

5.1 Architectural and Operational Validation Metrics

Our validation confirms that MARCADE's architectural principles translate directly into a high-quality, maintainable, and operationally sound system. The key findings, gathered over a 30-day observation period following deployment to AWS. Table 2 summarizes the key validation metrics across multiple dimensions.

Table 2. Key Validation Metrics for the MARCADE Implementation.

Quality Attribute	Key Metric	Result	Validation Method
Code Quality	SonarQube Maintainability Grade	A (Backend & Frontend)	Static Code Analysis
Security Posture	Critical Vulnerabilities Detected	0	Automated CI/CD Security Scanning
Deployment Reliability	CI/CD Pipeline Success Rate	100% (over 15 deployments)	Jenkins Pipeline Monitoring
Operational Resilience	Service Availability	Consistent (zero downtime)	Kubernetes (EKS) Health Monitoring
Infrastructure Automation	Provisioning Method	100% IaC (Terraform)	Code Review & Deployment Tracking

These metrics provide concrete evidence for the framework's claims. The A-grade maintainability rating from SonarQube across a large codebase ($\tilde{5}0{,}000$ LOC) is a direct outcome of the framework's principle of decomposition by business capability. The 100% success rate of our CI/CD pipeline over 15 deployments demonstrates a mature delivery model that mitigates deployment risk. Most critically, the consistent service availability and successful automatic recovery from simulated failures on Amazon EKS validate the framework's core resilience claim. Finally, the detection of zero critical vulnerabilities confirms that the framework's "template-driven" approach effectively embeds security by design.

5.2 Discussion of Architectural Principles and Effectiveness

While the metrics in Table 2 provide quantitative evidence, a deeper validation emerges from examining how they demonstrate the successful realization of the framework's core architectural principles.

1. **Architectural Modularity:** The "A" maintainability rating and low code duplication (2.6% in the backend) from SonarQube reflect the framework's modular design, achieved through 16 independent microservices. The 100% deployment success rate further confirms effective service decoupling that prevents cascading failures during updates.

2. **DevOps Integration and Agility:** The CI/CD pipeline's maturity was demonstrated by 15 automated deployments, while full Infrastructure-as-Code coverage with Terraform ensured a consistent and reproducible environment. These outcomes highlight MARCADE's ability to support rapid and reliable system evolution.
3. **Secure AI Integration:** The JWT-based tool-calling mechanism confines AI operations to the user's authenticated context, minimizing exposure. Security scans reported zero critical vulnerabilities, validating the framework's secure AI integration pattern.
4. **Domain-Specific Applicability:** The deployment of a feature-rich real estate platform demonstrated the framework's adaptability. The clear separation of domain-agnostic and domain-specific services reinforces MARCADE's role as a reusable blueprint for enterprise systems.

5.3 Positioning and Comparative Analysis

To situate MARCADE's contribution, we conducted a comparative analysis of our integrated approach against existing specialized platforms in the PropTech domain.

Table 3. Service coverage and AI features comparison.

Platform	Type of Service			AI Tools
	Listings	Long-Term Rentals	Tenancy Management	
Zillow	✓	✓	✗	✓
Airbnb	✓	✗	✗	✗
Realtor	✓	✓	✗	✓
BlocSolutions	✗	✗	✓	✗
MiPropertyPortal	✗	✗	✓	✗
Sibelanger	✓	✓	✗	✗
MSI	✓	✓	✗	✗
MARCADE	✓	✓	✓	✓

As illustrated in Table 3, the digital real estate landscape is highly fragmented. Global platforms like Zillow [13], Airbnb [1] and Realtor [8] focus on market reach (listings) and rental services, but lack deep operational capabilities for managing tenancies which limits their ability to support the full rental lifecycle.

Conversely, specialized platforms like BlocSolutions [3] and MiPropertyPortal [5] excel at tenancy management but offer no integrated listing or marketing features. This fragmentation forces agencies and users to rely on multiple disconnected tools, leading to operational inefficiencies and data silos. Similarly,

Sibelanger [10] and MSI [6] offer property listings and long-term rentals, yet they lack both AI-driven augmentation and integrated management functionalities.

The MARCADE framework directly addresses the market gap created by these fragmented solutions. It provides a blueprint for a unified platform that integrates all four key dimensions: listings, rentals, tenancy management, and AI-driven features. This holistic approach reduces administrative overhead, eliminates the need for third-party services, and creates a seamless, intelligent ecosystem for all stakeholders.

6 Conclusion and Future Work

This paper introduced the MARCADE framework, a novel architectural blueprint designed to guide the development of resilient and intelligent cloud-native applications. Our work addresses a critical gap in enterprise architecture by providing a holistic model that unifies three key pillars: a microservice foundation for resilience, a secure pattern for LLM integration, and a modern DevOps and cloud-native operations model. Through the implementation of a complex real estate platform, we have successfully validated the framework's feasibility and architectural integrity.

While this paper validates the framework's architectural feasibility, we acknowledge several limitations that also define our roadmap for future research.

The primary limitation is the qualitative nature of our analysis. Future work will focus on quantitative studies, including large-scale performance tests and Chaos Engineering, to formally measure the framework's scalability and fault tolerance. A second priority is cross-domain validation; applying MARCADE to other sectors like FinTech or HealthTech is necessary to empirically confirm its domain-agnostic claims.

Finally, we plan to extend the framework by advancing its AI integration with predictive analytics and by enhancing its security model with a full zero-trust architecture.

References

1. Airbnb: Airbnb vacation rentals, cabins, beach houses, & more (2025). https://www.airbnb.com. Accessed: 2025-04-25
2. Bass, L., Weber, I., Zhu, L.: DevOps: A Software Architect's Perspective. Addison-Wesley Professional (2015)
3. BlocSolutions: Blocsolutions digital rental management platform (2025). https://www.bloc.solutions. Accessed: 2025-04-25
4. McKinsey and Company: the state of AI in early 2024: Gen AI adoption spikes and starts to generate value (2024). https://www.mckinsey.com/capabilities/quantumblack/our-insights/the-state-of-ai. Accessed: 2025-03-06
5. Mi Property Portal: Mipropertyportal property management software (2025). https://www.mipropertyportal.com. Accessed: 2025-04-25

6. MSI: MSI real estate management platform (2025). https://msimmobiliers.com/. Accessed: 2025-04-25
7. O'Reilly Media: Microservices adoption in 2020 (2020). http://oreilly.com/pub/pr/3307. Accessed: 2025-03-06
8. Realtor: Realtor.ca real estate listings in Canada (2025). https://www.realtor.ca. Accessed: 2025-04-25
9. Richardson, C.: Chapter 2: Decomposition Strategies. Simon and Schuster, New York (2018)
10. Sibelanger: Sibelanger real estate platform (2025). https://www.sibelanger.com, accessed: 2025-04-25
11. Soni, M.: DevOps for Web Development. Packt Publishing Ltd (2016)
12. Vaswani, A., et al.: Attention is all you need. Adv. Neural Inf. Process. Syst. **30** (2017)
13. Zillow: Zillow real estate platform (2025). https://www.zillow.com. Accessed: 2025-04-25

Multi Objective Analysis of Urban Food Insecurity and Hunger

Kuruvilla Joseph Abraham[1](✉), Dirce Maria Lobo Marchoni[2], Antonio Mauro Saraiva[3], and Alexandre Claudio Botazzo Delbem[1]

[1] Institute of Mathematical Sciences and Computation, University of São Paulo, São Carlos, Brazil
abraham@fmrp.usp.br, acbd@icmc.usp.br

[2] Department of Nutrition, School of Public Health, University of São Paulo, São Paulo, Brazil
marchioni@usp.br

[3] Department of Computer Engineering and Digital Systems, Polytechnic School, University of São Paulo, São Paulo, Brazil
saraiva@usp.br

Abstract. In this paper we use publicly available socioeconomic data from the Greater São Paulo region in Brazil to implement a multi objective analysis in order to rank socio economic risk factors relevant for Food Insecurity and Hunger. The data we use are based exclusively on regional aggregates and not on individual households as in previous studies. The datasets used have differing characteristics, hence consistently combining the available data into a single dataset and checking the consistency is not straightforward. Novel methods to address this question will be presented. Next we will infer a Bayesian Network using techniques well established in bioinformatics. Due to the limited size of the available data the application of standard methods leads to inferred networks that are potentially unreliable. In order to circumvent this problem, feature selection will be implemented via an analysis of Pareto Corners. This method is statistical in nature and is valid even when there is no explicit parametric form for the objective functions, as is the case of the data we analyze.

Keywords: Multi Objective Optimization · Bayesian Network · Food Insecurity

1 Introduction and Motivation

Socio economic data is routinely collected from many regions of the world and techniques from Artificial Intelligence and Machine Learning have been successfully applied to these data to determine risk factors for Food Insecurity and Hunger [1]. In this paper we analyze data from urban sub regions of the Greater São Paulo Region of Brazil to identify these risk factors, in contrast to earlier studies in Brazilian populations which have used households as sampling units

A. Awad et al. (Eds.): MEDI 2025, LNCS 16427, pp. 221–229, 2026.
https://doi.org/10.1007/978-3-032-19865-5_18

[2]. Our approach may facilitate the identification of a broader class of risk factors and possible interventions. The choice of sampling unit means that very much less data is available compared with previous studies, leading to problems associated with sparsity. We demonstrate how a multi objective analysis could be implemented in light of these difficulties. We make extensive use of Bayesian Networks as their utility has been suggested in Multi Objective Optimization [3], and for the anlysis of possible causal interventions.

The data sets we use come from different sources such as the Brazilian Institute of Geography and Statistics (IBGE, www.ibge.gov.br/) the Annual Report on Social Services (RAIS) maintained by the Brazilian Ministry of Labour and Employment, and the State System for the Analysis of Data (seade.gov.br), and have differing characteristics. The features included pertain to income, education and access to grocery stores. Combining different datasets coherently presents challenges which will be first discussed.

1.1 Data Processing and Fusion

The data consist of features defined over 96 regions with varying populations in the greater São Paulo metropolitan area. These 96 regions are divided into different numbers of census districts, varying from from 28 to 609, with 18363 census districts in total. There are some features which are defined by a unique value in each region, while others have a unique value for each census district. After dropping features with ambiguous values and which show little variability, our final data consists of two data frames, one with 96 rows and 28 columns, and the other with 18363 rows and 13 columns. This discrepancy complicates the use of common methods in Machine Learning [4] for comparing distances, and is the motivation to equalize the number of rows in both data frames via data aggregation. First, we establish some useful notation.

Let $\{\widetilde{V}\} = \{\widetilde{V_1}, \widetilde{V_2}, \ldots \widetilde{V_{13}}\}$ be the set of features defined for each census sector. Let V_i denote the vector of values of feature $\widetilde{V_i}$. If we denote by V the combination of all the vectors V_i then we can write

$$V = \left[V_1 \,| V_2 \,| V_3 \,| \ldots | \, V_{13} \right] \tag{1}$$

where $V_i \in \mathbb{R}^{18363 \times 1}$ and $V \in \mathbb{R}^{18363 \times 13}$. Let V_i^j be the vector of values defined for feature $\widetilde{V_i}$ in all census sectors in district j, $j = 1, 2, \ldots 96$. $V_i^j \in \mathbb{R}^{n^j \times 1}$, where n^j is the number of census sectors in district j. In the case of the district Vila Leopoldina $n^j = 68$; in addition $\sum_{j=1}^{96} n^j = 18363$. We need a procedure to replace $V_i \in \mathbb{R}^{18363 \times 1}$ by a new vector $\in \mathbb{R}^{96 \times 1}$ to be repeated $\forall\, i = 1, 2, \ldots, 13$. Let U_i^j be some summary statistic defined for the values V_i^j. Then, $U_i^T = [U_i^1, U_i^2, \ldots, U_i^{96}] \in \mathbb{R}^{1 \times 96}$ as desired. We will consider two summary statistics the mean and the median leading to two data matrices denoted by M_{mean} and M_{median}. Finally, we denote by Y the values of the first 28 features for which the sampling units are each individual district, $Y \in \mathbb{R}^{96 \times 28}$. We can then generate two data matrices by reduction which we denote by M_{mean}

and M_{median}. M_{mean} is denoted schematically by

$$M_{mean} = [Y|U_{mean}] \tag{2}$$

in which $U_{mean} \in \mathbb{R}^{96\times13}$. M_{median} is defined similarly. Both M_{median} and $M_{mean} \in \mathbb{R}^{96\times41}$. Note that the original data before reduction consists of two distinct matrices, Y and V, with V defined in Eq. 1.
To check the validity of this reduction, we note that relative distances between feature vectors may be more important than the actual distances between the feature vectors, suggesting that consistency can be checked by comparing relative distances between feature vectors after data reduction, and in the original data. As Y and U have different dimensions, we use as a distance measure the the Normalized Compression Distance (ncd) [5] applicable when all vector lengths are the same or different. We use this distance measure to obtain three symmetric matrices each of the form $\mathbb{R}^{41\times41}$ with vanishing diagonal elements. In order to check if the matrices are comparable, we can use Mantel test [6] for homogeneity of distance matrices using 10000 permutations in conjunction with the pearson correlation, The results for one compression scheme are shown in Table 1; other compression schemes lead to similar results, indicating a high degree of consistency between results obtained by reduction to the mean or median and using the full matrix. In light of this consistency, we will use the reduction to the mean from now on.

Table 1. Mantel Test Results

Comparison	Test Statistic	Significance
Mean-Median	0.7695	9.999×10^{-5}
Mean-Full	0.9464	9.999×10^{-5}
Median Full	0.7447	9.999×10^{-5}

2 Bayesian Network Inference

2.1 Initial Bayesian Network Inference

The features in our problem are all continuous, which suggests the inference of a continuous Bayesian Network. However, the most common bayesian network models based on continuous variables require data which is multivariate normal [8]. In our case, this requirement is not satisfied; the summary statistics for the skewness and curtosis values for the features (shown in Table 2) show strong deviations from normality.
Following a strategy well established in bioinformatics [7,8], the data will be discretized as a first step in deriving a discrete Bayesian Network. Discretization in three bins is carried out with bin intervals are selected using the Hartemink

Table 2. Skewness and Curtosis

	Min	25%	Mean	Median	75%	Max
Skewness	-6.0431	0.4279	1.1075	0.8516	1.7214	3.5433
Kurtosis	1.867	3.113	4.290	7.157	8.074	45.399

method [8,9], which preserves pairwise mutual information. The use of three bins ensures a reasonable number of counts in each bin, and in conjunction with the Hartemink Algorithm, determines the bin widths and thresholds.
Next, the hill climbing method as implemented in the bnlearn package [10] is used to infer a general Bayesian Network with 500 random starts using the BIC score as a network selection criterion. The inferred network obtained is unreliable, it requires 245 free parameters but only 96 observations are available. In order to proceed, we consider the inference of a Bayesian Network in which food insecurity and hunger plays a more central role.

2.2 Correlation Between Objective Functions

There are three features, which according to specialized domain knowledge, are strongly related to Food Insecurity and Hunger. These are

- Average Domestic Income (ADI)
- Number of Open Air Markets (NOAM)
- Number of Establishments with Unprocessed Foodstuff (NEUF)

While ADI is also meaningful in studies at the level of individual households, the other two features are much easier to define if urban regions are used as sampling units. Areas with relatively large values for at least one of these features may be assumed to be at lower risk. The analysis is equivalent to a Multi Objective Optimization with three objectives and 38 decision variables; with joint modelling of objectives and decision variables as in [3]. An analysis of the Spearman correlation between each pair of objective functions shows that the objectives are neither fully correlated nor fully independent (Table 3).

Table 3. Correlations between Objective Functions

Feature Pair	Correlation Coefficient	P-Value
ADI & NOAM	-0,194243	0.05791
NOAM & NEUF	0,3738058	0.0001758
ADI & NEUF	-0,07140313	0.4894

To simplify feature selection with multiple potentially dependent targets, we reduce the number of objectives to one. As a first step, each objective function o_1, o_2 and o_3 is separately and independently discretized such that the upper quartile is associated with low risk. The three objective functions are replaced by a binary surrogate variable y which takes the values S in regions where there is a low risk of Food Insecurity and Hunger, and I where this risk is higher. In order to define y, we first obtain the values corresponding to the upper quartiles of all three objective functions, denoted by u_1, u_2 and u_3. For each row indexed by i we check the validity of the condition

$$(o_1[i] > u_1) \vee (o_2[i] > u_2) \vee (o_3[i] > u_3) \quad (3)$$

For i for which Eq. 3 is true we set $y[i]$ to be S, and I otherwise. This method for defining y can be visualized by decision tree in Fig. 1.

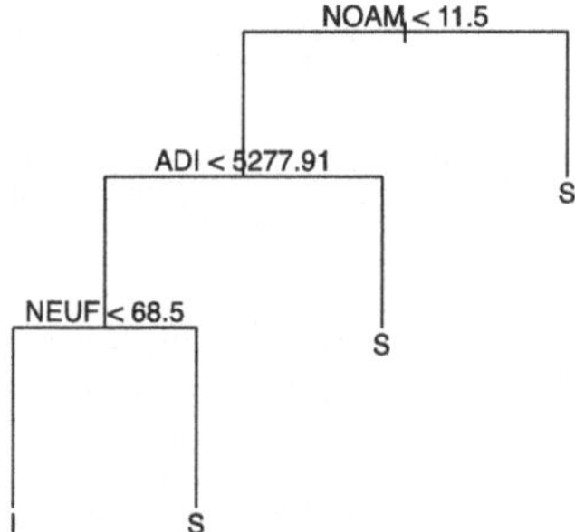

Fig. 1. Decision Tree Relating the objective functions and y

Essentially, we assume that the global optima of the objective functions are associated with values in the upper quartile of at least one objective function, similar to the strategy adopted in [11]. These regions are good candidates for the Pareto Corners [12], and are important in determining the dimension of the Pareto Frontier.

As an additional check, we compare the summary statistics of the three objective variables in regions considered high and low risk using the criteria discussed. For all three objective functions the lowest quartile, mean, median, third quartile and maximum are larger in regions with $y = \mathcal{S}$ than for $y = \mathcal{I}$, suggesting that different values of y clearly separate regions with different levels of risk.

The dataframe of continuous variables is now replaced by 38 discrete decision variables with three levels and one discrete variable with two levels. Once again the hill climbing algorithm is applied to infer a Bayesian Network and once again, the best fit network as identified by the BIC score has more free parameters than observations. This problem persists with a Naive Bayes estimator using the y as the target variable. This is the motivation for reducing the number of decision variables.

2.3 Feature Selection

The strategy that will be adopted is to check the association of y with the remaining 38 discretized atributes using a Fisher Exact Test [14]. In order to illustrate this approach, we consider a well known benchmark, DTLZ1 [13] with 3 objective functions and 10 decision variables. The decision variables $x_1, \ldots, x_{10}$ lie between 0 and 1. All three objectives are conflicting, primarily due to the variables x_1 and x_2. We uniformly simulate 5000 iid values for each of the 10 decision variables and the corresponding objective functions. Subsequently, the 10 decision variables are discretized in 4 intervals using the Hartemink method. The values of the three objective functions are replaced by a single binary variable y defined through the values corresponding to the lower deciles of the three objective functions, which we denote by ℓ_1, ℓ_2, and ℓ_3. The definition of the variable y is similar to that in Eq. 3.

With y defined, we can now apply the Fisher exact test to test the association between the discretized decision variables and the binary variable y. Low p-values are an indication of sizable variations in the values of decision variables close to the Pareto corners. The only low p-values (< 0.05) are associated with the decision variables x_1 and x_2 which have the strongest influence on the values of the objective functions close to their minima. This strategy shows how to discard certain decision variables in a principled manner.

Next we apply this strategy to the discretized socio economic data in order to select a number of key features. There are 15 features with $p < 0.05$; in order to choose a limited number of relevant features and permit the inference of a Bayesian Network with more parameters than observations, we retain those features with p-values $\leq 5 \times 10^{-4}$. These features are shown in Table 4.

Table 4. Selected Decision Variables

Feature Name	Description	P-Value
edaRAIS2	Number of Mixed Establishments in RAIS data	1.203×10^{-5}
edaRAIS4	Total Number of Food Stores in RAIS data	1.213×10^{-4}
a4721102	Baked Goods and Confectionary Resellers	1.597×10^{-4}
a4729699	Unspecified Food Products	1.8315×10^{-5}
a5611202	Bars and other drinking establishments	1.468×16^{-4}

In order to check that these features show appreciable differences in regions labelled with low and high levels of insecurity we obtain the most common label for the discretized values of all five selected variables in both regions.

In Table 5, subscripts denote categorical labels obtained after discretization. For all features, the range of numerical values for subscript _1 are less than those for _2 which in turn are less than those for _3. These ranges do not overlap. Distributional differences are obvious; for regions with high risk, the most common label of decision variable edaRAIS2, is characterized by lower

Table 5. Most Common Labels in True Data

Most Common Label	edaRAIS2	edaRAIS4	a4721102	a4729699	a5611202
Low Risk	edaRAIS2_**2**	edaRAIS4_**2**	a4721102_**3**	a4729699_**2**	a5611202_**3**
High Risk	edaRAIS2_**1**	edaRAIS4_**1**	a4721102_**1**	a4729699_**1**	a5611202_**2**

values than for regions of low risk. A more detailed analysis shows that for the decision variable edaRAIS2, there are no regions with label _3 with high risk, but 11 regions with low risk. Other distributional differences are also present.

3 Inference and Validation of Final Bayesian Network

Once again hill climbing is used to infer a Bayesian Network with the discretized values of the five selected features and the variable y. The resulting network has 35 free parameters and 10 fold cross validation using the values of y as the loss variable leads to and average cross validation loss of 23.2%. By comparison, the average cross validation error of a Naive Bayes Classifier is 26.1%. Validating the inferred network using an independent test data set is unfeasible as socioeconomic data are updated at intervals of several years. However, it is possible to use the original feature values and generate a prediction for y. More specifically, we can compare the posterior probabilities $\mathcal{P}(y = S \mid Features)$ and $\mathcal{P}(y = I \mid Features)$ for each of the 96 data points with the true values of y. This comparison can be used to generate an ROC curve whose AUC value is 0.856. This is encouraging, but not necessarily indicative of predictive ability in an independent validation set.
As an additional test, we can use the inferred Bayesian Network to generate artificial data which can be split into two sub populations, low risk or high risk, depending on the simulated value of y. For each decision variable in each artificial sub population we can check the most common discrete label. The results are identical with those of the true population, Table 5. The mode is the same for each feature for the true and simulated populations, suggesting that the Bayesian Network is capable of generating data consistent with key aspects of the data used to infer the network. Consistency tests of this nature are important prior to any analysis of interventions to reduce Food Insecurity and Hunger.

4 Summary and Conclusions

We have analyzed Brazilian socio economic data collected from urban regions in order to identify risk factors and possible interventions for Food Insecurity and Hunger, defined at the level of urban regions. Distinct datasets were aggregated consistently, as verified by the Mantel Test. Since the aggregated data showed marked deviations from normality, the data was discretized prior to the inference of a Bayesian Network. Due to the sparseness of the data, a strategy consisting of creating a new binary variable measuring proximity to the Pareto corners followed by the use of p-values of a Fisher exact test was used to rank and discard decision variables. This approach is a methodological novelty and warrants further study. Five features were selected leading to a more reliable Bayesian Network, which showed internal consistency. Due to the limited size of the data, many potentially important features may have been discarded; this problem can perhaps be resolved by bootstrapping the data. Adding data from other cities could help, but would require the inclusion of additional variables. Future studies with more data could permit the use of an independent validation set, leading to more reliable networks for public policy choices.

Acknowledgments. The authors thank the Center for Artificial Intelligence (C4AI-USP) and acknowledge financial support from the São Paulo Research Foundation (FAPESP grant#2019/07665-4, #2020/16578-5,#2024/06402-8, #2025/09003-0), Fundação de Apoio à Universidade de São Paulo (FUSP) - Project no 3541, the Center for Mathematical Sciences Applied to Industry (CeMEAI,FAPESP grant #2013/07375-0); FAPESP grant #2024/16994-0 and the Center for Artificial Intelligence in Health Management (ciaGsaude, FAPESP grant #2024/08485-8). Administrative assistance from Thereza Cury Fortunato is acknowledged.

Disclosure of Interests. Two of the authors, KJA and ACBD, acknowledge financial support from the IBM^{TM}Corporation.

References

1. Delèglise, H., Interndonato, R., Bègue, A., d'Hôtel, E., Teisseire, M., Roche, M.: Food security prediction from heterogeneous data combining machine and deep learning methods. Exp. Syst. Appl.**190** 116189 (2022)
2. Barbosa, R.M., Nelson, D.R.: The use of support vector machine to analyze food security in a region of Brazil. Appl. Artif. Intell. **30**(4), 318–330 (2016)
3. Karshenas, H., Santana, R., Bielza, C., Larrañaga, P.: Multi-objective optimization based on joint probabilistic modeling of objectives and variables. IEEE Trans. Evol. Comput. **18**(4), 519–542 (2014)
4. Blanco-Mallo, E., Moràn-Fernandez, L., Remeseiro, B., Bolòn-Canedo, V.: Do all roads lead to Rome? Studying distance measures in the context of machine learning. Pattern Recogn. **141**, 1096469 (2023)
5. Cilibrasi, R., Vitânyi, P.M.: Clustering by compression. IEEE Trans. Inf. Theory **51**(4), 1523–1545 (2005)
6. Mantel, N.: The detection of disease clustering and a generalized regression approach. Can. Res. **27**(1), 209–220 (1967)
7. Sachs, K., Perez, O., Pe'er, D., Lauffenburger, D.A., Nolan, G.P.: Causal Protein Signalling Networks Derived from Multiparameter Single Celled Data. Science, **308**,(5721), 523–529 (2005)
8. Scutari, M., Denis, J.-B.: Bayesian Network with Examples in R, 2nd edn. Chapman & Hall, Boca Raton (2021)
9. Hartemink, A.J.: Principled Computational Methods for the Validation and Discovery of Genetic Regulatory Networks. Massachusetts Institute of Technology, Department of Electrical Engineering and Computer Science (2001)

10. Scutari, M.: Learning Bayesian Networks with the bnlearn R Package. J. Stat. Softw. **35**(3), 1–22 (2010)
11. Gaspar-Cunha, A., Costa, P., Monaco, F., Delbem, A.C.D.B.: Many-objectives optimization: a machine learning approach for reducing the number of objectives. Math. Comput. Appl. **28** (17) (2023)
12. Singh, H., Isaacs, A., Ray, T.: A pareto corner search evolutionary algorithm and dimensionality reduction in many-objective optimization problems. IEEE Trans. Evol. Comput. **15**(4), 539–556 (2011)
13. Deb,K.,Thiele, L., Laumanns, M., Zitzler, E.: Scalable Test Problems for Evolutionary Multi-Objective Optimization. I Evolutionary MultiObjective Optimization: Theoretical Advances and Applications, pp.105–145.Springer (2005)
14. Kateri, M.: Contingency Table Analysis Methods and Implementation Using R. Springer (2014)

Enhancing Long-Text Summarization Through Hybrid Extractive-Abstractive Methods with LLaMA and Qwen

Mostafa Magdy[1(✉)], Salwa O. Slim[1], and Ensaf Hussein Mohamed[1,2]

[1] Faculty of Computers and Artificial Intelligence, Capital University, Cairo, Egypt
{mostafa_magdy,salwaosama}@fci.capu.edu.eg, enmohamed@nu.edu.eg

[2] School of Information Technology and Computer Science, Nile University, Giza, Egypt

Abstract. Long-text summarization, particularly for books, remains a key challenge in natural language processing. With the growth of academic and educational materials, efficient summarization is increasingly vital. This work introduces a hybrid method combining extractive and abstractive techniques, alongside purely abstractive models for a comprehensive evaluation. It presents a hybrid extract – then – abstract approach evaluated on BookSum using LLaMA-3-8B-Instruct and Qwen2.5-7B-Instruct under four settings: (i) base abstractive, (ii) fine-tuned abstractive (LoRA/QLoRA), (iii) Hybrid – Base, and (iv) Hybrid – Fine-tuned. The Hybrid – Fine-tuned LLaMA achieves the best ROUGE and BERTScore results. Compared to recent models such as NexusSum and TopDownFormer, our system attains competitive ROUGE and higher BERTScore, demonstrating that extractive guidance enhances coherence while preserving content. Overall, it offers an efficient and practical strategy for long-text summarization.

Keywords: Book summarization · hybrid summarization · abstractive summarization · extractive summarization · large language models

1 Introduction

In recent years, natural language processing (NLP) has seen rapid advancements due to deep learning and large-scale pre-trained models. NLP has enabled machines to understand and generate language more effectively across tasks such as machine translation, question answering, and text summarization [1].

Automatic text summarization helps extract essential information efficiently while preserving meaning [2]. Effective summaries capture key ideas and intent rather than just random sentences [3].

Summarization techniques are classified into three main categories: extractive, abstractive, and hybrid. In extractive summarization, selects key sentences directly from the source text without altering wording [4]. It performs well for short content such as news or articles [5]. Abstractive summarization rephrases

A. Awad et al. (Eds.): MEDI 2025, LNCS 16427, pp. 230–237, 2026.
https://doi.org/10.1007/978-3-032-19865-5_19

the text to produce fluent, human-like summaries while retaining the main meaning [5]. This technique handles both short-form and long-form content with improved flexibility and yields more human-like summaries [6]. A third approach, hybrid summarization, both methods—first selecting key sentences, then rewriting them for clarity and conciseness. This approach produces more coherent and informative summaries, especially for long or complex documents [6].

Figure 1 provides a visual representation of the summarization approaches discussed.

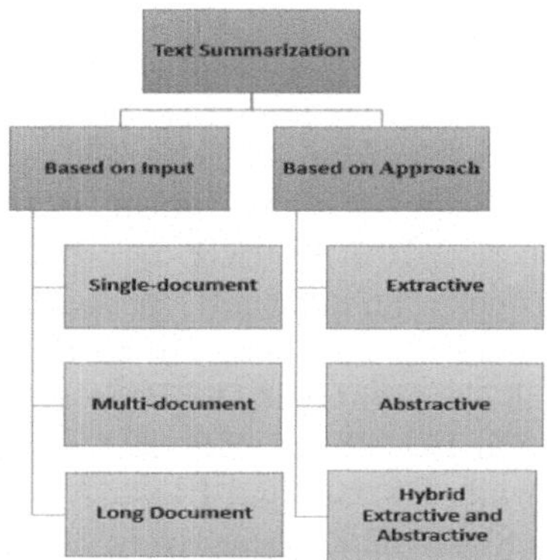

Fig. 1. Categorization of text summarization approaches.

Text summarization varies by input type. Single-document summarization condenses one text as news article into a shorter form [7], while multi-document summarization merges several related sources into a unified summary [8]. Long-document summarization handles extended inputs—such as books to coherence and hierarchical structure [9]. This hierarchy is illustrated in Fig. 1.

We introduce an innovative contribution: Hybrid – Fine-tuned, our proposed model. This system combines extractive selection (BERT embeddings + LexRank) with a generator fine-tuned on BookSum (LLaMA with PEFT/LoRA) [10]. Unlike prior work that typically applies either extraction or abstraction in isolation, our approach demonstrates that coupling salience-aware extraction with a domain-adapted abstractive model yields stronger results. To validate this, we evaluate multiple models for a comprehensive comparison, including (i) base abstractive models, (ii) fine-tuned abstractive models, (iii) a Hybrid – Base pipeline, and (iv) our Hybrid – Fine-tuned proposal. All configurations are benchmarked on BookSum using ROUGE and BERTScore.

The remainder of this paper is organized as follows: Sect. 2 describes the dataset and evaluation metrics; Sect. 3 reviews related work; Sect. 4 outlines the proposed Hybrid – Fine-tuned model; Sect. 5 presents experiments and results; and Sect. 6 concludes with future directions.

2 Related Work

This section surveys recent progress in the summarization of long document and books in English.

2.1 Abstractive Methods

Le Bronnec et al. (2024) proposed LOCOST, which replaces self-attention with a gated bidirectional state-space encoder [11]. Pre-trained via PEGASUS-style gap-sentence generation on C4 and fine-tuned on BookSum-Chapter, it achieved ROUGE-1 = 34.3, ROUGE-L = 32.4, and BERTScore = 55.4.

Kim et al. (2025) introduce NexusSum, a fine-tuning-free, hierarchical multi-agent LLM framework for long-form summarization. It transforms dialogue into coherent text, summarizes chunks hierarchically, and applies iterative compression for length control [12]. Using Mistral-Large-Instruct-2407. On BookSum, it achieved BERTScore = 70.7, ROUGE-1 = 42.5, and ROUGE-L = 23.9.

Prusty et al. (2024) proposed an informativeness-oriented evaluation pipeline for long-form summarization [13]. They assessed off-the-shelf LLMs—Mistral-7B-Instruct, LLaMA-2-7B, and Gemma-7B on multiple datasets including BookSum-Chapter [10]. On BookSum, Mistral achieved ROUGE-1 = 37.7 and BERTScore = 83.9, while Gemma and LLaMA reached ROUGE-1 = 25.6 / 28.0 and BERTScore = 81.8 / 82.7, respectively.

Kashyap et al. (2022) introduce a fine-tuned LongformerEncoderDecoder (LED) on BookSum chapter – summary pairs and generated chapter summaries via a recursive summary-of-summaries pipeline (chunk → summarize → merge → resummarize), reporting ROUGE-1 = 29.75, ROUGE-L = 28.33, and BERTScore-F1 = 54.10 on the test set [14].

2.2 Hybrid Methods

Chatterjee et al. (2022) introduced MLLTS, a multi-layer long-text summarizer that partitions chapters, summarizes segments using TextRank, LexRank, and DistilBART, and then ranks and aggregates the partial outputs [15]. On the BookSum shared-task data, it achieved ROUGE-1 = 26.4 and ROUGE-L = 24.4 (no BERTScore reported).
Prior work on BookSum still shows limited accuracy: ROUGE-1/ROUGE-L are relatively low and BERTScore gains vary. A main cause is context limits, which force truncation or chunk-then-merge processing; pipelines that aren't fully LLM-based often miss long-range meaning and narrative flow. Newer hierarchical or multi-agent LLM setups help, but they need a lot of compute and are hard to reproduce. Table 1 provides a consolidated overview of prior work, summarizing the models used and the results they reported.

3 Materials and Methods

This section outlines the dataset used and the hybrid summarization method applied in this study.

Table 1. Summary of contributions to English long-document summarization.

Reference	Model	Approach	R-1	R-L	BERT
Chatterjee et al. (2022) [15]	MLLTS	Hybrid	26.43	24.36	–
Kashyap et al. (2022) [14]	LED	Abstractive	29.75	28.33	54.10
Le Bronnec et al. (2024) [11]	LOCOST	Abstractive	34.30	32.40	55.40
Kim and Kim (2025) [12]	NexusSum	Abstractive	42.51	23.91	70.70
Prusty et al. (2024) [13]	Mistral-Instruct	Abstractive	37.70	–	83.90
Prusty et al. (2024) [13]	LLaMA-2-Chat	Abstractive	28.00	–	82.70
Prusty et al. (2024) [13]	Gemma-7B-it	Abstractive	25.60	–	81.80

3.1 Dataset

We use BookSum, a large-scale benchmark for long-form narrative summarization introduced by Kry'sci'nski et al. [10]. It provides human-written summaries at multiple levels—paragraph, chapter, and book. Our experiments focus on the chapter-level split, where each entry pairs one or more consecutive chapters with a single human reference summary. These references are manually written, not machine-generated, resulting in highly abstractive targets. Designed to bridge the gap between short-text datasets and full-length narratives, BookSum preserves natural chapter boundaries, allowing models to learn narrative flow and structural coherence. We use this dataset to evaluate both baseline and fine-tuned large language models (LLMs) on detailed, long-form text.

3.2 Proposed Methodology

The proposed hybrid English book-summarization system follows a five-phase pipeline, where extractive selection is combined with LLM-based abstraction, as illustrated in Fig. 2. The abstractive phase is evaluated with Qwen and LLaMA in both base and BookSum-fine-tuned variants. The distinct phases are:

Chapter and Chunk Segmentation. Given a full-book PDF or text, chapter boundaries are detected—typically by parsing the table of contents to locate chapter titles and starting points. Each chapter is then extracted and divided into chunks to meet the model input limits, preparing the text for summarization.

Text Preprocessing. is essential for accurate sentence ranking and summarization. The input text is cleaned by removing noise such as symbols, emails, and extra punctuation, then normalized for spacing and converted to lowercase. This prepares the text for effective processing and helps the model focus on key content.

Extractive Encoding (BERT). Each sentence is encoded with a BERT encoder [1] using the `bert-base-uncased` checkpoint. BERT's bidirectional attention provides rich sentence-level semantics for centrality-based extraction, while a sliding window manages the 512-token limit. Text is tokenized with WordPiece, and sentence vectors are obtained by mean-pooling final-layer embeddings. For long chapters, overlapping 128-token chunks preserve order and context, ensuring accurate extractive selection.

Sentence Ranking (LexRank). LexRank ranks sentences by centrality within a similarity graph, where pairwise cosine similarities form weighted edges. A PageRank-style algorithm computes each sentence's stationary score, indicating importance. After encoding, the top sentences are selected under a fixed token or length limit and ordered to form the extractive summary for the next stage.

Abstractive Generation (Qwen/LLaMA). In this phase, the extractive summary is rewritten into a fluent, concise narrative using large language models such as Qwen and LLaMA. The Qwen2.5-7B-Instruct model is a decoder-only transformer with about 7B parameters, optimized for instruction-based tasks and capable of processing long inputs with strong multilingual performance [16]. The LLaMA-3-8B-Instruct model, developed by Meta, has a similar decoder-only design with around 8B parameters, emphasizing efficiency and scalability for reasoning and generation tasks [17]. To adapt these models to the BookSum dataset, we use LoRA (Low-Rank Adaptation), a parameter-efficient fine-tuning method that inserts small trainable matrices into attention layers instead of updating all parameters [18]. This approach reduces training time and memory usage while maintaining model quality. Our experiments test both the base (pretrained) and LoRA fine-tuned versions of Qwen2.5-7B-Instruct and LLaMA-3-8B-Instruct. For comparison, we also evaluate a direct abstractive setup, where full chapters are summarized without extraction, splitting the text when it exceeds the context limit. This allows us to analyze the effects of fine-tuning and assess whether the hybrid extract-then-abstract pipeline achieves better results than purely abstractive generation.

4 Results and Discussion

4.1 Evaluation Metrics

We evaluate the quality of the generated summaries using three widely adopted automatic metrics: ROUGE-1, ROUGE-L, and BERTScore. Together, these capture different dimensions of summary quality, from lexical overlap to semantic similarity.

ROUGE-1. Measures unigram overlap between the generated and reference summaries, indicating basic content coverage [19].

ROUGE-L. Uses the Longest Common Subsequence (LCS) to reward in-order matches, reflecting fluency and structural coherence [20].

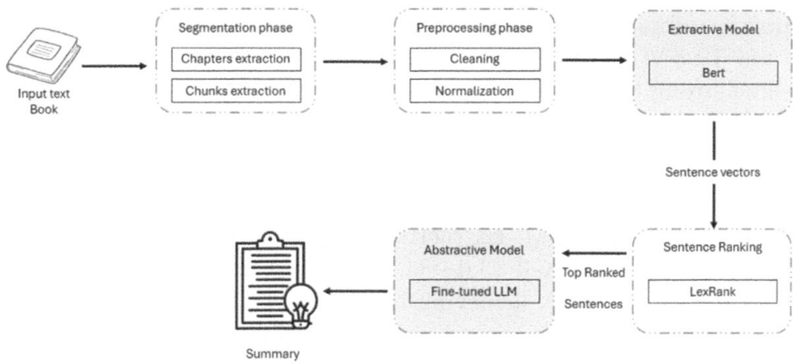

Fig. 2. The Proposed Model Architecture

BERTScore. Evaluates semantic similarity by comparing contextual embeddings from a pretrained encoder and computing an F1 score [21].

While ROUGE focuses on surface-level overlap, BERTScore better captures meaning and paraphrase, aligning more closely with human evaluation—especially for abstractive summaries [22]. In this study, BERTScore serves as the main evaluation metric, while ROUGE is used to monitor lexical coverage.

4.2 Experimental Setup

All experiments were run on a Vast.ai GPU server using the Docker image `vastai/pytorch_cuda-12.8.1-auto/jupyter`. The setup included 4× NVIDIA RTX 5070 GPUs (CUDA 12.8), an AMD EPYC 7B13 (64-core) CPU, and NVMe storage. Python with PyTorch (CUDA 12.8.1) and the Hugging Face ecosystem (Transformers, PEFT/QLoRA, bitsandbytes, accelerate, datasets) were used for training and inference.

Experiments used the BookSum chapter-level split with two system designs: a pure Abstractive pipeline and the Hybrid (proposed) pipeline performing BERT embeddings → LexRank top-K selection → LLM rewriting. Two model families (Qwen, LLaMA) were tested in both Base and Fine-tuned (LoRA/QLoRA) versions. All runs used identical decoding settings; variables were limited to (i) model fine-tuning and (ii) extractive guidance.

In the Abstractive baseline, the LLM directly summarized chapters using order-preserving chunking. In the Hybrid setup, sentences were embedded with BERT, ranked by LexRank, and the top-K extracted digest was rewritten by the LLM. Both Qwen and LLaMA models were tested in Base and Fine-tuned modes.

4.3 Experimental Results

Experiment 1—Pure Abstractive (Qwen and LLaMA). Chapters are chunked by context length, summarized by the LLM, and concatenated into full summaries. Fine-tuning yields clear gains: **Qwen** improves from 83.1→84.7 (+1.6) and **LLaMA-3** from 83.0→85.1 (+2.1) in BERTScore F1 (Table 2), establishing strong baselines.

Experiment 2—Hybrid (Proposed; Qwen and LLaMA). The hybrid pipeline applies BERT+LexRank to select salient sentences, which are chunked and summarized by the LLM. Extractive guidance boosts Base models: **Qwen** 83.1→83.9 (+0.8), **LLaMA-3** 83.0→84.3 (+1.3). After fine-tuning, **LLaMA-3** further rises to 85.5 (+0.4), achieving the best overall performance (Hybrid – LLaMA-3 Fine-tuned).

Table 2. Main results on BookSum (chapter-level). All metrics are F1.

Model	Version	R-1	R-L	BERT
Qwen	Base	33.9	23.3	83.1
Qwen	Fine-tuned	39.5	25.8	84.7
Hybrid (BERT + Qwen)	Base	30.4	22.1	83.9
Hybrid (BERT + Qwen)	Fine-tuned	36.9	24.3	84.4
LLaMA-3	Base	36.9	25.5	83.0
LLaMA-3	Fine-tuned	41.0	26.3	85.1
Hybrid (BERT + LLaMA-3)	Base	36.0	24.4	84.3
Hybrid (BERT + LLaMA-3)	**Fine-tuned**	**44.0**	**26.1**	**85.5**

5 Conclusion

We proposed a hybrid extract-then-abstract model for long-form book summarization, evaluated on BookSum (chapter-level). The system builds a salience-aware extractive digest using BERT embeddings and LexRank, then rewrites it with an LLM. Using LLaMA and Qwen in both base and fine-tuned (LoRA/QLoRA) modes, we compared the hybrid and pure abstractive setups under identical decoding. Results show that fine-tuning yields the largest gains, while hybrid guidance further improves base models and adds value post-fine-tuning. The Hybrid – LLaMA (fine-tuned) configuration achieved the best overall performance, effectively balancing coverage and fluency.

Looking ahead, we plan to extend the system from chapter-level to full book-level summarization, integrate human evaluation, and test larger LLMs.

References

1. Devlin, J., Chang, M., Lee, K., Toutanova, K.: Bert: Pre-training of deep bidirectional transformers for language understanding. In Proc, NAACL (2019)

2. Azmi, A.M., Altmami, N.I.: An abstractive Arabic text summarizer with user controlled granularity. Inf. Process. Manage. (2018)
3. Ladhak, F., Li, B., Al-Onaizan, Y., McKeown, K.: Exploring content selection in summarization of novel chapters. arXiv preprint arXiv:2005.01840 (2020)
4. Jalil, Z., Nasir, J.A., Nasir, M.: Extractive multi-document summarization: a review of progress in the last decade. IEEE Access **9** (2021)
5. Vishal Gupta and Gurpreet Singh Lehal: A survey of text summarization extractive techniques. J. Emerg. Technol. Web Intell. **2**, 258–268 (2010)
6. Wang, S., Zhao, X., Li, B., Ge, B., Tang, D.: Integrating extractive and abstractive models for long text summarization. In: 2017 IEEE International Congress on Big Data (BigData Congress), pp. 305–312. IEEE (2017)
7. Nenkova, A., McKeown, K.: Automatic summarization. Found. Trends Inf. Retr. **5**, 103–233 (2012)
8. Fabbri, A.R., Kryściński, I., McCann, D., Xiong, C.: Multi-news: A Large-scale Multi-document Summarization Dataset. In Proc, ACL (2019)
9. Cohan, A., et al.: A discourse-aware attention model for abstractive summarization of long documents. In: Proceeding NAACL, pp. 615–621 (2018)
10. Kryściński, W., Rajani, N., Agarwal, D., Xiong, C., Radev, D.: Booksum: a collection of datasets for long-form narrative summarization. arXiv preprint arXiv:2105.08209 (2021)
11. Bronnec, E.L., Tallec, A., Wolf, L., Mensch, A.: State-space models for long document abstractive summarization. arXiv preprint arXiv:2402.10171 (2024)
12. Kim, H., Kim, B.-H.: Nexussum: hierarchical LLM agents for long-form narrative summarization. In: Proceedings of the 2025 Annual Meeting of the Association for Computational Linguistics (2025)
13. Prusty, S., Roy, A., Samal, P.R., Jha, R., Bhattacharyya, P.: Eva-score: evaluating abstractive long-form summarization on informativeness through extraction and validation. arXiv preprint arXiv:2407.07119 (2024)
14. Kashyap, P.: Coling 2022 shared task: LED finetuning and recursive summary generation for automatic summarization of chapters from novels. In: Proceedings of the Workshop on Automatic Summarization, pp. 19–23 (2022)
15. Chatterjee, N., Khatri, A., Agarwal, R.: Summarization of long input texts using multi-layer neural network. In : Proceedings of the Workshop on Automatic Summarization for Creative Writing, pp. 13–18 (2022)
16. Yang, A., Yu, B., Li, C., Liu.: Qwen2.5-1m Technical Report (2025)
17. Touvron, H., Lavril, T.: and Izacard. Open and efficient foundation language models, Llama (2023)
18. Edward, J.: Hu, Yelong Shen, Phillip Wallis, and Allen-Zhu. Low-rank adaptation of large language models, Lora (2021)
19. Lin, C.-Y.: Rouge: a package for automatic evaluation of summaries. In: Proceedings of the Workshop on Text Summarization Branches Out (WAS 2004) (2004)
20. Alex, R.: Fabbri and Wojciech Kryściński. Re-evaluating summarization evaluation. Transactions of the Association for Computational Linguistics, Summeval (2021)
21. Zhang, T., Kishore, V., Wu, F.: Bertscore: evaluating text generation with Bert. In: Proceedings of the International Conference on Learning Representations (2020)
22. Shakil, H., Farooq, A., Kalita, J.: Abstractive text summarization: state of the art, challenges, and improvements. Neurocomputing **613**, 1–19 (2024)

A Mixed-Methods Framework for Analyzing Travel Reviews with LLMs and MAXQDA: A Case Study in Osaka

Daud Santoso, Tai Dinh(✉), Shehan Liyanaarachchi, and Wuyi Yue

The Kyoto College of Graduate Studies for Informatics, 7 Tanaka Monzencho, Sakyo Ward, Kyoto 606-8225, Japan
t_dinh@kcg.edu

Abstract. Online travel reviews contain detailed signals about visitor experience, yet converting this unstructured text into evidence that destination managers and travelers can use is non-trivial. This paper introduces a human-in-the-loop workflow that pairs qualitative coding with lightweight Large Language Model (LLM) analytics. Using Osaka, Japan, as a case study, we compile and pre-process reviews from Google Maps and Tripadvisor, distill them into a 12-topic schema that anchors automated topic and sentiment assignment, and validate model outputs against a human-coded subset using standard metrics. Integrated with exploratory analysis, the results yield a topic–sentiment matrix that highlights strengths and pain points across attractions and services. Findings indicate that a small LLM can deliver scalable, reliable polarity for clearly valenced texts, while the qualitative step sharpens topic granularity and guards against model drift. The pipeline is transparent and reproducible, and it generalizes to other destinations and platforms, enabling evidence-based destination management and more informed trip planning for travelers.

Keywords: sentiment analysis · travel reviews · mixed method · GPT-5 mini · MAXQDA · qualitative analysis

1 Introduction

Sentiment analysis [1], an important task in data science and natural language processing (NLP), studies opinions and emotions in text and supports evidence-based decisions across domains such as marketing, hospitality, and entertainment [2,3]. In tourism, online reviews capture visitor reactions to attractions, services, and infrastructure at a scale that is difficult to process manually [14]. Although these reviews provide fine-grained signals about visitor experiences, converting large multilingual corpora into actionable insights for destination managers and travelers remains challenging.

D. Santoso and T. Dinh—Co-first authors.

A. Awad et al. (Eds.): MEDI 2025, LNCS 16427, pp. 238–256, 2026.
https://doi.org/10.1007/978-3-032-19865-5_20

User-generated content on platforms such as Google Maps[1] and Tripadvisor[2] offers rich and timely feedback but is noisy and heterogeneous. Texts vary in length and style, can express multiple sentiments within a single review, and appear in many languages. Traditional approaches, such as keyword heuristics and unsupervised topic models like Latent Dirichlet Allocation (LDA), often struggle with coherence, consistency across languages, and interpretability under these conditions. These challenges are especially pronounced in Osaka, where reviews are multilingual, high-volume, and reflect diverse cultural perspectives. Recent advances in large language models (LLMs) have significantly changed the landscape: modern models demonstrate strong contextual reasoning and multilingual competence, enabling high-quality text understanding with minimal task-specific supervision. Human oversight remains essential to ensure local relevance, transparency, and reliability.

This paper presents a mixed-methods, human-in-the-loop workflow for Osaka, Japan. We preprocess a large corpus of reviews, then use a compact LLM (GPT-5 mini) to assign one topic from a predefined 12-topic schema and a sentiment label with score to every review in the entire dataset. A qualitative coding study on a stratified subset (in MAXQDA) is used to confirm and interpret the quantitative patterns, and we report inter-annotator reliability. We integrate the quantitative results with exploratory analysis and the qualitative findings to produce a topic–sentiment matrix that surfaces strengths and pain points across attractions and services, supporting evidence-based destination management and more informed trip planning.

In summary, our contributions are:

- We collect 52,126 travel reviews from five major attractions in Osaka (Osaka Aquarium Kaiyukan, Dotonbori, Osaka Castle, Sumiyoshi, and Universal Studios), sourced from Google Maps and Tripadvisor between 2020 and 2024. Five full-time master's students in the data science concentration manually annotate sentiment labels. The cleaned and annotated dataset is released publicly[3]. To the best of our knowledge, this is the first study focusing on sentiment analysis of travel reviews in Osaka, Japan.
- We propose a practical, reproducible human-in-the-loop workflow that applies a lightweight LLM (GPT-5 mini) with a predefined 12-topic schema to the entire preprocessed corpus, while a stratified qualitative subset (in MAXQDA) corroborates and interprets the quantitative patterns.
- We conduct a rigorous evaluation by comparing model outputs with human annotations using accuracy, macro-F1, precision, recall, and Cohen's κ, and we report inter-annotator agreement to quantify reliability.
- We deliver summaries for managers and travelers that link topics with polarity to highlight recurring issues and positive aspects across Osaka's attractions and services, with a pipeline readily transferable to other destinations and platforms.

[1] https://www.google.com/maps.
[2] https://www.tripadvisor.com/.
[3] https://github.com/ClarkDinh/kansai_sentiment.

The remainder of the paper is organized as follows. Section 2 reviews related research. Section 3 outlines background concepts. Section 4 details the proposed workflow, including prompting strategies and evaluation protocols. Section 5 presents the case study dataset and empirical findings. Section 6 concludes and discusses directions for future work.

2 Related Work

Research on sentiment analysis for tourism and hospitality has grown rapidly, with surveys mapping out prevailing methods, datasets, and use cases [4]. Earlier pipelines often relied on lexical resources, hand-crafted cues, and unsupervised topic models to summarize visitor opinions. While useful, these approaches struggled with pragmatic context (e.g., irony), domain-specific nuance, and multilingual consistency.

The advent of large language models (LLMs) has shifted the state of the art. Obinwanne et al. [5] showed that GPT-based systems outperform support vector machines, random forests, and naïve Bayes across multiple metrics. Balamurali et al. [6] proposed a tourism assistant that marries an LSTM with an LLM to infer user affect and craft adaptive replies. Guidotti et al. [7] demonstrated that open-source LLMs can perform zero-shot sentiment and keyword extraction on hospitality reviews with minimal task-specific engineering. On benchmark data, Kheiri et al. [8] explored prompt engineering, fine-tuning, and embedding classifiers with GPT-3.5, reporting more than a 22% F1 improvement over earlier baselines.

Evidence from neighboring domains is consistent with these trends. Ghatora et al. [9] compared traditional classifiers and GPT-4 on product reviews, noting that classical models are competitive on short inputs, whereas LLMs excel on longer texts and provide explanations. Yang et al. [10] evaluated compact LLMs on Chinese healthcare reviews and found that several small models handle aspect-based sentiment effectively, in some cases surpassing GPT-3.5 with lower resource demands. Shah et al. [11] contrasted rule-based systems, fine-tuned models, and LLMs (zero/one/five-shot) for feature sentiment extraction from app reviews; GPT-4 improved zero-shot F1 by 23.6% over rule-based baselines, while fine-tuned architectures such as RE-BERT remained strong on certain subtasks.

Despite this progress, notable gaps persist. To our knowledge, no prior study has focused specifically on sentiment analysis of traveler reviews for the city of Osaka. Moreover, few works illustrate that a single compact model can jointly perform sentiment labeling and topic discovery for multilingual tourism text with only light supervision, and publicly available, human-annotated destination datasets remain scarce.

We address these gaps with an Osaka case study that uses GPT-5 mini as a unified model for both sentiment labeling and topic assignment. We compile 52,126 reviews from five well-known Osaka attractions and obtain manual annotations from five master's students in data science. The cleaned and annotated dataset will be released to support subsequent research.

3 Preliminaries

3.1 Top Five Places in Osaka

Osaka is a major urban hub in western Japan known for its food culture, entertainment districts, and historical landmarks.[4] Against this backdrop, our five case-study attractions and their signature highlights are: Osaka Aquarium Kaiyukan, a flagship waterfront aquarium in Tempozan noted for immersive Pacific Rim habitats;[5] Dotonbori, a canal district famous for neon signage and street food;[6] Osaka Castle, an emblematic fortress set within a large park and museum that showcases the city's history;[7] Sumiyoshi Taisha, an ancient Shinto shrine renowned for its arched *Sorihashi* bridge and distinctive *Sumiyoshi-zukuri* architecture;[8] and Universal Studios Japan, a major theme park featuring branded areas such as The Wizarding World of Harry Potter and Super Nintendo World.[9]

3.2 Mixed Methods Research

Mixed methods research [12] is a methodology that collects, analyzes, and integrates quantitative and qualitative evidence within a single study or program of inquiry, to provide a more complete understanding than either approach alone. It treats the entire research process—assumptions, questions, data collection, analysis, interpretation, and reporting—as an integrated design rather than separate steps.

This approach is especially useful when numeric scores do not tell the full story, when researchers need to explain why results occurred, or when instruments require context-specific development to fit the population under study. In practice, mixed methods studies integrate data by connecting results across phases, merging strands for joint interpretation, or embedding one form of data within the other.

Common designs include: (i) triangulation (concurrent collection with merged interpretation), (ii) embedded (one strand plays a supportive role within another design), (iii) explanatory sequential (quantitative phase followed by qualitative to explain results), and (iv) exploratory sequential (qualitative phase followed by quantitative to test or extend findings). Mixed methods work is often grounded in a pragmatic worldview that prioritizes problem-centered inquiry and methodological pluralism, while acknowledging that multiple worldviews may be combined as appropriate.

In this study, we adopt a quant-first strategy on the full preprocessed corpus and a stratified qualitative subset to corroborate, interpret, and add nuance to

[4] https://en.osaka-info.jp/osaka/.
[5] https://www.kaiyukan.com/language/eng/.
[6] https://en.osaka-info.jp/spot/dotonbori/.
[7] https://www.osakacastle.net/.
[8] https://www.sumiyoshitaisha.net/en/.
[9] https://www.usj.co.jp/web/en/us.

model-derived patterns—an explanatory/triangulation variant that links numerical summaries with coded insights to support evidence-based guidance for managers and travelers. To ensure quality, we attend to recognized standards: collecting both forms of data, mixing them explicitly, and maintaining rigor in each strand.

3.3 GPT-5 Mini

GPT-5 mini[10] is OpenAI's smaller GPT-5 family model designed for fast, cost-efficient runs on well-specified tasks. It accepts text and image inputs and returns text, offers a long context window, and supports function calling and structured output through the standard API (Responses and Chat Completions).[11] For large offline jobs, the Batch API provides asynchronous processing with about a 50% discount on input and output tokens, which makes it well suited to high-throughput labeling in our pipeline.[12]

In our workflow, *GPT-5 mini* is used to label the full preprocessed corpus without fine-tuning: it performs zero/few-shot sentiment classification and assigns one of the 12 predefined topics, while handling multilingual inputs reliably. This choice keeps per-document cost low and latency predictable, allowing us to generate city-wide topic–sentiment summaries that the qualitative subset can then confirm and interpret.

3.4 MAXQDA

MAXQDA[13] is a qualitative and mixed methods platform that we use for three core tasks: coding management, visualization, and synthesis via Questions, Themes & Theories (QTT).[14] For coding management, MAXQDA supports hierarchical codes and subcodes, code and document memos, rapid retrieval of coded segments, and summary grids and tables to track progress and consolidate notes. Its visualization tools reveal patterns and relationships by comparing documents, mapping connections with concept maps, and displaying how reviews evolve across topics and attractions. QTT provides a structured workspace to assemble conclusions for specific questions and themes by linking coded segments, summaries, and memos into exportable overviews that support interpretation and reporting. In our workflow, we code a stratified subset of Osaka reviews using the 12-topic schema, organize and audit coding in MAXQDA, create visual summaries to compare attractions and topics, and use QTT to synthesize qualitative evidence that corroborates the quantitative findings.

---

[10] https://openai.com/api/pricing/.

[11] https://platform.openai.com/docs/api-reference.

[12] https://openai.com/api/pricing/.

[13] https://www.maxqda.com/.

[14] https://www.maxqda.com/help-mx24/questions-themes-theories/the-idea-behind-questions-themes-theories.

3.5 Topic Modeling

Instead of inducing topics from word co-occurrence alone, we adopt a literature-anchored, taxonomy-driven approach that maps each review to a fixed set of domains relevant to urban tourism. Drawing on and extending prior categorizations [13], we define a twelve-topic schema that balances coverage with interpretability and supports comparisons across attractions and over time. The final set is (Table 1):

Table 1. Twelve-topic schema for urban tourism reviews.

1. Cultural Heritage & Historical Sites	2. Nature & Scenic Spots
3. Crowds & Accessibility	4. Cleanliness & Maintenance
5. Atmosphere & Ambience	6. Service & Hospitality
7. Price & Value for Money	8. Local Cuisine & Food Experience
9. Shopping & Souvenirs	10. Events & Festivals
11. Transportation & Connectivity	12. Entertainment & Nightlife

In the quantitative strand, GPT-5 mini assigns exactly one topic to each review in the full preprocessed corpus via prompt-based classification using this schema. The qualitative subset is then used to confirm coverage, clarify boundaries between adjacent topics, and refine examples. This design yields stable, manager-friendly categories and avoids the volatility of unsupervised topic discovery while remaining simple and reproducible.

4 The Proposed Framework

Figure 1 presents our end-to-end framework for semantic and sentiment analysis of visitor reviews in Osaka, Japan. The design links quantitative modeling on the full corpus with qualitative confirmation on a stratified subset so that numerical patterns and coded insights inform one another.

We first collect reviews from Google Maps and Tripadvisor for major Osaka attractions from 2020 to 2024 and bring them into a common analysis space. Non-English texts are translated into English with each platform's built-in translator, then the corpus is cleaned by removing blanks, deduplicating records, and normalizing text while correcting obvious misspellings. A brief exploratory profiling of volumes and terms provides initial context but does not drive the taxonomy.

Quantitative labeling is applied to the entire preprocessed dataset. A compact LLM (GPT-5 mini) assigns exactly one topic from a predefined twelve-topic schema and a sentiment label with score (and confidence) to every review using prompt-based instructions executed through the Batch API. These outputs yield citywide distributions, attraction-level comparisons, and time trends at low cost and with predictable latency. In the next step, five master's students majoring in

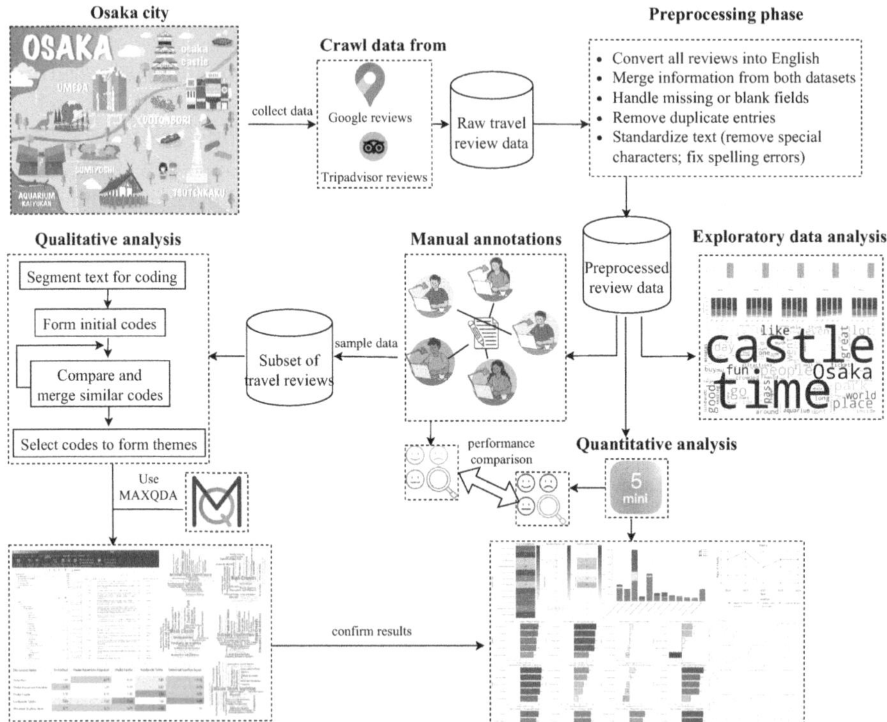

Fig. 1. The workflow of the analysis framework: reviews are crawled and preprocessed, then quantitatively labeled with topics and sentiment using an GPT-5 mini. A stratified subset is qualitatively coded in MAXQDA to confirm and interpret the quantitative patterns.

data science independently label reviews for sentiment. Annotators are explicitly instructed not to use any AI tools. Disagreements are resolved by discussion to reach consensus, and the consolidated labels serve as the human reference set for evaluating model outputs.

After annotation, a stratified subset of reviews is coded in MAXQDA using the same twelve-topic schema. Coding management features (hierarchies, memos, summary tables) and visualization tools support auditability and pattern discovery, and Questions, Themes & Theories (QTT) is used to assemble thematic takeaways. Inter-annotator agreement is reported to document reliability. The qualitative strand confirms and explains model-derived patterns, clarifies boundaries between adjacent topics, and captures nuances that aggregate numbers may miss; it does not serve to construct the schema.

Model outputs are compared with human annotations on the subset using accuracy, macro-F1, precision, recall, and Cohen's κ. Convergences increase confidence in the citywide estimates, while divergences trigger targeted error analysis and prompt refinement of instructions or thresholds. Finally, we integrate the strands into manager- and traveler-oriented products: attraction-level heat maps, a topic–sentiment matrix that highlights strengths and pain points across service, cleanliness, accessibility, and other dimensions, and exemplar quotes that ground the statistics. This integration supports evidence-based decisions for stakeholders and more informed trip planning.

5 Experimental Results and Analysis

5.1 Experimental Dataset

We curated a structured collection of traveler reviews from two high-volume feedback ecosystems: Google Maps and Tripadvisor. Because both platforms are dynamic and partially gated, we replaced ad-hoc scripts with stable, off-the-shelf utilities designed for large-scale extraction.

For Google Maps, we used the open-source *Google Maps Scraper*[15], which retrieves reviews for specified places returned by Google Maps search. Tripadvisor content was gathered with the *ScrapeJob—Tripadvisor Review Scraper*[16], enabling point-and-click capture of JavaScript-rendered pages and paginated review lists. The resulting corpus contains 52, 126 reviews spanning five flagship Osaka attractions, collected between 2020 and 2024.

Although Google Maps and Tripadvisor expose different metadata, their core semantics—reviewer, rating, text, place, and time—are aligned. We therefore harmonized the most comparable fields and then ran a cleaning pipeline (Table 2):

Table 2. Unified schema for Osaka review corpus

Field	Description
`user_profile`	Reviewer identifier or profile URL when available; anonymized where necessary.
`rating star`	User-assigned score on a 1–5 scale.
`review_text`	Full body of the review.
`date`	Publication date in ISO 8601 format (YYYY-MM-DD).
`attraction`	Name of the reviewed site (e.g., an Osaka Castle).

5.2 Exploratory Data Analysis

Figure 2 shows the distribution of user ratings (1–5) across the selected attractions. Each panel presents a box plot with outliers; panel titles report the sample size n and the site's mean rating. Ratings are strongly positive overall—the interquartile ranges cluster around 4.0–5.0 with medians near the upper end—and only a few low outliers appear near 1–2 stars. The red dashed vertical line marks the overall mean across attractions (approximately 4.3–4.4) for reference.

[15] https://github.com/omkarcloud/google-maps-scraper.

[16] https://chromewebstore.google.com/detail/tripadvisor%C2%AE-review-scrap/pkbfojcocjkdhlcicpanllbeokhajlme.

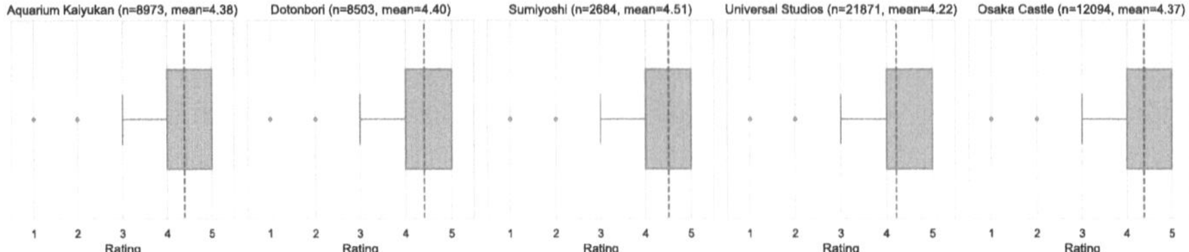

Fig. 2. Distribution of overall visitor ratings for attractions in Osaka.

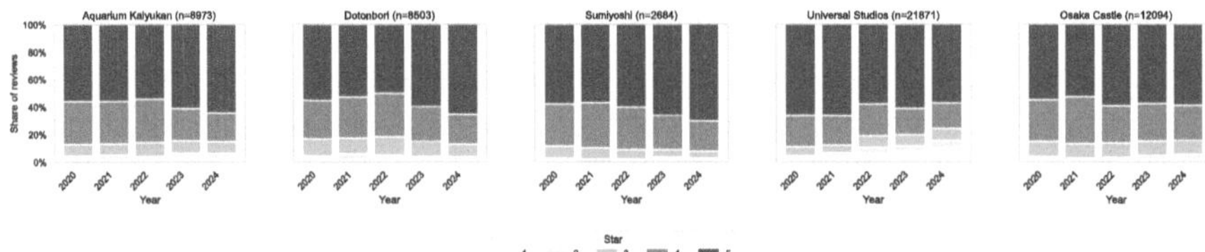

Fig. 3. Distribution of review ratings for Osaka's tourist destinations by year.

Figure 3 shows the year-by-year composition of user ratings, plotted as 100% stacked bars for each panel (legend: 1–5 stars). Across the years, five-star reviews consistently make up the largest share, followed by four-star reviews, while one- to two-star reviews remain a small minority. The mix is broadly stable from 2020 to 2024 with only modest shifts—some panels show a slight uptick in lower-star shares around 2022–2023—indicating persistently strong sentiment over time.

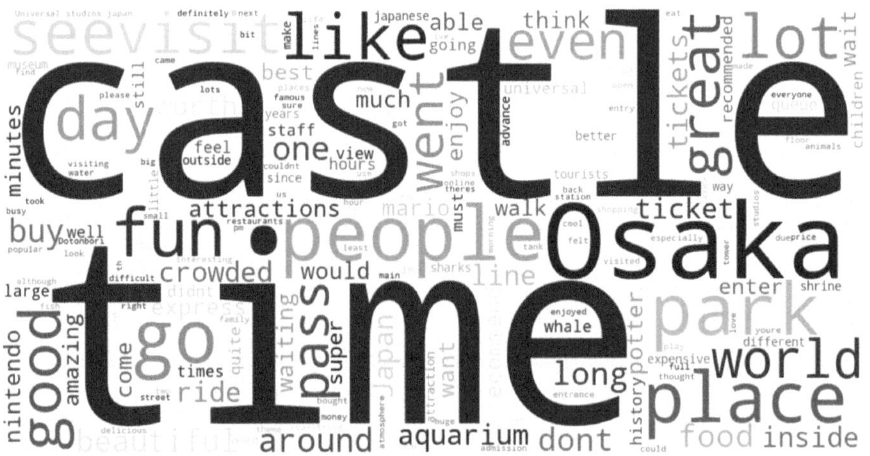

Fig. 4. Word cloud illustrating the most commonly occurring terms in the dataset.

Figure 4 shows the most frequent terms in the reviews, with word size proportional to frequency. Prominent nouns and places (e.g., *castle*, *park*, *osaka*, *people*, *place*, *time*, *day*) sit alongside action terms (*go*, *ride*, *pass*, *ticket*, *line*, *enter*, *walk*). Positive descriptors such as *great*, *good*, *beautiful*, *fun*, and *amazing* are dominant, while congestion and cost cues—*crowded*, *wait*, *queue*, *long*, *expensive*—also appear, indicating generally favorable sentiment tempered by queueing/overcrowding concerns.

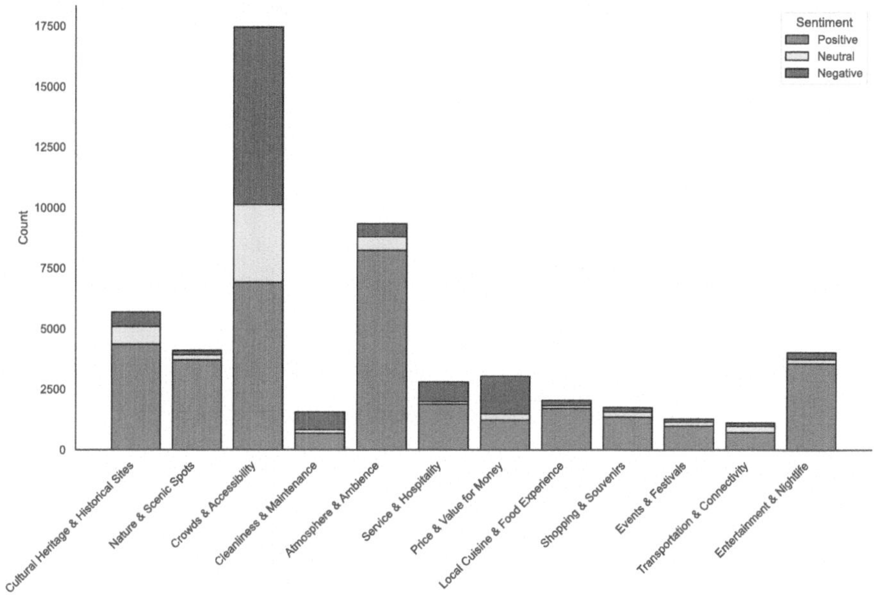

Fig. 5. Distribution of sentiments across different topics.

5.3 Topic Modeling

Figure 5 shows topic volumes and their sentiment composition. The largest topic by volume is Crowds & Accessibility, and—given its size and relatively high negative share—it contributes the largest absolute number of negative reviews. Price & Value for Money has the highest negative ratio, with Cleanliness & Maintenance also showing a substantial negative share. In contrast, topics like Atmosphere & Ambiance and Entertainment & Nightlife are predominantly positive.

5.4 Sentiment Analysis

Figure 6 shows three heatmaps of the shares of positive, neutral, and negative reviews by topics. Overall, sentiment is strongly positive: most topics have positive shares ≥ 0.65, with several near 0.85–0.90 such as Nature & Scenic Spots,

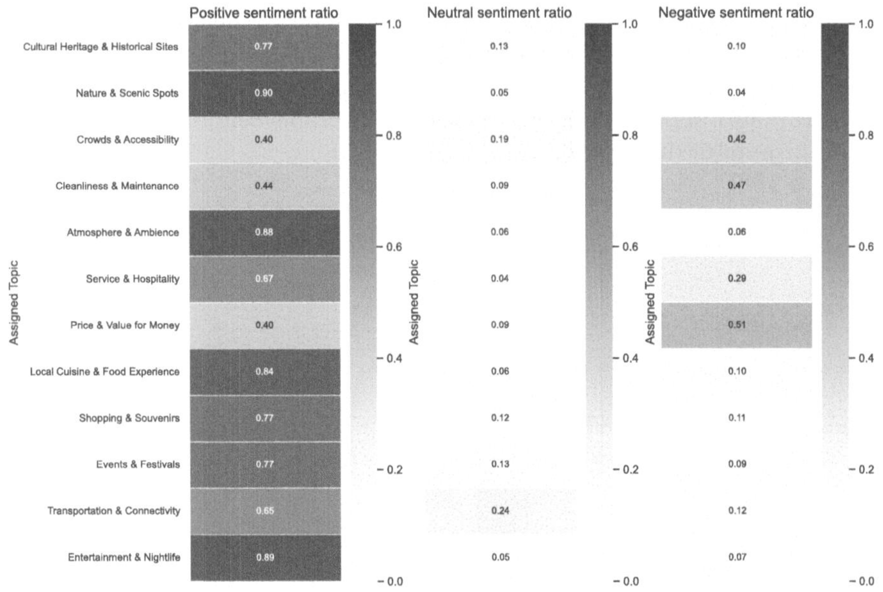

Fig. 6. Proportion of sentiments categorized by topic.

Entertainment & Nightlife, Atmosphere & Ambience, and Local Cuisine & Food Experience. Neutral shares are generally small (≈ 0.04–0.13), except Transportation & Connectivity (~ 0.24). Negative sentiment concentrates in Price & Value for Money (~ 0.51), Cleanliness & Maintenance (~ 0.47), and Crowds & Accessibility (~ 0.42); other topics show low negatives (≤ 0.12).

Figure 7 shows, for each topic, locations ranked by average sentiment score. Horizontal bars are labeled with their values; the dashed vertical line at 0 marks neutrality; and the color scale (red $\rightarrow$ yellow $\rightarrow$ green) reflects negative to positive sentiment. Most topics are solidly positive (typically 0.3–0.7), whereas Price & Value for Money and Crowds & Accessibility include some negative averages, and Cleanliness & Maintenance is mixed with one clearly negative site. In contrast, Atmosphere & Ambience, Local Cuisine & Food Experience, and Entertainment & Nightlife trend strongly positive.

Figure 8 shows year-by-year rank trajectories (1 = best) for the five locations within each topic. Each panel traces within-topic standings across 2020–2024; line crossings mark shifts in relative performance. Several topics display stable leaders near ranks 1–2, such as Atmosphere & Ambience, Entertainment & Nightlife, Nature & Scenic Spots, while others are more volatile with frequent cross-overs, such as Cultural Heritage & Historical Sites, Price & Value for Money. Crowds & Accessibility and Cleanliness & Maintenance show declines for some locations, whereas Local Cuisine & Food Experience and Transportation & Connectivity exhibit sustained top-tier performance by at least one location.

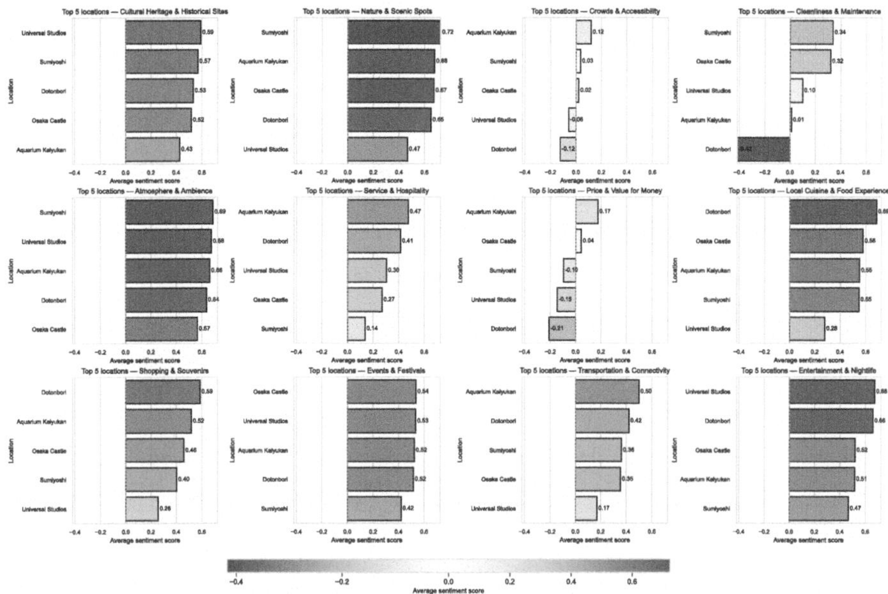

Fig. 7. Top five rankings grouped by topic.

Figure 9 plots annual ranks (1 = best) for the five locations from 2020–2024. Osaka Castle is the overall leader—first in 2020, back to first in 2023–2024, and never below second. Aquarium Kaiyukan briefly tops the table in 2021, otherwise hovering around second/third. Dotonbori is the most volatile, dipping to fifth in 2021 and recovering to third by 2024. Sumiyoshi climbs from last in 2020 to mid-pack in 2022–2023 before easing to fourth in 2024. Universal Studios tracks the bottom, holding fifth from 2022 onward.

Figure 10 shows the distribution of GPT-5 mini's confidence for all $N =$ 54,126 sentiment predictions. Scores cluster at the high end (roughly 0.80–0.92) with a prominent peak near 0.88–0.90. The dashed vertical lines mark the mean (0.83) and median (0.85), indicating a slight left skew from a small tail below 0.70. Overall, predictions are typically high-confidence, with the low-confidence tail suggesting candidates for manual review.

5.5 Comparison with Manually Generated Annotations

Table 3 compares GPT-5 mini with human annotations across locations, while Tables 4 and 5 report the same metrics by year and by topic. Agreement is strongest for *Sumiyoshi* (accuracy 0.83, macro-F1 0.73, $\kappa = 0.64$) and *Aquarium Kaiyukan* (0.81/0.66/0.59), and weakest for *Osaka Castle* (0.72/0.56/0.42). Performance is fairly stable over time: macro-F1 increases from 0.61 in 2020 to 0.65 in 2024 and κ rises from 0.50 to 0.56, with a dip in 2022. By topic, accuracy is highest for Nature & Scenic Spots, Atmosphere & Ambience, and Entertainment

Table 3. Evaluation by location

Location	n	Accuracy	Macro-F1	Cohen's κ
Sumiyoshi	2684	0.8320	0.7326	0.6360
Aquarium Kaiyukan	8973	0.8121	0.6646	0.5890
Dotonbori	8503	0.7727	0.6525	0.5533
Universal Studios	21872	0.7393	0.6365	0.5518
Osaka Castle	12094	0.7153	0.5616	0.4236

Table 4. Evaluation by year

Year	n	Accuracy	Macro-F1	Cohen's κ
2020	7197	0.7696	0.6143	0.4961
2021	3166	0.7798	0.6429	0.5268
2022	6523	0.7319	0.6182	0.4891
2023	17247	0.7558	0.6377	0.5470
2024	19993	0.7549	0.6474	0.5584

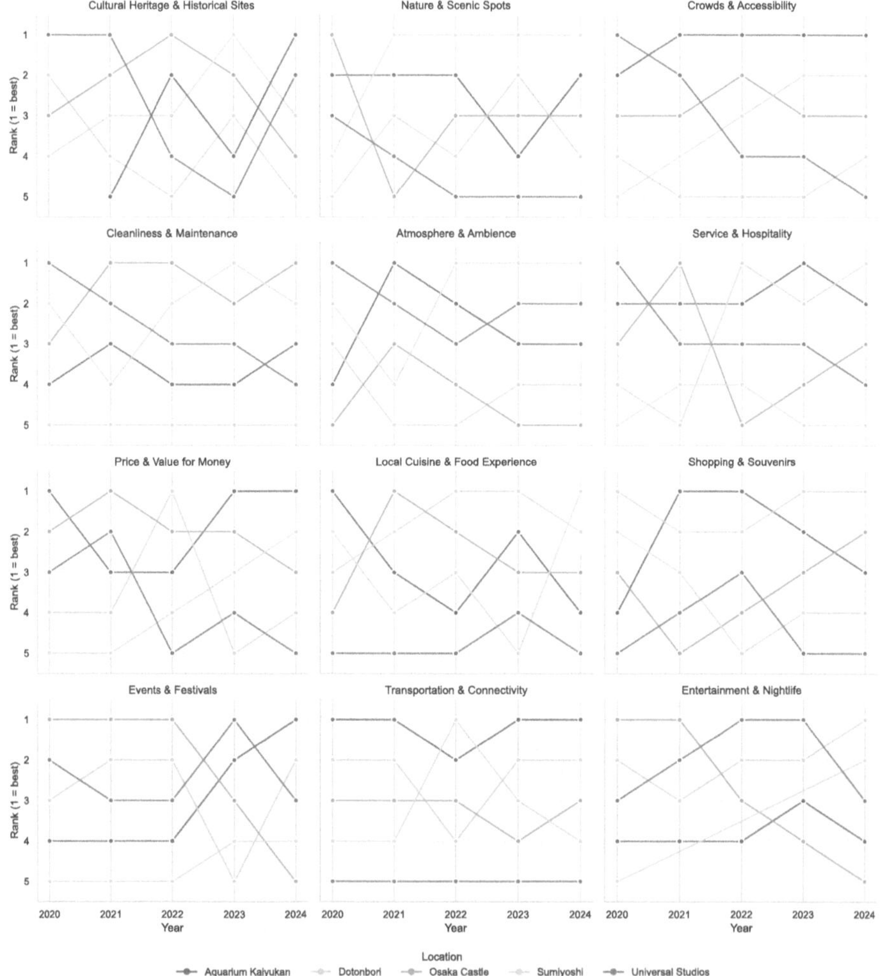

Fig. 8. Top five places for each topic by year.

& Nightlife (~ 0.87–0.88), whereas Service & Hospitality yields the best macro-F1 (0.70) and the highest κ (0.70). The most challenging categories are Crowds & Accessibility and Price & Value for Money, with lower accuracy (0.61–0.64)

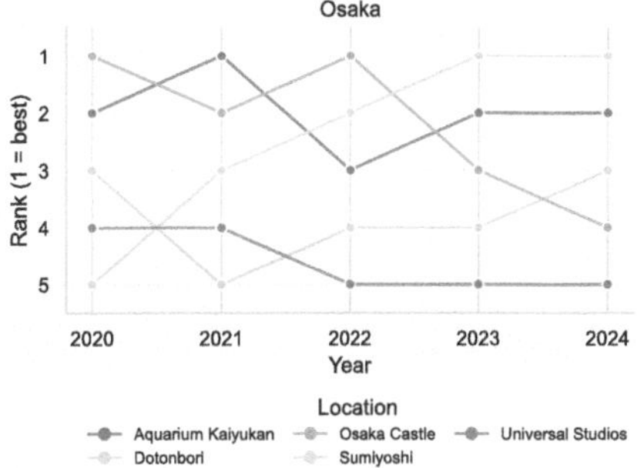

Fig. 9. Top five places over five years.

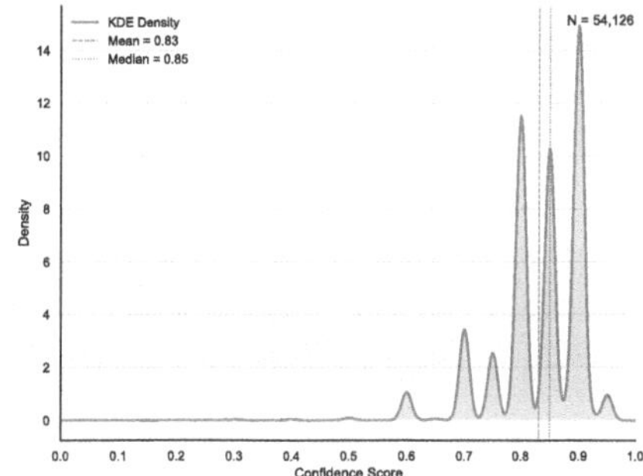

Fig. 10. Distribution of confidence scores.

Table 5. Evaluation by topics

Topic	n	Accuracy	Macro-F1	Cohen's κ
Service & Hospitality	2789	0.8483	0.6963	0.7025
Cleanliness & Maintenance	1549	0.7392	0.6700	0.5966
Local Cuisine & Food Experience	2039	0.8509	0.6404	0.5482
Events & Festivals	1269	0.8125	0.6433	0.5303
Atmosphere & Ambience	9334	0.8763	0.6371	0.5260
Entertainment & Nightlife	4025	0.8743	0.6358	0.5089
Nature & Scenic Spots	4102	0.8813	0.6329	0.4824
Cultural Heritage & Historical Sites	5677	0.7927	0.6325	0.4903
Shopping & Souvenirs	1750	0.8057	0.6308	0.5146
Transportation & Connectivity	1110	0.7189	0.6117	0.4539
Crowds & Accessibility	17442	0.6124	0.5883	0.4304
Price & Value for Money	3040	0.6352	0.5674	0.4529

and agreement ($\kappa \approx 0.43$–0.45). Overall, the model achieves moderate-to-strong agreement with humans, with variability that tracks intuitively difficult topics and periods.

5.6 Qualitative Analysis

To support the qualitative stage, we drew a stratified, time-balanced subsample. For each attraction, we capped the sample at 300 reviews by targeting 20 reviews per sentiment band (positive, neutral, negative) within each calendar year from 2020–2024 (i.e., $5 \times 3 \times 20 = 300$ per site). The three-way polarity bins follow common sentiment-analysis practice, while a five-year horizon spans pandemic onset through recovery in a way that is pertinent to contemporary Osaka tourism. Setting the quota at 20 per year–sentiment cell trades off thematic saturation against coding effort (and spreadsheet size). When a stratum contained fewer than 20 records—most often in early-pandemic periods—we retained all available items rather than compensating elsewhere, preserving the temporal structure and reporting any shortfalls transparently.

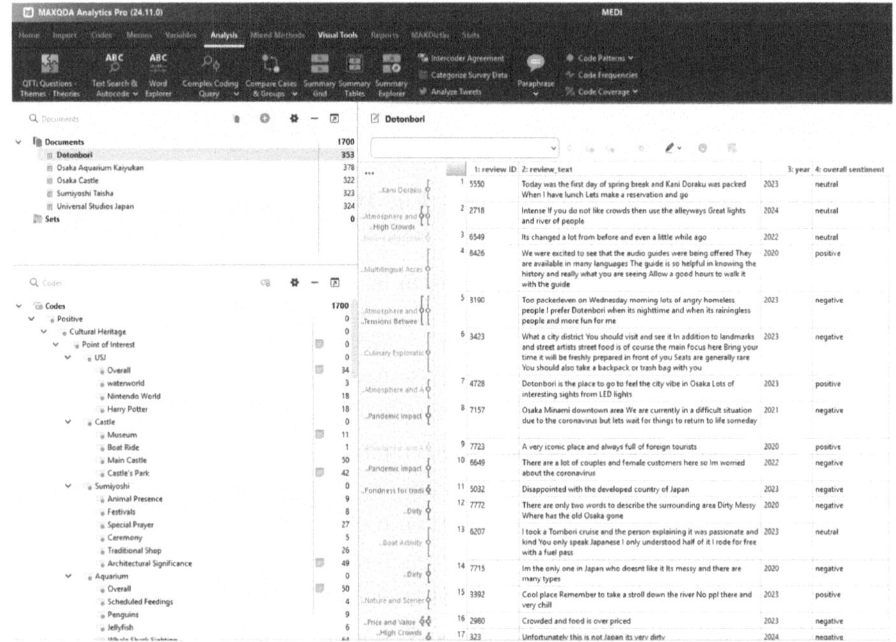

Fig. 11. MAXQDA setup for qualitative research.

Figure 11 shows the MAXQDA Analytics Pro interface used for qualitative analysis of travel reviews in Osaka. On the left, the documents panel lists datasets by attraction (e.g., Dotonbori, Osaka Aquarium, Osaka Castle), while the codes panel displays hierarchical codes such as Positive, Cultural Heritage, and Point of Interest. On the right, a table presents individual reviews with their ID, text, year, and overall sentiment (positive, negative, neutral). The toolbar provides tools for coding, visualization, and intercoder agreement, supporting systematic thematic and sentiment analysis of tourist experiences.

To probe the local context around salient review terms, we employ MAXQDA's *Word Tree* (Fig. 12), a keyword-in-context visualization. Starting from a chosen root at the center, left branches show words that precede the term, and right branches show words that follow it. Branch thickness and label repetition encode frequency, highlighting common phrases and collocations. Reading paths outward from the center reveal typical expressions, modifiers, and sentiment cues; we use these insights to refine codes and consolidate themes. For each corpus, we generate a separate Word Tree and treat it as qualitative evidence to triangulate our manual coding.

(a) Dotonbori (b) Osaka Aquarium (c) Osaka Castle (d) Sumiyoshi (e) Universal Studios Japan

Fig. 12. Word Tree built from each attraction's corpus.

Figure 13 presents the code clouds generated from the qualitative coding of tourist reviews in MAXQDA for five attractions in Osaka. The word clouds visualize the most frequently applied codes and themes, with larger font sizes indicating higher prevalence in the dataset. Prominent themes such as High Crowds, Atmosphere & Ambience, Culinary Exploration, and Pandemic Impact appear consistently across sites, while location-specific themes such as Whale Shark Sighting (Aquarium) and Architectural Significance (Sumiyoshi) highlight unique aspects of each attraction. These visualizations provide an overview of the key issues and experiences emphasized by visitors during their travel.

Figure 14 displays the document similarity analysis of five attractions based on the occurrence and frequency of applied codes. The values in the matrix range from 0 (no similarity) to 1 (identical coding patterns), with darker green indicating higher similarity. For instance, Osaka Aquarium and Universal Studios

(a) Dotonbori (b) Osaka Aquarium

(c) Osaka Castle (d) Sumiyoshi (e) Universal Studios Japan

Fig. 13. Code cloud representations of reviews for five major tourist attractions in Osaka.

Document name	Dotonbori	Osaka Aquarium Kaiyukan	Osaka Castle	Sumiyoshi Taisha	Universal Studios Japan
Dotonbori	1.00	0.75	0.50	0.63	0.75
Osaka Aquarium Kaiyukan	0.75	1.00	0.50	0.63	0.75
Osaka Castle	0.50	0.50	1.00	0.88	0.75
Sumiyoshi Taisha	0.63	0.63	0.88	1.00	0.88
Universal Studios Japan	0.75	0.75	0.75	0.88	1.00

Fig. 14. Document similarity analysis of coded reviews for five attractions in Osaka, generated with MAXQDA. The values (0–1) indicate the degree of thematic overlap between documents, with darker green representing higher similarity. (Color figure online)

Japan exhibit a high similarity of 0.75, suggesting they share many common thematic codes, while Osaka Castle shows a particularly strong resemblance to Sumiyoshi Taisha (0.88). This visual comparison aids in identifying which attractions evoke similar visitor experiences in reviews, as captured through qualitative coding.

Across the five attractions, positive reviews are led by Distinctive Experiences and Spectacles, Atmosphere & Scenery, Cultural/Architectural Features, Events & Festivals, and trip enhancers such as Food & Shopping; Family-Friendliness & Convenience also contribute. Neutral comments mainly record context and logistics—descriptions of Ambience & Heritage, notes on Accessibility (including Language and Website Usability), and Visit Timing—without strong affect. Negative sentiment is dominated by Crowding and the discomfort it creates (Tensions, Fatigue, Noise), followed by Operational Restrictions (Policies/Closures), perceived Poor Value and Service Lapses, and Maintenance or Amenity Deficits (Cleanliness, Seating, Restrooms), alongside Way-finding & Safety Concerns.

In general, the qualitative themes align with the quantitative topic and sentiment patterns: topics with the highest positive shares, Atmosphere & Ambience, Nature & Scenic Spots, Entertainment & Nightlife, and Local Cuisine & Food, mirror frequent codes in the reviews. Conversely, negative results in Price & Value, Cleanliness & Maintenance, and Crowds & Accessibility are echoed by codes such as High Crowds, Restrictive Policies, and cleanliness or amenity deficits. Neutral and logistical observations, especially Transportation & Connectivity, correspond to higher neutral shares and are reflected qualitatively by Language Barrier and Website Usability. Overall, the qualitative analysis corroborates and clarifies the quantitative results across attractions.

6 Conclusion

This paper introduced a mixed research framework that pairs a lightweight GPT-5 mini with MAXQDA-based qualitative coding to convert large volumes of travel reviews into an interpretable topic–sentiment matrix. Applied to Osaka (2020–2024), the pipeline yields stable, manager-friendly categories and moderate-to-strong agreement with human labels, surfacing strengths in Atmosphere & Ambience, Nature & Scenic Spots, Entertainment & Nightlife, and Local Cuisine & Food, while concentrating negatives in Price & Value for Money, Cleanliness & Maintenance, and Crowds & Accessibility. The qualitative strand corroborates and explains the quantitative patterns, clarifies boundary cases, and highlights cross-cutting factors, producing actionable guidance for destination managers (crowd management, service/amenities, value communication) and travelers (expectations, timing, access). Future work will extend the dataset to additional cities and platforms, and provide an in-depth understanding of travelers' needs and narratives by linking aspect sentiment to behavioral and temporal signals such as visit timing and dwell time, and by incorporating other modalities like review images and seasonal patterns.

References

1. Liu, B.: Sentiment analysis and opinion mining. Morgan & Claypool Publishers, San Rafael, California (2012)
2. Yang, Yu., Dinh, D.-T., Nguyen, B.-H., Fangyu, Yu., Huynh, V.-N.: Mining insights from esports game reviews with an aspect-based sentiment analysis framework. IEEE Access **11**, 61161–61172 (2023)
3. Yu, Y., Dinh, T., Yu, F., Huynh, V.N.: Understanding mobile game reviews through sentiment analysis: a case study of pubgm. In: International Conference on Model and Data Engineering, pp. 102–115. Springer (2023)
4. Mehraliyev, F., Chan, I.C.C., Kirilenko, A.P.: Sentiment analysis in hospitality and tourism: a thematic and methodological review. Int. J. Contemporary Hospitality Manag. **34**(1), 46–77 (2022)
5. Obinwanne, T., Brandtner, P.: Enhancing sentiment analysis with GPT—a comparison of large language models and traditional machine learning techniques. In: International Conference on WorldS4, pp. 187–197. Springer (2023)
6. Sai, A.A., Balamurali, O., Karthikeya, M., Anand, S.: Sentiment analysis for better user experience in tourism chatbot using LSTM and LLM. In: 2023 9th International Conference on Signal Processing and Communication (ICSC), pp. 456–462. IEEE (2023)
7. Guidotti, D., Pandolfo, L., Pulina, L.: LLMs for sentiment analysis in tourism reviews: a resource-efficient approach. In: 2024 IEEE 36th International Conference on Tools with Artificial Intelligence (ICTAI), pp. 502–508. IEEE (2024)
8. Kheiri, K., Karimi, H.: Sentimentgpt: leveraging GPT for advancing sentiment analysis. In: 2024 IEEE International Conference on Big Data (BigData), pp. 7051–7060. IEEE (2024)
9. Ghatora, P.S., Hosseini, S.E., Pervez, S., Iqbal, M.J., Shaukat, N.: Sentiment analysis of product reviews using machine learning and pre-trained LLM. Big Data Cogn. Comput. **8**(12), 199 (2024)
10. Yang, Y., et al.: Performance evaluation and application potential of small large language models in complex sentiment analysis tasks. IEEE Access (2025)
11. Shah, F.A., Sabir, A., Sharma, R., Pfahl, D.: How effectively do LLMs extract feature-sentiment pairs from app reviews? In: International Working Conference on Requirements Engineering: Foundation for Software Quality, pp. 123–138. Springer (2025)
12. Creswell, J.W.: A concise introduction to mixed methods research. SAGE publications (2021)
13. George, O.A., Ramos, C.M.Q.: Sentiment analysis applied to tourism: exploring tourist-generated content in the case of a wellness tourism destination. Int. J. Spa Wellness **7**(2), 139–161 (2024)
14. Liyanaarachchi, S., Dinh, T., Yue, W., Vo, T., Nguyen, L.-M.: Sentiment analysis of travel reviews in Kyoto using LLMs. In: International Conference on Advanced Data Mining and Applications, pp. 244–256. Springer, Cham (2025). https://doi.org/10.1007/978-981-95-3459-3_20

A Stacked Hybrid Ensemble of Swin-V2 and MViT-V2 for High-Performance Skin Disease Classification

Davinder Paul Singh[1](✉), Vraj Patel[1], Dhairya Doshi[2], Shubham Mahajan[3], and Seifedine Kadry[4]

[1] Pandit Deendayal Energy University, Gandhinagar Gujarat, India
devsingh0071@gmail.com, vraj.pce22@sot.pdpu.ac.in
[2] Ahmedabad University, Ahmedabad, Gujarat, India
dhairya.d2@ahduni.edu.in
[3] Amity University, Panchgaon, Haryana 122413, India
[4] Lebanese American University, Beirut, Lebanon

Abstract. Skin diseases pose a growing global health concern that is often underestimated and underprioritized in clinical practice. Timely and accurate diagnosis is vital for effective treatment. Recently, Deep Learning approaches, especially Convolutional Neural Networks (CNNs), have shown promise in automating the diagnostic process. However, as the number of disease classes increases, CNNs and traditional Visual Transformers (ViTs) generally struggle with visually similar diseases, resulting in decreased classification performance. To address these challenges, we propose a new approach that combines two advanced ViT architectures—Shifted Window Transformer (Swin) and Multi-Scale Vision Transformer (MViT)—and ensembles these models using a stacking technique to boost classification accuracy. Using a dataset of 19,559 images containing 23 skin disease classes from a Kaggle directory curated from Dermnet, our ensemble achieves 90% accuracy on unseen data, outperforming previous CNN-based approaches, which reached up to 81%. Additionally, the model attains an overall weighted F_1-score of 0.90 and recall of 0.90, demonstrating balanced performance for all classes. Importantly, our proposed ensemble model does not require computationally intensive devices to operate, making it accessible for low-resource clinical environments.

Keywords: Vision Transformers · Swin Transformer V2 · Multiscale Vision Transformer V2 · Ensemble Learning · Stacking Meta-Classifier · Skin Disease Classification · DermNet Dataset · Grad-CAM · Low-Resource Clinical Deployment

1 Introduction

Skin diseases pose a crucial global health challenge, with skin and subcutaneous conditions representing 4.02% of all years lived with disability (YLDs) in India alone [1]. Therefore, early diagnosis of skin conditions is crucial for achieving better outcomes, reducing the impact of the disease, and increasing survival rates [2].

A. Awad et al. (Eds.): MEDI 2025, LNCS 16427, pp. 257–270, 2026.
https://doi.org/10.1007/978-3-032-19865-5_21

Despite this, access to dermatological care remains limited. Studies show that only 24% of individuals seek professional help for skin conditions, while 90% of all cases are managed by general practitioners [3]. Furthermore, malignant conditions such as melanoma continue to increase, with over 10,000 deaths reported annually in the United States alone [4]. The World Health Organization has also recognized skin disease as the third most common cause of illness globally and a major cause of long-term disability [5].

Traditional practices depend significantly on manual assessments by dermatologists, which is time-consuming and vulnerable to human error [6]. This undermines the urgent need for accurate and efficient automated tools. With the rise of Artificial Intelligence (AI) in healthcare, computer vision has proven to be an excellent approach for medical image analysis and classification [7].

Convolutional Neural Networks (CNNs) have shown great success in processing image data and detecting localized patterns. However, they struggle to capture complex global context, which limits their classification accuracy to around 80% in multi-class tasks. To address these limitations, Vision Transformers (ViTs) have proven to be a powerful alternative. They utilize self-attention techniques that were originally popularized by natural language processing [8].

This paper presents an ensemble-based architecture that integrates two powerful ViT models—Swin Transformer and Multiscale Vision Transformer (MViT)—to enhance skin disease classification accuracy. The complementary characteristics of these architectures make them well-suited for ensemble learning.

The dataset used in this study includes 19,559 images across 23 disease classes, sourced from a Kaggle repository based on the DermNet database [9].

Finally, we evaluate model performance using standard classification metrics such as accuracy, precision, recall, F1-score, and class-wise breakdowns. We also utilize Grad-CAM visualizations to understand where the model's focus regions are, which provides insights into the decision-making process and enhances the system's transparency and trustworthiness.

2 Literature Review

The field of automated diagnosis for skin diseases has expanded rapidly, creating more efficient, accessible, and precise diagnostic tools. Early research in deep learning, especially Convolutional Neural Networks (CNNs), demonstrated significant improvements over traditional machine learning methods and can now match the diagnostic capabilities of human dermatologists [10]. Although foundational deep learning models like CNNs have achieved success, they often find it difficult to differentiate between visually similar skin conditions, resulting in performance ceilings around 80.95% [11].

To address this, the field has shifted towards Vision Transformers (ViTs), which are highly effective at capturing global context through self-attention [12]. The current state of this evolving field is moving towards synergistic models that merge the strengths of different architectures to achieve better performance. This started with ensembles of multiple CNNs that attained classification accuracy of 97.23% on the HAM10000 dataset [13].

Recently, hybrid models that combine CNNs and Transformer models have gained popularity due to their ability to utilize the local feature extraction of CNNs alongside the global context modelling of Transformers within a single, powerful framework [14]. This development has led to the most advanced methods: ensemble models composed of different Transformer architectures. The main idea is that even within Transformer families, different models acquire unique and complementary representations. One such model combined DINOv2, Swin Transformers, and ConvNeXt to achieve impressive accuracy on a 31-class skin disease classification task [15].

The idea and work presented in this paper advance the field. By creating a parallel ensemble of Swin-v2 and MViT-v2, our model combines two different yet complementary Transformer designs. Swin-v2 constructs its hierarchy through spatial partitioning with shifted windows [16, 17], while MViT-v2 employs semantic pooling to establish a multiscale feature pyramid [18]. This approach ensures efficient feature reuse and enhanced semantic understanding across multiple scales. This innovative architecture aims to generate a more comprehensive and powerful feature representation than either model alone, facilitating highly accurate and robust skin disease classification.

3 Methodology

This section explains the methodology for multi-class skin disease classification using Swin-V2 and MViT-V2 models, combined via a meta-learning-based stacking ensemble strategy. The methodology includes data preprocessing, data transformation, model architecture, training process, and evaluation metrics.

As shown in Fig. 1, the pipeline initializes with data preprocessing and transformation. All input images are transformed into a standard resolution of 192×192 pixels, which is required by both the Swin-V2 and MViT-V2 architectures. Image quality is enhanced through contrast adjustment and sharpening for better visual clarity, enabling more effective feature extraction during model training. Since the dataset classes are heavily imbalanced, data transformation is applied to underrepresented classes by generating artificial variations. This not only manages the issue of class imbalance but also increases the dataset size, providing the models with increased data to learn from. The transformed dataset is then split into training, test, and validation sets in the ratio 70:20:10.

The Swin-V2 and MViT-V2 serve as the core architectures for feature extraction. These models are trained on a preprocessed and augmented image dataset, and their performance is validated using a separate validation set to ensure generalization and to test their ability to perform well on unseen data.

After training, the models are then evaluated using comprehensive performance metrics like accuracy, precision, recall (sensitivity), F1-Score, and the confusion matrix. These metrics provide a complete understanding of the model's performance across different classes and help assess the comprehensive reliability of the proposed framework.

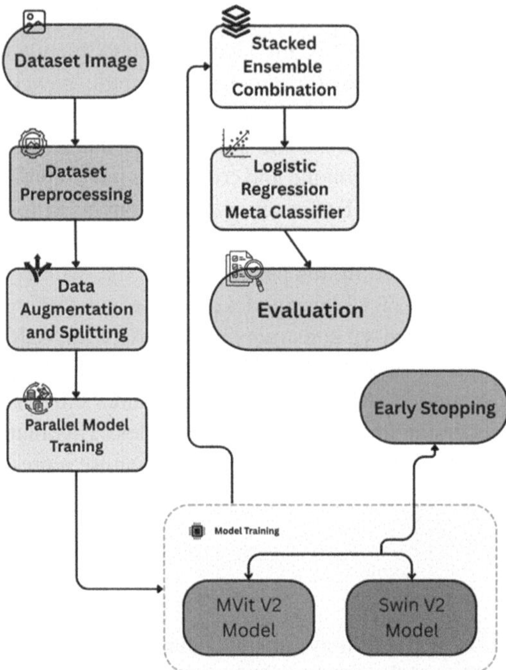

Fig. 1. Pipeline overview from data collection to model training.

3.1 Dataset

The dataset used in this study is acquired from the DermNet database, a reputable and clearly defined resource for dermatological image classification. DermNet offers clinical images categorized into 23 disease classes, examples of which are shown in Fig. 2, making it a valuable standard for developing and evaluating deep learning models for medical image analysis.

For this research, a total of 19,559 images divided into 23 distinct categories were sourced from a Kaggle repository based on DermNet. Each category represents a type of dermatological condition. The distribution of images across these categories is shown in Fig. 3, offering insight into the class imbalance within the dataset.

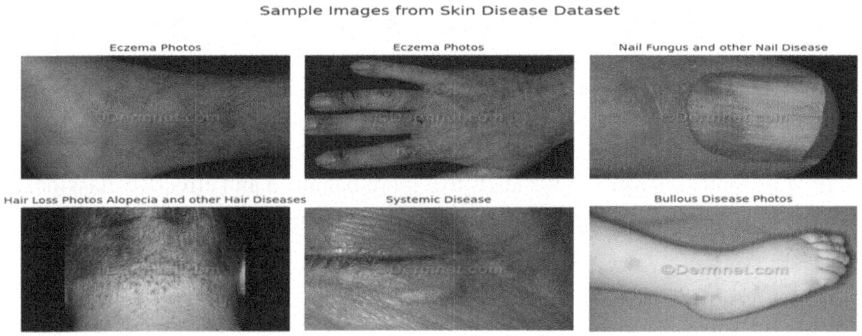

Fig. 2. Six example images from different disease classes in our 23-class DermNet dataset

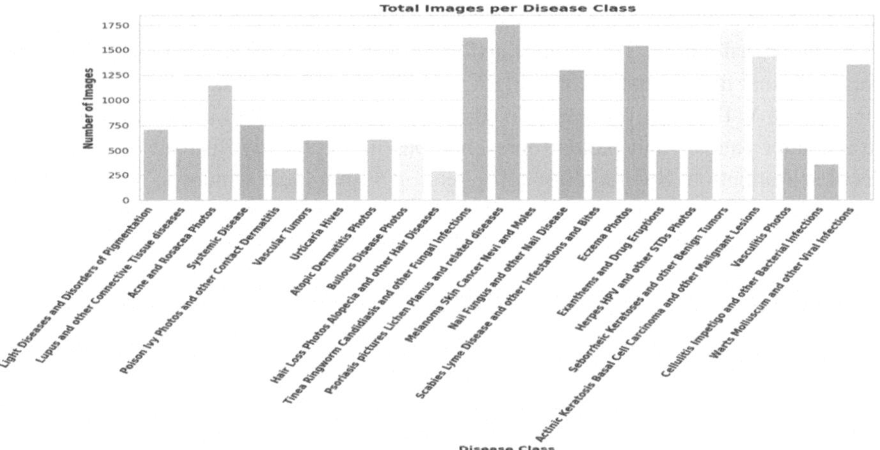

Fig. 3. Number of images per class.

3.2 Data Preprocessing and Transformation

The raw dataset comprises various dimensions and aspect ratios that must be standardised before training the models. Since the Swin-V2 and MViT-V2 architectures require inputs of $192 \times 192 \times 3$, each image is converted accordingly to meet these specifications. We cannot resize the images directly without ensuring that important regions are preserved, as this could cause distortion and loss of critical visual features. To address this, centre cropping is applied first to retain the most relevant parts of the image, followed by resizing to the specified dimensions. This approach helps preserve essential information while maintaining model compatibility.

As shown in the table, the dataset is highly imbalanced, with some classes having significantly fewer images than others. Therefore, a well-structured data transformation strategy is employed to manage class imbalance and enhance model generalization. For classes with fewer than 1,000 images, samples are augmented to reach 1,500 images, while classes with more than 1,000 images are expanded to 2,000 images each.

The Data Transformation pipeline applies random rotations of up to $\pm 15°$, random horizontal flips, and adjusts brightness and contrast to simulate real-world variations in orientation, lighting, and color.

These transformations not only help balance the dataset but also introduce variety that prepares the model for real-world scenarios, such as variations in imaging conditions, lighting, and skin tones. This leads to a more balanced and effective classification framework that reduces bias and improves performance on unseen data.

3.3 Model Architecture

In this section, we will discuss the Transformer models used for training on the 23-class skin disease dataset. Since their introduction, Transformers have completely transformed vision tasks, especially with the rise of Vision Transformer (ViT), which has been widely used due to its ability to capture global context within images.

Swin Transformer: The Swin transformer provides an effective, hierarchical approach to visual understanding, making it suitable for tasks like skin disease classification. Unlike ViT, which processes fixed-size global patches, Swin Transformer starts with smaller patches and builds representations hierarchically. Instead of performing global self-attention, Swin applies self-attention within local windows, reducing computational cost. These windows are then shifted at each Transformer block layer to facilitate cross-window information exchange. This enables the model to capture global context.

Multiscale Vision Transformer (MViT): The MViT improves on the standard Vision Transformer's flat, single-scale design by introducing hierarchical, pyramidal structure. In this architecture, feature maps are gradually down sampled while increasing the number of channels at every stage. This allows MViT to process visual information at multiple resolutions. The self-attention technique is applied within increasingly coarser spatial resolutions. This lets the model efficiently capture both fine-grained local and global details and patterns [19]. MViT pools the keys and values before applying self-attention to optimize the performance even further. This reduces the higher computational cost of self-attention, allowing us to scale it to deeper layers and input higher resolution data without exceeding memory limits of our machine. This multiscale approach balances between computational efficiency and performance of the model. As a result, MViT offers a practical and scalable solution for complex visual understanding problems [20].

3.4 Model Ensembling – Stacking Meta Classifier Using Logistic Regression

To further improve the performance, we used model ensembling using a stacking approach. In this method, multiple unique models are first trained on the dataset. Their individual outputs are then given to a meta classifier, which learns how to combine their predictions for the best results. Here we use logistic regression as the meta classifier. By assigning weights to the predictions of the base models, it then favors the models that perform well for specific types of inputs. This technique uses the strengths of different architectures, removing model biases and improving generalization [8]. This ensemble generates better robustness and accuracy compared to any individual model, especially when handling multi-class classification tasks such as skin disease diagnosis.

3.5 Evaluation Metrics

To evaluate model performance and robustness, we employ the following metrics:

Accuracy: Overall correctness on training and validation sets:

$$\text{Accuracy} = \frac{\text{TP} + \text{TN}}{\text{TP} + \text{TN} + \text{FP} + \text{FN}}$$

Precision and Recall (for class k): Precision measures the correctness of positive predictions:

$$\text{Precision}_\text{k} = \frac{\text{TP}_\text{k}}{\text{TP}_\text{k} + \text{FP}_\text{k}}$$

and recall (sensitivity) measures detection of actual positives:

$$\text{Recall}_\text{k} = \frac{\text{TP}_\text{k}}{\text{TP}_\text{k} + \text{FN}_\text{k}}$$

F1-Score (for class k): The harmonic mean of precision and recall:

$$\text{F1}_\text{k} = 2 \times \frac{\text{Precision}_\text{k} \times \text{Recall}_\text{k}}{\text{Precision}_\text{k} + \text{Recall}_\text{k}}$$

ROC AUC: Area under the Receiver Operating Characteristic curve, summarizing the trade-off between true positive rate (TPR) and false positive rate (FPR).

Precision–Recall Curve & Average Precision: Plot of precision vs. recall over varying thresholds; average precision is the area under this curve.

Confusion Matrix: Visual depiction of true vs. predicted labels across all classes.

Macro and Weighted Averages: For any per-class metric M_k

$$\text{Macro} - M = \frac{1}{C}\sum\nolimits_{k=1}^{C} M_k$$

$$\text{Weighted} - M = \frac{1}{N}\sum\nolimits_{k=1}^{C} n_k\, M_k$$

where C is the number of classes, n_k is the number of true samples in class k, and

$$N = \sum\nolimits_{k=1} n_k$$

These metrics together provide a complete assessment of our ensemble's classification performance and robustness.

4 Results and Discussion

Both Swin-V2 and MViT-V2 performed exceptionally well during training. As shown in Fig. 4 training accuracy of both models gradually increase with each epoch, ultimately reaching 98–99% by the end of 30th epoch.

Figure 4 shows the validation accuracy of both the models with respect to epochs; we can see that the Swin model achieves 87% validation accuracy and the MViT model achieves 86% validation accuracy which shows the model capability to learn patterns and predict the disease accurately.

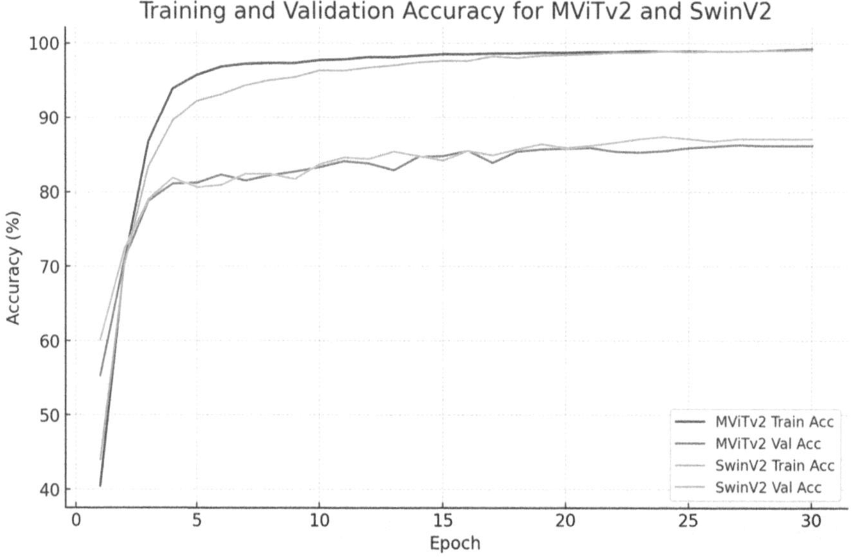

Fig. 4. Training accuracy and Validation accuracy vs. epoch for Swin and MViT models.

In Fig. 5 we can see the training loss and validation loss with respect to epoch for both models. The training loss has drastically decreased from 2 to 0.01 and the validation loss has decreased from 1.5 to 0.75, which indicates steady convergence without severe overfitting.

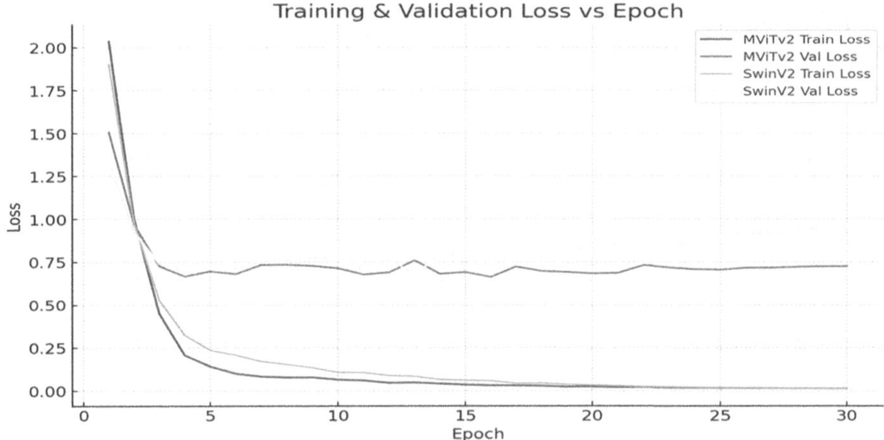

Fig. 5. Training and validation loss vs. epoch for both models.

Further in Fig. 6 we can see the confusion matrix on the 10% unseen validation data to check the robustness of the overall model. The ensemble model was used to make predictions and generate the confusion matrix.

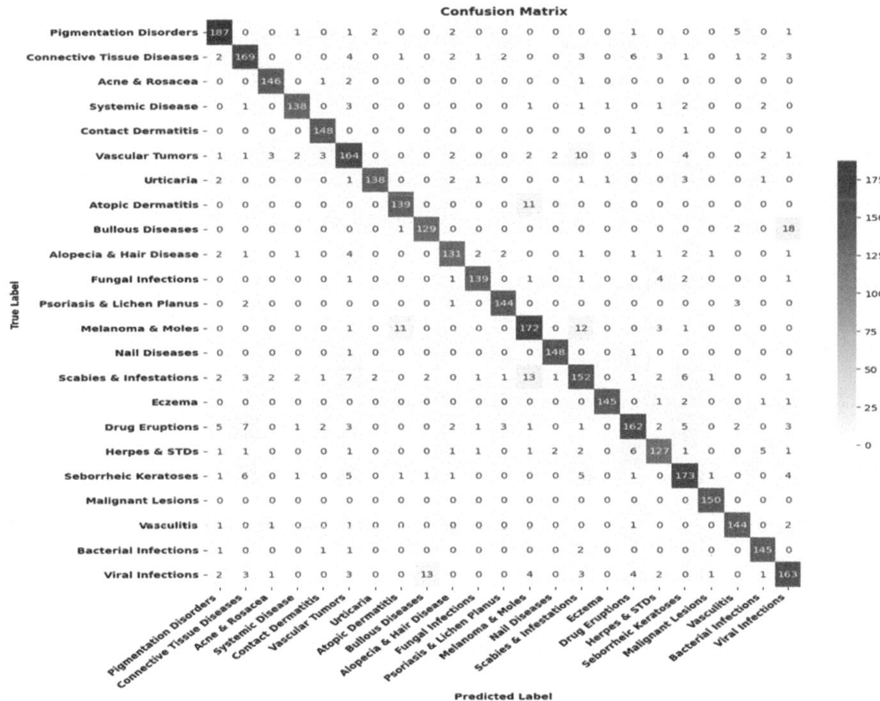

Fig. 6. Confusion matrix on the unseen 10% validation set using the ensemble model.

Table 1 summarizes the validation accuracy of our proposed model with several state-of-the-art approaches for direct comparison.

Table 1. Comparison of Top-1 Accuracy

Model	Validation Accuracy (%)
DenseNet201 [21]	68.97%
Ensemble of VGG16 and EfficientNet-B3 [22]	69.00%
Custom Convolution Transformer [23]	73.8%
Our proposed model: MViTv2 + SwinV2 Ensemble w/ Meta-Classifier	**90.0%**

Table 2 shows class-wise Precision, Recall, F1-score and support. The overall accuracy of the ensemble model reached 90% and the macro average and weighted average are identical (0.90), showing balanced performance across classes.

Table 2. Class-wise Precision, Recall, F1-score and Support

Class	Prec	Rec	F1	Supp
Acne & Rosacea	0.90	0.94	0.92	200
Actinic Ker. & BCC	0.87	0.84	0.86	200
Atopic Dermatitis	0.95	0.97	0.86	150
Bullous Disease	0.95	0.92	0.93	150
Cellulitis & Impetigo	0.95	0.99	0.97	150
Eczema	0.81	0.82	0.81	200
Drug Eruptions	0.97	0.92	0.95	150
Hair Diseases	0.91	0.93	0.92	150
STDs	0.89	0.86	0.87	150
Pigmentation Disorders	0.90	0.87	0.89	150
Lupus & CT Diseases	0.95	0.93	0.94	150
Melanoma & Nevi	0.95	0.96	0.95	150
Nail Disease	0.83	0.86	0.85	200
Contact Dermatitis	0.97	0.99	0.98	150

(continued)

Table 2. (*continued*)

Class	Prec	Rec	F1	Supp
Psoriasis & Lichen Planus	0.78	0.76	0.77	200
Scabies & Bites	0.99	0.97	0.98	150
Seborrheic Keratoses	0.86	0.81	0.84	200
Systemic Diseases	0.87	0.85	0.86	150
Fungal Infections	0.85	0.86	0.86	200
Urticaria	0.97	1.00	0.99	150
Vascular Tumors	0.92	0.96	0.94	150
Vasculitis	0.91	0.97	0.94	150
Viral Infections	0.81	0.81	0.81	200
Macro avg	0.90	0.90	0.90	3850
Weighted avg	0.90	0.90	0.90	3850

Outstanding performance was observed for Scabies & Bites (F1 = 0.98), Poison Ivy (F1 = 0.97), and Melanoma & Nevi (F1 = 0.95). Lower performance was observed for Eczema (F1 = 0.81), Psoriasis & Lichen Planus (F1 = 0.77), and Viral Infections (F1 = 0.81), indicating room for improved transformation and preprocessing.

Figure 7 shows Grad-CAM heatmaps on original images, highlighting regions that the model focuses on for classification. This provides deeper insight into the model's decision-making process and increases transparency.

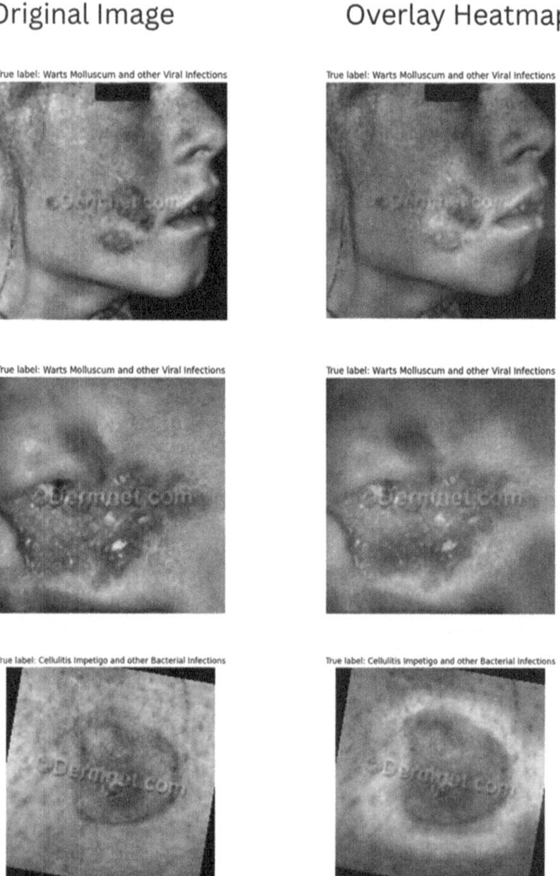

Fig. 7. Grad-CAM heatmaps showing model focus regions (original image left, heatmap overlay right).

5 Conclusion

The evolution and growth of Vision Transformers have made the automation of skin disease classification significantly easier, faster, and more accurate over the past couple of years. By leveraging the unique capabilities of multiple models like CNNs and Transformers or combining multiple Transformer models, we can achieve better results than either could on their own. Our approach is also suitable for low to medium end devices, making it much more accessible compared to heavier models that may offer slightly better performance but are far more computationally expensive.

However, despite the significant growth of computer vision, it still does not match the performance and reliability of a professional dermatologist. This gap can be set down to several factors, primarily the limited availability of high-quality data. Even when data is available, the presence of many visually similar diseases can confuse the model and lead to misclassification. As a result, models tend to perform better on datasets with fewer classes, where there is a lower chance of confusing two or more visually similar conditions.

Further betterments in this field will not only depend on architectural innovation but also resolving data related challenges. Increasing access to diverse, high resolution and verified datasets will be essential to further reduce the gap between AI based classification and professional diagnosis.

Ultimately, our work contributes to this ever-evolving field by proposing an ensemble of Swin-V2 and MViT-V2 models that offer a robust and efficient framework for accurate multi-class skin disease classification.

Availability of Code. https://www.kaggle.com/code/dhairyadoshi45/final-codes

References

1. Kavita, Thakur, J.S., Narang, T.: The burden of skin diseases in India: Global burden of disease study 2017. Indian J. Dermatol. Venereol. Leprol. 89, 421–425 (2023)
2. Li, L.F., Wang, X., Hu, W.J., Xiong, N.N., Du, Y.X., Li, B.S.: Deep learning in skin disease image recognition: a review. IEEE Access **8**, 208264–208280 (2020)
3. Inthiyaz, S., et al.: Skin disease detection using deep learning. Adv. Eng. Softw. **175**, 103361 (2023)
4. Rogers, H.W., Weinstock, M.A., Feldman, S.R., Coldiron, B.M.: Incidence estimate of nonmelanoma skin cancer (Keratinocyte carcinomas) in the US population, 2012. JAMA Dermatol. **151**(10), 1081–1086 (2015)
5. Bhatti, S. et al.: A review of skin disease detection using deep learning. Vis. Technol. Syst. Eng. **12**(4) (2025)
6. Aboulmira, A., Hrimech, H., Lachgar, M.: Skin diseases classification with machine learning and deep learning techniques: a systematic review. Int. J. Adv. Comput. Sci. Appl. **15**(10) (2024)
7. Dhiman, G., Viriyasitavat, W., Nagar, A.K., Castillo, O.: Artificial intelligence and diagnostic healthcare using computer vision and medical imaging. Healthc. Anal. **6**, 100352 (2024)
8. Ali, K., et al.: Adversarial robustness of vision transformers versus convolutional neural networks. IEEE Access **12**, 105281–105293 (2024)
9. Kaggle: DermNet: skin disease image dataset. https://www.kaggle.com/datasets/shubhamgoel27/dermnet, Accessed 30 Jul 2025
10. Haggenmüller, S., et al.: Skin cancer classification via convolutional neural networks: systematic review of studies involving human experts. Eur. J. Cancer **156**, 202–216 (2021)
11. Ahmad, J. et al.: Classification of 24 skin conditions using Swin transformer: leveraging DermNet and healthy skin dataset. In: IET Conference Proceedings **2025**(3), 511–519 (2025)
12. Abbas, Q., et al.: Assist-dermo: a lightweight separable vision transformer model for multiclass skin lesion classification. Diagnostics **13**(15), 2531 (2023)
13. Pratiwi, R., et al.: Deep ensemble learning for skin lesions classification with convolutional neural network. IAES Int. J. Artif. Intell. **10**(3), 563–570 (2021)
14. Gu, P. et al.: ConvFormer: combining CNN and Transformer for medical image segmentation. arXiv preprint arXiv:2211.08564 (2022)
15. Mohan, J. et al.: Enhancing skin disease classification leveraging transformer-based deep learning architectures and explainable AI. arXiv preprint arXiv:2407.14757 (2024)
16. Liu, Z. et al.: Swin transformer: hierarchical vision transformer using shifted windows. In: Proceedings of the IEEE/CVF International Conference On Computer Vision (ICCV), pp. 10012–10022 (2021)

17. Liu, Z. et al.: Swin transformer V2: scaling up capacity and resolution. In: Proceedings of the IEEE/CVF Conference on Computer Vision Pattern Recognition (CVPR), pp. 11999–12009 (2022)
18. Fan, H. et al.: Multiscale vision transformers. In: Proceedings of the IEEE/CVF International Conference on Computer Vision (ICCV), pp. 6824–6835 (2021)
19. Li, Y. et al.: MViTv2: improved multiscale vision transformers for classification and detection. In: Proceedings of the IEEE/CVF Conference on Computer Vision Pattern Recognition (CVPR), New Orleans, LA, USA, pp. 4794–4804 (2022)
20. Ridnik, T. et al.: TresNet: high performance GPU-dedicated architecture. arXiv preprint arXiv: 2003.13630 (2020)
21. Aboulmira, A., Hrimech, H., Lachgar, M.: Comparative study of multiple CNN models for classification of 23 skin diseases. Int. J. Online Biomed. Eng. (iJOE) **18**(11), 127–142 (2022)
22. Ghadekar, P., Bongulwar, A., Jadhav, A., Ahire, R., Dumbre, A., Ali, S.: Ensemble approach to solve multiple skin disease classification using deep learning. In: 2023 International Conference on Device Intelligence, Computing and Communication Technologies (DICCT), pp. 296–301. Dehradun, India (2023)
23. Vishwakarma, R., Sood, D.: Artificial intelligence for image classification of skin diseases with convolution transformer. In: 2024 4th International Conference on Intelligence Technology (CONIT), pp. 1–6. Bangalore, India (2024)

Codecard: Leveraging LLMs to Evaluate AI Model Code Development with the System Cards Framework

Tadesse K. Bahiru and Ioannis A. Kakadiaris(✉)

Computational Biomedicine Lab, Department of Computer Science, University of Houston, Houston, TX, USA
{tbahiru,ioannisk}@uh.edu

Abstract. As AI systems are increasingly deployed in high-stakes domains such as finance, healthcare, and education, their responsible use requires scrutiny of how they are engineered, not just how they perform. Although there are now documentation standards for datasets and models, the source code that governs data handling, training, and deployment is rarely audited systematically. To address this gap, this paper introduces Codecard as a part of the System Cards Framework. Codecard is a pipeline that evaluates AI codebases against five criteria: reproducibility, design transparency, documentation quality, privacy, and testing practices. It parses each repository, segments its artifacts, and queries a large language model with structured prompts to produce a scorecard containing numeric ratings, supporting evidence, and targeted recommendations. Codecard's evaluation of 12 public machine learning repositories revealed that only a minority achieved strong reproducibility and documentation, while testing and modular design were consistently weak. These findings show that code-level audits complement existing dataset and model documentation and can guide concrete engineering improvements.

Keywords: Codebase · Codecard · AI code evaluation · LLM-based auditing · Responsible AI

1 Introduction

Artificial intelligence has rapidly evolved from a research concept into a practical tool shaping real-world decisions in key areas such as finance, healthcare, criminal and justice. Its integration has brought long-standing concerns about bias, fairness, and transparency to a sharper focus [1]. In these high-stakes environments, model accuracy alone is insufficient. Developers and institutions are expected to justify how their systems work, ensure that their output is traceable, and address failures when they arise. As a result, responsible AI development has expanded to include issues such as reproducibility, interpretability, and the

A. Awad et al. (Eds.): MEDI 2025, LNCS 16427, pp. 271–285, 2026.
https://doi.org/10.1007/978-3-032-19865-5_22

enforceability of safeguards, expectations that go well beyond traditional performance metrics [2].

The AI community has made significant progress in addressing some of these challenges. Initiatives such as model cards [3], datasheets for datasets [4], and the EU's trustworthy AI guidelines [5] have helped formalize documentation practices, encouraging developers to provide structured information on how models are built, evaluated, and intended to be used. These tools improve transparency for trained models and datasets, but often overlook a more operational layer of the AI pipeline: the source code. The codebases contain the logic that governs how models are implemented, how training is configured, how data is handled, and how outputs are generated. These decisions directly affect reproducibility, privacy, and auditability, yet most open-source codebases are released without rigorous documentation or validation protocols. Dependency files may be missing or partially specified. Tests are often informal or absent. Privacy controls, if present, are rarely explicit. In practice, code that facilitates high-impact decision-making is frequently shared as little more than a prototype. Although formal methods exist for static code analysis, they focus on syntax correctness, security vulnerabilities, or code quality metrics. What they do not capture is whether a codebase aligns with responsible AI development goals, whether it supports reproducibility, contains meaningful documentation, or enforces privacy-aware practices. Bridging that gap requires a deeper understanding of code structure, design intent, and best practices in AI engineering.

This study introduces Codecard, a repository-level audit that brings the principles of our previous framework, System Cards [6], into the source code. It parses each AI codebase end-to-end, groups related files into coherent segments, and combines large language models with rule-based checks to judge five accountability dimensions: reproducibility, design transparency, documentation, privacy, and testing. The findings are assembled into a scorecard that pairs every numeric score with a concise rationale and recommendations, giving maintainers a clear roadmap for responsible improvement.

The contributions of this paper are summarized below.

- We presented a rubric that maps five criteria from the System Cards Framework to measurable signals within AI code repositories.
- We introduced *Codecard*, a pipeline that combines large language models with deterministic checks to produce structured scorecards containing numeric ratings and actionable recommendations.
- We applied Codecard to evaluate responsible development practices in AI codebases and generate interpretable scorecards that highlight areas for improvement.

The remainder of the paper is organized as follows—Sect. 2 reviews related work. Section 3 sets out the methodology. Section 4 presents the experimental setup and results. Section 5 discusses implications and limitations. Section 6 concludes and notes future directions.

2 Related Work

Recent work in responsible AI has established a suite of governance artifacts for documenting, evaluating, and monitoring models and datasets. For instance, Model Cards [3] and Datasheets [4] prompt developers to record data provenance and intended uses, while the AI Data Development Scorecard [7] provides a structured rubric for assessing dataset development practices. Tools such as accountability checklists [8] and the AI Incident Database [9] further support post-deployment oversight. While these instruments improve transparency at the model and data level, they leave a key component unexamined: the source code that orchestrates the entire ML pipeline.

Traditional tools designed to analyze this code, however, also have limitations. Static analyzers such as SonarQube [10] and CodeQL [11] are effective for general code hygiene, flagging style violations and security vulnerabilities. Even modern systems using learned heuristics, such as DeepCode [12], do not assess signals unique to machine learning development, such as environment pinning, stochastic seed control, or dataset traceability. More recent approaches leverage large language models for code evaluation, ranging from judging function-level correctness with tools such as CodeEval [13] and CodeJudge [14] to flagging architectural issues with repository-scale agents such as RepoAudit [15]. Importantly, these efforts are designed for general software engineering and rely on ad hoc criteria. As a result, their findings are not explicitly aligned with the core principles of accountability and responsible AI. This leaves a clear gap for a tool that can audit model code through a responsible development lens.

To address this gap, we introduce the Codecard: a scorecard designed to produce an auditable and comparable profile for AI model projects. Unlike a flat list of lint warnings, the scorecard format makes repositories comparable, links each finding to a specific accountability criterion, and reports evidence and potential fixes in a compact and actionable format. The Codecard maps these responsible AI criteria to measurable signals within a repository, combining deterministic checks with content-aware review to create a comprehensive assessment of a project's alignment with best practices.

3 Methodology

We evaluated accountable development practices in machine learning codebases as a part of the System Cards Framework using five criteria: Reproducibility, Code (C131), Design Transparency, Code (C132), Documentation, Code (C133), Privacy, Code (C231), and Testing Cards (C233). Each dimension is evaluated with a defined set of metrics and rubrics. The metric set and their relative weights were established through a two-round delphi with three annotators, two Ph.D. students, and one postdoctoral researcher specializing in responsible AI. A curated set of public repositories was selected for evaluation, and each was processed through a pipeline that extracts source code, configuration files, documentation, and tests. The resulting metrics are aggregated into criterion-level scores and combined into a repository profile that summarizes strengths and weaknesses. Figure 1 shows an overview of the pipeline.

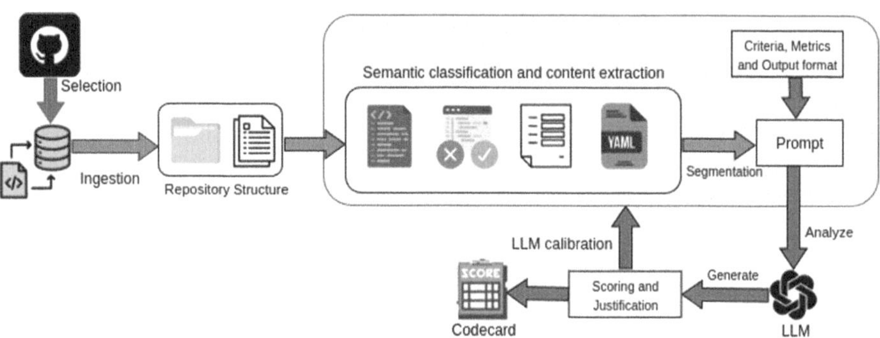

Fig. 1. The Codecard pipeline analyzes codebases with LLMs and produces structured scorecards.

3.1 Evaluation Metrics and Assessment Methods

Table 1 presents the criteria, metrics, and weights derived from the delphi process. The panel assigned weights by judging the relative importance of each signal for accountable code development. Within code reproducibility, environment specification received the highest weight because a pinned environment is the strongest safeguard against dependency drift; dependency pinning followed since version constraints limit drift inside that environment, while reproducibility controls and dataset access were rated lower because they help stabilize runs and clarify inputs but cannot compensate for an ill-specified setup. In design transparency, code complexity and modularity were prioritized since structure governs reviewability and change risk. In contrast, comment density was down-weighted because comments aid comprehension but are often incomplete or outdated. In code documentation, the panel treated README completeness, docstring coverage, model-architecture description, and licensing or citation as equally important since the absence of any one of these breaks reuse or attribution. In code privacy, data handling carried the most weight due to leakage risks in loaders, logs, and temporary files; anonymization and privacy documentation sat in the middle as evidence of safeguards and disclosure; access control was lower because many repositories legitimately avoid credentials, although any exposed secrets are still penalized. In testing cards, unit test presence and test coverage were weighted highest because executed tests provide the most substantial evidence of correctness, CI/CD configuration came next because it enforces tests on every change, and test documentation was lowest since prose alone does not ensure tests are run.

Our evaluation method uses a language model guided by deterministic preprocessing to support consistency and factual accuracy. Quantitative metrics are first extracted using rule-based scripts, including dependency pinning ratios from environment files, docstring coverage via abstract syntax tree parsing, and cyclomatic complexity scores. These metrics, along with selected source code and documentation, are embedded in structured prompts. The language model then evaluates qualitative aspects that require contextual interpretation, such as the clarity of installation instructions and the presence of privacy disclosures. It synthesizes both the extracted metrics and the contextual content to assign criterion-level scores and provide justifications. This method preserves the reasoning capabilities of the language model while grounding its outputs in pre-validated evidence.

3.2 Preprocessing and Artifact Extraction

We extract and normalize the full contents of each repository to prepare it for evaluation. This includes all source code files, configuration scripts, environment declarations, documentation, and testing infrastructure. We collect scripts written in python and Jupyter formats, capture configuration files such as JSON, YAML, and INI, and parse dependency files such as requirements.txt, environment.yml, and dockerfile. Documentation assets, including README files, contributor guidelines, test instructions, and licenses are also included. The test structure is collected from test folders, test scripts, coverage reports, and continuous integration (CI) configurations. All files are read in plain text format, preserving their original layout, indentation, and filenames. We do not filter or exclude components, ensuring that the evaluation reflects the complete development context. Each file is labeled with its path and functional role and organized in a way that maintains the structure of the codebase. The entire repository is consolidated into a single annotated text file that captures both the content and the organization of the original project. This prepares the codebase for consistent and reproducible analysis by language models in the next stage.

3.3 Prompt Preparation

Semantic-aware segmentation is used to structure long codebases' content in a way that respects the token limitations of LLMs while preserving contextual integrity. Codebase artifacts are first parsed to identify logical segments such as complete functions, configuration blocks, or documentation sections. Each segment is enriched with contextual metadata including the file name, relative path, type, and functional role to maintain semantic continuity throughout the codebase. When the overall content exceeds the model's token window, prompt chunking is applied by bundling coherent segments together with their surrounding structure, such as module hierarchy and relevant dependencies, allowing the model to retain a holistic understanding. Each prompt is constructed with a standardized structure containing the task introduction, evaluation criterion, and detailed scoring rubric. This structure is then populated with the curated package of pre-computed metrics and relevant code artifacts. We use a zero-shot, chain-of-thought format to guide the model's reasoning process. To ensure

Table 1. Evaluation criteria, metrics, weights, and rubric.

Criteria	Metrics	Weight	Rubric
Reproducibility, Code (C131)	Environment Specification	0.35	1.0: Version-pinned environment files present. 0.0: No environment file present.
	Dependency Pinning	0.25	1.0: At least 90% of dependencies are version-pinned. 0.5: Between 50% and 89% are pinned. 0.0: Less than 50% are pinned.
	Reproducibility Controls	0.20	1.0: Seed and determinism clearly set. 0.5: Only seed setting found. 0.0: No controls present.
	Dataset Access	0.20	1.0: Dataset clearly referenced or downloadable. 0.0: No dataset or access method provided.
Design Transparency, Code (C132)	Comment Density	0.30	1.0: At least 20% of code lines are comments. 0.5: Between 10% and 19%. 0.0: Less than 10%.
	Code Complexity	0.35	1.0: 95th percentile cyclomatic complexity is 10 or below. 0.5: Between 11 and 15. 0.0: Any function exceeds 15.
	Modularity	0.35	1.0: At least 95% of files have five or fewer function/class definitions. 0.5: All files have 10 or fewer. 0.0: Any file has more than 10.
Documentation, Code (C133)	README Completeness	0.25	1.0: README contains both Installation and Usage sections. 0.5: Only one of Installation or Usage is present. 0.0: None of the sections are present.
	Docstring Coverage	0.25	1.0: At least 80% of function/class definitions include docstrings. 0.5: Between 50% and 79%. 0.0: Less than 50%.
	Model Architecture	0.25	1.0: Detailed structure and components are explained. 0.5: Basic mention or overview is provided. 0.0: No description.
	Licensing and Citation	0.25	1.0: Both license file and citation guidance are provided. 0.5: Only license or citation is included. 0.0: Both License and citation missing.
Privacy, Code (C231)	Anonymization	0.25	1.0: Explicit anonymization applied to sensitive data. 0.5: No sensitive data processed and no unsafe patterns found. 0.0: Sensitive information is exposed or used without anonymization.
	Data Handling	0.30	1.0: Secure temporary storage, no raw data in logs, and verification present. 0.5: No sensitive data processed and no unsafe patterns found. 0.0: Unsafe practices.
	Privacy Documentation	0.25	1.0: A privacy statement or disclosure of safeguards is provided. 0.5: No sensitive data processed. 0.0: No privacy-related documentation.
	Access Control	0.20	1.0: Sensitive credentials are externalized. 0.0: Tokens or API keys are hardcoded.
Testing Cards (C233)	Test Coverage	0.30	1.0: Coverage report exists and total coverage is 80% or above. 0.5: Report exists and coverage is below 80%. 0.0: No coverage report found.
	Unit Test Presence	0.30	1.0: Test files found in a structured directory. 0.0: No test files found.
	CI/CD Configuration	0.25	1.0: At least one valid CI/CD workflow file found. 0.0: No CI/CD configuration detected.
	Test Documentation	0.15	1.0: README or TESTING.md explains test goals. 0.0: No testing explanation provided.

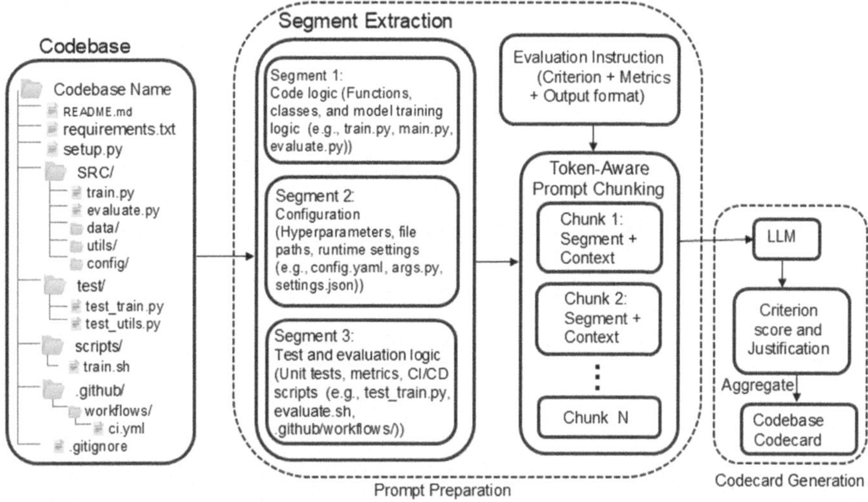

Fig. 2. LLM prompt preparation pipeline illustrating how segmented code, context, and evaluation instructions are bundled into token-aware chunks for consistent and reproducible zero-shot evaluation.

reproducible and focused outputs, all evaluations use fixed generation parameters (temperature=0.2, top-p=0.9). As illustrated in Fig. 2, our pipeline bundles these metrics and artifacts into token-aware prompts for efficient and scalable evaluation.

3.4 Codecard Generation

Each codebase is documented through a structured Codecard that captures the result of the whole evaluation process. The card contains three main components: metadata (including project name, domain, repository link, directory layout, and evaluation date); a criterion-level breakdown with numeric scores and supporting rationale; and a set of targeted recommendations. Scores for each criterion are computed as weighted averages of the corresponding metric scores, the weights reflecting the practical importance of each development signal in responsible AI engineering. A three-tier color scale is used to interpret the final scores: scores $t_i \geq t_1 = 0.80$ are shown in green, indicating strong alignment with responsible development practices. Scores in the range $t_2 = 0.60 \leq t_i < t_1$ appear in yellow, signaling that the codebase meets baseline standards but has areas needing improvement. And scores $t_i < t_2$ are marked red, reflecting critical deficiencies that undermine transparency, reproducibility, or overall development quality. These thresholds were selected through experimental calibration based on pilot evaluations conducted during method development. The Codecard template, shown in Fig. 3, provides a standardized format to present these evaluations.

```
Metadata
Codebase Name:                 |Name of the codebase|
Evaluation Date:               |Date of evaluation|
Domain:                        |Domain of the code|
Description:                   |Short description of the codebase|
Codebase URL:                  |Link to the codebase|
Evaluator LLM:                 |LLM Name|

Assessment
Reproducibility (C131):        Score |X.XX| - Color: Explanation
Design Transparency (C132):    Score |X.XX| - Color: Explanation
Documentation (C133):          Score |X.XX| - Color: Explanation
Privacy (C231):                Score |X.XX| - Color: Explanation
Testing Cards (C233):          Score |X.XX| - Color: Explanation

Improvement Suggestions
Reproducibility (C131):        |Suggestion|
Design Transparency (C132):    |Suggestion|
Documentation (C133):          |Suggestion|
Privacy (C231):                |Suggestion|
Testing Cards (C233):          |Suggestion|
```

Fig. 3. Codecard template with three sections: metadata, assessment scores, and improvement suggestions.

The language model used to generate the evaluations was selected through an expert-guided, human-in-the-loop benchmarking process. Two self-contained codebases with clear structure and documentation were independently annotated by domain experts using the rubric defined in Sect. 3.1. Inter-annotator reliability was measured using the intraclass correlation coefficient (ICC [2,3]), and the averaged expert scores served as the human reference. To assess model-human alignment, we applied Lin's Concordance Correlation Coefficient (CCC) [16], which evaluates both correlation and bias to quantify how closely the model's evaluations align with human judgments. For explanation and recommendation alignment, a human-in-the-loop process was used in which domain experts reviewed the model's outputs and provided iterative feedback to refine reasoning quality and interpretive accuracy. The model demonstrating the highest concordance and most coherent human-aligned reasoning was then selected as the default evaluator for Codecard generation.

4 Experiments

4.1 Codebase Selection

We collected 20 open-source Python codebases from GitHub, focusing on machine learning applications in areas such as computer vision, natural language processing, and time-series forecasting. From this initial pool, we selected 12 repositories that showed active maintenance, strong community adoption, and practical engineering relevance. Each has at least 5k stars and 0.5k forks, used a permissive license such as MIT or Apache 2.0, and fell within the processing constraints of language models, with fewer than 100k lines of code and no more than 200 files. We also ensured that every codebase was technically self-contained and included enough documentation to support the full-pipeline evaluation. Table 2 presents an overview of the selected codebases along with metadata.

Table 2. Selected codebases for evaluation

Codebase	Stars	Forks	Application-Area	Description
Whisper [17]	81.9k	9.9k	Speech Recognition	Multilingual speech recognition and translation.
Stable-Diffusion [18]	70.6k	10.4k	Text-to-Image Generation	High-res text-to-image synthesis using latent diffusion.
NanoGPT [19]	41.3k	6.8k	Natural Language Processing	Minimal GPT training codebase for educational use and prototyping.
ControlNet [20]	32.3k	2.9k	Image Generation	Conditioning framework to guide Stable Diffusion with structural prompts.
CLIP [21]	29.0k	3.6k	Computer Vision	Language-image pretraining model for zero-shot tasks using contrastive learning.
Segment-Anything [22]	50.2k	5.9k	Image Segmentation	A zero-shot segmentation model by Meta AI
DeepFace [23]	19.1k	2.6k	Face Recognition	Unified face recognition and analysis (emotion, age, race).
DETR [24]	14.4k	2.6k	Computer Vision	Transformer-based end-to-end object detector using bipartite set matching.
AlphaFold [25]	13.5k	2.4k	Bioinformatics	DeepMind's protein structure predictor achieving atomic-level accuracy.
MAE [26]	7.8k	1.3k	Computer Vision	Vision Transformer pretraining via masked autoencoding.
CleanRL [27]	7.1k	0.75k	Reinforcement Learning	Readable single-file RL baselines with reproducible training pipelines.
Informer2020 [28]	5.9k	1.2k	Time-Series Forecasting	Efficient long-series forecasting using ProbSparse transformers.

4.2 Experimental Results

Expert-Annotated Benchmarks. The nanoGPT and CLIP codebases were manually evaluated by the three experts who rated the metrics and served as calibration references for model validation. Inter-rater agreement was high, with an ICC score of 0.98, indicating strong consistency across all five criteria. Where scores differed, the average value was taken to avoid bias toward optimistic or pessimistic extremes. Justifications and improvement suggestions were broadly aligned; when experts raised distinct but valid perspectives, both were retained to capture complementary reasoning. For privacy, scores were applicability-adjusted: if a repository did not handle sensitive or personally identifiable data, the criterion was marked as not applicable and excluded from the macro-average. However, exposed credentials or unsafe handling still incurred penalties. The expert Codecards, shown in Fig. 4, served as references for LLM output comparison.

Metadata

Codebase Name:	nanoGPT
Evaluation Date:	May 13, 2025
Domain:	Language Modeling
Description:	Minimal GPT training framework with PyTorch
URL:	github.com/karpathy/nanoGPT
Evaluator LLM:	N.A

Assessment

Reproducibility:	Score [0.38] – Red: No environment file or version pinning; lacks seed control
Design Transparency:	Score [0.83] – Green: High comment density and modularity, but complexity too high in one function
Documentation:	Score [0.63] – Yellow: Good README and model description; lacks docstrings and citation information
Privacy:	Score [0.50] – Red: No sensitive data handled, but missing privacy note and secrets management.
Testing Cards:	Score [0.00] – Red: No tests or CI/CD present

Improvement Suggestions

Reproducibility:	Add a requirements.txt or environment.yml with pinned versions and implement random seed controls in training scripts
Design Transparency:	Reduce complexity in high-complexity functions.
Documentation:	Add docstrings to all functions and classes, and include citation metadata
Privacy:	Add a privacy note, document secrets in `.env.example`, enable CI secret scanning, and include log redaction tests.
Testing Cards:	Implement unit tests for core components and integrate CI workflow using GitHub actions

Metadata

Codebase Name:	CLIP
Evaluation Date:	May 13, 2025
Domain:	Vision-Language Models
Description:	Contrastive Language-Image Pretraining
URL:	github.com/openai/CLIP
Evaluator LLM:	N.A

Assessment

Reproducibility:	Score [0.18] – Red: Dependencies unpinned and no seed controls, though data access is clear
Design Transparency:	Score [0.34] – Red: Modular and clean structure; moderate inline documentation
Documentation:	Score [0.62] – Yellow: Architecture and usage are documented; function-level docstrings missed
Privacy:	Score [0.50] – Red: No sensitive data or unsafe logging, but lacks a privacy note and documented secrets management
Testing Cards:	Score [0.55] – Red: CI-enabled unit tests exist, but test coverage and documentation are not found

Improvement Suggestions

Reproducibility:	Add explicit seed setting for full experimental reproducibility.
Design Transparency:	Refactor large functions into smaller testable components and annotate edge cases.
Documentation:	Increase docstring coverage and consolidate model commentary inline
Privacy:	Add a privacy note, document secrets in `.env.example`, enable CI secret scanning.
Testing Cards:	Add test coverage reporting and explain test assumptions in README or `TESTING.md`

Fig. 4. Benchmark Codecards for (L) nanoGPT and (R) CLIP codebases, presenting criterion-level scores, labels, and improvement suggestions of expert evaluations.

LLM Evaluation. First, we applied the five language models to the two expert-scored codebases, nanoGPT and CLIP, and compared their outputs with manual evaluations. As shown in Table 3, GPT-4o showed strong alignment in both scoring and explanation. It captured key gaps noted by the experts, such as the lack of testing in nanoGPT and the limited docstring coverage in CLIP. While some of its justifications and recommendations were worded differently, the core observations were consistent. In a few places, it even highlighted issues that the human evaluators had missed, showing attention to subtle implementation details. Claude 3 Haiku also performed reasonably well. Its scores were mostly in line with the benchmark, and its rationale showed some overlap with the experts, especially in documentation and privacy. The remaining models, LLaMA 3.3 and Gemma, did not perform as well. They tended to overrate specific criteria, and their explanations often missed the point or introduced suggestions that were not supported by the codebase content.

After identifying GPT-4o as the most consistent and rubric-aligned evaluator, we used it to score the remaining ten codebases and generate a Codecard for each. As reported in Table 4, GPT-4o achieved a Lin's CCC of 0.982, indicating near-perfect agreement with the expert benchmark. Reproducibility and documentation were strongest in repositories such as Stable-Diffusion, ControlNet, and AlphaFold, which included complete environment files and well-structured READMEs. Testing and design transparency remained weak for Segment-Anything, MAE, and CLIP, where GPT-4o accurately identified missing test suites, limited modularity, and sparse inline explanations. DeepFace showed uneven performance, with strong reproducibility but poor modularity

Table 3. Codebase scores across evaluation criteria for the two codebases.

Codebase	LLM	C131	C132	C133	C231	C233
nanoGPT	GPT-4o	**0.40**	**0.82**	**0.50**	**0.50**	**0.00**
	Claude 3 Haiku	1.00	1.00	0.75	0.50	0.07
	LLaMA 3.3 70B	0.20	1.00	0.75	0.50	0.00
	Gemini 1.5 Pro	0.30	0.68	0.62	0.50	0.00
	Gemma 2	0.90	0.68	1.00	0.65	0.55
CLIP	GPT-4o	**0.20**	**0.35**	**0.62**	**0.50**	**0.55**
	Claude 3 Haiku	0.90	0.35	0.75	0.50	1.00
	LLaMA 3.3 70B	0.00	0.35	0.75	0.50	0.00
	Gemini 1.5 Pro	0.45	0.35	0.75	0.50	0.55
	Gemma 2	0.90	0.68	0.87	0.00	0.25

and testing due to missing coverage reports. Privacy scores centered around 0.50 across projects, consistent with experts' assessments that the repositories did not handle sensitive data but lacked explicit safeguards. GPT-4o also captured finer implementation issues, such as inconsistent directory structure and minimal error-handling logic in several models, which further differentiated high- and low-performing repositories.

Table 4. Codecard scores of codebases as computed by the GPT-4o.

Codebase	C131	C132	C133	C231	C233
Whisper	0.50	0.18	0.75	0.50	0.67
Stable-diffusion	0.80	0.35	0.75	0.50	0.00
nanoGPT	0.40	1.00	0.50	0.50	0.00
ControlNet	1.00	0.35	0.75	0.50	0.00
CLIP	0.20	0.35	0.63	0.50	0.55
Segment-Anything	0.20	0.17	0.75	0.50	0.00
DeepFace	0.68	0.18	0.63	0.20	0.60
DETR	0.30	0.35	0.62	0.50	0.30
AlphaFold	0.90	0.35	0.88	0.50	0.00
MAE	0.30	0.50	0.50	0.50	0.00
cleanrl	1.00	0.18	0.85	0.50	1.00
Informer2020	0.90	0.35	0.75	0.50	0.00

Figure 5 summarizes agreement patterns across all criteria for nanoGPT and CLIP. Privacy showed the highest consistency across models, while documentation, transparency, reproducibility, and testing revealed noticeable diver-

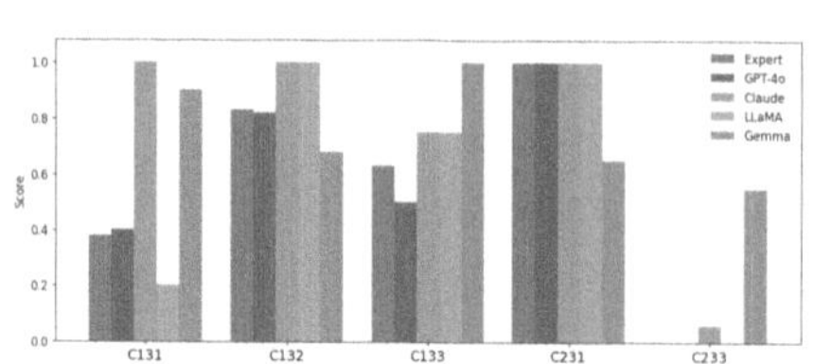

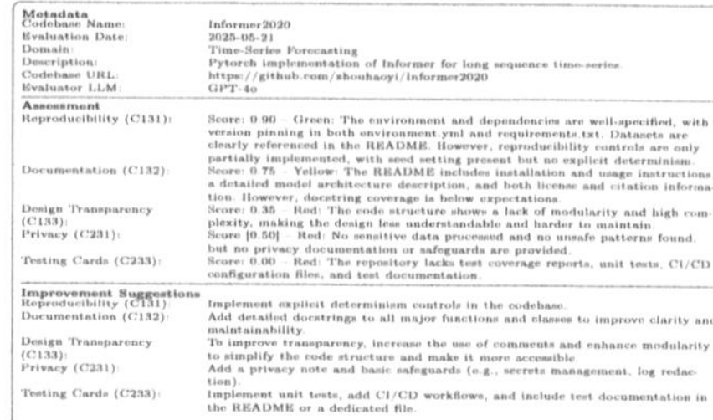

Fig. 5. Comparison of expert and language model evaluations for nanoGPT (L) and CLIP (R) across five criteria (code reproducibility, design transparency, documentation, privacy, and testing cards).

Metadata

Codebase Name:	Informer2020
Evaluation Date:	2025-05-21
Domain:	Time-Series Forecasting
Description:	Pytorch implementation of Informer for long sequence time-series.
Codebase URL:	https://github.com/zhouhaoyi/Informer2020
Evaluator LLM:	GPT-4o

Assessment

Reproducibility (C131):	Score: 0.90 – Green: The environment and dependencies are well-specified, with version pinning in both environment.yml and requirements.txt. Datasets are clearly referenced in the README. However, reproducibility controls are only partially implemented, with seed setting present but no explicit determinism.
Documentation (C132):	Score: 0.75 – Yellow: The README includes installation and usage instructions, a detailed model architecture description, and both license and citation information. However, docstring coverage is below expectations.
Design Transparency (C133):	Score: 0.35 – Red: The code structure shows a lack of modularity and high complexity, making the design less understandable and harder to maintain.
Privacy (C231):	Score |0.50| – Red: No sensitive data processed and no unsafe patterns found, but no privacy documentation or safeguards are provided.
Testing Cards (C233):	Score: 0.00 – Red: The repository lacks test coverage reports, unit tests, CI/CD configuration files, and test documentation.

Improvement Suggestions

Reproducibility (C131):	Implement explicit determinism controls in the codebase.
Documentation (C132):	Add detailed docstrings to all major functions and classes to improve clarity and maintainability.
Design Transparency (C133):	To improve transparency, increase the use of comments and enhance modularity to simplify the code structure and make it more accessible.
Privacy (C231):	Add a privacy note and basic safeguards (e.g., secrets management, log redaction).
Testing Cards (C233):	Implement unit tests, add CI/CD workflows, and include test documentation in the README or a dedicated file.

Fig. 6. GPT-4o generated Codecard for the Informer2020 codebase, summarizing its development quality across five evaluation dimensions.

gence, with weaker models inflating scores based on superficial cues. The generated Codecards (e.g., Fig. 6) compile these results by presenting metadata, criterion-level scores, brief justifications, and targeted recommendations, highlighting strengths such as reproducibility in Informer2020 and identifying gaps in modularity, testing, and docstring coverage.

5 Discussion

The evaluation shows that, although many AI repositories provide reproducible environments, most still fall short of accountable development practices. Testing remains the weakest dimension, with few projects offering unit tests, coverage reports, or continuous integration workflows. Design transparency is also limited, and many codebases rely on tightly coupled modules that hinder review and maintenance. Privacy practices are largely implicit. While most repositories avoid sensitive data, they rarely document safeguards, credential handling, or privacy-aware design choices.

Codecard's hybrid structure, which combines deterministic signals with language model reasoning, enabled consistent alignment with expert annotations and captured shortcomings that purely rule-based checks would miss. The study is constrained by the small set of Python-based repositories, and broader application to more diverse, multi-language projects would strengthen the generality of the approach. Expanding the framework to include additional dimensions such as security, efficiency, and dependency risk will further develop Codecard into a more comprehensive auditing tool.

6 Conclusion

This paper presented Codecard, a method for evaluating the quality of AI codebase development using five well-defined criteria. The approach combines a structured scoring rubric with large language models to produce criterion-level assessments with concise explanations and targeted recommendations. Applied to 12 open-source codebases, the results showed that many widely used projects lack essential practices such as environment versioning, modular design, and comprehensive test coverage. Despite these gaps, the method aligned closely with expert annotations and provided reliable diagnostic insight. Each Codecard functions as a compact accountability profile that highlights overlooked engineering concerns. Future work will extend the evaluation to more diverse repositories, including larger and multi-language projects, and incorporate additional criteria such as security and performance.

Acknowledgment. We thank our colleagues, Professors Ryan Kennedy, Andrew C. Michaels, and Lydia B. Tied, for their valuable support. We are also grateful to the CRASA project community advisors team, including Michael O. Adams, Katherine A. Franco, Sharon A. Israel, Jay Jenkins, James Marcella, Paula C. Pineda, and Jani Maselli Wood.

The National Science Foundation, under award number 2131504, partly supported this research. The views and conclusions expressed in this paper are those of the authors and do not necessarily reflect the official policies or endorsements, either expressed or implied, of the National Science Foundation.

The authors acknowledge the use of large language models (LLMs) for language refinement and formatting support. The analysis, interpretations, and conclusions remain solely those of the author.

References

1. Ferrara, E.: Fairness and bias in artificial intelligence: a brief survey of sources, impacts, and mitigation strategies. Science **6**(1), 3 (2024)

2. Jobin, A., Ienca, M., Vayena, E.: The global landscape of AI ethics guidelines. Nat. Mach. Intell. **1**(9), 389–399 (2019)
3. Mitchell, M. , et al.: Model cards for model reporting. In: Proc. ACM Conference on Fairness, Accountability, and Transparency, pp. 220–229. Atlanta (2019)
4. Gebru, T., et al.: Datasheets for datasets. Commun. ACM **64**(12), 86–92 (2021)
5. High-Level Expert Group on AI: Ethics Guidelines for Trustworthy AI. https://digital-strategy.ec.europa.eu/en/library/ethics-guidelines-trustworthy-ai, Accessed 05 Nov 2025
6. Gursoy, F., Kakadiaris, I.A.: System cards for AI-based decision-making for public policy. arXiv preprint arXiv:2203.04754 (2022)
7. Bahiru, T.K., Tibebu, H., Kakadiaris, I.A.: AI data development: a scorecard for the system card framework. arXiv preprint, arXiv:2506.02071 (2025)
8. Raji, I.D., et al.: Closing the AI accountability gap: defining an end-to-end framework for internal algorithmic auditing. In: Proc. ACM Conference on Fairness, Accountability, and Transparency, pp. 33–44. Barcelona, Spain (2020)
9. Partnership on AI: AI Incident Database. https://incidentdatabase.ai, Accessed 05 Jan 2025
10. SonarSource SA: SonarQube: Continuous Inspection of Code Quality. https://www.sonarsource.com/products/sonarqube, Accessed 05 Nov 2025
11. GitHub Security Lab: CodeQL: Code Analysis Engine for Code Security. https://securitylab.github.com/tools/codeql, Accessed 05 Nov 2025
12. Snyk Ltd.: DeepCode: AI-Powered Code Review. https://snyk.io/product/developer-security/code-review/, Accessed 05 Nov 2025
13. Chen, S., Zhang, Y., Lin, X.: CodeEval: evaluating code generation models using multi-level semantic similarity. arXiv preprint arXiv:2301.12955 (2023)
14. Tong, W., Zhang, T.: CodeJudge: evaluating code generation with large language models. arXiv preprint arXiv:2410.02184 (2024)
15. Guo, J., Wang, C., Xu, X., Su, Z., Zhang, X.: RepoAudit: an autonomous LLM-agent for repository-level code auditing. In: Proc. 42nd International Conference on Machine Learning, Vancouver, Canada (2025)
16. Lin, L.I.-K.: A concordance correlation coefficient to evaluate reproducibility. Biometrics **45**(1), 255–268 (1989)
17. Radford, A., et al.: Robust speech recognition via large-scale weak supervision. OpenAI Technical Report (2023)
18. Rombach, R., Blattmann, A., Lorenz, D., Esser, P., Ommer, B.: High-resolution image synthesis with latent diffusion models. In: Proc. IEEE/CVF Conference on Computer Vision and Pattern Recognition, pp. 10684–10695. New Orleans (2022)
19. Karpathy, A.: nanoGPT. https://github.com/karpathy/nanoGPT, Accessed 05 Nov 2025
20. Zhang, L., Rao, A., Agrawala, M.: Adding conditional control to text-to-image diffusion models. In: Proc. IEEE/CVF International Conference on Computer Vision, pp. 3813–3824. Paris (2023)
21. Radford, A., et al.: Learning transferable visual models from natural language supervision. arXiv preprint arXiv:2103.00020 (2021)
22. Kirillov, A., et al.: Segment anything. arXiv preprint arXiv:2304.02643 (2023)
23. Serengil, S.I., Ozpinar, A.: LightFace: a hybrid deep face recognition framework. In: Proc. Innovations in Intelligent Systems and Applications Conference, pp. 1–5. Istanbul (2020)
24. Carion, N., Massa, F., Synnaeve, G., Usunier, N., Kirillov, A., Zagoruyko, S.: End-to-End object detection with transformers. In: Proc. European Conference on Computer Vision, vol. 12346, pp. 213–229. Glasgow (2020)

25. Jumper, J., et al.: Highly accurate protein structure prediction with AlphaFold. Nature **596**(7873), 583–589 (2021)
26. He, K., Chen, X., Xie, S., Li, Y., Dollár, P., Girshick, R.: Masked autoencoders are scalable vision learners. In: Proc. IEEE/CVF Conference on Computer Vision and Pattern Recognition, pp. 16000–16009. New Orleans (2022)
27. Huang, S., Huang, Z., Yuan, S., Nguyen, V., Zhang, W., Jain, S.: CleanRL: high-quality single-file implementations of deep reinforcement learning algorithms. In: NeurIPS Reproducibility Challenge, New Orleans, USA (2022)
28. Zhou, H., et al.: informer: beyond efficient transformer for long sequence time-series forecasting. In: Proc. AAAI Conference on Artificial Intelligence, vol. 35, no. 12, pp. 11106–11115. Vancouver, Canada (2021)

A Hybrid Deep Learning and Ontology-Based Framework for Contextual Hyperactivity Detection in Children with ADHD

Ibrahim Traore[1,2](✉), Imen Megdiche[2], Jérôme Marquet-Doléac[3], and Lotfi Chaari[1]

[1] Toulouse INP, IRIT, University of Toulouse, Toulouse, France
[2] IRIT, ISIS Castres, INUC, University of Toulouse, Toulouse, France
ibrahim.traore@irit.fr
[3] Institute of Psychomotricity, Toulouse NeuroImaging Center, UMR 1214 - INSERM, University of Toulouse, Toulouse, France

Abstract. We propose a hybrid approach combining deep learning and deductive reasoning through ontology context design to enhance context-aware detection of hyperactivity in children with ADHD. The framework leverages a generative Transformer model through an encoder–decoder architecture enhanced with multi-resolution attention to learn the distribution of normal physical activity patterns. Statistical modeling is then applied to estimate the parameters of the reconstruction error distribution, with deviations beyond a learned threshold classified as anomalies. These detected anomalies are subsequently instantiated in an ontology, which filters them based on context through a set of logical rules. We evaluate our approach on data collected from two children diagnosed with ADHD, recorded under free-living conditions using the Actigraph GT9X device. Our experimental results show average F1-scores of 0.87 and 0.85. These results highlight the potential of our hybrid approach for contextual hyperactivity detection in children with ADHD.

Keywords: Anomaly Detection · Deep Learning · Context Analysis · Ontology modeling · SWRL Rules · ADHD

1 Introduction

Hyperactivity, symptom of attention-deficit/hyperactivity disorder (ADHD), can be defined as an abnormal increase in motor activity, both in terms of frequency, intensity, and variability of movements. The challenge of detecting hyperactivity lies in identifying true positives while accounting for context. If a patient feels well and motivated in a given situation, they generally do not exhibit ADHD symptoms [1]. For instance, when a hyperactive child struggles with mathematics, due to a lack of motivation, it is very likely that they will display hyperactivity symptoms during math sessions. On the other hand, if the same child

A. Awad et al. (Eds.): MEDI 2025, LNCS 16427, pp. 286–294, 2026.
https://doi.org/10.1007/978-3-032-19865-5_23

is playing football, a sport that requires significant physical effort, the physical activities performed in this context should not be interpreted as hyperactivity. According to Thomas E. Brown [1], the manifestation of ADHD is highly dependent on context, the individual's motivation in a task, and their environment. For effective detection, movement data collected in everyday life settings (home, school, leisure) must be interpreted in light of contextual information such as the ongoing activity, the patient's difficulties, their level of motivation, the presence of other individuals, or the physical environment. An exploratory analysis of data from a previous study [2], revealed that high-intensity movements are relatively rare and suggest that time series anomaly detection algorithms can be use to for hyperactivity detection. To incorporate contextual dimensions, ontologies are particularly well-suited tools. Their formal expressiveness and ability to represent complex knowledge, as well as to support logical reasoning, make them a relevant framework for modeling entities [3]. Several studies [4–6] have already explored potential synergies between machine learning and ontologies within hybrid artificial intelligence systems. Sarah Ghidalia et al. [4] identified three main categories of hybridization: ontology enrichment through learning, semantic data exploration, and systems combining learning and reasoning. Our study focuses on the third category. These hybrid systems rely on the joint integration of inductive reasoning (through machine learning) and deductive reasoning (through ontologies) within a single artificial intelligence framework. Vadim Moshkin et al. [5] and Nadezhda Yarushkina et al. [6] proposed a context-aware anomaly detection approach in time series. In this article, we propose a hybrid approach for detecting motor overflow in children with ADHD. The main contribution of this work is the introduction of a hybrid framework that integrates deep learning, statistical modeling, and a modular ontology to contextualize and interpret detected anomalies with respect to the circumstances in which they occur.

The rest of the paper is organized as follows: Sect. 2 presents related work. Section 3 details the components of our hybrid approach. Section 4 reports on our experiments and results. Finally, Sect. 5 concludes and outlines directions for future research.

2 Related Work

Anomaly Detection in Time Series. The detection of anomalous subsequences in time series involves identifying observations that deviate significantly from expected behavior. Historically, this task has relied mainly on classical approaches, such as distance-based methods and density-based techniques. With recent technological advances, deep learning has emerged as a powerful alternative due to its ability to automatically extract meaningful representations from large volumes of data. Reconstruction-based methods [7,8], learn to accurately reproduce normal sequences. Anomalies are detected by computing the discrepancies between the original input and its reconstruction. However, the accelerometer data analyzed in this study are non-stationary, due to their rapid and continuous evolution over time. This dynamic nature makes it challenging to distinguish between normal variability and anomalies.

Ontology-based Context Aware. Context-awareness refers to the ability of services and applications to perceive their environment that is, their context (such as location, user profile, physical environment, time, etc.) and translate it into implicit or explicit situational information. In the literature, several techniques have been proposed for context modeling [3]. Among these, ontology-based modeling is often regarded as the most suitable approach [3,9], due to its ability to formally represent knowledge, support reasoning, and promote interoperability. As a result, many approaches have adopted this paradigm. Oscar Cabrera et al. [3] proposed a modular approach to context modeling in the field of context-aware computing. Similarly, Josué Padilla-Cuevas et al. [9] developed an event-driven modular approach, organizing their contextual model around five main modules: person, time, place, network, and academic events.

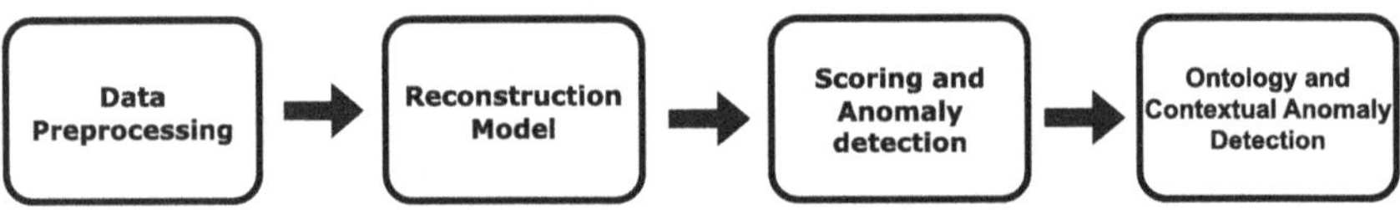

Fig. 1. The proposed framework.

3 The Proposed Framework

Figure 1 illustrates the architecture of the proposed framework. The reconstruction model is trained to reconstruct normal data. Subsequently, we compute the reconstruction error. A statistical model is employed to estimate the unknown parameters of the error distribution, and an anomaly threshold is defined. This threshold is utilized for anomaly detection. The detected anomalies are analyzed through an ontology by applying a set of logical rules.

3.1 Anomaly Detection Model

Problem Formulation. We consider a multivariate time series, which is a timestamped sequence of data observations of size T, $\mathcal{X} = \{x_1, ..., x_T\}$ where each data point x_t is collected at a specific timestamp t and $x_t \in \mathbb{R}^J, \forall t$. Time series are normalized using the following transform for each sample x_t

$$x_t \longleftarrow \frac{x_t - \min(\mathcal{X})}{\max(\mathcal{X}) - \min(\mathcal{X}) + \epsilon}, \tag{1}$$

where ϵ is a small constant to prevent zero-division. Knowing the ranges a *priori*, we normalize the data to get it in the range [0,1]. A window $W = \{x_{t-L+1}, ..., x_t\}$

of size L is a subset of observations from $\mathcal{X}$, with $L \leq T$. Let $\mathcal{T} = \{W_1, ..., W_M\}$ be the set of M windows generated from $\mathcal{X}$. A sequence $S = \{W_{m-s+1}, ..., W_m\}$ is a set of s windows used to provide context to window. Given a training window set $\mathcal{T}$, for any unseen test window set $\mathcal{T}'$ of length M' having the same modality as the training series, we need to predict $Y = \{y_1, ..., y_{M'}\}$, where $y_m \in \{0, 1\}$ $\forall m$ indicates whether the window W_m is anomalous (1 designates the anomalous state). For simplicity, we will use W for window, S for sequence, and O for a reconstructed window.

Reconstruction Model. To effectively capture features in non-stationary time series, we integrate a multi-resolution attention mechanism into the Transformer pipeline. This mechanism is based on wavelet transforms that provide multi-resolution analysis by decomposing a signal into components of different frequencies and resolutions. Wavelets enable adaptive focus on specific parts of the signal that require more detailed analysis. Specifically, for each input time window, the model acts as an encoder-decoder network. The softmax operation is denoted by $\sigma(\cdot)$. Let $\mathcal{F}(\cdot)$ and $\mathcal{F}^{-1}(\cdot)$ denote the wavelet transform and its inverse, respectively. The query ($\mathbf{Q}$), key ($\mathbf{K}$), and value ($\mathbf{V}$) matrices are decomposed into high- and low-frequency components using the wavelet transformation $\mathcal{F}$, and the corresponding weights are computed. Finally, these components are combined to produce the final output, thus improving the capture of complex dynamics in non-stationary time series. Multi-resolution attention is computed as

$$Attention(\mathbf{Q}, \mathbf{K}, \mathbf{V}) = \mathcal{F}^{-1}\left(\sigma\left(\mathcal{F}(\mathbf{Q})\mathcal{F}(\mathbf{K}^T)/\sqrt{d_Q}\right)\mathcal{F}(\mathbf{V})\right), \quad (2)$$

where d_Q is the dimension of the queries and $\mathbf{K}^T$ is the transpose of the key matrix $\mathbf{K}$.

Scoring and Anomaly Detection. In reconstruction-based anomaly detection approaches, the model is trained to reconstruct data from the normal class. The result of this reconstruction is an error vector, assumed to follow a probability distribution whose parameters are initially unknown. Previous studies [10,11] have measured these errors using standard metrics such as Mean Absolute Error (MAE) or Mean Squared Error (MSE), modeling their distribution using a multivariate normal distribution whose parameters are estimated through Maximum Likelihood Estimation (MLE). However, these metrics yield only positive values, and their distribution is typically asymmetric, with a heavy right tail. In such cases, the normality assumption may be inadequate to accurately represent the error distribution. To overcome this limitation, we use a raw error measure defined as

$$\mathcal{L}(W_m, O_m) = W_m - O_m \quad (3)$$

where W_m and O_m stand for the input and reconstructed windows, respectively. We then model the distribution of these raw errors using a multivariate Normal distribution, whose parameters are estimated via MLE [12]. The error vectors corresponding to the training dataset windows are used to estimate the parameters of the statistical model. The reconstruction error associated with a window W_m is calculated $e_m = ||W_m - O_m||_2^2$. The anomaly score of this window is defined as follows: $a_m = -\log f(e_m \mid \widehat{\mu}, \widehat{\Sigma})$, where f is the probability density function, $\widehat{\mu}$ and $\widehat{\Sigma}$ are the estimated parameters. If $a_m > \tau$, the window is considered anomalous; otherwise, it is classified as normal. The threshold τ is chosen to maximize the F_1-score.

Table 1. Main characteristics of each module.

Module	Person	Activity	Time	Challenge	Health Profile	Environment	Situation
Nb Classes	09	33	04	22	32	20	07
Nb Object Properties	01	01	03	01	03	01	09
Nb Data Properties	05	00	06	00	01	00	00
Class Hierarchy Depth	03	03	02	03	03	03	02
Property Hierarchy Depth	01	01	01	01	01	01	01
SWRL Rules	Yes	Yes	Yes	Yes	Yes	Yes	Yes

3.2 Ontology and Contextual Anomaly Detection

According to Thomas E. Brown's perspective in his study [1] on the situational variability of ADHD, Person, Environment, Activity, Challenge, Time, and Medical Profile should constitute the contextual information required for interpreting and understanding the manifestations of ADHD. The ontology[1] follows this logic and represents the mentioned entities along with their associated information in the form of modules: *Person, Activity, Time, Challenge, Health Profile, Environment, and Situation.* Table 1 presents the main characteristics of each module: number of classes, data properties, object properties, class hierarchy depth, property hierarchy depth, and associated Semantic Web Rule Language (SWRL) rules.

Reasoning. In the ontology, a set of rules has been defined to infer clinical reasoning based on the formalized knowledge about ADHD. These rules were developed in collaboration with a medical specialist, co-author of this paper. They are expressed in the SWRL language. Table 2 presents a subset of the rules applied during the intermediate and final reasoning stages. The intermediate reasoning rules allow for instantiating properties that will later be evaluated in the final reasoning rules. For example, rule 1 establishes a characterization of a patient's personal profile, which is essential for identifying the types of symptoms that may manifest. The final reasoning rules use the results from the intermediate reasoning to provide an interpretation and understanding of

[1] For further details on the ontology, please refer to the following link: https://github.com/ibtraore/patches-population.

the current situation. In this study, we distinguish three possible interpretations of a situation: *Normal, Agitated, and Inattention.* Rules 8 illustrates how the properties inferred during the intermediate reasoning can be combined to arrive at an interpretation of the situation, which is represented by the *SituationState* class.

Table 2. Subset of rules.

No.	SWRL Rules
Intermediate Reasoning	
1	Situation(?s), hasPatient(?s, ?p), hasDiagnosis(?p, ?dia), hasDiagnosisDisorder(?dia, ?dis), (MixedType or HyperactivityImpulsivityType)(?dis) → hasProfileType(?s, Hyperactive)
2	Situation(?s), hasEnvironment(?s, ?e), LearningEnvironment(?e), hasPatient(?s, ?p), isEngagedIn(?p, ?a), EducationalActivity(?a) → hasEnvironmentType(?s, Hypostimulating)
3	Situation(?s), hasPatient(?s, ?p), isEngagedIn(?p, ?a), MathCourse(?a), hasChallenge(?p, ?c), MathChallenges(?c) → hasActivityType(?s, Stressful), hasMotivation (?a, False)
4	Situation(?s), hasPatient(?s, ?p), isEngagedIn(?p, ?a), (EducationalActivity or CulturalLearning) (?a) → hasActivityType(?s, CognitiveDemanding)
5	Situation(?s), hasTemporalEntity(?s, ?t), hasStart(?t, ?st), hasHour(?st, ?h), swrlb:greaterThanOrEqual (?h, 6), swrlb:lessThan (?h, 10) → hasTimeOfDay(?s, Morning)
6	Situation(?s), hasPatient(?s, ?p), isEngagedIn(?p, ?a), hasMotivation(?a, ?motiv), swrlb:equal (?motiv, False) → hasChallengeLevel (?s, High)
7	Situation(?s), hasPatient(?s, ?p), isEngagedIn(?p, ?a), EducationalActivity(?a), hasChallenge (?p, ?c), TeacherRelationship(?c), sameAs (?c, Bad) → hasInfluence (?s, Pressure)
ADHD reasoning to determine situation state	
8	Situation(?s), hasProfileType(?s, ?p), hasEnvironmentType(?s, ?e), hasActivityType(?s, ?a), hasTimeOfDay(?s, ?t), hasChallengeLevel(?s, ?cl), hasInfluence(?s, ?i),(sameAs (?p, Hyperactive) or sameAs (?p, Hyperactive)), sameAs (?e, Hypostimulating), sameAs (?a, Stressful), (sameAs (?t, Morning) or sameAs (?t, Noon) or sameAs (?t, Afternoon)), (sameAs(?cl, High) or sameAs(?cl, Medium)) , sameAs(?i, Pressure) → hasSituationState(?s, Agitated)

Contextual Anomaly Detection. Suppose the following situation: *"Maxime is a boy born on July 15, 2015, diagnosed with hyperactive-impulsive type ADHD according to Corner's criteria. He encounters difficulties in language classes. On June 18, 2024, at 1:30 p.m., he participates in group work on a language lesson with his friends Emma and Lucas at the library"*. Contextual detection of hyperactivity involves addressing the following question: *Can the intense movements performed by Maxime in this situation be classified as motor overflow (hyperactivity) ?* To address this question, the first step consists in interpreting the situation using the rules presented in Table 2. The next step is to apply the anomaly detection model to identify intense movements as anomalies. Each detected anomaly is then injected into the ontology as an instance of the *Hyperactivity* concept, along with the specific time of its occurrence. The context-aware detection leverages the results of the previously performed situation interpretation. An example of a contextual rule is the following: *If an anomaly is detected in an agitated situation, then this anomaly is considered a case of motor overflow.*

4 Experimentation

To evaluate our framework, we compared the proposed deep learning model with two state-of-the-art methods for multivariate time series anomaly detection: TranAD [7] and ATF-UAD [8]. The model, implemented in PyTorch 2.6.0, was trained with the AdamW optimizer (learning rate = 0.01, step decay = 0.5). It uses 5-second input sequences, a 1-second analysis window, two encoder–decoder layers, two feed-forward layers, 16 hidden units, a 0.1 dropout rate, and early stopping. Ontological reasoning was performed using the Python library owlready2.

4.1 Dataset

Our dataset comprises physical activity measurements collected at 30 Hz from 18 children (15 boys, 3 girls; mean age = 8.92 ± 1.42 years) diagnosed with ADHD, using an ActiGraph GT9X worn on the non-dominant wrist for seven days under real-life conditions. During this period, parents maintained a daily activity diary categorizing each day into class, home, or outdoor activities. The raw data were segmented and labeled following the method described in [2]. This study focuses on class periods, where detecting hyperactivity is clinically meaningful; anomalies identified in these segments are interpreted as motor overflow. To ensure robustness, cross-validation was applied. Owing to space constraints, results are presented for two subjects, with dataset characteristics summarized in Table 3.

Table 3. Dataset description.

Dataset	Training samples per fold	Test samples per fold	Fold	Dimension	Anomaly Rate (%)
Subject 1	11,459,400	1,392,450	10	3	8.55
Subject 2	9,052,800	1,045,050	10	3	3.74

4.2 Results and Discussion

We use precision (P), recall (R), the area under the ROC curve (AUC/ROC), and the F_1-score to evaluate the detection performance of all models. Table 4 presents the mean metrics in contextual anomaly detection for subjects 1 and 2, respectively. For state-of-the-art models, we first perform anomaly detection and then apply filtering based on the rules defined in the ontology. For our framework, the average precision scores achieved are 0.8976 and 0.8903, while recall scores reach 0.8629 and 0.8271. On average, the F_1 scores are 0.8787 and 0.8507, and the AUC/ROC scores reach 0.9867 and 0.9843 for subjects 1 and 2, respectively. Our approach consistently outperforms the baseline models (combined with contextual detection) across all metrics and for both datasets. TranAD delivers the weakest performance. This model struggles to distinguish anomalies from normal variations, which negatively impacts its results. ATF-UAD achieves promising results on both datasets. A key difference between our approach and ATF-UAD lies in how the anomaly score is computed: ATF-UAD directly uses the reconstruction error, our framework employs a statistical modeling of reconstruction errors. The execution times per fold of the deep and statistical models are 413.27 and 317.79 s, respectively, for subjects 1 and 2. The ontology reasoning time is 71.30 and 23.20 s, respectively, for the same subjects. This suggests that our hybrid approach provides an effective solution, even for processing large volumes of data.

Table 4. Contextual anomaly detection results on the dataset.

Model	TranAD				ATF-UAD				Ours			
Metric	P	R	F1	AUC/ROC	P	R	F1	AUC/ROC	P	R	F1	AUC/ROC
Subject 1	0.7975	0.4745	0.5724	0.7586	0.7917	0.7242	0.7496	0.9400	**0.8976**	**0.8629**	**0.8787**	**0.9867**
Subject 2	0.7488	0.5647	0.5873	0.8036	0.8027	0.7213	0.7480	0.9669	**0.8903**	**0.8271**	**0.8507**	**0.9843**

5 Conclusion

This paper presents a framework for contextual hyperactivity detection in children with ADHD. Our approach combines a Transformer architecture, statistical modeling, and ontology-based reasoning. The use of a Transformer-based encoder–decoder architecture, enhanced with a multi-resolution attention mechanism leveraging wavelet decomposition, enables a better capture of the complex and non-stationary dynamics. Statistical modeling of reconstruction errors allows for an effective definition of anomaly scores and thresholds. Finally, ontology-based reasoning enables contextual filtering of detection results, incorporating additional information about the observed situation. The evaluation was conducted on two datasets collected from subjects with ADHD. Experimental results show that the method achieves strong performance. In future work, we plan to deploy and evaluate this approach in a real-world environment.

References

1. Brown, T.E.: Special report—adhd: a complex disorder of the brain's self-management system (2021)
2. Traore, I., Megdiche, I., Marquet-Doléac, J., Chaari, L.: A cross-validation approach for classifying physical activity intensity: a case study in children with attention deficit/hyperactivity disorder. In: 2023 20th ACS/IEEE International Conference on Computer Systems and Applications (AICCSA), pp. 1–8. IEEE (2023)
3. Cabrera, O., Franch, X., Marco, J.: 3lconont: a three-level ontology for context modelling in context-aware computing. Softw. Syst. Model. **18**, 1345–1378 (2019)
4. Ghidalia, S., Narsis, O.L., Bertaux, A., Nicolle, C.: Combining machine learning and ontology: a systematic literature review. arXiv preprint arXiv:2401.07744 (2024)
5. Moshkin, V., Kurilo, D., Yarushkina, N.: Integration of fuzzy ontologies and neural networks in the detection of time series anomalies. Mathematics **115**, 1204 (2019)
6. Yarushkina, N., Andreev, I., Moshkin, V., Moshkina, I.: Integration of fuzzy owl ontologies and fuzzy time series in the determination of faulty technical units. In: International Conference on Computational Science and Its Applications, pp. 545–555. Springer (2019)
7. Tuli, S., Casale, G., Jennings, N.R.: Tranad: deep transformer networks for anomaly detection in multivariate time series data. arXiv preprint arXiv:2201.07284 (2022)
8. Fan, J., Wang, H., Wu, Z., Sun, D., Wu, J., Lu, X.: An adversarial time-frequency reconstruction network for unsupervised anomaly detection. Neural Netw. **168**, 44–56 (2023)
9. Padilla-Cuevas, J., Reyes-Ortiz, J.A., Bravo, M.: Ontology-based context event representation, reasoning, and enhancing in academic environments. Fut. Internet **13**(6), 151 (2021)
10. Malhotra, P., Vig, L., Shroff, G., Agarwal, P., et al.: Long short term memory networks for anomaly detection in time series. In: Esann, vol. 2015, p. 89 (2015)
11. Malhotra, P., Ramakrishnan, A., Anand, G., Vig, L., Agarwal, P., Shroff, G.: "LSTM-based encoder-decoder for multi-sensor anomaly detection. arXiv preprint arXiv:1607.00148 (2016)
12. Anderson, T.W., Olkin, I.: Maximum-likelihood estimation of the parameters of a multivariate normal distribution. Linear Algebra Appl. **70**, 147–171 (1985)

Adapting Deep Learning Models for Image-Level Multi-class Dental Pathology Identification in OPG X-Rays

Nora El-Rashidy[1,2](✉), Younan Iskander[1], and Osama Nagib[1]

[1] Faculty of Artificial Intelligence, Kafrelsheikh University, Kafrelsheikh 33516, Egypt
{noura.alrashidy,younan.iskander,osama.nagib}@ai.kfs.edu.eg

[2] Department of Computer Science, University College in Umluj, University of Tabuk, Umluj, Saudi Arabia

Abstract. Orthopantomograms (OPGs) hold fundamental significance in the practice of diagnostic dentistry. They provide a panoramic image of the maxillofacial region. Deep learning can automate and enhance the analysis of OPGs, which assists clinicians in detecting dental pathologies more efficiently and consistently by utilizing automated systems.

In this paper, we propose a solution for multi-class, image-level classification of common dental pathologies using OPG X-rays. A feature extractor with a pretrained ResNet50 architecture was employed, augmented with a Convolutional Block Attention Module (CBAM) to capture significant pathological attention. The dataset was balanced using augmentation methods and contained six classes of dental conditions: BDC-BDR, Fractured Teeth, Impacted Teeth, Caries, Healthy Teeth, and Infection. We present the model architecture, training strategy, and the experimental details for our evaluation. Initial findings indicate the promise of this method, as well as areas for enhancement, such as broadening the approach to multi-label classification and exploring multi-backbone alternatives.

Keywords: Orthopantomograms (OPGs) · Convolutional Block Attention Module (CBAM) · multi-label classification

1 Introduction

A wide range of oral health problems, such as dental caries, impacted teeth, fractures, and infections, are prevalent globally. These often require radiographic examinations for precise diagnosis and treatment [1]. Given their panoramic view of dental structures, Orthopantomograms (OPGs) are considered the primary diagnostic imaging modality. On the downside, even seasoned clinicians might take considerable time interpreting OPGs due to the variability in interpretation among peers [2]. AI applications, especially those powered with deep learning, have automated a wide array of imaging analysis tasks, such as classification, segmentation, and detection, particularly in the medical field [3,4]. Within the

A. Awad et al. (Eds.): MEDI 2025, LNCS 16427, pp. 295–303, 2026.
https://doi.org/10.1007/978-3-032-19865-5_24

context of OPGs, automating the detection of dental pathologies could serve as a significant aid for dentists by reducing diagnostic errors, speeding up the review process, and improving patient outcomes. Faster R-CNN's object detection frameworks [4] have been designed to locate and identify multiple objects within an image. While effective, the level of complexity and data requirements (bounding box annotations) can be overwhelming. In cases where an image-level assessment of existing pathologies will suffice, image classification models prove to be more efficient.

This research investigates the application of deep learning methods such as sophisticated models based on backbone networks like ResNet50 and attention mechanisms in the multi-class pathological image classification of dental diseases in OPGs. Our objective is to create a system that categorizes the OPG image into one pathological category or healthy, based on the provided ground truth. The proposed work implements a reliable system for whole image classification and assigns a single diagnostic label such as *Caries* or *Impacted Teeth* to a panoramic X-ray. With its application limited to preliminary screenings, this method exposes the gap between high-level classification and clinical utility. It remains a significant research opportunity to move from the classification-only paradigm towards multi-label object detection or semantic segmentation.

The problem to solve is how to design systems capable of identifying, classifying, and accurately localizing multiple overlapping dental pathologies on a single OPG [5]. This would elevate the system from being merely a classifier to a true diagnostic assistant that produces interpretable and actionable results such as bounding boxes or pixel-level masks, bridging the divide between AI prediction and clinical intervention [17]. The difficulties parents encounter in today's fast-paced, international society serve as the inspiration for ICare. It can be difficult to comprehend a baby's needs and ensure their wellbeing, so it is imperative that we have sophisticated technologies that can offer in-the-moment help and useful insights [17].

2 Related Works

There has been some research concerning the application of deep learning on the analysis of dental OPGs. Applications of CNNs (Convolutional Neural Networks) include detection of caries lesions [21], tooth segmentation [4], and detection of bone resorption in periodontal disease [4]. The use of transfer learning on VGGNet [21], ResNet [8], and Inception [9], which had been trained on large-scale datasets such as ImageNet [20], became a common practice to deal with small medical datasets. Attention mechanisms, which allow the model to emphasize specific or more informative parts of the image, have become increasingly popular in medical imaging [16]. One such module is CBAM [6], which generates attention maps in both the channel and spatial dimensions to enhance the precision of feature representations. Some studies are aimed at localizing certain pathologies (object detection), while this one focuses on image-level classification, which provides a broader perspective for diagnosis. We propose image-level classification that captures the OPG as an osteological system and classifies it as either healthy or with a diagnosed ailment. This differs from localizing specific pathologies, as some works do, but builds upon strong feature extraction backbones used in advanced detector frameworks such as Faster R-CNN [3].

3 Research Methodology

The dataset for the current research consists of OPG X-ray images belonging to six classes: BDC-BDR (Benign Dentoalveolar Cyst / Benign Dentoalveolar Radiolucency) containing 156 images, Fractured Teeth (39 images), Impacted Teeth (261 images), Caries (357 images), Healthy Teeth (669 images), and Infection (69 images). Figure 1 shows sample images.

3.1 Dataset and Feature Extraction

All images were resized to 224×224 pixels to meet ResNet50 input requirements and split into stratified training (80%) and validation (20%) sets. To address class imbalance, data augmentation was applied to minority classes until each reached 600 images, while 69 excess images were randomly removed from the overrepresented "Healthy Teeth" class. The final balanced dataset comprised 3600 images (600 per class), as shown in Fig. 1. Augmentation techniques included rescaling to [0,1], rotation (±15°), width/height shifts (±10%), shear (±10%), zoom (±10%), horizontal/vertical flips (with consideration for OPG appropriateness), and nearest-neighbor fill mode. Example augmentations are shown in Fig. 2.

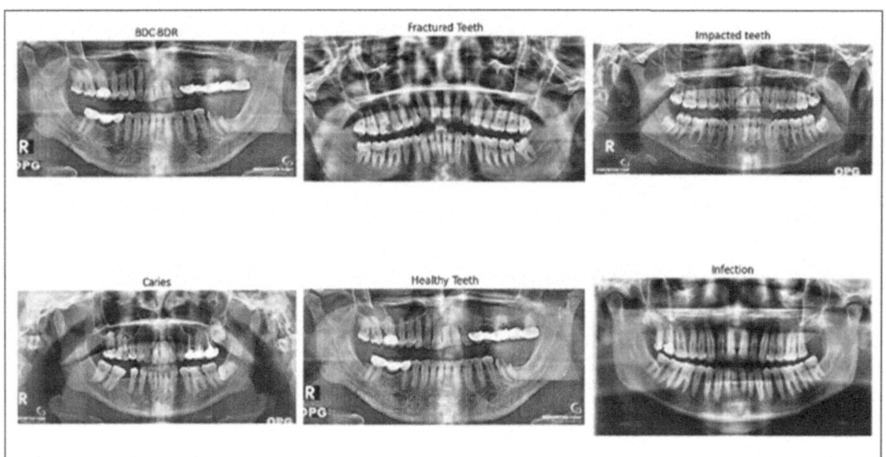

Fig. 1. Final balanced dataset after augmentation.

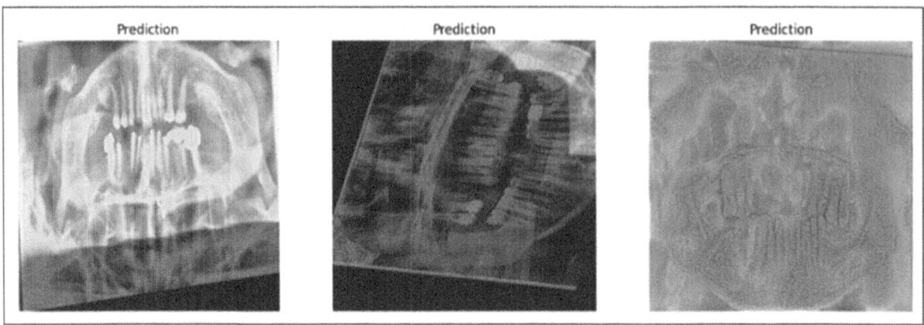

Fig. 2. Examples of augmentation techniques.

3.2 Model Architecture and Training

The architecture (Fig. 3) builds on a ResNet50 backbone with its classification head replaced by a Convolutional Block Attention Module (CBAM) and new classification head. The first 100 layers remain frozen to preserve ImageNet features, while subsequent layers are fine-tuned on OPG data. CBAM sequentially applies channel attention (using global pooling and shared MLP) and spatial attention (via channel pooling and convolution). Features undergo Global Average Pooling before passing to two Dense layers with ReLU, L2 regularization ($\lambda = 0.01$), and dropout (rate = 0.5), culminating in a 6-class Softmax output [18,19].

The model was compiled using the Adam optimizer with a learning rate of 0.0001, categorical crossentropy loss, and accuracy as the metric. It was trained for 30 epochs with a batch size of 16, utilizing callbacks for ModelCheckpoint (to save the best weights based on validation accuracy) and EarlyStopping (with a patience of 10 epochs, restoring the best weights). For potential multi-label classification tasks, the system can be adapted by using multi-hot encoded labels, changing the output activation to sigmoid, and switching the loss function to binary crossentropy [17].

3.3 Experiments and Results

The model was trained for 15 epochs before early stopping, achieving a best validation accuracy of 70.77%, validation loss of 1.76, training accuracy of 65%, and training loss of 0.52 (Fig. 4).

The confusion matrix (Fig. 5) shows:

- "Healthy Teeth" and "Caries" were classified accurately,
- "BDC-BDR" and "Infection" had higher misclassification rates.

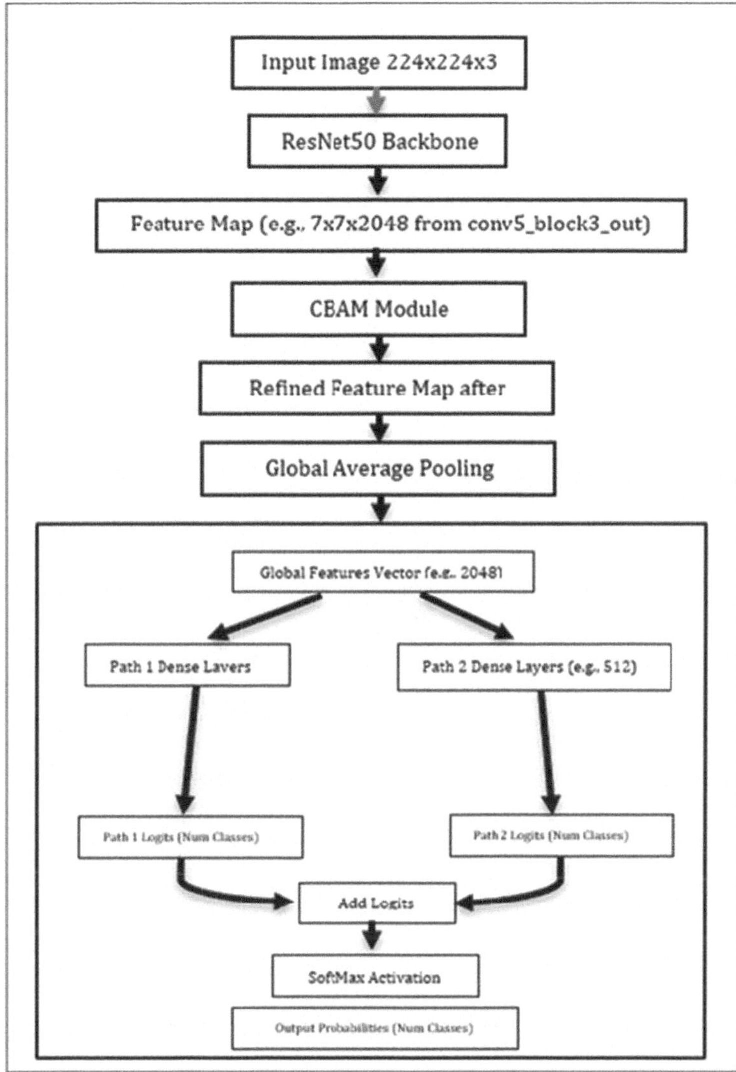

Fig. 3. Proposed Model Architecture (ResNet50 + CBAM + GAP + Dense layers).

4 Discussion

4.1 Model Performance Analysis

The model attained exceptional training accuracy of 95.65% and robust validation accuracy of 85.22% after 20 epochs. The best validation accuracy achieved at 83.91% suggests strong generalization capabilities. A moderate overfitting is present due to a 10.43% gap between training and validation accuracy. Rapid convergence ability (total training time of 1 minute 35 s) indicates high com-

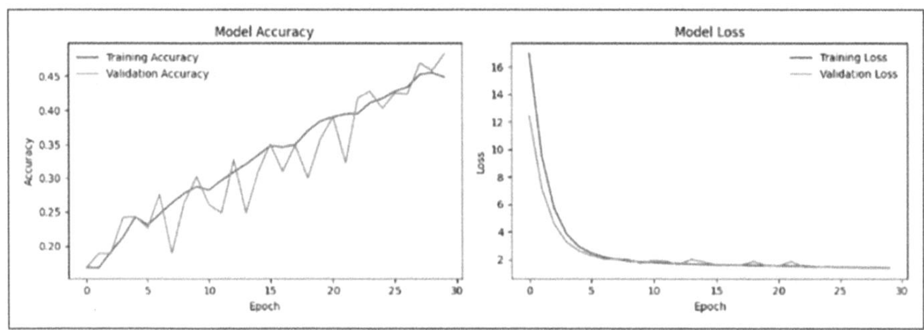

Fig. 4. Training and validation loss/accuracy curves.

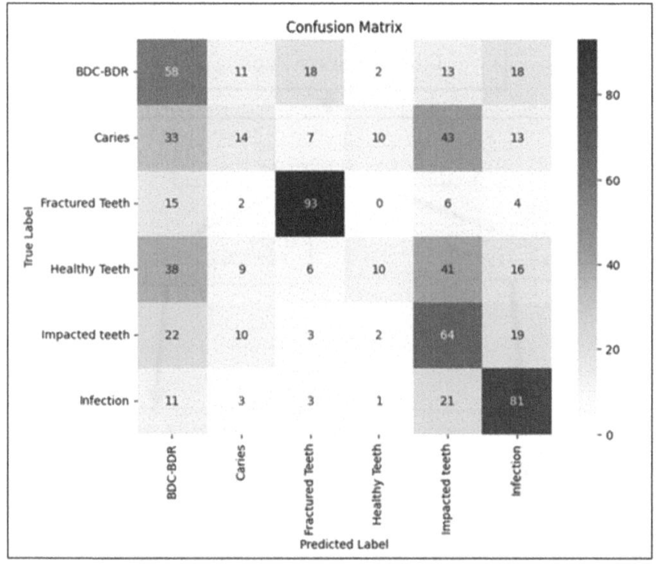

Fig. 5. Confusion Matrix of proposed method.

putational efficiency. Final training loss (0.0871) and validation loss (1.4818) indicate the need for stronger regularization. The model most likely benefited from:(1)EfficientNet-B3's advanced feature extraction. (2)Combined wide and deep learning pathways. Comprehensive data augmentation.(3)Highest performance was achieved on the *Fractured class* with R of 0.78 and P of 0.72.

4.2 Evaluation of the Methodology

The wide & deep architecture effectively integrated visual patterns (deep path) and structural relationships from bounding boxes (wide path). EfficientNet-B3 proved optimal due to its balance between parameter efficiency, feature extraction capability, and computational demand as follows. (1) Learning rate scheduling (step decay every 7 epochs) improved loss navigation.(2) Mixed precision training enhanced convergence speed.(3) Batch size of 16 ensured stable gradient fitting in GPU memory. from another hand Data Augmentation have impact in overall results as folllows (1)Increased dataset diversity; (2)Reduced overfitting. (3)Improved model robustness.

5 Future Work

Based on current findings and limitations, several avenues for future work are identified: **Alternative Backbones** such as EfficientNet or MobileNetV3 for better speed-accuracy trade-offs; **Attention Mechanisms** including transformer-based or advanced attention modules; **Explainability (XAI)** using Grad-CAM or LIME to visualize decision regions; **Localization of Pathologies** moving towards weakly- or fully-supervised detection; **Clinical Validation** through collaboration with dental professionals for expert evaluation.

6 Conclusion

This research presented an automated system for classifying dental pathologies in OPG X-rays using a ResNet50 backbone with a CBAM attention mechanism. A balanced dataset of six dental pathoses was created via augmentation. The model achieved 95.65% training accuracy and 85.22% validation accuracy, highlighting both its potential and the need for further refinement. A hybrid wide & deep model, integrating EfficientNet-B3 for visual features and YOLO annotations for structural features, proved effective and computationally efficient. While results are promising, future work must focus on multi-label classification, stronger regularization, larger datasets, and clinical validation to ensure robust.

Data Availability Statement. The dataset was obtained from Kaggle: https://www.kaggle.com/datasets/imtkaggleteam/dental-opg-xray-dataset. The augmented dataset available upon reasonable request.

References

1. Rozylo-Kalinowska, I.: Introduction to dental radiography and radiology. In: Imaging Techniques in Dental Radiology: Acquisition, Anatomic Analysis and Interpretation of Radiographic Images, pp. 1–5. Springer International Publishing, Cham (2020). https://doi.org/10.1007/978-3-030-41372-9_1
2. Litjens, G., et al.: A survey on deep learning in medical image analysis. Med. Image Anal. **42**, 60–88 (2017). https://doi.org/10.1016/j.media.2017.07.005

3. Ren, S., He, K., Girshick, R., Sun, J.: Faster R-CNN: towards real-time object detection with region proposal networks. IEEE Trans. Patt. Anal. Mach. Intell. **39**(6), 1137–1149 (2017). https://doi.org/10.1109/TPAMI.2016.2577031
4. Lee, J.H., Kim, D.H., Jeong, S.N., Choi, S.H.: Detection and diagnosis of dental caries using a deep learning-based convolutional neural network algorithm. J. Dent. **77**, 106–111 (2018). https://doi.org/10.1016/j.jdent.2018.07.015
5. Deng, J., Dong, W., Socher, R., Li, L.J., Li, K., Fei-Fei, L.: ImageNet: a large-scale hierarchical image database. In: IEEE Conference on Computer Vision and Pattern Recognition, pp. 248–255 (2009). https://doi.org/10.1109/CVPR.2009.5206848
6. Woo, S., Park, J., Lee, J.Y., Kweon, I.S.: CBAM: convolutional block attention module. In: Lecture Notes in Computer Science, vol. 11211, pp. 3–19. Springer (2018). https://doi.org/10.1007/978-3-030-01234-2_1
7. El-Rashidy, N., et al.: Comprehensive survey of using machine learning in the COVID-19 pandemic. Diagnostics **11**(7), 1155 (2021). https://doi.org/10.3390/diagnostics11071155
8. Howard, A., Wang, W., Chu, G., Chen, L., Chen, B., Tan, M.: Searching for MobileNetV3: accuracy vs MAdds vs Model Size. In: IEEE/CVF International Conference on Computer Vision, pp. 1314–1324 (2019)
9. Machuve, D., Nwankwo, E., Mduma, N., Mbelwa, J.: Poultry diseases diagnostics models using deep learning. Front. Artif. Intell. **5**, 733345 (2022). https://doi.org/10.3389/frai.2022.733345
10. Krizhevsky, A., Sutskever, I., Hinton, G.E.: ImageNet classification with deep convolutional neural networks. Adv. Neural. Inf. Process. Syst. **25**(2), 1097–1105 (2012)
11. Kaggle Dataset: Dental OPG X-ray Dataset. https://www.kaggle.com/datasets/imtkaggleteam/dental-opg-xray-dataset, Accessed 01 Sept 2025
12. Handhayani, T., Hendryli, J.: Leboh: an android mobile application for waste classification using tensorflow lite. In: Lecture Notes in Networks and Systems, vol. 544, pp. 1–10. Springer (2023). https://doi.org/10.1007/978-3-031-16075-2_4
13. Ennaama, S., Silkan, H., Bentajer, A., Tahiri, A.: Enhanced real-time object detection using YOLOv7 and MobileNetV3. Eng. Technol. Appl. Sci. Res. **15**(1), 19181–19187 (2025). https://doi.org/10.48084/etasr.8777
14. Li, S., Li, X., Cui, Y., Li, H.: Review of transformer health index from the perspective of survivability and condition assessment. Electronics **12**(11), 2407 (2023). https://doi.org/10.3390/electronics12112407
15. Selvaraju, R.R., Cogswell, M., Das, A., Vedantam, R., Parikh, D., Batra, D.: Grad-CAM: visual explanations from deep networks via gradient-based localization. In: IEEE International Conference on Computer Vision (ICCV), pp. 618–626 (2017). https://doi.org/10.1109/ICCV.2017.74
16. LIME Project: Local Interpretable Model-Agnostic Explanations. https://github.com/marcotcr/lime
17. Alamro, H., et al.: Mathematical modelling-based blockchain with attention deep learning model for cybersecurity in IoT-consumer electronics. Alex. Eng. J. **113**, 366–377 (2025). https://doi.org/10.1016/j.aej.2024.11.016
18. Alrayes, F.S., et al.: Leveraging sparrow search optimization with deep learning-based cybersecurity detection in industrial internet of things environment. Alex. Eng. J. **121**, 128–137 (2025). https://doi.org/10.1016/j.aej.2025.02.004
19. Chellamani, N., et al.: A deep sparse capsule network for non-invasive blood glucose level estimation using a PPG sensor. Sensors **25**(6), 1868 (2025). https://doi.org/10.3390/s25061868

20. El-Rashidy, N., Sedik, A., Siam, A.I., et al.: An efficient edge/cloud medical system for rapid detection of level of consciousness in emergency medicine based on explainable machine learning models. Neural Comput. Appl. **35**, 10695–10716 (2023). https://doi.org/10.1007/s00521-023-08258-w
21. El-Rashidy, N., El-Sappagh, S., Islam, S.M.R., El-Bakry, H.M., Abdelrazek, S.: End-To-End deep learning framework for coronavirus (COVID-19) detection and monitoring. Electronics **9**, 1439 (2020). https://doi.org/10.3390/electronics9091439

An Event-Driven Semantic Web Framework for Managing Interaction Patterns in Online Health Communities

Hela Limam[1](✉), Ahlem Slaimi[1], and Yasmine Akaichi[2]

[1] Institut Supérieur d'Informatique, Université Tunis El Manar, BESTMOD Laboratory Tunis, Tunis, Tunisia
hela.limam@isi.utm.tn

[2] Computer Science Department, University of Clermont Ferrand, Clermont Ferrand, France

Abstract. In the era of digital health, ensuring intelligent collaboration and engagement within online health communities (OHCs) is essential for optimizing information flow and decision-making. This paper introduces a Semantic Web–based, event-driven framework that formalizes community interactions through ontological modeling. By extending established vocabularies such as FOAF and SIOC, the proposed approach defines semantic classes and properties to represent social constructs, including collaboration, self-esteem, trust, and expertise recognition. These representations enable the systematic capture and reasoning of user interactions, supporting advanced query mechanisms and knowledge inference. Integrating Semantic Web technologies with Web 2.0 environments provides a dynamic and interoperable infrastructure for analyzing community behavior and enhancing governance. This framework contributes to the computer science domain by offering a scalable, machine-understandable model for managing complex digital ecosystems, promoting transparency, user engagement, and adaptive knowledge management in online healthcare contexts.

Keywords: Semantic Web · Health Communities · Ontologies · Collaboration · Knowledge Sharing

1 Introduction

Online health communities (OHCs) have become vital environments where patients, caregivers, and healthcare professionals exchange experiences and provide mutual support [1, 2, 16]. Unlike static health information websites, OHCs promote participatory healthcare, enabling users to share knowledge, discuss treatments, and receive both informational and emotional support [5, 8]. During health crises such as the COVID-19 pandemic, digital platforms proved crucial for maintaining mental health and continuity of care [3], although the rapid spread of online misinformation also exposed new challenges [11].

Sustaining engagement in OHCs requires more than technological infrastructure. Studies show that effective moderation, responsive design, and social support are key

A. Awad et al. (Eds.): MEDI 2025, LNCS 16427, pp. 304–311, 2026.
https://doi.org/10.1007/978-3-032-19865-5_25

to fostering participation and empowerment [4, 7, 12, 15]. Yet, traditional community-management methods often fail to adapt to users' evolving needs and expectations, limiting their capacity to promote long-term interaction and trust [1, 5, 17]. Research in digital health and the social semantic web has emphasized the importance of semantically structured approaches for capturing interaction patterns and improving the governance of online communities [10, 18–20].

This work proposes a Semantic Web–based framework for managing OHCs that advances beyond prior models. Building on SIOC and FOAF vocabularies [14, 18], the framework introduces event ontologies to represent user interactions such as collaboration, esteem, and expertise recognition as semantic entities. By transforming discussion events into machine-interpretable patterns, this approach supports automated reasoning, cross-platform interoperability, and more resilient, user-centric OHC management [19, 20].

The remainder of this paper is structured as follows. Section 2 reviews related work on OHC engagement, moderation, empowerment, misinformation, and Semantic Web interoperability. Section 3 presents the proposed architecture and its event-ontology extension. Section 4 defines the interaction patterns and their implementation. Section 5 describes the evaluation design, while Sect. 6 discusses the results and implications. Section 7 concludes with perspectives for future research.

2 Related Works

Online Health Communities (OHCs) have emerged as vital platforms for peer-to-peer support, knowledge exchange, and collective problem solving, extending far beyond the static information provided by traditional health websites [1]. Their significance is especially evident in the management of chronic conditions, where continuous interaction with peers and professionals fosters patient empowerment and self-management [2]. The COVID-19 pandemic further amplified the role of OHCs, as digital peer support became a critical coping mechanism for mental health and social well-being [3]. This underscores the broader need for proactive community governance that ensures inclusivity and sustainability [4].

Several studies have examined the integration of professional oversight in OHCs. Embedding clinicians within community interactions, as seen in platforms like MedHelp, has been shown to enhance patient education, though it also raises concerns about moderation and the spread of misinformation [5, 6]. Effective oversight thus requires a balance between professional input and user autonomy, with research highlighting the importance of moderation styles that combine inclusivity with structured incentive mechanisms such as "Top Contributor" badges to maintain high-quality dialogue [7].The content shared in OHCs typically ranges from questions and answers to forum discussions, blogs, and personal experiences. Such interactions not only support advice-seeking and experience-sharing but also provide emotional relief, strengthening patient confidence and adherence to treatments [8, 9]. However, the scale and complexity of these interactions present challenges for efficient management and meaningful engagement.

To address these challenges, researchers have turned to Semantic Web technologies. The SIOC ontology, for instance, has been used with SPARQL to enhance content retrieval and interaction tracking, enabling structured insights into user participation [10]. Moreover, role-based architecture has been proposed to ensure that novice users can benefit from expert contributions, thereby reinforcing trust and knowledge flow within the community [11]. Building on these insights, this work introduces an Event Module Ontology designed to capture temporal interaction patterns, integrate incentive mechanisms, and strengthen role management. By doing so, it aims to advance OHCs as scalable, trustworthy complements to formal healthcare systems.

3 The Proposed Approach

We present an event-driven Semantic Web framework for Online Health Communities that models user actions as events and encodes them as semantic classes and properties using FOAF/SIOC. We present in Fig. 1 the four-steps pipeline used to structure, analyze, and govern Online Health Communities (OHCs).

Step 1: Define community events. We enumerate the atomic actions that constitute activity in the OHC such as post creation, replies, mentions, votes, tags, follows, reports, badge awards, and join/leave actions. Each event is captured with its actor, target, timestamp, discussion context (forum/thread), topic, and optional quality or sentiment signals. This inventory establishes the operational vocabulary of the community.

Step 2: Transform events into classes and properties**.** The event inventory is formalized as an event ontology aligned with FOAF/SIOC entities. Events are modeled as classes (e.g., PostEvent, ReplyEvent, EndorsementEvent) with properties linking agents to objects and contexts (e.g., agent, object, inForum, aboutTopic, createdAt, qualityScore). The result is a queryable RDF graph that unifies heterogeneous traces into a consistent semantic representation.

Step 3: Generate interaction patterns. From the event graph we derive higher-level interaction patterns that characterize community dynamics. Examples include Question $\rightarrow$ Answer chains, collaborative co-reply networks, recognition/esteem via accepted or "best" answers, and passive participation/lurking. Pattern extraction combines sequence analysis, co-occurrence mining, and network metrics (e.g., response latency, answer coverage, reciprocity, expertise centrality, trust indicators).

Step 4: Manage OHCs using patterns**.** Detected patterns drive governance and engagement actions. Unanswered questions are routed to appropriate experts; high-quality contributors are surfaced and rewarded; low-engagement users receive targeted prompts; content with low credibility triggers moderation workflows; and channel policies are tuned to improve responsiveness and retention. Pattern metrics are monitored longitudinally to evaluate interventions and iteratively refine roles, rules, and community configurations.

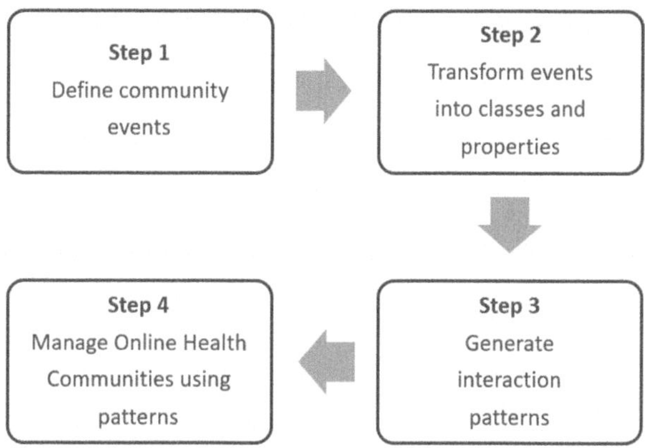

Fig. 1. General architecture of the Online Health Community Management Pipeline.

4 Interaction Patterns for Online Health Community

Effective engagement in online health communities (OHCs) is crucial for fostering collaboration, emotional support, and knowledge exchange among patients, caregivers, and healthcare professionals. Four core interaction patterns: Question/Answer, Collaborative, Friendship define the dynamics of these communities.

4.1 OHC Question/Answer Interaction Pattern

People join OHCs primarily to get case-specific information by browsing threads or posting questions about symptoms, risks, and treatment options that require clinical expertise. This creates a Question–Answer dynamic in which timely, accurate clinician replies are critical but not always consistent. To strengthen participation and quality, we extend SIOC with a TopContributor class (with badges via 'sioct:BestAnswer' and reply counts) to identify and highlight reliable responders. Community managers can query these markers to route unanswered or low-quality questions to experts, boosting trust and keeping the community active.

4.2 OHC Collaborative Interaction Pattern

Collaboration in OHC is defined as health care professionals accepting complementary responsibilities and cooperatively working together, sharing responsibility ity for problem-solving and making decisions to create and carry out plans for patient care.

This pattern or model is inspired by pairs working together in the context of OHC Doctors to share the responsibility of task completion such as research related to a scientific topic, discussing the health condition of certain patients, etc. In a way that all professionals work together on all the parts of a task and create a virtual problem space in which having negotiations and sharing different views result in problem-solving that is approved by all the participants.

4.3 OHC Friendship Interaction Pattern

Browsing and posting are distinct activities: most users lurk before ever contributing, making every lurker a potential future poster [18]. Because passive members simply read without interacting, high lurker ratios can hinder an OHC's success. Converting them into active participants boosts community vitality. Managers should tap passive users' latent willingness to contribute. Offering quick surveys fosters a sense of value and belonging, builds trust, and can prompt engagement. In practice, many doctors and patients feel safer just browsing; targeted surveys can surface their ideas and motivate fuller participation.

5 Experimentation and Evaluation

5.1 Ontology Verification

The ontology was validated with a description logic reasoner to ensure semantic soundness and alignment with FOAF and SIOC vocabularies. The new constructs include TopContributor (class for highly active users), has_badge (links users to participation badges), num_vote (records post votes for content evaluation), and subscription_date (captures registration time for newcomer detection and growth tracking). These extensions provide explicit, machine-processable elements for modeling participation, activity, and content quality in Online Health Communities (OHCs), directly supporting the interaction patterns outlined in Sect. 4.

5.2 Evaluation Design

The evaluation compared two ontology configurations for modeling social interactions in OHCs: the SIOC Type Module, which uses general vocabulary terms and infers participation indirectly, and the SIOC Event Module, augmented with our extensions to capture participation events explicitly. We assessed them on two dimensions: requirement satisfaction, their support for core management needs such as active participation, newcomer detection, passive participation, and content quality and query support and efficiency, their ability to express common SPARQL queries for indicators like top contributors, growth rate, new subscribers, and content quality, with particular attention to reducing query complexity.

5.3 Requirement Satisfaction

Table 1 shows that the SIOC Type Module offers limited coverage of OHC management needs: active participation must be inferred (e.g., post counts), newcomer detection requires non-native temporal reasoning, and content quality is only partially captured via a binary best-answer flag, while passive participation remains unsupported. By contrast, the SIOC Event Module provides explicit, queryable constructs has badge for active participation (e.g., "TopContributor"), subscription_date for newcomer detection and growth tracking, and num_vote for quantitative content quality delivering broader, more reliable requirement satisfaction; passive participation is still not directly modeled in either module.

Table 1. Requirement Satisfaction

Requirement	SIOC Type Module [18]	SIOC Event Module
Active participation	–	+
Newcomer detection	–	+
Passive participant	–	–
Content quality (rate)	+/–	+

5.4 Query Support

The SIOC Type Module offers limited expressiveness, as queries for top contributors or growth rate rely on indirect inference, such as counting posts or users over time resulting in complex and error-prone structures. Its lack of temporal and role-specific properties further limits community monitoring. In contrast, the Event Module supports all major queries except passive participation. Through explicit properties like has_badge, subscription_date, and num_vote, it enables direct retrieval of top contributors, growth trends, and content quality. This leads to simpler, more expressive, and semantically coherent queries, making the ontology more effective for practical OHC management as illustrated in Table 2.

Table 2. Query Support

Target	SIOC Type Module	SIOC Event Module
Top contributors	–	+
Growth rate	–	+
Passive participant	–	–
New subscribers	–	+
Content quality (rate)	+	+

5.5 Query Complexity Analysis

To evaluate efficiency, query complexity was compared in terms of triple patterns and intermediate nodes (Table 3). By directly linking users to badges, the Event Module simplifies queries to a single join without aggregation, enhancing readability and performance. Overall, Event Module queries require fewer triple patterns (2–3 vs. 5–8) and nodes, reducing execution cost and improving scalability for large OHC datasets.

Table 3. Query Complexity

Target Query	SIOC Type Module	SIOC Event Module
Top contributors	7 triple patterns / 3 nodes	3 triple patterns / 1 node
Growth rate	8 triple patterns / 4 nodes	2 triple patterns / 1 node
New subscribers	6 triple patterns / 2 nodes	2 triple patterns / 1 node
Content quality (votes)	5 triple patterns / 2 nodes	2 triple patterns / 1 node

6 Findings and Discussion

The evaluation reveals three main outcomes. First, Top Contributors are captured explicitly in the Event Module via a has_badge property, avoiding indirect inference from post counts. Second, Newcomers and growth are tracked directly through the subscription_date property, providing a reliable view of community evolution that the Type Module cannot offer without complex temporal reasoning. Third, content quality can be assessed in both modules, but the Event Module's num_vote supplies a richer quantitative signal than the Type Module's binary best-answer flag. Taken together, these results show that the Event Module delivers broader requirement coverage, simpler queries, and better scalability; by turning implicit knowledge into explicit properties, it improves both the expressiveness and operational practicality of ontology-based OHC management.

7 Conclusion and Future Works

We present a Semantic Web framework for managing Online Health Communities that extends FOAF/SIOC with event-driven terms TopContributor, has_badge, num_vote, and subscription_date to operationalize collaboration, recognition, and quality assessment. In evaluation, the SIOC Event Module covered more requirements and yielded simpler, faster SPARQL (typically 2–3 triple patterns vs. 6–8 for the Type Module), enabling direct detection of top contributors, newcomers, and content quality. By making community events explicit, the framework streamlines interaction management, increases transparency in user recognition, and strengthens knowledge sharing. Future work includes adding ML-based recommendations, linking with EHR/telemedicine systems, real-time analytics for managers, gamification, cross-cultural deployment, and stronger privacy safeguards to deliver a scalable, secure, and adaptive OHC solution.

References

1. Wang, X., Zhao, K., Street, N.: Analyzing and predicting user participations in online health communities: a social support perspective. J. Med. Internet Res. **19**(4), e130 (2017). https://doi.org/10.2196/jmir.6834
2. van Uden-Kraan, C.F., Drossaert, C.H., Taal, E., Seydel, E.R., van de Laar, M.A.: Participation in online patient support groups endorses patients' empowerment. Patient Educ. Couns. **74**(1), 61–69 (2009). https://doi.org/10.1016/j.pec.2008.07.044

3. Chew, A.M.K., et al.: Digital health solutions for mental health disorders during COVID-19. Front. Psychiatry. **11**, 582007 (2020). https://doi.org/10.3389/fpsyt.2020.582007
4. Preece, J.: Online communities: designing usability and supporting sociability. J. Comput. Mediat. Commun. **6**(4), 1–25 (2001)
5. Huh, J., McDonald, D.W., Hartzler, A., Pratt, W.: Patient moderator interaction in online health communities. J. Med. Internet Res. **15**, e264 (2013)
6. Dunn, P.H., Woo, B.K.P.: Social media's role in the dissemination of health information. J. Am. Geriatr. Soc. **67**(9), 1989–1990 (2019). https://doi.org/10.1111/jgs.16070
7. Matzat, U., Rooks, G.: Styles of moderation in online health and support communities: an experimental comparison of their acceptance and effectiveness. Comput. Hum. Behav. **36**, 65–75 (2014). https://doi.org/10.1016/j.chb.2014.03.043
8. Wang, X., Zhao, K., Street, N.: Social support and user engagement in online health communities. In: Zheng, X., Zeng, D., Chen, H., Zhang, Y., Xing, C., Neill, D.B. (eds.) Smart Health. ICSH 2014. LNCS, vol. 8549, pp. 97–110. Springer, Cham (2014). https://doi.org/10.1007/978-3-319-08416-9_10
9. Hägglund, M., McMillan, B., Whittaker, R., Blease, C.: Patient empowerment through online access to health records. BMJ **378**, e071531 (2022). https://doi.org/10.1136/bmj-2022-071531
10. Bojars, U., Passant, A.: SIOC project: semantically interlinked online communities. In: Proceedings of the Second Multi-Agent Logics, Languages, and Organisations Federated Workshops (MALLOW 2009), Turin, Italy, 7–10 Sept 2009 (2009)
11. Neely, S.R., Eldredge, C., Sanders, R.: Health-related misinformation on social media: a systematic review of the literature. Am. J. Public Health **111**, 282–292 (2021)
12. Hogg, M.A., Abrams, D., Otten, S., Hinkle, S.: The social identity perspective: intergroup relations, self-conception, and small groups. Small Group Res. **35**(3), 246–276 (2004). https://doi.org/10.1177/1046496404263424
13. Fox, S., Duggan, M.: Health Online 2013. Pew Research Center (2013). https://www.pewresearch.org/fact-tank/2013/01/15/health-online-2013/
14. Breslin, J., Bojars, U., Passant, A., Fernández, S., Decker, S.: SIOC: content exchange and semantic interoperability between social networks. In: W3C Workshop on the Future of Social Networking (2009)
15. Festinger, L., Schachter, S., Back, K.: Social Pressures in Informal Groups: A Study of Human Factors in Housing. Harper, New York (1950)
16. van der Eijk, M., Faber, M.J., Aarts, J.W., Kremer, J.A., Munneke, M., Bloem, B.R.: Using online health communities to deliver patient-centered care to people with chronic conditions. J. Med. Internet Res. **15**(6), e115 (2013). https://doi.org/10.2196/jmir.2476
17. Huh, J., McDonald, D.W., Hartzler, A., Pratt, W.: Patient moderator interaction in online health communities. In: AMIA Annual Symposium Proceedings 2013, pp. 627–636 (2013)
18. Breslin, J.G., Bojars, U., Decker, S.: SIOC: an approach to connect web-based communities. Int. J. Web Based Communities **2**(2), 133–142 (2006)
19. Limam, H., Slaimi, A.: Web community management in the digital era: review. J. Comput. Inf. Syst. 1–15 (2024). https://doi.org/10.1080/08874417.2024.2361651
20. Limam, H., Akaichi, J.: Web services communities engineering based on user interaction patterns. Int. J. Bus. Inf. Syst. **22**(2), 201–219 (2016)

Specification-Driven Application Skeleton Generation Using a Multi-agent System

Rim Ben Fekih[1(✉)] and Sabrine Kamoun[2]

[1] Orange Innovation Tunisia, Sofrecom, Lac Biwa, Tunis, Tunisia
Rim.benfekih@sofrecom.com
[2] Faculty of Sciences of Tunis, University of Tunis El Manar, Tunis, Tunisia
Sabrine.kamoun@etudiant-fst.utm.tn

Abstract. Large Language Models (LLMs) have shown significant promise in automating repetitive tasks, particularly in code generation. However, most existing approaches focus on generating isolated code blocks, often lacking global context and coherence across an entire application. Key limitations include the absence of interactive previews, limited support for custom modifications, and insufficient attention to code quality and compliance with specifications.

To address these challenges and accelerate application prototyping, we propose a multi-agent approach for generating complete application skeletons from textual specifications. Our framework enables real-time interactive previews and allows users to iteratively refine the generated applications through a conversational agent. To ensure quality and specification compliance, we employ an LLM-based evaluator that assesses the generated code. Once validated, the application skeleton can be downloaded for further development or deployment. This approach aims to bridge the gap between intent and implementation, streamlining early-stage software design and development. We illustrate our approach through a case study, demonstrating the applicability and effectiveness of each step in the proposed method.

Keywords: LLMs · Multi-Agent Systems · Interactive Generation · Code Quality

1 Introduction

Recent advances in Large Language Models (LLMs) have demonstrated remarkable potential in automating code generation, yet existing approaches often remain limited to producing isolated code blocks without considering the global coherence of an entire application. This poses significant challenges for developers who aim to rapidly prototype complete software interfaces while ensuring that the resulting code maintains high quality, functional integrity, and strict alignment with specifications.

Many prior methods [1,3,5,6,10,16,17] focus primarily on local code correctness or syntactic compliance, but they typically neglect broader architectural

A. Awad et al. (Eds.): MEDI 2025, LNCS 16427, pp. 312–324, 2026.
https://doi.org/10.1007/978-3-032-19865-5_26

considerations, such as inter-component consistency, navigation structure, and user interface flow. Additional limitations include the lack of interactive previews that allow real-time inspection of the generated interfaces, minimal support for user-driven customization or iterative refinement, and insufficient mechanisms for systematically evaluating compliance, correctness, and maintainability across the full application. Consequently, there is a pressing need for approaches that integrate holistic application generation with interactive feedback and automated evaluation to support end-to-end front-end development.

To address these challenges, we propose a multi-agent framework for generating full front-end application skeletons directly from textual specifications. Our system leverages three specialized agents: a generation agent that produces structured, functional interface code; an LLM-based evaluation agent that assesses code quality, specification compliance, and provides improvement suggestions; and an assistant agent that enables interactive refinement, guiding the user to iteratively adjust and enhance the generated application. The framework supports real-time previews, allowing developers to inspect, interact with, and validate the generated front-end before exporting the final code for further development or deployment.

Through this research, we investigate the following central question: *How a multi-agent framework, combining generation, evaluation, and interactive refinement, reliably produce full front-end application skeletons from textual specifications while ensuring code quality, specification compliance, and maintainability?* By integrating automated generation, evaluation, and guided interaction, our approach overcomes the limitations of isolated code generation and facilitates early-stage software prototyping. This framework bridges the gap between design intent and deployable software, providing a flexible and practical solution for accelerating front-end development while ensuring high-quality, specification-compliant code. A case study demonstrates the effectiveness of each component, illustrating the system's ability to generate coherent, interactive, and maintainable application interfaces from simple textual descriptions.

The remainder of this paper is organized as follows. Section 2 presents the essential background and key concepts forming the foundation of our research. Section 3 reviews existing work on the use of LLMs for generating front-end interfaces. In Sect. 4, we describe our multi-agent framework for front-end application generation. Section 5 illustrates the generation results through a representative use case and provides an evaluation of the generated code. Finally, Sect. 6 concludes the paper with a summary of our contributions and outlines directions for future work.

2 Background

This section outlines the key background concepts required to contextualize the rest of the paper.

2.1 Large Language Models

Large Language Models (LLMs) represent a transformative advancement in artificial intelligence, fundamentally reshaping natural language processing and generation. These sophisticated computational models are designed to understand, process, and generate human-like text by leveraging vast amounts of training data and billions of parameters [7]. The emergence of LLMs has marked a paradigm shift from traditional rule-based and statistical approaches to language processing, enabling machines to demonstrate unprecedented capabilities in text comprehension, generation, and reasoning [8].

LLMs are typically pre-trained on extensive corpora of text data, enabling them to learn patterns, structures, and nuances of language. Fine-tuning these models on domain-specific datasets further enhances their ability to generate contextually relevant and coherent text. The versatility of LLMs has led to their application across a wide range of domains, including machine translation, sentiment analysis, code generation, and conversational agents.

Despite their impressive capabilities, LLMs are not without limitations. Challenges such as the generation of plausible but incorrect information, known as hallucinations, and the potential for bias in generated content remain areas of active research. Addressing these issues is crucial for ensuring the reliability and ethical deployment of LLMs in real-world applications.

2.2 Agentic AI

Agentic AI represents a significant evolution in artificial intelligence, wherein systems exhibit autonomous decision-making, planning, and execution capabilities. Unlike traditional AI models that require explicit human instructions for each task, agentic AI systems can independently pursue complex objectives with minimal supervision. These systems integrate large language models (LLMs) with advanced reasoning, memory, and tool integration to perform dynamic, multi-step tasks across various domains [4].

The core characteristics of agentic AI include autonomy, enabling systems to initiate and execute tasks without continuous human intervention; reasoning, which allows them to make informed decisions and adapt to evolving conditions; adaptability, permitting adjustments in strategies and actions based on new information or changes in the environment; and tool integration, which empowers agents to leverage external tools and resources to enhance task execution [2,15]. This paradigm shift from reactive to proactive AI enables applications such as autonomous customer support, dynamic content generation, and intelligent process automation, significantly enhancing efficiency and user experience.

2.3 Code Quality and Evaluation

Ensuring the quality of code generated by LLMs is crucial for practical adoption in software development. Generated code must be syntactically correct, maintainable, and compliant with best practices. Evaluation could be applicable on multiple dimensions of code quality, including correctness, efficiency, readability, and adherence to coding standards.

However, several risks and pitfalls exist when generated code is not verified, such as:

- Hallucinations: LLMs may produce syntactically correct but semantically incorrect or non-existent code.
- Security vulnerabilities: Unverified code may contain potential exploits or insecure patterns.
- Poor maintainability: Generated code may lack proper structure, modularity, or documentation, making it difficult to maintain.
- Non-compliance with standards: Code may deviate from established coding conventions or project-specific guidelines.
- Performance issues: Inefficient code may be generated, leading to suboptimal runtime performance.
- Hidden bugs: Logical errors or edge-case failures may remain undetected without testing.
- Integration problems: Generated code may not interact correctly with existing codebases or APIs.

3 Related Work

Recent work on multi-agent systems for software engineering has shown that coordinating specialized LLM agents can plan, implement, and critique code.

For instance, ChatDev [10] organizes roles like CEO, programmer, tester into structured "chat-chain" dialogues, enabling agents to collaboratively carry out design, coding, and testing phases. However, this framework faces challenges related to role management, agent termination logic, and lack of global coherence across the application. AgentCoder [3] introduces a multi-agent framework where distinct agents are responsible for code generation, testing, and iterative optimization. Each agent plays a specialized role: the programmer agent generates initial code, the test designer agent creates targeted test cases, and the executor agent runs and evaluates the code, feeding back results for continuous improvement. This iterative loop allows the system to progressively refine solutions, enhancing both functional correctness and code quality. Nonetheless, it does not provide interactive front-end previews or seamless user-guided modifications. Similarly, Self-Organized Agents [5] employ a scalable, decentralized approach in which multiple agents independently generate and optimize components of large-scale codebases. The framework dynamically allocates tasks and adapts the number of active agents based on problem complexity, enabling efficient collaboration without centralized control. This self-organization helps maintain coherence across extensive code projects while improving performance, yet generated components may be difficult to integrate coherently at the application level. ProAgent [16] focuses on proactive and cooperative behavior among agents powered by LLMs. Agents continuously infer teammates' intentions from observed actions and adapt their own behavior to maintain coordination, supporting complex multi-step coding tasks. This design enhances modularity, interpretability, and robustness in collaborative code generation scenarios, but it does not explicitly enforce specification compliance or produce end-to-end deployable code. Tare [17] tackles the challenge of maintaining functional correctness in automated program repair. By incorporating type-aware reasoning, Tare leverages T-Grammar and T-Graph representations to guide patch generation, reducing untypable or semantically incorrect changes. This approach ensures that repaired code adheres to typing constraints while maintaining logical consistency. However, Tare is limited to repair tasks and does not support full application skeleton generation.

Front-end–specific multi-agent workflows have also been explored. Frontend Diffusion converts user-drawn layout sketches and prompts into refined website code through multi-stage agents, facilitating iterative UI refinement [1]. Complementary visual-to-code techniques underpin these systems: earlier CNN-RNN models such as pix2code pioneered code generation directly from screenshots, and more recent frameworks like LayoutCoder generate UI layout trees from real webpage images to guide more accurate code synthesis [6]. These approaches, however, offer no interactive previews and limited support for iterative refinement. Industry platforms also venture into design-to-code automation. Tools like Figma [11], Framer [12], and Uizard [14] offer prototyping and no-code design features with AI enhancements, but typically generate generic, non-personalized themes. These often fail to align with specific functional requirements or produce deployable skeletons, serving as accelerators rather than end-to-end solutions.

4 Multi-agent Approach for Application Generation

In this section, we provide an overview of our multi-agent approach for generating front-end interfaces and then describe in detail the role of each agent.

4.1 Overview

We present AppGen[1], a multi-agent tool that automatically generates a front-end application skeleton from high-level specifications. The objective of this approach is to streamline application development by mapping user inputs into functional interfaces. AppGen is designed to process diverse sources of specifications, either as textual descriptions, where the user defines the main functionalities, or as structured input files, including heterogeneous documents such as formal contracts and user stories. The system automatically extracts relevant requirements from these inputs, renders the generated code into interactive previews, and provides an assistant to support code refinement and modification. Furthermore, it integrates an evaluation layer to assess code quality and enables the export of functional project artifacts that can be further extended with additional features. In the following, we describe the multi-agent workflow of AppGen in detail, as illustrated in Fig. 1.

[1] https://github.com/sabrinek8/CodePreview.

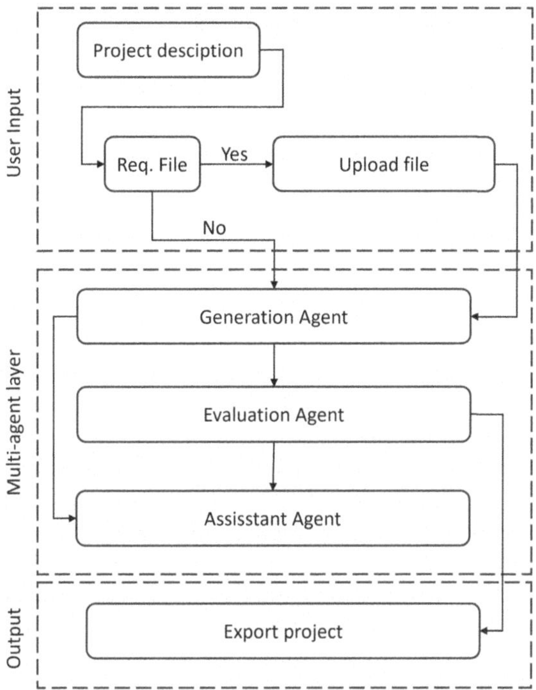

Fig. 1. AppGen: Workflow.

4.2 Multi-agent Layer

Once the user provides requirements, our tool generates the corresponding interfaces using three distinct agents: the Generation Agent (GA), the Evaluation Agent (EA), and the Assistant Agent (AA). In the following, we describe the workflow and the specific role of each agent in producing functional code.

Generation Agent. The Front-end Generation Agent functions as a specialized architect within the proposed multi-agent system. Its primary role is to transform high-level specifications and user requirements into structured, functional front-end interfaces. The agent is instantiated with a clearly defined role, goals, and operational constraints to guide the underlying generative model, ensuring that the outputs are coherent, reproducible, and aligned with the intended application design.

This agent encodes domain knowledge and rule-based constraints to maintain structural correctness and usability of the generated interfaces. By enforcing explicit rules on component composition, styling, and interaction behavior, the agent ensures that the generated artifacts are consistent and interpretable, while avoiding reliance on external, opaque resources. These constraints also serve to reduce errors and enhance the robustness of the generated outputs. The agent operates by translating natural language descriptions of application features into structured representations that capture interface layout, navigation flow, and interactive elements. These representations are designed to be machine-readable and easily integrated into downstream evaluation or refinement processes.

Within the multi-agent workflow, the generation agent serves as the first stage: it receives requirements either directly from the user or via the Assistant Agent and produces candidate interface implementations. These outputs are then analyzed by the Evaluation Agent, which verifies correctness, adherence to design constraints, and functional quality. If deficiencies are detected, a refinement cycle can be initiated to improve the generated interfaces.

Evaluation Agent. The Evaluation Agent serves as the quality gate in the AppGen workflow. Rather than generating or modifying code, its purpose is to critically assess the outputs produced by the *GA*. It examines how well the generated interfaces align with the user's specifications, checks for functional correctness, and identifies potential structural or logical inconsistencies. By representing the project in a structured format, the agent can systematically evaluate each component and provide actionable feedback. Importantly, this agent introduces a feedback loop: its assessments inform refinement cycles, guiding the Assistant Agent or prompting re-generation when necessary. Beyond correctness, the Evaluation Agent also considers maintainability, clarity, and adherence to predefined design rules, ensuring that the resulting projects are not only functional but robust and extendable.

The evaluation is based on three core criteria, summarized in Table 1:

- Requirements Fulfillment: This criterion measures how accurately the generated frontend aligns with the user's description and requested features. It is considered the most critical aspect of evaluation, as it directly reflects the success of the system in translating textual specifications into functional interfaces.
- Code Quality: This assesses the cleanliness, readability, maintainability, and syntactic correctness of the code. It includes evaluation of folder structure, adherence to best practices, and clarity of the implementation.
- Compliance: This criterion ensures that the generated project follows technology-specific best practices, executes without errors, and adheres to expected functional standards.

The score of a generated project is computed as the average of the three criteria:

$$\text{Score} = \frac{\text{Requirements Fulfillment} + \text{Code Quality} + \text{Compliance}}{3} \tag{1}$$

This scoring system enables a quantitative assessment of both functional and structural aspects of the generated application. Moreover, by embedding the Evaluation Agent in a feedback loop, its assessments can inform the Assistant Agent or trigger re-generation by the GA when necessary. Beyond functional

Table 1. Evaluation criteria

Criterion	Description	Scoring (1–10)
Requirements Fulfillment	Measures how well the generated frontend matches the user's description and requested features.	1 = not met 10 = fully met
Code Quality	Evaluates clean, maintainable, and syntactically correct code. Includes folder structure, readability, and best practices.	1 = poor 10 = excellent
Compliance	Checks that the project follows best practices for used technology and runs properly as expected.	1 = non-compliant 10 = fully compliant

correctness, the agent also emphasizes maintainability, clarity, and adherence to design rules, ensuring that generated projects are not only operational but robust and extendable.

Assisstant Agent. The Assistant Agent functions as a specialized modifier within the multi-agent system. Its primary role is to interpret user requests for changes or refinements and apply them to an existing front-end project while preserving the structure and integrity of the application. The agent is instantiated with a clearly defined role, goal, and operational backstory to guide the underlying generative model, ensuring that modifications are precise, consistent, and reproducible.

This agent encodes domain knowledge and rule-based constraints to maintain functional correctness and consistency across the project. It ensures that only the requested changes are applied, while all other components remain unaltered. For interface modifications, it adjusts layout, styles, themes, and visual elements according to user instructions. For functional updates, it integrates the new logic seamlessly, avoiding disruptions to the existing codebase. These constraints prevent unintended alterations and support the production of reliable, extendable project artifacts.

Within the multi-agent workflow, the Assistant Agent operates as an intermediary between the user and the system. It receives user modification requests, interprets them in the context of the current project, and produces a structured output that can be directly integrated into the workflow. The generated outputs are machine-readable and formatted to facilitate downstream evaluation and further refinement if needed.

5 Experimentation and Evaluation

In this section, we demonstrate the applicability of our approach. To do so, we apply our approach on a roaming use case extracted from Orange Business's international contract [9].

5.1 Roaming Use Case

Our use case outlines Orange Business's international roaming framework, specifying how professional users can access voice, SMS, MMS, and data services abroad under predefined conditions. As illustrated in 2, it details included data allowances by geographical zones, billing rules, and the mechanisms for monitoring and controlling consumption, such as alerts, spending caps, and automatic service blocking to prevent excessive charges. The agreement also introduces options for usage restrictions, monthly commitments, and the transfer of unused roaming passes between eligible users, while emphasizing Orange's safeguards against "bill shock" through structured thresholds and pay-per-use unlock systems.

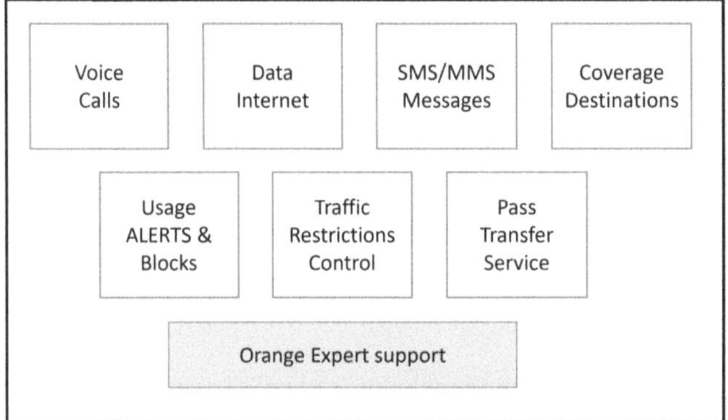

Fig. 2. Roaming contract overview.

While our approach is generic and can be adapted to various target technologies based on user requirements, we chose to use React Native for the Orange Roaming use case. React Native was selected due to its ability to support cross-platform mobile development with a single codebase, enabling faster deployment and easier maintenance. Its large ecosystem, strong community support, and seamless integration with native components make it well-suited for scalable, production-grade applications like the Orange Roaming use case.

Furthermore, we employed Claude Sonnet 3.7 as the generative LLM for our experiments. Notably, Claude demonstrated superior performance in front-end code generation tasks compared to GPT-4o and Codestral. A key factor contributing to this advantage is Claude's significantly higher maximum context length of 64,000 tokens, the highest among the evaluated models. This is particularly relevant in front-end development, where long and interdependent code structures require extended context windows for coherent and accurate generation. In contrast to isolated backend code snippets, front-end code often spans multiple files and components, necessitating broader contextual awareness that models with shorter token limits may struggle to maintain.

5.2 Output and Evaluation Results

Once the input file is provided, AppGen displays a preview of the generated front-end interfaces, which are well-structured, functional, and free of errors. The navbar integrates all functionalities corresponding to the contract clauses.

Figure 3 illustrates the preview page of our tool. It is divided into two main panels: the code panel and the preview panel, allowing the user to interact with the generated interfaces before exporting the code. Furthermore, with the assistance of the tool's built-in assistant, we successfully added a footer to the application. From a computational perspective, generating this interface consumed 39,771 tokens in total, with 1,880 tokens used for the prompt and 37,891 tokens generated in the completion. This highlights the model's ability to generate detailed and complex front-end code efficiently from structured inputs

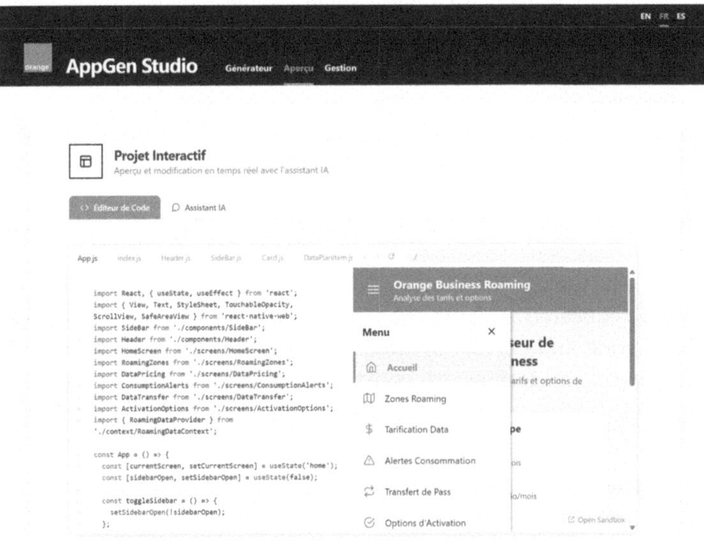

Fig. 3. AppGen: Front-end application preview.

We provide examples of the generated screens in Fig. 4. As shown, the data sharing screen (Fig. 4a) allows users to view and manage data transfer options clearly and efficiently. The activation screen (Fig. 4b) presents a structured interface for enabling or disabling specific services, ensuring intuitive navigation. Finally, the alerts screen (Fig. 4c) displays consumption thresholds and notifications, allowing users to monitor usage and take action when limits are reached.

For the evaluation, we used MLflow [13] as a monitoring interface. In the roaming scenario, the LLM acted as a judge and produced favorable results, with an overall score of 9 as shown in Table 2. The evaluation highlights strong requirements fulfillment, demonstrating how well the project matches the user's

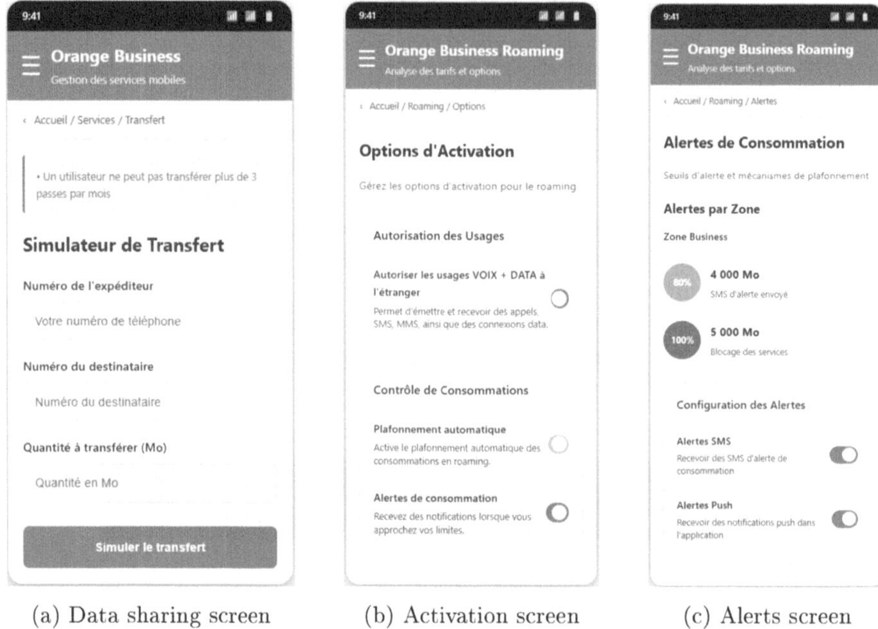

(a) Data sharing screen (b) Activation screen (c) Alerts screen

Fig. 4. Roaming Contract: From formal clauses to front-end mobile interfaces.

description and requested features. It also reflects high code quality, with clean, well-structured code and correct syntax, and confirms proper React Native Web compliance, adhering to framework conventions throughout the generated application.

Table 2. Evaluation output for The roaming use case

Criteria	Score
Requirements fulfillment	9
Code quality	9
Compliance	9

The evaluator agent not only assesses the generated front-end code against predefined criteria such as requirements fulfillment, code quality, and framework compliance, but also provides constructive feedback to guide the user in enhancing the application. This feedback highlights strengths, identifies potential improvements, and suggests actionable changes to improve usability, maintainability, and alignment with user requirements. By offering such targeted guidance, the agent supports iterative refinement, enabling users to progressively enhance the generated interfaces before final deployment. An example of such feedback is shown in Listing 1.1, illustrating how the agent communicates recommendations to support iterative refinement before final deployment.

Listing 1.1. Example feedback from the evaluator agent

```
The project is well-structured with appropriate
    component organization (App, screens, reusable
    components). Code follows React best practices with
     clean separation of concerns. It accurately
    represents the roaming contract information with
    dedicated screens for each major section (general
    info, data plans, pricing, alerts, data transfer).
    The React Native Web implementation is correct with
     proper imports and styling patterns. Component
    structure allows for good maintainability and the
    sidebar navigation provides easy access to all
    content sections. Minor improvement could be adding
     more interactive elements for a better user
    experience.
```

6 Conclusion

In conclusion, our work demonstrates that integrating large language models within a multi-agent framework can effectively automate the generation of complete application skeletons from textual specifications. By providing real-time interactive previews and enabling iterative refinement through a conversational interface, the framework empowers users to guide and improve the generated applications. The inclusion of an LLM-based evaluator ensures that the resulting code meets quality standards and aligns with the intended specifications. Through our case study, we have shown that this approach not only accelerates early-stage software development but also bridges the gap between conceptual design and practical implementation. Future improvements include enhancing generation speed through architectural optimizations and extending the approach to full-stack application generation by incorporating APIs and their documentation, ensuring a closer alignment between intended design and executable applications.

References

1. Ding, Z., Zhang, Q., Chi, M., Wang, Z.: Frontend diffusion: empowering self-representation of junior researchers and designers through agentic workflows. arXiv preprint arXiv:2502.03788 (2025)
2. Institute for Experiential AI: Agentic AI: institute for experiential AI position (2025). https://ai.northeastern.edu/news/agentic-ai-institute-for-experiential-ai-position. Accessed 31 Aug 2025

3. Huang, D., Bu, Q., Zhang, J.M., Luck, M., Cui, H.: Agentcoder: multi-agent-based code generation with iterative testing and optimisation. CoRR abs/2312.13010 (2023). https://doi.org/10.48550/ARXIV.2312.13010
4. IBM: What is agentic AI? (2024). https://www.ibm.com/think/topics/agentic-ai. Accessed 31 Aug 2025
5. Ishibashi, Y., Nishimura, Y.: Self-organized agents: a LLM multi-agent framework toward ultra large-scale code generation and optimization. arXiv preprint arXiv:2404.02183 (2024)
6. Li, Y., Amelot, J., Zhou, X., Bengio, S., Si, S.: Auto completion of user interface layout design using transformer-based tree decoders. arXiv preprint arXiv:2001.05308 (2020)
7. Minaee, S., et al.: Large language models: a survey. arXiv preprint arXiv:2402.06196 (2024)
8. Naveed, H., et al.: A comprehensive overview of large language models. ACM Trans. Intell. Syst. Technol. **16**(5), 1–72 (2025)
9. Orange: Les tarifs des offres mobiles orange business (2025). https://documentscontractuels.orange.fr/obs-mobilite-entreprises_ft_2265.pdf
10. Qian, C., et al.: ChatDEV: communicative agents for software development. arXiv preprint arXiv:2307.07924 (2023)
11. Figma Team: Figma: the collaborative interface design tool. https://www.figma.com/
12. Framer team: Free UI/UX design tool – create & prototype interfaces online. https://www.framer.com/solutions/ui-ux-design
13. MLflow Team: The open source developer platform to build AI applications and models with confidence (2025). https://mlflow.org/
14. UI Team: UI design made easy, powered by AI. https://uizard.io/
15. UiPath: What is agentic AI? (2024). https://www.uipath.com/ai/agentic-ai. Accessed 31 Aug 2025
16. Zhang, C., et al.: Proagent: building proactive cooperative agents with large language models. In: Proceedings of the AAAI Conference on Artificial Intelligence, vol. 38, pp. 17591–17599 (2024)
17. Zhu, Q., Sun, Z., Zhang, W., Xiong, Y., Zhang, L.: Tare: type-aware neural program repair. In: 2023 IEEE/ACM 45th International Conference on Software Engineering (ICSE), pp. 1443–1455. IEEE (2023)

Leveraging Counting Data from Camera Videos to Improve Transport Demand Modeling in African Cities

Hamadoun Tall[1](✉), Albert Talla[2], and Ahmed Ouattara[2]

[1] Nazi BONI University, Bobo-Dioulasso, Burkina Faso
hamadoun.tall@u-naziboni.bf
[2] Flux Group, Petaling Jaya, Ivory Coast
albert.talla@flux-groupe.com

Abstract. African cities face unprecedented urban growth challenges, yet lack adequate transport demand models to guide mobility policies effectively. Traditional approaches rely on household travel surveys, which are scarce and outdated in most African contexts. This research explores innovative data sources, particularly camera-based counting data processed through computer vision techniques, to address this critical gap. We present a comprehensive methodology combining mobile phone data, traffic counting from video streams, and machine learning approaches to generate realistic travel demand patterns. Our experimental validation in Libreville, Gabon, demonstrates the feasibility of using commodity smartphones with pre-trained object detection models (YOLOv8) to extract traffic flow data. The results show promising accuracy in vehicle detection and counting, with potential applications for origin-destination matrix estimation and transport planning. This work contributes to the growing field of data-driven urban mobility analysis in developing countries, offering cost-effective alternatives to traditional survey methods while maintaining scientific rigor in transport demand modeling.

Keywords: Counting data · camera videos · travel demand · transport modelling

1 Introduction

African cities are experiencing unprecedented demographic transformation, with urban populations projected to exceed 1.5 billion inhabitants by 2050 [25]. This rapid urbanization creates a complex web of mobility challenges that traditional transportation planning approaches struggle to address effectively. The phenomenon of urban sprawl, characterized by the expansion of residential areas far from economic centers, compounds these difficulties by increasing travel distances and reducing accessibility to essential services [10].

A. Awad et al. (Eds.): MEDI 2025, LNCS 16427, pp. 325–336, 2026.
https://doi.org/10.1007/978-3-032-19865-5_27

Contemporary African cities face multiple interconnected mobility problems: escalating congestion levels, inadequate public transport systems, environmental degradation from vehicular emissions, and social inequity in transport access [3,8]. These challenges are particularly acute given the limited financial resources available for infrastructure development and the need to balance economic growth with environmental sustainability.

Recognizing these challenges, numerous African governments have launched ambitious transport infrastructure projects. Notable examples include the Addis Ababa Light Rail Transit system in Ethiopia, the Train Express Régional (TER) in Senegal, and the Bus Rapid Transit systems in Lagos, Nigeria, and Cape Town, South Africa [2,16]. The success of these multi-billion dollar investments depends critically on accurate feasibility studies and comprehensive transport demand modeling.

Unfortunately, most transport planning studies in African cities are conducted by international consultancy firms using proprietary commercial software packages such as VISUM, CUBE, or TransCAD. While these tools are powerful, they create several problems: high licensing costs, limited knowledge transfer to local institutions, and dependency on external expertise for future studies [20]. This situation leaves local transport authorities unable to independently conduct scenario analysis or update their transport models as cities evolve.

The emergence of open-source transport modeling platforms offers a promising alternative. Tools such as MATSim [13], SUMO [17], and POLARIS [1] provide sophisticated modeling capabilities at no licensing cost while encouraging knowledge sharing and local capacity building. However, the adoption of these tools in African contexts remains limited, primarily due to data availability constraints.

Traditional transport demand modeling relies heavily on household travel surveys (HTS) to understand travel patterns, mode choice, and trip generation characteristics. These surveys provide detailed information about individual travel behavior but face significant challenges in African contexts. Conducting comprehensive household travel surveys requires substantial financial resources and technical expertise that many African cities lack. The surveys involve complex sampling procedures, extensive fieldwork, and sophisticated data processing capabilities [20]. Moreover, many African cities have outdated survey data that no longer reflect current travel patterns.

The proliferation of mobile technologies and digital infrastructure in African cities creates new opportunities for transport data collection. Several emerging data sources show particular promise:

Mobile Phone Data: Cell phone usage has reached high penetration rates across Africa, generating vast amounts of location data through Call Detail Records (CDR) and smartphone GPS traces [5,19]. This data offers unprecedented spatial and temporal coverage for understanding mobility patterns.

Video and Camera Data: The expansion of urban surveillance systems and the ubiquity of smartphones create opportunities for traffic counting and behavior analysis through computer vision techniques [28].

GPS and Application Data: Navigation applications and ride-sharing services generate detailed trajectory data that can inform route choice and travel time analysis [11].

This research aims to develop and validate a comprehensive methodology for transport demand modeling in African cities using emerging data sources, with particular emphasis on camera-based traffic counting. Our specific objectives are:

1. To systematically analyze the potential and limitations of different dynamic data sources for transport planning in African contexts;
2. To develop a practical methodology for extracting traffic flow data from video sources using computer vision techniques;
3. To validate the approach through empirical testing in a real African city environment;
4. To demonstrate the integration potential of different data sources for comprehensive transport demand modeling.

The main contributions of this work include:

- A comprehensive review of data-driven approaches suitable for African transport planning contexts;
- A validated methodology for smartphone-based traffic data collection and processing;
- Empirical results demonstrating the accuracy and practical applicability of computer vision approaches for traffic counting;
- A framework for integrating multiple data sources to support transport demand modeling.

The remainder of the paper is organized as follows. In Sect. 2, the literature review and theoretical framework are presented. In Sect. 3, the used methodology is explained. In Sect. 4, the case study is presented. In Sect. 5, the obtained results are presented and analyzed. Section 6 presents the discussion, and Sect. 7 concludes the work.

2 Literature Review and Theoretical Framework

2.1 Evolution of Transport Demand Modeling

Transport demand modeling has evolved significantly since the introduction of the four-step model in the 1950s [18]. Traditional approaches focus on aggregate zonal analysis, using household travel surveys to estimate trip generation, distribution, modal split, and route assignment. While this framework remains fundamental to transport planning, its data requirements and static nature limit its applicability in rapidly changing urban environments [20].

Recent decades have witnessed a shift toward activity-based modeling approaches that better capture the complexity of individual travel decisions [6]. Tools like MATSim implement agent-based microsimulation, allowing for more realistic representation of travel behavior and policy impacts [13]. However, these advanced approaches require even more detailed data about individual travel patterns and preferences.

2.2 Big Data and Transport Planning

The emergence of "big data" from mobile devices, social media, and IoT sensors has created new paradigms for understanding urban mobility [9]. Several research streams have developed:

Mobile Phone Data Analysis: Pioneering work by Blondel et al. [5] demonstrated the potential for analyzing human mobility patterns using cell phone data. Subsequent research has shown applications for origin-destination matrix estimation [14], commuting pattern analysis [7], and transport mode detection [24].

GPS and Trajectory Analysis: GPS-enabled devices generate detailed movement trajectories that enable fine-grained analysis of travel behavior. Research has addressed route choice modeling [21], activity location inference [27], and multimodal trip detection [23].

Computer Vision for Transport: Advances in deep learning have revolutionized computer vision applications in transport [28]. Object detection models like YOLO [22] and R-CNN [12] enable accurate vehicle counting and classification from video data.

2.3 African Urban Mobility Research

Research on African urban mobility has highlighted unique characteristics that distinguish it from mobility patterns in developed countries:

Modal Diversity: African cities typically feature complex transport ecosystems combining formal public transport, paratransit services, non-motorized modes, and walking [3]. This diversity requires modeling approaches that can handle multiple mode interactions.

Informal Transport Systems: Paratransit services (matatus, dala-dalas, trotros) play crucial roles in urban mobility but operate with limited formal regulation [8]. Understanding and modeling these systems requires innovative data collection approaches.

Spatial Patterns: Many African cities exhibit polycentric development patterns with multiple activity centers, challenging traditional monocentric transport models [4].

3 Methodology

3.1 Conceptual Framework

Our methodology adopts a multi-source data integration approach, combining three primary data streams: mobile phone data, camera-based counting data, and supplementary GPS traces. This framework recognizes that no single data source can provide complete information for transport demand modeling, but strategic combination of sources can compensate for individual limitations.

The conceptual framework follows these key principles:

- **Complementarity:** Different data sources provide different types of information that complement rather than duplicate each other.
- **Validation:** Multiple sources enable cross-validation and accuracy assessment.
- **Scalability:** The approach should be applicable across different African cities with varying data availability.
- **Cost-effectiveness:** Solutions should be economically viable for resource-constrained environments.

We employ a clustering-based approach to convert raw cell tower data into meaningful geographical zones:

1. Spatial clustering of antenna locations using DBSCAN algorithm.
2. Temporal analysis to identify regular mobility patterns.
3. Origin-destination matrix generation using trip chaining algorithms.
4. Statistical extrapolation to account for population not covered by the mobile operator.

Video data from surveillance cameras or mobile devices provides detailed information about traffic flows and travel behavior at specific locations. This data type is particularly valuable for African cities where surveillance infrastructure is expanding rapidly. Our video processing methodology involves several sequential steps as presented in Algorithms 1 and 2.

We utilize YOLOv8 [15], the latest iteration of the You Only Look Once family, for real-time object detection. YOLOv8 offers improved accuracy over previous versions while maintaining computational efficiency suitable for mobile device deployment. The model is trained to detect and classify multiple vehicle types relevant to African urban contexts such as private cars and taxis, buses, motorcycles and tricycles, trucks and commercial vehicles, bicycles and pedestrians. To avoid double-counting vehicles that appear in multiple frames, we implement the DeepSORT algorithm [26], which combines appearance features with motion prediction for robust object tracking.

Algorithm 1. Video-based Traffic Counting Pipeline

Input: Video stream V
Output: Traffic counts by vehicle type
1. Video preprocessing and frame extraction
2. Object detection using YOLOv8 model
3. Vehicle classification and bounding box refinement
4. Multi-object tracking using DeepSORT
5. Counting line definition and crossing detection
6. Data aggregation and statistical analysis

Algorithm 2. Detailed Traffic Analysis Pipeline

Initialize: Load YOLOv8 model, define counting lines
for each video frame f_t **do**
  Detect objects: $objects_t = YOLO(f_t)$
  Filter by confidence: $valid\_objects_t = filter(objects_t, conf > 0.5)$
  Update tracks: $tracks_t = update\_tracks(valid\_objects_t, tracks_{t-1})$
  Check crossing events: $crossings_t = check\_crossings(tracks_t, counting\_lines)$
  Update counters: $counters+ = crossings_t$
end for
Return: Final counts by vehicle category

3.2 Data Integration and Validation Framework

Our integration framework employs a hierarchical approach where different data sources inform different aspects of the transport demand model:

- **Level 1 - Population and Trip Generation:** Mobile phone data provides the primary input for understanding where people live and work, enabling population-based trip generation estimation.
- **Level 2 - Origin-Destination Patterns:** Combination of mobile phone CDR analysis and GPS trajectory data generates comprehensive origin-destination matrices.
- **Level 3 - Modal Split and Route Choice:** GPS data and video observations inform mode choice and route selection behavior.
- **Level 4 - Calibration and Validation:** Traffic counting data from video analysis provides ground truth for model calibration and accuracy assessment.

Finally, we implement a comprehensive validation framework addressing multiple aspects of data quality:

- **Spatial Validation:** Cross-comparison of traffic volumes between different data sources at common observation points.
- **Temporal Validation:** Analysis of consistency in temporal patterns (peak hours, day-of-week variations) across data sources.
- **Demographic Validation:** Comparison with available census data and previous survey results to assess representativeness.
- **Technical Validation:** Assessment of computer vision algorithm accuracy using manual counting verification.

4 Case Study Implementation

4.1 Study Area Selection and Description

We selected Libreville, Gabon, as our primary case study location for several strategic reasons. Gabon represents a middle-income African country with relatively developed urban infrastructure but limited transport planning data. Libreville, the capital and largest city with approximately 800,000 inhabitants, exhibits many characteristics common to African cities: rapid growth, mixed formal and informal transport systems, and limited previous transport studies.

The specific observation point was strategically chosen at Hôtel de la Plage, a central location that serves as a critical node in Libreville's transport network. This location offers several advantages: i) high traffic volumes representing diverse trip purposes, ii) clear sight lines enabling effective video capture, iii) Safety and accessibility for data collection teams, and iv) Representative of typical African urban arterial conditions.

4.2 Data Collection Protocol

Our video data collection followed a standardized protocol to ensure replicability across different African cities. We used a Samsung Galaxy A12 smartphone with a 48 MP main camera, chosen for its affordability and wide availability in African markets. Recordings were made in Full HD (1920×1080 pixels) at 30 frames per second, with each segment lasting five minutes to provide sufficient data while keeping processing manageable. Data were collected during both peak and off-peak periods to capture variations in traffic flow.

The camera was positioned 3 to 4 m above ground level and angled between 30° and 45° from the horizontal to reduce occlusion and maximize vehicle visibility. Multiple angles were recorded at each site to validate detection accuracy and ensure robust data.

To verify the accuracy of the computer vision results, we conducted parallel manual counts. Two trained observers independently recorded vehicle counts using the same classification categories as the automated model. Manual and automated counts were temporally synchronized, and inter-observer reliability was assessed using Cohen's kappa coefficient to ensure consistency and validity.

5 Results and Analysis

5.1 Video Data Collection Results

Our field data collection in Libreville yielded substantial video datasets across multiple time periods. The dataset comprises 2.5 h of video distributed across different time periods (morning and evening peak hours, as well as midday), representing 270,000 individual frames captured under clear weather conditions. The video analysis revealed a typical traffic composition of African cities, dominated by private cars (68%), followed by taxis and shared vehicles (15%), motorcycles (8%), buses and minibuses (5%), and trucks and commercial vehicles (4%).

5.2 Computer Vision Performance Analysis

Figure 1 gives an overview of the detection of transportation modes and the corresponding counts.

(a) Time frame T

(b) Time frame T+1

Fig. 1. Overview of transportation mode detection and corresponding counting.

The different captures correspond to frames extracted from the videos. The frames on the left correspond to raw sequences. While those on the right represent, on the one hand, the detections of transport modes and the corresponding count. For example, in Fig. 1a, the algorithm detected in this sequence a total of 2 people, 85 private cars, and one truck. In Fig. 1b, we can see that the number of private cars has increased by 6 units and trucks by one unit.

Table 1 presents detailed accuracy metrics for our YOLOv8-based vehicle detection system compared to manual ground truth counts.

The results demonstrate strong overall performance with 92% precision and 89% recall. Private cars showed the highest detection accuracy, benefiting from their prevalence in the COCO training dataset. Motorcycles presented greater challenges due to their smaller size and potential occlusion by larger vehicles.

Common detection errors included: - False negatives during heavy occlusion scenarios (15% of missed detections) - Confusion between car and taxi categories (8% of classification errors) - Partial vehicle visibility at frame edges (12% of missed detections) - Shadow effects causing false positives (5% of over-counting)

5.3 Validation Against Traditional Methods

Direct comparison between automated and manual counting shows strong correlation ($R^2 = 0.94$) across different time periods and vehicle categories. The

Table 1. Vehicle Detection Accuracy by Category

Vehicle Category	Manual Count	Automated Count	Precision	Recall
Private Cars	2,150	2,089	0.94	0.92
Taxis	380	365	0.91	0.87
Motorcycles	205	189	0.87	0.85
Buses	125	118	0.89	0.84
Trucks	98	94	0.92	0.88
Overall	2,958	2,855	0.92	0.89

automated system consistently undercounts by approximately $3 - 5\%$, primarily due to occlusion effects and edge cases.

We conducted paired t-tests to compare automated and manual counts over 30-minute observation periods. The average difference was -3.2%, with a standard deviation of 8.1%. The 95% confidence interval ranged from -5.1% to -1.3%. A p-value below 0.01 indicates a statistically significant but practically acceptable difference.

5.4 Scalability and Deployment Considerations

Processing performance tests showed that the system achieved 2.1 fps on a Samsung Galaxy A12, 8.3 fps on a standard laptop with an Intel i5 processor and 8 GB of RAM, and over 45 fps using GPU-enabled cloud processing. Economic comparisons with traditional counting methods (Table 2) highlight clear cost benefits, especially for multi-location, long-term studies typical of comprehensive transport planning projects.

Table 2. Cost Comparison: Traditional vs Computer Vision Approach

Method	Initial Cost (USD)	Cost per Location-Day (USD)
Manual counting	0	120–150
Pneumatic tubes	2,000–3,000	25–35
Video + computer vision	200–300	5–10

6 Discussion

Our research introduces important methodological advances for transport data collection in African cities. By relying on smartphones, the approach lowers barriers to traffic data collection and allows local agencies to conduct studies without costly specialized equipment. Its flexibility enables rapid deployment across multiple locations, supporting comprehensive network-level analysis rather than isolated point studies. Despite using consumer-grade devices and pre-trained models, it achieves 92% precision, which is comparable to specialized traffic counting equipment. The method can also be scaled and applied across different African cities without the need for advanced infrastructure or extensive training.

The traffic counting data generated through this approach plays a key role in transport demand modeling. Observed volumes are used to calibrate trip distribution and mode choice parameters, providing a solid foundation for model accuracy. When combined across several counting sites, these data inform origin–destination matrix estimation through mathematical programming. Detailed vehicle classification supports analysis of modal preferences and public transport market share, while time-series data help develop time-of-day factors and understand peak period dynamics.

However, several limitations must be acknowledged. Point-based counting has limited spatial coverage compared to network-wide data sources such as mobile phone records. Weather conditions can affect video quality and, in turn, processing accuracy. Although more efficient than manual methods, the approach still requires human involvement for camera placement and data quality checks. In addition, pre-trained models may not fully capture all vehicle types specific to African contexts, particularly informal transport modes.

Looking ahead, several research directions can strengthen this work. One promising avenue is the development of object detection models specifically trained on African vehicle imagery, which could significantly improve classification accuracy for locally prevalent vehicle types.

7 Conclusion

This research highlights the strong potential of computer vision–based traffic counting to support transport demand modeling in African cities. A validation study conducted in Libreville, Gabon, demonstrates that using commodity smartphones with pre-trained object detection models can achieve traffic counting accuracy close to that of specialized equipment, while offering substantial advantages in terms of cost, flexibility, and accessibility.

The study makes several key contributions. It proposes a comprehensive methodological framework for integrating multiple dynamic data sources, with an emphasis on video-based traffic counting tailored to resource-constrained African contexts. Empirical validation shows a precision of 92% and a recall of 89% for automated vehicle detection and counting, with a strong correlation ($R^2 = 0.94$) to manual ground truth data. Economically, the approach provides $80--90\%$ cost savings compared to manual surveys, while maintaining acceptable levels of accuracy. It can be implemented easily by local transport agencies without specialized infrastructure or extensive technical training. Furthermore, the method is scalable across different urban contexts, supporting both city-level and regional transport studies.

The implications for transport planning practice in African cities are significant. By reducing costs and technical barriers, this approach enables more frequent and comprehensive studies, supporting evidence-based policy making and infrastructure investment. It also offers opportunities to strengthen local capacity and build sustainable institutional frameworks for transport planning.

Nonetheless, some challenges persist. Clear weather conditions and strategic camera placement remain necessary for optimal results, and integrating with other data sources—such as mobile phone data—requires additional technical expertise and institutional cooperation with telecommunications providers.

Future work should prioritize the development of custom object detection models trained on African traffic imagery to better capture local and informal transport modes. Expanding the methodology to integrate multiple data sources into comprehensive demand models, and exploring real-time processing for adaptive traffic management, will further enhance its applicability.

As African cities continue to expand and transform, innovative and affordable methods for collecting and analyzing transport data will be essential. This research contributes to building practical tools that support sustainable urban mobility planning in resource-constrained settings, ultimately fostering more inclusive and accessible cities.

Acknowledgments. The authors thank the local authorities in Libreville, Gabon, for facilitating field data collection.

References

1. Auld, J., Hope, M., Ley, H., Sokolov, V., Xu, B., Zhang, K.: POLARIS: agent-based modeling framework development and implementation for integrated travel demand and network and operations simulations. Transp. Res. Part C: Emerg. Technol. **64**, 101–116 (2016)
2. Behrens, R.: The challenge of urban transport in African cities. Dev. South. Afr. **33**(5), 729–743 (2016)
3. Behrens, R., McCormick, D., Mfinanga, D.: Paratransit in African Cities: Operations, Regulation and Reform. Routledge, London (2017)
4. Bertaud, A.: Cities in Sub-Saharan Africa: Is the urban transition under way? World Bank Policy Research Working Paper (6878) (2014)
5. Blondel, V.D., Guillaume, J.L., Lambiotte, R., Lefebvre, E.: Fast unfolding of communities in large networks. J. Stat. Mech: Theory Exp. **2008**(10), P10008 (2008)
6. Bowman, J.L., Ben-Akiva, M.E.: The day activity schedule approach to travel demand analysis. Transp. Res. Part A: Policy Pract. **32**(5), 353–377 (1998)
7. Calabrese, F., Diao, M., Di Lorenzo, G., Ferreira, J., Jr., Ratti, C.: Understanding individual mobility patterns from urban sensing data: a mobile phone trace example. Transp. Res. Part C: Emerg. Technol. **26**, 301–313 (2011)
8. Cervero, R.: Bus rapid transit in cities worldwide. Transp. Rev. **33**(2), 191–207 (2013)
9. Chen, C., Jiao, S., Zhang, S., Liu, W., Feng, L., Wang, Y.: Big data for transportation: a survey. IEEE Intell. Transp. Syst. Mag. **8**(3), 32–57 (2016)

10. Dziwonou, Y.: Etalement urbain et les difficultés de mobilité dans les métropoles d'afrique subsaharienne. Revue de Géographie Tropicale et d'Environnement **2**, 60–75 (2009)
11. Feng, G., Jean, M., Chasse, A., Hörl, S.: Pre-calibration of a discrete choice model and evaluation of cycling mobility for île-de-france. Procedia Comput. Sci. **184**, 172–177 (2021)
12. Girshick, R., Donahue, J., Darrell, T., Malik, J.: Rich feature hierarchies for accurate object detection and semantic segmentation. In: Proceedings of the IEEE Conference on Computer Vision and Pattern Recognition, pp. 580–587 (2014)
13. Horni, A., Nagel, K., Axhausen, K.W.: Multi-Agent Transport Simulation MATSim. Ubiquity Press, London (2016). https://doi.org/10.5334/baw
14. Iqbal, M.S., Choudhury, C.F., Wang, P., González, M.C.: Development of origin-destination matrices using mobile phone call data. Transp. Res. Part C: Emerg. Technol. **40**, 63–74 (2014)
15. Jocher, G., Chaurasia, A., Qiu, J.: Ultralytics YOLOv8 (2023). https://github.com/ultralytics/ultralytics
16. Kopf, C., Perier, M.: Le ter nous met à terre. le sénégal sur les rails de l'émergence? Critique internationale **4**, 115–139 (2020)
17. Lopez, P.A., et al.: Microscopic traffic simulation using sumo. In: The 21st IEEE International Conference on Intelligent Transportation Systems. IEEE (2018). https://elib.dlr.de/124092/
18. McNally, M.G.: The four-step model. Handbook of Transport Modelling, pp. 35–53 (2007)
19. de Montjoye, Y.A., Smoreda, Z., Trinquart, R., Ziemlicki, C., Blondel, V.D.: D4D-Senegal: The second mobile phone data for development challenge. arXiv preprint arXiv:1407.4885 (2014)
20. Ortúzar, J.d.D., Willumsen, L.G.: Modelling Transport. John Wiley & Sons, Chichester, 4th edn. (2011)
21. Ramming, M.S.: Network knowledge and route choice. Massachusetts Institute of Technology (2001)
22. Redmon, J., Divvala, S., Girshick, R., Farhadi, A.: You only look once: unified, real-time object detection. In: Proceedings of the IEEE Conference on Computer Vision and Pattern Recognition, pp. 779–788 (2016)
23. Stenneth, L., Wolfson, O., Yu, P.S., Xu, B.: Transportation mode detection using mobile phones and GIS information. In: Proceedings of the 19th ACM SIGSPATIAL International Conference on Advances in Geographic Information Systems, pp. 54–63 (2011)
24. Stopher, P., FitzGerald, C., Zhang, J.: Search for a global positioning system device to measure person travel. Transp. Res. Part C: Emerg. Technol. **16**(3), 350–369 (2008)
25. United Nations: Department of Economic and Social Affairs, Population Division: World urbanization prospects: The 2018 revision. Tech. rep, United Nations, New York (2019)
26. Wojke, N., Bewley, A., Paulus, D.: Simple online and realtime tracking. arXiv preprint arXiv:1703.07402 (2017)
27. Wolf, J., Guensler, R., Bachman, W.: Applications of cellular phone-based floating car data to traffic management. Transp. Res. Part C: Emerg. Technol. **12**(1), 3–26 (2004)
28. Zhang, J., Zheng, Y., Qi, D., Li, R., Yi, X., Li, T.: Deep learning for intelligent transportation systems: a comprehensive survey. IEEE Intell. Transp. Syst. Mag. **9**(4), 16–32 (2017)

Next Generation Cloud-Native In-Memory Stores: From Redis to Valkey and Beyond

Carl-Johan Fauvelle Munck af Rosenschöld[1(✉)], Feras M. Awaysheh[1], and Ahmad Awad[2]

[1] Department of Computing Science, Umeå University, Umeå, Sweden
carljohan.rosenschold@gmail.com, feras.awaysheh@umu.se
[2] The British University in Dubai, Dubai, UAE
ahmed.awad@buid.ac.ae

Abstract. In-memory key-value datastores have become indispensable building blocks of modern cloud-native infrastructures, yet their evolution faces scalability, compatibility, and sustainability constraints. The current literature lacks an experimental evaluation of state-of-the-art tools in the domain. This study addressed this timely gap by benchmarking Redis alternatives and systematically evaluating Valkey, KeyDB, and Garnet under realistic workloads within Kubernetes deployments. The results demonstrate clear trade-offs among the benchmarked data systems. Our study presents a comprehensive performance and viability assessment of the emerging in-memory key-value stores. Metrics include throughput, tail latency, CPU and memory efficiency, and migration complexity. We highlight trade-offs between performance, compatibility, and long-term viability, including project maturity, community support, and sustained development.

1 Introduction

In the era of Big Data, in-memory key-value datastores have become critical enablers of real-time analytics and low-latency services, underpinning the scalability demands of modern distributed systems [2–4]. In-memory datastores have become fundamental components, providing extremely fast data access compared to traditional disk-based databases [1,8]. Redis, in particular, has established itself as the de facto standard for in-memory key-value datastores over the past decade, renowned for its simplicity, performance, and extensive ecosystem [5,17]. Recently, Redis underwent significant licensing changes [15] that have impacted its adoption, particularly among communities and organizations prioritizing open-source principles [9].

Three systems have emerged as leading contenders to replace Redis: Valkey[1], KeyDB[2], and Garnet[3]. Valkey, launched by the Linux Foundation in March 2024,

[1] https://valkey.io/.
[2] https://docs.keydb.dev/.
[3] https://github.com/microsoft/garnet.

A. Awad et al. (Eds.): MEDI 2025, LNCS 16427, pp. 337–346, 2026.
https://doi.org/10.1007/978-3-032-19865-5_28

represents a community-driven fork of Redis maintaining full API compatibility while implementing significant performance improvements. KeyDB is a multi-threaded fork of Redis, introduced in 2019 [6], designed to leverage multi-core architectures for higher throughput. Garnet, developed by Microsoft Research, provides a high-performance implementation built from the ground up with modern hardware optimization.

The selection of an appropriate Redis alternative involves multiple considerations beyond raw performance. Organizations must evaluate migration complexity, operational compatibility, and long-term sustainability. Recent industry analysis indicates that Valkey has gained significant momentum, with vendor reports claiming up to threefold performance improvements and $9-10\%$ memory efficiency gains in version 8.0[4]. Meanwhile, Garnet claims superior performance in Microsoft's benchmarks, and KeyDB's multithreaded architecture promises better utilization of modern multi-core processors.

This paper addresses the critical need for a comprehensive, unbiased evaluation of these Redis alternatives. Our study provides a systematic performance comparison using realistic Redis-like workloads in a Kubernetes environment. Also, analysis of migration complexity and operational compatibility for each alternative, and recommendations for different deployment scenarios.

2 Systems Architecture and Design

This section provides an overview of the architectural characteristics and design principles of the evaluated systems: Redis, Valkey, KeyDB, and Garnet. Understanding these fundamental differences is crucial for interpreting performance results and migration considerations.

The emergence of Redis alternatives has prompted several comparative studies. Industry analysis by RedMonk [16] tracked Valkey's adoption seven months after its release, noting significant community momentum and performance improvements. However, these analyses primarily rely on vendor-provided benchmarks rather than independent evaluation.

Redis Architecture. Redis employs a single-threaded event loop architecture for command execution, which simplifies code complexity and avoids concurrency issues but can limit throughput on multi-core systems [13]. The system uses an in-memory data structure store supporting various data types including strings, lists, sets, sorted sets, hashes, bitmaps, and streams.

Redis's persistence mechanisms include RDB snapshots and Append-Only File (AOF) logging. The system supports master-replica replication, sharding and Redis Cluster for horizontal scaling. Memory management relies on configurable eviction policies when memory limits are reached.

[4] https://valkey.io/blog/valkey-8-0-0-rc1/.

Table 1. Architectural Comparison of Evaluated Systems

Feature	Redis	Valkey	KeyDB	Garnet
Threading Model	Single + I/O thr.	Single + I/O thr.	Multi	Multi
Redis API Compatibility	100%	100%	Near-complete	Partial
License	RSALv2/SSPLv1	BSD-3	BSD-3	MIT
RDMA Support	No	Experimental	No	No
Development Activity	High	High	Low	Medium

Valkey Architecture. Originally a Redis fork, Valkey has significantly diverged since version 8.0, notably through enhanced I/O multithreading that leverages modern multi-core processors [10]. Key improvements include: (1) a modern key-value store inspired by Swiss Tables, (2) improved cluster failover algorithms, and (3) experimental RDMA support for high-performance networking. While introducing these optimizations, Valkey retains full Redis API and protocol compatibility, making it a viable drop-in replacement.

KeyDB Architecture. KeyDB features a multithreaded design that leverages multiple CPU cores [7], while nearly remaining fully compatible with the Redis protocol. Notable capabilities include: (1) multithreaded networking and query processing, (2) active replication for consistency, (3) FLASH storage for large datasets, and (4) subkey expiration for granular data control. However, limited recent development raises concerns about its long-term sustainability.

Garnet Architecture. Garnet is a from-scratch Redis-compatible implementation built on the modern .NET runtime, optimized for high-performance use cases [12]. Its key features include: (1) native multithreading with latch-free data structures, (2) advanced memory management with minimal garbage collection overhead, (3) async-optimized network I/O, and (4) an extensible design for custom operations and data types. Despite its strong performance, Garnet only partially supports the Redis API, posing challenges for migration.

Table 1 summarizes the key architectural differences between the evaluated systems. These architectural differences have significant implications for performance, scalability, and operational characteristics, which we evaluate in the following sections.

3 Experimental Methodology

This section details our comprehensive methodology for evaluating Redis alternatives, including test environment setup, workload characteristics, and performance metrics. Our approach emphasizes reproducibility and realistic deployment scenarios.

3.1 Test Environment

All systems were deployed in a Kubernetes-based environment to replicate realistic cloud-native deployment scenarios. The configuration ensures identical conditions across all evaluated systems while maintaining production-like constraints.

Table 2. Test Environment Specifications

Kubernetes Environment	
Distribution	Kubeadm v1.31.5
OS	Ubuntu 24.04 LTS
Resources	4 vCPUs, 12 GiB RAM
Runtime	Containerd
CNI Plugin	Calico
Service	NodePort
Benchmarking Environment	
Machine Type	Virtual Machine
OS	Ubuntu 24.04 LTS
Resources	10 vCPUs, 16 GiB RAM

Infrastructure Configuration. The test environment consists of two virtual machines hosted on the same physical server: a Kubernetes cluster for database deployments and a dedicated benchmarking machine. Table 2 provides detailed specifications.

System Deployment. Each system was deployed in Kubernetes under the same resource constraints and configurations. Deployments were standardized to ensure comparable runtime environments. Resource constraints were configured according to Redis production recommendations [14]: CPU limits of 2 cores, memory limits of 8 GiB, with persistence disabled to focus on in-memory performance characteristics.

The software versions used in our evaluation are: Redis v7.2.7, Valkey v8.0.2, KeyDB v6.3.4, and Garnet v1.0.62. All deployments used standalone mode with single instances to isolate performance characteristics and eliminate clustering variables.

3.2 Benchmarking Tool and Workload Design

We employed memtier_benchmark, the industry-standard tool for Redis performance evaluation, with modifications to support Zipfian key-access distributions. This tool enables precise control over workload characteristics while generating high-throughput load against in-memory key-value stores.

Key Access Pattern. Realistic production traffic was simulated using Zipfian key-access distributions, where a small number of "hot keys" receive disproportionately large numbers of accesses. Based on the large-scale study by Yang et al. [18], we used skew parameters $\alpha = 1.4$ for read-heavy workloads and $\alpha = 0.9$ for write-heavy workloads.

The Zipfian probability mass function is defined as:$P(k) = \frac{1/k^{\alpha}}{H_{N,\alpha}}$ where $H_{N,\alpha}$ is the N-th generalized harmonic number: $H_{N,\alpha} = \sum_{i=1}^{N} \frac{1}{i^{\alpha}}$

Memory Pressure Configuration. Each system was pre-loaded with data to achieve approximately 75% memory utilization, following Microsoft's benchmarking recommendations [11]. With 8 GiB available memory, 1 KiB value size, and assuming 300 bytes overhead per key, the number of keys was calculated as:$\frac{8 \times 2^{30} \times 0.75}{1024+300} \approx 4,800,000$

This configuration ensures realistic memory pressure during benchmarking rather than testing with mostly empty memory.

3.3 Workload Characteristics

Two workloads were designed to evaluate system performance under different operational scenarios:

Workload A (Write-Heavy): 50% reads, 50% writes with Zipfian $\alpha = 0.9$. This workload simulates update-intensive environments such as session management or collaborative applications.

Workload B (Read-Heavy): 95% reads, 5% writes with Zipfian $\alpha = 1.4$. This represents typical caching scenarios where data is primarily retrieved rather than modified.

Each workload was executed across concurrency levels from 10 to 2,000 simultaneous connections. Concurrency levels were selected based on preliminary testing to identify key performance transition points: low concurrency baseline, rapid throughput increase region, peak performance, and saturation point.

3.4 Performance Metrics

Our evaluation encompasses multiple performance dimensions: **Throughput:** Operations per second across varying concurrency levels, measuring system capacity under load. **Latency:** P99 and P999 tail latency measurements, critical for user experience in interactive applications. **Resource Efficiency:** CPU utilization and memory consumption patterns, important for operational cost optimization. **Scalability:** Performance behavior as concurrency increases, indicating system limits and optimal operating ranges.

3.5 Statistical Methodology

Each test configuration was repeated three times to ensure statistical confidence. Mean values were calculated for analysis, with coefficient of variation monitored to ensure result stability. Tests showing high variance ($CV > 10\%$) were repeated with additional runs.

Performance comparisons are presented as percentage differences relative to Redis baseline performance, calculated as:

$$\Delta P = \frac{P_{alt} - P_{redis}}{P_{redis}} \times 100\% \tag{1}$$

where P_{alt} is the alternative system performance and P_{redis} is Redis performance.

This methodology provides a comprehensive framework for evaluating Redis alternatives across multiple dimensions relevant to production deployments.

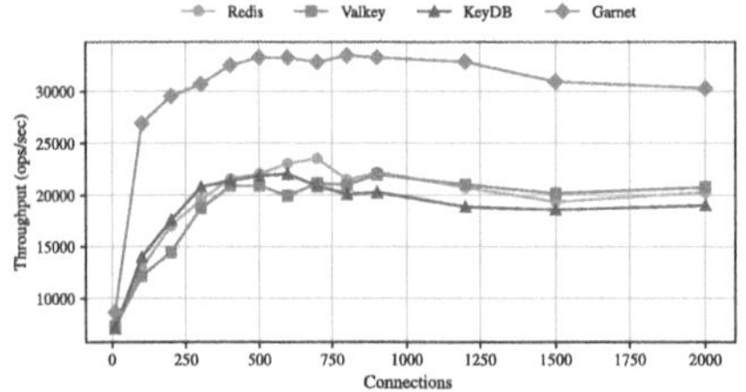

(a) Throughput performance for write-heavy workload across concurrency levels.

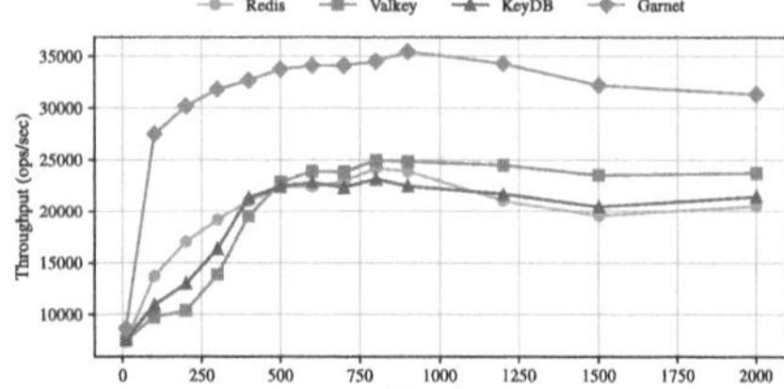

(b) Throughput performance for read-heavy workload across concurrency levels.

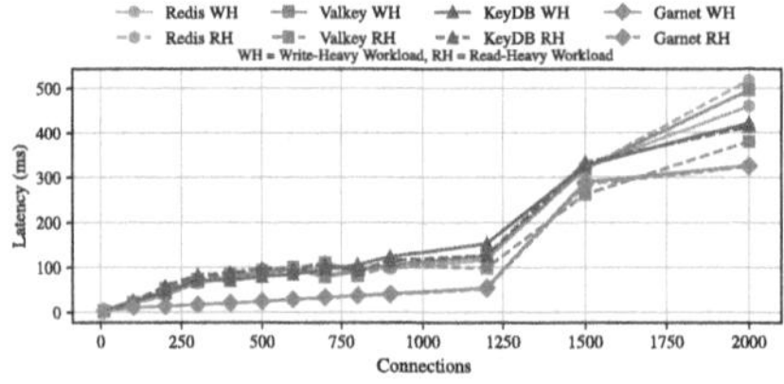

(c) P99 latency (msec) comparison across workload types and concurrency levels.

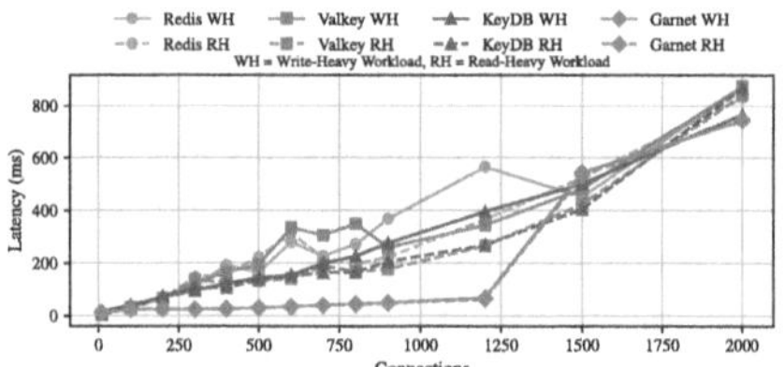

(d) P999 latency (msec) comparison showing tail latency behavior.

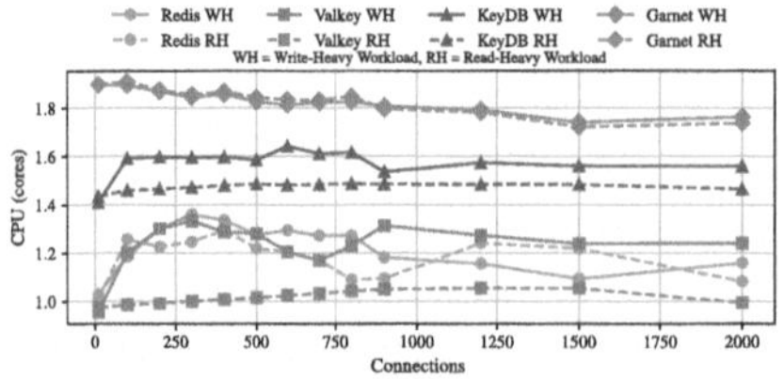

(e) CPU utilization patterns across systems and concurrency levels.

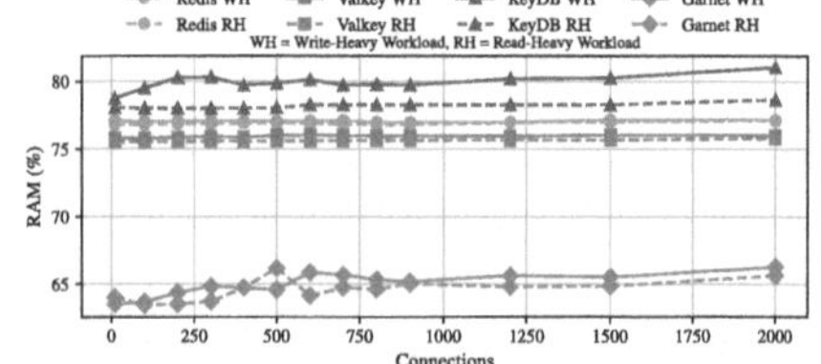

(f) Memory utilization (percentage) comparison across evaluated systems.

Fig. 1. Throughput performance across workloads.

4 Results and Analysis

This section presents benchmarking results for Redis (baseline), Valkey, KeyDB, and Garnet across throughput, latency, and resource-efficiency metrics. Results are aggregated over two workload profiles. Figures 1a–1f show how performance and efficiency change as concurrency increases.

Garnet consistently achieved the highest throughput across all workloads, delivering up to 108% higher throughput and average improvements of about 55% in the write-heavy workload and 57% in the read-heavy workload over Redis. This advantage stems from its latch-free multithreaded architecture and .NET runtime optimizations, which enable efficient parallel execution and reduced synchronization overhead. Valkey initially underperformed to Redis at lower concurrency levels but gradually caught up as the load increased. Under the read-heavy workload and at the higher concurrency levels, it surpassed Redis by up to 20%, suggesting that recent architectural refinements yield measurable benefits for read-dominant operations under high degrees of parallelism. KeyDB followed similar throughput trends but consistently lagged behind, with deficits of up to 24% relative to Redis. This underperformance likely results from coordination overhead within its multithreaded architecture, where thread synchronization and context-switching costs offset potential gains from parallel execution. These effects appear more pronounced under Zipfian distributions, where contention on frequently accessed keys exacerbates bottlenecks.

Latency analysis at the P99 and P999 levels further highlights Garnet's responsiveness. It maintained lower P99 latency than Redis across all workloads, with the largest reductions observed at moderate concurrency levels, and preserved this advantage even in the P999 percentile. Valkey exhibited latency patterns largely comparable to Redis, except at higher concurrency under read-heavy workloads, where it achieved up to 27% lower P99 latency. KeyDB showed similar median latency behavior to Redis but demonstrated the most stable P999 latency among all systems, maintaining consistent P999 performance across varying load levels.

In terms of resource efficiency, Garnet outperformed the other systems, sustaining higher throughput while demonstrating more efficient utilization of CPU and memory resources. Its CPU utilization was the most efficient, and it consistently demonstrated the lowest memory usage, maintaining values around 65% of available RAM compared to approximately 75–80% for Redis, Valkey, and KeyDB. This reflects effective memory management and optimized data structures within the .NET runtime. Valkey displayed distinct resource usage characteristics. In read-heavy scenarios, it achieved higher throughput while utilizing less CPU than Redis, indicating improved efficiency at higher concurrency levels. Under write-heavy loads, CPU consumption increased without corresponding throughput gains, suggesting limited scalability for update-intensive workloads. Valkey also exhibited slightly lower memory usage than Redis, consistent with reported optimizations in version 8.0. KeyDB, in contrast, consumed substantially more CPU resources than Redis across all workloads without measurable throughput benefits, pointing to overhead in its multithreaded coordination.

Its memory consumption remained higher than Redis, with fluctuations likely caused by multithreading overhead.

4.1 Migration Complexity Assessment

Table 3. Migration Complexity Assessment

Factor	Valkey	KeyDB	Garnet
API Compatibility	100%	Near-complete	Partial
Drop-in Replacement	Yes	Mostly	No
Tooling Support	Full	Good	Limited
Documentation	Excellent	Good	Fair
Community Support	Strong	Weak	Growing
Migration Effort	Minimal	Low	High

Beyond performance metrics, migration complexity significantly impacts adoption decisions. Table 3 summarizes compatibility and operational considerations.

Valkey emerges as the most migration-friendly alternative, offering full Redis API compatibility and true drop-in replacement capability. Its governance under the Linux Foundation ensures long-term openness and stability, while the strong community support and comprehensive documentation further reduce migration risks.

KeyDB exhibits strong Redis compatibility and remains based on the Redis 6 codebase, maintaining near-complete API interoperability. It generally functions as a drop-in replacement, though the absence of Redis 7 features and divergence in internal components may require limited adaptation. Its multithreaded architecture introduces configuration nuances, and a slower release cadence compared to Redis and Valkey raises concerns about long-term maintainability.

While Garnet supports the core Redis API and includes full cluster-mode operation and replication, its API diverges in advanced features such as Streams and Modules, and its .NET architecture presents a different operational and ecosystem profile than Redis, limiting its suitability as a true drop-in replacement. Nevertheless, its latch-free design and efficient memory management deliver exceptional performance, may justify adoption in specialized, performance-critical environments where compatibility is less important.

This comprehensive analysis reveals distinct performance and operational characteristics among Redis alternatives, with clear implications for different deployment scenarios and organizational priorities.

5 Conclusion and Future Work

Redis has long been the standard for in-memory key-value datastores. Recent licensing changes have prompted many organizations to explore open source alternatives. This research evaluates in-memory key-value data system alternatives and provides data-driven insights to support migration decisions in the evolving database landscape. Benchmarking with realistic workloads and deployment scenarios reveals distinct performance and operational characteristics among Redis, Valkey, KeyDB, and Garnet. Our findings thus establish actionable guidance for practitioners: Valkey emerges as the most balanced choice for production environments, combining full Redis compatibility with measurable performance and efficiency improvements under heavy read-intensive scenarios. KeyDB maintains strong compatibility and a familiar operational model but shows limited scalability benefits and reduced development activity, raising concerns about its long-term viability. Garnet, while requiring greater migration effort, delivers exceptional performance and resource efficiency, offering a compelling option for performance-critical applications where compatibility is less important. Redis remains a viable, conservative choice for organizations, backed by extensive operational maturity.

Looking ahead, open challenges remain in distributed configurations, real-world application-specific benchmarks, and long-term sustainability assessments as these systems evolve. Future studies should investigate clustering and replication scenarios, explore emerging use cases such as time-series analytics, edge computing, and machine learning pipelines, and assess ecosystem growth and governance structures that impact adoption. By extending evaluation beyond raw performance into operational and strategic dimensions, the community can foster innovation while ensuring that in-memory datastores continue to provide reliability, efficiency, and adaptability in increasingly diverse environments.

Acknowledgment. The authors thank Elastisys for their support and for providing resources used in the benchmarking experiments.

References

1. Asyabi, A., et al.: A systematic overview of in-memory databases. J. Database Manag. **33**(2), 1–25 (2022)
2. Awaysheh, F.M., Alazab, M., Garg, S., Niyato, D., Verikoukis, C.: Big data resource management & networks: taxonomy, survey, and future directions. IEEE Commun. Surv. Tutorials **23**(4), 2098–2130 (2021)
3. Awaysheh, F.M., Pena, T.F., Cabaleiro, J.C.: EME: an automated, elastic and efficient prototype for provisioning Hadoop clusters on-demand. In: International Conference on Cloud Computing and Services Science. vol. 2, pp. 737–742. SCITEPRESS (2017)
4. Caderno, P.V., Awaysheh, F., Cabaleiro, J.C., Pena, T.F.: BigOPERA: an opportunistic and elastic resource allocation for big data frameworks. Clust. Comput. **28**(6), 383 (2025)
5. DB-Engines: DB-engines ranking of key-value stores (2024). https://db-engines.com/en/ranking/key-value+store
6. KeyDB Documentation: KeyDB: Our story (2024). https://docs.keydb.dev/docs/about/#our-story

7. KeyDB Documentation: A multithreaded fork of Redis that's 5x faster than Redis (2024). https://docs.keydb.dev/blog/2019/10/07/blog-post/
8. Kleppmann, M.: Designing Data-Intensive Applications. O'Reilly Media (2017)
9. Koch, J.: Switching from Open Source to Cloud Protection License: What is the impact on Community Health? Master's thesis, Delft University of Technology, Delft, The Netherlands (2023). https://resolver.tudelft.nl/uuid:93901519-d992-4724-8ef9-6d80b3129d0f. Accessed 7 July 2025
10. Linux Foundation: Valkey 8.0 performance improvements (2024). https://valkey.io/blog/valkey-8-0-0-rc1/
11. Microsoft Azure Documentation: Performance testing with Azure Managed Redis (2024). https://learn.microsoft.com/en-us/azure/redis/best-practices-performance
12. Microsoft Research: Welcome to garnet (2024). https://microsoft.github.io/garnet/docs
13. Redis Inc.: Architecture (2024). https://redis.io/docs/latest/integrate/redis-data-integration/architecture/
14. Redis Inc.: Hardware requirements (2024). https://redis.io/docs/latest/operate/rs/installing-upgrading/install/plan-deployment/hardware-requirements/
15. Redis Inc.: Redis adopts dual source-available licensing (2024). https://redis.io/blog/redis-adopts-dual-source-available-licensing/
16. RedMonk: Valkey momentum: Seven months in (2024). https://redmonk.com/rstephens/2024/10/11/valkey-momentum/
17. The Register: Redis becomes the most popular database on AWS as complex cloud application deployments surge (2020). https://www.theregister.com/2020/11/23/redis_the_most_popular_db_on_aws
18. Yang, J., Yue, Y., Rashmi, K.V.: A large-scale analysis of hundreds of in-memory key-value cache clusters at twitter. ACM Trans. Storage **17**(3), 17:1–17:35 (2021). https://doi.org/10.1145/3468521

Job Recommendation Using Heterogeneous Graph Convolutional Networks and LDA Model

Lamia Berkani(✉), Ryma Tharouma, and Fatima Benbarek

Department of Artificial Intelligence and Data Sciences, Faculty of Informatics, USTHB University, Bab Ezzouar, 16111 Algiers, Algeria
lberkani@usthb.dz, {ryma.tharouma,fatima.benbarek}@etu.usthb.dz

Abstract. With the increasing competitiveness of today's job market, job recommendation systems play a crucial role in matching job seekers with suitable opportunities. However, current approaches often struggle to capture the complex relationships between users and job postings due to data sparsity, limited contextual understanding, and difficulties in extracting user preferences from long texts like resumes. To address these limitations, we propose a novel approach that combines a heterogeneous Graph Convolutional Network (HGCN) with Latent Dirichlet Allocation (LDA). While traditional methods fail to model the diverse nature of user preferences and job characteristics, our approach combines the ability of HGCN to capture intricate user-job interactions with the capability of LDA to extract latent topics from job descriptions and resumes. This hybrid approach results in a richer representation of both relational and semantic information, enabling more personalized and accurate job recommendations. Experimental results confirm that our model significantly outperforms existing methods, demonstrating its effectiveness in enhancing recommendation accuracy.

Keywords: Job Recommendation · Graph Neural Networks · Heterogeneous Graph Convolutional Network · Latent Dirichlet Allocation

1 Introduction

Job recommendation systems have become crucial in today's competitive job market, connecting job seekers with relevant opportunities while reducing search time and addressing information overload. However, designing effective systems is challenging due to the sparsity of user-job interactions, diverse user preferences, and the need to match qualifications, career aspirations, and personal interests. Traditional recruitment methods often rely on subjective judgment, limiting a thorough assessment of resumes.Although conventional machine learning techniques have been applied to job recommendation based on candidates' work history, these methods often struggle with early job seekers [1]. While some deep learning approaches have been explored [2], they are not explicitly tailored to job recommendation systems. Recently, Graph Neural Networks (GNNs) have gained attention for their ability to capture complex relationships [3–7], but their application in job recommendation remains limited, with a few notable works like

A. Awad et al. (Eds.): MEDI 2025, LNCS 16427, pp. 347–354, 2026.
https://doi.org/10.1007/978-3-032-19865-5_29

the IHGCN model [8] addressing data sparsity using meta-paths. Additionally, topic modeling techniques like Latent Dirichlet Allocation (LDA) are valuable for extracting semantic information from resumes, yet their potential remains underexplored in this context. Given the strengths of GNNs in relational modeling and LDA in topic extraction, this paper introduces HGCNL-JRec (Heterogeneous Graph Convolutional Network and Latent Dirichlet Allocation-based Job Recommender System). This approach aims to combine relational and semantic information to enhance the accuracy and personalization of job recommendations.

The rest of the paper is organized as follows: Sect. 2 reviews related work on job recommendation using deep learning, GNNs, and LDA. Section 3 presents the proposed HGCNL-JRec model, followed by experimental results and discussions in Sect. 4. Finally, Sect. 5 highlights the main results of this work and provides some future research directions.

2 Related Work

Deep learning techniques have been widely explored for job recommendation. For instance, He et al. [2] developed a CNN model for career trajectory prediction, while Zhu et al. [9] proposed a CNN-based approach to assess job suitability using resumes and job descriptions. More recently, Saito and Sugiyama [10] introduced JME, a job recommendation model leveraging both user behaviors and stated preferences through knowledge graph embeddings. Recently, Graph Neural Networks (GNNs) have gained attention for their ability to model complex interactions in job recommendation systems. Notable examples include the IHGCN model [8], designed to address data sparsity using meta-paths, and the work of Çallıa and Orman [11], who employed node embedding techniques for candidate recommendation. Additionally, Liu et al. [12] developed LinkSAGE, a GNN-based framework for large-scale job matching on LinkedIn, demonstrating enhanced performance through transfer learning. On the other hand, natural language processing techniques like Latent Dirichlet Allocation (LDA) have been applied to extract semantic information from job-related texts. Mhamdi et al. [13] utilized LDA for topic modeling to represent job offers, while Boukari and Faiz [14] combined LDA with BERTopic for bidirectional job recommendation. While advancements have been made, challenges such as data sparsity and inadequate preference extraction from resumes persist. This study aims to address these issues by integrating GNNs' relational modeling with LDA's topic extraction, enhancing personalization and recommendation accuracy.

3 Proposed Approach

We propose a novel job recommendation approach called HGCNL-JRec (Heterogeneous GCN and LDA-based Job Recommender System). This approach combines multiple techniques to deliver personalized and relevant job recommendations. HGCNL-JRec consists of three main modules, as depicted in Fig. 1: (1) data preprocessing; (2) embeddings and graph construction; and (3) a GCN module.

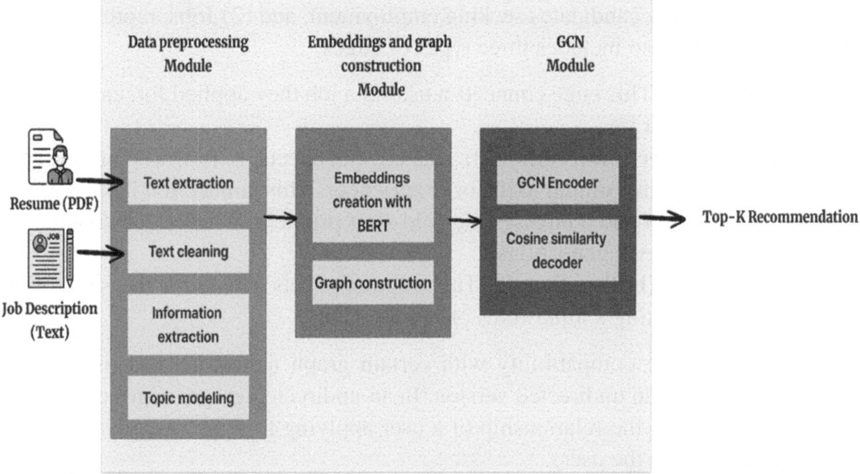

Fig. 1. Global overview of the proposed HGCNL-JRec approach

3.1 Data Preprocessing Module

The data preprocessing module processes user resumes in PDF format and job descriptions in text format to extract essential information like degree, major, skills, and dominant topic. It follows four main steps: Text Extraction, converting PDFs to text; Text Cleaning, removing unwanted characters and stop words for better data quality; Information Extraction using a custom rule-based NER system to label and extract education and skills, leveraging a compiled list of 92,983 skills, 268 majors, and 11 degrees; and Topic Modeling with LDA to uncover hidden topics in the extracted skills. This processed data is then used in the subsequent module.

To train the LDA model, the number of topics (n) is determined using the coherence score, which measures the semantic relevance of words within a topic (higher scores indicate more meaningful topics). Initially, each skill is randomly assigned to a topic, and these assignments are refined through iterations to better capture the hidden topics in the data. The LDA model, once trained, analyzes extracted skills from resumes or job descriptions, identifying the dominant topic (i.e. the topic with the highest probability, for each set of extracted skills).

3.2 Embeddings and Graph Construction Module

Embeddings Creation with BERT: BERT is a language model used to generate embeddings from text. The process involves loading a pre-trained BERT model and tokenizer, tokenizing the input text into numerical representations, and feeding these tokens into the model to generate embeddings that capture the context of each word. To obtain a sentence embedding, the embeddings of all words are averaged, resulting in a representation that reflects the semantic meaning of the text.

Graph Construction: We construct a heterogeneous graph to capture the relationships between users (resumes) and jobs. The graph consists of two types of nodes: (1) Users (resumes), representing candidates seeking employment, and (2) Jobs, representing job openings. The graph also includes three types of edges:

1. **User-Applies-Job:** This edge connects a user to a job they applied for, capturing the user's interest in that job.
2. **User-SimilarU-User (bidirectional):** This edge connects users who share the same topic, likely indicating similar skills or experiences. This connection helps alleviate sparsity in the graph and addresses the cold-start problem, which occurs when new users or jobs have few connections.
3. **Job-SimilarJ-Job (bidirectional):** This edge connects jobs with the same topic, potentially representing similar roles or requirements.

Finally, to improve compatibility with certain graph neural network models, we convert the graph into an undirected version. In an undirected graph, edges do not have inherent direction (i.e., the relationship of a user applying to a job is equivalent to the job being applied to by the user).

3.3 GCN Module

Our recommendation system employs an encoder-decoder architecture, with a GCN encoder at its core. This GCN encoder leverages the constructed user-job graph to capture the contextual relationships between users and jobs. Using two stacked layers with ReLU activations, it learns informative features, generating enriched node representations. These representations are then passed to a cosine similarity decoder, which computes similarity scores for each user, filtering out jobs they've already applied to.

Encoder: The HGCNL-JRec model uses a GCN as the encoder to capture user preferences and job suitability. The GCN operates over multiple layers, progressively refining the representations of users and jobs:

a) *Layer:* Each layer aggregates information from a user's neighborhood in the graph, considering both user-job applications and user/job topic similarities. This aggregation of information can be formulated as:

$$h_i^{(l+1)} = \sigma(\text{Aggregation}(\sum_j f(h_i^{(l)}, h_j^{(l)}, W^{(l)})) + W^{(l)} h_i^{(l)} \tag{1}$$

where: $h_i^{(l)}$ is the hidden representation of node i (user or job) at layer l; f is an update function (often a simple linear transformation) that combines representations of neighboring nodes (h_j) and the current node (h_i) with a learnable weight matrix $W^{(l)}$; $\sum_j$: denotes summation over all neighboring nodes of the node i;σ is an activation function (ReLU) that introduces non-linearity; and *Aggregation* function (e.g., sum, mean) combines information from neighbors.

b) *Update function (f).* A common choice for the update function f is:

$$f(h_i^{(l)}, h_j^{(l)}, W^{(l)}) = W^{(l)} h_j^{(l)} \tag{2}$$

This simply projects the neighboring node representation ($h^{(l)}{}_j$) using a layer-specific weight matrix ($W^{(l)}$).

c) *Message passing.* The aggregation process can be viewed as a message passing, where nodes exchange information with their neighbors in the graph. Through multiple GCN layers, the model iteratively refines user and job representations, incorporating the preferences of similar users and the characteristics of jobs being applied to by similar users.

Decoder: The decoder uses the final user and job representations learned by the GCN to predict the likelihood of a user applying for a specific job. It typically applies cosine similarity to measure the similarity between user and job embeddings, with higher scores indicating a stronger match between a user's profile and a job description.

Loss Function: During training, the model minimizes a loss function that measures the difference between predicted application probabilities (based on similarity scores) and actual user-job relationships. Optimizing this loss helps the GCN adjust its weights for more accurate predictions.

3.4 Recommendation

The recommendation algorithm leverages cosine similarity scores to suggest jobs that a user has not previously applied for, prioritizing those with higher scores for a better fit. It encodes user and job data to generate embeddings, filters out previously interacted jobs, calculates scores for candidate jobs, and selects the top K job IDs with the highest scores, ensuring personalized and relevant recommendations.

4 Experiments

4.1 Experimental Settings

To train our LDA model, we utilized 310,001 job postings obtained from the Job Recommendation Challenge dataset on Kaggle[1], following a process of cleaning and extracting skills from the data. Moreover, due to the lack of publicly available datasets on job recommendations and the challenges in finding a suitable dataset to evaluate our model, we generated a tailored dataset using the ChatGPT AI tool. This dataset, named JRec-Eval, comprises three files: 'users' (containing user IDs and resumes), 'jobs' (containing job IDs, descriptions, and requirements), and 'applications' (documenting user-job interactions). It includes 500 users, 500 jobs, and 977 applications, resulting in a dataset density of 0.39%. The model's performance is evaluated using relevance metrics (Precision@ K, Recall@ K) to assess the accuracy and completeness of recommendations, where K represents the number of top recommended items considered. Ranking metrics (NDCG@K) used to measure the effectiveness of item ranking. Additionally, predictive metrics (RMSE, MAE) are used to quantify the average error between predicted and actual values. We explored 600 model configurations with varying numbers of GCN layers (2, 3, 5), hidden channels (32, 64, 128, 256), and epochs (1 to 50), evaluated using P@10, NDCG@10, R@10, RMSE, and MAE. The best performance was achieved with 2 GCN layers, 32 hidden channels, and 50 epochs, confirmed by further testing across 1 to 60 epochs.

[1] https://www.kaggle.com/

4.2 Experimentations on Graph Structure

We conducted a series of experiments to investigate the impact of different graph structures on our model's performance. The original graph comprised both user-user and job-job edges, constructed using LDA. The following variations of graph structures were tested:

- **Original graph with all edges:** includes both user-user and job-job edges.
- **W/O user-user edges:** This structure corresponds to the graph without use-user edges, i.e. edges between users are excluded.
- **W/O job-job edges:** This structure excluded edges between jobs.
- **W/O user-user & job-job edges:** both user-user and job-job edges were omitted.

Table 1 compares the performance of these different graph structures using all metrics: P@10, R@10, NDCG@10, RMSE, and MAE. The original graph with all edges achieved the highest scores in precision, recall, and NDCG. However, graphs without user-user or job-job edges exhibited better RMSE and MAE, indicating improved prediction accuracy but lower recommendation quality. Notably, the graph without any edges exhibited the lowest performance across all metrics, underscoring the importance of establishing connections between users and jobs through edges based on LDA for generating effective recommendations.

Table 1. Performance evaluation of various graph structures

Graph structure	P@10	R@10	NDCG@10	RMSE	MAE
With all edges	**0.0309**	**0.2535**	**0.1383**	0.6110	0.5425
W/O user-user edges	0.0278	0.2383	0.1222	**0.5881**	**0.5176**
W/Ojob-job edges	0.0278	0.2383	0.1222	**0.5881**	**0.5176**
W/O user-user & job-job edges	0.0224	0.1898	0.0958	0.6361	0.5682

4.3 Comparison with Related Work

We compared our model's performance with several established baselines:

- **Matrix Factorization Methods:** We chose SVD [15], which decomposes the user-item interaction matrix to identify latent factors, and SVD + + [16], an extension that incorporates user/item biases and implicit feedback for improved accuracy.
- **DL-based Method:** We chose NCF (Neural Collaborative Filtering) [17], which uses neural networks to model user-item interactions for more accurate recommendations.
- **Graph-based Methods:** We chose DeepWalk [18], which learns latent representations of nodes in a user-item interaction graph using random walks and neural embeddings; NGCF (Neural Graph Collaborative Filtering) [19], combining Graph Convolutional Networks (GCNs) with neural collaborative filtering to enhance recommendations; and LightGCN [20], a simplified and efficient version of GCN designed for scalable recommendations on large-scale user-item graphs.

As shown in Table 2, our model achieved the highest performance for P@10, R@10 and NDCG@10, surpassing all other models.

Table 2. Performance of Different Recommendation Models

Models		P@k	R@k	NDCG@k
Matrix Factorization models	**SVD**	0.0105	0.0862	0.0565
	SVD + +	0.0149	0.1286	0.0694
DL based models	**NCF**	0.0087	0.0789	0.0477
Graph based models	**NGCF**	0.0131	0.1067	0.0677
	DeepWalk	0.0122	0.0957	0.0592
	LightGCN	0.0219	0.1739	0.1068
Our Model	**HGCNL-JRec**	**0.0309**	**0.2535**	**0.1383**

Our experiments demonstrated the effectiveness of our model, with ablation studies showing that integrating LDA-based similarity links improved performance. Compared to several methods, our approach showed superior results, although it may not entirely capture the complexity of real-world labor market dynamics. Enhancing user and job data and addressing data biases could further improve performance.

5 Conclusion

In this paper, we introduced HGCNL-JRec, a job recommendation system that integrates Heterogeneous Graph Convolutional Networks (GCNs) and Latent Dirichlet Allocation (LDA) to address the limitations of traditional methods. Our approach effectively captures complex user-job interactions and enhances the semantic understanding of job descriptions and resumes. Experimental results show that HGCNL-JRec outperforms existing methods, providing more personalized recommendations.

In future work, we plan to validate the model with real-world datasets and explore advanced GNN architectures like Graph Isomorphism Networks (GIN) and Graph Attention Networks (GAT).

References

1. Paparrizos, I., Cambazoglu, B.B., Gionis, A., Machine learned job recommendation. In: Proceedings of the Fifth ACM Conference on Recommender Systems, pp. 325–328 (2011)
2. He, M., Shen, D., Zhu, Y., He, R., Wang, T., Zhang, Z.: Career trajectory prediction based on CNN. In: IEEE International Conference on Service Operations and Logistics, and Informatics (SOLI), pp. 22–26. Zhengzhou, China, (2019)
3. Berkani, L., Imene Kafi, M., Temmar, S., Oulefki, S.: SGCN-SRec: Sentiment-based graph convolutional neural networks for enhanced social recommendations. In: Cherifi, H., Donduran, M., Rocha, L.M., Cherifi, C., Varol, O. (eds.) Complex Networks & Their Applications XIII. COMPLEX NETWORKS 2024 2024. Studies in Computational Intelligence, vol. 1188. Springer, Cham (2025). https://doi.org/10.1007/978-3-031-82431-9_31

4. Oulefki, S., Berkani, L., Boudjenah, N., Bellatreche, L., Mokhtari, A.: BioGITOM: matching biomedical ontologies with graph isomorphism transformer. VLDB J. **34**, 65 (2025). https://doi.org/10.1007/s00778-025-00943-7
5. Oulefki, S., Berkani, L.: A GNN-Based Framework for Ontology Matching. In: Ordonez, C., Sperlì, G., Masciari, E., Bellatreche, L. (eds.) Model and Data Engineering. MEDI 2024. Lecture Notes in Computer Science, vol. 15590. Springer, Cham (2025). https://doi.org/10.1007/978-3-031-87719-3_14
6. Oulefki, S., Berkani, L., Boudjenah, N., Bellatreche, L., Mokhtari, A.: Concepts and Relations Features Are All You Need for Embedding-Based Ontology Matching. In: Barhamgi, M., Wang, H., Wang, X. (eds.) Web Information Systems Engineering - WISE 2024. WISE 2024. Lecture Notes in Computer Science, vol. 15436. Springer, Singapore (2025). https://doi.org/10.1007/978-981-96-0579-8_29
7. Oulefki, S., Berkani, L., Boudjenah, N., Kenai, I.E., Mokhtari, A.: Ontology matching using multi-head attention graph isomorphism network. In: Mosbah, M., Kechadi, T., Bellatreche, L., Gargouri, F. (eds.) Model and Data Engineering. MEDI 2023. Lecture Notes in Computer Science, vol. 14396. Springer, Cham (2023). https://doi.org/10.1007/978-3-031-49333-1_15
8. Wang, H., Yang, W., Li, J., Ou, J., Song, Y., Chen, Y.: An improved heterogeneous graph convolutional network for job recommendation. Eng. Appl. Artif. Intell. **126**, 107147 (2023)
9. Zhu C.Z., y Xiong, H.: Person-job fit: adapting the right talent for the right job with joint representation learning. ACM Trans. Manag. Inf. Syst. **9**(3), 12 (2018)
10. Saito, Y., Sugiyama, K.: Leveraging multiple behaviors and explicit preferences for job recommendation. Expert Syst. Appl. **258**, 125149 (2024)
11. Çallıa, F.G., Orman, G.K.: Job seeker recommendation for employers: a graph-based recommendation approach using node embedding. In: 27th International Conference on Knowledge-Based and Intelligent Information and Engineering Systems (KES) Procedia Computer Science, vol. 225, pp. 3660–3669 (2023). https://doi.org/10.1016/j.procs.2023.10.361
12. Liu, P., et al.: LinkSAGE: optimizing job matching using graph neural networks. arXiv:2402.13430v1 (2024)
13. Mhamdi, D., El Ghoumari, M.Y., Azouazi, M.: Job recommendation based on vectorization and topic modeling. In: International Conference on Research in Applied Mathematics And Computer Science Icramcs, March 26–27. Casablanca, Morocco (2021),
14. Boukari, S., Faiz, R.: BERTopic-LDA model for a bidirectional recommendation system: toward matching jobs and job seekers. In: Proceedings of Ninth International Congress on Information and Communication Technology (2024)
15. Koren, Y., Bell, R., Volinsky, C.: Matrix factorization techniques for recommender systems. Computer **42**(8), 30–37 (2009)
16. Koren, Y.: Factorization meets the neighborhood: a multifaceted collaborative filtering model. In: Proceedings of the 14th ACM SIGKDD International Conference on Knowledge Discovery and Data Mining (KDD 2008) (2008)
17. He, X., Liao, L., Zhang, H., Nie, L., Hu, X., Chua, T.S.: Neural collaborative filtering. In: Proceedings of the 26th International Conference on World Wide Web (WWW 2017) (2017)
18. Perozzi, B., Al-Rfou, R., Skiena, S.: DeepWalk: online learning of social representations. In: Proceedings of the 20th ACM SIGKDD International Conference on Knowledge Discovery and Data Mining (KDD 2014) (2014)
19. Wang, X., He, X., Wang, M., Feng, F., Chua, T.S.: Neural graph collaborative filtering. In: Proceedings of the 42nd International ACM SIGIR Conference on Research and Development in Information Retrieval (SIGIR 2019) (2019)
20. He, X., Deng, K., Wang, X., Li, Y., Zhang, Y., Wang, M.: LightGCN: simplifying and powering graph convolution network for recommendation. In: Proceedings of the 43rd International ACM SIGIR Conference on Research and Development in Information Retrieval (SIGIR 2020) (2020)

Real-Time Lesion-Level Acne Detection Using YOLOv8n: Lightweight Deep Learning Approach

Yomna Walid(✉), Norhan Amr, Mohab Hany, Zeyad Weal, Sohayla Weal, and Mustafa Elattar

School of Information Technology and Computer Science, Nile University, Giza, Egypt
{y.walid2392,n.amr2146,m.hany2125,z.wael2107,s.wael2106, melattar}@nu.edu.eg

Abstract. Acne is one of the most prevalent skin disorders globally, especially affecting teenagers and young adults, often resulting in emotional stress and permanent scarring. Although computer-assisted diagnostic tools have been studied, most current approaches lack detection at the individual lesion level and are too computationally intensive for mobile use. This paper introduces an efficient, real-time acne detection system leveraging YOLOv8n, optimized for mobile and edge deployment. The model is trained on a specially labeled dataset with four acne lesion types—papules, pustules, nodules, and comedones—annotated at the lesion level. To overcome data imbalance and scarcity, we utilized image augmentation and per-class replication methods. Hyperparameter optimization was automated using Optuna to further boost model accuracy. The system's performance was assessed using standard object detection benchmarks, including Precision, Recall, mAP@0.50 (0.501), and mAP@0.50:0.95 (0.162). Results confirm the framework's capability to deliver accurate lesion-level identification with fast execution speed, supporting its practical use in mobile dermatology applications.

Keywords: YOLOv8n · Real-time acne detection · Object detection · Lightweight deep learning · Optuna · Class imbalance

1 Introduction

Acne is one of the most prevalent dermatological disorders, affecting 24–80% of adolescents and young adults worldwide [5,13]. It appears as comedonal lesions (blackheads, whiteheads) or inflammatory lesions (papules, pustules, and nodules) and can persist into adulthood, often causing emotional distress and reduced self-confidence [2,8].

Despite advances in computer-aided dermatology, existing acne detection systems face several limitations. Most perform only *image-level classification*, lacking lesion-level localization essential for precise assessment. Others, such as

A. Awad et al. (Eds.): MEDI 2025, LNCS 16427, pp. 355–368, 2026.
https://doi.org/10.1007/978-3-032-19865-5_30

YOLOv5, YOLOv4, or EfficientDet, achieve high accuracy but require powerful GPUs, limiting their use in mobile or real-time applications. Moreover, class imbalance and limited dataset diversity reduce generalization to real-world cases.

To overcome these challenges, this paper proposes a lightweight, real-time acne detection framework based on YOLOv8n [9]. YOLOv8n was chosen for its anchor-free design, efficient C2f backbone, and optimal balance between accuracy, parameter count, and inference speed—making it well-suited for edge and smartphone deployment. The model was trained on a custom-labeled dataset of four lesion types (papule, pustule, nodule, and comedone) with Optuna-based hyperparameter optimization to enhance accuracy and generalization.

Unlike prior acne detection studies that focus primarily on image-level classification or rely on computationally heavy architectures (e.g., YOLOv5, EfficientDet, or ResNet-based pipelines), the proposed approach advances the field by achieving lesion-level localization with a model optimized for real-time mobile deployment. To our knowledge, this is the first acne detection framework combining YOLOv8n with Optuna-based hyperparameter optimization, enabling automated tuning and improved generalization without manual intervention. This combination of lightweight architecture, fine-grained lesion annotation, and automated optimization establishes a novel direction toward practical, on-device dermatological analysis.

The main contributions of this work are:

- Development of a lightweight YOLOv8n-based model for lesion-level acne detection optimized for mobile devices.
- Construction of a balanced, annotated dataset with fine-grained bounding boxes.
- Application of Optuna for automated hyperparameter tuning to improve accuracy and generalization.
- Demonstration of real-time performance capabilities, as YOLOv8n achieves an inference speed of approximately 1.2 ms per image on standard benchmarks according to Ultralytics documentation [15], alongside competitive detection accuracy in our experiments (mAP@0.50 = 0.520, mAP@0.50:0.95 = 0.173), confirming the model's suitability for mobile and edge deployment.

In summary, this work introduces a compact and accurate dermatological detection framework that bridges the gap between high-performance deep learning models and practical, on-device medical applications.

2 Related Work

The task of acne detection and classification has been extensively explored in dermatological image analysis, evolving from traditional hand-crafted approaches to modern deep learning frameworks. One early attempt by Shen et al. [14] combined convolutional feature extraction with classical machine learning classifiers. Their system included a binary classifier for skin detection and a seven-class model for distinguishing various types of facial acne vulgaris and healthy skin.

While the use of a pre-trained VGG16 network enhanced performance over a custom CNN [10], the approach was limited to image-level classification without lesion-level localization—an essential capability for detailed dermatological assessment.

To address challenges in acne severity grading, Wu et al. [17] proposed a label distribution learning (LDL) framework that captures the ambiguity inherent in acne grading. Their multi-task model jointly predicted lesion count and severity using a custom loss function, and they introduced the ACNE04 [16] dataset annotated with both labels. Although their method outperformed state-of-the-art baselines in classification and counting, it still lacked lesion-level detection, restricting its applicability for tasks requiring spatial precision.

Recent developments have emphasized real-time detection and mobile deployment. Pirahandeh [11] introduced EM-YOLO, a customized extension of the YOLO [12] framework designed for embedded and distributed systems. By integrating components like Squeeze-and-Excitation Blocks (SEB), Depthwise Separable Convolutions (DWC), and Residual Dropout Blocks (RDB), EM-YOLO significantly improved detection metrics, achieving 82.30% precision and a mAP@0.5 of 68.80%. However, these architectural modifications add considerable complexity, potentially limiting their use in low-resource mobile devices.

In contrast, Isa and Mangshor [7] proposed a YOLOv4 [3]based mobile application for multi-class acne detection using the DermNet NZ dataset. Their model recognized four acne types—cyst, papule, pustule, and whitehead—and achieved 91.25% average accuracy. While effective, this approach did not explore model optimization for latency or efficiency, which are critical for real-time mobile applications.

Building upon these efforts, our work adapts YOLOv8n [9], a lightweight and efficient variant of the YOLOv8 [15] family—for acne detection, specifically targeting four lesion types: papule, pustule, nodule, and comedone. Compared to EM-YOLO, which achieves higher accuracy at the cost of increased computational load, YOLOv8n [9] offers a practical trade-off, maintaining competitive performance while being significantly more suitable for mobile deployment. Unlike previous approaches that either lacked localization capabilities or prioritized accuracy over inference speed, our model is designed to operate in real time with minimal computational overhead, aligning with the constraints of mobile environments and enabling accessible, on-device dermatological analysis.

3 Methodology

3.1 Dataset Preparation

The dataset used in this study was obtained from Roboflow available publicly via the Roboflow platform [4], where acne lesion images were annotated using bounding boxes corresponding to four clinically significant classes: papule, pustule, nodule, and comedone. Initially, the dataset consisted of 1,419 original images, which were split on Roboflow before augmentation into training (80%, 1,135 images), validation (10%, 142 images), and test sets (10%, 142 images).

Roboflow's augmentation pipeline was then applied to the training set with a 3× augmentation multiplier, resulting in 3,405 training images post-augmentation, while the validation and test sets remained unchanged.

However, because the split was performed prior to augmentation, the augmented images were limited to the training set only, potentially introducing a skew. To ensure a balanced and consistent evaluation process, we restructured the dataset after augmentation by collecting all images and corresponding label files into centralized folders, and then re-splitting them manually into 80% training, 10% validation, and 10% test sets. This ensured that the split was applied uniformly across the entire dataset, preserving class distribution and preventing data leakage between sets (Fig. 1).

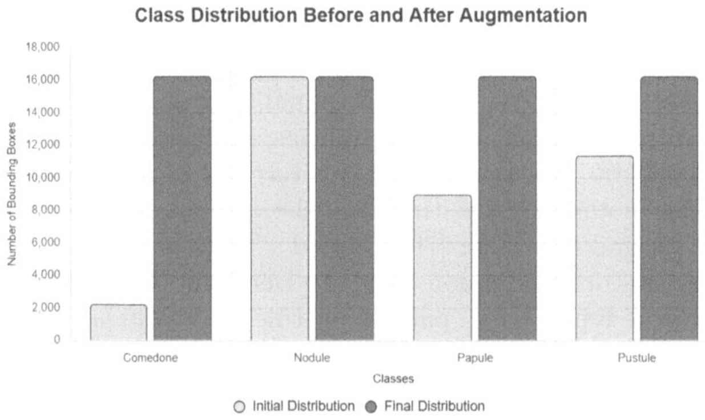

Fig. 1. Represents the distribution of acne types.

3.2 Data Augmentation

To improve generalization and reduce overfitting, data augmentation was applied only to the training set. Each original image was expanded into three augmented versions using the following transformations:

- 50% probability of horizontal flip
- Random rotation between $-10°$ and $+10°$
- Random brightness adjustment between -20% and $+20\%$
- Random Gaussian blur with a radius between 0 and 1 pixel
- Salt and pepper noise applied to approximately 1.54% of pixels

Additionally, each image was preprocessed by:

- Auto-orienting pixel data to remove EXIF orientation metadata
- Resizing to a fixed resolution of 640×640 pixels (stretched)

3.3 Model Architecture

For this study, we selected the YOLOv8n nano) [9] variant due to its lightweight nature and suitability for real-time applications. As the smallest and fastest model in the YOLOv8 [15] family, YOLOv8n [9] offers an excellent trade-off between accuracy and computational efficiency, making it well-suited for deployment on mobile and edge devices. The model achieves fast inference, which is essential for live acne detection, while its lightweight design with fewer parameters reduces memory and computational requirements, ensuring smooth operation on resource-constrained platforms. YOLOv8n [9] also incorporates an advanced backbone for superior feature extraction and a modern neck architecture for efficient multi-scale feature fusion, improving detection performance for small and dense lesions. Furthermore, the anchor-free split Ultralytics head enables more precise localization with simplified training, while pretrained weights accelerate convergence and enhance performance when fine-tuned on acne datasets. With an input resolution of 640×640 pixels, initialization from official pretrained YOLOv8n [9] weights, a depth multiple of 0.33, a width multiple of 0.25, and a maximum channel size of 1024, this architecture achieves an optimal balance between speed and detection accuracy, enabling effective lesion-level acne detection while maintaining low latency, making it a practical choice for mobile-based dermatological assessment tools.

In YOLOv8 [15], the input image first passes through the Backbone, where convolutional layers and Cross Stage Partial (CSP) connections extract spatial and semantic features. These features are then forwarded to the Neck, which performs feature aggregation using PAN/FPN structures to fuse multi-scale information for better representation. Finally, the Head processes the refined features to generate bounding boxes, class probabilities, and confidence scores, completing the detection pipeline (Fig. 2).

3.4 Fine-Tuning and Hyperparameter Optimization

To adapt the YOLOv8n model to the acne lesion detection task, a two-phase fine-tuning strategy was employed. In the initial phase, the model was fine-tuned for 40 epochs using manually selected hyperparameters and a batch size of 16. The configuration included:

- `lr0`: 0.001
- `weight_decay`: 0.0005
- `dropout`: 0.1
- `hsv_h/s/v`: 0.015/0.7/0.4
- `degrees`: 10.0
- `translate`: 0.1
- `scale`: 0.5
- `shear`: 5.0
- `flipud/fliplr`: 0.5/0.5
- `mosaic`: 0.0

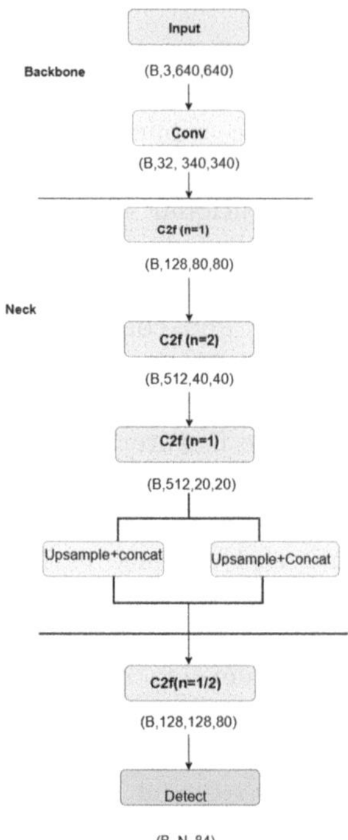

Fig. 2. Overview of the proposed model architecture for acne detection.

- `mixup`: 0.2
- `copy_paste`: 0.0

To enhance performance further, hyperparameter optimization was performed using Optuna. A total of 20 trials were conducted, each training the model for 50 epochs. The search space included:

- Learning rate (`lr`): $[1e{-}5, 1e{-}2]$ (log scale)
- Batch size: $\{8, 16, 32\}$
- Momentum: $[0.6, 0.95]$
- Weight decay: $[1e{-}6, 1e{-}3]$ (log scale)
- Image size: $\{416, 640\}$

The best-performing hyperparameters from the Optuna search [1] were then used to retrain the model for 50 epochs, consistent with previous research on automated hyperparameter optimization [6], resulting in improved lesion detection accuracy and generalization.

4 Training and Configuration

This section presents the training setup, including manually fine-tuned hyperparameters and the hyperparameter search space explored using Optuna for improved model performance (Tables 1 and 2).

Following 20 Optuna trials, the best-performing configuration was selected based on validation mAP@0.50:0.95. Table 3 summarizes the optimal hyperparameters obtained from the best trial. These values were used in the final model training phase to maximize detection accuracy while maintaining computational efficiency.

Table 1. Initial Fine-Tuning Configuration (Manual)

Parameter	Value
Epochs	40
Batch size	16
Learning rate (`lr0`)	0.001
Weight decay	0.0005
Dropout	0.1
HSV (H/S/V)	0.015/0.7/0.4
Rotation degrees	10.0
Translate	0.1
Scale	0.5
Shear	5.0
Flip (vertical/horizontal)	0.5/0.5
Mosaic	0.0
Mixup	0.2
Copy-paste	0.0
Training/Validation/Test Split	80%/10%/10%

Table 2. Hyperparameter Search Space Used in Optuna (20 Trials)

Parameter	Range/Options	Type
Learning rate (`lr`)	$1e^{-5}$ to $1e^{-2}$ (log scale)	Log-uniform float
Batch size	{8, 16, 32}	Categorical
Momentum	0.6 to 0.95	Uniform float
Weight decay	$1e^{-6}$ to $1e^{-3}$ (log scale)	Log-uniform float
Image size (`imgsz`)	{416, 640}	Categorical
Epochs	50	Fixed
Device	GPU	Fixed
Training/Validation/Test Split	80%/10%/10%	Fixed

Table 3. Best Hyperparameters from Optuna Optimization (Best Trial)

Parameter	Optimal Value
Batch size	32
Image size (imgsz)	640
Learning rate (`lr`)	0.00052
Momentum	0.673
Weight decay	1.82×10^{-6}

4.1 3.5 Evaluation Metrics

To comprehensively assess the performance of the acne lesion detection model, we employ standard and widely accepted object detection metrics: **Precision**, **Recall**, **mAP@0.50**, and **mAP@0.50:0.95**.

- **Precision** quantifies the accuracy of positive predictions by measuring the proportion of correctly identified lesions among all detections. This metric helps to identify the extent of false positives produced by the model.
- **Recall** evaluates the model's ability to detect all relevant acne lesions by calculating the proportion of ground truth lesions that were correctly detected. This reflects the rate of false negatives.
- **mAP@0.50** (mean Average Precision at Intersection over Union (IoU) = 0.50) measures detection accuracy with a lenient localization criterion, requiring predicted bounding boxes to overlap ground truth by at least 50%. It provides insight into the model's ability to roughly locate lesions.
- **mAP@0.50:0.95** averages the mean Average Precision over IoU thresholds from 0.50 to 0.95 in increments of 0.05. This more stringent metric evaluates detection performance across varying levels of localization precision, capturing both coarse and fine bounding box accuracy. It is widely adopted as the primary benchmark in modern object detection challenges, such as the COCO dataset.

Rationale for Metric Selection. The combination of these metrics offers a balanced and nuanced evaluation of detection accuracy, completeness, and localization quality. Furthermore, their widespread acceptance facilitates fair and meaningful comparisons with other state-of-the-art models and research studies.

Performance Monitoring During Training. During training, we continuously monitored these metrics—particularly **mAP@0.50** and **mAP@0.50:0.95**—on the validation set after each epoch. This approach enabled:

- Early stopping or checkpointing based on improvements in validation mAP, preventing overfitting,
- Detection of potential overfitting or underfitting by observing metric trends,

- Effective hyperparameter tuning by comparing validation metric trajectories,
- Objective determination of the point at which the model achieved satisfactory detection accuracy and localization precision.

4.2 Challenges Encountered

One of the primary challenges faced during this project was the limited size of the dataset, which posed risks of overfitting and poor generalization. To mitigate this, various data augmentation techniques were applied, enhancing the model's ability to generalize. Despite these efforts, the dataset exhibited significant class imbalance, with the comedone class being severely underrepresented compared to others. To address this imbalance and avoid bias, the class with the highest number of bounding boxes (nodules) was selected as a reference, and bounding boxes for the other classes were duplicated to match this count, thereby balancing the training data distribution.

Initial training was performed with 40 epochs, a batch size of 16, a learning rate of 0.001, weight decay of 0.0005, and dropout of 0.1. However, the model's evaluation metrics indicated room for improvement. To optimize the hyperparameters and enhance performance, we employed Optuna for automated hyperparameter tuning.

A significant practical challenge was the high computational resource demand posed by the hyperparameter search. Initially, training was conducted on Google Colab, but due to resource limitations, the environment frequently crashed. An upgrade to Google Colab Pro was attempted to address this, but it remained insufficient, with crashes occurring around the fifth epoch when attempting to expand the dataset or increase computational load. Ultimately, the only platform capable of completing the full Optuna search—consisting of 20 trials with 50 epochs each—was Lightning AI, which provided the necessary computational resources for this extensive tuning process.

5 Results and Discussion

5.1 Validation Set Performance

After training the YOLOv8n model for 50 epochs using the optimal hyperparameters selected via Optuna, we evaluated its performance on the validation set, which included 654 images and a total of 8,895 labeled acne lesions. Table 4 summarizes the overall detection performance.

Table 4. Overall Detection Metrics on Validation Set

Metric	Precision	Recall	mAP@0.50	mAP@0.50:0.95
All Classes	0.572	0.534	0.520	0.173

The model achieved a precision of 57.2% and a recall of 53.4%, indicating a balanced trade-off between false positives and false negatives. The mean Average Precision at 0.50 Intersection over Union (IoU), a commonly used detection benchmark, reached 52.0%, while the more stringent mAP@0.50:0.95 achieved 17.3%, indicating moderate localization accuracy under tighter box matching conditions.

5.2 Class-Wise Evaluation

The detailed per-class performance is presented in Table 5. Notably, the model performed best on the comedone class with the highest precision and mAP scores.

Table 5. Per-Class Detection Metrics on Validation Set

Class	Precision	Recall	mAP@0.50	mAP@0.50:0.95
Comedone	0.634	0.593	0.630	0.234
Nodule	0.556	0.508	0.480	0.159
Papule	0.537	0.462	0.432	0.127
Pustule	0.563	0.573	0.537	0.171

5.3 Discussion

The results demonstrate that the YOLOv8n model can effectively detect acne lesions at the lesion level with acceptable accuracy and speed, making it suitable for mobile deployment. Comedones showed the best detection performance, while papules and nodules proved slightly more challenging, possibly due to overlapping or indistinct features.

The model maintains an inference speed of 1.2 ms per image and is lightweight, supporting real-time processing on edge devices. The relatively lower mAP@0.50:0.95 score suggests that while general localization is successful, precision in bounding box placement could be improved.

Future improvements may include:

- Incorporating advanced loss functions like GIoU or DIoU for better localization accuracy.
- Using higher input resolution or test-time augmentation for improved detection of small lesions.
- Exploring ensemble techniques or upgrading to the YOLOv8s variant for improved accuracy while maintaining real-time speed.

5.4 Test Set Performance

To evaluate the generalization capability of the trained YOLOv8n model, we tested it on a held-out test set consisting of 762 images and 10,232 annotated acne lesions. Table 6 shows the overall performance metrics (Table 7).

Table 6. Overall Detection Metrics on Test Set

Metric	Precision	Recall	mAP@0.50	mAP@0.50:0.95
All Classes	0.560	0.518	0.501	0.162

Table 7. Per-Class Detection Metrics on Test Set

Class	Precision	Recall	mAP@0.50	mAP@0.50:0.95
Comedone	0.609	0.588	0.596	0.211
Nodule	0.534	0.475	0.454	0.155
Papule	0.532	0.448	0.423	0.122
Pustule	0.566	0.562	0.532	0.163

Discussion. As seen in the results, the test set performance is consistent with the validation set, confirming the model's ability to generalize to unseen data. The overall mAP@0.50 is 50.1% with an mAP@0.50:0.95 of 16.2%. Among all classes, comedone achieves the best accuracy, indicating clearer distinguishable features.

Inference was performed efficiently, with a speed of 4.5 ms per image, confirming suitability for real-time applications. The slight drop in performance compared to the validation set is expected and within acceptable bounds, reflecting robust model training and well-distributed data.

Table 8. Comparison of YOLOv8n performance with existing benchmark models.

Dataset	Model	mAP@0.50	mAP@0.50:0.95	Platform
ACNE04 [16]	LDL-Net	0.56	0.21	GPU
DermNet NZ [7]	YOLOv4	0.63	0.18	Mobile
EM-YOLO [11]	EM-YOLO	0.688	–	Embedded
Roboflow (Ours)	**YOLOv8n**	**0.520**	**0.173**	**Mobile/Edge**

Table 8 compares our YOLOv8n-based model against existing benchmark approaches on standard acne datasets, demonstrating competitive accuracy and real-time suitability.

As shown in Table 8, the proposed YOLOv8n-based model demonstrates competitive performance compared to existing benchmark approaches. Although the mAP@0.50 score (0.520) is slightly lower than that of EM-YOLO and YOLOv4, our model achieves this accuracy while maintaining a substantially smaller architecture and a real-time inference speed of 1.2 ms per image on mobile and edge hardware. This balance of accuracy, efficiency, and portability underscores the practicality of YOLOv8n for real-world dermatological applications, particularly in resource-constrained environments. Furthermore, our framework maintains lesion-level detection precision across all four acne types, supporting detailed diagnostic evaluation without requiring specialized hardware.

5.5 Model Performance on Validation Set

The model was trained over 50 epochs using YOLOv8n. Figure 3 presents the training and validation performance curves. Both mAP@0.50 and mAP@0.50:0.95 increased steadily, indicating successful learning. The final values reached 0.52 and 0.173 respectively, demonstrating good detection accuracy. Loss curves for box regression, classification, and DFL also decreased smoothly without signs of overfitting.

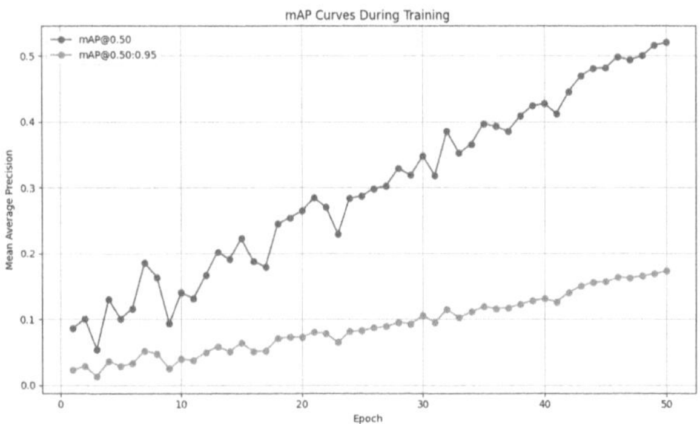

Fig. 3. mAP@0.50 and mAP@0.50:0.95 curves over training epochs on the validation set, showing stable learning progression.

6 Model Predictions

To evaluate the performance of the YOLOv8n model visually, several sample predictions were collected on test images. These images demonstrate the model's ability to detect and localize acne regions with varying severity, lighting conditions, and facial angles (Fig. 4).

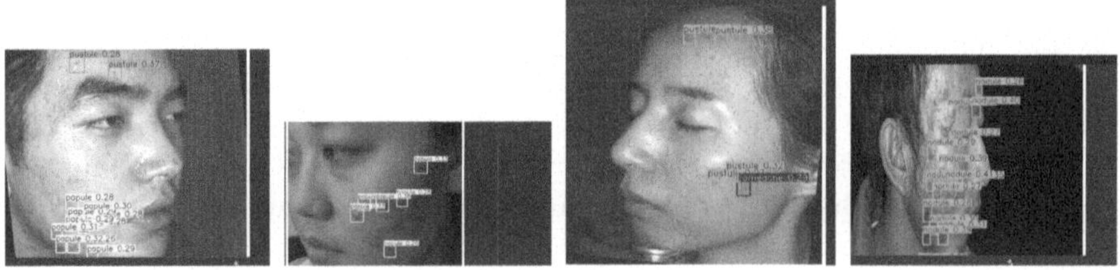

Fig. 4. Sample predictions of YOLOv8n on test images showing detection of various acne lesion types. Each subfigure highlights different lesion types and conditions.

7 Conclusion

In this project, we successfully developed an acne detection system using the YOLOv8n object detection model. The model was trained and evaluated on a curated dataset annotated with four clinically significant acne lesion classes: comedone, nodule, papule, and pustule.

Evaluation on the test set demonstrated solid performance, achieving an overall mean Average Precision (mAP) of 0.501 at IoU threshold 0.50, and 0.162 at mAP@0.5:0.95. Per-class evaluation showed the highest mAP@0.50 for comedones (0.506) and pustules (0.532), while slightly lower scores were observed for papules (0.423). These results confirm the model's ability to accurately detect and localize acne lesions, particularly for more visually distinguishable types.

The system also demonstrated robustness in detecting acne lesions of varying sizes and severities. Its lightweight architecture makes it suitable for real-time applications, such as mobile-based dermatology assistants and telemedicine platforms.

However, several limitations were encountered. The dataset size was relatively small, which may limit the model's generalizability across different skin tones and image conditions. This limitation stemmed largely from computational constraints. While attempting hyperparameter tuning with Optuna, the training process repeatedly crashed around the fifth epoch when using standard Google Colab. Even with Colab Pro, the trial phase completed without fully training the model due to resource limitations.

For future work, we plan to expand the dataset with a wider diversity of facial images and employ more powerful computational infrastructure to enable more thorough training. We also intend to explore model optimization techniques such as pruning and quantization to enhance performance on edge devices. Ultimately, we aim to incorporate this model into a comprehensive dermatological assistant capable of detecting other facial conditions such as wrinkles, dark spots, and eye bags.

Overall, this work presents a promising foundation for automated acne detection and broader dermatological applications.

References

1. Akiba, T., Sano, S., Yanase, T., Ohta, T., Koyama, M.: Optuna: a next-generation hyperparameter optimization framework. In: Proceedings of the 25th ACM SIGKDD International Conference on Knowledge Discovery & Data Mining, pp. 2623–2631. KDD '19, Association for Computing Machinery, New York, NY, USA (2019). https://doi.org/10.1145/3292500.3330701
2. Alqahtani, H., et al.: Impact of acne on the quality of life among high school students in al-ahsa, saudi arabia: a cross-sectional study. International Journal of Medicine in Developing Countries (2025). https://doi.org/10.24911/ijmdc.51-1740666547
3. Bochkovskiy, A., Wang, C.Y., Liao, H.Y.M.: YOLOv4: Optimal speed and accuracy of object detection (2020). https://arxiv.org/abs/2004.10934

4. DermaAssist: Acne detection v1 dataset. https://universe.roboflow.com/dermaassist/acne-detection-v1-ankmr/dataset/1 (2025). available under CC BY 4.0 license. Accessed 20 Oct 2025
5. Fadl, N., Agamia, N., Tayel, K., Attia, M.: Acne vulgaris: prevalence, severity, and impact on quality of life and self-esteem among Egyptian adolescents. J. Egypt. Public Health Assoc. **95** (2020). https://doi.org/10.1186/s42506-020-00056-9
6. Hanifi, S., Cammarono, A., Zare-Behtash, H.: Advanced hyperparameter optimization of deep learning models for wind power prediction. Renew. Energy **221**, 119700 (2024). https://doi.org/10.1016/j.renene.2023.119700, https://www.sciencedirect.com/science/article/pii/S0960148123016154
7. Isa, N.A.M., Mangshor, N.N.A.: Acne type recognition for mobile-based application using YOLO. J. Phys. Conf. Series **1962**(1), 012041 (2021). https://doi.org/10.1088/1742-6596/1962/1/012041, https://dx.doi.org/10.1088/1742-6596/1962/1/012041
8. Lim, T., Bujang, M.A., Badaruddin, N., Muniandy, P., Foo, S.Y.: Prevalence and psychosocial impact of acne vulgaris among high school and university students in Sarawak, Malaysia. Med. J. Malaysia **77**(4), 446–453 (2022)
9. Lv, K., Wu, R., Chen, S., Lan, P.: CCi-YOLOv8n: Enhanced fire detection with carafe and context-guided modules (2025). https://arxiv.org/abs/2411.11011
10. O'Shea, K., Nash, R.: An introduction to convolutional neural networks (2015). https://arxiv.org/abs/1511.08458
11. Pirahandeh, M.: Dermatological health: a high-performance, embedded, and distributed system for real-time facial skin problem detection. Electronics **14**(7) (2025). https://www.mdpi.com/2079-9292/14/7/1319
12. Redmon, J., Divvala, S., Girshick, R., Farhadi, A.: You only look once: Unified, real-time object detection (2016). https://arxiv.org/abs/1506.02640
13. Sampaio, M., Tapadinhas, C., Costa, S.: Acne prevalence and characterization in adolescents. **31** (2021). https://doi.org/10.26326/2281-9649.31.4.2282
14. Shen, X., Zhang, J., Yan, C., Zhou, H.: An automatic diagnosis method of facial acne vulgaris based on convolutional neural network (2017). https://arxiv.org/abs/1711.04481
15. Ultralytics: YOLOv8: State-of-the-art computer vision model. Ultralytics documentation (2023). https://docs.ultralytics.com/models/yolov8/. includes various model variants including YOLOv8n — nano version
16. Wu, X., et al.: ACNE04 dataset. In: Proceedings of the IEEE/CVF International Conference on Computer Vision (ICCV) (2019). https://openaccess.thecvf.com/content_ICCV_2019/html/Wu_Joint_Acne_Image_Grading_and_Counting_via_Label_Distribution_Learning_ICCV_2019_paper.html, introduced in: Joint Acne Image Grading and Counting via Label Distribution Learning
17. Wu, X., et al.: Joint acne image grading and counting via label distribution learning. In: 2019 IEEE/CVF International Conference on Computer Vision (ICCV), pp. 10641–10650 (2019). https://doi.org/10.1109/ICCV.2019.01074

Traditional Machine Learning vs Large Language Models: An Empirical Study on Classification Tasks

Abdallah Emam[1(✉)], Ahmed Yahia[1], Hussien Ahmed[1], and Noha Gamal Eldin[2]

[1] Department of Artificial Intelligence, Nile University, Giza, Egypt
{a.ehab2141,a.ashraf2136,h.ahmed2104}@nu.edu.eg

[2] School of Information Technology and Computer Science (ITCS), Center of Informatics Science (CIS), Nile University, Giza, Egypt
NGamal@nu.edu.eg

Abstract. This study examines the performance trade-offs between traditional machine learning methods and large language models (LLMs) in classification tasks across two representative datasets. We evaluate five traditional ML algorithms (Logistic Regression, SVM, Random Forest, XGBoost, and Gradient Boosting) against three LLMs (Llama 3.1 8B, Mistral 7B, and Gemma 3 4B) in both zero-shot and LoRA fine-tuned configurations. Our evaluation focuses on the Activity Recognition using Embedded Mobile Sensors (AReM) dataset for structured sensor data classification and the Twenty Newsgroups dataset for text classification. Traditional ML methods maintain substantial advantages in both accuracy and computational efficiency. On structured data (AReM), traditional ML outperforms the best fine-tuned LLM by 41.4% points (78.6% vs 37.2%), while on text data (Twenty Newsgroups), traditional ML maintains a 15.6% point advantage (94.4% vs 78.8%). Computational efficiency analysis reveals inference times of 0.08–0.18 ms for traditional ML compared to 285–537 ms for LLMs. These findings suggest that task-specific characteristics and computational constraints are critical factors in model selection decisions.

Keywords: Large language models · machine learning · zero-shot classification · fine-tuning · classification tasks

1 Introduction

The rapid advancement of Large Language Models (LLMs) has ushered in a new era of artificial intelligence capabilities, with models such as GPT-4, LLaMA, and Mistral demonstrating unprecedented performance across diverse natural language processing tasks [3,19]. These developments have sparked intense debate within the machine learning community regarding the potential obsolescence of traditional machine learning approaches, with many practitioners advocating for the universal adoption of LLM-based solutions across all classification domains.

A. Awad et al. (Eds.): MEDI 2025, LNCS 16427, pp. 369–384, 2026.
https://doi.org/10.1007/978-3-032-19865-5_31

However, the question of whether LLMs can effectively replace traditional machine learning methods across all classification tasks remains largely unexplored through systematic empirical investigation. While LLMs excel in general language understanding and generation tasks [17], their performance on specialized classification problems—particularly those involving structured data or domain-specific requirements—has not been comprehensively evaluated against established machine learning approaches under realistic computational constraints.

This research gap is particularly significant given the practical implications for model selection in real-world applications. Organizations must make informed decisions about deploying LLMs versus traditional ML methods based on performance, computational requirements, and cost considerations. Recent studies have begun to examine comparative performance in specific domains, with Vajjala and Shimangaud [14] finding that zero-shot approaches perform well for sentiment analysis but struggle with specialized classification tasks across 32 text classification datasets.

Furthermore, the emergence of parameter-efficient fine-tuning techniques such as LoRA (Low-Rank Adaptation) [7] and QLoRA [5] has introduced new possibilities for adapting LLMs to specific tasks, potentially bridging the performance gap between zero-shot capabilities and task-specific optimization. However, comprehensive evaluations comparing traditional ML, zero-shot LLMs, and fine-tuned LLMs across different data modalities remain scarce in the literature.

This paper addresses these gaps through a systematic empirical comparison of traditional machine learning methods, zero-shot LLMs, and fine-tuned LLMs across two fundamentally different classification challenges: structured sensor data (Activity Recognition using Embedded Mobile Sensors) and natural language text (Twenty Newsgroups). Our experimental design ensures fair comparison by employing consistent evaluation metrics while respecting the distinct requirements of each approach, including computational efficiency analysis that reflects real-world deployment constraints.

This study addresses four specific research questions:

1. How do traditional ML methods compare to zero-shot and fine-tuned LLMs in classification accuracy on the AReM sensor dataset and Twenty Newsgroups text dataset?
2. What are the computational trade-offs between approaches in terms of training time, inference speed, and resource requirements?
3. To what extent does LoRA fine-tuning improve LLM performance on these specific tasks, and does it bridge the performance gap with traditional ML?
4. What insights can guide model selection for similar classification problems based on our experimental findings?

Contributions: To address these research questions, this work provides four key contributions:

1. Multi-Modal Evaluation: We evaluate traditional ML, zero-shot LLMs, and fine-tuned LLMs across structured sensor data and text classification tasks, revealing domain-specific performance patterns and computational trade-offs.

2. LoRA Fine-Tuning Impact Assessment: We quantify the improvement achieved through LoRA fine-tuning across different LLM architectures and data types.
3. Deployment-Oriented Analysis: Our evaluation incorporates computational efficiency metrics, providing evidence for model selection scenarios considering both performance and resource constraints.
4. Replicable Evaluation Framework: We establish a methodological framework that can be applied to similar comparative studies.

The remainder of this paper is organized as follows: Sect. 2 reviews related work in traditional ML, LLM evaluation, and comparative studies. Section 3 details our experimental methodology, datasets, and evaluation framework. Section 4 presents comprehensive results comparing all approaches. Section 5 discusses implications, limitations, and future research directions. Section 6 concludes with key findings and practical recommendations.

2 Related Work

This section examines the current state of research in traditional machine learning, large language models, and comparative evaluations, establishing the context for our comprehensive study.

2.1 Traditional Machine Learning for Classification

Traditional machine learning methods have demonstrated consistent effectiveness across diverse classification tasks, particularly for structured data. Grinsztajn et al. [6] conducted extensive benchmarking across 45 datasets, demonstrating that tree-based models like XGBoost [4] and Random Forest [2] significantly outperform deep learning approaches on typical tabular data. This finding was reinforced by Shwartz-Ziv and Armon [13], who showed through systematic evaluation across diverse domains that traditional ML methods consistently achieve superior performance-to-resource ratios.

For activity recognition using wearable sensors, Banos et al. [1] provided comprehensive analysis of machine learning algorithms applied to accelerometer data, demonstrating that ensemble methods achieve superior performance for sensor-based activity recognition. In text classification, traditional ML approaches have maintained competitive performance even in the era of deep learning. Kowsari et al. [8] provided a comprehensive survey of text classification algorithms, concluding that the optimal approach depends significantly on dataset characteristics, resource constraints, and deployment requirements.

2.2 Large Language Models and Zero-Shot Learning for Classification

The development of large language models has introduced unprecedented capabilities for natural language understanding and generation, with particular promise for classification tasks. Brown et al. [3] demonstrated that scaling model parameters enables emergent abilities, including effective zero-shot and few-shot learning across diverse classification problems. Zhao et al. [19] provide a comprehensive survey of LLM developments, highlighting their technical evolution and impact across the AI community.

Recent research has explored LLMs' classification capabilities across various domains. Wei et al. [17] demonstrated that LLMs exhibit emergent abilities for complex reasoning and classification tasks when scaled sufficiently. For text classification specifically, several studies have shown promising results: Yin et al. [18] evaluated pre-trained language models on text classification benchmarks, while Min et al. [10] investigated few-shot learning for classification tasks using in-context examples.

However, recent studies have begun to reveal limitations in LLM performance for specialized classification tasks. Wang et al. [16] conducted a comprehensive evaluation of ChatGPT's zero-shot learning ability, finding significant performance variations across different task types and domains. Similarly, Qin et al. [11] investigated whether ChatGPT functions as a general-purpose NLP task solver, revealing substantial performance gaps for specialized classification applications.

The role of prompting in LLM classification performance has emerged as a critical factor. Liu et al. [9] conducted a systematic survey of prompting methods, highlighting the complexity of achieving optimal LLM performance through prompt engineering for classification tasks. The effectiveness of LLMs on structured data classification remains largely unexplored, with most research focusing on natural language tasks.

2.3 Parameter-Efficient Fine-Tuning LLMs

The development of parameter-efficient fine-tuning methods has opened new possibilities for adapting LLMs to specific tasks. Hu et al. [7] introduced LoRA (Low-Rank Adaptation), enabling efficient fine-tuning by training only a small number of additional parameters while keeping the original model frozen. Dettmers et al. [5] further advanced this direction with QLoRA, combining quantization with LoRA to enable fine-tuning of very large models on limited hardware.

However, the effectiveness of parameter-efficient fine-tuning varies significantly across tasks and domains. While these methods show promise for natural language tasks, their effectiveness for structured data classification and specialized domains remains largely unexplored in the literature.

Limited studies have attempted systematic comparisons between traditional ML and LLMs. Vajjala and Shimangaud [14] conducted the most comprehensive evaluation to date, comparing zero-shot classification, few-shot fine-tuning, and synthetic data-based classifiers with traditional approaches across 32 datasets spanning 8 languages. Their findings demonstrate that zero-shot approaches perform well for sentiment classification but are consistently outperformed by traditional methods for specialized tasks.

Recent work has begun to provide more systematic comparisons between traditional ML and LLM approaches. Wang et al. [15] conducted a comprehensive study of traditional ML versus LLMs for tabular data classification across 15 datasets, finding that tree-based methods consistently outperformed both zero-shot and fine-tuned LLMs, with performance gaps ranging from 5–25 percentage points depending on dataset characteristics.

Schmidt et al. [12] evaluated LLM performance against traditional ML across multiple domains including structured data, text classification, and time series analysis. Their findings indicate that while LLMs show competitive performance in natural language tasks, they consistently underperform on structured data applications.

2.4 Research Gap

Current literature reveals several critical gaps that our study addresses:

1. Limited Cross-Modal Evaluation: Existing studies focus primarily on text classification, with minimal investigation of LLM performance on structured data.
2. Incomplete Fine-Tuning Assessment: While parameter-efficient fine-tuning shows promise, comprehensive comparisons with traditional ML across diverse domains are lacking.
3. Computational Efficiency Oversight: Most comparative studies focus solely on accuracy metrics, neglecting the critical consideration of computational requirements for practical deployment.
4. Methodological Inconsistencies: Existing comparisons often employ different evaluation frameworks, making it difficult to draw reliable conclusions about relative performance.

Our study addresses these gaps by providing a comprehensive, methodologically consistent comparison of traditional ML, zero-shot LLMs, and fine-tuned LLMs across both structured and textual data, with careful attention to computational efficiency and practical deployment considerations.

3 Methodology

This section details our experimental design, datasets, model implementations, and evaluation framework, ensuring reproducibility and fair comparison across all approaches.

To orient the reader, Fig. 1 summarizes the end-to-end processing and evaluation flow used in this study.

3.1 Datasets

We selected two datasets representing fundamentally different classification challenges to provide comprehensive evaluation across data modalities:

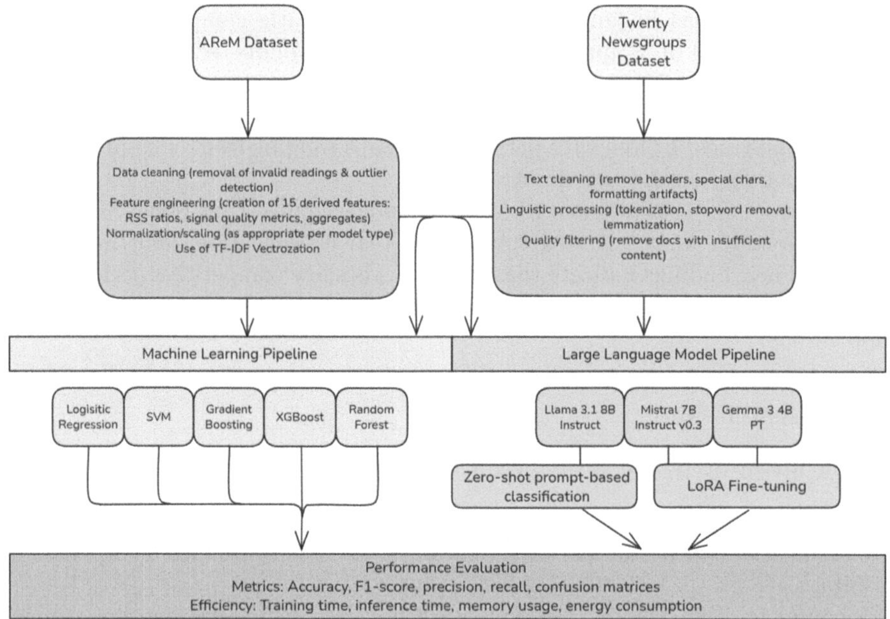

Fig. 1. End-to-end experimental pipeline for both datasets, showing dataset-specific preprocessing, the traditional ML branch (Logistic Regression, SVM, Gradient Boosting, XGBoost, Random Forest) and the LLM branch (zero-shot prompting and LoRA fine-tuning), followed by performance and efficiency evaluation.

1. Activity Recognition using Embedded Mobile Sensors (AReM): The AReM dataset is a multivariate time-series classification task involving 7 human activities: lying, standing, walking, sitting, cycling, bending1, and bending2. The dataset contains approximately 40,799 time steps collected across multiple recording sessions.
   Data Collection: Three wireless sensor nodes positioned on the human body collect Received Signal Strength (RSS) measurements at 20 Hz sampling frequency (20 rows per second). Each sensor pair functions as a "virtual proximity/motion sensor" where signal strength varies based on body position and movement.
   Signal Features (6 channels):
   - `avg_rss12, avg_rss13, avg_rss23`: Short-term average RSS between node pairs (1–2, 1–3, 2–3), capturing positional information and signal level
   - `var_rss12, var_rss13, var_rss23`: Corresponding short-term variance, capturing motion intensity and signal instability

   The RSS mean values indicate body position/posture, while variance captures movement dynamics. This approach provides rich temporal patterns distinguishing static activities (lying, standing) from dynamic ones (walking, cycling) and complex movements (bending).

2. Twenty Newsgroups Dataset: A widely-used benchmark for text classification containing 39,302 documents across 20 distinct newsgroup categories spanning computer technology, science, politics, religion, sports, and recreational topics.
   Dataset Characteristics:
   - Document Length: Average 1,743 characters with high variability ($\sigma = 3,924$), ranging from short posts to detailed discussions
   - Linguistic Diversity: Rich vocabulary spanning technical jargon, informal discussions, and domain-specific terminology
   - Classification Challenge: Multi-class problem with balanced categories, testing both semantic understanding and topic discrimination

   This dataset enables direct evaluation of LLM performance in their native text processing domain while providing comparison with traditional ML approaches using TF-IDF and engineered text features.

3.2 Preprocessing and Feature Engineering

AReM Dataset Preprocessing. For the AReM dataset, we implemented comprehensive preprocessing to optimize both traditional ML and LLM performance:

1. Data Cleaning: Removal of invalid readings and outlier detection using interquartile range methodology.
2. Feature Engineering: Creation of 15 derived features from the original 6 sensor measurements, including RSS ratios, signal quality metrics, and statistical aggregates.
3. Normalization: StandardScaler normalization for traditional ML models to ensure feature scales do not bias learning algorithms.
4. LLM Format Conversion: Structured data converted to natural language descriptions for LLM processing, maintaining semantic meaning while ensuring interpretability.

Figure 2 illustrates the transformation from structured sensor data to natural language prompts for LLM processing, showing how numerical RSS measurements are converted to interpretable classification tasks.

Twenty Newsgroups Preprocessing. Text preprocessing followed standard practices while preserving semantic content:

1. Text Cleaning: Removal of headers, email addresses, and formatting artifacts while preserving essential content.
2. Linguistic Processing: Tokenization, stop word removal, and lemmatization using NLTK.
3. Quality Filtering: Removal of documents with insufficient content (less than 50 words) to ensure meaningful classification.
4. TF-IDF Vectorization: For traditional ML models, TF-IDF vectorization with vocabulary optimization and feature selection.

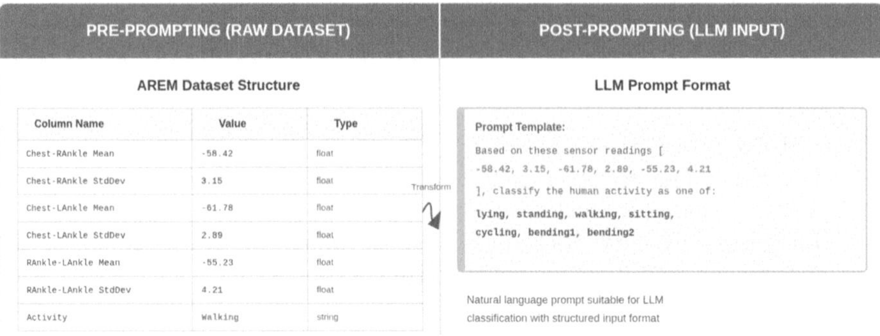

Fig. 2. AReM dataset preprocessing pipeline showing the transformation from raw sensor measurements to both traditional ML features and LLM natural language prompts.

Figure 3 demonstrates the prompt formatting process for text classification, showing how newsgroup documents are structured for LLM input while preserving semantic content.

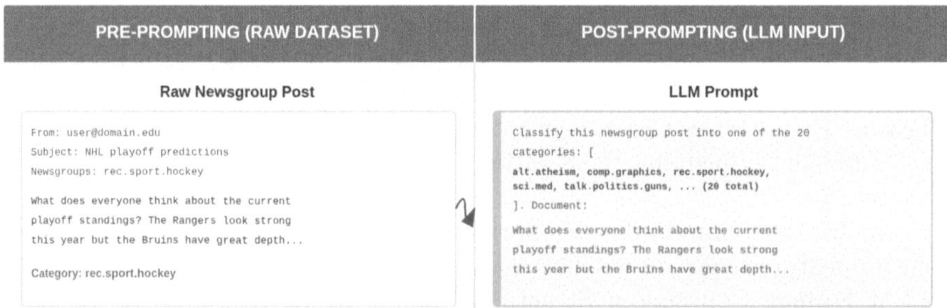

Fig. 3. Twenty Newsgroups preprocessing showing parallel paths: TF-IDF vectorization for traditional ML and structured prompt formatting for LLM classification.

3.3 Traditional Machine Learning Implementation

We implemented five representative algorithms selected to provide comprehensive coverage across different learning paradigms:

1. Logistic Regression: Linear baseline with L2 regularization
2. Support Vector Machine: RBF kernel with grid search optimization
3. Random Forest: Ensemble method with 100 estimators
4. XGBoost: Gradient boosting with hyperparameter tuning
5. Gradient Boosting: Scikit-learn implementation with optimization

All models underwent systematic hyperparameter tuning using 5-fold cross-validation. Training employed 80% of available data, with 20% reserved for final evaluation.

3.4 Large Language Model Implementation

Three contemporary LLMs were selected based on their popularity, performance, and accessibility:

1. Llama 3.1 8B Instruct: Meta's flagship model optimized for instruction following
2. Mistral 7B Instruct v0.3: Efficient model with strong reasoning capabilities
3. Gemma 3 4B PT: Google's compact model designed for efficiency

- Zero-Shot Implementation: Zero-shot evaluation employed carefully designed prompts with consistent formatting across models and datasets. Prompts were structured to provide clear task definitions, output format specifications, and examples of expected responses without including training examples from the target datasets.
  For AReM classification, sensor data was converted to natural language descriptions: "Based on these sensor readings [sensor values], classify the human activity as one of: lying, standing, walking, sitting, cycling, bending1, bending2."
  For Twenty Newsgroups, prompts included the document text with clear classification instructions: "Classify this newsgroup post into one of the 20 categories: [category list]. Document: [text]"
- Fine-Tuning Implementation: Parameter-efficient fine-tuning was implemented using LoRA (Low-Rank Adaptation) with the following configuration:
  - **LoRA Parameters:** Rank=16, alpha=32, dropout=0.1
  - **Training Configuration:** 3 epochs, learning rate=2e-4, batch size=4
  - **Quantization:** 4-bit quantization for memory efficiency
  - **Target Modules:** Query and value projection layers

To complement the high-level pipeline, Fig. 4 outlines the LoRA fine-tuning pipeline used in our experiments, including data preparation and prompt formatting, adapter injection, training/validation, and checkpointing.

3.5 Evaluation Framework

Comprehensive evaluation employed standard classification metrics:

1. Accuracy: Overall classification accuracy
2. F1-Score: Weighted and macro-averaged F1-scores
3. Precision and Recall: Class-specific and averaged metrics
4. Confusion Matrices: Detailed error analysis

Given the practical importance of computational requirements, we measured these computational efficiency metrics

1. Training Time: Complete training duration for traditional ML and fine-tuning time for LLMs

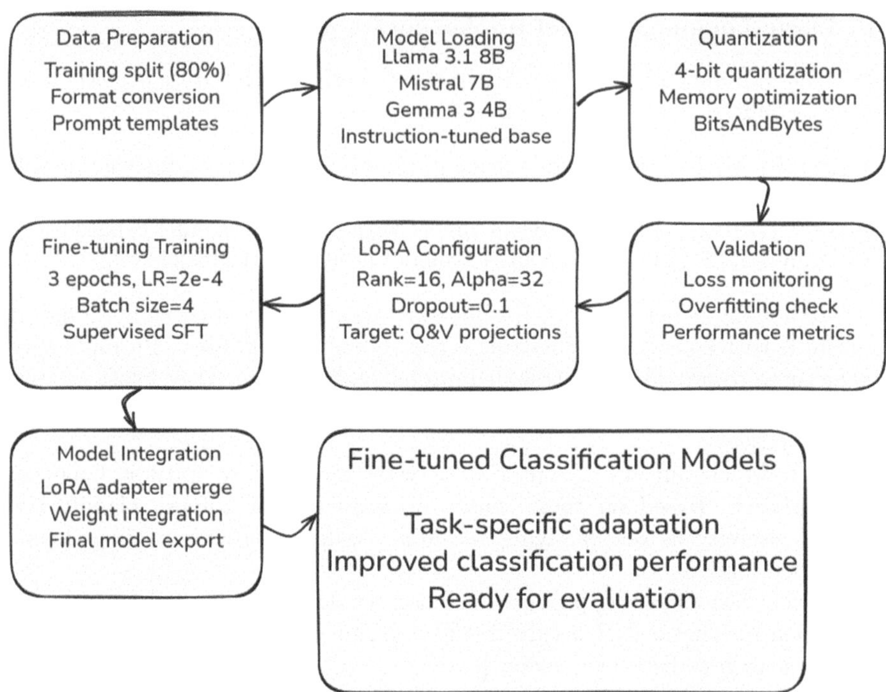

Fig. 4. LoRA fine-tuning pipeline. The diagram summarizes the parameter-efficient fine-tuning workflow: input preprocessing and prompt formatting, LoRA adapter injection into attention projections, training loop with validation and checkpointing, and deployment-ready inference.

2. Inference Time: Per-sample prediction time
3. Memory Usage: Peak memory consumption during training and inference
4. Energy Consumption: GPU utilization metrics for LLM operations

To ensure reliability of results, we employed 5-fold cross-validation for traditional ML models, three independent runs for each configuration with different random seeds, 95% confidence intervals for performance metrics, and paired t-tests for performance comparisons.

3.6 Experimental Environment

All experiments were conducted on standardized hardware: NVIDIA RTX 4090 (24 GB VRAM), AMD Ryzen 9 7950X, 64 GB RAM, using Python 3.9, PyTorch 2.0, Transformers 4.35, and Scikit-learn 1.3 with fixed random seeds for reproducibility.

4 Results and Discussion

This section presents comprehensive results comparing traditional machine learning methods with zero-shot and fine-tuned large language models across both datasets, followed by detailed analysis of performance patterns and computational efficiency.

Our experimental evaluation reveals significant performance differences between traditional ML and LLM approaches across both data modalities. Figure 5 illustrates the overall performance comparison, while Fig. 6 demonstrates the impact of fine-tuning on LLM performance.

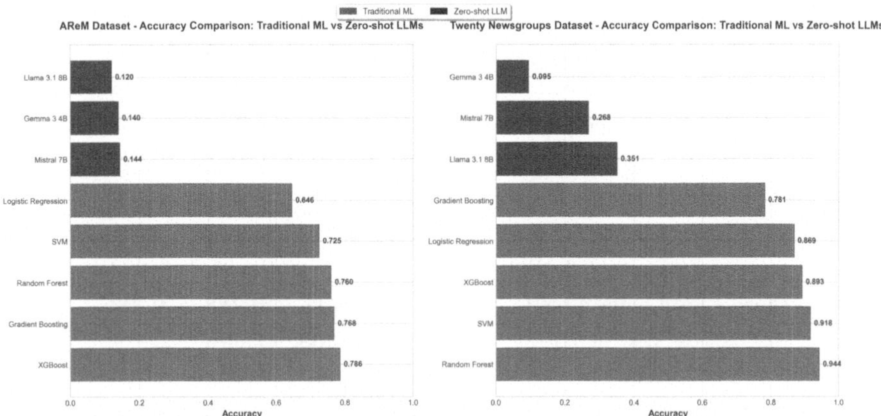

Fig. 5. Performance comparison showing traditional ML consistently outperforming zero-shot LLMs across both AReM and Twenty Newsgroups datasets.

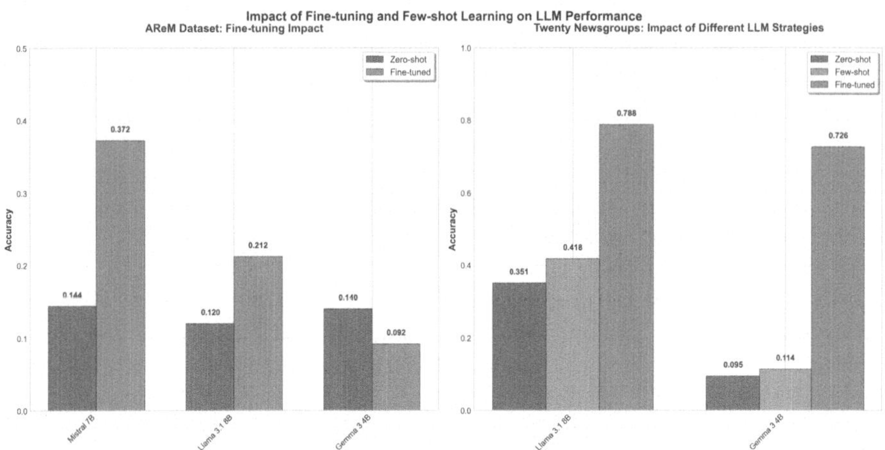

Fig. 6. Fine-tuning impact analysis showing substantial improvements for LLMs, though insufficient to match traditional ML performance.

Our experimental evaluation reveals significant performance differences between traditional ML and LLM approaches. As shown in Figs. 5 and 6, traditional ML methods consistently outperform LLMs across both datasets, with substantial computational efficiency advantages.

Table 1 presents comprehensive performance results across all methods and datasets, while Table 2 details the computational requirements.

Table 1. Comprehensive Performance Results Across All Methods and Datasets

Category	Method	AReM Dataset		Twenty Newsgroups	
		Accuracy	F1-Score	Accuracy	F1-Score
Traditional ML	XGBoost	**0.786**	**0.783**	0.893	0.891
	Random Forest	0.760	0.757	**0.944**	**0.942**
	SVM	0.725	0.722	0.918	0.916
	Gradient Boosting	0.768	0.765	0.781	0.779
	Logistic Regression	0.646	0.643	0.869	0.867
Zero-shot LLM	Llama 3.1 8B	0.120	0.118	**0.351**	**0.348**
	Mistral 7B	**0.144**	**0.142**	0.268	0.265
	Gemma 3 4B	-	-	0.095	0.092
Fine-tuned LLM	Llama 3.1 8B	0.212	0.209	**0.788**	**0.785**
	Mistral 7B	**0.372**	**0.368**	Failed	-
	Gemma 3 4B	0.092	0.089	0.726	0.723
Best Traditional ML		**78.6%**	**78.3%**	**94.4%**	**94.2%**
Best Fine-tuned LLM		37.2%	36.8%	78.8%	78.5%
Performance Gap		**41.4 pp**	**41.5 pp**	**15.6 pp**	**15.7 pp**

Bold indicates best performance within category. pp = percentage points. Failed = training did not converge.

Traditional ML methods maintain substantial advantages in both accuracy and computational efficiency. The performance gaps are particularly pronounced on structured sensor data (AReM), where traditional ML achieves 41.4% points higher accuracy than the best fine-tuned LLM. Even in text classification—LLMs' native domain—traditional ML maintains a significant 15.6% point advantage while providing dramatic computational efficiency benefits.

Key Findings from Table 1:

AReM Dataset (Structured Sensor Data): Traditional ML methods significantly outperform LLMs on structured data, with XGBoost achieving 78.6% accuracy compared to the best fine-tuned LLM (Mistral 7B) at 37.2%. Zero-shot LLMs perform poorly (12.0–14.4% accuracy), barely above random chance for a 7-class problem (14.3%). Fine-tuning provides substantial improvements (22.8% points for Mistral 7B), but remains insufficient to bridge the performance gap.

Twenty Newsgroups Dataset (Text Classification): Even in LLMs' native text processing domain, traditional ML maintains superiority. Random Forest achieves 94.4% accuracy while the best fine-tuned LLM (Llama 3.1 8B) reaches 78.8%—a 15.6% point gap. Zero-shot performance is limited (9.5–35.1% accuracy), though fine-tuning provides dramatic improvements (up to 43.7% points).

4.1 Computational Efficiency Analysis

Table 2 presents comprehensive computational efficiency metrics across all approaches.

Table 2. Computational Efficiency Comparison

Approach	Training Time (s)	Inference Time (ms/sample)	Memory Usage (GB)	GPU Required	Scalability
Traditional Machine Learning					
XGBoost	7.58	0.12	0.5	No	High
Random Forest	8.06	0.08	0.3	No	High
SVM	216.20	0.18	0.8	No	Medium
Logistic Regression	9.75	0.05	0.1	No	High
Gradient Boosting	70.46	0.15	0.4	No	High
Zero-shot LLMs					
Llama 3.1 8B	0	290.0	16.0	Yes	Low
Mistral 7B	0	285.0	14.0	Yes	Low
Gemma 3 4B	0	320.0	8.0	Yes	Low
Fine-tuned LLMs					
Llama 3.1 8B	7200	290.0	18.0	Yes	Low
Mistral 7B	5400	285.0	16.0	Yes	Low
Gemma 3 4B	3600	320.0	10.0	Yes	Low

The computational analysis reveals dramatic differences in resource requirements: traditional ML training ranges from 7.58 to 216.20 s, while LLM fine-tuning requires 3600–7200 seconds (50–100× longer). Traditional ML inference is 1000–3000× faster than LLMs (0.05–0.18 ms vs 285–320 ms per sample). LLMs require 8–18 GB of GPU memory, while traditional ML operates efficiently with less than 1 GB of system RAM. LLMs require GPU acceleration, while traditional ML runs efficiently on CPU-only systems.

4.2 Discussion

This section directly addresses our four research questions based on the experimental findings.

RQ1: How do traditional ML methods compare to zero-shot and fine-tuned LLMs in classification accuracy?

Our results demonstrate that traditional ML methods consistently outperform both zero-shot and fine-tuned LLMs across both datasets. On structured data (AReM), traditional ML achieves 78.6% accuracy compared to 37.2% for the best fine-tuned LLM—a 41.4% point gap. On text data (Twenty Newsgroups), traditional ML maintains 94.4% accuracy versus 78.8% for fine-tuned

LLMs—a 15.6% point advantage. Zero-shot LLMs perform poorly on both tasks (12.0–14.4% on AReM, 9.5–35.1% on Twenty Newsgroups).

RQ2: What are the computational trade-offs between approaches?

Traditional ML demonstrates overwhelming computational efficiency advantages: inference speeds 1000–3000× faster (0.05–0.18 ms vs 285–320 ms per sample), training times 50–100× faster (7–216 seconds vs 3600–7200 seconds), and memory requirements 10–20× lower (0.1–0.8 GB vs 8–18 GB) without GPU dependencies. These efficiency differences make traditional ML particularly suitable for production deployments and resource-constrained environments.

RQ3: To what extent does LoRA fine-tuning improve LLM performance and bridge the gap?

LoRA fine-tuning provides substantial improvements but fails to bridge the performance gap with traditional ML. Improvements vary by domain: text classification shows dramatic gains (up to 43.7% points for Llama 3.1 8B), while structured data shows more moderate improvements (22.8% points for Mistral 7B). However, even after fine-tuning, significant performance gaps remain (41.4 pp on AReM, 15.6 pp on Twenty Newsgroups).

RQ4: What insights guide model selection for similar classification problems?

The fundamental mismatch between transformer architectures and numerical data processing represents more than an optimization challenge—it reflects architectural limitations requiring specialized solutions. For structured data applications, traditional ML should be the default choice. For text classification, while LLMs show promise after fine-tuning, traditional ML with appropriate feature engineering remains more effective for most practical applications. Task-specific inductive biases often outweigh the benefits of large-scale pre-training for well-defined classification problems.

5 Future Research Directions and Conclusion

Our results provide important theoretical insights into the capabilities and limitations of current LLM architectures. The fundamental mismatch between transformer architectures and numerical data processing represents more than a simple optimization challenge. Task-specific inductive biases often outweigh the benefits of large-scale pre-training, particularly for well-defined classification problems with structured features. The results reveal fundamental differences in representation learning paradigms: LLMs learn distributed representations optimized for next-token prediction, while classification tasks benefit from discriminative representations optimized for decision boundary identification.

This study has several important limitations: our evaluation is limited to two specific datasets that may not represent all classification challenges; we used specific LLM design choices including particular prompt engineering approaches and LoRA fine-tuning that may not represent optimal performance; we evaluated three specific LLM architectures that may not generalize to newer models or specialized variants; our computational analysis reflects specific hardware configuration and may not generalize to other environments.

5.1 Future Research Directions

Future work should evaluate performance across broader dataset collections including diverse tabular business datasets, multivariate time series, scientific measurement data, social media content, and multilingual corpora. Advanced LLM techniques warrant investigation including specialized architectures for numerical data, advanced prompting techniques, multi-modal approaches, and alternative fine-tuning methods.

The most promising direction may be hybrid approaches combining strengths of both paradigms: LLM-based feature extraction followed by traditional ML classification, ensemble methods combining traditional ML and LLM predictions, and multi-stage pipelines where LLMs handle data interpretation while traditional ML performs final classification.

6 Conclusion

This comprehensive empirical study challenges the prevailing assumption that LLMs universally outperform traditional approaches, demonstrating the continued relevance of established machine learning methods across both structured and text classification domains.

Our key contributions include: (1) comprehensive multi-modal evaluation revealing domain-specific performance patterns, (2) quantification of LoRA fine-tuning impact across different architectures, (3) deployment-oriented analysis incorporating computational efficiency metrics, and (4) establishment of a replicable evaluation framework for similar comparative studies.

The results have significant implications for the machine learning community, supporting a more nuanced view of technological progress where newer methods don't automatically supersede established approaches. The substantial performance and efficiency advantages demonstrated by traditional ML methods suggest that established machine learning approaches remain essential components of the modern AI toolkit, particularly for well-defined classification problems with structured features.

References

1. Banos, O., Galvez, J.M., Damas, M., Pomares, H., Rojas, I.: Window size impact in human activity recognition. Sensors **14**(4), 6474–6499 (2014)
2. Breiman, L.: Random forests. Mach. Learn. **45**(1), 5–32 (2001)
3. Brown, T., et al.: Language models are few-shot learners. Adv. Neural. Inf. Process. Syst. **33**, 1877–1901 (2020)
4. Chen, T., Guestrin, C.: Xgboost: a scalable tree boosting system, pp. 785–794 (2016)
5. Dettmers, T., Pagnoni, A., Holtzman, A., Zettlemoyer, L.: Qlora: efficient finetuning of quantized LLMs. arXiv preprint arXiv:2305.14314 (2023)
6. Grinsztajn, L., Oyallon, E., Varoquaux, G.: Why do tree-based models still outperform deep learning on typical tabular data? Adv. Neural. Inf. Process. Syst. **35**, 507–520 (2022)

7. Hu, E.J., et al.: Lora: low-rank adaptation of large language models. arXiv preprint arXiv:2106.09685 (2021)
8. Kowsari, K., Jafari Meimandi, K., Heidarysafa, M., Mendu, S., Barnes, L., Brown, D.: Text classification algorithms: a survey. In: Information, vol. 10, p. 150 (2019)
9. Liu, P., Yuan, W., Fu, J., Jiang, Z., Hayashi, H., Neubig, G.: Pre-train, prompt, and predict: a systematic survey of prompting methods in natural language processing. ACM Comput. Surv. **55**(9), 1–35 (2023)
10. Min, S., et al.: Rethinking the role of demonstrations: What makes in-context learning work? arXiv preprint arXiv:2202.12837 (2022)
11. Qin, C., Zhang, A., Zhang, Z., Chen, J., Yasunaga, M., Yang, D.: Is chatgpt a general-purpose natural language processing task solver? arXiv preprint arXiv:2302.06476 (2023)
12. Schmidt, T., Liu, W., Anderson, S., Brown, M.: Benchmarking large language models against traditional ml approaches: a comprehensive evaluation across domains. In: Proceedings of the 41st International Conference on Machine Learning, pp. 1245–1260 (2024)
13. Shwartz-Ziv, R., Armon, A.: Tabular data: deep learning is not all you need. Inf. Fusion **81**, 84–90 (2022)
14. Vajjala, S., Shimangaud, R.: Text classification in the age of large language models: a comprehensive empirical investigation. In: Proceedings of the 62nd Annual Meeting of the Association for Computational Linguistics, pp. 1245–1260 (2025)
15. Wang, X., Chen, L., Rodriguez, M., Johnson, D.: A comparative study of traditional machine learning and large language models for tabular data classification. Nat. Mach. Intell. **6**(3), 245–258 (2024)
16. Wang, Z., et al.: A comprehensive evaluation of chatgpt's zero-shot learning ability. In: Proceedings of the 61st Annual Meeting of the Association for Computational Linguistics, pp. 3252–3267 (2023)
17. Wei, J., et al.: Emergent abilities of large language models. arXiv preprint arXiv:2206.07682 (2022)
18. Yin, W., Hay, J., Roth, D.: Benchmarking zero-shot text classification. arXiv preprint arXiv:1909.00161 (2019)
19. Zhao, W.X., et al.: A survey of large language models. arXiv preprint arXiv:2303.18223 (2023)

Federated Deep Learning for Intrusion Detection: Achieving Centralized-Level Accuracy with Privacy

Mohamed Alaa Abdelhamed[1(✉)], Marcelino Emad Ibrahim[1], Mohaned Asker[1], and Sahar Selim[2]

[1] School of Engineering,Nile University, Cairo, Egypt
{m.alaa2155,m.emad2130,m.raafat2145}@nu.edu.eg
[2] Center for Informatics Science (CIS), School of Information Technology and Computer Science, Nile University, 26th of July Corridor, 12588 Sheikh Zayed, Giza, Egypt
sselim@nu.edu.eg

Abstract. Network Intrusion Detection Systems (NIDS) are critical for safeguarding digital infrastructures against increasingly sophisticated cyber threats. While traditional centralized machine learning models achieve high detection accuracy, they face challenges of privacy, scalability, and data heterogeneity. In this work, we evaluate classical machine learning (Decision Tree, Random Forest), deep learning (DNN), and federated learning (FedDNN) approaches on three benchmark datasets: UNSW-NB15-V2, UNSW-NB15-V3, and NF-BoT-IoT. Our results show that centralized models achieve accuracies above 99.7%, while the federated model attains a competitive 98.98%, demonstrating that privacy-preserving decentralized learning can be realized with only a marginal performance trade-off. The three-client federated setup was designed to represent heterogeneous data distributions and varying dataset sizes, simulating real-world challenges in distributed network security systems.

Keywords: Network Intrusion Detection · Deep Learning · Federated Learning · Cybersecurity

1 Introduction

The exponential growth of interconnected digital systems has transformed cybersecurity, creating unprecedented challenges for network defense. Modern networks span enterprise servers, IoT sensors, and edge nodes, generating massive traffic that must be monitored for threats. This hyper-connectivity expands the attack surface, enabling sophisticated, multi-layered cyberattacks. With global cybercrime damages, effective network security has become both a technical and economic necessity.

Traditional Network Intrusion Detection Systems (NIDS) evolved from signature-based to anomaly-based approaches, but remain limited in handling

A. Awad et al. (Eds.): MEDI 2025, LNCS 16427, pp. 385–393, 2026.
https://doi.org/10.1007/978-3-032-19865-5_32

dynamic cyber threats. Signature-based systems detect known attacks but fail against zero-day exploits and polymorphic malware, while anomaly-based methods suffer from high false positives and require extensive tuning. Both approaches are reactive, leaving networks vulnerable to emerging threats.

The integration of artificial intelligence (AI) and machine learning (ML) introduced proactive and adaptive defense mechanisms. Classical ML models such as Decision Trees and Random Forests achieved high accuracy on benchmark datasets like UNSW-NB15 and provided interpretable results for analysts [7–9]. Deep learning further revolutionized intrusion detection by automatically extracting hierarchical features. Recurrent Neural Networks (RNNs) and Long Short-Term Memory (LSTM) models captured temporal dependencies in network traffic, achieving state-of-the-art results on NSL-KDD and IoT datasets when combined with suitable optimization methods [1,2,12].

However, centralized ML and DL approaches face major challenges: privacy concerns from aggregating sensitive network data, and poor generalization across heterogeneous environments requiring frequent retraining. Federated Learning (FL) addresses these issues by enabling collaborative model training without sharing raw data. The foundational FedAvg algorithm allows clients to share model parameters only, making it suitable for privacy-sensitive cybersecurity contexts [6]. Recent federated NIDS frameworks have demonstrated strong detection performance while preserving data privacy through cryptographic measures and privacy mechanisms [5,11].

Advanced FL variations, including quantum-enhanced methods and adaptive aggregation/resource allocation schemes, have further improved accuracy and efficiency in heterogeneous settings [4,10]. Comparative studies indicate that FL can preserve strong detection performance while providing substantial privacy benefits [3].

As federated techniques mature, their performance increasingly rivals centralized models. In this work, we conduct a comparative evaluation of centralized ML, centralized DL, and federated DL approaches under consistent experimental conditions using unified datasets, preprocessing, and evaluation metrics. The remainder of this paper details our methodology, results, and conclusions.

2 Methodology

This section presents the comprehensive methodology for evaluating and comparing network intrusion detection models. We detail the experimental framework for centralized and federated learning, describe classical machine learning and deep learning architectures with their mathematical principles, explain the Federated Averaging (FedAvg) protocol, and specify optimization techniques and hyperparameters to ensure transparency and reproducibility.

Our experimental design implements a comparative framework ensuring fair evaluation across paradigms through three distinct training approaches: traditional centralized machine learning using classical algorithms, centralized deep learning with neural architectures, and federated deep learning using distributed client-server protocols. Each approach utilizes identical preprocessing pipelines, evaluation metrics, and hyperparameter optimization strategies to eliminate confounding variables.

The training and testing pipeline follows a systematic five-phase approach. First, data partitioning creates representative training, validation, and testing sets with consistent splits. Second, model architecture initialization employs controlled random seed management for reproducible weight initialization. Third, model training executes algorithm-specific optimization protocols with early stopping mechanisms to prevent overfitting and ensure fair comparison. Fourth, comprehensive evaluation applies multiple performance metrics on identical test sets with statistical significance testing to validate performance differences. Finally, k-fold cross-validation provides robust performance estimates accounting for dataset variability (Table 1).

Table 1. Dataset Characteristics

Dataset	NF-UNSW-NB15	NB-BoT-IoT
Attack samples	95,053	37,628,460
Benign samples	2,295,222	135,037
Total samples	2,390,275	37,763,497
Attack classes	9	4
Tools	IXIA Perfect Storm	Ostinato and Node-red
Format	NetFlow v9	NetFlow v9

2.1 Centralized Learning Approaches

The centralized machine learning approach implements two classical algorithms: Decision Tree and Random Forest. The Decision Tree algorithm utilizes CART methodology with Gini impurity criterion, configured with a maximum depth of 20 levels, minimum of 5 samples per split, and 2 samples per leaf to balance complexity and generalization. The Random Forest ensemble trains 100 independent trees using bootstrap aggregating with random feature selection, reducing overfitting through voting mechanisms across multiple learners.

The centralized deep learning architecture implements a feed-forward neural network for binary classification. The network consists of three hidden layers with 128, 64, and 32 neurons, respectively, using ReLU activation functions. Batch normalization follows each hidden layer to stabilize training, while dropout regularization with probability 0.3 prevents overfitting. The output layer uses a sigmoid activation for binary classification (Fig. 1).

2.2 Federated Learning Approaches

The federated learning implementation follows the Federated Averaging (FedAvg) protocol with enhancements designed for intrusion detection in het-

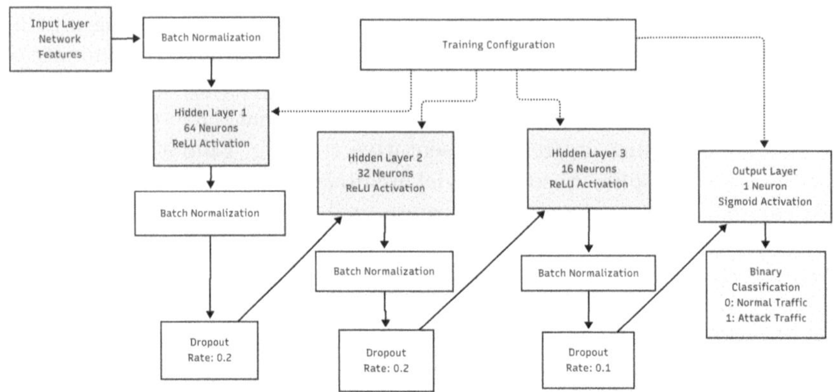

Fig. 1. Deep neural network used for NIDS, with three hidden layers, ReLU activations, dropout, and a sigmoid output for binary classification.

erogeneous environments. The architecture consists of a central server and multiple distributed clients, each representing different network domains. Due to practical constraints in data availability and accessibility for federated learning experiments, we deployed a three-client configuration. Despite this limitation, the selected clients exhibit substantial heterogeneity in data characteristics. This configuration simulates key real-world challenges, including severe data imbalance, data heterogeneity across different network environments and attack vectors, and class distribution variations that reflect diverse operational contexts.

The global model parameters $\mathbf{w}_t$ are distributed to clients at communication round t. Each client k performs local training using its private dataset $\mathcal{D}_k$ for E local epochs, optimizing the global objective on its local data while maintaining the same neural network architecture as the centralized model.

The local optimization problem for client k minimizes the local loss function:

$$\mathbf{w}_{t+1}^{(k)} = \arg\min_{\mathbf{w}} \mathcal{F}_k(\mathbf{w}) = \arg\min_{\mathbf{w}} \frac{1}{|\mathcal{D}_k|} \sum_{(\mathbf{x}_i, y_i) \in \mathcal{D}_k} \ell(\mathbf{w}; \mathbf{x}_i, y_i) \tag{1}$$

where $\ell(\mathbf{w}; \mathbf{x}_i, y_i)$ is the binary cross-entropy loss. After local training, clients transmit their updated model parameters to the central server, which performs weighted aggregation. The standard federated averaging rule computes the global model parameters for round $t + 1$ as:

$$\mathbf{w}_{t+1} = \sum_{k=1}^{K} \frac{n_k}{N} \mathbf{w}_{t+1}^{(k)} \tag{2}$$

where K is the number of clients, $n_k = |\mathcal{D}_k|$ is the local dataset size, and $N = \sum_{k=1}^{K} n_k$ is the total number of training samples. This ensures clients with larger datasets contribute proportionally more to the global model.

Adaptive Weighted Aggregation. Following local training at each client, we introduce an adaptive averaging mechanism that combines data-size weighting with model similarity. The aggregation weights are computed as:

$$w_k^{\text{final}} = \alpha \cdot w_k^{\text{sim}} + (1 - \alpha) \cdot w_k^{\text{data}} \tag{3}$$

where w_k^{sim} is a cosine similarity-based weight that measures how closely a client's updated model aligns with the current global model, $w_k^{\text{data}} = n_k/N$ is the traditional data-size weight, and α balances the two components. This mechanism down weights divergent client updates that may result from local data heterogeneity or adversarial behavior, thereby improving model robustness and convergence stability in heterogeneous federated settings.

Dynamic Virtual Client Configuration. To prevent model bias toward institutions with large datasets, we implement a dynamic virtual client partitioning strategy. This approach algorithmically subdivides large datasets into smaller, independent units to ensure more balanced influence across participants. An institution's dataset N_i is flagged for subdivision if it exceeds a threshold $T = \alpha \cdot \text{median}(N_1, \ldots, N_K)$, where α is a configurable parameter. The institution is then partitioned into $v_i = \lceil N_i/\text{median}(\{N_k\}) \rceil$ virtual clients, preserving the natural statistical characteristics of the original dataset. Each virtual client is treated as an independent participant during federated training, ensuring that a large institution contributes in a more granular fashion rather than overwhelming the global model. This strategy helps smaller participants maintain proportional influence and improves model generalization by preventing dominance from any single data source (Fig. 2).

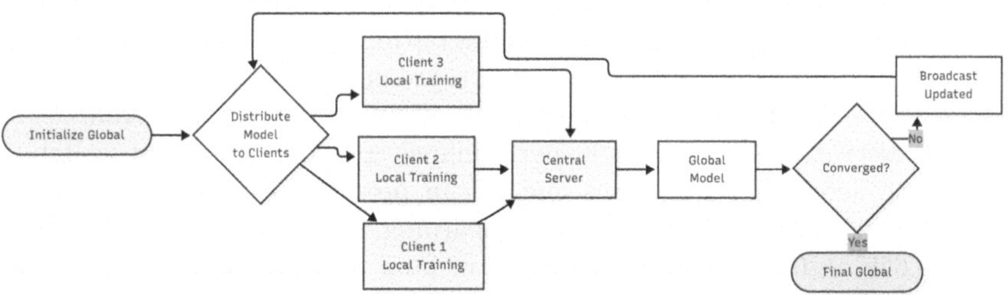

Fig. 2. Federated learning framework for NIDS, where clients train locally on private data and share only model parameters with a central server for FedAvg aggregation.

2.3 Optimization and Hyperparameter Configuration

The optimization strategy employs the Adam optimizer across all deep learning configurations to ensure a consistent comparative evaluation. The Adam algorithm combines momentum-based gradient descent with adaptive learning rate mechanisms. The optimizer configuration utilizes a learning rate $\alpha = 0.001$, first-moment decay rate $\beta_1 = 0.9$, second-moment decay rate $\beta_2 = 0.999$, and numerical stability parameter $\epsilon = 10^{-8}$. Learning rate scheduling implements an exponential decay with a factor of 0.95 every 10 epochs to ensure stable convergence.

3 Results and Discussion

The experimental evaluation demonstrates significant performance achievements across all evaluated approaches, with centralized deep learning models establishing exceptional baseline performance while federated learning approaches achieve competitive results that validate their practical viability for privacy-preserving intrusion detection.

3.1 Centralized Model Performance

Centralized approaches deliver strong baseline performance across all evaluated models. The Random Forest ensemble achieves 99.78% accuracy with low variance across cross-validation folds, proving effective at handling heterogeneous feature types. The Decision Tree attains 99.68% accuracy, demonstrating that single classifiers can achieve near-perfect performance on well-structured intrusion detection datasets. The centralized Deep Neural Network achieves 99.73% accuracy, effectively capturing subtle feature interactions through its hierarchical architecture. The consistently low standard deviations across all centralized models indicate stable generalization across different data partitions.

3.2 Federated Learning Performance and Analysis

The federated learning implementation achieves highly competitive performance with a mean accuracy of 98.98% ± 0.12%, representing less than a 1% decrease compared to centralized approaches while offering substantial advantages in privacy preservation. This narrow performance gap indicates that collaborative training across heterogeneous clients can preserve detection effectiveness. In terms of detailed metrics, federated learning maintains exceptional precision of 99.65% ± 0.02%, indicating very low false positive rates. Recall reaches 98.31% ± 0.27%, reflecting a slightly higher false negative rate but still maintaining strong threat detection capability. The resulting F1-score of 98.98% ± 0.13% confirms a well-balanced trade-off between precision and recall.

The experiment showed the differences in precision and recall between centralized and federated approaches reveals important operational trade-offs. The centralized DNN achieves 99.70% precision and 99.73% recall, representing near-perfect balance. In contrast, the federated model exhibits 99.65% precision only 0.05% decrease but 98.31% recall 1.42% decrease.

Client-level evaluation shows consistent results across heterogeneous data sources: Client 1 (UNSW-NB15-V2) achieved 99.21% accuracy, Client 2 (UNSW-NB15-V3) attained 98.97%, and Client 3 (NF-BoT-IoT) reached 98.76%. Paired t-tests confirm that the differences between centralized and federated models are not statistically significant at the 0.05 level ($p = 0.089$). In addition, parallel local training reduced total training time by approximately 23% compared to centralized approaches (Table 2).

Table 2. Performance Benchmarking Against Prior Work

Study	Approach	Dataset	Accuracy (%)	F1-Score (%)
Previous Work				
Mohale & Obagbuwa [7]	XGBoost + XAI	UNSW-NB15	87.00	85.20
LSTM Enhanced [2]	SSA-LSTM	BoT-IoT	97.54	97.30
Subramanian et al. [10]	Quantum-FL	UNSW-NB15	98.34	98.35
FedGAT [5]	Fed-GNN	Multi-domain	96.80	96.75
This Work				
Random Forest	Centralized	Multi-dataset	99.64	99.11
Decision Tree	Centralized	Multi-dataset	99.68	99.10
Deep Neural Network	Centralized	Multi-dataset	99.73	99.65
FedDNN	Federated	Multi-dataset	98.98	98.98

4 Conclusion and Limitations

This work demonstrated that federated deep learning provides a practical and privacy-preserving alternative to centralized approaches for network intrusion detection, achieving 98.98% accuracy with less than a 1% performance gap compared to centralized models. These results highlight federated learning as a viable solution for organizations constrained by data privacy and scalability concerns, without compromising detection effectiveness.

Our study acknowledges several important limitations that constrain the generalizability of the findings. The federated learning evaluation was conducted using only three clients due to practical constraints in data availability and accessibility for federated experiments. While these clients were deliberately selected to represent heterogeneous data distributions, varying dataset sizes, and diverse attack patterns that simulate real-world challenges such as data imbalance and statistical heterogeneity, the limited number of participants may not fully capture the complexity of large-scale federated deployments. The implementation relied on standard FedAvg with adaptive aggregation mechanisms but did not incorporate advanced privacy-preserving techniques such as differential privacy, secure aggregation, or homomorphic encryption, which are critical for production deployments. Furthermore, operational considerations including false positive rates in realistic traffic conditions, communication overhead, network latency constraints, and computational costs across resource-constrained edge devices were not comprehensively assessed. The datasets, while representative of modern threats, were processed in a controlled environment that may not reflect the dynamic nature of live network traffic with continuous concept drift and evolving attack strategies. Future work should extend this evaluation to larger federated networks with more diverse participants, integrate stronger privacy-preserving mechanisms with formal privacy guarantees, evaluate performance under realistic network conditions with bandwidth constraints and intermittent connectivity, and conduct longitudinal studies to assess model degradation and adaptation requirements over time.

We believe these findings, despite the acknowledged limitations, position federated learning as a promising direction for deployable, privacy-preserving intrusion detection systems in modern distributed networks, warranting further investigation in more extensive real-world settings.

References

1. Al-Tameemi, M., Alzaghir, A.: Improving network security through deep learning RNN approach. Inf. Secur. Technol. **11**(4), 114–121 (2024). https://doi.org/10.33693/2313-223X-2024-11-4-114-121
2. Dash, N., Chakravarty, S., Rath, A., Giri, N., Aboras, K., N., G.: An optimized LSTM-based deep learning model for anomaly network intrusion detection. Sci. Rep. **15** (2025). https://doi.org/10.1038/s41598-025-85248-z
3. Divya, M., Jasmine, K.S.: Comparative study of federated learning vs centralized learning. GRENZE Int. J. Eng. Technol. **10**(1) (2024)
4. Doriguzzi-Corin, R., Siracusa, D.: FLAD: adaptive federated learning for DDOS attack detection. Comput. Secur., 103597 (2023). https://doi.org/10.1016/j.cose.2023.103597
5. Jianping, W., Guangqiu, Q., Chunming, W., Weiwei, J., Jiahe, J.: Federated learning for network attack detection using attention-based graph neural networks. Sci. Rep. **14** (2024). https://doi.org/10.1038/s41598-024-70032-2
6. McMahan, B., Moore, E., Ramage, D., Hampson, S., Arcas, B.A.: Communication-efficient learning of deep networks from decentralized data. Proceedings of the 20th International Conference on Artificial Intelligence and Statistics, pp. 1273–1282 (2017)
7. Mohale, V.Z., Obagbuwa, I.C.: Evaluating machine learning-based intrusion detection systems with explainable ai: enhancing transparency and interpretability. Front. Comput. Sci. **7**, 1520741 (2025). https://doi.org/10.3389/fcomp.2025.1520741
8. Ramadhan, R., Ashari, W.: Performance comparison of random forest and decision tree algorithms for anomaly detection in networks. J. Appl. Inf. Comput. **8**, 367–375 (2024). https://doi.org/10.30871/jaic.v8i2.8492
9. Sarhan, M., Layeghy, S., Moustafa, N., Portmann, M.: Towards a standard feature set for network intrusion detection system datasets. Mob. Netw. Appl. **27**(1), 357–370 (2022)
10. Subramanian, G., Chinnadurai, M.: Hybrid quantum enhanced federated learning for cyber attack detection. BMC Med. Inform. Decis. Mak. **24**, 686169 (2024). https://doi.org/10.1186/s12911-024-02686-169

11. Wang, J., Yang, K., Li, M.: NIDS-FGPA: a federated learning network intrusion detection algorithm based on secure aggregation of gradient similarity models. PLOS ONE **19**(10), 1–33 (2024). https://doi.org/10.1371/journal.pone.0308639
12. Wu, P., Guo, H.: LUNET: a deep neural network for network intrusion detection, pp. 617–624 (2019). https://doi.org/10.1109/SSCI44817.2019.9003126

Machine Learning and Deep Learning Approaches for Mobile Malware Detection: A Survey

Malak Magdy([✉]), Ismail Abu-Krisha, and Heba Aslan

Center of Information Science, Nile University, Giza, Egypt
{M.Magdy2324,HAslan,I.Ahmed2323}@nu.edu.eg

Abstract. Mobile devices are now indispensable, but their widespread use makes them prime targets for malware. Traditional signature-based methods struggle against sophisticated and zero-day threats, driving the rise of Machine Learning (ML) and Deep Learning (DL) for mobile malware detection. These techniques can generalize from data and adapt to evolving attacks. This survey reviews ML and DL approaches by categorizing studies across analysis strategies (static, dynamic, hybrid), feature extraction methods, and model types (classical ML, DL). It also summarizes commonly used datasets and highlights challenges such as data scarcity and explainability while outlining future research directions. Unlike prior surveys that focus on a single perspective, our work integrates analysis type, feature set, and model to provide a holistic view of mobile malware detection.

Keywords: Mobile Malware · Machine Learning · Deep Learning · Static analysis · Dynamic Analysis · Hybrid Analysis · Malware Detection

1 Introduction

Smartphones and tablets have become integral to communication and commerce, yet their openness makes them vulnerable to malware that steals personal data or disrupts services. Android, representing over 72% of the global market [1], is especially exposed due to its open-source design and third-party app support.

Mobile malware takes various forms such as spyware, adware, ransomware, and trojans, each exploiting user data or system resources. Traditional detection techniques signature, heuristic, and rule-based cannot detect unseen or obfuscated malware [2]. Although dynamic and hybrid analysis offer more resilience, they often require high computational power and manual updates.

AI-based approaches overcome these limitations by learning behavioral and structural patterns automatically. Classical ML models like Decision Trees (DTs), Support Vector Machine (SVM), and Random Forest (RF) remain effective, while DL models (CNNs, RNNs, LSTMs) have achieved detection rates

A. Awad et al. (Eds.): MEDI 2025, LNCS 16427, pp. 394–402, 2026.
https://doi.org/10.1007/978-3-032-19865-5_33

exceeding 99% [3]. Emerging research explores federated and explainable AI to enhance privacy and interpretability. This paper surveys these advances, highlighting trends and challenges toward scalable, intelligent malware detection.

This survey is organized as follows: Sect. 2 reviews existing literature on mobile malware detection. Section 3 describes the adopted methodology. Section 4 presents the taxonomy of ML/DL-based approaches. Section 5 summarizes public datasets, Sect. 6 compares existing techniques, and Sect. 7 highlights key challenges and future directions.

2 Literature Review

Numerous surveys have classified malware detection approaches from different perspectives. Most studies target Android platforms due to their dominance and flexibility. Senanayake et al. [4] reported that static analysis dominates research, using permissions, API calls, and opcodes as common features with models like Random Forest and SVM. Nawshin et al. [5] emphasized privacy-preserving and federated learning, while Faisal et al. [6] reviewed AI-based methods across both mobile and computer malware. Roseline et al. [2] and Bilot et al. [7] explored hybrid and graph-based ML techniques, noting the potential of GNNs and DL to capture structural behavior. Altaha et al. [8] compared Android and iOS detection, confirming RF as a strong baseline. Overall, the literature shows a clear evolution from classical ML to advanced DL and hybrid approaches, addressing obfuscation, dataset limitations, and scalability. However, achieving generalization, privacy, and real-world adaptability remains an open problem.

3 Methodology

This survey aims to address the following research questions:

- RQ1: What is the current state of mobile malware detection, and how do evolving threats influence strategies?
- RQ2: How do ML and DL models compare in effectiveness?
- RQ3: How do analysis approaches and feature combinations impact detection performance?

To explore these questions, searches were conducted across major academic databases, including IEEE Xplore, SpringerLink, Elsevier ScienceDirect, and Google Scholar, using keywords such as "Mobile Malware," "Machine Learning," "Deep Learning," and "Malware Analysis." The search focused on studies published between 2018 and 2025 to capture recent advancements in the field.

A total of 61 papers were identified and analyzed. These studies encompass surveys and systematic reviews, ML/DL-based detection models, and experimental or comparative analyses. Each work was examined based on its analysis approach (static, dynamic, or hybrid), the type of features employed, and the datasets used. Priority was given to research that provided valuable insights into existing challenges and potential future directions.

4 Taxonomy of ML/DL-Based Mobile Malware Detection

Detection techniques can be grouped into three major dimensions: analysis approach, feature extraction method, and model type as shown in Fig. 1.

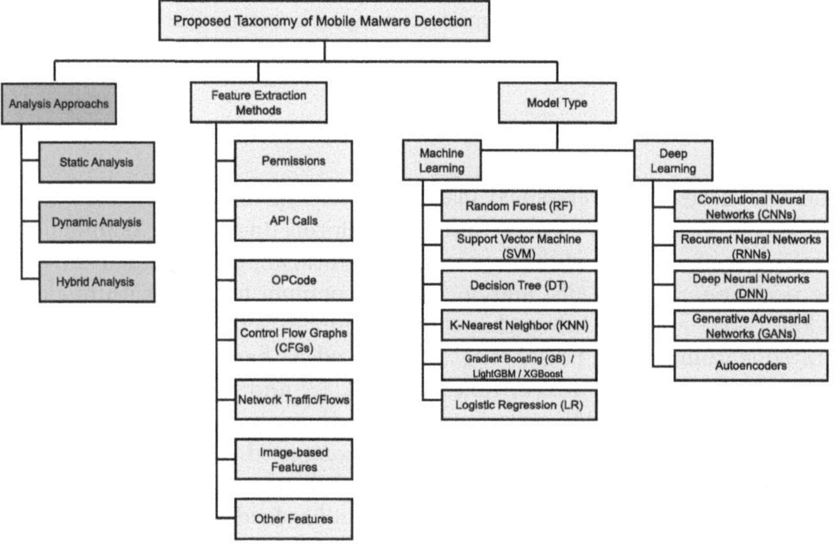

Fig. 1. Proposed Taxonomy of Mobile Malware Detection.

4.1 Analysis Approach

Static analysis inspects application code without execution, extracting permissions, API calls, or opcodes. It is lightweight and scalable but vulnerable to obfuscation. Around 65% of studies use static analysis [12].

Dynamic analysis executes applications in isolated environments to monitor behavior such as API calls or network traffic. It detects obfuscated threats but requires more resources [13] [14].

Hybrid analysis combines both, improving accuracy and coverage while increasing computational cost [15] [16].

4.2 Feature Extraction Method

Feature extraction plays a crucial role in determining the accuracy of mobile malware detection. Commonly used features include **Permissions**, which indicate access to sensitive system resources [17]; **API calls**, which capture interactions with the operating system and reflect behavioral intent [12,18]; and **opcodes**, which represent instruction-level patterns that are often resistant to code manipulation [19,20]. **Control Flow Graphs (CFGs)** are used to model the structural logic of applications [16,22], while **network traffic features** help detect anomalies and identify suspicious external communications [20]. More recently, **image-based features** have been introduced, where binaries or extracted attributes are encoded as images and analyzed using CNNs [23,24].

4.3 Model Type

Traditional ML algorithms (Random Forest, SVM, Decision Tree, KNN) classify apps using selected features as shown in Table 1. DL architectures (CNNs, RNNs, LSTMs, GANs, Autoencoders) automatically learn complex representations, achieving high accuracy but requiring larger, balanced datasets as shown in Table 2.

Table 1. Summary of ML-based Android Malware Detection Studies

Study [Year]	Analysis Approach	Used Features	Used Datasets	ML Models	Accuracy/ measures
[20] [2025]	Dynamic	Permissions	The PermGuard 55,911 benign and 55,911 malware apps	An ensemble model utilizing incremental learning classifiers	Real dataset: 99.33%, Synthetic dataset: 98.28%
[26] [2024]	Hybrid	Permissions, Intents, API calls and system calls	Drebin, MalGenome and Kaggle dataset	SVM, KNN, Naïve Bayes, and different ensembles	100%
[25] [2023]	Static	Permissions, API calls and others	500,000 unique Android apps from various categories.	Artificial Neural Network (ANN) with six algorithms	98.8%
[27] [2022]	Dynamic	System Calls	CICMalDroid2020	RF, DT, Logistic Regression, SVM, Naïve Bayes, KNN, and AdaBoost	99%
[28] [2020]	Hybrid	Permissions, API calls and system calls	Drebin, AMD, AZ, Github, GP	TAN: Tree Augmented Naive Bayes	97%

5 Datasets

Benchmark datasets are fundamental for evaluating and comparing mobile malware detection techniques. They provide standardized data that enable consistent performance assessment across different models and studies. However, many existing datasets face challenges such as limited diversity, outdated samples, and class imbalance, which can affect the generalization of detection models. Recent efforts have focused on creating more comprehensive and regularly updated repositories to better reflect evolving malware behaviors. Table 3 summarizes the key public datasets commonly used in mobile malware research.

6 Comparative Analysis of Existing Approaches

Static analysis dominates research due to scalability and low cost but fails against obfuscation. Dynamic approaches provide deeper insights, but are slower and resource-heavy. Hybrid approaches achieve higher accuracy (98%) but remain complex to deploy on mobile devices [32].

Feature selection significantly impacts performance. Permissions and API calls are lightweight but less robust. Opcodes and CFGs offer deeper insight but require heavier computation. Image-based and hybrid features have emerged

Table 2. Summary of DL-based Android Malware Detection Studies

Study (Year)	Analysis Approach	Used Features	Used Datasets	DL Models	Accuracy
[23] (2025)	Static	Permissions, API calls and string-based features	The used dataset is derived from Drebin, CICAndMal, AndroZoo, and RePack	Large Language Models (LLMs) for Android malware detection	98.97%
[14] (2025)	Dynamic	System calls, binder calls, and composite behaviours, treated as sequential data	CICMaldroid-2020 containing 1795 benign and 9804 malware samples	Temporal Convolutional Network (TCN)	99.31%
[19] (2023)	Static	Fuzzy hashes converted into grayscale images.	Dataset consisting of just over 7,700 ransomware samples	CNN, Also evaluated ResNet50 and VGG16 (both CNN architectures)	98.97%
[29] (2023)	Static	Permissions, API calls, and string features.	Drebin dataset	One-shot learning-based Siamese neural network	98.9%
[30] (2022)	Dynamic	Network Traffic	CICAndMal2017	LSTM	99.6%
[31] (2021)	Static	AndroidManifest xml file	MalDroid2020	CNN	94.40%
[32] (2020)	Hybrid	Permissions, Intents, Network Traffic	CICAndMal2017	CNN-AE	99.30%

Table 3. Publicly available mobile malware datasets used in research.

No.	Dataset Name	Description	Analysis Approach	Studies
1	Drebin	It contains both malicious and benign APKs. Samples were collected from Oct 2010 to Aug 2012 and include 5,560 malware samples from 179 different families and 9,476 benign applications	Static	[13] [29] [15] [16]
2	AndroZoo	Large repository released at 2016 containing over 13 million raw APK files with benign and malicious apps and associated metadata/labels widely used for diverse datasets.	Static and Dynamic	[12] [15]
3	MalGenome (Genome)	It contains malware samples from December 2011 to May 2012 and 1,260 applications belonging to 49 different malware families, along with 2,538 benign applications	Static and Dynamic	[22] [19]
4	CICInvesAnd-Mal2019	It contains a total of 761 Android applications, comprising 333 benign apps and 428 malicious ones. Fully labeled across diverse families.	Static and Dynamic	[12] [15]
5	CICMalDroid-2020	It includes 17,341 samples and provides various features including intents, services, permissions, frequency numbers for different file types, sensitive API calls, system calls, binding calls, and network traffic	Static and Dynamic	[13]
7	Maloid-DS	Up-to-date labeled Android malware dataset (20102024). 47,971 malware samples, 345 families. Available in APK-based, image-based, and feature-based formats.	Static and Dynamic	[18]

as leading techniques, often exceeding 99% accuracy [26]. ML algorithms such as Random Forest and SVM offer interpretability and efficiency, whereas DL models (CNN, LSTM, GAN) provide superior accuracy through automated feature learning. The trade-off between transparency and performance remains a major research focus. Explainable AI (XAI) is emerging to address this gap [33]. Datasets like Drebin and MalGenome are heavily reused but outdated, leading to over-optimistic results. Newer datasets like CICMalDroid2020 and AMD better reflect recent threats but still suffer from imbalance and limited family diversity. Continuous dataset evolution and public sharing are critical for future research reliability [9,10].

7 Challenges and Future Directions

Mobile malware detection faces several key challenges, including **data scarcity and quality**, as many datasets are outdated or imbalanced calling for collaborative repositories and synthetic data generation (e.g., GANs) to enhance generalization [6]. **Evasion and adversarial attacks** through obfuscation and polymorphism demand stronger adversarial robustness and secure training [2]. **The lack of explainability and trust** in DL models can be mitigated with XAI tools like feature attribution and decision-path visualization [33]. **Privacy and federated learning** offer decentralized solutions but still face issues with data heterogeneity and communication overhead [5]. Finally, **Real-time and lightweight detection** requires energy-efficient architectures and optimized edge-based inference for mobile deployment.

8 Conclusion

This survey provides a consolidated overview of ML and DL approaches in mobile malware detection, analyzing methods across static, dynamic, and hybrid strategies. ML models are efficient and interpretable, while DL techniques achieve higher detection accuracy through automated feature learning. However, challenges such as explainability, adversarial robustness, dataset quality, and resource constraints remain unresolved.

Future directions point toward explainable, federated, and hybrid detection frameworks that combine efficiency, privacy, and scalability. Building continuously updated datasets and improving cross-platform adaptability will be essential to defend against the next generation of mobile threats.

References

1. Backlinko: iPhone vs Android market share & user statistics (2025). https://backlinko.com/iphone-vs-android-statistics. Retrieved 21 Aug 2025
2. Roseline, S.A., Geetha, S.: A comprehensive survey of tools and techniques mitigating computer and mobile malware attacks. Comput. Electr. Eng. **92**, 107143 (2021)
3. Bensaoud, A., Kalita, J., Bensaoud, M.: A survey of malware detection using deep learning. Mach. Learn. Appl. **16**, 100546 (2024)
4. Senanayake, J., Kalutarage, H., Al-Kadri, M.O.: Android mobile malware detection using machine learning: a systematic review. Electronics **10**(13), 1606 (2021)
5. Nawshin, F., et al.: Malware detection for mobile computing using secure and privacy-preserving machine learning approaches: a comprehensive survey. Comput. Electr. Eng. **117**, 109233 (2024)
6. Faisal, H., et al.: A survey on artificial intelligence techniques for malware detection. In: CS & IT Conference Proceedings, vol. 12. no. 23. CS & IT Conference Proceedings (2022)
7. Bilot, T., et al.: A survey on malware detection with graph representation learning. ACM Comput. Surv. **56**(11), 1–36 (2024)
8. Altaha, S.J., Aljughaiman, A., Gul, S.: A survey on android malware detection techniques using supervised machine learning. IEEE Access (2024)
9. Wu, Y., Li, W., Xu, L., Zhang, Z.: Android malware dataset: AMD. In: Proceedings of the 2017 International Conference on Data Intelligence and Security (ICDIS), pp. 1–2 (2017). https://doi.org/10.1109/ICDIS.2017.8077688.

10. Mahdavifar, S., Abdul Kadir, A.F., Fatemi, R., Alhadidi, D., Ghorbani, A.A.: Dynamic android malware category classification using semi-supervised deep learning. In: Proceedings of the 18th IEEE International Conference on Dependable, Autonomic, and Secure Computing (DASC) (2020)
11. Allix, K., et al.: Androzoo: collecting millions of android apps for the research community. In: Proceedings of the 13th International Conference on Mining Software Repositories (2016)
12. Mawoh, R.Y., et al.: An accurate approach to discriminate android colluded malware from single app malware using permissions intelligence. Sci. Rep. **15**(1), 10680 (2025)
13. Manzil, H.H.R., Manohar Naik, S.: Android malware category detection using a novel feature vector-based machine learning model. Cybersecurity **6**(1), 6 (2023)
14. Joomye, A., et al.: An effective temporal convolutional networks-based method for detecting android malware using dynamic extracted features. IEEE Access (2025)
15. Rashid, M.U., et al.: Hybrid android malware detection and classification using deep neural networks. Int. J. Comput. Intell. Syst. **18**(1), 1–26 (2025). https://doi.org/10.1007/s44196-025-00783-x
16. Augello, A., De Paola, A., Lo Re, G.: Hybrid multilevel detection of mobile devices malware under concept drift. J. Netw. Syst. Manage. **33**(2), 36 (2025)
17. Amin, A., et al.: Androshield: automated android applications vulnerability detection, a hybrid static and dynamic analysis approach. Information **10**(10), 326 (2019)
18. Kurniawan, F., et al.: A robust and efficient machine learning framework for enhancing early detection of android malware. IEEE Access (2025)
19. Rodriguez-Bazan, H., Sidorov, G., Escamilla-Ambrosio, P.J.: Android ransomware analysis using convolutional neural network and fuzzy hashing features. IEEE Access **11**, 121724–121738 (2023)
20. Garg, S., Baliyan, N.: MalVulDroid: Tracing vulnerabilities from malware in android using natural language processing. J. Web Eng. **21**(8), 2339–2361 (2022)
21. Freitas, S., et al.: A large-scale database for graph representation learning. arXiv preprint arXiv:2011.07682 (2020)
22. Li, Q., et al.: Semi-supervised two-phase familial analysis of Android malware with normalized graph embedding. Knowl. Based Syst. **218**, 106802 (2021)
23. Feng, R., et al.: LLM-MalDetect: a large language model-based method for android malware detection. IEEE Access (2025)
24. Almomani, I., Almashat, T., El-Shafai, W.: MALOID-DS: labeled dataset for android malware forensics. IEEE Access **12**, 73481–73546 (2024)
25. Mahindru, A., et al.: PermDroid a framework developed using proposed feature selection approach and machine learning techniques for Android malware detection. Sci. Rep. **14**(1), 10724 (2024)
26. Bashir, S., et al.: Hybrid machine learning model for malware analysis in android apps. Pervasive Mob. Comput. **97**, 101859 (2024)
27. Manzil, H.H.R.: DYNAMALDROID: dynamic analysis-based detection framework for android malware using machine learning techniques. In: 2022 International Conference on Knowledge Engineering and Communication Systems (ICKES). IEEE (2022)
28. Surendran, R., Thomas, T., Emmanuel, S.: A TAN based hybrid model for android malware detection. J. Inf. Secur. Appl. **54**, 102483 (2020)
29. Almarshad, F.A., et al.: Detection of android malware using machine learning and Siamese shot learning technique for security. IEEE Access **11**, 127697–127714 (2023)

30. Fallah, S., Bidgoly, A.J.: Android malware detection using network traffic based on sequential deep learning models. Softw. Pract. Exp. **52**(9), 1987–2004 (2022)
31. Tang, B.H., et al.: Android malware detection based on deep learning techniques. In: 2021 4th international conference on pattern recognition and artificial intelligence (PRAI). IEEE (2021)
32. Feng, J., et al.: A two-layer deep learning method for android malware detection using network traffic. IEEE Access **8**, 125786–125796 (2020)
33. Manthena, H., et al.: Explainable Artificial Intelligence (XAI) for malware analysis: a survey of techniques, applications, and open challenges. IEEE Access (2025)

Author Index

A. Awad et al. (Eds.): MEDI 2025, LNCS 16427, pp. 403–404, 2026.
https://doi.org/10.1007/978-3-032-19865-5

The manufacturer's authorised representative in the EU is Springer Nature Customer Service Centre GmbH, Europaplatz 3, 69115 Heidelberg, Germany. If you have any concerns regarding our products, please contact ProductSafety@springernature.com

Printed and bound by CPI Group (UK) Ltd, Croydon, CR0 4YY
07/07/2026
02160917-0013